READING
MEDIEVAL
CULTURE

Robert Hanning

Photo by Barbara Hanning

READING MEDIEVAL CULTURE

Essays in Honor of Robert W. Hanning

Edited by

ROBERT M. STEIN

and

SANDRA PIERSON PRIOR

UNIVERSITY OF NOTRE DAME PRESS
Notre Dame, Indiana

Manufactured in the United States of America

Library of Congress Cataloging-in-Publication Data
Reading medieval culture : essays in honor of Robert W. Hanning /
edited by Robert M. Stein and Sandra Pierson Prior.
    p.   cm.
Includes bibliographical references and index.
ISBN 0-268-04111-3 (acid-free paper)
    1. Civilization, Medieval.   2. Literature, Medieval—History and criticism.
I. Stein, Robert M., 1943–   II. Prior, Sandra Pierson.   III. Hanning, Robert W.
    CB351.R395   2005
    909.07—dc22

2005012540

∞ *This book is printed on acid-free paper.*

CONTENTS

ACKNOWLEDGMENTS

A project as large as this necessarily incurs many debts, and we have been fortunate in the support and assistance we have received. We are grateful to the Department of English and Comparative Literature at Columbia University for their grant to support this book. We are much indebted to both Jeffrey J. Cohen and the anonymous second reader for the University of Notre Dame Press for their careful reading and helpful suggestions, and to Barbara Hanrahan for her enthusiastic support of this project. To Katherine Olson: our gratitude for assistance with research and especially for her expert work on the genealogical chart for "Women in the Shadows of the *Divine Comedy*." To Mary Agnes Edsall, we owe a special thanks for helping us find the cover image. Above all, we are indebted to all our contributors for their energy and enthusiasm and to the person who inspired us all, Robert W. Hanning.

READING
MEDIEVAL
CULTURE

INTRODUCTION

ROBERT M. STEIN AND
SANDRA PIERSON PRIOR

The Work of Robert Hanning
and the Work of This Book

T his book honors Robert W. Hanning on the occasion of his sixty-fifth birthday and retirement from Columbia University, where he studied as an undergraduate and graduate student, and where—as Professor of English and Comparative Medieval Literature since 1964—he has been a mentor and guide for several generations of scholars. Through his teaching and prolific writing he has significantly shaped the development of the profession at large. The book consists of entirely new work, written expressly for the occasion by a select group of Hanning's students, colleagues, and friends.

In an age of ever more narrow specialization within the academy, Hanning's work is marked by its enormous scope. It has engaged all of the significant periods of medieval literary production—Anglo-Saxon England, the so-called twelfth century Renaissance, the Age of Chaucer—and it has addressed very large historical and cultural questions through the examination of a wide range of texts in several quite diverse genres, languages, and cultural settings. Moreover, this work has often taken up matters of large significance from a unique and unexpected angle of vision that has set the agenda for much fruitful further study. Hanning's first book, *The Vision of History in Early Britain,* has been foundational for the study of medieval historiography. It demonstrated how methods of textual interpretation from within the disciplinary framework of literary criticism could be brought to bear on texts that, until that time, had been read only by professional historians as more or less distorted windows onto the world of the past. By asking new questions and providing new and powerful tools for analysis, *The Vision of History* almost single-handedly created the field that has become one of the prime growing points of medieval studies. After almost forty years, the book still remains the essential starting point for any work on medieval historiography. *The Individual in Twelfth-Century Romance,* which appeared about ten years after *The Vision of History,* situated twelfth-century vernacular romance, primarily the courtly romances of Chrétien de Troyes, within the large international framework of twelfth-century intellectual culture. To read the discussions of courtly romance dating from before and after this book is a revelation: Hanning's was an important voice in shifting attention from narrow questions of source-study and philology to the interactions between vernacular fictions and the social and cultural world that produced them and to which they artistically respond. At this time, with his colleague Joan Ferrante, he translated the *Lais* of Marie de France, making the most important work of an outstanding artist fully available for the first time to a non-Francophone audience. At the moment, Hanning is completing a book on Chaucer and Boccaccio. His lectures at Columbia and on other campuses—including the biennial lecture presented to the New Chaucer Society's 1998 meeting in Paris—and his many published articles have marked him for at least the last fifteen years as an acknowledged leader in Chaucer studies. Throughout his career, Hanning has also regularly written on Anglo-Saxon culture, Old English poetry, and medieval English drama, as well as producing a number of articles on Italian culture and literature. This includes work not only on Boccaccio, but also on such high Renaissance figures as Ariosto and Castiglione.

Hanning is first and foremost a powerfully attentive reader of texts, from whom anyone can always take a lesson in how to read. His awareness of the manifold ways that language always says more than, other than, and even precisely the contrary of what it ostensibly intends to say allies him not only with the Anglo-American New Critics who were his teachers but more directly with the contemporary theoretical tendencies in the profession that we can loosely call deconstruction. At the same time, Hanning is equally aware of the checks and constraints on the free flow of signification: while certain that language speaks in spite of itself, Hanning is concerned with the determinate social situation in which language always speaks—words are addressed by particular speakers to particular audiences in an attempt to accomplish something equally particular. The most important element in his work—and indeed what we consider to be the intellectual center of this collection—is Hanning's sense of the flow and circulation of the discourses of the social world. While Hanning has for the most part focused on the "high" genres of courtly romance, history, and the work of Chaucer, he reads them in the context of social discourse—the language of the marketplace, of penitence and confession, and of love-casuistry. Throughout, there is the direct confrontation with the instrumentality of language: language is not only a means to share information, it is a tool to get something done. And his engagement with the instrumentality of language—with the questions "who speaks?" "to what end?" "with what motive?" (including of course the unacknowledged and the disavowed motive)—is the source of the ultimate humanity of Hanning's work: his sense that the great works of medieval literature register, in no matter how mediated a way, the lives of the people who produced them and for whom they were produced.

When we began to plan this Festschrift, several colleagues suggested that, given the difficulty these days of finding a publisher for a collaborative volume, and given the large number of Hanning's articles that have never been reprinted, it might be wiser to edit a volume of his selected essays as a way of honoring him. While we think that this is a good and practical idea and, in fact, would love to see such a volume (for much of his work deserves reprinting and wide availability), we have proceeded with our original idea of a Festschrift precisely in order to demonstrate the contemporary legacy of Hanning's work. The way that Hanning has, throughout his career, brought together impulses that are often at war within the discipline—close reading and cultural studies, or engagement with high culture and concern for the language of ordinary people, to mention only two—strikes us as particularly exemplary in our own "post-theoretical" moment of historicizing literary studies. While addressed to a rich variety of primary sources, the essays in this collection are united in their search to account for the complex ways in which these sources are situated in their own time, mediated historically to us through other texts and other readers, and, finally, are read within the context of our own social questions and disciplinary structures. This is a most important demonstration of the ample relevance of Hanning's work to our own time. It is with this understanding of Hanning's rich and distinctive career that we have designed a Festschrift in his honor. We have gathered essays by a prestigious array of scholars whose work represents most of the major areas of scholarship and criticism to which Robert Hanning has so brilliantly and significantly contributed.

When Hanning began his work examining the chronicle sources for the history of early Britain, medieval chronicles were used only for documentary purposes. Hanning was perhaps the first scholar to recognize that reading medieval chronicles presented a general historiographical problem larger than the question of their factual reliability. In the first instance, this is an aspect of the literary critical problem raised by any realistic narrative, for in its claim to truthfully represent something that happened independent of the confines of the narrative, historical writing requires the reader's assent to its own formal techniques of representation. This requirement, presented by any narration that claims to be true, is met with particular urgency by medieval historical narratives precisely because, in at least two ways, they so completely stand outside the canons of truth that produce the regular operations of contemporary professional historical practice. Most obviously, many of the events they narrate—miracles, prodigies, portents—are literally beyond belief; less obviously, but even more importantly, the medieval writers' own systems of historical reasoning have themselves been relegated to the sphere of the irrational and superstitious by our notions of action and logical causality. And the same historical process that thus places the Middle Ages on the far side of an epistemological divide also gives rise to the canons of our own practices of reading and interpretation.[1] In *The Vision of History in Early Britain*, Hanning attacked the problem of representation directly by using the techniques of literary critical close reading to interrogate the historians' own narrative protocols, not to look beyond their credulousness in order to pry unquestionably true "facts" out of the structure of their unbelievable narratives, but rather to understand what their own shaping power of narration could tell us about the processes and procedures of medieval cultural and intellectual life.

If Hanning's first book demonstrated the usefulness of literary criticism for understanding the significance of historical writing, his second, *The Individual in Twelfth-Century Romance*, addressed the social and cultural work done by medieval romance, which has been read since at least the eighteenth century as the most fanciful of fictional genres, a species of pure aesthetic play far removed from any engagement with the social world.[2] Stimulated by the work of R. W. Southern's *Making of the Middle Ages*, whose final chapter "From Epic to Romance" took the image of the quest as a master trope for understanding the broad cultural transformations of the twelfth century, Hanning investigated the structures of vernacular romance writing as expressive of new organizations of activity, new places felt to be of particular significance by their contemporaries. From this perspective romance and historiography form two sides of the same coin: writing in both genres proves to be an attempt to understand secular processes in a world increasingly perceived to be obedient to secular imperatives—the need for territorial control, the activity of the marketplace, and the desire for individual happiness in the here-and-now are their objects of immediate attention.

The contributors to the first section of our volume take up questions of narrative representation in active dialogue with Hanning's foundational work in the fields of historiography and romance. In both genres, the sense of identity—whether conceived of as individual, national, or religious—comes into being by means of complex narrative operations that simultaneously produce it and register it as if already accomplished, simply waiting to be represented. While the passage of time is the fundamental material of narrative, it is time in relation to some kind of determinate imaginative space that provides the framework for historiographic representation as well as for the critical understanding of the contemporary scholar. Nicholas Howe accordingly sets the stage for several recurrent themes of this volume in his look at the precipitates of time in the physical space of Jarrow—medieval monastery, nineteenth-century shipyard, twentieth-century petrochemical and industrial landscape—from the perspective of "Bede's World," a historically reconstructed eighth-century village. This is a space whose visual particularities are the outcome of a specific historical trajectory. The beginning of that trajectory in the eighth-century monastery that produced one of the central texts of English self-definition, Bede's *Historia Ecclesiastica Gentis Anglorum,* is peculiarly marginal to the main historical development of Jarrow as an industrial center for the British Empire and its postcolonial present. And for Howe, this spatio-temporal field of alternating centers and margins is also an image of the contemporary medievalists' own encounter with their complex subject matter, a past mediated to the present by means of the same historical transformations in culture and society that both bring the present into being in its specificity and transform the past into an object whose existence is always partial and spectral, always a *re*construction and outcome of critical work.

Howe is concerned with the traces of the past within the present; Monika Otter examines textual places where the medieval historian imagines the future. By exploiting the Virgilian technique of "retrospective prophecy"—where, by setting the "present" of the narrative before the present moment of composition, things that have already come to pass can be foreseen in prophetic vision—the historian can enlist the future for narrative closure. What Otter finds, however, is that many of these moments of prophecy, such as Geoffrey of Monmouth's inclusion of Merlin's prophecies or Edward the Confessor's vision of the Seven Sleepers, serve rather to open narrative possibilities to alternative outcomes and thus to register an anxiety about the epistemological status of the fleeting present, ever receding into historical memory and graspable only in its vanishing. The most evocative attempt to allay that anxiety is Henry of Huntingdon's invocation of a future without resorting to tropes of prophecy; rather, Henry addresses a reader of the next millennium, in the year 2135 to be precise, and implores that reader, whom, he says, he has mentioned "long before you are to be born," to pray for him who will "already be dust by your time." If, as Howe shows us, Bede's Christianity is a place "occupied by believers who maintain themselves as a community through the simultaneous observance of the same set of practices," Henry here has imagined the permanence of that community as an infinitely full space of time, a structure of permanent rememberance. For just as he asks that the reader of 2135 pray for him, so he hopes that reader will be remembered and prayed for by the people of 3125, and so on, into the next millennium and the next, in a triumph of narrative over death and over the loss of the past.

For Sarah Spence, the space of a religious practice, the very material Church of Saint-Denis, provides the ground for a complex narrative of time involving a relation between texts as well as between the occupants of the "same" space at different times. Suger uses the well-known rhetorical terminology of *amplificatio* to describe his own plans to rebuild the church of Saint-Denis, and by so doing, Spence argues, puts himself into a direct relation with Hilduin, the Abbot of Saint-Denis who first translated the texts of the Pseudo-Dionysius, wrote his life, and built a new chapel to house his relics. Suger thus transforms himself into a figure of historical mediation, and he does this by deploying in his writing the casuistry of love and desire, that great "invention" of the twelfth century and principal subject matter of the genre of romance. In Suger's desire, the body of the saint, the text of his works, and the chapel that houses his remains all are forged into a unity that is precisely representative of the present moment filled with the living remains of the past: texts, commentaries, translations, spiritual treasure. And Suger's experience—represented, as Spence shows, by the dynamic figure of a woman rushing forward toward the altar over the heads of the multi-tudinous crowd—is its measure.

Charlotte Gross throws the problem of time and narrative into sharp philosophical relief by examining the equally dynamic and innovative intel-lectual work of William of Conches. William and his Chartrian associates addressed in their philosophical work the same set of relations between time and space that Spence, Otter, and Howe see as variously animating the texts they study; and it is striking in this regard that William produced his philo-sophical writing under the patronage of Angevin princes—themselves im-portant patrons both of romance and of the earliest vernacular historiogra-phy. Gross shows us some of the results of the Chartrians' reasoning: among them, a desacralized nature, understandable entirely from the perspective of immediate relations of causality; and a tight relation between time and space, in that time is the measure of space, both in motion and at rest. In brief, the world of history and romance, the world of secular processes unfolding in time and space, becomes in the work of William and his associates in Chartres the object and outcome of scientific inquiry.

One of the key insights of Hanning's later work on Chaucer and Boc-caccio is the observation that discourses are social products that circulate and are thus always available for use by people other than their original users; they are available, as well, for new and often subversive purposes. Thus, to cite only one well-known example, Chaucer's innkeeper, Harry Bailly, can speak "like a lawyer" to enforce his governance of the storytelling game. And in so doing, as Bakhtin reminds us, Chaucer puts the discourse itself on display so that we can understand its properties and its effects.[3] Several of the contributors to this first section of the volume have brought this insight to bear on historiography and romance in a variety of ways. Each in their own way, they reveal the extreme complexity in the interplay between textual production, dissemination, and the social use of the discourses that texts embody.

Nancy Partner attends to the way that the hagiographical narrative of the life of Christina of Markyate is disrupted by another, unwritten narrative, a counterlife in another voice. This is the story of Theodora (Christina's ac-tual baptismal name), which, read in the elisions and tensions of the text, re-veals the discourse of a "tradition-bound society deeply discomfited by non-conformity." For just as the hagiographical "life" of Christina is celebratory, the unwritten "life" of Theodora is one of discontent. It is the story of a strong-willed young woman whose vague defiances of the conventions of a society that, as Partner puts it, "placed all official authority in the hands of males," finally become channelled into a monastic profession by circumstance and by the male authority she was forced to use for her own ends. Partner demonstrates that Theodora was not merely a passive victim of male power: she was able to use the prevailing norms and available discourses of her time and place to fashion a life for herself that ran precisely against prevailing norms, one "following no institutional model and accepting no external supervision." Yet, as the stresses on the narrative surface of Christina's unfinished official *Vita* reveal, this is a life won not without a certain psychic cost.

Partner notes how, in the circulation of discourses and narrative protocols, life sometimes imitates art; Marshall Leicester, too, is concerned with the way people can themselves be experts in the discursive possibilities made available by art. His powerful reading of Marie de France's *Lais* shows us how Marie's characters are not "innocent embodiments of the experience of 'falling in love' that happens to be expressed in the conventional forms and styles of twelfth-century romance," but rather are themselves expert users of the amatory discourses of romance that they knowingly and strategically deploy to try to get what they want. And in the voices of the officially "bad girls" of Marie's *Lais*—the wife of the *bisclavret*, for example, or La Fresne's mother, or especially Guenevere in "Lanval"—Leicester hears a particular form of feminine discontent. This voice registers the work of social power that romance discourses perform precisely by using romance discourse against itself. Leicester considers the figure of the androgynous white hind, who, wounded, wounds Guigemar and speaks to him dismissively, as the starting point for meditating on the discourses of romance "as techniques people use to negotiate their interests in the register of desire, and their desires in accordance with their interests."

Partner and Leicester each use a psychoanalytic approach to reveal the fissuring and incompletion of official narrative discourses—hagiography and romance—and discern in them a play of opposition and resistance to the social normativity that these genres naturalize. Christopher Baswell's contribution moves from questions of the individual to those of the group and to the ideological forces at play in the presumed unities of an official national language and an officially national identity as they play out in the polyglot and class-striated reality of fourteenth-century England. To do this, Baswell considers the figures of Brutus and of Arthur, two central mythic heroes of British and then English national identity, in two late medieval vernacular translations: Trevisa's translation of Higden's Latin *Polychronicon* and the English renderings of the anonymous Anglo-Norman prose *Brut* chronicles. Baswell situates these translations—and the very material books that disseminate them—in the social contest over the meaning of the English vernacular: a vehicle on the one hand for royal ambitions, both dynastic and imperial, and on the other, for Lollard insurgency.

Finally Suzanne Akbari looks also at this same conflict as it plays out in romance, between "Lancastrian efforts to promote a distinctively English national identity through official use of the English language" and "Lollard efforts to employ the vernacular in preaching, at trial, and in the study of the Bible." In the romance of *Richard Coer de Lion* and its strange episodes of cannibalism, on the one hand, and eucharistic devotion on the other, Akbari sees an assertion of English national identity emerging from the particular combination of religious and royal authority wielded by the Lancastrian regime, one in which secular and spiritual authority were integrated to an extraordinary degree in response to the Lollard challenge. Akbari thus reads the romance as a dynamic social artifact, an instrument that both participated "in the forging of an idea of the nation . . . and disseminated it across a broad reading community."

The last two sections of this volume address two areas of Hanning's work: Chaucer and Italian art and literature. In his articles of the 1970s and 1980s, Hanning brings to Chaucer studies the topics and methods of his work on historiography and romance: careful analysis of the language of texts, enriched by intertexts from pagan antiquity and from other medieval genres and traditions, and a focus on narrative structures and representations as a means for discovering the workings of medieval culture. For example, Hanning's 1986 article, "Chaucer's First Ovid: Artistic Transformation and Poetic Tradition in the *Book of the Duchess and the House of Fame*" concludes that: "Chaucer as a working poet, is simultaneously a hostage to his tradition—a victim of *fama*—and the perpetrator of *fama*'s mischief."

In the 1980 essay "The Struggle between Noble Designs and Chaos: The Literary Tradition of Chaucer's Knight's Tale," Hanning revisits Muscatine's claim that "the history of Thebes had perpetual interest for Chaucer as an example of the struggle between noble designs and chaos."[4] Hanning's essay looks at sources for the Knight's Tale in Statius and Boccaccio and concludes that Chaucer omits all "of Boccaccio's self-consciously literary epic trappings" and instead "confronts the paradoxes inherent in chivalry" (530).

An earlier essay on the Prioress and the Wife of Bath examines not only the Middle Ages' misogynist views, both learned and popular, but also the idealized female roles of Christian tradition.[5] Hanning reminds us that "both impulses, of course, effectively dehumanize their object, and they suggest that a basic inability to confront woman as person and individual was endemic to [medieval European] culture" (581): Hanning thus helped usher in a fuller context for studying gender issues in medieval literature in general and Chaucer in particular.

The articles foreshadow Hanning's subsequent turn to the analysis of social discourses and performances. His recent work on *The Canterbury Tales* and *The Decameron* focuses on the competing discourses performed both by speakers within the fiction and by tellers of the fictions. While still working with language structures found in courtly and learned literature, Hanning has been drawing on both his work in medieval drama and performance and also on materials like confession manuals, sermon collections, and merchants' diaries. Hanning has characterized the confrontations that arise among the Canterbury pilgrims as a kind of "parlous play"—much like the diabolic inversion and parody performed by the demons in the religious drama he has studied. These performed rivalries among the pilgrims are playful because, Hanning claims, they occur "through the 'holiday' medium of story . . . perilous because, despite their holiday disguise, words spoken in anger have the power to rend the social fabric of the ad hoc compaignye."[6]

His work on Boccaccio reveals a similar trajectory, for Hanning has been examining the ways that both Boccaccio and Chaucer depict their imagined communities. These storytelling communities are contingent and ad hoc, unlike the monasteries, schools and universities, and courts that formed the institutional sites for histories and romances. They thus bring their creators to a different kind of poetics, what Hanning calls a "lapsarian poetic." He calls the social paradigms at work in *The Decameron* and *The Canterbury Tales* lapsarian, *not* postlapsarian, in order to highlight the absence in them of any earlier Edenic society. Their poetics are lapsarian as well. As Hanning puts it, "corresponding to the lapsarian social constructions of these texts is a lapsarian poetic that highlights the fiction-making rhetorical virtuosity and discourse manipulation of their imagined communities."[7]

The contributors to the section on Chaucer in this book draw on a wide range of resources—from feminist theory and queer studies to careful historicizing through the examination of a range of literary and archival texts.

Like Hanning in his most recent work, these essays focus especially on social discourses as performed, manipulated, and challenged in Chaucer's narratives. Peter Travis examines an instance of Chaucer's questioning of cultural presumptions, in this case "the logocentric and phallocentric presumptions of a complex European aesthetic tradition," which Patricia Parker has defined and characterized as the "virile style."[8] The virile style, going back to Roman writers and continuing through the early Modern period, prizes a Spartan style of robust and plain language, as opposed to a language and a style it always characterizes as flaccid, effeminate, and degenerate. While Chaucer dramatizes and parodies the sexual obsessions in the Host's over-the-top praise of the Nun's Priest's physique and thereby exposes the tradition's anxiety about masculinity and its concomitant misogynist assumptions, Travis concludes that "there is no evidence that [Chaucer] is committed to killing [the tradition] off *tout court.*"

Gendered poetics and masculine identity also figure in Margaret Pappano's and William Askins's contributions. Pappano's essay examines Robyn the Miller's appeal to the Reeve as his "leve brother," an appeal that remains always suspect throughout *The Canterbury Tales.* Pappano claims that, in the Miller's Prologue and Tale, Chaucer exposes "the impossible and fantastical notion of masculinity that underlies the guilds' language of fair exchange." And because both Nicholas the clerk and Alisoun the wife triumph over John the Carpenter, Pappano sees in the Miller's Tale a breakdown of the fraternal system. For while Robyn's address to the Reeve would claim that they are united in a fraternity of married, and presumably cuckolded, men, the tale's actual "cohesive fellowship" is that of the officially celibate clerks who join together at the end in laughter over the Carpenter's fate. Thus, Pappano concludes that "while Chaucer seems to reproduce the masculinist biases of [the Miller's] system, he also subjects it to the destabilizing power of its very constituent others—women, clerics, apprentices."

The power to limit membership in their brotherhood to married men is but part of the larger hegemonic control exerted by craft guilds, and, in turn, by the merchants and civil servants connected to the wool trade who stood resolute against outsiders and what the English, in their statutes and other writings, saw as foreigners' deceitful, greedy, effete, and corrupt ways. Pappano shows that, in guild statutes, "foreigners" included anyone not admitted to the guild (such as unmarried women, clerics, or servants); but, as Askins argues, the "foreigners" most threatening to much of Chaucer's English audience were the Flemish. Rather than Thopas' social class, Askins concludes that what is primarily mocked and burlesqued in the tale's hapless hero is his Flemish identity: his name, his heraldic sign, his birthplace, his obsession with money and coinage, even his ineptitude as a chivalric warrior and lover. No doubt popular poetry's lack of craft is mocked in Chaucer the pilgrim's silly and "drasty" tale, but popular social and political views are equally, if more subtly and complexly, at issue as well.

Poetics for Chaucer is a matter both of craft and of context, as illustrated by the essays of George Economou and Elizabeth Robertson, both of whom examine Chaucer's poetics—Economou vis-à-vis Langland and Robertson in a comparison with James I's *Kingis Quair.* Economou focuses on *makyng,* the craft of the two poets (who, scholars increasingly suspect, knew each other), and Robertson focuses on the poetics of married love. Working with the growing assumption that Chaucer knew and drew upon *Piers Plowman* for other parts of the *Canterbury Tales* as well as for the General Prologue—Economou investigates the implications of Chaucer's readings of his fellow poet as borrowings, adaptations, or translations that shed light on both poets' views of their craft. Langland dramatizes himself as a minstrel of God (a lowly person but an exalted mission), while Chaucer places himself in the ranks of the canonical poets of Europe, past and present. And, in a last word in the Parson's Prologue—wherein, as many fail to note, "rym" is held in almost as low regard as the versifying of "'rum, ram, ruf,' by lettre"—Chaucer, or at least his pilgrim Parson, "seconds the skeptical attitudes towards Will's making" that are voiced by Imaginative (in B12) and Reason and Conscience (in C5). The pairing of the two English versifying forms by the pilgrim Parson places Chaucer and Langland in "a fellowship of makers" who reveal both pride and misgivings about their craft.

Elizabeth Robertson compares the Wife of Bath's Tale to James I's *Kingis Quair,* the latter being the author's self-conscious homage to Chaucer. The Wife of Bath begins her tale with a rape and concludes it with a fairytale ending of a blissful marriage. James I's poem, honoring his forthcoming marriage, surprisingly includes a recollection of his own rape/abduction as a child, a recollection that initiates a meditation on the story of Philomela's rape. Rape and marriage, as Robertson demonstrates, were closely linked in law and society, owing to the emphasis on property and the general lack of concern for individual desire. Ultimately and in different ways, James I and Chaucer both address this cultural problem: Chaucer in social structures and James in the forms of love poetry that tended to deny agency to women.

In the only essay in the Chaucer section that directly analyzes the portrayal of a female character, Laura Howes situates Chaucer's Criseyde in two competing contexts: the conventions of courtly romance predicating the behavior of a lady in love; and the discursive formations of Chaucer's own society governing a young, marriageable woman. Howes argues that Chaucer has had all the male characters and voices in the poem—from Calchas and Pandarus to Troilus and the narrator—betray Criseyde, a betrayal that Chaucer the poet engineers by making her an obedient daughter, as fourteenth-century women were enjoined to be, rather than a faithful beloved, as was expected of romance heroines. Such a collision draws attention to the problems of late medieval England's views towards women, in the culture's idealizations of the feminine, whether that of saint or courtly lady, as well as in the institutions, laws, and values that were meant to keep women in their assigned places.

What these essays all address are aspects of Chaucer's poetics that Hanning has been studying for several decades: they examine Chaucer's poems in relation to the texts of the past and his contemporaries, and in relation to the social and economic worlds of the writer and his characters and storytellers. The last two essays in this section address Chaucer's reception in the centuries between James I and the late twentieth century. John Ganim, working in the field of late nineteenth- and early twentieth-century medievalism, focuses on the responses of Virginia Woolf and William Morris to Chaucer. In often surprising ways, both Woolf and Morris find in Chaucer's poems connections to their infamous love lives, and they draw on medieval tales and readers as meditations for their own work. In the *Kelmscott Chaucer,* which Morris produced with the collaboration of Burne-Jones, the illustrations focus on chivalry and women in distress and often draw on other myths and narratives—the Tristan/Iseut and Lancelot/Guinevere stories, preeminently. Ganim argues that Morris relies on Chaucer "as a kind of fetish that wards off the confusions of the sexual and political present"—and also as an inspiration for innovative creation. Unlike Morris, Woolf reads Chaucer as a straightforward and unselfconscious poet. But like Morris, she too turns to him as a welcome refuge from modern poetry and modern life. At the same time, she implicates the fifteenth-century reader of Chaucer, John Paston, in an earlier version of her semi-autobiographical portrait of Vita Sackville-West in *Orlando.* Ganim reminds us how the late nineteenth century and early twentieth century often blurred the distinctions "between an academic interest in Chaucer and that represented by a more general readership."

Perhaps the single most decisive event in the twentieth century's separation of the scholarly and the academic world from the rest of Chaucer's
readers was the 1940 publication of Manly and Rickert's edition of *The Canterbury Tales*. Yet, while the work itself is decidedly "academic," even scientific, drawing as it did on techniques of cryptography, it was not any more
divorced from the personal lives and values of its authors, John Manly and
Edith Rickert, than was William Morris's Kelmscott Chaucer or Virginia
Woolf's John Paston—quite the contrary, as Sealy Gilles and Sylvia Tomasch show in the final essay of this section. Manly and Rickert found in
Chaucer a model of rectitude—"democratic, plain-spoken, honest, efficient,
entrepreneurial, and thoroughly professional"; and yet their "ideal bourgeois" proved unreliable and ultimately failed them, as surely as did their scientific methods, which never yielded the longed-for archetype of the text
for *The Canterbury Tales*.

Our final section of essays, set in the context of Italian late medieval and
Renaissance culture, brings us to an area central to Hanning's current work
on Boccaccio and Chaucer. Going back at least as far as his collaboration
with his colleague David Rosand on a team-taught course in Italian renaissance art and poetry and on their 1978 Symposium on Castiglione (out of
which came the collection of essays, *Castiglione: The Ideal and the Real in
Renaissance Culture*), Hanning's long-standing interest in the art and literature of the Italian Renaissance is yet one more way in which his work has
so consistently challenged the academy's boundaries of time, place, culture,
and language. The four essays in this section of our book—two on literature
and two on art and theories of art—thus form a fitting conclusion to our
tribute to Hanning's work and inspiration.

Reception and translation of cultures across geographical space and languages figure in Warren Ginsberg's essay comparing the Franklin's Tale
with Boccaccio's *Filocolo*. Using Walter Benjamin's term "modes of meaning," Ginsberg points to all the aspects of Menedon's *quistione* that are peculiar to Boccaccio's time and place, aspects that Chaucer may not have fully
understood. Whereas Menedon's question turns upon the gendered identity of upper-class Italian men, the Franklin's Tale depends more upon identity based upon rank, a central and explicit concern in Chaucer's England.
Gender anxiety is displaced from the man to the woman, for Dorigen's grief
and anxiety over the black rocks, we suspect, are connected to her unarticu-
lated resentment that she is powerless, not just over rocks but over men, and
especially over her husband. Perhaps no fantasy is more disenchanted in

Chaucer than that of the power of courtly ladies in love—Criseyde, Dorigen, and others suffer in silence at the critical moments of their lives.

Suppression of the feminine and the female voice would not seem to be a problem in Dante's *Divine Comedy*, at least not in Purgatory or Paradise; but the reality of political relations in church and state means that, for Dante, the good that women might do is thwarted by the men who hold the seats of power, while the women stand on the sidelines or in the shadows. In her essay, Joan M. Ferrante provides a rich context for two passages in the *Comedy* (Purg.7.128, Par.6.133–35) in order to argue for the importance of four barely mentioned women of the House of Savoy. Mothered by a queen significantly named Beatrice, the four daughters of Raymond of Berengar, "ciascuna reina" (each a queen; Par.6.133), took active roles in contemporary affairs. These queens, together with their mother and other powerful women in thirteenth-century Europe, stand alongside the leading ideal women of the *Comedy*: St. Clare, Matelda, and Dante's Beatrice. While the latter speak for and, for the most part, represent spiritual ideals, the women in the shadows of Dante's poem remind us of women's familial, political, and diplomatic accomplishments—everything from managing property and finances while husbands were absent, to restoring, maintaining, and consolidating political power. And yet for all the achievements Dante's historical women can claim in terms of their "work for the cause of peace and empire," Ferrante suspects that Dante is suggesting that "the men undermined their efforts or failed to carry them through."

By providing us with new material by and about women who were politically powerful in Dante's time, Ferrante creates a rich historical context for our reading of the *Comedy*—a context that, at least in part, would have been immediately apparent to Dante's original audience—thus awakening us to some aspects of Dante's poem that are peculiar to his time and place. In the centuries that followed, in the flowering of Italian humanism across all the arts, contemporary writers and observers of that culture were using terms and concepts of one discipline to provide contexts for understanding others. Our last two essays in this book analyze specific instances of such translation across disciplines and modes of thought, as well as across time and cultures.

Joseph A. Dane traces the often contradictory, sometimes simply confusing, reception and adaptation of the theories of perspective developed in the Italian Renaissance. Starting with Alberti's formula in the fifteenth-century *De Pictura*, Dane reminds us that, while the author clearly admits to his borrowing and application of mathematic principles, "not as a mathematician but as a painter," Alberti's translation of those principles into the context of aesthetics was subsequently carried back into more practical scientific contexts, in manuals of architecture, for example. Other writers' applications and considerations, especially regarding curvilinearity, produced a wide variety of models and interpretations, often quite at odds with each other and not surprisingly reaching radically different judgments on the value of the models.

David Rosand brings the volume to a close by considering the discussion of painting in Castiglione's *Libro del Cortegiano* and its afterlife in a variety of early modern contexts. In Castiglione's dialogue, texts of classical antiquity and contemporary discourses drawn from both the workshop and literary pedagogy are deployed and rearranged, as Rosand demonstrates, to grant painting a noble place among the liberal arts. In the writings of the next generations, the high value accorded to art in Castiglione's text and the connections made there between painting and an idealized notion of civility constitute the framework within which works of visual art and the craft of the artist are appreciated and analyzed. Through the texts of Vasari and his lesser known contemporaries, the work of the visual artist—considered as creative process and as visual product—became a central constituent of Renaisssance aesthetic culture and, indeed, of the notion of culture itself. But Rosand's argument does not stop at this cultural conclusion, important as it is. We have long since learned to read Castiglione's book as something much more complex than "a mere book of manners"; now Rosand discovers in it the emergence of the language of visual culture itself, in what he calls "the clearest articulation of sensitivity to the *art* of painting from the High Renaissance." No other writer, Rosand argues, articulated with such critical precision the qualities that contemporaries recognized in Raphael and in the art of Raphael. In formulating those qualities as he does, Castiglione makes them appear with stunning clarity—the line, "una linea sola non stentata [a single, unforced line]," leaps forth as a miraculous achievement: simultaneously the trace of the artist's body, the signifier in his creation, and the sign and being of art itself. In that formulation, the act of human creativity receives its highest value.

The essays in this volume consider texts crossing both geographical and epistemological borders and situate them in multiple contexts of reception spanning over a thousand years. Yet they are all united, as Robert Hanning's own work has been united, by an engagement with a set of questions involving the place of artistry in culture and social life and by a complex methodology that attempts to elucidate that place by seeing it in multiple frames: texts never float free but come into being within a network of other texts and reading practices. Language, too, needs to be understood as a complex social transaction among different discourses in practical use in a polyglot world. Thus reading is always highly mediated; reading practices are historically constructed artifacts that change over time; and artistic production is always situated in an inexhaustible number of contexts—literary, social, cultural, and discursive. To examine these multiplicities by an act of reading, the essays in this volume directly follow Hanning's example, participate in conversation with his work, and in so doing, honor him on the occasion of his sixty-fifth birthday.

Notes

1. Michel de Certeau has addressed this same epistemological problem with regard to writing the religious history of the seventeenth century. See Michel de Certeau, *The Writing of History*, trans. Tom Conley (New York: Columbia University Press, 1988), 117–46.

2. Hegel's treatment of romance as pure fantasy is paradigmatic for some of the most significant literary theory of the twentieth century, including the work of Mihail Bakhtin, Georg Lukács, and Erich Auerbach. See G. W. F. Hegel, *Aesthetics: Lectures on Fine Art*, trans. T. M. Knox, 2 vols. (Oxford: Clarendon Press, 1975), 1:517–602, 2:1040–1113.

3. See especially "Discourse in the Novel," in M. M. Bakhtin, *The Dialogic Imagination: Four Essays*, trans. Caryl Emerson and Michael Holquist, ed. Michael Holquist, University of Texas Press Slavic Series, no. 1 (Austin: University of Texas Press, 1981).

4. Charles Muscatine, *Chaucer and the French Tradition* (Berkeley: University of California Press, 1957), 190.

5. "From EVA to AVE to Eglentyne and Alisoun: Chaucer's Insight into the Roles Women Play," *Signs* 2 (1977): 580–99.

6. "'Parlous Play': Diabolic Comedy in Chaucer's Canterbury Tales," in *Chaucerian Comedy*, ed. Jean Jost (New York: Garland, 1994), 303.

7. From the introduction to *Lapsarian Poetics: Coping with an Imperfect World in* The Decameron *and* The Canterbury Tales (nearing completion). We thank Robert Hanning for allowing us to quote from his work in progress.

8. Patricia Parker, "Virile Style," in *Premodern Sexualities*, ed. Louise Fradenburg, Carla Freccero, and Kathy Lavezzo (New York: Routledge, 1996).

I. THE PLACE OF HISTORY AND THE TIME OF ROMANCE

1

NICHOLAS HOWE

From Bede's World
to "Bede's World"

Few men can have spent more years or worked more hours on the same
spot than Bede did; and to me at least the site of the monastery at Jarrow,
where he lived and died, is one of the most moving things in England.

—R. W. Southern[1]

This study has at its center a site in Northumbria that has been known since at least the eighth century C.E. as Jarrow, or *Ingyruum* in Latin and *On Gyrwum* in Old English.[2] There Bede lived his life in a monastery until he died in 735; there in the late nineteenth century, Palmer's Shipyard prospered as one of the engines of British industrialism; and there during the depression years of the 1930s, unemployment was endemic after the shipyard was driven into insolvency by a man named McGowan. In 1936, two hundred seven unemployed men and women left from there on a march for London to protest against conditions on the Tyneside. Carrying banners reading "Jarrow Crusade," they were led by their local M.P., Ellen Wilkinson, who was known among the Geordies as "Wee Ellen" or "Red Ellen" for the color of her hair and her politics. She would later write her account of the place under the title *The Town That Was Murdered: The Life-Story of Jarrow*.[3] Years later in 1976, a journalist named Guy Waller who accompanied the marchers remembered tersely: "There was a saying in Jarrow, probably still is to this day, St Bede founded it, Sir Charles Mark Palmer built it and McGowan buggered it." [4] There too in Jarrow, in the 1990s, a historical recreation of various Anglo-Saxon buildings was established, not far from St. Paul's Church, and called "Bede's World." [5]

Throughout Bede's historiography runs an abiding concern with senses of place, whether conceived of as geography or topography. This claim may seem at first to run counter to the usual reason for venerating Bede as a writer, namely, his skill at shaping time to the demands of religious practice and historical narrative through both his work on the computus and his use of *anno domini* dating for the *Historia Ecclesiastica*.[6] His sense that time matters, that it must be shaped to a coherent and eschatologically meaningful order, that it must emplot the events it records—all this has made him seem like something of our contemporary as a historian. For unlike his immediate predecessors in the narrating of Christian history, such as Jordanes or Gregory of Tours, Bede writes with a chronology that is recognizably our own: his 449, 597, and 731 belong to the same continuum as does our 2004.[7] While we may evade or disguise this recognition by tagging our years C.E. rather than A.D., we also know that our choice of tag is finally less significant than is our use of the same rolling count of years. Indeed, C.E. is a convenient designation: it may refer to "Common Era," as standard usage has it, but it retains for a medievalist the figurative sense of "Christian Era."

The work of computus, and specifically the setting of a canonical date for the annual celebration of Easter, is most immediately a matter of reading time so that a liturgical calendar for the entire year can be fixed, then promulgated, and finally observed.[8] Yet the reason for setting this date has everything to do with Christendom as a place occupied by believers who maintain themselves as a community through the simultaneous observance of the same set of practices. That the great religious controversy recorded in the *Historia Ecclesiastica* should center on methods for calculating the Easter date is neatly emblematic of Bede's sense of place; for it demonstrates that questions of time acquire their significance—and also their answers—within the literal and cognitive realms of place. Put more simply, the Synod of Whitby, a debate about which custom should be accepted for dating Easter, became significant in Bede's telling because it is a question that had to be settled with reference to the newly converted region that would come to be known as *Engla lond*.[9] Whether the practice to be followed should be of Irish or Roman provenance became a matter of dispute because the region in question had not previously been Christian. A theological argument about the computus thus became a political matter. The controversy at Whitby arose because conversion in the early Middle Ages was comprehended through the measure of place: that the inhabitants of a city or tribal kingdom or geographical region had entered Christendom by accepting the faith.

Bede's account of the debate at Whitby establishes that the most compelling argument for the Roman practice—as advanced by that party's spokesman, the priest Wilfrid—was based on geography. As Wilfrid argued against the Irish position advocated by Colman, he cited the use of the Roman practice not just in Rome or even in Italy or Gaul but virtually everywhere else in Christendom:

> hoc Africam, Asiam, Aegyptum, Greciam et omnem orbem, quacumque Christi ecclesia diffusa est, per diuersas nationes et linguas uno ac non diuerso temporis ordine geri conperimus.[10]

> We learned that it was observed at one and the same time in Africa, Asia, Egypt, Greece, and throughout the whole world, wherever the Church of Christ is scattered, amid various nations and languages.

Against this uniformity of practice, Wilfrid can cite as exceptions only the Picts and Britons, who alone in all the world follow an unorthodox custom because, as he says, they live in the two remotest islands in the ocean or, more exactly, not even everywhere in them (*cum quibus de duabus ultimis Oceani insulis, et his non totis*). And from there, he adds scornfully and decisively for his argument, they resist the practice of the rest of the world: "contra totum orbem stulto labore pugnant." Wilfrid functions, in this debate, as the spokesman for Roman orthodoxy and thus as the mouthpiece for Bede's ecclesiastical politics and geography. His is the voice charged with rejoining those distant islands and their people to the center of the Christian world by establishing the proper practice for dating Easter.

Demarcating the world as he knew it, designating it as Christian or pagan terrain, as converted or yet-to-be converted, is fundamental to Bede's sense of his work as a historian and as a biblical commentator in the service of religious orthodoxy.[11] Bede offers us the necessary facts by which to appreciate his concern with place in a brief autobiographical statement that concludes his *Historia Ecclesiastica*. There he demonstrates that a sense of place need not depend on wide travel, as is thought necessary in our time, but rather can be based on a contemplative regimen by which the observer detaches himself from the immediate circumstances of physical reality:

> Qui natus in territorio eiusdem monasterii, cum essem annorum VII, cura propinquorum datus sum educandus reuerentissimo abbati Benedicto, ac deinde Ceolfrido, cunctumque ex eo tempus uitae in eiusdem monasterii habitatione paragens, omnem meditandis scripturis operam dedi, atque inter obseruantiam disciplinae regularis, et cotidianam cantandi in ecclesia curam, semper aut discere aut docere aut scribere dulce habui.[12]

> I was born in the territory of this monastery. When I was seven years of age I was, by the care of my kinsmen, put into the charge of the reverend Abbot Benedict and then of Ceolfrith, to be educated. From then on I have spent all my life in this monastery, applying myself entirely to the study of the Scriptures; and, amid the observance of the discipline of the Rule and the daily task of singing in the church, it has always been my delight to learn or to teach or to write.

This passage has customarily been taken as evidence for Bede's devotion to the Benedictine ideal of *stabilitas loci,* and so undoubtedly he intended it to be read. But he did so in the fullest sense: that ideal meant staying in a place so that one could better contemplate the mysteries of God's Creation as revealed in Scripture and providential history, and then write about them in commentaries and histories and lives of abbots and saints. *Stabilitas loci* meant focusing on the essential matter of place by abjuring the distractions of travel or aimless wandering in the mapped world.[13] As proof that he had honored this ideal throughout his life, Bede added a list of his writings to this autobiographical sketch. Indeed, that bibliography is his autobiography, the record of a lifetime spent in monastic scholarship.

Bede says that he lived "in this monastery" (*in eiusdem monasterii habitatione*) since he was a young boy and offers a general sense of its location when he speaks, in the previous sentence, of belonging to a "monasterii beatorum apostolorum Petri et Pauli, quod est ad Uiuraemuda et Ingy-ruum." That he does not further locate Wearmouth and Jarrow for an au-dience not familiar with Northumbrian geography is no mystery but simply the economy of a good writer who relies on his readers to remember a pas-sage that appeared a few chapters earlier in Book Five. In his account of the Pictish king Nechtan's desire to convert to Christianity, Bede embeds the site of his home monastery into the political and ecclesiastical geography of his narrative:

> Siquidem misit legatarios ad uirum uenerabilem Ceolfridum, abbatem monasterii beatorum apostolorum Petri et Pauli quod est ad ostium Uiuri amnis, et iuxta amnem Tina in loco qui uocatur Ingyruum. . . .[14]

> So he sent messengers to the venerable Ceolfrith, abbot of the monas-tery of the apostles St. Peter and St. Paul, one part of which stands at the mouth of the river Wear and the other part near the river Tyne in a place called Jarrow.

Bede's message here could hardly be clearer. His monastery was the recipient of Nechtan's request because it was named for two great apostles, because it observed Roman practices, because it was the seat of a great missionary abbot, and because it was located on the near frontier between Christian En-gland and pagan Pictland. Or, more implicitly, because Jarrow and Wear-mouth, as centers of apostolic missions, were becoming a new Rome set at the end of the road that led from the papal city to Northumbria.

We know that Bede did travel in Northumbria on rare occasions to gather material for his *Historia Ecclesiastica;* he went as far afield as a day or two's journey to such religious centers as Lindisfarne and York to examine documents and interview those who had known, or known reliably about, the heroic pioneers of the Northumbrian conversions. But he otherwise showed none of the desire or willingness for travel that marked his predecessors at Jarrow and Wearmouth. Most notably, Bede was utterly unlike Benedict Biscop who seemed to have journeyed ceaselessly between Rome and the Continent so that he could bring back books and other necessary materials to set a monastic culture firmly in place in Northumbria.[15] Bede, by contrast, reminds one of nothing so much as the Sinologist mentioned in passing in one of John LeCarré's novels: the man who knew everything there was to know about China but who had never crossed the English Channel and who was, in the world of espionage, considered all the more expert for maintaining that distance.

The portrait of Bede I am suggesting—the man who understood the importance of place in history and exegesis but who knew only one place in his adult life—has its origins in Robert Hanning's revelatory *Vision of History in Early Britain.* Writing of Benedictine monasticism in the time of Bede as "the great paradox of Christian Europe," Hanning ponders further how it was that "Britain, an island far from the traditional center of European civilization, should witness a vigorous rebirth of Christian social ideals and their artistic expression."[16] For Hanning, the answer lies largely in the wide-ranging work of conversion effected first by Roman missionaries on the island of Britain and then later by missionaries from that same island who ventured back to the Continent.[17] Missionary work in the centuries following the Age of Migration across northern Europe was of necessity defined as movement through space, as turning specific places from pagan error to Christian truth. It was concerned less with the saving of individual souls than with the winning of regions and their populations. If, by a more skeptical reading, missionary Christendom was a kind of deferred or even deformed version of Roman empire building, in which pope superseded emperor and politics morphed into religion, the means for measuring the success of both remained geographical: how many people in how much territory does one control?

Bede's sense of geographical history, of narrative deployed through place, must also be read as a legacy of Roman empire building. That sense of the world was tied directly to the fact that Bede lived on a distant and isolated island. Ultimately, Bede's knowledge of geography derived from Pliny the Elder's *Naturalis Historia,* though it was mediated and complicated by having reached him through a series of Christian writers. Hanning's phrase—"an island far from the traditional center of European civilization"—encapsulates the vision of Britain within that long tradition of geographical study. Bede offers a particularly memorable expression of that tradition in the opening sentences of the first book of his *Historia Ecclesiastica:*

> Brittania Oceani insula, cui quondam Albion nomen fuit, inter septentrionem et occidentem locata est, Germaniae Galliae Hispaniae, maximis Europae partibus, multo interuallo aduersa. Quae per milia passuum DCCC in boream longa, latitudinis habet milia CC, exceptis dumtaxat prolixioribus diuersorum promontoriorum tractibus, quibus efficitur ut curcuitus eius quadragies octies LXXV milia conpleat.[18]

Britain, once called Albion, is an island of the ocean and lies to the
north-west, being opposite Germany, Gaul, and Spain, which form the
greater part of Europe, though at a considerable distance from them. It
extends 800 miles to the north, and is 200 miles broad, save only where
several promontories stretch out further and, counting these, the whole
circuit of the coastline covers 4,875 miles.

By beginning in this way, by writing in Latin to place the island in relation to
the Continent, Bede pays homage to his predecessor who was at once natural
historian, civil servant, and admiral of the Roman fleet. Indeed, Bede's key
phrase here—*inter septentrionem et occidentem*—derives directly from the
Naturalis Historia and is the position of someone looking, like Pliny or Isidore of Seville, from the Mediterranean toward Britain. Bede opens his *Historia* with this vantage point to identify where Britain/Albion/England
appears on the mental map of Christendom because that is the great theme
of his work. Within a few chapters of Book I, Bede will shift his vantage
point and write as one looking from the island south towards Rome and the
remains of the old empire rather than (as in his opening) looking north. Had
he opened with this other perspective, his first sentence would have spoken
instead of Britain in terms of what lies to its southeast. Bede's world is thus,
at least at the start of his *Historia,* shaped by a consciousness of Rome, seat
of empire and papacy, as the center of the world inhabited by human beings.
    From reading Pliny, from accepting the orientation of a Latin geogra-
phy that took Rome as its vantage point, Bede knew that he lived in the far
north. That knowledge was not simply a neutral matter relating to the points
of the compass. For it came to Bede not as a bundle of facts and names but
as an implicit theory of geographical representation in which his home island appeared as somewhere like the back of beyond. After describing the
Rhine delta, Pliny writes:

Ex adverso huius situs Britannia insula clara Graecis nostrisque moni-
mentis inter septentrionem et occidentem iacet, Germaniae, Galliae,
Hispaniae, multo maximis Europae partibus magno intervallo adversa.
Albion ipsi nomen fuit, cum Britanniae vocarentur omnes de quibus
mox paulo dicemus.[19]

Opposite to this region lies the island of Britain, famous in the Greek
records and in our own; it lies to the north-west, facing, across a wide
channel, Germany, Gaul and Spain, countries which constitute by far

the greater part of Europe. It was itself named Albion, while all the islands about which we shall soon speak were called the Britains.

Pliny's reference to Britain lying to the northwest follows, quite strictly, from his cartographic exposition in Books III and IV of the *Naturalis Historia;* in them, he organizes geography as a coherent and decipherable body of knowledge by constructing a catalogue that begins with the Straits of Gibraltar and then moves place by contiguous place in a predictable direction through the remainder of the known world until it reaches, as here, Britain.[20] Beyond lies only the remoter region of Thule, which is, for Pliny, less of the northern world than it is *beyond* the northern world. Pliny's cartographic sequence with Britain at its virtual end does suggest a remoteness that comes with being located on the far frontier of empire. For Bede, that meant his monastery at Jarrow and Wearmouth lay at the end of the long road north from Rome.

The setting of Britain in the far northwest that we find in Pliny is echoed in Isidore of Seville's *Etymologiae,* where he explains that Britain is an island in the ocean and lies across the water from Gaul and Spain:

> Brittania Oceani insula interfuso mari toto orbe divisa, a vocabulo suae gentis cognominata. Haec adversa Galliarum parte ad prospectum Hispaniae sita est.[21]

> Britain, an island in the ocean, cut off from all the rest of the world by the intervening sea, has taken its name from that of its people. It is situated opposite the territory of the Gauls and faces Spain.

That Isidore uses Pliny's placement of Britain is noteworthy in this context because his *Etymologiae* served as the essential cultural encyclopedia of the early medieval west, and nowhere more so than in Anglo-Saxon England.[22] Put another way, reading Pliny's geography through Isidore was another form of religious conversion: the map of the pagan empire could also serve the purposes of a Christian exegete and historian.

The crucial next stage in the worldview that Bede inherited from his predecessors may be located in Gildas' *De Excidio Britanniae.* Writing in a sixth-century Britain marked by warfare between the Christian Celts resident on the island and the pagan Anglo-Saxons invading it, Gildas endows this element of northern remoteness with a theological and moral resonance that will be registered throughout Bede's *Historia*. From the north looking south, Gildas says:

> Brittannia insula in extremo ferme orbis limite circium occidentemque versus divina, ut dicitur, statera terrae totius ponderatrice librata ab Africo boriali propensius tensa axi. . . .[23]

> The island of Britain lies virtually at the end of the world, towards the west and the north-west. Poised in the divine scales that (we are told) weigh the whole earth, it stretches from the south-west towards the northern pole.

The sacralizing of geography in this passage takes a more explicit form as Gildas tells of the first conversion of the British during the reign of Tiberius:

> Interea glaciali frigore rigenti insulae et velut longiore terrarum secessu soli visibili non proximae verus ille non de firmamento solum temporali sed de summa etiam caelorum arce tempora cuncta excedente universo orbi praefulgidum sui coruscum ostendens radios suos primum indulget, id est sua praecepta, Christus.[24]

> Meanwhile, to an island numb with chill ice and far removed, as in a remote nook of the world, from the visible sun, Christ made a present of his rays (that is, his precepts), Christ the true sun, which shows its dazzling brilliance to the entire earth, not from the temporal firmament merely, but from the highest citadel of heaven, that goes beyond all time.

With these passages, Gildas changed radically the way in which those on the island, whether Britons or Anglo-Saxons, looked south; for he established that looking south toward Rome and the Holy Land was the way to divine illumination. More historically, looking in that direction was to locate in Rome and its empire the source for the conversion of the Britons.[25]

Gildas knew he was in the north because he had read Roman authorities; he knew he belonged to their north, a position he exploited with great force to animate his jeremiad. Indeed, he recognized that it was entirely to his rhetorical advantage to occupy the northern edge of Latin, Mediterranean Christianity because it was a place of peril, just as he also had his own sense of north as the place whence came the barbarian invaders. In his historicized and sacralized geography, the north functions as a shifting signifier: it is, at once, Britain, the place of benighted belief; and also Germania, the source of danger for those who live to the south. Even the north, it would seem, needs to demonize its own form of the north.

More generally, as these passages in Gildas reveal, the creation of a British and then (through Bede) of an Anglo-Saxon geographical identity was calibrated on accepting Rome's vantage point. The Britons, and later the English, learned to see themselves as the Romans saw them: on the northwest, far off, in the regions of cold and spiritual darkness. That Gildas was a Briton, and very much neither Angle nor Saxon, reminds us that ethnicity was not a determining factor for those who saw their native island as being on the northern edge of the world. Instead, it was religion and its attendant culture that gave these writers (whether by origin Celtic or Germanic) this sense of northern isolation. The perspective of north looking south belonged to those who were Christian in their faith and Latin in their learning. The continuity of that identity from the sixth to the eleventh century, across enormous political and linguistic changes, explains how it is that Wulfstan in his *Sermo ad Anglos* of 1014 could invoke Gildas in a manner that reads as all but inevitable.[26] Both Gildas and Wulfstan occupied the same Christian north because—and there is no paradox here—they both feared the incursions of outsiders from a north that lay beyond. If north was the compass point from which Anglo-Saxons learned to expect danger, it was also the region in which they would experience the peril of falling into sin and thus of violating their covenant with God, as was proven in another narrative context by Isaiah 14:12 ff. on the fall of Satan. North was not a fixed point in this turning world. The long duration for that sense of the north in Anglo-Saxon England, from Gildas to Wulfstan, owes a great deal to the canonizing influence of Bede's *Historia Ecclesiastica*.

The *Historia* begins with the perspective of Roman geography that sets Britain in the northwest, but it then shifts to assume the perspective of the Anglo-Saxon gaze looking back at Rome. Where this shift of vantage from Rome to Britain is first registered in the *Historia* can be debated, although I would argue that it has certainly been accomplished no later than the concluding sentence of the sixth chapter of Book One. Here, after relating the persecutions of Christians led by Diocletian and Maximianus Herculius, Bede writes: "Denique etiam Brittaniam tum plurima confessionis Deo deuotae gloria sublimauit. [In fact Britain also attained to the great glory of bearing faithful witness to God.]"[27] Bede can only claim Britain as a site of martyrdom by looking south toward the source of the persecutions in Rome and Constantinople. Or, put another way, Bede manifests his vantage as a writer not merely by describing events in Britain but also by tracing them to their causes. To understand what happens in the world of Britain one must look south.

Bede's technique for opening the *Historia*—his choice to look at the island from Rome—may be compared anachronistically but usefully to a filmmaker's establishing shot that begins from afar and then moves in to the actual location of the film. In each case, the opening establishes the relation of the work's setting to the world elsewhere; and in each, once that relation has been established, the *auteur* can shift point of view so that what had been the object of the gaze becomes in turn the vantage of sight. Using a different theoretical idiom, Uppinder Mehan, in dialogue with David Townsend, makes a similar point: "What intrigues me is how Bede is able to represent himself, while adopting the perspective of the metropolitan center, so as not to be entirely abject."[28]

Bede could adopt this perspective without rendering himself abject because he understood, first, that Christian history was continuing to spread outward from the Roman metropole to the far reaches of Britain, and because he understood, further, that it was his life's work to contribute to that missionary work, as biblical exegete and expert in computus, and later as historian. Being on the periphery was proof for Bede of his lifework's importance. If in a moment of doubt he ever thought of himself as abject, he had only to think of one of the great heroes of his *Historia*. For Gregory the Great had wished, before he became pope, to dedicate himself to converting the far frontier of Britain and was persuaded to remain in Rome only by the intervention of the city's inhabitants who would not allow him to leave. As Bede notes, therefore, one of Gregory's first acts as pope was to send Augustine of Canterbury and his missionary companions to further the work he himself could not accomplish.[29] Being in the metropole was, by the logic of the missionary's calling, to be peripheral rather than central because no work remained to be done there.

This vision of the world as demarcated by the places of conversion has its origins in the New Testament, especially the Gospels, the narratives of Christ's life and the deeds of the apostles. That vision finds its fullest expression in Bede's corpus in, predictably enough, what is arguably his least original work and one of his earliest (probably 702–3 A.D.). His *De Locis*

Sanctis is not so much a traveler's account or itinerary as it is a handbook for the reader of holy scripture. Derived from such earlier authorities as Adamnan, Bede's Latin work surveys the Holy Land to give a sense of the hagiographical as well as topographical reality of the place. Taken in the abstract, as a disembodied text, it could serve any reader of Latin anywhere in Christendom because it has no vantage point of its own; it does not tell one how to get to the Holy Land from England or anywhere else, but instead presumes one is already there, as a traveler, whether actual or readerly, a pilgrim or an exegete. In that respect, it bears a striking resemblance to tourist guidebooks of our time that have no concern with how their readers get to Bangkok or London or Buenos Aires: all that matters is that they are in Bangkok or London or Buenos Aires. In another respect, however, Bede's *De Locis Sanctis* is utterly unlike a tourist guidebook of our time because its assumption that its readers are on site, gazing at the places and buildings it describes, is a kind of exegetical fiction. That is, readers of Bede's *De Locis Sanctis* are more likely to be in the Holy Land because they are reading scripture than because they have made a pilgrimage.

Indeed, much of what makes the *De Locis Sanctis* so interesting as a text today, despite its derivative nature, is that it should work so hard to evoke the physical setting of the Holy Land. Bede is at great pains, if only as a redactor of inherited material, to make the Holy Land seem the world where Christ and his followers walked; to evoke it as a landscape of rock and vegetation, rather than simply a circuit of memorable religious sites. Bede's work is particularly noteworthy for its description of Holy Land topography; it summons up the physical actuality of the place for those who will never make the journey there in person. Thus it says, for instance, of the territory surrounding Jerusalem:

> Circa Hierusalem aspera ac montuosa cernuntur loca. Hinc quoque septentrionem uersus usque ad Arimathiam terra petrosa et aspera per interualla monstratur, ualles quoque spinosae usque ad Thamnicam regionem patentes. Ad Caesaream uero Palestinae ab Aelia quamuis aliqua repperiantur angusta et breuia aspera loca, praecipue tamen planities camporum interpositis oliuetis. Distant autem LXXV milibus passuum. Longitudo uero terrae repromissionis a Dan usque Bersabee tenditur spatio CLXV milium, ab Ioppe usque Bethlehem XLVI milibus.[30]

> Around Jerusalem one can see rough and mountainous places. North of here, as far as Arimathea, one can also see rocky and rough land in

places. The valleys which extend up the region of Thamna are also full of thorns. But between Aelia and Caeserea of Palestine, there are mostly level plains with olive groves here and there, although one may occasionally see short stretches of rough terrain. Now Aelia and Caeserea are 75 miles apart. In fact, the length of the promised land from Dan to Beersheba is 165 miles; 46 miles from Joppa to Bethlehem.

The operative verb of this passage—*cernuntur*—participates in the genre of the work: it is meant to endow readers with the sense of vision that would enable them to transcend the distance between where they read and where they read about. In that same way, Bede includes ground plans for various sites in the Holy Land such as the Lord's Tomb, the Church of Golgotha, the Church of Constantine, and the church atop Mt. Zion where the Last Supper was held and where Mary died.[31] In this way, readers can follow his descriptions of architecture and visualize the spatial relationships that are so difficult to register in prose. Some historians of English cartography count these ground plans as the earliest surviving maps from that nation; ironically if appropriately, given Bede's standing as the founder of English historiography, these are images of places far distant from that island.[32]

The purpose of this passage, and many others like it in *De Locis Sanctis*, is not so much to aid in the exegesis of a specific scriptural quotation as it is to make the distant and, for northern readers, exotic terrain around Jerusalem part of their spiritual landscape. To read the Bible in a responsive and thoughtful manner requires this grounding in landscape, this specifying of olive trees and thorns, mountains and valleys, as well as the designation of distances in terms that would enable an English reader to measure the sacred landscape mentally. That the Roman mile could serve as an accurate and comprehensible unit of measure for the distance between Dan and Beersheba, as well as it would for the distance between Jarrow and Lindisfarne, is another legacy of the Roman Empire.

Bede's *De Locis Sanctis* opens with Jerusalem and then proceeds in an orderly fashion outward to surrounding regions such as Bethlehem and Jericho, then Mount Tabor and Damascus, and finally Alexandria and Constantinople. The inclusion of these last two cities may seem a bit surprising; but they belong in the work because, as Bede explains, they were among the sites visited by the Gallic bishop Arculf who later, through the force of a contrary wind, found himself beached on the island of Britain. There he dictated his account of the holy places to Adamnan and thereby became the source for Bede's little book.[33] That Arculf found himself stranded in Britain would not have seemed the result of a malevolent nature to Bede but rather the workings of a divine providence intent on enlarging the knowledge of the world available to those who inhabited that cold and northern island.

In this way, Bede's *De Locis Sanctis* stands as the textual equivalent of a pilgrimage object such as the "Reliquary Box with Stones from the Holy Sites of Palestine," one of the treasures of the Vatican Museum. This sixth- or seventh-century wooden box, measuring 9 ½ x 7 ¼ x 1 ⅝ inches, is decorated with a cycle of pictures showing scenes from Christ's life and contains actual stones from the holy sites where these same scenes took place. It is, quite literally, an object of memory designed to bring the terrain and history of the Holy Land back to wherever its pilgrim-owner returned home from his journey. No wonder that Diane De Drazia should say: "This painted box, though modest in scale, is one of the most evocative and compelling objects to have survived from early Palestine, indeed from the whole of the early Christian world."[34] Bede's *De Locis Sanctis* is, in this analogy, a textual reliquary that closes the distance between the original center of Christian belief and the distant north. His text is a guide for diminishing the remoteness of the island, and thus its distance from the warming rays of Christ the sun. When read knowingly as the work of Bede, and in the company of his *Historia,* the *De Locis Sanctis* acquires a precise place of origin because its authority resides in it being recognized as the work of that English scholar. For those who turned to the *De Locis Sanctis* after the *Historia Ecclesiastica,* this tour of where Jesus and his apostles walked would have read as the record of a writer looking south to render it vivid to those in the north.

A work like *De Locis Sanctis* may not be a masterpiece or even particularly original, but it nonetheless has its place in the world of Bede's writing because it supplies the information that every reader of the Bible would need—but that only a traveler could be expected to know firsthand. That it surveys a distant landscape explains its value and also suggests the reason why Bede should offer relatively little material of a similar nature in his *Historia Ecclesiastica,* beyond its opening chapter. For the part of the world surveyed there would not have been at all exotic or distant to his Anglo-Saxon readers. To them, it would instead have been homeground, native soil, the site of their own religious history and identity. It was a place of elm and hawthorn, not olive and thorn. Placing the *De Locis Sanctis* beside the *Historia Ecclesiastica* demonstrates how the demands of genre affect the ways in which Bede writes a sense of place. The history of his own island requires less topographical information than does his account of the Holy Land; the account of the Holy Land requires less global positioning than does the history of his own island.

These differences in the handling of place should not be allowed, however, to obscure a fundamental aspect of Bede's geography, regardless of which part of the world he surveys. For a writer like Bede, cartography is essentially a narrative rather than a visual technique.[35] He locates places not by pointing to them on an illustrative map but by setting them in an ordered sequence beginning with a well-defined site and then moving outward. This technique is not original to Bede; he inherited it, as I have suggested, from the tradition exemplified by Pliny's *Naturalis Historia*. Places for Bede, therefore, have no absolute location as fixed by longitude and latitude; they exist instead in relation to each other. To tell where a place is, one must in this cartography tell the sequence of places that lead to it. Or, in the idiom of our jokes about places, you can only get there from here by going through all of those other places.

With this idiom comes the possibility of narrative. A sequence of places is not for Bede simply a list of names, such as appear on a modern subway map. They contain instead an implicit story that must be interpreted by the reader. Perhaps the most striking expression of this belief in Bede's work appears in a letter he wrote in about 716 to Acca, bishop of nearby Hexham in Northumbria. Acca had turned to Bede for assistance in reading the list of resting places occupied by the Israelites as they made their exodus from Egypt into the promised land (Numbers 33:1–49). Acca seems to have wondered if there was a meaningful relation between the forty-two resting places and the forty-two years of the journey: did this mean that each was occupied by the Israelites for a year? Bede explains that there was no such neat symmetry and then turns to the question that intrigues him:

Ubi diligentius intuendum quare legislator tanta solertia trium annorum conscripto catalogo reliquas maluerit praeterire silentio, ita ut tanto temporum vel potius saeculorum spatio distincta mansionum loca sub contextu continuae narrationis quasi mox subinvicem succedentia connectat: Egressique de Hebrona castra metati sunt in Asiongaber. Inde profecti venerunt in desertum Sin, haec est Cades. Egressi de Cades, castra metati sunt in monte Hor.[36]

Here we ought to consider more carefully why the lawgiver [Moses] who had so diligently composed a catalogue of three of the years preferred to pass over the rest in silence, in such a way that he fastened the distinct locations of the resting-places of such greater periods of time (or rather ages) into the form of a continuous narrative, as though they were following in turn, one right after another: And departing from Abronah they encamped at Ezion-geber. Going on from there, they came into the desert of Zin (that is, Kadesh). Departing from Kadesh, they encamped at Mount Hor.

Bede's reading of this passage in Numbers as a series of place-names that form a narrative is an obvious instance of narrative cartography, such as I have traced elsewhere in his work as well as in that of his predecessors. We can find strikingly similar instances in Anglo-Saxon texts, such as the itinerary of Bishop Sigeric's journey in the 990s from Rome to the English Channel that appears in British Library Cotton Tiberius B. v. along with much other geographical material.[37]

Bede's reading of Numbers is, however, notable for being foregrounded so explicitly, for being (in our idiom) so precisely theorized within the larger context of biblical hermeneutics. Under the pressure of doing exegesis, of instructing a superior in the ecclesiastical hierarchy, Bede sets out a means for understanding places so that they form a sequence within providential history. The passage in Numbers is not a jumbled list of names from a badly read map; instead, it contains the great biblical story of the flight from oppression and entrance into the chosen land. That Numbers 33 should have produced so theorized a reading of its geography is not at all surprising, for rarely does a sense of place so underlie both the literal and the allegorical Christian readings of a biblical passage as does this written map of the Exodus. Nowhere in his letter to Acca does Bede explicitly relate this passage and its larger context of the Israelites' migration to the ancestral experience of his own people. To have done so would probably have taken him, as far as we can judge, beyond the terms of Acca's original query. But one cannot help remembering that the great mythmaker of the Anglo-Saxon migration was none other than Bede in his *Historia Ecclesiastica*.[38]

Place matters in Bede's writing as the setting for history, though not simply in the obvious sense of being the location where events happen over the generations. More crucially, place becomes setting in Bede's work because it allows him to contain the layers of the past that he must register to achieve his ends as historian and exegete. Place becomes a device for ordering narrative because it enables the writer to establish the necessary relation between events from different periods. Put most reductively, a sense of place allows the historian to contain the vagaries of chronology within the framework of a fixed, identifiable location. That sense of place can be demarcated in various forms, depending on the work that must be done. For exegetical geography, Bede follows the path that Jesus and His Apostles walked. For the history of the *gens anglorum*, Bede works within an island territory circumscribed by the sea. He thus describes his most famous work as *Historiam ecclesiasticam nostrae insulae ac gentis in libris V*,[39] and he is careful to specify in its second sentence the measure of that island's circumference.

By a certain reckoning glance, Bede's world now survives as eleven acres of recreated Anglo-Saxon structures in Jarrow on the south bank of the Tyne. The site is a short walk from St. Paul's Church, once part of the monastery where Bede lived his adult life. For those versed in the history of several different eras, this is hallowed ground. The site of "Bede's World" is entered through a visitor center which has, to quote the official brochure, "paved courtyard, central atrium and pool, reflecting the Continental style of architecture."[40] With its light-colored stucco finish and design reminiscent of Rome, this building is meant to suggest the Mediterranean world that was home to the missionaries who ventured north to convert the Angles and Saxons.[41] The modern visitor thus enters a recreated Anglo-Saxon village through the portal of Roman culture, a telling allusion to the importance of Bede as local hero, but also an acknowledgment that the Anglo-Saxons were themselves practiced in looking south toward Rome. Or, to put it in different terms, the Mediterranean style of this building is meant to establish the seriousness of the historical project: "Bede's World" will not be a fantasy theme park of the Dark Ages with blue-faced warriors and wizards chanting spells. In this vision of Bede's world, there is nothing pagan.

The recreated village is surrounded by a high earthen wall planted with trees that will in time provide a kind of wooded barrier separating the site from its immediate surroundings. The buildings inside the wall are recreations based on serious archaeological research and include a timber hall, a monastic cell, a bakehouse, and several animal shelters and barns.[42] The grounds are planted with various crops that would have been cultivated in eighth-century England: grains such as spelt, emmer, and barley; vegetables such as onions, radishes, garlic, parsnips, cabbages, and turnips; as well as useful plants such as woad and medicinal herbs. As the information sheet distributed at the site explains: "On the farm we keep the following primitive breeds of animals: Greylag geese; Bantams; Dexter cattle; Pigs; Goats; Sheep including Soay, Hebridean, North Ronaldsay, Shetland, Herdwick, Portland and Manx Loghtan breeds. Apart from the goats these are all close in size and colouration to the animals that would have been kept by the Anglo-Saxons for wool, eggs, meat and leather."[43] Another telling measure of authenticity is the aroma of manure, for the site is not sanitized as are most recreated farm villages in the United States.

On the earthen wall at its northern point, that is, where it is closest to the Tyne, stands a monumental cross made in 1996 – 97 by Keith Ashford. Not an exact copy of any surviving Anglo-Saxon monumental cross, it is a pastiche of their typical elements: biblical images, vine scrolls, beasts, an archer. Ashford's cross also contains an image that would have been as puzzling to the Anglo-Saxons as some of those on the Ruthwell Cross are to us today: the figure of "a welder at work on a boat keel." This image is a quiet acknowledgment that the setting of "Bede's World" is not eighth-century Northumbria but a parcel of twentieth-century "derelict industrial land." For as you stand today on that earthen wall near Ashford's cross, you look out at one of the most industrialized landscapes ever created by human beings. In one direction, there is a large tank-farm holding petrochemicals; in another, there are large yellow construction cranes looming over the replica cross. Rows of electrical pylons with their high-tension lines tower overhead. Across the River Don, along the eastern edge of "Bede's World," is a vast parking lot packed with new Nissan automobiles from a nearby factory that are waiting to be loaded onto cargo ships for export. Beyond, on the horizon, you can see the outlines of huge shipyards and collieries along the River Tyne. This is an industrial landscape of coal and iron, of forging metal into ships that made nineteenth-century Britain the greatest empire Europe had known since the fall of Rome. In its time, through World War I, it was one of the most prosperous areas of industrial England, with skilled and good-paying jobs. Most of those who lived in Jarrow worked in Palmer's Shipyard or depended on it indirectly for their livelihoods.

Looking at the landscape today from atop the embankment at "Bede's World" can seem at first utterly disconcerting. For what is this bucolic village doing amid a landscape of industrial decline and human suffering? Modern gestures, such as adding a welder making a boat to the replica cross or displaying a mural of the Jarrow Crusade in the museum at "Bede's World," seem only to exaggerate the incongruity. If the site of "Bede's World" is geographically correct, its surroundings seem so utterly alien as to destroy any possibility of authenticity. How can the history of twelve hundred years ago be understood on this site? A monument to the passing of British industrialism, to the loss of a working-class culture of skilled craft unions — that seems far more appropriate for this setting. By contrast, "Bede's World" would seem better sited anywhere in the Northumbrian countryside, perhaps within walking distance of Lindisfarne or Hexham.

Or so the site seemed to me as I wandered around it on an overcast day in May 2000. There were very few visitors there, so I could photograph the village without people obscuring the scene. After a while, it became something of a challenge to photograph the various parts of the village in ways that would visually echo the surrounding industrial landscape. Thus, a round hut of wattle and daub could be seen as having the same outline as the petrochemical tank behind it, and Ashford's cross looked stunning in profile as it soared upward amid a forest of yellow cranes and electrical pylons. These visual jokes were my way of deconstructing whatever pretensions "Bede's World" might have had to historical authenticity.

Sometimes, though, the scholar's purism misses the point. As I talked with a man tending the grounds, another way of thinking about "Bede's World" emerged. After telling me about the work that remained to be done on the site, he added that he had grown up nearby as the son of a shipyard worker on the Tyne. He spoke about a pedestrian tunnel beneath the river that came out a short distance away in Jarrow; it was built so workers could cross over to the shipyards from Newcastle. It had, he said, the longest wooden escalators in the world, and workers were practiced at shooting their bicycles off them as they reached the top. In the middle of that replica Anglo-Saxon village, the history that seemed most intensely alive to me at the moment belonged to the earlier twentieth century. Even though I could walk in five or ten minutes to St. Paul's Church with its eighth-century chancel, the Age of Bede seemed far distant. But the site released in my mind another play of time. That a place could hold in suspension two radically different moments in British history separated by twelve hundred years — agricultural village and industrial landscape — taught a way to think about Bede's world. For he traced in his *Historia Ecclesiastica* a cultural shift as profound as that from village to shipyard, though it took only a century or so. As he recorded the transition in Britain from pagan to Christian, Bede set his history in place.

To argue that Northumbria has some essentialist claim on history as its defining quality in both the eighth and the twentieth centuries would push the point of this study too far. Yet as one reads writers trying to define the character of contemporary northern England, such a claim or one very like it appears regularly and acquires a certain plausibility. The scriptwriter Alan Plater remarks, in a searching essay entitled "The Drama of the North-East": "Memory becomes history becomes legend, and writers are the stewards in charge of the process. In the North-East, we have long memories and a massive burden of history." [44] His frame of reference is meant to include writers of the last seventy years or so, but to speak in this geographical setting of "long memories and a massive burden of history" is also to invoke Bede. We can find similar ideas in the opening paragraph of a more theorized essay by Stuart Rawnsley on "Constructing 'The North': Space and a Sense of Place": "It [the North of England] is a reified landscape which encapsulates various rhetorical interpretations of the past and the present, of classes and cultures, and of geographical and topological features of a large area of England. No other region has such an intensified 'sense of place.'" [45] With a few minor adjustments of idiom, such as specifying "Northumbria" and replacing "classes and cultures" with "religions and tribal regions," this passage would certainly not have puzzled Bede. He might even have enjoyed its heavily Latinate diction.

If there is an abiding sense of the north as a historically distinct place, as Plater and Rawnsley suggest in very different ways, it owes more than a little to the example set by Bede. For he is always known there, and rarely anywhere else, as St. Bede. That honorific, bestowed by his native region and not by distant Rome, suggests that if he is to be considered the patron saint of anything, it should be of the ways human beings locate their history through a sense of place.

Notes

An early version of this study was read at the August 2001 meeting of the International Society of Anglo-Saxonists in Helsinki. For comments and suggestions, I am most grateful to Rosemary Cramp, Roberta Frank, Christopher A. Jones, Stacy Klein, and Ursula Schaefer.

1. R. W. Southern, "Bede," in his *Medieval Humanism and Other Studies* (Oxford: Basil Blackwell, 1984), 1–8, at 1.
2. For the Latin spelling, see *Bede's Ecclesiastical History of the English People*, ed. Bertram Colgrave and R. A. B. Mynors (Oxford: Clarendon Press, 1981), 532 (*His-*

toria Ecclesiastica V.21); for the Old English spelling, see *The Old English Version of Bede's Ecclesiastical History of the English People*, ed. Thomas Miller (London: Trübner, 1890), E.E.T.S., o.s. 110:468. For the etymology of Jarrow from the tribal name *Gyrwe* from "an old word for 'mud' or 'fen' found in OE *gyr*, ON *gior* 'mud'," that is, from the people who lived in fens or muddy districts, see Eilert Ekwall, *The Concise Dictionary of English Place-Names* (Oxford: Clarendon Press, 1960), 268, s.n. "Jarrow."

3. Ellen Wilkinson, *The Town That Was Murdered: The Life-Story of Jarrow*, Left Book Club (London: Victor Gollancz, 1939).

4. Quoted in the invaluable study by Tom Pickard, *Jarrow March* (London: Allison and Busby, 1982), 35. Additional information about the history of Jarrow and Northumbria in the nineteenth and twentieth centuries can be found in three fine volumes: Robert Colls and Bill Lancaster, eds., *Geordies: Roots of Regionalism* (Edinburgh: Edinburgh University Press, 1992); Norman McCord and Richard Thompson, *The Northern Counties from AD 1000* (London: Longman, 1998); and Neville Kirk, ed., *Northern Identities: Historical Interpretations of 'The North' and 'Northernness'* (Aldershot: Ashgate, 2000).

5. For a virtual tour of "Bede's World," go to its website at www.bedesworld.co.uk.

6. Among the numerous studies of Bede's historiography, see Gerald Bonner, "Bede and Medieval Civilization," *Anglo-Saxon England* 2 (1973): 71–90; R. A. Markus, "Bede and the Tradition of Ecclesiastical Historiography," Jarrow Lecture, 1975; and Jan Davidse, "The Sense of History in the Works of the Venerable Bede," *Studi Medievali* 23 (1982): 647–95.

7. For further on these issues, see the indispensable study by Walter A. Goffart, *The Narrators of Barbarian History (A.D. 550–800)* (Princeton: Princeton University Press, 1988), 235–328.

8. For Bede and the computus, see *Bedae: Opera de Temporibus*, ed. C. W. Jones (Cambridge, Mass.: Medieval Academy of America, 1943); and *Bede: The Reckoning of Time*, trans. Faith Wallis (Liverpool: Liverpool University Press, 1999).

9. For Bede's narrative of the Synod of Whitby, see *Historia Ecclesiastica* III.25; Colgrave and Mynors, 294–309.

10. *Historia Ecclesiastica* III.25; Colgrave and Mynors, 300–301.

11. Among various studies of Bede and geography, see J. M. Wallace-Hadrill, "Bede's Europe," Jarrow Lecture, 1962; James Campbell, "Bede's Words for Places," in his *Essays in Anglo-Saxon History* (London: Hambledon Press, 1986), 99–119; and, more generally, Della Hooke, "The Anglo-Saxons in England in the Seventh and Eighth Centuries: Aspects of Location in Space" and "Discussion," in *The Anglo-Saxons from the Migration Period to the Eighth Century: An Ethnographic Perspective*, ed. John Hines (Woodbridge: Boydell Press, 1997), 65–99.

12. *Historia Ecclesiastica* V.24; Colgrave and Mynors, 566–67.

13. For studies of this ideal with reference to Anglo-Saxon England, see Christopher A. Jones, "Envisioning the *Cenobium* in the Old English *Guthlac A*," *Mediaeval Studies* 57 (1995): 259–91; and Roberta Frank, "Old English *Ancor* 'anchor': Transformation of a Latin Loanword," in *Medieval Reconstructions: Germanic Texts and Latin Models*, ed. Antonina Harbus and Karin Olsen, Germania-Latina IV (Gröningen: 2001), 7–27.

14. *Historia Ecclesiastica* V.21; Colgrave and Mynors, 532–33.

15. For Benedict Biscop, see Peter Hunter Blair, *The World of Bede* (Cambridge: Cambridge University Press, 1990), 155–83. Sister Benedicta Ward has usefully pointed, in this regard, to Bede's praise of Benedict Biscop for traveling so extensively. That he did so, Bede notes, freed others from that sort of work. See her "Preface" to *Bede: A Biblical Miscellany*, trans. W. Trent Foley and Arthur G. Holder (Liverpool: Liverpool University Press, 1999), xv. For Rome and the Anglo-Saxon Church, see J. M. Wallace-Hadrill, "Rome and the Early English Church: Some Questions of Transmission," in his *Early Medieval History* (Oxford: Blackwell, 1975), 115–37; and Éamonn Ó Carragáin, "The City of Rome and the World of Bede," Jarrow Lecture, 1994.

16. Robert W. Hanning, *The Vision of History in Early Britain: From Gildas to Geoffrey of Monmouth* (New York: Columbia University Press, 1966), 64 and 65.

17. See further, Nicholas Howe, *Migration and Mythmaking in Anglo-Saxon England* (Notre Dame, Ind.: University of Notre Dame Press, 2001), 108–42.

18. *Historia Ecclesiastica* I.1; Colgrave and Mynors, 14–15.

19. Pliny the Elder, *Natural History*, trans. H. Rackham (Cambridge, Mass.: Harvard University Press, 1969), 2:196–97. *NH* IV.xvi.

20. See further, F. W. Walbank, "The Geography of Polybius," *Classica et Mediaevalia* 9 (1947): 155–82; and Nicholas Howe, "In Defense of the Encyclopedia Mode: on Pliny's *Preface* to the *Natural History*," *Latomus* 44 (1985): 561–76.

21. *Isidori Hispalensis Episcopi: Etymologiarum sive Originum*, ed. W. H. Lindsay (Oxford: Clarendon Press, 1911), XIV.vi.2.

22. See the numerous references to the *Etymologiae* in Helmut Gneuss, *Handlist of Anglo-Saxon Manuscripts: A List of Manuscripts and Manuscript Fragments Written or Owned in England up to 1100* (Tempe: Arizona Center for Medieval and Renaissance Studies, 2001), MRTS 241; and William D. McCready, "Bede and the Isidorian Legacy," *Medieval Studies* 57 (1995): 41–73.

23. *Gildas: the Ruin of Britain and Other Works*, ed. and trans. Michael Winterbottom (London: Phillimore, 1978), 16 and 89; *De Excidio Britanniae* 3.1.

24. *Gildas: the Ruin of Britain*, 18 and 91; *DEB* 8.1.

25. See Hanning, *The Vision of History*, 44–62; and Neil Wright, "Gildas' Geographical Perspective: Some Problems," in *Gildas: New Approaches*, ed. Michael Lapidge and David Dumville (Woodbridge: Boydell, 1984), 85–105.

26. Dorothy Bethurum, ed., *The Homilies of Wulfstan* (Oxford: Clarendon Press, 1957), 261–75; and Howe, *Migration and Mythmaking in Anglo-Saxon England*, 8–20.

27. *Historia Ecclesiastica* I.6; Colgrave and Mynors, 228–29.

28. Uppinder Mehan and David Townsend, "'Nation' and the Gaze of the Other in Eighth-Century Northumbria," *Comparative Literature* 53 (2001): 1–26, at 7.

29. *Historia Ecclesiastica* II.1; Colgrave and Mynors, 134–35.

30. For the Latin text, see *Itineraria et Alia Geographica* (Turnholt: Brepols, 1965), Corpus Christianorum Series Latina 175, 1:261; for the translation, see *Bede: A Biblical Miscellany*, 12. This CCSL volume also contains the text of Adamnan's *De Locis Sanctis*, 177–234. See also *Adamnan's De Locis Sanctis*, ed. Denis Meehan (Dublin: Dublin Institute for Advanced Study, 1958).

31. For these ground plans, see *Itineraria et Alia Geographica*, 2:2–5, 256, and 258.

32. Catherine Delano-Smith and Roger J. P. Kain, *English Maps: A History* (Toronto: University of Toronto Press, 1999), 8–12.

33. *Itineraria et Alia Geographica*, 18:4–5, 279–80.

34. Robert P. Bergman and Diane De Grazia, *Vatican Treasures: Early Christian, Renaissance, and Baroque Art from the Papal Collections* (Cleveland: Cleveland Museum of Art, 1998), 31; for illustrations, see 30–33.

35. For the concept of narrative cartography, see Nicholas Howe, "An Angle on This Earth: Sense of Place in Anglo-Saxon England," *Bulletin of the John Rylands Library of Manchester* 82 (2000): 1–25.

36. For the Latin text, see J.-P. Migne, ed., *Patrologia Latina* 94:701 (quoted from the online version); for the translation, see *Bede: A Biblical Miscellany*, 33.

37. Francis P. Magoun, Jr., "An English Pilgrim-Diary of the Year 990," *Mediaeval Studies* 2 (1940): 231–52. See further, Blake Leyerle, "Landscape as Cartography in Early Christian Pilgrimage Narratives," *Journal of the American Academy of Religion* 64 (1996): 119–43.

38. Howe, *Migration and Mythmaking in Anglo-Saxon England*, 49–71; and Patrick Wormald, "The Venerable Bede and the 'Church of the English,'" in *The English Religious Tradition and the Genius of Anglicanism*, ed. Geoffrey Rowell (Nashville, Tenn.: Abingdon, 1992), 13–32.

39. *Historia Ecclesiastica* V.24; Colgrave and Mynors, 570.

40. "Bede's World—Where History Was Made," printed brochure available from "Bede's World."

41. Personal communication from Rosemary Cramp, August 2001, International Society of Anglo-Saxonists, Helsinki, Finland.

42. For the archaeology of Jarrow, see Rosemary Cramp, "Monkwearmouth and Jarrow: The Archaeological Evidence," in *Famulus Christi: Essays in Commemoration of the Thirteenth Centenary of the Birth of the Venerable Bede*, ed. Gerald Bonner (London: SPCK, 1976), 5–18; and also her more general study, "The Northumbrian

Identity," in *Northumbria's Golden Age*, ed. Jane Hawkes and Susan Mills (Stroud, England: Sutton, 1991), 1–11.

43. "Bede's World—Where History Was Made," 3–4.

44. Alan Plater, "The Drama of the North-East," in Colls and Lancaster, *Geordies: Roots of Regionalism*, 71–84, at 83.

45. Stuart Rawnsley, "Constructing 'The North': Space and a Sense of Place," in Kirk, *Northern Identities*, 3–22, at 3.

2

MONIKA OTTER

Prolixitas Temporum

Futurity in Medieval Historical Narratives

W riting in the late twelfth century, Walter Map finds himself be-
mused by one of the basic paradoxes of time and our experience
of it: despite its apparent neatness, the commonsense system
containing past, present, and future is stubbornly asymmetrical. We can reasonably talk about the past one hundred years as "our times" ("nostra modernitas"), if we define "living memory" ("recens et manifesta memoria")
somewhat generously; but we cannot do so for the next one hundred. They
are mathematically just as far away from us as the last one hundred, but so
dissimilar in texture, so dissimilar with respect to our intellectual and intu-
itive grasp of them, that it just does not make sense to include them in "nostra modernitas." "For," Walter concludes somewhat elliptically, "the past
belongs to narration and the future to divination."[1] In identifying this paradox of linear time, Walter anticipates Émile Benveniste, who says that the
speaker's present—the only time that feels fully "real"—is the axis around
which all our subjective as well as linguistic sense of time is organized. But he
also notes that the past seems more palpable than the future. In most if not
all languages, the future tense as a grammatical category develops considerably later, and remains much less developed, than the past tense. This, he
says, echoing Augustine, seems to correspond to lived experience, in which

the past registers as "real" and differentiated, whereas the future is outside our grasp, devoid of concrete data or lived events, and "does not temporalize itself except as an expectation of experience."[2]

Both Benveniste and Walter Map want to see time as linear, hinging on the axis of the speaker's present, which would suggest symmetry; yet they notice, as they try to elaborate, that the symmetry does not work. Both, moreover, locate the difficulty in memory and narrativity. Even when we conceptualize it as linear, time assumes concreteness and reality for us only insofar as it is filled with events we can recall, reexperience, narrate. When he says that only experience will "temporalize" time, Benveniste goes so far as to imply that, in our subjective experience, the future barely registers as "time" at all—certainly not, as Walter puts it, as "our time." If the speaker's present is an axis, then, or a hinge, it is a strange one, articulating not two equivalent chunks of time but the concrete sequence of the past on one side, and the emptiness of the future on the other.[3]

It is worth stressing that, despite appearances to the contrary, the problematic term is not really the future but the present. The philosophical reflections and narrative contortions we are about to consider are prompted not by a burning intellectual desire to know what will come to pass, or by a practical wish to be forewarned, but rather by an uneasiness about one's own limited and precarious epistemological position. This uneasiness—odd and possibly disturbing for any self-aware historian—comes to a head for a historian who, like Walter Map, tries to chronicle "nostra modernitas." The historian who writes about his own time brings the narrated sequence of events right up to his own moment, and therefore to a bizarre, unsatisfying halt—a dead stop but not an end: nothing is finished, there is no closure, yet there is an absolute cut-off beyond which the historian cannot see or narrate. The writer knows, or assumes, that things will carry on beyond this moment; indeed, that is happening even as he tries to bring his history to a close. As he would have learned from Augustine, the present moment, being an extensionless juncture between future and past, is extremely evanescent, always receding into the past even as we try to wrap our minds around it. Therefore, while the cut-off of the future is absolute, it is also, in another sense, arbitrary and artificial: why should today rather than tomorrow, or even *this* moment, rather than *this*, be the end point? It is only the writer's own person, his own consciousness, that provides both what closure there is *and* continued openness toward the future.

If the writer continues this train of thought to its logical conclusion, he will be uncomfortably reminded of his own death. Only the end of his person and of his consciousness—that is, the writer's death—could bring the narrative to closure, and even then only a provisional, contingent one: a premature closure that provides little in the way of meaning. What is one man's death in relation to "nostra modernitas," let alone the history of the world? The writer's dilemma, therefore, has a textual as well as a personal aspect; or, rather, the personal and the textual merge. To stay alive—to ward off dwelling on his own death—and to keep the history from closing prematurely become one and the same. The text has to be kept open, and the false closure of the present has to be overcome. The best way to do this is to invoke the future, even though it cannot be properly narrated, only gestured at.

In what follows, I will address three Latin histories from the late eleventh and early twelfth centuries that use futurity to sketch a way around the dead stop of the present.[4] Two of them, Geoffrey of Monmouth's *Historia Regum Britanniae* and the anonymous *Life of King Edward Who Rests at Westminster*, construct futurity through prophecy, which Walter Map maintains is the natural and appropriate cognitive mode for apprehending the future. Henry of Huntingdon's *Historia Anglorum* takes a different approach, attempting to reach into the future while foregoing prophecy altogether. Yet the impulse behind Henry's fascinating and curious experiment is recognizably the same as in the two prophetic texts: he wants to gain some narrative purchase on the future and extend the present, but in a purely conceptual way, unadulterated, as it were, by narrative matter. In this way, he helps throw into sharper relief what in the prophetic texts may remain hidden beneath the spectacular narrative events and barely rise to the text's surface.

In all three histories, the future segment is an insert, which interrupts the history somewhere in mid-narrative—not, interestingly, at the end. All three emphatically set off that prophetic insert, marking it as a foreign element in the text; yet they also stress its centrality to the text's meaning. Like Derrida's supplement, the insert is almost self-contained yet not truly detachable; it is part of the narrative but also somehow out of it. Forecasting events-to-come is not the point: none of these future segments, not even the Prophecies, seem to predict anything in a strict sense; they are ambiguous, vague, or pseudo-precise—or, in Henry's case, ingeniously devoid of any propositional content whatsoever. Despite or because of their narrative blankness, they serve as *mises-en-abyme* of the main text: miniaturizations, mirrors, focal points.[5] But they also explode the text's temporal and logical boundaries. And, in variously enlisting other speakers and the reader in the narrating, they also disrupt the text's normal directionality and hierarchy of author and audience. Thus, in deconstructing some of the most defining parameters of historical narrative, they defy closure and keep the history open.[6]

Merlin's Prophecies have been characterized as the off-center center of Geoffrey of Monmouth's *History of the Kings of Britain.* Merlin acts as a kind of John the Baptist to King Arthur's Jesus. Conspicuously inserted shortly before the appearance of Arthur, Merlin's Prophecies gesture toward Arthur, while recapitulating and anticipating the past and future of the entire narrative, as well as an indefinite stretch of time beyond its temporal limits. The *Historia,* as Schirmer and Pähler recognized, has two centers. The climax of the action is clearly the reign of Arthur and its end. The Prophecies, despite their inserted status, are a "structural center," a central point of reference for the entire text. This double focus, and the threads spun between these two obliquely related centers, gives the work its peculiar tension and dynamism.[7] Robert W. Hanning, in his pioneering chapter on Geoffrey of Monmouth, first explained why and how the Prophecies are central: Merlin, a kind of parodic historian figure, provides a mirror-in-the-text, a miniaturization or condensation, but also a parody of what the work as a whole does. Merlin the Historian has special, yet limited, insight into the history he narrates, and he both does and does not control its course: he narrates it, yet he is (presumably) bound to a "real" sequence of events outside his control. That he is controlled by an alien spirit and not necessarily free to prophesy whenever he chooses is emblematic of his limitations.[8]

On a simple level, the figure of Merlin solves the future problem instantly and elegantly, by the oldest prophetic trick in the book: antedating the prophecy, setting its utterance at some point in the past, so that at least part of its "future" is past from our perspective.[9] This permits manipulation of the text's temporal structures. The ploy is the easiest way of solving Walter Map's and Benveniste's axis problem: by shifting the axis, locating the present of a fictional speech earlier than the "now" of narration, it is indeed possible to have a before and after, in a way that our own present does not allow. Moreover, the ploy allows the writer to sneak past his own present without even acknowledging it. All the prophecies refer, of course, to future events from Merlin's point of view; but some will register as already "fulfilled" in the reader's mind. Some prophecies appear to relate to events later in the *Historia,* and readers in Geoffrey's time would presumably have identified these as readily as we do (for example, the Boar of Cornwall is Arthur). Other prophecies, to mid–twelfth-century readers, will quite clearly point to events within their living memory (the lion's cubs that are transformed into fish are the children of Henry I who perished in the wreck of the White Ship)—well past the temporal limits of the *Historia*, but still past from the reader's point of view. Still other prophecies, not so easily identifiable, may be presumed to be still unfulfilled and still to come, particularly the most apocalyptic ones, such as rivers boiling and constellations fighting in the sky. Some events, then, are within the temporal limits of the text; others are in the text's future but the reader's past; still others are in the reader's future, and the difference among the categories is far from clear. There is no obvious temporal hinge in the Prophecies. By thus blurring the reader's present and his own, Geoffrey has managed to leapfrog over himself and narrate into the future in an apparently smooth sweep, without even signaling the cutoff point that is his own present.

This temporal trick also contributes to the dizzying openness of the Prophecies. They are, as Tatlock dismissively puts it, "imaginative to the point of lunacy."[10] Like much lunacy, Merlin's language and mode of referring to events are spectacularly obscure but also curiously precise, creating the impression that we should be able to make the correct connections if we were in the know:

> Bos montanus caput lupi assumet dentesque suos in fabrica Sabrinae dealbabit. Associabit sibi greges Albanorum et Kambriae, quae Tamensem potando siccabunt.

> A Mountain Ox shall put on a Wolf's head and grind its teeth white in the Severn's workshop. The Ox will collect round itself the flocks of Albany and those of Wales; and this company will drain the Thames dry as it drinks.[11]

Even those readers who believe that each prophecy, however obscurely, does intend a precise referent and is ultimately translatable, are unable to decipher them all; and the dominant experience of reading them is awe and disorientation. Readers drift in and out of understanding the text, or believing that they do, recognizing certain landmarks and being at sea the rest of the time.[12] The prophecies are referentially and chronologically wide open, even "empty"—not in the sense that nothing is being said (if anything, all too much is being said), but in the sense Wolfgang Iser intends with his "blanks" or "Leerstellen": "empty," indeterminate spaces in the text that invite and even require each reader to plug in his or her own interpretive contribution.[13] The prophecies invite attempts at interpretation but also frustrate them. Despite their tone of finality and authoritative explanation, Merlin's Prophecies do not provide interpretive closure but rather open up the text to indefinite further glossings and elaborations.

The temporal disjuncture of the Prophecies is underscored by the curious way in which they are inserted into the main text. Geoffrey sets them off, in mid-narrative, with an explanation and a separate dedicatory letter.[14] Having introduced Merlin, Geoffrey leaves him precariously suspended on the verge of a prophetic trance to deliver his auctorial intervention. It may well be the case that, as Geoffrey suggests, the Prophecies were originally conceived and circulated separately.[15] But whether that bit of textual history is real or fictional, Geoffrey, rather than smoothly integrating the insert, chooses to mark the insertion point. The Prophecies, according to Geoffrey's account, did not simply preexist the *Historia* but have interrupted its composition, somewhat to the historian's annoyance and inconvenience. He even contrives to say so twice, first outright and then in the self-quotation of his dedicatory epistle to Bishop Alexander of Lincoln:

Nondum autem ad hunc locum historie perveneram, cum, de Merlino divulgato rumore, compellebant me undique contemporanei mei prophetias ipsius edere. . . . Coegit me, Alexander Lincolliensis praesul, nobilitatis tuae dilectio prophetias Merlini de britannico in latinum transferre, antequam historiam perarassem, quam de gestis regum Britannorum inceperam. Proposueram enim illam prius perficere istudque opus subsequenter explicare.

I had not yet reached this point in my story when Merlin began to be talked about very much, and from all sorts of places people of my own generation kept urging me to publish his Prophecies. . . . Alexander, bishop of Lincoln, my admiration for your noble behaviour leaves me no other choice but to translate the "Prophecies of Merlin" from the British tongue into the Latin, before I have finished the history which I had already begun of the deeds of the kings of the Britons. My intention had been to complete the other work first, and only then to have devoted myself to the present one.[16]

With this surprisingly ungracious dedication, Geoffrey very strongly marks the present moment, his as well as ours.[17] He stops himself short *at this very point* where we have now arrived, to back up and compose the enigmatic prophetic epitome of his *Historia,* which in its fluid way reaches up to and well beyond the present moment in the text, and indeed well beyond the outer temporal limit marked by the end of the text.

And yet, despite these contortions and despite the conspicuous double framing (an introduction to an introductory letter that leads into the Prophecies proper), at the end of the Prophecies there is no corresponding apparatus. Merlin ends his speech, and without transition we segue right into the reactions of Vortigern and his people. The Prophecies thus are part of the narrative sequence; if they were omitted, there would be a noticeable lacuna in the text. (Wace, who refuses to recount the Prophecies in his translation of Geoffrey, has to fill the lacuna with his explicit refusal to translate them.[18]) At the same time, the Prophecies are clearly marked as a foreign, even disturbing element; they are an inserted text, both a translation and a self-quotation; they are thus at least double- if not triple-voiced, spoken by the character Merlin, written down by an anonymous Welsh chronicler, and also written (on a previous occasion) by Geoffrey, and now reiterated by him. In one way, they do preexist the *Historia:* they are, or claim to be, a translation of a preexisting text. But, by needing to be translated, they also interrupt the *Historia's* composition. Thus, insofar as the Prophecies are a miniature version of the *Historia,* in the original Welsh version they anticipate the *Historia,* and the *Historia* has to be seen as their elaboration and fulfillment; yet Geoffrey must also actively compose them, summarize his own *Historia* that is halfway written. Geoffrey has compounded and confounded the distinction between original and translation, source and derivation, and even simple chronology.

At the same time, the Prophecies anticipate and overwrite the *Historia's* ending. They are apocalyptic in tone and imagery. As Hanning says, the prophecies end by spinning out of control, by dissolving auctorial control and tending towards narrative entropy, long before we get anywhere near the end of the book, even before the central Arthurian segment.[19] At the book's real end, by contrast, there is no such chaos or dissolution. There is a definite sense of an ending; there is decline and despair; but the author remains firmly in control. The prophecies counterpoint this apparently controlled ending with an implied apocalyptic ending, but they locate it at an indeterminate point in the future, well past the present tense that is the end of the narrative, well past the writer's (or reader's) present tense. The prophecies are a soft center, to which all the book's events refer and in which they are grounded, though in a curiously vague way. They are also an absolute yet soft ending: everything melts and dissolves, spins out of control. Yet it is not clear when this will happen, except that it is not *now* (as Merlin speaks); or *now* (at the end of the narrative, as the Britons under Yvor and Yni sink into obscurity and the Saxons establish themselves); or *now* (as Geoffrey ends his *Historia* with a facetious address to contemporary fellow historians)—or *now*, as we are reading it. Nor is it clear what relationship they bear to the promised end of Christian eschatology. Thus, despite their apocalypticism, Merlin's Prophecies in all senses undermine closure, temporal or interpretive; all we can do is continue to spin off endless glosses and commentaries, all unverifiable—and that is precisely their purpose.[20]

The *Vita Aedwardi Regis,* emphatically a book about contemporary events, uses a prophetic insert as a kind of escape mechanism. The *Vita Aedwardi* is a very idiosyncratic biography, hagiography, and history of Edward the Confessor; and perhaps even more of his wife Edith and her family, including her brother Harold, the loser of the battle of Hastings. It was written, literally, right around the Norman Conquest: begun in 1065 and finished in 1067, it was composed, or purports to have been composed, simultaneously with the cataclysmic events that form its main subject; and it makes an issue of that simultaneity. In an earlier essay, I concentrated on the difficulty of narrating catastrophe even as it is happening.[21] Here, I am interested in the text's future dimension. King Edward, portrayed as an ethereally saintly, though hapless figure, prophesies several times, the most famous instance being his deathbed prophecy of the "green tree." My object here, however, is the other major prophecy in the text, which, unfortunately, may not be original to it. Frank Barlow has examined its precarious textual status in detail: he is fairly certain that the Seven Sleepers episode as we have it is an interpolation made around 1100; it is impossible to say whether the original text had the episode at all or in what form.[22] With these strictures in mind, we can nonetheless postulate a revised *Vita Aedwardi Regis,* ca. 1100, with an interpolated Seven Sleepers. In fact, in analogy to our other two texts, interpolation is eminently appropriate: someone, though not necessarily the author, has decided to insert a prophecy that interrupts the narrative and explodes its boundaries.

Here is a brief summary of this curious episode. In 1060, Edward, who was never known to laugh, suddenly laughs. Asked by his startled courtiers what is so funny, he explains: "For more than 200 years the Seven Sleepers have rested on their right sides in a cave on Mount Cheilaion at Ephesus;

but just now, after we started dinner, they have turned on to their left sides and will lie thus for seventy-four years." During those seventy-four years, he predicts, apocalyptic disasters will befall. When asked, he further explains who the Seven Sleepers are, narrating the well-known legend, which was extraordinarily widespread in both western and eastern Christendom as well as in Islam.[23] The Seven Sleepers were Christians under the Emperor Decius. They hid from persecution in a cave and, with God's help, slept right through the danger, awaking only 272 years later. Edward then gave their names and "described their appearances and characters as though they had always been his comrades" ("retulit eis formas eorum et qualitates acsi eius semper fuissent sodales"). Messengers are dispatched to Ephesus to verify the story, and find everything as the king has said.[24] There follows—in the voice of the author—a long, sweeping survey of disasters throughout the known world, beginning with France, then the Roman Empire, the popes, Byzantium, the Crusade, and finally England.[25]

Quite apart from the question of interpolation, this episode is clearly and explicitly an inserted story, with multiple layers of elaboration. In the first place, the old and far-ranging motif of the Prophetic Laugh creates a frame that allows for the insertion of the Seven Sleepers legend. In fact, that would seem to be its only function: compared to the analogues cited by Lewis Thorpe, the story here is virtually a blind motif.[26] It is usually far better motivated in terms of the surrounding narrative. The laugher and prophet are always either demonic or mad, or both. He is an outsider, on an antagonistic or even hostile footing with the community to which he prophesies. Merlin, in the *Vita Merlini*, even uses his mysterious laugh to obtain promises from his captors in exchange for his prophetic explanation. The prophetic laugh, in these analogues, is truly "sardonic," directed at human blindness (the beggar sitting on a buried treasure without knowing it), at short-sighted and futile preparations for the future (the man who buys shoes, not knowing that he will not live to wear them), or at the hypocrisy of polite society that hides its shameful secrets (the queen whose adultery is unknown to her husband). In the *Vita Aedwardi*, however, none of these motivations quite obtains. Edward is a king, not some mad outsider, and he is prophesying to his own people. Far from demonic, he is cast as pious, poised for official sainthood. Since he is predicting disaster not only for the entire world but especially for his own realm, he would seem to have little reason for glee or sarcasm. All that remains of the Prophetic Laugh motif here is its framing function for a riddling prophecy, which in turn stands in need of prophetic elaboration.

For the king's vision itself is quite empty of future reference. It is, actually, not future-oriented at all, and arguably tautological: the king miraculously knows that his *sodales*, the Seven Sleepers, have turned over, and this is then confirmed by messengers. The turning of the Seven Sleepers, here as in its Muslim analogues, undeniably implies some great significance of apocalyptic proportions, as does the king's knowledge of it.[27] But that significance is entirely uncertain, and not initially at issue; it is not even alluded to in the messengers' charge or in their report upon returning.

The actual prophecy—seventy-four years of disaster—is already an interpretation, a commentary by the king on this initial vision. This prophecy, predicting generalized disaster everywhere, is hugely unspecific—much like Merlin's Prophecies, an invitation to commentary and interpretation. On the other hand, there is one element that acts as a retardant for such commentary. Ironically, the only precise detail, the duration of seventy-four years, appears to be pseudo-precise, a random number. At any rate, no one has been able to discover any possible significance for that number; no particular event or point in time seems to be intended.[28] Pseudo-precise time calculations are a hallmark of the Seven Sleepers story, and while they may appear as gratuitous obfuscation in most of the Christian renderings of the legend, they are far from gratuitous in the Islamic branch of the tradition.[29] If the King Edward episode is based, however indirectly, on an Islamic source, then his knowledge of the Sleepers' names and other details would seem to have apocalyptic overtones in and of itself. In the Qur'an, the uncertainty about the length of the Sleepers' sleep, or even the precise number of sleepers, is a central issue; the point of the episode seems to be, among other things, an injunction against claiming or seeking to know what only God knows.[30] In this tradition, then, commentary appears to be invited only to be instantly and explicitly forbidden. In the much weaker, possibly no longer understood reflex of this motif in the Christian versions, the pseudo-precise number acts not as a prohibition, but a discouragement to elaboration: the number, however randomly derived, is a given.

But other aspects of the prophecy very much invite interpretation. The first installment follows right away, in the voice of the narrator, no longer prophetic but retrospective, verifying the prophecy's fulfillment of the first few years of disaster:

Quid de Anglia dicam? Quid posteris referam? Ve tibi est Anglia que olim sancta prole fulsisti angelica, sed nunc pro peccatis ualde gemis anxia. Naturalem regem tuum perdidisti et alienigeni bello cum ingenti tuorum sanguine fuso succubuisti. Filii tui miserabiliter in te occisi sunt et consiliarii principesque tui uincti seu necati uel exhereditati sunt.

And what shall I say about England? What shall I tell generations to come? Woe is to you England, you who once shone bright with holy, angelic progeny, but now with anxious expectation groan exceedingly for your sins. You have lost your native king and suffered defeat, with much spilling of blood of many of your men, in a war against the foreigner. Pitiably your sons have been slain within you. Your counsellors and princes are bound in chains, killed, or disinherited.[31]

King Edward's prophecy has thus occasioned its first batch of interpretations on the spot, first by himself, then by the narrator. If Barlow's reconstruction of the episode's textual history is correct, the text as we have it (or can reconstruct it) already represents several layers of accretions to this commentary. Further elaborations are clearly invited: the Seven Sleepers insertion functions precisely as a *Leerstelle*, a locus for generating future glosses.

More importantly, perhaps, the episode offers a kind of desperate consolation by simply pointing us to the future—any future. The narrator has projected a point—apparently precise, yet really random—in the medium-term future, well beyond the end of his history and the end of his own life and that of his contemporary readers. In a text so intimately concerned with simultaneity and temporal coincidence, in which the writer is overtaken by the events he hopes to chronicle and feels trapped in his present, this prophecy seems not so much a forecast of future events as a kind of eject button, a desperate attempt to propel oneself, and the history, past the utterly bleak present moment—anything to escape, no matter where we touch down again. Precisely because of its imprecise or nonexistent reference, the prophecy helps this highly inconclusive text avoid what seems like a most undesirable closure.

Henry of Huntingdon's attempt at future historiography is distinctive in that it is *not* prophetic. He predicts nothing, openly or covertly. He does not invent or speculate. Yet he ingeniously and hauntingly opens his *Historia Anglorum* up to the future, and emphatically involves us in the exercise. The *Historia*'s originality is much easier to appreciate now that Diana Greenway's full edition has restored to it the pieces that the nineteenth-century editor for the Rolls Series deemed "not historical."[32] Henry inscribes himself in his work in various ways, signaling the year of his birth, the death of his father, and other personal dates; he incorporates all sorts of tracts, letters, and poems. He works on the *Historia* continuously through his lifetime: Greenway identifies six more or less clear-cut redactions between 1129 and 1155.[33] The later versions contain an "epilogue" that begins with this energetic flourish:

> Hic est annus qui comprehendit scriptorem. Annus tricesimus quintus regni gloriosi et inuictissimi regis Anglorum Henrici. Annus lxix ab aduentu Normannorum gentis temporibus excellentissime nostris in Angliam. Annus ab aduentu Anglorum in Angliam dcciii. annus ab aduentu Britannorum ad hanc eandem insulam inhabitandam ii M. et cc et lxv. Annus ab initio mundi v M. et ccc et xvii. Annus gratie Mcxxxv.
>
> Hic est igitur annus ille a quo scriptor historie suam uoluit etatem a sequentibus computari.

This is the year which contains the writer. The thirty-fifth year of the reign of the glorious and invincible Henry, king of the English. The sixty-ninth year from the arrival in England, in our own time, of the supreme Norman race. The 703rd year from the coming of the English into England. The 2,265th year from the coming of the Britons to settle in the same island. The 5,317th year from the beginning of the world. The 1,135th year of grace.

This, then, is the year from which the writer of the History wished his age to be reckoned by posterity.[34]

It scarcely matters that, according to the editor's notes, not all the figures make sense.[35] What matters is the grand gesture of dating, the more noteworthy because Henry is not normally very interested in dates, tending to suppress the A.D. dating even where his sources have it.[36] This emphatic dating and self-inscription, the attempt to nail down the present moment and the writer's own place in it, seems to me an attempt not only to mark the passing of time and the inevitable end of the world, but also to arrest that passing and delay the end, to carve out some space for the world, for time, for the present.

The label "epilogue" is editorial,[37] but the piece was originally conceived as the actual end of the book. As we have seen, it is dated, emphatically, 1135.

But, interestingly, as the *Historia* grew, Henry chose not to update the epilogue or to move it to wherever the new end of the work was. He did change the date once, from 1130 to 1135, but then left it alone through many subsequent reworkings over two decades. And although King Henry I died late in that same year, Henry did not update the epilogue even in that respect, although in the post-1135 redactions a detailed account of the king's death immediately precedes this passage.[38] As his history grows beyond and around it, Henry keeps the 1135 date fixed, sealed off, a bit like the "time capsule" schoolchildren are sometimes encouraged to make and to dig up a year later, in order to experience a sense of "history." This school exercise, as we shall see, is a fairly precise analogy to what Henry is up to.

The first move (not unlike Geoffrey's in stopping himself right before Merlin's Prophecies) is to mark the present tense and the simultaneity of writing with what is being narrated. The point seems to be to solidify the writing, as it were, to create a kind of plenitude of experience that can only be guaranteed by a personally experiencing subject—albeit a very stylized one. (Henry is hardly interested in his own unique subjectivity here, but rather in subjectivity as a general concept.) His lived presence, his memory, and even his physical body concretize and thereby underwrite the realness of the present time.

Henry's next move is to get beyond that present moment; and he enlists us, his readers, in a quite unsettling way. First, in a classic *ubi sunt*, Henry looks back a thousand years to the year 135: where are—he goes down the list—the kings, the bishops, the nobles . . . of that year? Do we even know their names? As always, he does not forget to address himself, the Archdeacon of Huntingdon ("loquar ad meipsum"): where are the archdeacons? Can you name even one archdeacon alive in 135 A.D.? No matter how hard they tried to distinguish themselves, Henry observes, these people did not live on in historical memory any more than their horses did.[39]

So far, the rhetoric of the passage is familiar and unsurprising. But then Henry projects one thousand years forward: "Now I speak to you who will be living in the third millennium, around the 135th year."[40] We modern readers, even though we are still over a century away from 2135, may well feel spoken to directly. But Henry does not have much of a message for us, except to let us know that he has anticipated our existence and to remind us of the passage of time. His experiment in historical writing, utterly devoid of any particular events, evidently addresses the same fundamental difficulty recognized by Walter Map and Émile Benveniste: how can the historian overcome his odd limitation—his view being cut off right in front of his nose, as it were—how can he extend his reach into the future? It is a bold and unusual experiment, and Henry has to improvise: what tense does one use? Whose eyes, perspective, vantage point? He is clearly *not* aiming at prophecy or prediction; he does not care to guess what will happen; so what does one even write *about?*

Henry solves the perspective problem by addressing "us," his future readers, enlisting our subjectivity in his meditation. The result is an interestingly compounded and contorted perspective. The *ubi sunt* "where are they who came before us?" becomes an *ubi fuerimus,* a *quo deuenerimus,* where will *we* be—what *will have* become of *us* by *your* time? He points out to us the oddity of his having thought of us so far ahead of time: could we please return the favor, he asks, by praying for him?

> Nunc autem qui tanto tempore antequam nascamini de uobis mentionem iam uestro tempore puluis in hoc opere feci, si contigerit— quod ualde desiderat anima mea—uestras ut in manus hoc opus meum prodeat, precor ut Dei clementiam inexcogitabilem pro me miserrimo exoretis. Sic et pro uobis orent et impetrent qui quarto uel quinto millenario cum Deo ambulabunt, si generatio mortalium tamdiu protelabitur.

> Now, however, I, who will already be dust by your time, have made mention of you in this book, so long before you are to be born, so that if—as my soul strongly desires—it shall come about that this book comes into your hands, I beg you, in the incomprehensible mercy of God, to pray for me, poor wretch. In the same way, may those who will walk with God in the fourth and fifth millennia pray and petition for you, if indeed mortal man survives so long.[41]

We are to validate his existence even as he has validated our existence by postulating it—even though he himself will have turned to dust by the time we come around. And, lest we become too smug by seeing ourselves as the teleological end of all of this, he invites us to perform the same exercise ourselves: let us think of the people of 3135, and imagine them thinking of us, and so on to 4135, 5135, etc. This is hypothetical history writing, historiography in the future perfect, without the slightest bit of forecasting in it; indeed, it is historiography without events or narrativity. Henry here has abandoned the *narracio* proper to historical writing, and does without the *divinacio* Walter Map says is proper to future events. All that matters is the formal reach past the present moment, a perspectival trick to secure a hold on the future.

That this exercise is indeed about holding off closure is confirmed by the ensuing argument about the end of the world and the length of time— "prolixitas temporum" is Henry's phrase.[42] Anticipating objections that surely the world will already have ended by all those future dates, Henry explicitly rejects various millenarian models, both Christian and Jewish. He acknowledges we cannot be sure, but he decidedly does not believe the end of the world is imminent, or even anywhere close. Subjectively, he says, time ends for each of us when we die. Objectively, he is confident that it will continue for quite some time. If the time before Christ (*ante legem* and *sub lege*) prefigures the time after Christ (*sub gratia*), then surely the time *sub gratia* has to be at least as long as the time that prefigured it:

> Multo amplius durabit ueritas quam figura, lux quam umbra, significatio quam significans, tempus gratie quam tempus legis.

> Truth will endure much longer than symbol, light than shadow, the thing signified than what signifies it, the time of grace than the time of law.[43]

Apart from assuring us that we have plenty of time left, Henry here also structures history, both objectively and subjectively, and ingeniously moves its axis around. Invoking Christ as the big, epochal turning point in history— the one that marks before and after, even to us today—Henry, by his insistence on 1135, also posits his own present and turning point. Just as one's personal end of time comes with one's death, so one's present and therefore one's hinge in time comes whenever one happens to be—in this case 1135. His refusal to update it only underlines the randomness of this positing, but also its importance.

In a final move, Henry explicitly brings together the objective end of time and one's own personal end of time, one's death:

> Tamdiu uero in temporum prolixitate moratus sum, ut precogitemus, cum tanto spacio in sepulchris putrescentes memoriam omnium, que ex corporibus procedere possunt, nos amittere necesse sit, ut illam gloriam et honorem et probitatem et opulentiam et dignitatem et nominis

claritatem, que in Deo est, sudantes appetemus. Hanc cum adeptus fueris
habes et semper habes. Mundanam cum adeptus fueris ut aqua uase tere-
brato defluit et nichil habes.

I have dwelt at some length on the question of the extent of time. This
was because we shall lie decaying in our tombs for such a long time that
we shall necessarily lose the memory of all bodily activities, and therefore we should think about it in advance, in order to work hard at seeking the glory, honour, goodness, wealth, dignity, and fame of name that
are in God. When you have gained this glory, you have it and will always
have it. When you have gained worldly glory, it will flow away like water
from a broken pitcher, and you have nothing.[44]

I am deliberately quoting Greenway's translation unedited, although I would
tend to translate differently here: if hers is a mistranslation, it is a brilliantly
suggestive one. The original reads, "memoriam omnium, que ex corporibus
procedere possunt, nos amittere necesse sit." Surely this is *memoria* in an
objective sense—the memory that survives of us, that which is remembered
of us—not in a subjective sense, "that which we remember."[45] That is, the
fame of all those things we did that "can come from [our] bodies" will be
forgotten. But, on the other hand, Greenway is right: it does sound just the
way she translates it. As we lie in our graves, we will forget our bodily activities, and we need to do our thinking before that happens.[46] In Henry's
own case this surely means that he must write while he can—his only chance
to gain fame ("memoria") in my translation; in Greenway's translation, his
only chance to put his body, consciousness, and memory to use to produce
thought, or a history. The logic of Henry's "because" ("I have dwelled on the
extent of time . . . *because* we shall lie decaying in our tombs . . .") is also sug-
gestively ambiguous. In the first place it must surely be read as straightforward *contemptus mundi:* Henry is stressing the *prolixitas temporum* to remind
us that our deaths will last much longer than our lives, and hence all worldly
glory will pass, as his *ubi sunt/ubi fuerimus* has shown. On the other hand,
it can also be read as an anxious plea for more time, or a self-reassurance
that there is still plenty of time.[47] Elsewhere in the epilogue, Henry ambiguously characterizes the present year as the one "in which we are leading our
lives [*uitam ducimus*] or—to put it more appropriately—*mortem sustine-
mus,*" which Greenway renders as "we are holding back death."[48] This could
be read as a pessimistic comment: we do not truly live, but just barely stave

off death. Or it can be read, perhaps, not as optimistic but as desperately heroic. Living is the very action that holds back death, a tautological statement (as long as we live, we do not die) that is either banal or profound, or most likely both. At its most profound, as we have seen, it means that by living we delay the end of history and the world, just as by reading, interpreting, and reinterpreting, we delay the end of the text.

It is not too surprising, then, that Henry should be so intent on delaying closure, personally and universally. He does this, in part, by resolutely inscribing himself in the text. It is his own life, his memory, and even his own body that guarantee the truth and substance of the present, as the transitional point between past and future, those vastly asymmetrical chunks of time. The very intrusion of a speaker who marks his own present has a subtle deconstructive effect in such macro-historic reflections. Henry's self-inscription in 1135, as he makes clear, both mimics and displaces the epochal divide of salvation history. By thus counterpointing the divinely instituted timeline from creation to doomsday with human and subjective time, he subverts its continuity, its teleology, its divinely sanctioned meaning.

Not that Henry wants to obliterate that greater narrative, or its orthodox readings; he could not do so if he tried, any more than he can prevent his own death or the end of the world. But he can defer both the temporal and the interpretive closure; and that is what prophecy and future reference do for all three historical narratives. Prophecy by definition gestures toward certitude, highest authority, and ultimate meanings. That would seem especially true in a historiographical culture beholden to an unquestioned master narrative, which guarantees both its ultimate outcome and its ultimate meaning. R. W. Southern argues that prophecy in medieval historiography, far from being the most iffy and speculative element, as it may appear to us, is therefore the most reliable, most authoritative, most self-evidently true and meaningful form of historical insight.[49] Yet (as Southern also recognizes) by enabling and inviting uncertain, provisional, and multiple interpretations, prophecy also distances and defers this ultimate truth. Henry's experiment in creating pure futurity, without actual prophetic content, is another and maybe even more radical way of achieving the same effect: he has stretched his own historiographical reach and delayed the closure of his text—and thereby of history. In that sense this historian of *contemptus mundi* is surprisingly life-affirming. Even though the end of (his) history inevitably conjures up thoughts of death, he has managed to extend the space allotted to time. We may conclude by returning to Walter Map, whose thoughts also turn to death as he muses on the present and on the dilemma of a writer caught up in the present. Writers, he complains, get no respect in their own lifetime; to be an "auctoritas" you have to be dead—"the present generation will look down upon me because I am still living." But, he says, that cannot be helped, "quia uiuere uolo"—"I want to live."[50]

Notes

1. "Nostra dico tempora modernitatem hanc, horum silicet centum annorum curriculum, cuius adhuc nunc ultime partes extant, cuius tocius in his que notabilia sunt satis est recens et manifesta memoria, cum adhuc aliqui supersint centennes, et infiniti filii qui ex patrum et suorum relacionibus certissime teneant que non viderunt. Centum annos qui effluxerunt dico nostram modernitatem, et non qui veniunt, cum eiusdem tamen sint racionis secundum propinquitatem, quoniam ad narracionem pertinent preterita, ad diuinacionem futura." Walter Map, *De Nugis Curialium: Courtiers' Trifles*, ed. and trans. M. R. James, rev. C. N. L. Brooke and R. A. B. Mynors (Oxford: Clarendon, 1983), 122–24.

2. "Ne se temporalise qu'en tant que prévision d'expérience" (my translation). Émile Benveniste, "Le langage et l'expérience humaine," in *Problèmes de linguistique générale* (Paris: Gallimard, 1972), 2:67–78, here 76.

3. Augustine, who is more or less palpably behind all these reflections, somewhat avoids the asymmetry of time by locating all time in subjective experience, with past ("memoria") and future ("expectatio") being "extensions of the mind," and the present merely the extensionless point at which expectation passes into memory. *Confessions*, Book XI; see also Paul Ricoeur, *Time and Narrative*, trans. Kathleen McLaughlin and David Pellauer (Chicago: Chicago University Press, 1984), 1:5–30; and Jean-Claude Schmitt, "Appropriating the Future," in *Medieval Futures: Attitudes to the Future in the Middle Ages*, ed. J. A. Burrow and Ian P. Wei (Woodbridge: Boydell, 2000), 4.

4. Geoffrey de Monmouth, *Historia Regum Britanniae, La légende Arthurienne, Première partie: Les plus anciens textes*, ed. Edmond Faral (Paris: Honoré Champion 1929), 3:63–303; and the translation by Lewis Thorpe, *The History of the Kings of Britain* (Harmondsworth: Penguin, 1966). *Vita Aedwardi Regis qui apud Westmonasterium requiescit: The Life of King Edward Who Rests at Westminster*, ed. and trans. Frank Barlow (Oxford: Clarendon, 1992). Henry, Archdeacon of Huntingdon, *Historia Anglorum: The History of the English People*, ed. and trans. Diana Greenway (Oxford: Clarendon, 1996).

5. The classic formulations of this concept are Lucien Dällenbach, *The Mirror in the Text*, trans. Jeremy Whiteley with Emma Hughes (Cambridge: Polity Press,

1982); and Robert W. Hanning, "Poetic Emblems in Medieval Narrative Texts," in *Vernacular Poetics in the Middle Ages*, ed. Lois Ebin (Kalamazoo, Mich.: Medieval Institute, 1984), 1–31.

6. For a related discussion of "embedded narratives" in medieval fiction, see Rebecca S. Beal, "Ending in the Middle: Closure, Openness, and Significance in Embedded Medieval Narratives," *Annali d'Italianistica* 18 (2000): 175–98.

7. Walter Schirmer, *Die frühen Darstellungen des Arthurstoffes* (Cologne: Westdeutscher Verlag, 1958), 13; Heinrich Pähler, "Strukturuntersuchungen zur Historia Regum Britanniae des Geoffrey of Monmouth" (doctoral dissertation, University of Bonn, 1958), 127 and 159–60.

8. *The Vision of History in Early Britain: From Gildas to Geoffrey of Monmouth* (New York: Columbia University Press, 1966), 154, 171. This idea has since been elaborated and modified by various commentators; among others, R. Howard Bloch, *Etymologies and Genealogies: A Literary Anthropology of the French Middle Ages* (Chicago: University of Chicago Press, 1983), 1–5; Martin B. Shichtman and Laurie A. Finke, "Profiting from the Past: History as Symbolic Capital in the *Historia Regum Britanniae*," *Arthurian Literature* 12 (1993): 8–9, 29–35; and Kimberly Bell, "Merlin as Historian in Geoffrey of Monmouth's *Historia Regum Britanniae*," *Arthuriana* 10 (2000): 14–26.

9. J. S. P. Tatlock, *The Legendary History of Britain: Geoffrey of Monmouth's Historia Regum Britanniae and Its Early Vernacular Versions* (Berkeley: University of California Press, 1950), 404; Jan Ziolkowski, "The Nature of Prophecy in Geoffrey of Monmouth's *Vita Merlini*," in *Poetry and Prophecy: The Beginnings of a Literary Tradition*, ed. James Kugel (Ithaca, N.Y.: Cornell University Press, 1990), 158. Benveniste notes that written texts, unlike spoken utterances, permit such complications of deixis ("Le langage," 77).

10. Tatlock, *Legendary History*, 416. The formulation is apt, despite the heartfelt contempt and overt anti-Celtic bias that prompted it.

11. Faral, *Historia Regum Britanniae*, 198; Thorpe, *History of the Kings of Britain*, 180.

12. On the commentary tradition, which started as soon as the *Historia* became available, see Jean Blacker, "Where Wace Feared to Tread: Latin Commentaries on Merlin's Prophecies in the Reign of Henry II," *Arthuriana* 6.1 (1996): 36–52; Jacob Hammer, "A Commentary on the *Prophetia Merlini*," *Speculum* 10 (1935): 3–30 and 15 (1940): 409–31; Caroline D. Eckhardt, *The Prophetia Merlini of Geoffrey of Monmouth: A Fifteenth-Century English Commentary* (Cambridge, Mass.: Medieval Academy of America, 1982), 10–15. Orderic Vitalis, who excerpted and glossed the Prophecies perhaps as early as 1135, did believe that each could be assigned a specific meaning; but he explicitly invited further interpretations, for which his own were only a prompt and example: "Some part of it has, I know, already been fulfilled in past events; and unless I am mistaken more will be proved true with sorrow or joy by

future generations. Men well read in histories can easily apply his predictions. . . . After this fashion wise men may clearly decipher the rest." Orderic Vitalis, *The Ecclesiastical History*, ed. and trans. Marjorie Chibnall (Oxford: Clarendon, 1978), 6:386–89.

13. Wolfgang Iser, *The Act of Reading: A Theory of Aesthetic Response* (Baltimore: Johns Hopkins University Press, 1978), 182–203. This is not to deny that the prophecies and their glossings had considerable political potency. See, for instance, Shichtman and Finke, "Profiting from the Past"; Blacker, "Where Wace Feared to Tread"; Michael J. Curley, "A New Edition of John of Cornwall's *Prophetia Merlini*," *Speculum* 57 (1982): 217–28; and, for a different set of prophecies and their political permutations, Phyllis B. Roberts, "Prophecy, Hagiography, and St. Thomas of Canterbury," in Burrow and Wei, *Medieval Futures*, 67–80.

14. Lewis Thorpe's Penguin translation, which divides the *Historia* into "parts" and typographically emphasizes the breaks thus created, unfortunately mutes the impact of this startling interruption (*History of the Kings of Britain*, 170).

15. For different views on this controversial question, see Caroline D. Eckhardt, "The *Prophetia Merlini* of Geoffrey of Monmouth: Latin MS Copies," *Manuscripta* 26 (1982): 167–76; Neil Wright, ed., *The Historia Regum Britannie* (Cambridge: D. S. Brewer, 1985), xi–xii; Lewis Thorpe, "Orderic Vitalis and the Prophetia Merlini of Geoffrey of Monmouth," *Bulletin bibliographique de la Société internationale Arthurienne* 29 (1977): 191–208; Tatlock, *Legendary History*, 418–21.

16. Faral, *Historia Regum Britannie*, 189–90; translation in Thorpe, *History of the Kings of Britain*, 170.

17. See Tatlock, *Legendary History*, 403.

18. *Wace's Roman de Brut: A History of the British*, ed. and trans. Judith Weiss (Exeter: University of Exeter Press, 1999), 190–91, lines 7535–42; see Jean Blacker, "'Ne vuil sun livre translater': Wace's Omission of Merlin's Prophecies from the Roman de Brut," in *Anglo-Norman Anniversary Essays*, ed. Ian Short (London: Anglo-Norman Text Society, 1993), 49–59; and Blacker, "Where Wace Feared to Tread." Interestingly, one scribe just as explicitly reinstates the prophecies in the Wace manuscript he is copying: answering Wace's first-person intervention, "Ne vuil sun livre translater," he counters, "Mais jeo Wilhelme vus dirai / Des altres prophecies ço ke je sai. . . ." *Wace's Roman de Brut*, 190 n. 2. By marking the (incomplete) suppression of the Prophecies with the placeholder of his refusal, then, Wace just barely kept them alive but enabled others to reactivate them. On the treatment of the Prophecies (omissions and reframings) in various Latin manuscripts of the *Historia Regum Britanniae*, see Julia C. Crick, *The Historia Regum Britannie of Geoffrey of Monmouth: Dissemination and Reception in the Later Middle Ages* (Cambridge: D. S. Brewer, 1991), 4:102–3.

19. Hanning, *Vision of History*, 172.

20. Anne Berthelot makes a similar case for the "prophecies de Merlin" that appear in the thirteenth-century Arthurian cycles: "Discours prophétique et fiction:

Les systèmes de brouillage dans la prophétie médiévale," *Poétique* 70 (1987): 181–91. R. W. Southern, "Aspects of the European Tradition of Historical Writing 3: History as Prophecy," *Transactions of the Royal Historical Society*, 5th ser., 22 (1972): 159–80, while stressing the authoritative and conclusive connotations of medieval prophecy, also describes, as a necessary complement, the open-ended and bewildering process of interpretation (162). See note 49 below.

21. "1066: The Moment of Transition in Two Narratives of the Norman Conquest," *Speculum* 74 (1999): 565–86.

22. A leaf is missing at that point in the unique manuscript, BL Harley Ms. 526. In a tentative reconstruction of the missing segment, Barlow supplies text from later works that rework and/or interpolate sections of the *Vita Aedwardi*. By meticulous detective work and logical reasoning, he is able to show that *some* version of the Seven Sleepers must have been included in a revision of the original *Vita Aedwardi*—and most likely in Harley 526—by the early 1080s. The text he derives from Bodleian Ms. Bodley 297 (a twelfth-century Bury St. Edmunds manuscript in which a large chunk of *Vita Aedwardi* is interpolated verbatim into "Florence" of Worcester's *Chronicon ex chronicis*) cannot, from the events it alludes to, be earlier than ca. 1100, and on stylistic grounds it does not appear to be by the author of the *Vita Aedwardi*. Barlow, *The Life of King Edward*, lxi–lxiii; and Frank Barlow, "The Vita Aedwardi (Book II); the Seven Sleepers: Some Further Evidence and Reflections," *Speculum* 40 (1965): 385–97.

23. The best and most comprehensive study remains Michael Huber, *Die Wanderlegende von den Siebenschläfern: Eine literargeschichtliche Untersuchung* (Leipzig: Harrassowitz, 1910). On its important place in Islamic worship and tradition, see Louis Massignon, "Les 'Sept Dormants': Apocalypse de l'Islam," *Analecta Bollandiana* 68 (1950): 245–60; and Norman O. Brown, "The Apocalypse of Islam," in *The Qur'an: Style and Content*, ed. Andrew Rippin (Aldershot: Ashgate, 2001): 355–80.

24. Barlow, *The Life of King Edward*, 102–7.

25. Ibid., 107–11.

26. "Merlin's Sardonic Laughter," in *Studies in Medieval Literatures and Languages*, ed. W. Rothwell, W. R. J. Barron, David Blamires, and Lewis Thorpe (Manchester: Manchester University Press, 1973): 323–39. Besides Geoffrey of Monmouth's *Vita Merlini*, Thorpe discusses an early Christian Greek text and a Rabbinical text; then, two later texts directly or indirectly dependent on the *Vita Merlini:* the *Estoire de Merlin* from the Vulgate Cycle and the *Roman de Silence*.

27. The Sleepers figure prominently in Sura 18 of the Qur'an ("The Cave"), which has been called the "Apocalypse of Islam" (Massignon, "Les 'Sept Dormants.'" Brown, "The Apocalypse of Islam," takes issue with the label, not denying that the sura is apocalyptic but rather arguing that the entire Qur'an is.) The latter part of the same sura concerns the wall built to contain Gog and Magog, another prominent apocalyptic theme in both Islamic and Christian traditions. The Qur'an specifically

mentions God's turning the Sleepers from the right to the left as one of the miraculous aspects of the story (Sura 18, verse 18), and the motif was later expanded in the Islamic tradition. Massignon gives three examples from Muslim historiography of the turning of the Sleepers, combined with the motif of a ruler sending a delegation to verify a rumor or vision thereof ("Les 'Sept Dormants,'" 285). In one of them, a second delegation is sent to check on the status of Gog and Magog.

28. The prophetic incident is datable to 1060; counting seventy-four years from 1060 puts us in 1134 which appears to have no particular resonance, numerological or otherwise. The obvious speculation that we might be dealing with a retroactive prophecy first composed in or around 1134 to "predict" some specific event in that year is ruled out by William of Malmesbury's use of the same figure, seventy-four years, even though he is writing in the early 1120s, well before the prophecy's deadline. (Barlow, *The Life of King Edward*, 104, note 261).

29. Huber, *Wanderlegende*, 14–16, 102.

30. Massignon, "Les 'Sept Dormants,'" 249. In later Islamic tradition, reciting the names of the Sleepers appears to have acquired mystical, apotropaic properties—also a highly suggestive motif here.

31. Barlow, *Vita Aedwardi*, 108–11.

32. *The History of the English by Henry, Archdeacon of Huntingdon*, ed. Thomas Arnold, Rolls Series 74 (London: Longman, 1879), x–xxx.

33. Greenway, *Historia Anglorum*, lxvi–lxxvii.

34. Ibid., 494–95.

35. Ibid., 495, note 2.

36. Ibid., lxiii–lviv.

37. Ibid., 494, note 1.

38. Ibid., 490–93 and lxxi–lxxiv.

39. "Cogitemus autem de his qui in primo millenario circa hanc etatem, id est circa annum centesimum tricesimum quintum fuerunt, quid deuenerint. . . . Dicant nunc reges et duces, tiranni et principes, prelati et consules, tribuni et presides, magistratus et uicecomites, bellicosi et fortes—qui tunc temporis sui ordinis et professionis fuerint. . . . Loquar ad meipsum. Dic, Henrice, dic huius auctor historie, qui fuerint illius temporis archidiaconi? . . . Si aliquis eorum causa laudis et glorie aliquid laboris presumpserit, cum iam nulla super eo possit esse memoria maior quam super equo uel asello suo, cur in uanum miser animum suum afflixit? Quid ualuerunt qui ad hoc deuenerunt?" Ibid., 494–97.

40. "Ad uos igitur iam loquar qui in tercio millenario, circa centesimum tricesimum quintum annum, eritis. Cogitate de nobis, qui modo clari uidemur. . . . Cogitate, inquam, quo deuenerimus." Ibid., 496–97.

41. Ibid. For a somewhat analogous maneuver in Dante's *Commedia*, see Piero Boitani, "'Those Who Will Call This Time Ancient': The Futures of Prophecy and Poetry," Burrow and Wei, in *Medieval Futures*, 51–65.

42. Greenway, *Historia Anglorum*, 498–99.

43. Ibid. Henry claims to have heard this argument in private conversation from Herbert Losinga—indeed quotes it verbatim as the bishop's words.

44. Ibid., 498–501. In the 1135 redaction, where the "epilogue" was in fact the end of the book, these were the memorable last words: the entire *Historia* quite stunningly ended with the phrase, "nihil habes."

45. Cf. the use of memoria a few pages earlier, in the "ubi sunt" passage cited at n. 39 ("cum iam nulla super eo possit esse memoria").

46. There may also be a reminiscence of Psalm 6:6. Asking God to spare him from death, the Psalmist reminds God, "For there is no one in death, that is mindful of thee."

47. Nancy Partner, while arguing that *contemptus mundi* is the chief theme of Henry's historiography, also points out how ambivalent that *contemptus mundi* is (*Serious Entertainments: The Writing of History in Twelfth-Century England* [Chicago: University of Chicago Press, 1977], 11–48).

48. Greenway, *Historia Anglorum*, 494–95.

49. Southern, "Aspects of the European Tradition," 159–80. Even more categorically in this vein, Marjorie Reeves, "History and Prophecy in Medieval Thought," *Medievalia et Humanistica*, n.s. 5 (1974), 51–75; and Schmitt, "Appropriating the Future," 16–17.

50. *De Nugis Curialium* 36–37.

3

SARAH SPENCE

"What's Love Got to Do with It?"

Abbot Suger and the Renovation of Saint-Denis

To introduce Suger, abbot of Saint-Denis from 1122 until his death in 1151, in the context of beauty would not surprise anyone: Suger's struggles with the aesthetic are what, for many, put him on the map. Whether or not his renovation of the church of Saint-Denis is in fact to be seen as the origin of the Gothic—because of its glorious attention to light, in particular—Suger's fascination with the beautiful permeates his work, both verbal and visual.[1]

To mention Suger in the context of love, however, might provoke a less credulous response. Beauty is one thing—there are ways to justify even an excessive interest in the material—but love is another. Even if the church of Saint-Denis and the writings of Suger speak to an aesthetic sensibility, what is there to suggest that the erotic deserves attention? Surely it is a stretch to look at a building and writings about that building, and to see someone weighing in on the role and importance of love. Yet I will argue that love has everything to do with Suger's decision to renovate the choir of Saint-Denis. Far from being removed from the debate on love that dominates the literary and philosophical writings of his time, Suger is deeply involved, using both his building and his texts to make a statement on the nature and importance of love. Moreover, while the commentaries on the Song of Songs offer up an often-cited locus for the intersection of the erotic with the architectural, Suger grounds his argument in a very different set of texts.

Amplificatio est res; res est amplificationum

On the face of it, Abbot Suger's decision to renovate the choir of Saint-Denis seems relatively straightforward:

> Nono decimo administrationis nostrae anno, cum novo operi in anteriori ecclesiae parte libenter et fideliter desudassemus . . . subito sanctorum Martyrum domnorum et protectorum nostrorum amor et devotio nos ad augmentandam et amplificandam superioris ecclesiae partem capitalem rapuit.[2]

> In the nineteenth year of our administration, after we had applied ourselves duly and faithfully to the front part of the church with the new construction, . . . the love and devotion for our holy Martyr, lord and protector, suddenly drove our chapter to augment and amplify the back part of the church.

Having reworked the front of the church, Suger argues, he turned his attention to the back. The questions that plague much of the rest of his writings—of the need or desire for luxury, of the importance of light and beauty, of the centrality of the visible and material to the finished work—are not even hinted at here. With one part completed, Suger turned to the other.

Conrad Rudolph has demonstrated how the artistic program Suger initiated, which enabled him to transform the church from a dark, low example of the Carolingian to an airy, color-saturated prototype of the Gothic, involved, finally, a series of elaborate defenses: "by the time that Bernard of Clairvaux himself attended the consecration ceremony for the east end [Suger] had developed a complex system of claims to justify that program."[3] Rudolph's revisionist readings of these justifications point away from an anti-Cistercian bias and pseudo-Dionysian light mysticism and towards a "middle-ground solution to the question of an acceptable monastic art [which] at the same time retain[s] and even increase[s] the previous level of the sensory saturation of the holy place."[4]

It seems equally likely that Suger's initial decision—to finish the job at hand—must have entailed defenses of its own. The church Suger is driven to enlarge and amplify is, after all, no less than the shrine of the patron saint of France. To enlarge it means to change the external, even metonymic representation of that saint. Suger's motivation for such a renovation, while not as detailed or even perhaps as polemical as his subsequent decisions to increase the "sensory saturation" of the building, nonetheless required radical and even questionable decisions on his part. Underlying the bald statement that he wishes to complete what he started, then, lies an unanswered question of motivation: how and why did he do this?

The "why" has been addressed elsewhere: Robert Hanning's argument about the tension evident in these texts between Suger the showman and Suger the curator speaks to this, as does my own work on the centrality of the body and the tangible to Suger.[5] But the "how"—Suger's own justification, to himself and others, of such radical change—remains unexplored.

The fullest explanation Suger explicitly provides is in the *De Consecratione:*

Gloriosus et famosus rex Francorum Dagobertus, vir etsi in regni administratione magnanimitate regia conspicuus, nihilominus tamen Ecclesia Dei devotus, cum ad declinandam patris sui Clotharii intolerabilem iram Catulliacum vicum aufugisset, et sanctorum Martyrum ibidem quiescentium effigies venerandas, tanquam pulcherrimos viros niveis vestibus comptos, servitium suum requirere et auxilium promittere incunctanter voce et opere comperisset, basilicam Sanctorum regia munificentia fabricatum iri affectu mirabili imperavit. Quam cum mirifica marmorearum columnarum varietate componens, copiosis purissimi auri et argenti thesauris inaestimabiliter locupletasset, ipsiusque parietibus et columnis et arcubus auro textas vestes margaritarum varietatibus multipliciter exornatas suspendi fecisset, quatinus aliarum ecclesiarum ornamentis praecellere videretur et, omnimodis incomparabili nitore vernans et omni terra pulchritudine compta, inaestimabili decore splendesceret: hoc solum ei defuit quod quam oporteret magnitudinem non admisit. Non quod aliquid ejus devotioni aut voluntati deesset, sed quod forsitan tunc temporis in primitiva Ecclesia nulla adhuc aut major aut aequalis existeret, aut quod brevior fulgorantis auri et splendorem gemmarum propinquitati arridentium oculorum acutius delectabiliusque refundendo ultra satis quam si major fabricaretur irradiaret.

Hujus brevitatis egregiae grata occasione, numerositate fidelium crescente et ad suffragia Sanctorum crebro confluente, tantas praefata basilica sustinere consuevit molestias, ut saepius, in solemnibus videlicet diebus, admodo plena per omnes valvas turbarum sibi occurrentium superfluitatem refunderet, et non solum intrantes non intrare, verum etiam qui jam intraverant praecedentium expulsas exire compelleret.[6]

When the glorious and famous King of the Franks, Dagobert, notable for his royal magnanimity in the administration of his kingdom and yet no less devoted to the Church of God, had fled to the village of Catulliacum in order to evade the intolerable wrath of his father Clothaire the Great, and when he had learned that the venerable images of the Holy Martyrs who rested there—appearing to him as very beautiful men clad in snow-white garments—requested his service and unhesitatingly promised him their aid with words and deeds, he decreed with admirable affection that a basilica of the Saints be built with regal magnificence. When he had constructed this [basilica] with a marvelous variety of marble columns he enriched it incalculably with treasures of purest gold and silver and hung on its wall, columns and arches tapestries woven of gold and richly adorned with a variety of pearls, so that it might seem to excel the ornaments of all other churches and, blooming with incomparable luster and adorned with every terrestrial beauty, might shine with inestimable splendor. Only one thing was wanting in him: that he did not allow for the size that was necessary. Not that anything was lacking in his devotion or good will; but perhaps there existed thus far, at that time of the Early Church, no [church] either greater or [even] equal in size; or perhaps [he thought that] a smallish one—reflecting the splendor of gleaming gold and gems to the admiring eyes more keenly and delightfully because they were nearer—would glow with greater radiance than if it were built larger.

Through a fortunate circumstance attending this singular smallness—the number of the faithful growing and frequently gathering to seek the intercession of the Saints—the aforesaid basilica had come to suffer grave inconveniences. Often on feast days, completely filled, it disgorged through all its doors the excess of the crowds as they moved in opposite directions, and the outward pressure of the foremost ones not only prevented those attempting to enter from entering but also expelled those who had already entered.

I quote this passage at length since the diction is telling. First, it is worth noting the *munificentia* Suger ascribes to the earlier church, a sumptuousness that supports Rudolph's dismissal of Panofsky's anti-Cistercian claims:[7] by the time this text was written, at least, beauty was not a problem for the abbot.

Rather, Suger's professed interest lies in redeeming the building from its *brevitas*.[8] The word is striking; one would expect instead a term like *angustia*.[9] Coupled with the earlier description of the renovation as amplification, the project starts to assume an identifiable, if unexpected, profile. Taken together, *amplificatio* and *brevitas* are rhetorical terms and, as Edmond Faral has demonstrated at length, key rhetorical terms in the twelfth and thirteenth centuries. Citing Geoffrey of Vinsauf, Evrard and John of Garland, Faral demonstrates that "l'amplification et l'abréviation tiennent dans les arts poétiques une place importante. . . . L'amplification est la grande chose; elle est la principale fonction de l'écrivain." [10] Chief among these is clarifying the meaning of a text through glossing (*interpretatio* or *expolitio*).

For Suger to refer to the renovation of his building in rhetorical rather than architectural terms is to suggest a strong identification between church and text. Such a glissage is not wholly surprising, given that Suger was author to both projects. But, in his description, Suger hints at another reason why these two efforts might be viewed together: the desire to expand the church, he says in the *Chartes*, derived from a love for "Martyrum domnorum et protectorum nostrum," Saint-Denis, or Pseudo-Dionysius, who was, as Suger reminds us elsewhere, present to him in two forms: in his martyred bones and in his writings, including the neoplatonic *Celestial and Ecclesiastical Hierarchies* and the treatise on *Divine Names*.[11] While the influence of these writings on the particulars of Suger's artistic program has been disputed by Rudolph and others, knowledge of these texts by Suger has not.

If we accept that Suger's identification of the renovation as textual amplification was intentional and rooted in the fact that Saint-Denis himself is present as both text and building, then the question we aim to address, how Suger justified his decision to renovate, should perhaps be approached in terms of this intersection. In other words, if his renovation is, as Suger suggests, to be understood in textual terms, then perhaps a look at the textual tradition surrounding the works of Pseudo-Dionysius will provide insight into Suger's justifications for renovation.

Surgetne Pseudo-Dionysius verus, si vis?

As part of a diplomatic effort in the ninth century, the royal court of Louis the Pious received from the Byzantine emperor Michael II a copy of the writings of Pseudo-Dionysius, which traveled from East to West in the luggage of a royal ambassador. This manuscript, BN 437, also included the scholia of Maximus. Emperor Louis requested (PL 104, cols. 1326D–1328D) that Hilduin, abbot of Saint-Denis from 815–840, translate the Greek texts into Latin and write a life of the author. Hilduin, trained in the school of Alcuin and so somewhat versed in Greek, responded with both, of which we will discuss the last first.[12]

The purpose of the life of Saint-Denis (PL 106, cols. 23D–50B) is to establish that Dionysius, who debated with Saint Paul in Greece, converted, and was ultimately named archbishop, is the same person as Saint-Denis, patron saint and martyr of Paris.[13] The text hinges on a parallel the author draws between Paul and Dionysius: even as Paul traveled to Rome and was martyred, so Dionysius "Lutetiam Parisiorum, Domino ducente, pervenit, doctrina praeclarus, miraculis coruscans, et virtutum signis, quae Atheniensium magister Paulo docente didicerat, Galliis ministravit" ["arrived in Paris, led by the Lord, knowledgeable of doctrine, brandishing miracles and signs of virtue, which the Athenian teacher had learned from Paul, and ministered to the Gauls" (col. 40A)]; he also was eventually martyred for his teachings.

The document begins with a glorious description of ancient Athens, home to pagan beauty and teachings until the ministries of Paul; it ends with an equally evocative description of the location where Pseudo-Dionysius, together with Rusticus and Eleutherius, was martyred and buried, and where the original basilica was built to enshrine their bodies: "Quorum memoranda et gloriosissima passio e regione urbis Parisiorum in colle qui ante mons Mercurii, quoniam inibi idolum ipsius principaliter colebatur a Gallis, nunc vero mons Martyrum vocatur, sanctorum Domini gratia, qui ibidem triumphale martyrium perpetrarunt" ["Of whose memorable and most glorious passion in the region of Paris on the hill which was mount Mercury, since an idol of Mercury was originally worshipped there by the Gauls, now is truly called Mount Martyrs, by the grace of those blessed of the Lord who endured the triumphal martyrdom" (col. 50B).] Not only does Hilduin succeed in establishing the identity of the two who are named Denis as one, he uses this opportunity to provide a model of *translatio* and the movement of culture from East to West, a movement reenacted in the transfer of the manuscript from Constantinople to Paris. There is a subtle dynamic at work here: not only does Hilduin grant Saint-Denis the authority of the second-century Dionysius (and the authorship of all his writings); he also ascribes to him the legacy of antiquity and thereby grants to Paris the historical riches of Athens. It is worth noting that the story begins on a hill in Greece and ends on a hill in Gaul, suggesting yet another parallel between the two.

The vita provides further useful information for our purposes. In its insistence that Dionysius, Pseudo-Dionysius, and Saint-Denis are the same, it argues as well for viewing the texts and body together. This is a critical step: given that, in fact, the writings are of one person and the bones of another, it creates a precedent for viewing the two together. It is perhaps for this reason that, in the vita, the martyrdom is described in as much detail as the writing, from the decapitation to the miraculous recovery of the saint whose: "exanime corpus viventis currere more, et hominem jam mortuum recto gressu incedere. Sed quanquam sit mirum, non est tamen difficile, praeciso capite, sanctissimi viti corpus angelico ministerio in modum viventis ambulare ["the dead body began to run, in the fashion of a living man, and the dead man to walk with even step. Although this is miraculous it is not difficult, even given the decapitated head, for the body of a very holy man to walk like the living with the help of the angels" (col. 47D)].[14]

Having established the identity of Saint-Denis, Hilduin sets out to confirm that identity by means of two actions that establish an important precedent for Suger: translating the writings of Pseudo-Dionysius and building a new chapel *ante pedes,* or "against the feet of the martyrs," to the east of the eighth-century apse.[15] Although Hilduin's translation is almost immediately superseded by the significantly more accurate version by John Scot, it nonetheless remains that Hilduin, as abbot of Saint-Denis, memorialized the saint and his writings through both a building and a text. Not only does he confirm the identification between Pseudo-Dionysius and Saint-Denis, but he reaffirms it by himself authoring a translation and overseeing construction of a building. The "real" Saint-Denis exists both in East and West, and in word and body: Hilduin's translation of his texts parallels exactly his oversight of the building of the chapel, since the two correspond to the saint's dual form and thus mark them with authorial sameness. While Suger's text ascribes the building that is too small, though beautiful, to Dagobert, the very fact that he describes it in rhetorical terms suggests the presence—and precedent—of Hilduin, author and abbot.

This is where Suger's word-choice is, I would argue, particularly telling; for it places him into this "genealogical" line as well. The section of the church Suger proposes renovating in his nineteenth year as abbot is none other than Hilduin's chapel.[16] Given that *amplificatio* and *brevitas* together refer to rhetorical expansion and diminution, Suger's decision to expand the building not only reinforces the notion that the building should be seen as a text but suggests that his own role be taken as that of glossator. Even as Hilduin had established a link between Denis the word and Denis the body, so Suger, in his drive to justify the expansion of the church, turns to a well-established tradition, the glossing of text, as a model for renovation. The works of Pseudo-Dionysius, of course, offered the perfect analogue, since they had been glossed first by John Scot and then, more importantly, by Hugh of Saint Victor.

... *tructam in lacte* (with apologies to Henry David Thoreau and Sir Arthur Conan Doyle)

The most graphic description of Suger's argument for renovation comes in a passage the abbot must have been fond of, since he repeats it, with variation, in three texts:

> Videres alios ab aliis graviter conculcari, et, quod multi discrederent, pronitas mulierculas, super capita virorum tanquam super pavimentum incedendo, niti ad altare concurrere, pulsas aliquando et repulsas et pene semimortuas vivorum miserantium auxilio in claustrum ad horam retrocedentes, pene extremo spiritu anhelare. ("Chartes," *Oeuvres,* 357–58)

> You would see some men gravely trodden by others and, which few could believe, little women leaning forward and walking over the heads of men as if on a pavement, if not running to the altar, pushed forward and back, half-dead receding into the cloister with the aid of the barely living, almost breathing their last.

> ... et videbamus et sentiebamus importunitatem (exigebat enim loci angustia ut mulieres super capita virorum, tanquam super pavimentum, ad altare dolore multo et clamoso tumultu currerent).... (*De Administratione* 25, *Abbot Suger,* 42–43)

... the inadequacy which we often saw and felt (for the narrowness of the place forced the women to run toward the altar upon the heads of the men as upon a pavement with much anguish and noisy confusion)....

Videres aliquando (mirabile visu), quod innitentibus ingredi ad venerationem et deosculationem sanctarum reliquiarum, Clavi et Coronae Domini, tanta congestae multitudinis opponebatur repugnantia, ut inter innumera populorum millia ex ipsa sui compressione nullus pedem movere valeret, nullus aliud ex ipsa sui constrictione quam sicut statua marmorea stare, stupere, quod unum supererat, vociferare. Mulierum autem tanta et tam intolerabilis erat angustia, ut in commixtione virorum fortium sicut prelo depressae, quasi imaginata morte exsanguem faciem exprimere, more parturientium terribiliter conclamare, plures earum miserabiliter decalcatas, pio virorum suffragio super capita hominum exaltatas, tanquam pavimento adhaerentes incedere (*De consecratione 2, Abbot Suger,* 86–89)

At times you could see, a marvel to behold, that the crowded multitude offered so much resistance to those who strove to flock in to worship and kiss the holy relics, the Nail and Crown of the Lord, that no one among the countless thousands of people because of their very density could move a foot; that no one, because of their very congestion, could [do] anything but stand like a marble statue, stay benumbed or, as a last resort, scream. The distress of the women, however, was so great and so intolerable that [you could see] how they, squeezed in by the mass of strong men as in a winepress, exhibited bloodless faces as in imagined death; how they cried out horribly as though in labor; how several of them, miserably trodden underfoot [but then], lifted by the pious assistance of men above the heads of the crowd, marched forward as though clinging to a pavement....

In this extraordinary description of just how cramped the quarters were, several things stand out: the rhetorical thrust of the passage, given the number of similes used, and the peculiar, striking image of the women walking over the heads of men. Most of the similes are biblical and, as such, are of a piece (drawn, for example, from Genesis, Song of Songs, and Esther). The one simile that is not—"tanquam pavimentum"—is also the one associated with the movement of the women, a fact that draws further attention to their action.

The link between these women and textual *amplificatio* is not immediately apparent. If Suger can justify his renovation on the grounds that the building of St.-Denis deserves the same expansive treatment as his text, then why insist on these women and their seemingly very tangible presence in this way? The focus Suger places on the description of these women would urge a closer look at their textual history. All three descriptions of these women involve the phrase, "over the heads of men" (*super capita virorum* or *hominum*). While the phrase *super capita hominum* is used by Pseudo-Dionysius in his discussions of certain church rituals,[17] in none of these examples is there reference to walking over the heads of men, merely the passing of things overhead. Even more strikingly, each of these discussions refers to men, not women. Women walking over the heads of men does not appear.[18]

But in Greek, its use is somewhat more notorious. "Krata androon" is the tag phrase used by Agamemnon of the female offspring of Zeus, Delusion (*Ate*), in his allegory that sets the context for his apology to Achilles:

πρέσβα Διός θυγάτηρ Ἄτη, ἣ πάντας ἀᾶται,
οὐλομένη· τῇ μέν θ' ἁπαλοὶ πόδες· οὐ γὰρ ἐπ' οὔδει
πίλναται, ἀλλ' ἄρα ἥ γε κατ' ἀνδρῶν κράατα βαίνει
βλάπτουσ' ἀνθρώπους· κατὰ δ' οὖν ἕτερόν γε πέδησε.

Eldest daughter of Zeus is Ate that blindeth all—a power fraught with bane; delicate are her feet, for it is not upon the ground that she fareth, but she walketh over the heads of men, bringing men to harm, and this one or that she ensnareth.[19]

As Agamemnon tells it, Ate originally tricked only the gods; Zeus, angry after being deceived by Hera, threw Ate out of Olympus and caused her to inflict her harm only on humans.

Plato quotes this passage, but in a very different context. In the *Symposium*, Agathon describes love in the following terms:

νέος μὲν οὖν ἐστί, πρὸς δὲ τῷ νέῳ ἁπαλός· ποιητοῦ δ' ἔστιν ἐνδεὴς
οἷος ἦν Ὅμηρος πρὸς τὸ ἐπιδεῖξαι θεοῦ ἁπαλότητα. Ὅμηρος γὰρ
Ἄτην θεόν τέ φησιν εἶναι καὶ ἁπαλήν—τοὺς γοῦν πόδας αὐτῆς
ἁπαλοὺς εἶναι—λέγων

τῆς μένθ' ἁπαλοὶ πόδες· οὐ γὰρ ἐπ' οὔδεος
πίλναται, ἀλλ' ἄρα ἥ γε κατ' ἀνδρῶν κράατα βαίνει.

καλῷ οὖν δοκεῖ μοι τεκμηρίῳ τὴν ἁπαλότητα ἀποφαίειν, ὅτι οὐκ ἐπὶ σκληροῦ βαίνει, ἀλλ' ἐπὶ μαλθακοῦ. τῷ αὐτῷ δὴ καὶ ἡμεῖς χρησώμεθα τεκμηρίῳ περὶ Ἔρωτα ὅτι ἁπαλός. οὐ λὰρ ἐπὶ λῆς βαίνει οὐδ' ἐπὶ κρανίων, ἅ ἐστιν οὐ πάνυ μαλακά, ἀλλ ἐν τοῖς μαλακωτάτοις τῶν ὄντων καὶ βαίνει καὶ οἰκεῖ. ἐν λὰρ ἤθεσι καὶ ψυχαῖς θεῶν καὶ ἀνθρ-ώπων τὴν οἴκησιν ἵδρυται, καὶ οὐκ αὖ ἑξῆς ἐν πάσαις ταῖς ψυχαῖς, ἀλλ' ᾗτινι ἂν σκληρὸν ἦθος ἐχούσῃ ἐντύχῃ, ἀπέρχεται, ᾗ δ' ἂν μαλα-κόν, οἰκίζεται. ἁπτόμενον οὖν ἀεὶ καὶ ποσὶ καὶ πάντῃ ἐν μαλακω-τάτοις τῶν μαλακωτάτων, ἁπαλώτατον ἀνάγκη εἶναι. (195C–196A)

So then he is young, and delicate withal: he requires a poet such as Homer to set forth his delicacy divine. Homer it is who tells of Ate as both divine and delicate; you recollect those delicate feet of hers, where he says—

> Yet delicate are her feet, for on the ground
> She speeds not, only on the heads of men.

So I hold it convincing proof of her delicacy that she goes not on hard things but on soft. The same method will serve us to prove the delicacy of Love. Not upon earth goes he, nor on our crowns, which are not very soft; but takes his way and abode in the softest things that exist. The tempers and souls of gods and men are his chosen habitation: not indeed any soul as much as another; when he comes upon one whose temper is hard, away he goes, but if it be soft, he makes his dwelling there. So if with feet and every way he is wont ever to get hold of the softest parts of the softest creatures, he needs must be most delicate.[20]

In Plato, Ate is introduced not as Delusion, the Pandora-like figure she is in Homer, but instead as an instance of the importance of poetic troping and as a *comparanda* for Love. Whereas Ate earned the great honor of being described by Homer, Love, an even greater god, has yet to find his poet. Whereas Ate is fine and delicate, love is even more so. Ate thus becomes, in the context of Plato's work, Love's forerunner, especially in the context of poetic treatment. Moreoever, she serves to define him: if Ate gets x, then Love deserves x + 1.[21]

That this same passage was known in the twelfth century cannot be shown directly.[22] However, indirect evidence that it was available in some form is suggested by a passage in Hugh of Saint Victor's commentary on

Pseudo-Dionysius' *Celestial Hierarchies* (PL 175, cols. 1037A-1044E). When love enters your heart, Hugh explains:

> et ad intimum cordis tui . . . pertingit; tunc intrat in te ipse, et tu quoque intras ut maneat scilicet vel subsitat extra apud te, vel in portis tuis, vel in atriis tuis; sive ante ostium domus tuae, . . . usque ad thalamum perveniat, et cubiculum ingrediatur, et usque ad interiora penetret, et in intimis tuis requiescat. Adhuc amplius dicam . . . ut nihil apud te durum aut rigidum inveniat virilis truculentiae. Sed totum liquefiat, et mollescat igne dilectionis.

> and reaches your innermost heart, then it enters into you and you also enter so that it can either remain or squat outside yourself, either on your doorstep, or in your courtyard or before the door of your house, . . . [let him] come all the way to your bed, and let him enter your bedroom, and penetrate all the way to the innermost sanctum and let him rest in your intimacy. About this I should add . . . that he should find nothing about you that is hard or rigid with virile ferocity. But all should be liquified and made soft with the fire of love.

which echoes Agathon's description, quoted above, of Love, who dwells neither on earth nor on our heads, because they are not soft, but lives instead in "the softest things that exist," seeking out the souls of gods and men of delicate temperament. As a result, Love proceeds with caution, so that "with feet and every way," he is able to get hold of "the softest parts of the softest creatures."

The composite description of love—as tender, as dwelling in the house of the heart, and as not tolerating anything hard—at the very least triangulates this passage to a source in the *Symposium*, the same one that seems to lie behind Suger's description of the women walking over head. [23] Moreover, Suger's passage would seem to comment on Hugh's: if love needs a soft home—softer, Plato says, than the heads of men—then the women running overhead are preparing the way for love, even as Ate does for Love in Plato. While this does not prove that the passage from Plato was known to Hugh and Suger, sometimes, as Thoreau says, circumstantial evidence can be very compelling. It is worth noting that the women in Suger's passage cry out as if in labor, like Eve after the fall; on this evidence alone, the women can be seen as forerunners to Love, a reading reinforced by the passage from Hugh.[24]

festinat renovari

The extent of Hugh of Saint Victor's influence on Suger's artistic program has been explored in detail by Rudolph, who reaches the conclusion that the "major stimulus toward the meaning and the means of Suger's program" was provided in large part by the "cooperation and innovation of Hugh of St-Victor," especially his commentary on *The Celestial Hierarchy.* [25] The same is true, I would argue, of Suger's renovation of the abbey church, where Hugh provides both meaning, through his particular gloss on Pseudo-Dionysius, and means, by the very fact of glossing. Like Hugh, Suger glosses, and his glosses often seem to respond to Hugh's.

Suger's description of the women walking overhead provides yet another, even more interesting, example of this influence. What is perhaps most striking about these women is the fact that they are moving, unlike the other people who close in around them. The purpose of Suger's repeated description of this scene is to show how crowded and immobile the congregation was, on feast days in particular; the lack of movement is what is stressed throughout, underscoring the argument that the need for renovation is predicated on a lack of room to move. But the women are shown walking, above the heads of men, in a passage that established the need to renovate the choir.

Once again Hugh of Saint Victor's commentary on the *Celestial Hierarchies* provides insight into Suger's passage. Later in the passage discussed above, Hugh draws the following connection between love and motion:

> Et quid amor? . . . Ubi fervorem, et calorem amor habuit; vel potius, ubi amor sine calore, et fervore fuit? Ambulantes et amantes, incendentes et ferventes, quid dixerunt de Jesu, quem audierunt, et non cognoverunt in via? Ambulabant enim et movebantur, impatientia dilectionis acti, quia si starent non amarent. (PL 175, col. 1037B)

> And what of love? . . . Where love is, there is drive and heat; or rather, where love is not, is without heat and drive? They who were walking and loving, burning and driving, why did they speak about Jesus, whom they heard and did not recognize on the road? [26] They were walking and they were moved, driven by the impatience of love, since if they stood still they would not love.

In the nineteenth section of Pseudo-Dionysius's treatise on naming God, *De divinis nominibus,* in the context of a critical discussion on the nature of love, Pseudo-Dionysius argues that God, as love, is Himself the basis of such motion: "Ipsum autem eum dilectum et cupitum vocant . . . cupiditatem autem iterum et dilectionem, . . . cupidialem motionem simplicem";[27] that motion is an attribute of love, perceived both literally and figuratively. Love needs and creates room to rise.

Yet here Pseudo-Dionysius adds a further layer: glossing, he argues, is a form of such motion: "Ὅταν δὲ ὁ νοῦς διὰ τῶν αἰσθητῶν ἀνακινεῖσθαι σπεύδῃ πρὸς θεωρητικὰς νοήσεις. While the translation of this line by John Scot reads "Cum vero anima per sensibilia *removeri festinat* ad contemplabiles invisibilitates," Hilduin's reads "Quando autem mens sensibilibus *renovari festinat* ad theoriticas intelligentias" (emphasis mine). In classical Latin, *renovare* means "renew" or "refresh," a sense it still retained in Hilduin's time; by Suger's time the term has come to mean "renovate" or "refashion"; it is the term Suger himself uses to discuss various building projects in the *Administratione* and the *Testamentum*.[28]

In the section of the *De Consecratione* in which Suger describes his decision to renovate, he writes:

> . . . sola Dei omnipotentis ineffabili misericordia praefatae molestiae correctioni sanctorum Martyrum dominorum nostrorum suffragio raptus, ad augmentationem praefati loci toto animo, tota mentis affectione accelerare proposuimus: qui nunquam, si tanta, tam necessaria, tam utilis et honesta non exigeret opportunitas, manum supponere vel cogitare praesumeremus. (*De Consecratione*.2)

> . . . then, impelled to a correction of the aforesaid inconvenience only by the ineffable mercy of Almighty God and by the aid of the Holy Martyrs our Patron Saints, we resolved to hasten, with all our spirit and all the affection of our mind, to the enlargement of the aforesaid place— we who would never have presumed to set our hand to it, nor even to think of it, had not so great, so necessary, so useful and honorable an occasion demanded it.

Suger "sets his hand" to the renovation of the "enlargement of the aforesaid place"—*loci* or "topoi"—rhetorical and architectural once again. Yet it is the phrase "ad augmentationem toto animo, tota mentis affectione accelerare" that is particularly striking in this context, since it speaks of an urgency toward augmentation, or renovation, and suggests a link between motion and *amplificatio* that echoes Pseudo-Dionysius, especially via Hilduin's

translation. For Hilduin, unlike John Scot, describes progress toward illumination in architectural terms: he explains that the mind hastens to renovate
itself through explanation, through gloss. Suger's phrase, even as it echoes the
action of the women over head, also paraphrases the phrase *festinat renovari*
from Hilduin's translation.

The history of Hilduin's translations of the works of Pseudo-Dionysius
is far from clear. The perceived superiority of John Scot's translation meant
that Hilduin's version receded almost immediately into the shadows. The
commentary of Hugh of Saint Victor, for example, is keyed to John Scot's
translation, as are most if not all of the later translations of the works of
Pseudo-Dionysius. Yet Hilduin's translation remained an item of enough
interest that it was transcribed periodically. Gabriel Théry located two
extant manuscripts, one a fifteenth-century Belgian (MS 756 – 57 Bibliothèque Royale de Bruxelles), the other a twelfth-century French (MS 15645
Bibliothèque Nationale), from which he established the text of his edition.[29] Philippe Chevallier includes the Hilduin translation in his edition of
the works of Pseudo-Dionysius as the earliest of nine Latin translations of
the texts.[30] The very fact that, like Suger after him, Hilduin was both abbot
of Saint-Denis and, more importantly, directly involved with celebrating
the saint's dual identity gives cause to look hard at his translation of Pseudo-
Dionysius. Moreover, the existence of a twelfth-century copy from a northern French provenance suggests the possibility that Suger had this copy made,
perhaps from Hilduin's original that had been deposited at Saint-Denis.
Fidelity to the Greek would, from many angles, be less important than preserving or even establishing a precedent to Suger's own efforts; if anything, the idiosyncracies of Hilduin's texts may be more telling than the lack
of accuracy. Moreover, where Hilduin uses an architectural term to refer
to a rhetorical process, Suger does the reverse, gesturing toward Hilduin's
metaphoric use of *renovari* in his own use of a rhetorical one, *augmentationem.*[31]

Michael Riffaterre has argued that when a word jumps out of its stylistic register it functions as an "ungrammaticality," which signals the presence
of an intertext, a second text that will provide the context for the unexpected
word choice.[32] Suger's use of *accelerare . . . ad augmentationem* sends us back
to Hilduin's version of Pseudo-Dionysius' text, where we find a complementary passage that expands upon Suger's choice of rhetorical terminology. Not
just the word itself, then, but the passage as a whole—with its argument that
gloss, like love, involves motion—should be brought to bear on Suger's

intent here. The urgency to augment, like the drive to renovate, is brought about, as the full passage from Pseudo-Dionysius explains, by the fact that love needs room to move.

Suger's echo of Hilduin's phrase, which is then reified in the movement of the women overhead, serves as a further commentary on and response to the passage from Hugh of Saint Victor. In both the original of Pseudo-Dionysius and in the commentary by Hugh of Saint Victor, love is affiliated with motion; in particular, with room to move. But it is Hilduin's translation in particular that provides Suger with a two-edged motivation for renovation that is rooted in the Dionysian conception of love as motion. Movement is not only essential to love, as Hugh argues, it is essential to both glossing and renovation, as Hilduin's translation suggests.[33] Using Hilduin, Suger expands Hugh's commentary and understanding of love to include glossing and so renovation. The women walking overhead are thus twice Love's precursors: their very ability to move indicates what the others still lack, even as the hardness of the pavement-like heads they run on suggests a place where love would not yet thrive.

Poetria in motu

The unrenovated church, which keeps its faithful from moving forward, hinders the fostering of love. But the women are able to move over the heads of men, even in the unrenovated church, because they are textual fragments, icons from the textual tradition that demonstrate how amplification could provide the motive and means for increase. The heightened poetry of the passage points to a metatextual tradition that not only comments on metaphor but illustrates as well the significance of motion and love in both textual and spatial terms.

Suger finds in the commentary tradition a language of love that enables him to justify his will to renovate and expand. Hilduin's translation, together with the commentary of Hugh of Saint Victor, provides motivation for the renovation. The women running overhead serve as a trope that enables Suger to present his architectural decisions in textual terms, and, more specifically, in terms that entail necessity and enable him to argue for expansion. The renovation of Saint-Denis is in fact an act of love for the saint—"sanctorum Martyrum domnorum et protectorum nostrorum amor et devotio nos ad augmentandam et amplificandam superioris ecclesiae partem capitalem rapuit"—since love, like interpretation, needs room to grow and move. The image of Tina Turner in concert evoked by the title of this paper is perhaps more apt than her lyrics, unless we, with apologies to Suger, gloss them to read: "what's love but the sacred plan of motion."

Notes

I am indebted to my colleagues Richard A. LaFleur and Erika Hermanowicz: Rick for advice on the subheadings, Erika for help with those overhead.

1. There is a similar bias in the criticism of his work: see, e.g., Erwin Panofsky, "Introduction," *Abbot Suger: On the Abbey Church of St.-Denis and its Art Treasures* (Princeton: Princeton University Press, 1946); Otto von Simson, *The Gothic Cathedral* (Princeton: Princeton University Press, 1962); *Abbot Suger and Saint-Denis*, ed. Paula Gerson (New York: Metropolitan Museum of Art, 1986), sections 5 and 6; Philippe Verdier, "Réflexions sur l'esthétique de Suger," *Etudes de civilisation médiévale, IXe au XIIe siècles: Mélanges offerts à Edmond-René Labande* (Poitiers: C.É.S.C.M., 1984), 699–709; André Moisan, "Suger de Saint-Denis, Bernard de Clairvaux et la question de l'art sacré," *Le Beau et le laid au Moyen Âge* (Aix-en-Provence: Centre universitaire d'études et de recherches médiévales d'Aix , 2000), 385–99.

2. *Chartes* 10, in *Oeuvres complètes de Suger,* ed. A. Lecoy de la Marche (Paris: Reynouard, 1867), 356–57.

3. Conrad Rudolph, *Artistic Change at St.-Denis* (Princeton: Princeton University Press, 1990), 75.

4. Ibid., 74–75.

5. Robert W. Hanning, "Suger's Literary Style and Vision," in Gerson, *Abbot Suger and Saint-Denis,* 145–50; Sarah Spence, *Texts and the Self in the Twelfth Century* (Cambridge: Cambridge University Press, 1996), 19–53. See also Peter Diemer, "Abt Suger von Saint-Denis und die Kunstschätze seines Klosters," in *Beschreibungskunst—Kunstbeschreibung,* ed. Gottfried Boehm and Helmut Pfotenhauer (Münich: Fink, 1995), 177–216.

6. *De Consecratione* 2; text and translation from Panofsky, *Abbot Suger,* 86–87.

7. In addition, Hilduin's description, at the close of the life of Saint Denis, states that "basilicam super pretiosorum martyrum corpora, magno sumptu . . . construxerunt" (PL 106, col. 49C).

8. Hanning ("Suger's Literary Style") argues for seeing the threat of narrowness as a threat of theft, in temporal as well as spatial terms.

9. So, for example, the description given of Suger's accomplishments in his *Vita:* "ex veteri novam, ex angusta latissimam, ex tenebrosiore splendidem reddarent ecclesiasm" (*Oeuvres,* 391).

10. Edmond Faral, *Les arts poétiques du XIIe et du XIIIe siècle* (Paris: Champion, 1971), 61. While Faral focuses on *amplificatio* and *brevitas* as stylistic features of good writing, it is clear from his discussion and examples that these are fundamentally explicative processes (62 ff.).

11. As Panofsky summarizes: "Fusing the doctrines of Plotinus and, more specifically, Proclus with the creeds and beliefs of Christianity, Dionysius the Pseudo-Areopagite . . . combined the neoplatonic conviction of the fundamental oneness and luminous aliveness of the world with the Christian dogmas of the triune God, original sin and redemption" (19). See also Grover A. Zinn, Jr., "Suger, Theology, and the Pseudo-Dionysian Tradition," in Gerson, *Abbot Suger and Saint-Denis*, 33–40. For a discussion of the influence of Pseudo-Dionysius on another significant work by Suger, the *Vita Ludovici*, see Gabrielle Spiegel, "History as Enlightenment: Suger and the *Mos Anagogicus*," in *The Past as Text: The Theory and Practice of Medieval Historiography* (Baltimore: Johns Hopkins University Press, 1997), esp. 170–77.

12. Gabriel Théry, "Introduction," in *Études Dionysiennes*, 2 vols. (Paris: Vrin, 1932–37); Foss, *Über den Abt Hilduin von St. Denis und Dionysius Areopagita* (Berlin: Gaertner, 1886).

13. Dionysius is the name of the historic figure Eusebius reports as having debated with St. Paul; Pseudo-Dionysius is the name given to the author of works reputedly, but not actually, written by this figure.

14. The decapitation is likewise worthy of note: "Talique ad Dominum meruere professione migrare, ut amputatis capitibus adhuc putaretur lingua palpitans Jesum Christum Dominum confiteri" (col. 46D). Perhaps Hilduin had it wrong, and Saint-Denis was actually the patron saint of academics.

15. See Sumner McKnight Crosby, *The Royal Abbey of Saint-Denis from Its Beginnings to the Death of Suger, 475–1151* (New Haven: Yale University Press, 1987), chapter 4.

16. Ibid., 89.

17. See, for example, John Scot's commentary on the *Ecclesiastical Hierarchies* (PL 122, cols. 1098C–1101B).

18. A woman traveling overhead does occur in Vergil, where the native Italian fighter, Camilla, at the end of *Aeneid* 7, is described as "illa vel intactae segetis per summa volaret / gramina nec teneras cursu laesisset aristas, / vel mare per medium fluctu suspensa tumenti / ferret iter celeris nec tingeret aequore plantas" (*Aen.* 7.808–11). Yet this, too, does not correspond fully to Suger's passage, since Camilla explicitly does not set foot on anything, especially not heads. On the sources for the Camilla story, see Barbara Weiden Boyd, "Virgil's Camilla and the Traditions of Catalogue and Ecphrasis (*Aeneid* 7.803–17)," *American Journal of Philology* 113 (1992): 213–34.

19. Homer, *Iliad* 19. 91–94. Text and translation from Loeb.

20. Text and translation from Loeb.

21. That this passage from Homer was picked up by even later commentators is clear from Lucian who, in his *Essays on Portraiture*, shows how the passage has become almost aphoristic:

οὐδεὶς λὰρ ἄν φθονήσειε τῷ ὑπερέχοντι, ἢν μετριάζοντα ἐπὶ τοῖς εὐτυχή-
μασιν αὐτὸν ὁρᾷ καὶ μὴ κατὰ τὴν τοῦ Ὁμήρου Ἄτην ἐκείνην ἐπ' ἀνδρῶν
κράατα βεβηκότα καὶτὸ ὑποδεέστερον πατοῦντα·

Nobody will envy the man above him if he sees him behaving with moderation amid his successes and not, like Homer's Ate, treading on the heads of men and crushing whatever is feebler. (Text and translation from Loeb)

22. There was definitely no direct knowledge of the *Symposium* as a whole before the 1430s when a partial translation by Leonardo Bruni appeared. There are a certain number of quotations and allusions known through Cicero, Apuleius, and Augustine, among others; this particular passage does not appear in those. For more on this, see Stephen Gersh, *Middle Platonism and Neoplatonism: The Latin Tradition* (Notre Dame, Ind.: University of Notre Dame Press, 1986); Edouard Jeauneau, *Lectio Philosophorum* (Amsterdam: Hakkert, 1973); James Hankins, *Plato in the Italian Renaissance* (Leiden: Brill, 1994).

23. Especially movement over the head, or superior movement. Pseudo-Dionysius' own neoplatonism, of course, would suggest that such a Platonic echo was entirely feasible, perhaps from some lost commentary. Plotinus' tractate on love (*Enneads*, book 5), while not referring to this passage in particular, does certainly allude to the discussion of love in the *Symposium*. See Hermann Friedrich Müller, *Dionysios. Proklos. Plotinos* (Münster: Aschendorff, 1918); Stephen Gersh, *From Iamblichus to Eriugena* (Leiden: Brill, 1978).

24. One would expect, in this context, reference to the Song of Songs. Suger does, indeed, make frequent allusion to Solomon's temple in his descriptions of the new church. However, nothing in the biblical text connects Solomon's temple with crowding and lack of motion. There is a sermon by Augustine—one of the ones only recently discovered—that tantalizingly discusses many of the issues relevant here, including crowding and need for charity. It does not, however, mention any of the texts at play in Suger's passage. François Dolbeau, "Nouveaux sermons de saint Augustin pour la conversion des paiens et les donatistes (III)," *Revue des Études Augustiniennes* 38 (1992): 50–79.

25. Rudolph, *Artistic Change*, 75. See also 70: "[I]t may be that Hugh's commentary on *The Celestial Hierarchy* suggested to Suger his defense of external materialism on the basis of Pseudo-Dionysian thought. . . . Hugh's theology was one which, while tinted with Pseudo-Dionysian thought, was fundamentally Augustinian. And it was Augustinian Christology and exegetical method that, with an ele-

ment of Pseudo-Dionysianism, were apparently refracted through Hugh to form the conceptual bases of the west central portal and the Allegorical Window, two of the most central artworks of the program. . . . That is, the west portal or any of the other artworks at St-Denis are not illustrations of Hugh's writings, but rather his writings are a relatively complex indicator of his role in the determination of various aspects of the art program in that they relate his specific approach to the general subjects presented."

26. Luke 24:13–32.

27. *De div nom.*, 19; *Études dionysiennes,* 213; *Dionysiaca,* 221–22. He quotes Hierotheus' gloss on the Song of Songs: "Cupiditatem seu divinam seu angelicam seu intelligibilem aut animalem aut naturalem si dixerimus, coadunalem quamdam et continealem intelligimus virtutem, superna quidem moventem providentiam inferiorum, conscripta iterum ad communialem convenientiam, et novissima ac subdita ad meliorum et superjacentium conversionem" (225).

28. "Easque et redditus earum thesaurario ad renovandas et augmentandas ecclesiae hujus palliaturas, in sempiternum contulimus" (*De administratione,* 23); "in aedificatione magnae et charitativae domus hospitium, in reparatione et renovatione dormitorii et refectorii, et in augmentatione . . . thesauri" (*Testamentum*).

29. *Études dionysiennes,* 2 vols. (Paris: Vrin, 1932). The twelfth-century manuscript was corrected following John Scot; the fifteenth-century one following other versions, including those by John Scot and Sarrazin. It is interesting to note that in the twelfth-century version, the passage under consideration here, found on folio 79v[a], has not been corrected, even though it does not correspond to the John Scot translation.

30. Philippe Chevallier, *Dionysiaca: Recueil donnant l'ensemble des traductions latines des ouvrages attribués au Denys l'Areopagite* (Paris: Desclée, 1937). See also Martin Grabmann, "Ps-Dionysius Areopagita in lateinischen Übersetzungen des Mittelalters," in *Beiträge zur Geschichte des christlichen Altertums und der Byzantinischen Literatur: Festgabe Albert Ehrhard,* ed. Albert Koeniger (Bonn: Kurt Schroeder, 1922), 180–99.

31. Panofsky, *Abbot Suger,* 88–89. Note also that Hilduin's translation of *nous* asserts the separation of mind and soul, while John Scot's does not. I have revised Panofsky's translation of *animus* to reflect what I feel is Suger's intended meaning of spirit and mind, not soul (*animus* versus *anima*).

32. Michael Riffaterre defines "ungrammaticality" as the type of semantic indirection that distorts representation through deviant grammar or lexicon: "The ungrammaticalities spotted at the mimetic level are eventually integrated into another system. As the reader perceives what they have in common . . . the new function of the ungrammaticalities change their nature, and now signify as components of a different network of relationships." *Semiotics of Poetry* (Bloomington: Indiana University Press, 1978), 2, 4.

33. Another striking difference between Hilduin and John Scot, especially in the present context, is that Hilduin consistently misconstrues πτοιῶν as ποδῶν, and thus introduces feet into the text where they do not occur in either the original Greek or other Latin translations. So, for instance, chapter 6 of the *Ecclesiastical Hierarchies* reads, in Hilduin: "Quidam, vero, sicut adhuc *ab adversariis pedibus* inviriliter timente et virtutifactis sermonibus eos quodam confortante" (emphasis mine), where John Scot, more correctly, reads "a contrariis tumultibus." Given the significance of walking, and even feet, in the passage under consideration in Suger, the difference is suggestive.

4

CHARLOTTE GROSS

Time and Nature in Twelfth-Century Thought

William of Conches, Thierry of Chartres, and the "New Science"

I n his gloss on Plato's *Timaeus*, written in the second quarter of the twelfth century, the natural philosopher William of Conches defines time as "the measure of changing things according to rest and motion" ("dimensio more et motus mutabilium rerum"). For time, William writes, is measured according to the rest of things in place and their movement from place to place.[1] If definitions of time offer vantage points on different ways of looking at the world — on what Thomas Kuhn, in his influential account of scientific revolutions, has called paradigms — then William's original definition signals an important paradigm shift in western thought.[2]

For Plato, who views time as "the moving likeness of eternity" (*Tim.* 37d), the fluctuating world of temporal things is an inferior copy of the eternal, intelligible, and unchanging world of forms: the immutable is valued over the mutable.[3] In contrast, Aristotle's first concern is the motion of the physical world. Conceiving nature as a principle of motion and change (*kinesis*), he views time as an aspect of movement as measured by the human observer — "the number of motion in respect of 'before' and 'after'" (*Physics*

219b1–2).[4] Finally, at the start of the Christian tradition, Augustine's psychological account of time reveals a profound concern for the world of the
spirit: he describes time as a *distensio animi*, a distension or extension of the
measuring mind.[5] In his commentaries on Genesis, Augustine also associates
time with the motion and change of the physical world; yet he never sur-
mounts the spiritual inquietude evoked by the impermanence and incon-
stancy of temporal things.[6]

In the larger context of these foundational paradigms, William's original definition of time signals an important change in ways of looking at the
world: most simply, in the twelfth century, time becomes an aspect of nature. As M.-D. Chenu has shown in his classic study, the twelfth-century
"discovery of nature"—and the concomitant "discovery of time" that is the
main subject of this paper—is characterized by a new understanding of the
natural order as self-sufficient, uniform in its operations, and penetrable by
human reason.[7] Possessing a new sense of control over the material world—
held to be created expressly to minister to human *indigentia*—the twelfth
century desacralizes nature, proclaiming both the intelligibility of the natural world and the efficacy of human inquiry: "In all things," writes William of Conches in his early *Philosophia Mundi*, "a reason must be sought."[8]
Thus, whereas Augustine holds that the time of the physical world is regulated directly by God, in the twelfth century natural philosophers like William of Conches and Thierry of Chartres view time as an empirical aspect
of an autonomous nature, a consistent and predictable feature of natural secondary causation.[9] As these new attitudes develop, the old Augustinian inquietude about temporality is replaced by a new confidence in the regu-
larity of the temporal order—the Chartrian master Bernard of Chartres,
for example, derives *tempus* from *temperat*, explaining that time controls, orders, and distinguishes all things.[10] While the natural philosophers or *phisici*
of the twelfth century continue to draw upon Augustine's account of time in
the physical world—his commentaries on Genesis are "read and reread"—
they significantly revise his conceptions of time and nature.[11] In the first part
of this paper, I want to argue that, for Augustine, time in the natural world
is regulated by an omnipotent Creator. Thus William's definition of time—
"modern" in the twelfth-century sense of the term, an aspect of a newly
discovered nature—marks the emergence of a fresh paradigm in western
thought.

But from another perspective, William's definition of time as a measure of motion is "modern" insofar as it appears to anticipate the reception

of Aristotle's *Physics,* generally dated in the late twelfth or early thirteenth century.[12] Both in associating time with motion—especially locomotion—and in insisting that time must be quantified by an observer, William's definition is strikingly Aristotelian. Having treated nature as a principle of motion, in *Physics* 4 Aristotle advances the view that time is the countable aspect of motion—"movement insofar as it admits of enumeration" (219b1–5). As he adds, time is the measure of "what is moved and what is at rest, the one *qua* moved, the other *qua* at rest . . ." (221b14–18).[13] We do not know whether William had access to a translation of Aristotle's *Physics.* But as long ago as 1909, the distinguished historian Pierre Duhem suggested that William of Conches, Thierry of Chartres, and Gilbert of Poitiers all were familiar with Aristotelian doctrines of movement, place, and the motion of the spheres, either through a translation of *Physics* 4 or a commentary thereon, available at Chartres during the first half of the twelfth century.[14] As recent research finds increasing evidence of the "new science" in the twelfth century—that is, Aristotelian treatises on natural philosophy—William's definition invites us to inquire whether twelfth-century discussions of time and nature not only anticipate but also establish an intellectual foundation for the reception of Aristotle. As I will argue, the recognition of temporal change as process—evident in the writings of both William and Thierry—marks an essential aspect of a developing concept of nature receptive to the new science and Aristotelian thought, where nature is defined as a principle of process (*kinesis*).[15] In this sense, the natural philosophers of the twelfth century not only revise the old Augustinian paradigm, but also stand on the threshold of further changes in ways of looking at the world.

A paradigm shift is said to occur when a like-minded scientific community, engaged upon a single set of problems, becomes aware of anomalous data not congruent with previously accepted theories; controversy and ultimately a shift in professional commitments ensue.[16] According to traditional accounts of historians of science, such a Kuhnian change in ways of looking at the world begins in the twelfth century, when scholars reject the intellectual status quo and take direct action to acquire the scientific heritage of the past: translations of Aristotle from the Greek and Arabic, as Edward Grant writes, contain "an overpowering and comprehensive scientific view of the cosmos that [is] wholly new to the West."[17]

As Joan Cadden has shown, however, the institutional framework, authoritative texts, and even constitution of natural philosophy develop only gradually during the course of the twelfth century; for example, William of

Conches composes his *Dragmaticon* not in the schools but under secular patronage.[18] If study of the *Timeaus* creates a "like-minded" textual community among natural philosophers of the twelfth century—for as Kuhn observes, new paradigms do not arise from many competing theories—the
Kuhnian "discovery of anomaly" and the concomitant assimilation of the
new science occur only gradually and in diverse contexts and ways.[19] According to Bernard Dod, although most of Aristotle's works are translated
in the twelfth century, manuscript evidence suggests that these texts were
not thoroughly studied or widely circulated until the thirteenth century.[20] Yet
Aristotelian influence is clearly present: as early as 1125, William of Conches
reads translations of Arabic and Greek medical works in the cathedral library at Chartres; by 1160, scholars in northern France annotate translations
by James of Venice of the *Physics* and *Metaphysics*.[21] As Andreas Speer has
argued in an important essay, the roots of the reception of Aristotle are to
be found in the twelfth century—not simply in the work of translation, but
in the intellectual themes taken up by twelfth-century thinkers that both reflect and stimulate interest in the new science.[22] Nor are the textual bases of
these themes entirely lacking: for example, when Thierry of Chartres defines
natural science as the study of bodies in motion and subject to change, he
draws upon Aristotle's *Physics* and *Metaphysics* as transmitted by Boethius.[23]
In this article, I will argue that twelfth-century discussions of time and nature are both shaped by currents of the new science and play a role in its
further reception. My discussion will focus on William and Thierry as representatives of those twelfth-century thinkers: the *phisici* who, inspired by Platonic cosmology, turn to available sources of the "new science" in developing
a natural philosophy.[24]

Augustine: Time and the Physical World

While some modern commentators have given primacy to Augustine's psychological account of time in *Confessions* 11—which they read as signifying that time is mind-dependent—Augustine in fact conceives time far less
narrowly. As he writes in his mature commentary on Genesis, time depends
on the motion of *both* spiritual (that is, mental) *and* physical creation (*De
Gen.* 5.5.12).[25] In the early Christian paradigm that emerges from his several discussions of Genesis, time in the physical world is regulated directly
by God—a view ultimately deriving from his doctrine of creation *simul.*

Wishing to distinguish sharply and irrevocably between time and eternity, Augustine teaches that God made all the works of the six days at once, some actually and some potentially, in a single atemporal instant.[26] The subsequent temporal development of living things—plants, animals, and humans—is mediated by the causal reasons, bits of intelligibility placed in matter at first creation. Derived from Stoic and, more importantly, from Plotinian tradition, these intelligible reasons—the *rationes causales*—not only make possible a simultaneous creation—the eternal God does not work in time—but also have important consequences for Augustinian concepts of time and nature.[27]

First, the reasons direct the motion of creation and thus guarantee temporal order, an inherent "before" and "after" independent of any observer; for example, a tree leafs out, flowers, and bears fruit in fixed and successive temporal intervals.[28] In ordering the motion, sequence, and time of things, the reasons ensure the stability and continuity of creation. All things arise, develop, and perish in due course and according to kind; as Augustine writes, a grain of wheat does not produce a bean, nor a bean a grain of wheat (*De Gen.* 9.17.31). Second—and here Augustine's concept of nature begins to emerge—the causal reasons work to restrict creative causality to God alone, in effect eliminating secondary efficient causes. In a well-known passage, Augustine observes that "we do not call parents the creators of men," since the causal reasons, not human agents, regulate birth and growth (*De Trin.* 3.8.13; cf. *De Civ.* 22.24; 1 Cor. 3.7). For Augustine, all causal power is concentrated in God: were divine governance to lapse, he writes, all creation would cease to exist (*De Gen.* 4.12.22).

Finally, although on first examination the causal reasons suggest a concept of natural law—a provision for the regular operation of things according to their nature—Augustine's treatment of miracles points to a different view. As he explains in his treatise on Genesis, the causal reasons contain a "double potentiality," so that any and all effects can be drawn forth from created things, according to divine will (*De Gen.* 9.17.32). R. A. Markus has therefore persuasively argued that, for Augustine, the distinction between "natural" processes and miraculous events tends to be blurred.[29] Miracles are not against nature but a part of it, since for God, "nature is that which he has made" (*De Gen.* 6.13.24).[30] For example, in changing water to wine, writes Augustine, God had no need of vine, grape, earth, sun, moisture, or the passage of time—as he asks, "Did the Creator of time have need of time's assistance?" (*De Gen* 6.13.24; cf. John 2.10). Thus, while Augustine's treatises on Genesis seek to discover "a rational order in nature," the causal reasons ultimately work against the notion of natural law.[31]

In sum, according to this early Christian paradigm, natural secondary causes are not autonomous or efficacious, nor are natural processes like fermentation consistent or predictable. Time is not an aspect of nature, but is instead regulated directly by an omnipotent Creator. That is, while Augustine holds that time always *accompanies* motion and change, it is not produced by these—it is not an epiphenomenon of nature.[32] Rather, time is a creature made by God, effected by the causal reasons, and regulated by continued divine governance: "He rested in order to create subsequently, by administering these things, the order of time and temporal things" (*De Gen.* 7.28.42). For time itself "moves according to the numbers received atemporally at first creation" (*De Gen.* 4.35.52).

William of Conches: Time and Nature in the Twelfth Century

In his dialogue on natural philosophy, *The Dragmaticon*, the twelfth-century thinker William of Conches also takes as illustrative example the process of wine making. But unlike Augustine, who finds divine omnipotence as much in the production of wine from grapes as in the miracle at Cana, William, as Chenu observes, distinguishes between the works of nature and God.[33] The Creator makes the four elements and souls *ex nihilo* and produces miracles such as virgin birth; nature perpetuates species by producing "like from like" (*Drag.* 1.7.2–3).[34] Most importantly, William emphasizes that nature works gradually and in time: "When nature creates [*operatur*]," he writes, "she brings forth something rough and confused at first, and then gradually forms and divides it"—for example, in wine making, nature carries the heavy sediment to the lowest part of the wine vat over a period of time.[35]

William's definition of nature—"a force implanted in things producing like from like"—derives from a well-known passage in Calcidius.[36] But his *account* of natural processes—in this example, fermentation—is indebted to Constantine the African, whose eleventh-century translations from the Arabic transmitted Greek medical and scientific traditions to the West. In the *Dragmaticon*, as in his earlier Timaean gloss, William's concern for the temporality of natural processes draws our attention to the new ideas of nature and time emerging in twelfth-century thought. As Dorothy Elford observes in her comprehensive study of the *Dragmaticon*, William supplements

Plato to arrive at "a far more dynamic picture of the world."[37] For example, he explains the indissolubility of the world body not only by its harmonious elemental proportion (*Tim.* 32c–e; cp. *Glosae* 64–65), but also by the balanced alternation of elemental changes in the seasonal cycle (*Drag.* 2.6.3).[38] Thus to explain the world in terms of ordered and temporal processes is to move towards a paradigm compatible with the "new science"—towards an Aristotelian view of nature as "a principle of process and change" (*Physics* 200b1–2).

According to the classic thesis of Tullio Gregory, the twelfth-century idea of an autonomous, self-moving, and operant nature—"a life-giving force implanted in things" (*vis rebus insita, Glosae* 37)—first develops from William's efforts in his Timaean gloss to accommodate to Christianity the Platonic world soul: "a life-giving spirit implanted in things" (*spiritus rebus insitus, Glosae* 71). As the *anima mundi* confers life and motion upon all things, so—according to William and many of his contemporaries—nature as a purely cosmological principle works to initiate and guarantee the *natura rerum*.[39] While founding their cosmologies on a transcendent Trinitarian Cause, William and Thierry of Chartres thus give unprecedented importance to what they call the material cause of creation—the four elements.[40] Unlike Augustine, who taught a simultaneous creation, natural philosophers of the twelfth century hold that the world and its creatures were made in the course of time, through the work of secondary causes and natural processes.[41] According to William's Timaean gloss, for example, God created [*creavit*] the different species of animals from a mixture of earth and water, heated to boiling by the fiery nature of the stars (*Glosae* 52). In the later *Dragmaticon*, however, nature not only assists the Creator but is represented as fully autonomous: "[T]he surface of the earth, muddy from the water lying on it [and] boiling from the heat, produced *from itself* [*ex se*] various kinds of animals" (my emphasis; 3.4.3).

For his reliance on "naturalistic" accounts of creation, William was attacked in 1141 by the Cistercian monk William of St. Thierry, who condemned him as "*homo physicus.*"[42] Yet in his early Timaean gloss (ca. 1130), William had argued that for God to work through nature does not derogate divine power, since He gives to each thing the nature (*natura*) by which it works (*Glosae* 52). Even more strongly, he declares that the will of God can act *against* natural law, *contra naturam rerum* (*Glosae* 114).[43] In contrast, in the later *Dragmaticon*—even while affirming that divine power is without limit—William suggests that the interconnection of the elements is such that their natures could not have been created otherwise by God (2.4.1–6). As Dorothy Elford observes, a new tension emerges between the themes of divine omnipotence and the autonomy of nature: although in the *Dragmaticon* William explicitly retracts all views condemned by the Church, "the *vires naturae* have, if anything, a greater autonomy."[44]

From this twelfth-century "discovery of nature" follow several consequences for ideas about time. With the new attention to secondary causes, time becomes an integral aspect of both individual natures and the larger patterns ensured by natural law. Insofar as natural processes are uniform and predictable, so too is time regular and quantifiable. The twelfth-century cosmologist Clarembald of Arras, a pupil of Thierry of Chartres, indeed argues that time is an *accident* of the physical world, having being only from mutable natures.[45] This view differs notably from that of Augustine, who considers time a creature. Second, whereas for Augustine space (the condition of bodies) is distinct from and inferior to time (the condition of spirits), the twelfth century firmly associates time with distance and space (*De Gen.* 8.20.39)—a distinctly Aristotelian view which, as Jacques LeGoff observes, marks "an innovation more revolutionary than is initially apparent."[46] Third, a significant number of natural philosophers of the twelfth century, including William and Thierry of Chartres, conceive nature as a principle of unending continuity and therefore hold the world to be perpetual.[47] Finally, as these natural philosophers become increasingly attentive to temporal process in the physical world, they move towards an Aristotelian concept of nature as a principle of motion and change; to the extent that they do so, they tend to encounter and address the problems of the *Physics*: causation, matter, motion, the infinite, place and void, and, of course, time itself.[48]

The New Science in the Twelfth Century

In thus transforming the old Augustinian paradigm—in developing new views of nature and time—the natural philosophers of the twelfth century stand on the threshold of further changes in ways of looking at the world. Side by side with a Calcidian definition of nature, for example, Thierry of Chartres also cites Aristotle's definition from *Physics* 2: "Nature is a principle of movement [and rest] in things in themselves and not accidentally."[49] As Marie-Thérèse d'Alverny has observed, "[I]gnorance of the 'Libri naturales' and 'Metaphysica' during the early Middle Ages was not as complete as is frequently assumed."[50] If we search the twelfth century for possible sources of

Aristotle and the new science, three areas suggest themselves. First, twelfth-century philosophers find an admixture of Aristotelian thought in Middle Platonists like Boethius, Calcidius, Macrobius, and Martianus Capella, thought which they easily assimilate to newly available scientific texts. As we have seen, William and Thierry find Aristotelian concepts of nature, motion, and cause in Boethius.[51] Second, these philosophers received Greek science in medical and scientific treatises and commentaries from the school of Salerno: for instance, a corpus of five medical treatises—including eleventh-century translations of Hippocrates, Theophilus, and Galen—was available in the cathedral library at Chartres during the second decade of the twelfth century.[52] Also found at Chartres during the same period are Salernitan commentaries on the *Articella*—as this collection of medical treatises came to be called—that draw extensively and explicitly on Aristotle's *Physics* and *De Generatione*.[53] Finally, natural philosophers may have had access to translations of the "new Aristotle" made by the cleric James of Venice, the earliest of the twelfth-century translators.

James, a prolific translator of both the scientific and logical works of Aristotle, worked in the second quarter of the twelfth century.[54] The oldest manuscript of his translation of the *Physics* (with *De Intelligentia, De Anima,* and *De Memoria*), from the library at Mont-Saint-Michel, was copied and profusely annotated in the same region around 1160.[55] As Lorenzo Minio-Paluello has shown, "a centre of interest in the 'new' Aristotle, which produced the first known attempt at Latin exegesis and at propagation of these works," existed in northern France around 1160.[56] Minio-Paluello associates this scholarly activity with the circle of Robert of Torigny, Abbot of Mont-Saint-Michel, and Richard Bishop, Archdeacon of Coutances. Like William of Conches, Richard was a former teacher of John of Salisbury, whose *Metalogicon* (1159) contains the first known quotation from the *Posterior Analytics* in the translation of James.[57] As William spent his last years in the household of Geoffrey Plantagenet, Duke of Normandy, where he wrote the *Dragmaticon*, it is tempting to speculate that this natural philosopher advanced the reception of Aristotle in his native Normandy. But there is no evidence that William (who died ca. 1154) drew on James's translation of the *Physics* for his discussions of time.[58] Rather, my goal is more general: to suggest that natural philosophers of the twelfth century, as they assimilate, transform, and build upon available texts, make possible the further reception of the new science. To what extent do they frame issues in ways influenced by or receptive to Aristotelian thought?[59] To investigate—if not answer—this question, I turn to William's contemporary, Thierry of Chartres.

Thierry of Chartres: Time, Nature, and the New Science

The ideas of Thierry of Chartres about time must be inferred from his discussions of nature, matter and form, and motion—related issues which for twelfth-century readers adumbrate the concerns of the *Physics*. Thierry's well-known hexameron, a reading of Genesis according to natural science—*secundum phisicam*—describes creation as the work of secondary causes.[60] Writing before 1140, Thierry holds that God created matter from nothing, in the first instant of time; thereafter, the formation and adornment of the world were effected naturally (*naturaliter*) and in time by autonomous elemental interactions initiated by the motion and heat of fire (*SD* 9). Like William, Thierry views creation as a temporal process: defining each of the six days of Genesis as a single complete revolution of the fiery heavens, he suggests that the physical order of creative nature is a temporal order as well (*SD* 4). According to Thierry's naturalistic account of the six days, certain powers (*virtutes*) and seminal causes, placed in the elements by God, regulate both the production of creatures and the temporal order of creation (*SD* 17).[61]

Yet having explained the works of Genesis according to natural law or *ordo naturalis,* Thierry adduces causes beyond the physical universe (*SD* 9).[62] Thus in the second half of his hexameron, the twelfth-century cosmologist argues that the "power of the maker" (*virtus artificis*)—equally the "spirit" of Genesis 1.2, the Holy Spirit, and the Timaean world soul—works in created matter to give form and motion to all things (*SD* 17). In effect, Thierry's treatment of the *virtus artificis* parallels William's earlier development, from an understanding of the Platonic world soul, of the concept of an autonomous nature that helps to initiate and guarantee the *natura rerum.* In Thierry's hexameral account of an informing and motive spirit, immanent and operant in creation, we find an early version of the concept of nature he would later develop in his mature theological commentaries.

This concept of nature is indebted to Aristotle and derived from Boethius, whose theological works transmit two notions basic to the *Physics:* nature as a principle of motion or change (*kinesis*) and nature as form. First, commenting on Boethius' *Contra Eutychen,* Thierry defines nature as "a principle or cause of movement of things in themselves [*per se*] and not accidentally" (*Abbr.* 1.59–61; cp. *Physics* 200b10–13).[63] The twelfth-century cosmologist emphasizes that "per se" must be understood to mean "from creation and by nature"—*ex creatione et natura*: that is, he thus firmly rejects Aristotle's notion of an eternal world (*Abbr.* 1.63). As Thierry explains, the causes of motion are implanted in the elements at creation, so that (for example) fire is naturally carried upward and earth downward—an interpretation suggesting that the *virtutes* of his earlier hexameron are Aristotelian in origin (*Abbr.* 1.62–66).[64] Second, Thierry follows Aristotle in defining nature as form (cp. *Physics* 193b8–10). As he explains, the Aristotelian definition refers not to form abstracted from matter, but to what the twelfth-century thinker calls enmattered forms (*formas immateriatas*), the "images" by which an actual thing is either "this" or "that."[65] These forms or "images" are imperfect, like a circle drawn in water, because of the mutability of matter (*Lect.* 2.20). Without abandoning Boethius' Christian-Neoplatonic ontology, then, Thierry restates this ontology in Aristotelian terms: when matter, or the aptitude for receiving different states, is conjoined with form to produce actually existing things, "possibility is led forth to act" (*Comm.* 2.28).[66] Working from Boethius, Thierry at length arrives at a definition of nature both influenced by Aristotle and congenial to Aristotelian thought: "Nature is the form in matter without which difference could not exist" (*Comm.* 2.45; cp. *Physics* 193a30–31).[67]

Finally, like Aristotle, Thierry holds that all motion and change arise from the conjunction of matter and form (*Comm.* 2.11).[68] Form is itself immutable; but mutability is introduced by the conjoined matter. The "enmattered forms" studied by the natural scientist are material, in motion, and changeable (*Lect.* 2.19–21; cf. *Physics* 237a17–20). As Thierry observes in his *Commentary on De Trinitate*, whatever is natural is in motion, and all motion and change take place in time. Elsewhere, he draws on *De Consolatione* to describe time as movement through interminable successions (*Comm.* 2.11; *Lect.* 4.72).[69] As Stephen Gersh has shown, the Aristotelian influences present in Thierry's account of form and matter are derived from Calcidius.[70] Yet the twelfth-century philosopher's *application* of his Boethian and Calcidian sources to formulate a concept of nature—the "enmattered forms" of changing and temporal things—is itself original. Eulogized by a contemporary as "Aristotle's worthy successor," Thierry develops to a remarkable degree a metaphysical framework for natural philosophy.[71]

Epilogue: Towards the New Science

"In almost everything concerning physics," writes William of Conches, "Aristotle contradicts Plato" (*Drag.* 3.5.1). Where Middle Platonists tend to combine the two philosophies, natural philosophers of the twelfth century show an awareness of difference—a Kuhnian perception of anomaly—that surely facilitates the reception of the new science.[72] On the other hand, as Cadden has shown, the development of natural philosophy during the twelfth century "reveals not a smooth and inevitable trajectory toward university-based Aristotelian science but a matrix of diverse and competing possibilities."[73] As a brief epilogue to this discussion of time and nature, I want to illustrate the variety of ways in which twelfth-century thought both anticipates and influences the development of the new science. I turn again to William of Conches.

In his Timaean gloss, William draws upon Constantine the African to define an element as "the simplest and least part of a body" (*Glosae* 58).[74] What we see in the world around us are things made up of elements—or, to use William's innovative term, *elementata*. The elements themselves do not exist independently, although the mind is able to perceive them independently through a process of analysis (*Glosae* 163).[75] When, in his later *Dragmaticon*, William again takes up the vexed issue of the elements, he interrogates his revised definition—"an element is what is first in the constitution of a body, and last in its breaking down"—to pose deliberately unanswerable questions (*Drag.* 1.6.2). How can a least particle exist, he asks, if magnitude is infinitely divisible? If minimal particles *do* exist, are they perceived by the senses or by intellect? If by intellect (as William consistently holds), how can these particles constitute three-dimensional bodies (*Drag.* 1.6.3–13)? As Elford persuasively argues, a Neoplatonic ontology cannot fully account for the element-particles, a class of entities corporeal by nature but in experience insensible and perceptible only to intellect.[76]

Characteristically, William offers linguistic solutions to his puzzles about the elements; for example, he resolves the first by redefining the term "infinite." Similarly, he explains the formation of perceptible bodies from the imperceptible element-particles by distinguishing a "transferred philosophical" sense of "body" from ordinary linguistic usage. The element-particles, he holds, are both simple bodies and nondimensional entities—a seemingly untenable position (*Drag.* 1.6.12–13).[77] Yet if, as L. M. de Rijk writes, for the twelfth century "thought and language were taken to be related . . . to reality in their elements and structure," then William's logico-semantic approach to natural science is not easily dismissed.[78] Questioning accepted categories of thought, William's conundrums suggest that natural scientists of the twelfth century are searching for new ways of looking at the world.

Far from undermining the worth of William's contribution, then, his logico-semantic approach to problems of physics extends Cadden's thesis that the twelfth-century philosopher turns to the trivium to develop and advance natural philosophy. As William himself writes, linguistic considerations may be brought to bear on philosophical issues, "For not signification alone, but the mode of signifying [*modus significandi*] makes truth or falsehood."[79] His own innovative definitions of time are a case in point. In his glosses on Boethius, Macrobius, Priscian, and Plato, William offers both a "general" definition of time—"the measure of changing things according to rest and motion"—and a "total" definition—"that interval [*spatium*] that begins and ends with the world" (*Glosae* 94). Significantly, William's "general" definition proves sufficiently congenial to the new science to be cited nearly verbatim by the thirteenth-century thinker Robert Grosseteste— himself a commentator on Aristotle's *Physics*—who (like William) defines time as "the measure of the movement of changeable things."[80] Equally important, William uses his "total" definition of time to construct a linguistic argument showing that Plato and Aristotle held the world to have had a beginning *with* time.[81] This argument, as Richard Dales has shown, mediates the reception of Aristotle. That is, in the thirteenth century, William's "total" definition becomes the most widely accepted defense of Aristotle's doctrine of the eternity of the world—and is indeed condemned in 1277 along with other "double truths."[82]

Finally, in his glosses on Priscian's *Institutiones grammaticae* (c. 1125), William elaborates his conception of time. Here he distinguishes between a "simple" and "compound" present, the former a single moment or point, the latter a temporal continuity—a notion not unlike the Aristotelian "now," which is said both to divide and to give continuity to time (cf. *Physics* 200a1–12).[83] As Karin Fredborg has shown, a significant portion of William's glosses on Priscian are copied verbatim by Petrus Helias in his widely circulated *Summa Super Priscianum* (ca. 1140). Significantly, the thirteenth century thus receives William's teachings on time in both works of natural science and in a logico-grammatical treatise.[84] "Who will exclude [grammar] from the threshold of philosophy," writes John of Salisbury, "save one who thinks that philosophizing does not require an understanding of what has been said or written?"[85] The achievement of natural philosophers like William and Thierry lies not only in their innovative discussions of time and nature, not only in their energetic pursuit of the new science, but also in the breadth and scope of their vision. As these few examples suggest, in

the twelfth century the boundaries between natural science and the arts of
the trivium are more fluid than generally conceived. William's definitions
of time invite us to rethink the ways in which natural philosophers of the
twelfth century encounter and transmit new ways of looking at the world—
and to widen our own vision so that we may undertake further and more
comprehensive studies of the development of natural science.

Notes

1. *Guillaume de Conches: Glosae Super Platonem* 94, ed. Edouard Jeauneau (Paris:
Vrin, 1965), 176. William also includes this "general" definition of time in his glosses
on Boethius, Macrobius, and Priscian. All translations are mine; all citations are according to the *capitula* established by Jeauneau.

2. Thomas Kuhn, *The Structure of Scientific Revolutions*, 3rd ed. (Chicago:
University of Chicago Press, 1962), 6–7. On the originality of William's definition,
see *The Didascalicon of Hugh of St. Victor*, trans. Jerome Taylor (New York: Columbia
University Press, 1961), 185 note 5.

3. *Plato's Cosmology: "The Timaeus" of Plato*, trans. F. M. Cornford (Indianapo-
lis: Bobbs-Merrill Company, 1975), 98. All references are to this edition and are cited
parenthetically.

4. *Physics*, trans. R. P. Hardie and R. K. Gaye, in *The Basic Works of Aristotle*,
ed. Richard McKeon (New York: Random House, 1941), 292. All references are to
this edition and are cited parenthetically.

5. *St. Augustine's Confessions* (Cambridge, Mass.: Harvard University Press,
1912; reprint, 1977), 2:268–69.

6. See my "Augustine's Ambivalence About Temporality: His Two Accounts
of Time," *Medieval Philosophy and Theology* 8 (1999): 129–48.

7. M.-D. Chenu, *Nature, Man, and Society in the Twelfth Century*, ed. and
trans. Jerome Taylor and Lester K. Little (Chicago: University of Chicago Press,
1968), 1–44. The topic of "nature" is too broad for discussion here; see, for example,
Richard C. Dales, "A Twelfth-Century Concept of the Natural Order," *Viator* 9
(1978): 179–92, who defines "naturalism" as the view "that the physical universe operates in a uniform and rational manner; that it is autonomous and self-sufficient; . . .
that it is intelligible; and that it is . . . worth studying in its own right"; and D. M.
Armstrong, *What Is a Law of Nature?* (Cambridge: Cambridge University Press,
1983).

8. In his early Boethian gloss, William compares the world to a house prepared for man (see excerpts in J. M. Parent, *La Doctrine de la création dans l'école de
Chartres: étude et textes* [Paris: Vrin, 1938], 124–36); in his Timaean gloss, he argues
that the world was made to minister to human need or *indigentia* (*Glosae* 48). See

Philosophia Mundi, 1.23, "In omnibus rationem esse quaerendam," cited in Chenu, *Nature, Man, and Society,* 11 note 21.

9. William of Conches (fl. 1120–54), pupil of Bernard of Chartres, probably taught at both Chartres and Paris. He composed glosses on Boethius, Macrobius, Priscian, and Plato, as well as the innovative *Philosophia* (ca. 1125) and *Dragmaticon* (1145–49), studies of natural philosophy. Thierry of Chartres (fl. 1120–56), an influential teacher at Chartres and possibly Paris, was Chancellor of Chartres in the 1140s. He composed commentaries on Cicero, Boethius, and an original cosmological treatise, *De sex dierum operibus* (ca. 1135). Thierry is also known for a collection of texts for teaching the liberal arts, the *Heptateuchon*. On William and Thierry, see Peter Dronke, ed., *A History of Twelfth-Century Philosophy* (Cambridge: Cambridge University Press, 1988), 308–27; 358–85; and references below.

10. Paul Edward Dutton, ed., *The Glosae Super Platonem of Bernard of Chartres* (Toronto: Pontifical Institute of Mediaeval Studies, 1991), 42.

11. Chenu, *Nature, Man, and Society,* 72.

12. On the translation and reception of the *Physics,* see Bernard Dod, "Aristoteles Latinus," in *The Cambridge History of Later Medieval Philosophy,* ed. Norman Kretzmann, Anthony Kenny, and Jan Pinborg (Cambridge: Cambridge University Press, 1982), 45–98.

13. For William's understanding of Aristotle's categories of motion (generation/corruption; increase/decrease; transformation of quality; according to place), see *William of Conches: A Dialogue on Natural Philosophy,* ed. Italo Ronca and Matthew Curr (Notre Dame, Ind.: University of Notre Dame Press, 1997), 32. All citations from the *Dragmaticon* are to this edition.

14. Pierre Duhem, "Du temps où la scholastique latine a connu la Physique D'Aristote," *Revue de Philosophie* 9 (1909), 163–78. He writes: "Il semble maintenant certain que Thierry de Chartres et Gilbert de la Porrée ont eu connaissance des doctrine d'Aristote sur le lieu et le mouvement locale . . . [et] que Guillaume de Conches s'est également inspiré de ces doctrines" (177).

15. Sarah Waterlow, *Nature, Change, and Agency in Aristotle's Physics: A Philosophical Study* (Oxford: Clarendon, 1982), 93–96, translates the Greek *kinesis* (motion) as "process." Twelfth-century thinkers, I will argue below, increasingly adopt the Aristotelian view that "nature is a principle of process and change" (*Physics* 200b12).

16. Kuhn, *Structure of Scientific Revolutions,* 5–7.

17. Edward Grant, *Physical Science in the Middle Ages* (Cambridge: Cambridge University Press, 1977), 15–19.

18. Joan Cadden, "Science and Rhetoric in the Middle Ages: The Natural Philosophy of William of Conches," *Journal of the History of Ideas* (1995): 1–24.

19. Margaret Gibson, "The Study of the *Timaeus* in the Eleventh and Twelfth Centuries," *Pensiamento* 25 (1969): 249–60, points out that we do not know why study of the *Timaeus*—the text unifying twelfth-century thought—was reopened in the eleventh century.

20. Dod, "Aristoteles Latinus," 46 – 53. Dod adds that "[m]any early manuscripts have undoubtedly perished, so the full story will never be known" (53).

21. On medical treatises at Chartres, see Charles Burnett, "The Contents and Affiliation of the Scientific Manuscripts Written at, or brought to, Chartres in the Time of John of Salisbury," in *The World of John of Salisbury,* ed. M. Wilks (Oxford: Blackwell, 1984); on a center of interest in the new Aristotle in northern France ca. 1160, see Lorenzo Minio-Paluello, "Iacobus Veneticus Grecus: Canonist and Translator of Aristotle," in *Opuscula: The Latin Aristotle* (Amsterdam: Adolf M. Hakkert, 1972).

22. Andreas Speer, "The Discovery of Nature: The Contribution of the Chartrians to Twelfth-Century Attempts to Found a *Scientia Naturalis,*" *Traditio* 52 (1997): 135 – 51; see also his "Reception-Mediation-Innovation: Philosophy and Theology in the 12th Century," in *Bilan et perspectives des études médiévales: Actes de premier congrès européen . . . ,*" ed. J. Hamesse (Louvain-la-Neuve, 1994), 129 – 49. For a related argument, see Peter Dronke, "New Approaches to the School of Chartres," *Annuario de estudios medievales* 6 (1969): 117 – 40.

23. See Thierry of Chartres, *Commentum super Boethii librum De Trinitate* 2.9 – 11, in *Commentaries on Boethius by Thierry of Chartres and His School,* ed. Nikolaus M. Häring (Toronto: Pontifical Institute of Mediaeval Studies, 1971), 71: "Quamvis autem forme rerum in sua quidem natura sint inmutabiles phisicus tamen mutabilitatem earum in materia considerat. . . . Formas enim considerat [physica] in materia. Unde motus i.e. mutabilitas." According to S. Cohen, *Aristotle on the Nature of Incomplete Substance* (Cambridge: Cambridge University Press, 1996), 21, Aristotle distinguishes physics, which treats things in motion and not separable from matter, from mathematics, which treats objects separable from matter and motion, at *Meta.* 6.1 and *Physics* 2.2193b31 – 34. For Thierry's source, see Boethius, *De Trinitate* 2.

24. In his *Dragmaticon,* William of Conches claims to "set down the view of natural scientists (*phisici*) concerning substances" (1.7.5). As I suggest above, the *phisici* of the twelfth century—in modern scholarship variously called cosmologists, cosmogonists, natural scientists or philosophers, and teacher-philosophers—constitute a twelfth-century scientific community in the Kuhnian sense, sharing common texts, terminology, definitions, methods, and concerns. With William and Thierry, this community includes, for example, Adelard of Bath, Hermann of Carinthia, Clarembald of Arras, and Bernard Silvestris—the latter three pupils of Thierry who dedicate works to him. Many modern studies point to shared terminology and common sources and concerns; see, for example, Theodore Silverstein, "Guillaume de Conches and Nemesius of Emessa: On the Sources of the 'New Science' of the Twelfth Century," in *Henry Austyn Wolfson Jubilee Volume on the Occasion of His Seventy-Fifth Birthday* (Jerusalem: American Academy for Jewish Research, 1965), 2:719 – 34; Theodore Silverstein, "ELEMENTATUM: Its Appearance among the Twelfth-Century Cosmogonists," *Medieval Studies* 16 (1954): 156 – 62;

and Italo Ronca, "The Influence of the *Pantegni* on William of Conches's *Dragmaticon*," in *Constantine the African and 'Ali Ibn Al-'Abbas Al-Magusi: The Pantegni and Related Texts*, ed. Charles Burnett and Danielle Jacquart (Leiden: Brill, 1994), 274–75.

25. *La Genèse au sens littéral*, ed. P. Agaësse and A. Solignac, vols. 48–49 of *Oeuvres de Saint Augustine* (Paris: Brouwer, 1972): "Motus enim si nullus esset vel spiritalis vel corporalis creaturae . . . nullum esset tempus omnino" (*De Gen.* 5.5.12). My translations are indebted to J. H. Taylor, trans., *Saint Augustine: The Literal Meaning of Genesis*, 2 vols. (New York: Newman Press, 1982).

26. On creation *simul*, see for example, *De Gen. ad Litt.* 4.33.51–52. On the potential existence of things as *rationes causales*, see *De Gen. ad Litt.* 5.23.45, 6.6.10; and *De Trin.* 3.9.16.

27. On the reasons as intelligible "numbers" implanted in corporeal things, see *De Gen. ad Litt.* 4.33.51–52; 5.7.20; 6.5.8; 6.6.10–11. Owing to the mechanism of the causal reasons, God rests and acts at the same time (*De Gen.* 5.23.46; 6.11.18). On the Plotinian origins of the causal reasons, which pertain to the intelligible order, see John J. O'Meara, *Understanding Augustine* (Dublin: Four Courts Press, 1997), 122–23; on the Stoic *logoi spermatikoi*, see Marcia Colish, *The Stoic Tradition from Antiquity to the Early Middle Ages* (Leiden: E. J. Brill, 1990), 31–32.

28. This phrase—"certis dimensionibus temporum"—is from an early formulation of the notion of causal reasons, *De Mus.* 6.17.57.

29. R. A. Markus, "Augustine: God and Nature," in *The Cambridge History of Later Greek and Early Medieval Philosophy*, ed. A. H. Armstrong (Cambridge: Cambridge University Press, 1967), 395–405.

30. Cf. *De Civ. Dei* 21.8: "How can an event be contrary to nature . . . since the will of the great Creator assuredly is the nature of every created thing?"

31. O'Meara, *Understanding Augustine*, 117. For a differing view, see Christopher Kaiser, *Creational Theology and the History of Physical Science* (Leiden: Brill, 1997), 42–43, who argues that the causal reasons develop the "autonomy of nature."

32. See John M. Rist, *Augustine: Ancient Thought Baptized* (New York: Cambridge University Press, 1994), 83.

33. Chenu, *Nature, Man, and Society*, 41–42.

34. Ronca and Curr, *William of Conches*, 18. Cf. *Glosae Super Platonem* 37: "Opus nature est quod similia nascuntur ex similibus, ex semine vel ex germine. Et est natura vis rebus insita similia de similibus operans."

35. For discussion of editorial emendation here, see Ronca, "The Influence of the *Pantegni*," 274–75. Whereas, in the Timaean gloss, William insists that the elements were ordered at first creation, in the *Dragmaticon* he uses the wine vat as an analogy for "a literal state of primal chaos," presumably to give more prominence to secondary causes; see Dorothy J. Elford, "Developments in the Natural Philosophy of William of Conches: A Study of His 'Dragmaticon' and a Consideration of Its Relationship to the 'Philosophia,'" Ph.D. diss., Cambridge University, 1983, 53–61.

36. See Calcidius, *Commentarius* 23, in *Timaeus a Calcidio Translatus Commentarioque Instructus*, ed. J. H. Waszink, 73: "Omnia enim quae sunt vel opus Dei sunt, vel naturae, vel naturam imitantis hominis artificis."

37. Elford, "Developments," 86.

38. Ibid., 85–86; see *Dragmaticon* 2.6.1–12.

39. For this argument, see Tullio Gregory, *Anima Mundi: La filosofia di Guglielmo di Conches e la Scuola di Chartres* (Florence: Sansoni, 1955), 184–88; and esp. Tullio Gregory, *Platonismo medievale: studi e ricerche* (Rome: Istituto storico italiano, 1958), 135–50.

40. Chenu, *Nature, Man, and Society*, 26. Twelfth-century cosmologists know of Aristotle's four causes through Boethius.

41. See my "Twelfth-Century Views of Time: Three Reinterpretations of Augustine's Doctrine of Creation *Simul*," *Journal of the History of Philosophy* 23, 3 (1985): 325–38.

42. On William of St. Thierry's accusations and criticism, see Elford, "Developments," 28; and Ronca, "The Influence of the *Pantegni*," 272.

43. For William, the word *natura* usually designates the "peculiar being" (*proprium esse*) of a thing; this passage affords a noteworthy use of the term *natura* to designate natural law: "Natura enim exigit ut omne compositum in componentia possit resolvi" (*Glosae* 114).

44. Elford, "Developments," 68–72.

45. See *Tractatulus Super Librum Genesis* 37, in *The Life and Words of Clarembald of Arras*, ed. Nikolaus M. Häring (Toronto: Pontifical Institute of Mediaeval Studies, 1965), 242: "[N]imirum cum tempus habeat esse in aliquo et per aliquid quoniam accidens est, non est per se creatum sed illis, quae ei causae sunt, concreatum."

46. Jacques LeGoff, *Time, Work, and Culture in the Middle Ages* (Chicago: University of Chicago Press, 1980), 34. See also Carlo Cipolla, *Clocks and Culture: 1300–1700* (1967; New York: W. W. Norton, 1978), 37–75.

47. These include, for example, Bernard of Chartres, Bernard Silvestris, and Clarembald of Arras; see my "The Idea of the Perpetual in Twelfth-Century Philosophy and Poetry," *Medievalia et Humanistica*, n.s. 26 (Rowman and Littlefield, 1999), 119–36.

48. Cf. Aristotle, *Physics* 200b12–25: "Process [*kinesis*] is held to belong to the class of continuous things, and the infinite makes its appearance first and foremost in the continuous.... Moreover, there cannot be process without place and void and time." I follow here the translation of Waterlow, *Nature, Change, and Agency*, 93.

49. Thierry of Chartres, *Abbreviatio Monacensis Contra Eutychen* 1.59–64, in Häring, *Commentaries on Boethius*, 450: "NATURA EST MOTUS PRINCIPIUM . . . PER SE ET NON PER ACCIDENS." Thierry finds this Aristotelian definition in Boethius' *Contra Eutychen*. According to Häring, the *Abbreviatio Monacensis* is "an abridgement of Thierry's lectures" of unknown date (34–38). All citations from Thierry's commentaries are to this edition; all translations are mine.

50. Marie-Thérèse D'Alverny, "Translations and Translators," in *Renaissance and Renewal in the Twelfth Century*, ed. Robert Benson and Giles Constable (Toronto: University of Toronto Press, 1991), 436–37, note 66.

51. On Middle Platonism and Aristotle, see esp. Stephen Gersh, "Platonism—Neoplatonism—Aristotelianism," in Benson and Constable, *Renaissance and Renewal*, 512–34. Burnett, "The Contents and Affiliation," observes that Chartrian thinkers typically assimilated new texts to the "old science" of Boethius, Calcidius, Macrobius, and Martianus Capella—for example, in *De Essentiis*, Hermann of Carinthia combines the "old philosophy" of Middle Platonism with the "new science" of Abu Ma'shar, Ptolemy, and others (136–37).

52. The translation movement in western Europe was initiated by Constantine the African and Alfanus of Salerno (second half of eleventh century); as scholars now emphasize, nineteenth-century accounts of the transmission of Greek science focused incorrectly on the Arabic tradition (d'Alverny, "Translations and Translators," 422–27). On the corpus of medical treatises at Chartres (MS. 160), translated in eleventh-century Salerno, see Burnett, "The Contents and Affiliation," 128–29. The *Articella* (as this collection came to be called) includes the *Ysagoge ad artem Galeni* by Johannicius; the *Aphorisms* and *Prognostics* of Hippocrates; *De urinis* by Theophilus; and *De pulsibus* by Philaretus; the Chartrian manuscript substitutes Constantine's *Pantegni* for Galen's *Ars Parva*. Chartres 171 consists of commentaries to the *Articella*; both manuscripts (Chartres 160 and 171) were destroyed during World War II. On William's use of these and related treatises, see Silverstein, "Guillaume de Conches and Nemesius," in *Wolfson Jubilee*, 2:719–34; and Ronca, "The Influence of the *Pantegni*," 274–74.

53. See Danielle Jacquart, "Aristotelian Thought in Salerno," in *A History of Western Philosophy*, ed. Peter Dronke (Cambridge: Cambridge University Press, 1988), 407–28, who identifies and enumerates Aristotelian citations in Salernitan commentaries on the *Ysagoge ad artem Galeni;* and Burnett, "The Contents and Affiliation," 128–29. Burnett's careful study of manuscripts in the cathedral library at Chartres offers real evidence that a center of learning, receptive to the "new science," flourished at Chartres in the first half of the twelfth century. This position was questioned by R. W. Southern in his "Humanism and the School of Chartres," in *Medieval Humanism and Other Studies* (Oxford: Oxford University Press, 1970); among many responses to Southern are essays by Dronke (1969); Häring (1974); Burnett (1984); Wetherbee (1988); and Speer (1997). The present study concurs with Southern's subsequent observation that natural philosophers of the twelfth century were obliged to go beyond the *Timaeus;* see his *Platonism, Scholastic Method, and the School of Chartres* (Reading, England: University of Reading, 1979), 1–41.

54. On James of Venice, see Dod, "Aristoteles Latinus," 54–56; and Minio-Pauello, "Iacobus Veneticus Grecus." There are 139 surviving manuscripts of the *Physics* in the translation of James.

55. Minio-Paluello, "Iacobus Veneticus Grecus," 217.

56. Ibid., 218.

57. Ibid., 215–18. As Minio-Paluello hypothesizes, "John of Salisbury knew of the arrival of James' . . . translation of Aristotelian works; these texts had come into the hands of people like Robert of Torigny and Richard Bishop; the oldest copies preserved derive from manuscripts which reached Normandy about 1160; the notes, considered authoritative enough to be repeatedly copied, were the work of such scholars as Richard Bishop and others of the same circle."

58. The *Dragmaticon* is a dialogue between "the Duke of Normandy" and "a Philosopher." See Cadden, "Science and Rhetoric," 20–24, who argues that "William detached his work on natural philosophy from the standard production of scholarly texts, and attached it to a secular setting." William was tutor to Geoffrey's two sons, the elder of whom became Henry II of England.

59. According to cognitive learning theory, understanding of known data— in this case, fragments of the new science—facilitates the reception of new information. Of course, diverse interpretations of Aristotle were current; thus William excoriates certain contemporaries as "unworthy of serving in Aristotle's kitchen," complaining of their self-serving distortions of Aristotelian concepts (*Drag.* 3.5.1). On this passage, see Elford, "Developments," 101–7.

60. Thierry of Chartres, *Tractatus de Sex Dierum Operibus*, in Häring, *Commentaries on Boethius*, 555–75. All citations are to this edition; all translations are mine.

61. Thierry calls fire "quasi artifex et efficiens causa" (*SD* 17); on the Stoic *ignis artifex* in Hippocratic and Galenic tradition, see Tullio Gregory, "La Nouvelle Idée de Nature et de Savoir Scientifique au XII Siècle," in *The Cultural Context of Medieval Learning*, ed. J. E. Murdoch and E. D. Sylla (Dordrecht-Holland: D. Reidel Publishing, 1975), 198–200. The notion of seminal causes is adapted from Augustine.

62. Dales, "A Twelfth-Century Concept of the Natural Order," lists as one criterion of "naturalism" that "no cause outside the [physical world] need be invoked to explain its workings" (180). Yet for thinkers like Thierry, nature and theology are not separable, as the trinitarian discussion of his hexameron suggests (*SD* 31–47). On this issue, see also Dronke, "New Approaches," 135–37.

63. Thierry, *Abbreviatio Monacensis Contra Eutychen* 159–61, in Häring, *Commentaries on Boethius*, 450: "NATURA EST MOTUS PRINCIPIUM i.e. causa motus. . . . Et subiungitur secundum SE i.e. non ex accidente veniens sed ex creatione insitum. Et hoc dicit secundum SE ET NON PER ACCIDENS."

64. Readers differ on the extent to which Thierry's hexameron reflects the new science. Duhem, "Du temps où la scholastique," sees in Thierry's account of elemental motion "an exact summary of Aristotelian physics" (170); in contrast, Étienne Gilson, *A History of Christian Philosophy in the Middle Ages* (New York: Random House, 1954), 145–47, argues that Thierry's "kinetic explanation of the elements" is "the work of a man who did not know Aristotle's physics."

65. According to Aristotle, a thing is said to be what it is by virtue of the fulfillment of form rather than the potentiality of matter (*Physics* 193b8–10). On *formas*

immateriatas, see Thierry, *Lectiones* 2.19–21: "Natura enim vocatur forma inmateria. Et phisica FORMAS inmateriatas CONSIDERAT CUM MATERIA: numquam abstrahendo formas ab ipse materia." In contrast, mathematics investigates forms in themselves through mental abstraction; see Boethius, *De Trin.* 2. On the Boethian concept of images or "forms in body," which only *resemble* incorporeal form, see *De Trin.* 2.

66. Thierry, *Comm.* 2.27–29. For Thierry's ontology, an elaboration of the Boethian formula "Omne namque esse ex forma est" (*De Trin.* 2), see *Comm.* 18–28.

67. Thierry, *Comm.* 2.45: "Materia namque informis est. Natura vero forma est in materia sine qua differens nichil potest esse."

68. R. J. Hankinson, "Philosophy of Science," in *The Cambridge Companion to Aristotle* (Cambridge: Cambridge University Press, 1995), 116. Thierry, *Comm.* 2.11: "NATURALIS inquit IN MOTU. . . . Omnis itaque mutabilitas ex coniunctione forme prouenit et materie: non quod ex forma mutabilitas sed ex mutabilis materie natura proueniat."

69. See Thierry, *Lect.* 4.72: "[N]ostrum presens QUASI CURRENS TEMPUS FACIT i.e. interminabilem successionem." This last description of time derives from Boethius, *De Consolatione* 5, pr. 6.

70. Gersh, "Platonism," 521–23.

71. Cited in Peter Dronke, "Thierry of Chartres," in *A History of Western Philosophy*, ed. Peter Dronke (Cambridge: Cambridge University Press, 1988), 359.

72. See, for example, Gersh, "Platonism," who writes that Middle Platonists "set the pattern of combining the two philosophies [i.e., Platonism and Aristotelianism] into a coherent whole" (531). On the consistent efforts of Calcidius to combine Plato and Aristotle, see J. C. M. Van Winden, *Calcidius on Matter, His Doctrines and Sources* (Leiden: Brill, 1959), 76–77 *et passim*.

73. Cadden, "Science and Rhetoric," 3.

74. "Constantinus igitur in *Pantegni* sic deffinit elementum: Elementum est simpla et minima alicuius corporis particula, simpla ad qualitatem, minima ad quantitatem" (*Glosae* 58). The second part of the definition ("simpla ad qualitatem . . .") originates with William.

75. On this term, see Silverstein, "ELEMENTATUM," 156–62.

76. Dorothy Elford, "William of Conches," in Dronke, *A History of Western Philosophy*, 316–17.

77. See Elford's discussion in "William of Conches," 314–17. She concludes that "William has overreached himself" in holding the element-particles to be bodies without three dimensions.

78. L. M. de Rijk, "Origins of the Theory of the Property of Terms," in Kretzmann et al., *The Cambridge History of Later Medieval Philosophy*, 161. See also Elford, "William of Conches," who writes that "[t]he limitations of [William's] approach are obvious" (317).

79. William of Conches, *Glosae Super Priscianum* 2.14, cited in Edouard Jeauneau, "Deux rédactions des gloses de Guillaume de Conches sur Priscien," reprinted

in Edouard Jeauneau, *Lectio Philosophorum: Recherches sur l'école de Chartres* (Amsterdam: Hakkert, 1973), 361: "Non enim sola significatio sed modus significandi facit veritatem vel falsitatem." As Karin Fredborg notes in "The Dependence of Petrus Helias' *Summa Super Priscianum* on William of Conches' *Glosae Super Priscianum*," *Université de Copenhague: Cahiers de l'Institut du moyen-âge grec et latin* 11 (1973): 30–31, William uses the term "modus significandi" rather loosely here.

80. For William's definitions, see his glosses on Plato, cap. 94: "Totalis vero talis est: tempus est spacium illud quod cum mundo incepit et cum mundo desinet: que diffinitio, quia toti convenit et nulli parti, dicitur totalis." See also *Robert Grosseteste on the Six Days of Creation*, 5.12.3, trans. C. F. J. Martin (Oxford: Oxford University Press, 1996), 174. James McEvoy, *The Philosophy of Robert Grosseteste* (Oxford: Clarendon Press, 2000), 82, notes that Grosseteste's marginal glosses of the *Physics* were copied out after his death by an unknown hand.

81. On this linguistic argument, see my "Curious Grammatical Argument Against the Eternity of the World," *Proceedings of the PMR Conference* 11 (Villanova, Pa.: Augustinian Hist. Institute, 1986), 127–33.

82. R. C. Dales, *Medieval Discussions of the Eternity of the World* (Leiden: Brill, 1990), 27–31.

83. See Ronca and Curr, "William of Conches," 181 note 49; see also William's discussion "de tempore" as included in Petrus Helias, *Summa Super Priscianum*, ed. Leo Reilly (Toronto: Pontifical Institute of Mediaeval Studies, 1993), 1:489–90.

84. See Fredborg, "The Dependence of Petrus Helias' *Summa Super Priscianum*," 1–45.

85. John of Salisbury, *Metalogicon* 1.21, trans. Daniel D. McGarry (1955; reprint, Westport, Conn.: Greenwood Press, 1982), 61–62.

5

NANCY F. PARTNER

Christina of Markyate and Theodora of Huntingdon

Narrative Careers

C hristina of Markyate is a saint. She is listed in the *The Oxford Dictionary of Saints*, the compilation including all the English saints first published in 1978 by David Hugh Farmer. The listing notes optimistically "some traces of a cult" and a possible feast day of 5 December.[1] So she made the cut by the Bollandists and passed the scrutiny of the 1969 reform of the Roman Calendar—as she well deserved to do, having enjoyed actual existence in the body on this earth (from about 1096/8 to at least the mid-1150s), which is more than one can say for any number of holy mirages who were dropped from the Calendar. The *Oxford Dictionary* entry consists of a précis of her life written by a contemporary monk of St. Albans. This has come to be fairly well known, especially among feminist scholars: Christina came from a rich Anglo-Saxon family in the town of Huntingdon, made a vow of virginity at about age fourteen, repelled an attempted seduction by the bishop of Durham (her aunt's ex-lover), then won a prolonged war of wills against her parents and a man named Burthred, who was their candidate for Christina's husband. She escaped from home to live as a sort of anchoress and eventually as abbess of her own nunnery at Markyate, close to her hometown. C. H. Talbot, whose 1959 edition and translation of Christina's *Vita* became an early fixture in the canonical texts of women's history, found that Christina's family did not leave as many traces as the high status claimed by her biographer might suggest; but her father, two brothers, and two sisters are attested to in records outside the narrative. One brother and one sister entered religious life, and one brother and one sister remained in secular society—all of them staying near hometown Huntingdon.[2] The historical, verifiable foundation for the literary-spiritual character of Christina is a woman who was a product of, and all her life a part of, local, small-town society. She came from a family of urban respectability, a gild merchant family. They were frequent visitors to monasteries, socially visible, well connected, and susceptible to gossip and reputation damage, as all such families were in medieval towns. The leading motifs in the twelfth-century *Vita* are Christina's virginity and her steadfast defense of it against the worldly and corrupt wishes of parents, predatory men, and certain Church authorities. Readers informed by late twentieth-century feminism, sensitized to signs of resistance to the engulfing patriarchy of earlier centuries, may read into this text a proto-feminist allegory of autonomous self-determination and defiance of patriarchy. That reading may be a bit anachronistic, but it has the virtue of endowing this saint with humanity.[3]

The Latin *Vita*, by a monk of St. Albans who knew the adult Christina and her family and friends personally and who was "in the loop" of local gossip networks, is a fascinating and oddly shaped book: part biography, part apology, defensive, aggrandizing, evasive, and struggling to sound like conventional hagiography. Although writing during the lifetime of his subject, the monk of St. Albans seems to have been assembling the sort of materials that are supposed to culminate in a spiritually edifying death completed by postmortem miracles. The author signals the long-established *topoi* of saints' lives in arranging his material: prenatal signs of spiritual distinction experienced by the saint's mother; precocious piety as a small child; reverence for the virgin state as soon as she could understand this subject; dedication to God; a series of challenges to her spiritual stability posed by immoral people, worldly temptations, lustful men, and the baser parts of her own human nature; supernatural encouragement in the form of visions; feats of ascetic endurance; and preternatural powers of insight and prophesy. But the book was never finished; it just stops, and there is no sign that it was ever completed in now lost manuscripts. A biography, however reverently intended and however many dream visions and spiritual heroics it records, cannot count as hagiography until the death is registered and postmortem proofs as well. This literary life stops, unfinished, with its subject in full vigor of life, in acrimonious engagement with her world. One of the last fully recorded incidents involves Christina's quarrel with a neighbor over taking salad greens from his garden. The business of her life is still ongoing and, so to speak, in mid-sentence by any measure of narrative or historical completion. In fact, Christina lived some thirteen years or more beyond the end point of her *Vita*.

Although the author stalwartly takes the side of Christina throughout, there is a hectic quality, a beleaguered and defensive tone to this text that has always invited me into a different kind of reading—a reading against the *littera* but strictly tracing textual signals and structures to what, I think, is a fuller human life, a thicker narrative, there, but incompletely suppressed. Without violating the standards of rigorous historical understanding, we can refocus the textually foregrounded information and bring forward the social context and the severe social conflicts of Christina's life: an even more interesting life than the hagiographic conventions her author used to elevate and protect, subdue, and disguise her.

With no futher evidence than the narrative *Vita* itself, I have always thought that any historically informed reader, aware of the pervasive disciplines of family authority, gender hierarchies, and the narrow limitations on female self-assertion in medieval society, especially the close-knit and self-surveying society of small-scale urban life, would have to notice that something nearly always feels "wrong" in Christina's biography. There is a palpable disconnect between the events described and the author's insistent coaching of the reader's attitude; we, the readers, are pushed heavily into casting Christina as pure-minded victim, and casting nearly everyone else around her as mean-spirited and crudely self-gratifying.

Working out the details of this reading, I read Rachel M. Koopmans' article, "The Conclusion of Christina of Markyate's Vita," surely the most important piece of scholarship on the *Vita* since Talbot's edition. In specific terms, Koopmans addresses the questions that ripple out from a few salient facts: that the sole manuscript of the incomplete *Vita* was summarized only into much later texts and apparently was never copied. Koopmans proves that this incomplete story is not an accident of manuscript destruction or transmission failure.[4] The admiring near-hagiography was one among many extravagant gifts from Abbot Geoffrey of St. Albans, her powerful but controversial patron whose death in 1146 effectively dissolved the narrow band of support Christina enjoyed at St. Albans and its environs. Except to her patron and a circle of special friends, Christina seems to have been an embarrassment, a financial drain, and a cause of internal rancor at St. Albans.[5] Carefully analyzing and collating information from the *Gesta Abbatum,* Koopmans traces an internal history of factionalism and furious power struggles in St. Albans, all stemming from Abbot Geoffrey's relations with Christina. After his death the *Vita* project came to a halt; after her death no one completed the *Vita,* and no one, apparently, treated her as a saint: "no church or altar dedications in her honour, no liturgy composed for her feast day, no artwork commissioned for her cult, no reports of miracles at her tomb . . . no record of where her body was buried, much less any indication that her relics were revered."[6] And in a sense, precisely for these reasons, Koopmans regards this *Vita,* "a text which had little or no impact on its contemporaries," as particularly valuable to us, one which "well repays close scrutiny today" precisely for what it unwillingly reveals about the forces that governed religious culture of the twelfth century.[7] The kind of textual reading I am offering in this essay, laying out what the text "unwillingly reveals," only rarely finds itself meeting virtual proofs of the more traditional kind.

The uncompleted text itself, left in a rawer, less discrete state than its author probably intended, retains the legible signs of its own internal pressures, its struggle for narrative coherence. Koopmans' reconstruction of the furious divisions within the monastery of St. Albans over its abbot's slavish (so it seemed to many) fondness for a woman of dubious repute offers out-of-text substantiation and an exact historical setting for the implicit cluster of problems recognizable in the Christina narrative. Here is one case where narrative theory—or a reading built by bringing to the foreground the legible incoherencies, social illogic, and evasions of the text—is actually supported and given credence by outside evidence attesting to the circumstances in which this book was half-created and abandoned. My reading examines this phenomenon from the inside, so to speak, using the basic strategies of narrative theory to map the textual topography, the pattern of selections, and the implicit rejections with which the partisan author tried to construct a serene and convincing *Vita.* The passage of time has been kind to this book; social and cultural change have worked in its favor. The admiration the Christina story elicits from sympathetic readers now has a way of blinding us to the sheer level of difficulty she presented to her biographer as hagiographic material.[8]

From a narrative "arm's-length" distance, Christina's *Vita* reads almost like hagiography, especially if you let yourself fall into the author's intention and become the Sympathetic Reader demanded by the silently inscribed, insistent reading instructions inviting you to merge with the point of view of narrator and subject. But just a small shift in perspective, with reading eyes adjusted to a different frequency of information—medieval small-town life and its decorums—brings into focus a different book written in the same words.

> In the town of Huntingdon there was born into a family of noble rank a maiden of uncommon holiness and beauty. Her father's name was Autti, her mother's Beatrix. The name which she herself had been given in baptism was Theodora, but later on, through force of circumstance, she changed it to Christina.[9]

Theodora and Christina are introduced and baptized, as it were, in the same sentence; but from that first mention of the adopted name—Christina—the narrative insistently asserts the life of *Christina,* holy virgin and aspirant saint, a persona created through the combined efforts of author and subject with the collaboration of ourselves—as obliging readers in the text. The very next sentence: "Even before the maiden's birth she was chosen as a servant of God . . . ," speeds us right into this construct and (we note on a second reading) right past the fact that we are never to be told exactly *when* "later on," or under *what* compelling circumstances (*ex necessitate,* but what necessity?) she discarded her baptismal name.[10] So what happened to Theodora, born and banished in the same sentence; and what if we perversely decide to want to read the life of Theodora of Huntingdon? Saintly Christina of Markyate occupies the florid insistent narrative foreground, always lapped in biblical allusions and quotations no matter what she does. But the recalcitrant Theodora of Huntingdon, stubborn and difficult in narrative as in life, refuses to be totally effaced; and her inconsistencies, complex desires, and equivocal ambitions shadow the pious conventions and drive the narrative to account for and defend some uncomfortable realities. In literary terms: *genre*—hagiography—gives us Christina; *narrative analysis* gives us Theodora.

The creation of Christina was a collaborative effort that also included various partisans among the St. Albans monks, her siblings, and notably her mother, Beatrix—who, long years after her anger with the exasperating teenage Theodora had faded, enthusiastically cooperated in turning her memories into saint material for the monk who was honoring her daughter (now a local celebrity), and thus her family, with a book. We have to presume that when Beatrix recounted her memories to the biographer, she did not know how nasty his treatment of her would be. So Beatrix's ordinary anxiety and heightened piety, her multiplied devotions just before always-dangerous childbirth, are turned in obliging retrospect into exalted premonitions about the infant she was carrying. Her prenatal encounter with a white dove, which flew to her as if it were tame and let itself be handled (probably because it was *tame,* someone's pet bird escaped from its cage), works as well as anything could. "As she told me herself," the narrator says, attaching elaborate and formulaic conclusions to this tiny authenticating device: the child would be holy, protected by the Virgin Mary, detached from worldliness, and so forth.[11] Sometimes life does imitate literature.

Theodora's decision for lifelong virginity is the narrative pivot around which most of the significant plot turns, and so its provenance and authentication are crucial to the *Vita,* as they were crucial to the turmoil and confusion of her adolescence. After some anecdotes about the girl's childish piety, we are told about her special relationship with Sueno, an elderly canon of St. Mary's, Huntingdon, who was her unofficial religious teacher. As the narrator tells us about Sueno's teaching, he writes: "Porro virguncula statuit integritatem suam Deo servare . . . ," which C. H. Talbot translates as: "Furthermore, as the maiden had decided to preserve her virginity for God . . . ,"[12] Sueno supported her decision with various advice and encouragement. *Virguncula* indicates a female child, not just a virgin female, but the really interesting word is the bland, neutral little adverbial connector of this dependent clause. *Porro,* or "furthermore" as Talbot renders it, can also modify as an adverb, a time emphasizer, indicating a time in the future or the past. So another possible translation would read: "the little girl had *long ago* decided to devote her virginity to God," thus underscoring even more the curious narrative elision here. Either way, we only learn of the most important decision of Theodora's life *after* it had been made, at some vague time and no particular place in a child's life, a momentous non-event slipped without comment into the middle of a paragraph. What ought to be a major hagiographic topos, elaborated with lingering dramatization, is treated as a narrative embarrassment covered by a flurry of platitudes attributed to Sueno, and a single anecdote in which Theodora rebukes some unnamed man for making a stupid dirty joke in her presence.[13] The text isolates Theodora from her natural and inevitable social setting of home and family, crowded rooms, and observant relatives and friends. In this supremely important life-altering decision, we hear only of a young girl and an adult man unrelated to her, something contemporaries would find very odd and hardly reassuring. No one else attests to her early self-dedication. This passage is crowded with the silenced voices of everyone who had known Theodora in her early years and found no reason to think that she had special aptitude for religious dedication.

The Vow

There would be no reason to include that dubious material if it weren't for the worse problem of her alleged "vow," the act that would be legally and morally central to everything that followed. This action, in contrast, is located as specifically as possible: Theodora accompanies her family to visit St. Albans on her birthday; she is filled with religious enthusiasm there, and "the following day" in the church at the vill of Shillington where they had spent the night, she offered a penny at the altar after the gospel and made a silent vow of lifelong virginity ("saying in her heart"), making mental reference to the penny as a symbolic token of surrender of her virginity to God.[14] Theodora seems to have been about fourteen at this time. This action is so thoroughly elaborated and precisely rendered in the text that it can almost distract a reader's attention from the fact that the crucial action (the vow itself) is invisible, inaudible, and unverifiable. She went to church; the priest was saying mass; she approached the altar; she offered a penny; [she thought various things silently]. The authenticating business, the narrative busyness, of sequential visible actions covers and envelops the invisible action and distracts us from the fact that no one else is named as witness or as confidant, although a girl traveling in a family party surely did not attend church alone. The author slips fictionally into interior knowledge and impersonation of Theodora's thoughts, which is narratively vivid but not an argument to convince anyone not already convinced.[15] Silenced skeptics stand behind this scene, insisting: "I was there; nothing happened; she said nothing about it; she behaved just as usual."

Personal sanctity in medieval society was not a matter of theological technicalities or even, always, miracles. For the most part, saints were popularly recognized, not made by any official procedure. The definition that best grasps this is the one offered by Dom David Knowles who defines a medieval saint as "one who appeared to those who knew him best as a pure reflection of Christ, and as such able in a strength not his own to transcend the limits of human virtue and endurance."[16] This captures the essentials of the matter in a way that postpones official recognition to its after-the-fact status, while it foregrounds the small group and near neighborhood realities of medieval life. Those post-antique saints who were recognized for their way of life, not their deaths, were saints because of the conviction of others, because of the feeling they aroused in people that they were doing and being something different and something more than other religiously motivated people. This response, affirming personal sanctity, whatever its local form and expression, did not have to be unanimous (Bernard of Clairvaux, for example, had his enemies); but there had to be a strong convinced core among "those who knew him best." Theodora never really achieved this in a lifetime spent mainly in a locality thickly populated with relatives and lifelong acquaintances, and combating this dubiousness that clung to her reputation is evident in the tone and emphases of the biography. The sainthood of Christina was a product of the passage of time, the passing away of many talkative local people, the resolution and oblivion of the internal discord at St. Albans, in short, the persistence of the partisan fragment of biography and the flaking away of its social context. The defense of virginity, organizing topos of the *Vita*, finally emerged in self-authenticating spiritual isolation as it never could have done in the lifetime of a bourgeois girl.

In her life story, Theodora was badly in need of support. The respectable Sueno is quickly brought into the narrative as witness and support. Theodora tells him about the vow and he "confirmed" her vow: "*votum virginis coram Deo confirmavit.*"[17] What exactly does this mean? How does one do this? If she merely told him she *had* made a vow, then how could he actually "confirm" an act he had not witnessed? Or did she make her vow over again, this time audibly, in his presence? If so, why is this not specifically asserted? Does "confirm" here come down to "express his approval" and nothing more? And more importantly, to contemporary mores, why were her parents not consulted or informed? Whose decision was this? If Sueno, as a respected religious advisor, actually thought a girl of a prominent family, nearing marriageable age, had made such a binding, life-altering vow, why would he make no effort to advise and influence her family to place her in a suitable monastery? This is an acutely serious problem both for social morality and for narrative persuasion. Keeping the narrative busy, voluble, and tightly focused on private exchanges between Theodora and the canon Sueno is a way of deferring and avoiding the social context of female religiosity, avoiding it in narrative exclusions as it was never avoidable in life.

To open and specify these critical weaknesses in Theodora's story is not to be mean-spirited or merely to debunk. These events were taking place in the early twelfth century, among the social elite of a small town, in a family powerful and well-connected but also socially exposed, not above ridicule and loss of reputation. In this small world, her world, Theodora was first and above all a daughter, living with and subject to the authority of her parents. The way the narrative diminishes her familial life, undermines her father's proper authority, and foregrounds her confidential relations with canon Sueno was not guaranteed to win over all readers. Keeping secrets from parents, sharing secrets with a man not her father, no matter how venerable, would look hopelessly bad to all but the most convinced admirers. Willfulness, impropriety, defiance, and disobedience were not easily tolerated in female minors. Sueno's behavior in encouraging her would be judged as, if possible, even more reprehensible.

After this elaborate moral drama, there follows—nothing. This is a problem, both narrative and moral, to account for two or three years with nothing remotely hagiographic to tell. In one hurried sentence, it is admitted that Theodora in effect did nothing after this life commitment to indicate to anyone that she had any intentions different from other girls of her class and age: "remained peacefully in her father's house" is the way this is evasively put.[18] In other words, she lived the ordinary life of the urban upper classes. The narrative conflates the period of some few years into one sentence and as quickly as possible distracts the reader's attention with the far more satisfying drama of the lecherous bishop of Durham who tried to seduce her after a dinner party in her aunt's house. But Theodora's family and Huntingdon neighbors would never have been so obligingly hustled past the long-observed life of a girl they thought they knew. Looking back from the uproar of her later refusal to marry, observers would have noted her contradictory behavior, frequent participation in pleasures, entertainments, and expense, luxurious clothes, no announced vocation for a religious life as a nun, and a suspicious-looking association with a man who supported her in defiance of parents.

The Men Who Loved Theodora

Here we might take advantage of the fact that we have read to the end of this book and note that an enduring and life-determining motif of Theodora's personality has already been established: that her life found its impetus and personal style through a series of intense, emotionally fraught relationships with men who were strongly moved (usually attracted, sometimes angrily fixated, never indifferent or bored) by her. Shorn of the narrator's distractions and uncritical admiration, Theodora's early religious life consists in exchanging exciting confidences of a romantically self-dramatizing nature with an adoring religious mentor who thinks she is quite wonderful. Away from him she apparently seemed just like other upper-class girls. She wielded great personal power over men. Her biographer says that she was beautiful, and her early self-assurance and ease with men seem the style of an indulged but well-protected beauty. Consider her subsequent relations with her would-be seducer, the bishop of Durham, who could not stop offering her valuable things after his drunken pass was rejected, and with her fiancé, Burthred, who plainly was hopelessly infatuated with her. For all the author's efforts, Burthred is never convincingly portrayed as a phallic threat: his characteristic moment is when he pathetically grabs Theodora's cloak as she shrugs out of it and departs with a cutting remark.[19] The hermit Roger adopted her as an acolyte, a truly astonishing action, and he imprudently kept her in his house at considerable risk to his reputation. Consider the bishops on whom she made such strong impressions once they had met her, with Thurston of York exerting himself as protector and giver of special personal favors. The unnamed Important Man who almost became her lover was a besotted suppliant to her, not an aggressor. Most importantly, there was Abbot Geoffrey of St. Albans, with whom she initiated an enduring love affair, chaste surely (she was still of childbearing age), but too intense and intimate, and entirely too public. Rachel Koopmans finds evidence that the dynamic of this relation was "that Geoffrey was more influenced by and enamoured with Christina than she with him."[20] Her father, Autti, who figures in modern scholarship, just as he does in the *Vita*, as a patriarchal oppressor, favored and indulged Theodora so much that she carried the keys to the household cash box all through their clash of wills over the marriage, and even in its hostile reported form, his anger sounds like baffled love. Her father's own chaplain carried messages for her.[21] The boy servant, Loric, risked his safety helping her run away and could not resist a compliment: "I wish I could have you with me outside the town." Theodora was suitably affronted and embarrassed, but remembered the incident for her biographer years later.[22] And we should not forget to include the anonymous monk who worked so devotedly to create the exalted Saint Christina out of the exacting, trouble-attracting, alluring Theodora. Obviously a society that placed all official authority in the hands of males accounts for some of this pattern, but there is no Theodora-evidence that she ever tried to create a life for herself separate from men who appealed to her. She refused Archbishop Thurston's pressing advice that she enter even the most socially exclusive of nunneries. Theodora was an intense and compelling personality, organized around a strongly erotic and heterosexual charge of excitement, which was (in an odd but, I suspect, not infrequent way) only intensified when her first dubious enthusiasm for virgin purity was turned by a crescendo of mishaps into an irrevocable commitment.

The famous episode of Bishop Ranulf Flambard's attempted seduction of Theodora in the course of a dinner party at the home of Alveva, Theodora's aunt and Ranulf's ex-mistress, is one of those behaviors which has grown more pruriently shocking with the passage of time and the secularization of society than it probably seemed in its own moment. Unchastity in bishops could not, in itself, have been notable, although the growing acceptance of post-papal reform strictness seems to have impelled Ranulf Flambard to give up Alveva, with whom he had children, when he was promoted to the bishopric of Durham.[23] The bishop always stayed in Alveva's new marital household in Huntingdon when he traveled to London, and he socialized with her family, whom he knew well. While everyone else was still at table, Ranulf and Theodora were in a bedroom where he asked her for sex. Even the narrator finds he has to admit that the overture was verbal and not violent: "sollicitavit." The only thing he touched was her sleeve.[24] Theodora, feeling it futile to call her parents, who had gone to bed, and afraid that rejection would provoke him to violence, tricked the bishop with a false promise and locked him in the room.

Here, the narrative challenge for the author, an exceptionally difficult one, is to isolate Theodora in the bishop's bedroom without impugning her character. The basic strategy is to make the man entirely aggressive and the girl (hitherto so precociously thoughtful and strong willed) entirely passive, indeed, narratively nonresponsible, in charge of no active verbs. Therefore, he desires her; he plans a trick; "he had the unsuspecting girl brought to his room" (as opposed to inviting her from the dining hall where she and her parents would have been); he had members of his own household there; he gave a "secret sign," and everyone else left the room; he laid his hand on her sleeve and spoke. The element most needing to be glossed over is characteristically sunk into one dependent clause: "when it was getting dark."[25] The uncomfortable and nearly incorrigible fact, given the purpose of this narrative, was that Theodora had willingly gone to the bishop's room and had stayed a very long time at his private party, making no attempt to leave. Only at the very end, does she recover her personal and narrative agency to be quick-witted, talkative, assertive, and bold in thwarting her seducer. We are given a strenuous recasting of what had to appear daring and provocative behavior, a girl careless of her reputation, making trouble with her family's most valuable connection.[26]

In the aftermath of whatever it was that happened between Bishop Ranulf Flambard and Theodora in Aunt Alveva's guest room, the bishop offered her expensive presents and brought forward a suitor for Theodora who was very acceptable to her parents. Everything henceforth turns on the nature of this courtship/betrothal, which has to be presented in a hostile light, as an aggressive and degraded self-seeking plot among Ranulf Flambard, Burthred the suitor, and Theodora's parents. Therefore, the bishop's motivation as matchmaker is cast as a psychologically exciting but wholly implausible act of displaced lust, defloration by proxy, motivated by revenge.

This prurient idea attributed to the bishop (that someone, *anyone*, must penetrate the girl) is an important narrative fulcrum to justify all her later actions. It is set up by the dramatic detail of Theodora's escape from the bedroom, locking the bishop inside; the direct dialogue between them ("allow me to bolt the door"); and several heavy-breathing, impossible-to-substantiate assertions about the bishop's subsequent frame of mind: "eaten up with resentment," "avenge the insult," "made a fool by a young girl," "a slave to lust and malice," and his purported mania to deprive her of virginity "either by himself or by someone else."[27] I find it curious that so many sophisticated modern readers have accepted this bizarre explanation, which makes no sense, psychologically or socially. Ranulf's imputed sense of sexual deprivation and personal rejection would hardly find compensation in imagining Theodora in the arms of a younger, presumably more attractive, wealthy husband whom, for all he knew, she might have welcomed and loved. And the monk's overwrought accusations (and too many modern readers) entirely overlook the signal fact that the bishop had no clue about any vows of dedicated virginity—no one except the canon Sueno knew about that.

The extremely odd idea of sex-by-proxy as revenge is offered to substitute an exciting and distracting alternative to a motivation and a narrative sequence that every ordinary twelfth-century observer would have found quite obvious: that is, offering a rich, well-born suitor with powerful friends to a family with several daughters to provide for is an act of friendship, generosity, and great good will. The narrative keeps the focus limited to the tense and sexy relations between Ranulf and Theodora, even though we have been told that Ranulf's good friend of long-standing was her father, Autti. Assuming that the usual hierarchies of family importance, of generational and masculine status, were in effect here, and assuming that Autti and Beatrix knew that something improper had occurred between the bishop and their daughter, to *whom* was the rich suitor being offered? To her parents, of course, and to Alveva as an act of apology and respect, an exertion of patronage and favor, to restore good relations between old friends. Reparation is a far more plausible idea than displaced sexual revenge in this situation.

Malo Casta Manere

Here finally, in response to the marriage proposal supported by her family, Theodora for the first time announces her vow of virginity. "And when they asked the reason [for rejecting the marriage]: 'Malo respondit casta manere. Nam et votum feci.'"[28] Talbot's translation is: "She replied: 'I wish to remain single, for I have made a vow of virginity.'" A simpler, more literal rendering captures the characteristic Theodora better: "I want to remain chaste. And I've even made a vow." And then the people hearing her made fun of, derided her "temeritatem," her "rashness" in Talbot's word choice; but our modern usage of "temerity," adding a note of audacity, is suggestive, and Samuel Johnson's eighteenth-century "unreasonable contempt of danger" is even better. We should not forget that the dialogue was written by the monk of St. Albans, and that Theodora was not speaking Latin. But even trying to portray her in the best light at all times, he renders her as being both vague in her intentions (remaining *casta*) and impertinent (flatly announcing her *votum*, made all by herself, a surprise to her nearest relations).

In subsequent passages, she is portrayed as steadfast and courageous, her family as hectoring and bullying, and Burthred as mindlessly persistent. The passage of time is unclear, but apparently over a year passes in this manner—mainly occupied with persuasion, gifts, and promises of more bribes, interspersed with heated quarrels in which Theodora more than holds her own. Theodora remains steadfast—until she changes her mind. She agrees to marry Burthred, at church, before her family. "How it happened I cannot tell," says the narrator, prudently taking the narrative "fifth." Narratives are selective; life is linear. Filling that momentous year with its most minimal contents has Theodora living the ordinary life of a girl of her class, accepting her parents' gifts, wearing pretty clothes, attending their parties, and—this is important—regularly seeing Burthred, her suitor, because this was acceptable behavior in northwestern Europe, and the narrator has nothing to say to the contrary. In the course of this year, Burthred apparently thought that he was not being entirely and unconditionally rejected; he was there at church with her, on what seems an ordinary occasion, when "she yielded (at least in word) and on the very day Burthred was betrothed to her."[29] Words were what made legal marriages.[30]

Although betrothed and possibly married (the narrator is signally confused about this detail because betrothals were legally binding), Theodora remained living with her parents, renounced her betrothal, and restated her desire for a virgin life. And here I want to make it clear in this reading that I do agree that *both* Theodora and Christina, as it were, did not want this marriage. However, "Christina-reasons" are doctrinaire and exalted, while "Theodora-reasons" seem closer to the resentment at being pushed around that a self-willed person very accustomed to having her own way might display. In all the flurry of recriminations and domestic chaos that ensues, it is easy (*it is made easy*) to overlook the signal fact (and significant narrative embarrassment) that in the twelfth century, *being chaste* in the sense of unmarried and sexually uninitiated (as she said she wanted to "remain") was not, in itself, a religious career for either a woman or a man. When Theodora gave as her reason for rejecting a desirable marriage: "I want to remain chaste. And I've even made a vow," everyone found this ridiculous at first, which the author presents as callous meanness. But it *was* ridiculous from their point of view. Dedicated celibacy required an institutional setting of some sort. The anchoress and anchorite who lived near Huntingdon and later gave shelter to Theodora were only metaphorically alone: they are described as having houses, servants, companions, and sources of income. No religious institution was ever suggested by Theodora, and if anyone else proposed this obvious idea, we are not told about it. But there was no secular life option for an unmarried woman of Theodora's class, or none that any of her acquaintance would conceive that she wanted. What she declared she wanted, "to remain chaste," did not exist socially unless she intended a life of dependency with her parents or one of her married siblings.[31] Her eventual running away from home and concealment with a local anchoress, and later with Roger the anchorite, were improvised expedients of desperation, as her legal and social options closed off and her angry stubbornness hardened. Nonetheless, here Theodora and Christina converge in displaying the one quality they unequivocally shared: brave and defiant, single-minded perseverence in a course once taken.

At this point I should interject that Theodora is, of course, a narrative construct as much as Christina, or both are equally historical to some degree. I do not want to deconstruct one only to reify the other, but one of these female characters does have a better claim to past actuality. Reading the *Life* this way is like creating a negative from a photograph. If the surface of the text read "positively" gives us the discourse of a certain post-papal reform exaltation of virginity, reading in "negative" reveals the discourse of a tradition-bound society deeply discomfited by nonconformity and any threat to hierarchies of family and gender. But the narrative is often discomfited itself by Theodora's intermittent conformity. The narrator tells us that she was kept under rigid supervision and restraint and then depicts scenes of guildhall banqueting, festivities at home, chats with a girlfriend, and numerous instances of messages carried back and forth by servants. Theodora goes out anywhere she chooses; she always has money to spend. The only real restraint seems to have been on her friendship with Sueno, for which her parents had ample reason.

Even the startling episodes in which her parents colluded in letting Burthred into her bedroom, presumably to force her to have intercourse and thus reconcile her to living with her husband, were far more cruel in intention than in commission. Somehow, on all three occasions, she was forewarned and prepared to defend herself successfully. On the first night, Theodora entertained a docile Burthred with a sermon on the virtue of chastity: "Do not take it amiss that I have declined your embraces. . . . I will go home with you: . . . ostensibly as husband and wife, but in reality living chastely in the sight of the Lord. . . . in three or four years time we will receive the religious habit and offer ourselves to some monastery which providence shall appoint." After some hours of this, "the young man eventually left the maiden." Aside from the comical aspect, which no one seems to notice, this scene is startlingly like the episode in Book I.47 of Gregory of Tours' *History of the Franks,* in which a bride persuades her husband on their wedding night to live chastely with her.[32] The second, and more chilling attempt was when Burthred and unnamed others entered her room, finding her again awake, aware, and resourceful in hiding herself. The psychologically gripping effect of the scene is entirely the product of the author's fictional capacity to merge his narrative self with that of Christina imagining herself dragged out of hiding, stared at and surrounded, threatened and destroyed.[33] But none of this happened. No one found her and nothing happened. The *Vita* version is entirely Theodora's version, without corroboration, although she said many people were involved.

Once Theodora left the protection of her father's house to reside, first, with a female religious authority, and next with Roger at his hermitage, she had embarked on a career that permitted no alternatives or second thoughts. She may, by this action, have so shamed her father before his peers that he could not take her back. It seems clear enough from the awkward materials that make up the *Vita* that she had no clear idea of a religious life, that the defiant pathos of "I want to remain chaste," which speaks so poignantly to us, was a gesture in the direction of nothing her society could allow, or even picture. It is not at all clear what remaining *casta* could have meant to Theodora, in 1114, in Huntingdon. But this inchoate rebellion and vague defiance of convention were channeled by circumstance into something closer to a steadfast purpose modeled after her first protectors, and she eventually found herself, still only in her late twenties, in possession of the hermitage Roger had left her, returned to the familiar country neighborhood and towns, and the known religious map of her girlhood.

Gossip

The narrator clearly knew the mature Theodora (he speaks of having had dinner with her); knows the neighborhoods of Markyate (which became her own convent when she could finally be persuaded to take vows), Huntingdon, and St. Albans; and he added his book to the plentiful local talk about her.[34] For the true narrative motif organizing the Return-to-Markyate portion of the *Vita* is gossip.

The narrator cannot leave behind the subject of gossip and rumors, which he feels it necessary to acknowledge in colorful but vague language, condemning the apparently many persons who spoke openly, disrespectfully, and often about her. A great deal of this hostility concerned her relations with Geoffrey, abbot of St. Albans. With her accustomed self-confidence in dealings with men, Theodora had initiated personal contact with Abbot Geoffrey. She influenced the settlement of some disputed matters between the abbot and his monks, and she became a close and influential friend of the abbot. Although her establishment of Markyate was in bad financial shape, Geoffrey took over the financial management of Theodora's house and improved the conditions there, using the resources of St. Albans, much against the will of his monks. The friendship between Theodora and Geoffrey aroused hostile gossip and jealousy; some of her friends were rejected or ignored by her and grew angry and did not hesitate to say what they thought of her.

The narrator reports that several of her enemies were stricken with illness or driven to great unhappiness through envy, although no details are offered about the circumstances. He consistently speaks of her detractors in the plural. She seems to have provoked controversy, hostility, suspicion, and contempt among a substantial number of (unnamed) people who debunked her spiritual pretentions, accused her of venality and sharp business practice, and loudly suspected that something improper was going on between herself and Abbot Geoffrey. Relations between the two provoked a lot of frank suspicion that they were carrying on a sexual affair, and the abbot's reputation suffered as well as Theodora's. Whatever the truth of the matter, it is clear that many people disliked and distrusted her and felt no hesitation at speaking quite openly about her, so her controversial reputation was well known. The monk mentions even the common people being influenced by talk about her. We hear that she had bad relations with a neighbor in a dispute over taking salad herbs from his garden; far from trying to mend the quarrel, Theodora cultivated her grudge against him. Her detractors included many monks, notably the monks of St. Albans who were bitterly divided over her influence with their abbot. But as the existence of this *Vita* makes clear, she also had fervently loyal friends, a circle of favorites, confidants, dependents, no doubt led by Abbot Geoffrey, reinforced by her wealthy family supporting their relatives: two sisters at Markyate, a brother at St. Albans. But the narrative lingers over this matter of her reputation at surprising length, denouncing her enemies, detailing various visions that proved her complete innocence to one or another doubter, building pious rhetoric around the topic—although characteristically light on the specific accusations.[35]

If one follows the traces of narrative response to implicit pressures, asking simple questions about what sequence of demands is generating the course of narrative topics, then it seems clear that much of this book is dedicated to justifying Theodora's motives and behavior while answering or counterattacking her detractors, especially as narrative time moves closer to the present tense of the author's and his subject's lives. The narrative-constructing pressures make this a rather odd book: something like a defense attorney's counter-attack awkwardly laminated to a hagiographer's celebration. Once stripped of the devotional rhetoric and the lavish and omniscient recounting of her visionary experiences, this narrative emerges as a counternarrative, built over and against, in antiphonal relation to another story—one prevailing in the vicinity of twelfth-century Huntingdon, prevailing in contemporary public opinion, but unwritten and thus ephemeral.

I started by stating that Christina of Markyate is a saint. Do I still count Christina of Markyate as a saint? Yes, of course. Sainthood, so far as I know, is an official status conferred within institutional auspices of the Roman Catholic Church, according to criteria generated by an institution. She has been admitted to that distinction by the gatekeepers empowered to confer it, and I wouldn't dream of second-guessing the Bollandists. If this sounds rather cool and bureaucratic, I would remind readers that there are very few saints who can satisfy a modern taste for warm and cozy religion.

And Theodora? Freed for a moment from the grip of the hagiographical ambitions of her *Vita,* she emerges very interestingly: a woman of compelling sexual attraction to men, which she indulged fully at an emotional level in a lifelong series of intense and important relationships: men wanted to do things for her and she directed this impulse. She liked personal power and freely exerted her influence wherever she could make it felt; she was strong-willed, arrogant, controlling, and probably held a grudge quite well. She was interesting and clever, impressive and rather seductive; she aroused strong reactions, her acquaintances dividing into loyal partisans and angry detractors. Against convention and against the odds, she made a life for herself following no institutional model and accepting no external supervision. And with the passage of time and massive social change, she has found her cult—as anyone who has taught this text to students in late adolescence knows. When Theodora says, "I want to remain chaste," they hear her speaking for herself and wanting to form and follow her own wishes—more a hero than a saint; but that is the cult for which her *Vita* had to wait eight centuries. At the core of the Christina/Theodora amalgam we recognize a girl struggling desperately to keep some options open against massive social forces that would hurry her from docile childhood to marital constraints before she had a chance at a single autonomous life decision. We might remember that human lives acquire the saturated, coherent, univocal meaningfulness of *saint,* a specific cultural construct, by the same means that mere events during a stretch of time acquire the meaningful coherence of *narrative:* by a process of selection, suppression, emphasis, and repetition. Saints, like narratives, are made, not born.

Notes

1. David Hugh Farmer, *The Oxford Dictionary of Saints* (Oxford: Clarendon Press, 1978), 77–78, in which Christina's religious identity is simply "virgin."

2. *The Life of Christina of Markyate: A Twelfth-Century Recluse,* ed. and trans. C. H. Talbot (Oxford: Clarendon Press, 1959), 10–12.

3. Here, unsurprisingly, Robert Hanning has led the way in seeing Christina foremost as a woman living at a particular moment and place: *The Individual in Twelfth-Century Romance* (New Haven: Yale University Press, 1977), 34–50.

4. Rachel M. Koopmans, "The Conclusion of Christina of Markyate's Vita," *Journal of Ecclesiastical History* 51 (2000): 663–98. This scrupulously thorough and incisively argued essay addresses the questions about Christina without apology or special pleading; Koopmans asks, and answers, many of the hardest questions about the manuscript, its provenance and transmission (or lack of it), without allowing contemporary admiration for this unconventional medieval woman to distort her sense of twelfth-century realities.

5. Ibid., 683–85, especially the financial aspects of Abbot Geoffrey's reliance on Christina's advice.

6. Ibid., 665.

7. Ibid., 698.

8. Scholarship on the *Vita* has been strong and interesting, especially on the themes of mystical experience, the marginal or semi-institutional lives of hermits, and the special difficulties faced by women with religious vocations. Good examples are Christopher Holdsworth, "Christina of Markyate," in *Medieval Women,* ed. Derek Baker (Oxford: Basil Blackwell, 1978), 185–204; and Sharon Elkins, *Holy Women of Twelfth-Century England* (Chapel Hill: University of North Carolina, 1988). There is, however, a strong tendency for modern readers to take all their reading cues from the narrative stance of the text and look at Christina and her world from one partisan point of view, never questioning narrative assertions that support her cause.

9. Talbot, *The Life of Christina,* 35.

10. Ibid.

11. Ibid., 34–35: "Porro columba cum pregnante muliere sicut ipsa michi retulit."

12. Ibid., 36–37.

13. Ibid., 37–39: Sueno "extolled the glory of virginity, the difficulty of preserving it," and Theodora peremptorily told off the unnamed man who joked about lust in her presence.

14. Ibid., 39–41.

15. The full license permitted to medieval writers of the nonfiction genres to incorporate fictional techniques (omniscience, impersonation, interior knowledge, direct dialogue, etc.) is used by the monk of St. Albans to good effect in this book. His most important efforts are given to rendering his subject's interior states of

mind and emotion as vividly as possible; so at the church at Shillington, Christina's interior thoughts are voiced: "For to Thee as a surrender of myself I offer this penny . . . ," ibid., 41.

16. David Knowles, *The Monastic Order in England* (Cambridge: Cambridge University Press, 1940), 60.

17. Talbot, *The Life of Christina,* 41.

18. Ibid. Her reportable activity during this period was being happy "that she could grow from day to day in holy virtue and in the love of supernatural things."

19. Ibid., 72–73.

20. Koopmans concludes that the rumors of a sexual relationship between Christina and Geoffrey of St. Albans were widespread and commonplace among the laity and religious community: "In an age when Bernard of Clairvaux warned that a man could not lie down with a woman without having sex with her, it is little wonder that Geoffrey's monks suspected a sexual relationship between Christina and their abbot," Koopmans, "The Conclusion," 682–83. We might also note that specific acts of sexual intercourse are not necessary to an erotic love affair, and their absence is no guarantee of innocence.

21. Talbot, *The Life of Christina,* 69: "She sent two persons of great authority, namely Sueno the canon and her father's chaplain, to her husband to ask him to release her."

22. Ibid., 87: her affronted reaction was chiefly class snobbery ("it was beneath her dignity as a daughter of Autti to be found in the open countryside with such a youth"), because she was the one giving orders: "go and tell your master to prepare two horses. . . ."

23. Sir Richard Southern's portrait of Ranulf Flambard is balanced, vivid, and sympathetic, with good reason given: in *Medieval Humanism and Other Studies* (Oxford: Basil Blackwell, 1970), 183–205.

24. Talbot, *The Life of Christina,* 43.

25. Ibid. This is, of course, another of the fictionalized scenes where narrative omniscience takes us through walls to make us invisibly present.

26. In a very interesting article, R. I. Moore reexamines the Ranulf/Christina event and suggests that Ranulf might have been offering Christina the same position in his life that her aunt, Alveva, had previously occupied. I tend to think that Ranulf's decision to part with Alveva, arranging a good marriage for her at Huntingdon when he became bishop of Durham, shows that the relatively new standard of clerical celibacy (or at least the avoidance of clerical marriage) was becoming the norm. See R. I. Moore, "Ranulf Flambard and Christina of Markyate," in *Belief and Culture in the Middle Ages,* ed. Richard Gameson and Henrietta Leyser (Oxford: Oxford University Press, 2001), 231–35.

27. Talbot, *The Life of Christina,* 43.

28. Ibid., 44–45.

29. Ibid., 47.

30. A thorough and subtle examination of the variant marriages and vows in the Christina *Life*, with their legal and spiritual statuses, is Thomas Head, "The Marriages of Christina of Markyate," *Viator* 21 (1990): 75–101.

31. The personal status of unmarried women is examined in a superb book of essays, *Singlewomen in the European Past, 1250–1800*, ed. Judith M. Bennett and Amy M. Froide (Philadelphia: University of Pennsylvania Press, 1999). See especially Maryanne Kowaleski, "Singlewomen in Medieval and Early Modern Europe: The Demographic Perspective," 38–81. Single women were far more common than we tend to suppose; but single status varied greatly according to social status, wealth, time, and place. Marriage was commonly considered the best option, if available; and a girl like Theodora, without livelihood skills, not raised to wage work, and not likely to receive her dowry for her personal use, was not making a demand her family could comprehend.

32. Talbot, *The Life of Christina*, 50–51. The author composes an eloquent little speech for Theodora, depicting the spiritual glory of a chaste marriage. Compare the rather similar episode in Gregory of Tours' *History of the Franks*, Book I.47, in which a noble bride on her wedding night persuades her husband to accept a life of chastity, allow her to keep her valued virgin state, and win salvation for both of them. Gregory of Tours, *History of the Franks*, trans. Lewis Thorpe (Middlesex, England: Penguin Books, 1974), 95–97.

33. I have discussed this scene, in terms of its fictional technique at the service of narrative persuasion and the striking advances of fictional realism in medieval historical narrative, in "Medieval Histories and Modern Realism: Yet Another Origin of the Novel," *Modern Language Notes* 114 (1999): 866–68.

34. Talbot, *The Life of Christina*, 191: "On another occasion, as we were sitting at table with the maiden of Christ. . . ."

35. Ibid., 173–79.

6

H. MARSHALL LEICESTER, JR.

The Voice of the Hind

*The Emergence of Feminine Discontent
in the* Lais *of Marie de France*

I n this essay I want to suggest some protocols for a way of reading the *Lais* of Marie de France. I will focus on a certain voice that can intermittently be found in them, and an anamorphosis, or displaced angle of viewing/reading, that is, I think, potentially transformative for the interpretation of the individual *lais* and the collection as a whole. In keeping with my title, I call the perspective I have in mind "the voice of the hind" and begin the analysis with an examination of that curious magical figure, at once central and marginal to the action, in *Guigemar.*

I

Immediately after we have been introduced to the hero of the *lai,* his country, lineage, upbringing, and unnatural indifference to love (*G.* 1–68), he is seized by a desire to hunt; and in the course of his hunting, he encounters the game that will change his life: "Tute fu blaunche cele beste, / Perches de cerf ont en la teste" (*G.* 91–92; A completely white beast, / With deer's antlers on her head). Firing at her, Guigemar is himself wounded by the rebound of his arrow; and as both hunter and prey lie wounded, the hind begins to speak:

"Oï! Lase! Jo sui ocise!
E tu, vassal, ki m'as nafree,
Tel seit la tue destinee:
Jamais n'aies tu medecine,
Ne par herbe, ne par racine!
Ne par mire, ne par poisun
N'avras tu jamés garisun
De la plaie k'as en la quisse,
De si ke cele te guarisse
Ki suffera pur tue amur
Issi grant peine e tel dolur
K'unkes femme taunt ne suffri,
E tu referas taunt pur li;
Dunt tuit cil s'esmerveillerunt
Ki aiment e amé avrunt
U ki pois amerunt aprés.
Va t'en de ci, lais m'aveir pés!"
                    (G. 106–22)

"Alas, I'm dying!
And you, vassal, who wounded me,
this be your destiny:
may you never get medicine for your wound!
Neither herb nor root,
neither physician nor potion
will cure you
of that wound in your thigh,
until a woman heals you,
one who will suffer out of love for you,
pain and grief
such as no woman ever suffered before.
And out of love for her, you'll suffer as much;
the affair will be a marvel
to lovers, past and present
and to all those yet to come.
Now go away, leave me in peace!"

It is striking that, after this dense and extended presentation, noticeable in so relatively short a poem from a writer typically committed to bald statement and narrative economy, the hind disappears, never to be seen again. She is an early example of what might be called "conspicuous *surplus*," a richly suggestive source of potential signification that is linked (in Marie's Prologue to the *Lais*) to what the ancients left undeveloped in the *matiere* they handed down to us, and linked as well (in the lovemaking of Guigemar and his lady) to the *jouissance*, as well as the *solas*, of eros. Though, as I'll argue, her voice resonates throughout the collection, narratively the hind is the merest device to move the plot of the *lai* forward, killed off, as she herself notes, to set the hero on the path to love. As a magic talking animal, she is a marker of Romance, one of those manifestations from the Other World who tell us that our lives are allegories of love. She is there to take a complex but determinate part in Guigemar's self-reflexive wounding, the stalking-deer of what will turn out to have been his discovery of desire; and she is there to tell him the kind of story he is in, the particular bundle of romance clichés about faithful love and suffering that will turn out to have made him memorable to the *Bretun*. The hind is burdened with and occluded by the Symbolic, the discourse that has always already structured our experience of the Real; and she is therefore a hapless bearer of the future anterior, the known-before-it-happens.

What I find most interesting about the hind, however, is her resistance to being made the vehicle of so much portentousness, whether of the romantic *Bretun* or of poststructural psychoanalytical me. The resistance is most concentrated, perhaps, in her final bitter dismissal of Guigemar, "Va t'en de ci, lais m'aveir pés!" Hovering somewhere between relief at the discharge of her obligatory message and a need to be alone with the pain her involvement in this man's affairs has caused her, the comment adds a different sort of *surplus*, a tone of what we now call "attitude," to her narrative function, stressing her detachment from it, her dislike of it and of those responsible for it, and her independence in a kind of suffering the message itself does not declare. It is a sentiment that can be heard to echo behind situations as superficially diverse as those of the lady in *Yonec* and of Guildeluec in *Eliduc*, although it is only glancingly relevant to anyone else in *Guigemar*.[1]

But once we begin to attend to it, the ways the hind exceeds her place in this *lai* begin to multiply. Her horns and her fawn mark an instability of gender identity at once powerfully tempting to interpretation—I'll resist for now—and difficult to bring home very clearly to the story of Guigemar. More immediately productive is the fact that her prediction of what will happen to the hero does not quite jibe with the course of the story. At a very general level, the question of whether the love and suffering Guigemar and his

lover feel and undergo for each other are really such as were never seen before and a marvel to lovers for all time is at least subject to debate and interpretation. To take it seriously, rather than as an instance of the general romance category into which adventures of this kind fall, would need at least as
much interested contestation as, say, the question of whether a given woman
is really better—"De cors, de vis e de beauté, / De enseignement e de bunté"
(*Lanval* 301–2)—than Guenevere or not. More immediately, however, the
abduction of the hind and her wound into the Symbolic is marked by the
bodily *surplus* the change of register leaves behind. That is, the hind and
Guigemar both begin with real physical injuries, however framed by marvels,
and the hind is left, as far as we know, to die of hers. For Guigemar, however,
his injury is quite rapidly transformed into the wound of love, a metaphorical illness whose physical register ("plaie dedenz cors / E si ne piert nïent
defors": "a wound in the body, / and yet nothing appears on the outside," *G.*
483–84) enters into discourse and is subject to its processes, like the boasting
of "vilain curteis" and the laws of feudal service (*G.* 485–95). Though it takes
several hundred lines for this transformation to be completed in the plot of
the *lai*, Guigemar already has it fully under rhetorical control by the time he
first wakes up to tell his story to the lady of the tower. He has received such
a wound, he tells her:

> Jamés ne quid estre sané.
> La bise se pleinst e parlat:
> Mut me maudist, e si urat
> Que ja n'eüsse guarisun
> Si par une meschine nun,
> Ne sai u ele seit trovee.
> (*G.* 320–24)

> ... I've given up hope of being cured.
> The hind complained and spoke to me,
> cursed me, swore
> that I'd never be healed
> except by a girl;
> I don't know where she might be found.

The leading nature of this recital is confirmed a moment later with the mock-
innocence of Guigemar's conclusion, "Bele dame, pur Deu vus pri, / Cun-
seillez mei, vostre merci!" ("Beautiful one, I beg you for God's sake, please

advise me!" *G.* 533–34). The lady shows that she has understood the message behind the narrative by launching at once into an impassioned denunciation of her husband (*G.* 336–58). She then conceals Guigemar from the husband and his agents using surplus food saved from her own meals (*G.* 375–79), and waits for him to heal.

"De sa plaie nul mal ne sent" (*G.* 383). Henceforward the healing of the physical wound takes a back seat to the developing love between the two protagonists, a process the *lai* follows with loving attention to the psychological and rhetorical skill the lovers use in deploying their affecting conventional laments to themselves and each other, and the "brief debate," whose "delightfully spurious reasoning," as Hanning and Ferrante note (p. 57), brings them together. I mean this disenchanted summary to suggest the extent to which the *lai* attends to its characters less as innocent embodiments of an experience of "falling in love," which happens to be expressed in the conventional forms and style of twelfth-century romance, than as knowledgeable users and performers of those conventions. Guigemar is, of course, looking for shelter and for tending for his wound, but he is aware of where such things are likely to lead in the circumstances; he may well be aware also, since he is used to being propositioned ("Plusurs l'en [d'amer] requistrent suvent" *G.* 63), that his charms—"sages e pruz" (*G.* 43) as he is—are his strongest cards in winning help. The lady, similarly, at least knows that this pitiable and handsome young man is more interesting than anything else going on in her life at the moment.[2] It is not necessary to make these people deliberately calculating in order to register the deftness of their practical consciousness of how to "go on" in conventionally recognizable situations. One might put it rather that, like Le Fresne, they can make effective improvisatory use of the signifying resources of their world and its furniture, and, like Equitan, can put themselves in the way of occasions of desire without having to take full note of their own agency in the matter.

Such a perspective, one that attends to various forms of narrative and descriptive *surplus* in the *lais* as traces of the material interests and agency of the social actors within them, allows one of the central themes of the collection: the examination of the uses of stories, to be read as Marie de France's psychology and socioanthropology of her culture's technologies of desire. The conventions, narremes, and tropes, the exquisite pains and elegant marvels of *fin amor* and romance are represented in the poem as techniques people use to negotiate their interests in the register of desire and to negotiate their desires in accordance with their interests. What justifies my char-

acterization of Marie's project in such general and abstract terms is precisely
the systematic and cumulative character of the representation; and this will
bring us back to the hind.

Guigemar and his lady build their romance by a kind of Freudian *An-
lehnung* on a real physical wound that is symbolized and transcended, leaving its literal and bodily character and consequences back with the hind.
The pattern is a general one in the *lai,* a pattern set up even before the hind
appears in it, insofar as the poem begins with an extended account of historical, geographical, genealogical, and political detail—King Hoel of Leon-
nais and his vassal Oridial; the mother and sisters, education and travels of
the latter's son Guigemar—which is never used again. One effect of making
the episode with the hind the point of transition for the journey to the Other
World (which is to say the abstraction into romance of what might otherwise
be, say, a story about a problem of feudal succession and the provision of an
heir)[3] is that it sets up the borderline between the Real of the body and its
Symbolic representations as the site of a *gendered* differentiation in the experience of eros and its difficulties, which is then played out in the rest of the
lais. That is, the difference I have been developing between the hind's real experience of bodily rupture and Guigemar's complex interpretive engagement
with an increasingly symbolized lack, is the first instance in the *Lais* of a consistently developed difference in the way the structuring of desire weighs on
women and on men.

Many of the Francophone writers of the early courtly period,[4] in taking
notice of the derangements, in both fields, that arise from linking the circulation of economic resources to the vicissitudes of erotic life—the aspect
of arranged marriage as the main material source of *fin amor*—take note as
well of the fact that the burdens of these derangements fall more heavily on
women. In *Guigemar,* this differential appears most plainly in the careers of
Guigemar and his lady after their affair is discovered and he is expelled by her
husband. It is not simply that she must wait and he must seek, in accordance
with general romance stereotypes. To begin with, it is noticeable that Guigemar does *not* seek for her, and it is made more noticeable by the energy with
which he engages in the politics of renouncing his fealty, raising an army,
and conducting a siege to regain her once his hand has been forced by her
rediscovery and the issues of male and feudal competition imported into
the story by Meriaduc (*G.* 840–80). The knotted shirt that is the sign of his
attachment to her is, unlike the knotted belt from him that she wears, detachable. Guigemar has a special officer, "Un chamberlenc . . . / Ki la chemise

ot a garder" ("A chamberlain . . . / who was in charge of the shirt," *G.*
796–97), who produces it on demand (I imagine a silken pillow) for the
widely famed social occasions when "Il n'i ad dame ne pucele," throughout
Brittany, "Ki n'i alast pur asaier" ("all the women and girls came to try their
luck," *G.* 652–53).[5] One cannot help noticing that this ritual supplies Guigemar with a perfect excuse for continuing to live in the way that he did before
he met the hind, but now without the criticisms for indifference to love that
he received before, and apparently without pressure to marry. The possibility
that the shirt has more significance for him as a convenient symbolic defense
against unwanted involvements in the present than as a living trace of the
lady herself is strengthened by the fact that Guigemar does not recognize
her when she does turn up, even after she has successfully undone the knot
(*G.* 801–14).

In order to convince himself that it is really she, Guigemar invokes a
signifier of identity that sticks to the lady the way the wound sticks to the
hind—and it is not a belt: "'Lessiez mei vostre cors veeir!'" ("'Let me see
your body!'" *G.* 818). This "request" is made in open court, and not for the first
time.[6] The lady wears Guigemar's belt under her clothes, and it apparently
serves as a physical warden of her chastity, since it frustrates Meriaduc's attempt to rape her:

> Il [Meriaduc] la receit entre ses braz,
> De sun bliaut trenche les laz:
> La ceinture voleit ovrir,
> Mes n'en poeit a chief venier
>
> (737–40)

> He took her in his arms,
> cut the laces of her tunic.
> and tried to open the belt.
> But he didn't succeed.[7]

If this assault is, as one hopes, at least conducted in private, the brief but startling account of Meriaduc's reaction to his failure sounds like an all-too-
public way of socializing his losses: "Puis n'ot el païs chevalier / Que il n'i
feïst essaier" (*G.* 741–42), "There wasn't a knight in the region / Whom he
didn't summon to try his luck." The *lai* consistently focuses on both the in-
vasive publicity of the lady's exposure and the apparent failure of the characters to remark it.

In *Guigemar* the insistence of a woman's body as a marker for the actuality of female oppression, begun in the episode of the hind and kept running in the adventures of the belt, is not directly acknowledged. Along with the other forms of more realistic political violence that start to push through the surface of a happy ending—delayed just a little too long—the situation of Guigemar's lady remains mostly tacit, a *surplus* that presses on the margins of the romance plot. The further progress of the *Lais* can be read as the gradual explicit rendering of this theme in the central characters and action, thereby giving body and voice in the tales to a perspective we first bruited in the hind. *Guigemar* already suggests Marie's sense of the unbalanced construction of gender roles in her society, such that the dominant (or in our current jargon, hegemonic) view of feminine protest, where it is not simply disregarded, is negative. The practical consequence in the early *Lais* is that the voice of the hind is given to what are, in conventional terms, "bad girls": the seneschal's wife in *Equitan,* the mother in *Le Fresne,* the werewolf's wife in *Bisclavret,* and Guenevere in *Lanval.* I will attempt to move quickly through the first three of these, before looking more closely at the queen.

II

One implication of male ideological domination of romance as a technology of desire is that the *Bretun* who supplied Marie with her material were, mostly unconsciously, male chauvinists, and this prejudice is nowhere more evident than in *Equitan.* The basic story of the plot by a wife and her lover to kill her husband is close enough to modern tales like *Double Indemnity* and *The Postman Always Rings Twice* to warrant its characterization as a *lai noir,* especially when that plot is enacted in an atmosphere of obsessive and slightly perverse sexuality. The poem concentrates on powerful bodily sensations in a way unique in medieval literature, first in its association of the lovers' sexual trysts with Equitan's practice of being bled, and then by the *amour fou* of their impulsive sexual embrace on the husband's bed when the latter steps out of the room,[8] leading, on his return, to the immediate deaths by scalding that their action courts. Equitan is a pursuer of intense experiences at the boundaries of pleasure and pain, and he does so in the company of what looks like a classic *femme fatale.* Hanning and Ferrante take note of the "doggedly didactic tone" of the *lai* (p. 69); and though most of their paraphrase of the poem's stern moralizing concentrates, quite properly, on

Equitan, the poem begins by sketching a recognizably *noir* apportionment of blame. Equitan is one whose love "n'unt sen ne mesure" (*Eq.* 18, is "without sense or moderation"), but everyone knows that it is the nature ("mesure,") of love "Que nuls n'i deit reisun garder" (*Eq.* 20, "that no one involved with it can keep his head"); and if we are looking for the cause of the great public damage that arose from this affair, "Femme espuse ot li seneschals / Dunt puis vint el païs granz mals" (*Eq.* 29–30: "This seneschal took a wife / through whom great harm later came to the kingdom"). After all, before that unlucky marriage and its exciting consequences, Equitan pursued his hunting and hawking in peace, and the seneschal took—the poem spends four lines on it—excellent care of the kingdom.

I take this moralized plot and its lesson to be the *lai* the *Bretun* made of the *aventure* they heard. In the virtual origin the poem projects, the story takes both its didactic tendency and its covert prurience from the guilty fantasies of the folk imagination; and the structure it gave to those events was relayed to Marie, though she heightens both tendencies to the point of discomfort as a way of stressing them. Her own *relais*, however, presses back against the overt moralizing of the official surface of the tale to reimagine the *aventure* in the discursive detail of its dramatization. As with Meriaduc and Guigemar, Equitan's homosocial relationship with the seneschal (which in this case, as noted, predates the advent of the wife) is foregrounded, first by the fact that the king desires her ("la coveita," a word the Decalogue itself applies to a neighbor's goods as well as his wife) sight unseen (*Eq.* 41). The *lai* next focuses on the deliberation with which Equitan plans his hunting trip to put himself in the way of an encounter with his vassal's wife (*Eq.* 43–50), so that when he begins his stock love-soliloquy with "'Allas, fet il queils destinee / M'amenet en ceste cuntree?'" (*Eq.* 65–66: "'Alas,' he says, 'what destiny / led me to these parts?'"), its performed and self-serving character is evident. This framing context brings forward, as well, how much more the soliloquy is focused on the seneschal than on the lady, and the extent to which it is transgression and the prospect of its discovery rather than her actual erotic attractions that excite him, since that prospect is its main theme. By the end of the passage, it is clear that if the *Bretun* were inclined to blame the lady for this *aventure*, they took their cue from Equitan, who is the first (in this story anyway) to blame the insatiable sexuality of a woman he knows nothing about for his own desire: "'Suls ne la peot il pas tenir[9] / Certes, jeo voil a li partir!'"(*Eq.* 87–88: "'he certainly can't hold her all by himself, / and I'm happy to share the burden with him!'").

It is this persistent concentration on the aggressive agency that Equitan cloaks in the performance of abject *fin amor,* that makes the lady's responses to him into the voice of the hind rather than the cold calculation of a *femme fatale.* She registers with complete clarity the power differential between them, the freedom it gives to his situation, and, with the hind's savvy about how things go, the anxieties that must beset hers:

"Vus estes reis de grant noblesce;
Ne sui mie de teu richesce
Qu'a mei vus deiez arester
De druërie ne d'amer.
S'aviez fait vostre talent,
Jeo sai de veir, ne dut nïent,
Tost m'avrïez entrelaissiee
J'en sereie mut empeiriee."
                    (*Eq.* 121 – 28)

"You're a king of high nobility,
and I'm not at all of such fortune
that you should single me out
to have a love affair with.
If you get what you want from me
I have no doubt of it:
you'll soon get tired of me,
and I'll be far worse off than before."

Her assessment is entirely correct. Because we know that he does not really mean it, Equitan's counter to her appraisal of the class (and gender) difference between them—"Ne me tenez mie pur rei, / Mes pur vostre humme e vostre ami. . . . Vus seiez dame e jeo servanz, / Vus orguilluse e jeo preianz" (*Eq.* 170 – 71, 175 – 77: "Don't think of me as your king, / but your vassal and your lover. . . . You be the lord and I'll be the servant—You be the proud one and I'll be the beggar")—sounds like his fantasy of a role-reversal sex game. I suggested earlier that Equitan's intensest *jouissance* (with typical concentration on sensation, the text notes what makes him "trembler," 69, and his "friçuns," 109) comes from self-dramatizing his transgressions, in a flirtation with discovery. The lovers' exchange of rings after the wife gives in (*Eq.* 181), surely likely to be noticed by her husband, continues this practice, as does the king's aggressive refusal to wed, which draws—which is *meant* to draw—the attention and protest of his people (*Eq.* 197–201).[10] Thus, by the time she speaks again, the text's concentration on her anxiety brings out, in a situation where she must make the best of a coerced intimacy with no other resource than the king's pleasure, how little of her own pleasure the wife gets from it, as opposed to the complex pleasures Equitan does:

> Quant ele pout a lui parler
> E el li duit joie mener,
> Baisier, estreindre e acoler,
> E ensemblë od lui juer,
> Forment plura e grant deol fist.
> 　　　　　(*Eq.* 205–9)

> So when she next had the chance to speak to him—
> when she should have been full of joy,
> kissing and embracing him
> and having a good time with him [od lui juer][11]—
> she burst into tears, making a big scene.

The plot to murder the husband that arises from the wife's statement of her anxiety is proposed to her by Equitan: "'Si vostre sire fust finez, / Reïne e dame vus fereie'" (*Eq.* 226–27, "'If your husband were dead, / I'd make you my lady and my queen'"). When she dutifully comes up with the details, the exchange between them reads as a series of attempts on her part to gain the security of some admission of complicity from him ("Legier serait a purchacier [her husband's death], / *Pur ceo k'il li vousist aidier*" *Eq.* 236–37, emphasis added: "It would be easy to arrange / *if he were willing to help her*"). However, she is frustrated by the bland cruelty of his refusals of complicity: "Ja cele *rien ne li dirrat* / Que il ne face *a sun poeir*," (*Eq.* 238–39, "there was *nothing she could demand of him* / that he wouldn't do, *if he possibly could*," emphasis added); and "Li reis li ad tut *graanté* [as if she had asked him a favor] / Qu'il en ferat *sa volonté*" (*Eq.* 261–62, "The king promised her / that he'd do *just as she wished*," emphasis added).[12]

At the end of the *lai,* Equitan engineers the culmination of his pleasure in dramatizing his malfeasances, his hatred and contempt of himself for doing these things and of others for letting him get away with them, his delight in taking chances and in intense sensations, and the power of his love and hatred for the seneschal—all bound up in the advance planning and controlled improvisation that sends him into the tub of boiling water. In tending so carefully to his own poetic justice, Equitan would seem to have evoked from the *Bretun* pretty much the response he sought: "Tels purcace le mal d'autrui / Dunt tuz li mals revert sur lui" (*Eq.* 309 – 10, "he who plans evil for another / may have that evil rebound back on him"), making himself into an example for the ages of a wickedness to savor and denounce.[13] What escapes this wrap-up in Marie's telling, and in the oddly suspended last line of the *lai*, is the sense she develops of the wife as the stalking-horse and victim of the king's project, made so by his power, his malice, and his indifference to her, "la dame ki tant l'ama" (*Eq.* 314, "the lady who loved him so much").

III

Both of the women who carry the voice of the hind in the next two *lais* in the collection share with the wife in *Equitan* this feeling of being caught out on a limb, surrounded and overwhelmed by the forces of social convention and public opinion. Indeed, the lady who will become the mother of Le Fresne brings about her own humiliation through her ill-judged invention, "oant tute sa gent" (*LeF.* 30, "for all her household to hear"), of an improbable and slanderous sex-fact that is also sufficiently compelling as gossip to circulate throughout Brittany (*LeF.* 49 – 52). As a result, "Mut en fu la dame haïe" (*LeF.* 53, "The slanderous wife was hated for it") by every woman who heard the story, and by her husband as well.

This instance of Marie's interest in how stories get started and how they circulate is glossed by the circumstances of her story's invention and reception. The imprudent factoid—that the conception of twins is caused by intercourse with more than one man—is generated by the very public generosity of a neighbor knight whose wife has just borne twin boys and who sends a messenger to tell his neighbor, surrounded by his household at dinner, that he will name one of them after him and give it to him to foster. The neighbor's way of announcing his good fortune, "Que sa femme ad deus fiz eüz: / De tant de force esteit creüz" ("that his wife had had two sons— / by so much was his power increased," translation altered and emphasis added), is crucial to understanding the situation. This is a *don contraignant* or prestation, an aggressive gift that enforces social subordination and imposes an obligation, as the receiver-lord's immediate attempt to hold his place in the potlatch by rewarding the messenger with a "bel cheval" confirms (*LeF.* 23–24).[14] It is another instance of the way men in the world of these poems use their women to play power games with each other; and the wife's attack on the other messenger of this aggression, the neighbor's wife—because it strikes indirectly but powerfully at the imputedly cuckolded husband—*blows the cover* of a social transaction everyone else is trying to keep tacit. Her own husband's potential difficulties with his neighbor are reason enough for his response; but the hostility of "tutes les femmes" is testimony to their awareness of the social power of even so implausible a tale. Thus their hostility is readily traceable to the way the wife's story threatens to make them even more vulnerable than they already are to the unpredictability of their own bodies and to the rumor-mill in the game of shame and dishonor. The wife notes as much, in the voice of the hind, in the complaint she delivers when, conceiving twins in her turn, she is betrayed by her own biology to the consequences of her story: "'Mis sire e tuz sis parentez / Certes jamés ne me crerrunt, / Des que ceste aventure orrunt'" (*LeF.* 76–78, "'My lord and all his kin / will never believe me / when they hear about this bad luck'").

The rest of the *lai* details the steps that are taken over the course of a generation to contain the effects of this too-open-speaking and to return the management of conflict to the level of the tacit. The poem is in large part about noble female support networks and the manipulation of symbolic objects, and it celebrates the cultural resources—everything from a convenient wet nurse to a bishop in one's pocket—that allow the negotiation of interests and desires through deals and exchanges of real and symbolic capital.[15] This is not the place for a full reading of the *lai;* let it suffice to note the most complex moment in the poem: when Le Fresne places the unique birth-garment, whose provenance her guardian-abbess has told her, on the marital bed that is about to receive her lover Gurun and his new bride, her unacknowledged sister La Codre. As the text makes clear, this is a triumph of practical consciousness. Le Fresne need tell herself and others no more than that the coverlet the servants had placed there "N'ert mie bons, ceo li sembla" (*LeF.* 401, "it seemed to her poor stuff"). The rest can be left to luck, supported by the powerful network of significations the cloth carries and participates in.

Nor is it only her mother and sister who are potentially to be caught up in the weave of this symbolic nexus. What if Le Fresne has shared something of what she knows about the cloth—whatever that is—with Gurun? What message will it carry to him when he brings his bride to bed and finds it there? Does not the coverlet hang suspended between moral blackmail, reminding him and others of how he has treated the previous occupant of this bed, and the veiled threat of how much trouble might still be made by the woman, intimate enough in his life to have put the cloth there, who has—so far—chosen not to make it?[16] The aggressive deployment of innocence and virtue shadowed here is, like the other instances of potential conflict in the tale, not allowed to emerge into the open scandal Fresne's mother incautiously provoked.[17] But Fresne's garment barely covers the world of such things as marital tension and status competition, the disposal of inconvenient daughters, the collusion of guardians in the sale of mistresses, and the expedient annulment of inexpedient marriages. One might put it that the garment is a cover story that allows the appearance of moral resolution in an objectively amoral world. It is Fresne's ability to keep the insistent pressure of this world both present and tacit that enables her to manipulate it so brilliantly, since, as her mother's rash sounding of the voice of the hind shows, it is just such carefully maintained universal silence about what they are really doing that allows everyone to keep on doing it.

IV

Marie's reading of women's situation in the *Lais* emerges sequentially and cumulatively. The meaning of the fate of the werewolf's wife in *Bisclavret* comes clear in the light of the demythologizing context supplied for its romance events by the previous poems in the collection. The surface of the tale is implacably stacked against her; but, as early as her initial questioning of her husband's absences, we can find some intertextual support for a more mundane, and more interesting, reading of her situation. Hanning and Ferrante note that the *lai* "prompts our initial sympathy with the wife's reaction of fear and loathing when she learns that her husband is [a werewolf]" (p. 101); and certainly her reported reaction—"Ne voleit mes lez lui gesir" (*Bisc.* 102, "she never wanted to sleep with him again")—supplies one of the *lai*'s characteristically infrequent but telling touches of emotion and action connected to the immediacy of the body; although one notes, as well, its purchase in domestic rather than public life.

This response to her husband's potential savagery, however, is balanced by the implications of his more domesticated inflection of wolf nature.[18] When her husband informs her that what he does in wolf-form is to go hunting, we have at a minimum the previous examples of Guigemar and Equitan to remind us that men in the world of these poems do not need the impetus of lycanthropy to absent themselves for days on end from the society of their women. We can even suspect that the wife's discontent might not be hers alone: "Mes d'une chose ert grant ennui, / Qu'en la semeine le perdeit / Tres jurs entiers, qu'el ne saveit / U deveneit ne u alout" (*Bisc.* 24–27: "but one thing was very vexing to her: / during the week he would be missing / for three whole days, and she didn't know / what happened to him or where he went").[19]

I find one of the most striking features of this *lai* to be the considerable time it spends narrating the initial conversation between the couple, in which both announce themselves reluctant to speak their true feelings to the other for fear of losing love (*Bisc.* 29–62). I see the passage as a recuperation of many of the odd silences, conspicuous omissions, and unexplained bits of pregnant behavior throughout the *lais* that are so characteristic a feature of Marie's laconic style, because, if we let the scene speak beyond its immediate place here, it allows us to bring these gaps home to the characters whenever they occur. Things that might otherwise have to be ascribed to ineptitude or the conventions of fable and romance become more compelling if they are seen as the symptoms of a world in which people have fairly good, if not fully formulated, practical intimations of what they are doing to one another and even better reasons for not acknowledging these intimations to themselves or others. Such a perspective, for example, adds further complexity and bite to the already complex political reasons for Eliduc's continuing refusal or inability, in the final *lai* of the collection, to reveal to Guilliadun that he is married. That said, *Bisclavret* demonstrates in spades the uneven distribution of pressures and consequences for men and women of acting on one's feelings. "If I told you who I really am or how I really feel, you would leave me" needs to be qualified by the realities of social power to include the rider "if you could." The balance of the story is given over to a demonstration of just how hard it is for a woman to escape a husband with whom she can no longer bear to sleep.[20]

From this perspective, it is not so much the particular details of the mechanism that will strand her husband in werewolf form that ask for attention, suggestive though those are, as it is the alliance the wife has to accept in order to carry them out. It is true that *Bisclavret* shares with *Le Fresne* a world of latent cultural resources that can be activated at need: there is always a courtly lover pining in the wings for his turn. However, the way the poem spends time on the wife's dealings with a man—"Ele ne l'aveit unc amé / Ne de s'amur aseüré" (*Bisc.* 107–8, "She'd never loved him at all, / nor pledged her love to him"), not only offering him her body and her love but extracting an oath from him and then, as it were in return, marrying him,[21]—stresses how much trouble she has to take, and how much she has to agree to in an attempt to feel secure. A committed and socially embedded treachery is the first price of her body's safety.

One consequence of the initial domestication of the *bisclavret* in the poem is the consistent displacement of violence away from the werewolf, though just enough of the *frisson* attached to violence is allowed to show through to make the displacement conspicuous. Thus the hounds who first detect the *bisclavret* in the woods when they are loosed, run him down "Tant que pur poi ne l'eurent pris / E tut deciré e maumis" (*Bisc.* 143–44, "Until they were just about to take him / and tear him apart"), at which point his timely obeisance to the king rescues him and finds him a place at court. When the knight who has married his former wife appears at court, the werewolf attacks "As denz li prist, vers lui le traït. / Ja li eüst mut grant leid fait" (*Bisc.* 199–200, "sank his teeth into him, and started to drag him down. / He would have done him great damage"), only to be frustrated by the Old French equivalent of "*bad* doggie!": "Ne fust li reis ki l'apela, / D'une verge le manaça." (201–2, "if the king hadn't called him off / and threatened him with a stick").[22]

The third instance of displaced violence of this sort is both edgier and more illuminating, because it makes clear where the violence displaced *from* the wolf is displaced *to*. Rather than follow the displacement line by line, let me just narrate it in an impersonal—though perhaps not an entirely impartial—voice: (1) a woman is attacked by a usually tame, but occasionally unruly, pet wolf, and her nose is bitten off. (2) Rather than kill the wolf—or at least threaten to punish it, as has been done on previous occasions—an explanation for the incident is sought by torturing the victim until, "Tant par destrece e par poür" (*Bisc.* 265, "out of fear and pain"), she confesses that the wolf is her former husband, a werewolf, whom she has imprisoned in wolf form by hiding his clothes, with the help of her present husband.[23] (3) On the basis of this likely story, the clothes are sent for;[24] but when they are offered to the animal, it pays no attention to them (*Bisc.* 275–80). (4) Undeterred by this seeming disconfirmation, the men of the court conduct the wolf, along with the clothes, to a private chamber in order to spare him the shame of public nudity should he be moved to change into a man. I do not mean to ignore the "facts" of the *bisclavret's* situation—what was indeed done to him by his wife, though I have tried to suggest that the human situation might have more than one reading—but it does seem to me that the events of the end of the *lai* make eminently clear the lengths to which the king and court are prepared to go in his behalf, and their lack of concern for the wife, in circumstances where they have far less information than we.

The conclusion of the poem, with its account of the fate of the wife and her descendents, once again benefits from an intertextual reading. Banished with her husband, she lives on to have many descendents who were

> . . . bien cuneü
> E del semblent e del visage:
> Plusurs des femmes del lignage,
> C'est veritez, senz nes sunt neies
> E sovent ierent esnasees.
> (*Bisc.* 310–14)

> . . . widely known
> for their appearance:
> several women of the family
> were actually born without noses,
> and lived out their lives noseless.

Though the myth of the werewolf lends itself generically to the individual and psychological thematics of the wolf within—what Hanning and Ferrante call "the forces of bestiality that exist within human nature" (p. 101)— the actual violence in the tale is predominantly social and judicial, and, in the narrow sense, rational. The wife is not directly subjected to further bodily harm in these terms, but her extended punishment is conducted in this register; and to trace its connections with other moments in the *Lais* is to gain a more precise measure of its costs as well as a clearer idea of Marie's sense of the social meanings of stories. The voice of the hind proposes a darker inflection of Hanning and Ferrante's benignly inflected, but by no means inaccurate, contention that "In *Bisclavret* Marie argues that human beings are defined not only by their inherent potential for good or evil but also by their fellow humans' responses of trust or fear" (p. 104). In my hearing of her, the hind might say that human beings are defined by the way people choose to take them *regardless* of their inherent potential for good or evil or any other "true nature" they may have, that audiences control the stories that they get themselves told. The wife's punishment itself has certain similarities to the imprudent sex-fact invented by Le Fresne's mother, in that it is the sort of improbable but titillating and memorable tale about generation that is ready-made for popular oral transmission. Marie frequently registers this kind of improbability by overprotesting its veracity, as here, or by distancing herself from the received traditional *lai* as the source of otherwise unattested events "ceo m'est avis, si cum j'entent" (*Bisc.* 220), perhaps "as I understand from what I'm told." This is the kind of thing a family (and indeed women in general, if they are thinking about their husbands along certain lines) can be tarred with where it really counts—in the realm of gossip and entertainment beyond the reach of judicial punishment *or* its redress. It is a fate feared by Fresne's mother and actually suffered by the seneschal's wife in *Equitan*, she of the "neis bien asis" (*Eq.* 36, "well-shaped nose"); and the strongest image for it is an intertextual extension of one of the moments of apparently arrested violence in *Bisclavret*. I have in mind the brief mention of the king's dogs, who are just prevented from tearing the *bisclavret* apart (143–44, see above). The pack connects back to the opening of *Guigemar*, where a similar image, which is associated with the poet's defense of her own activity and which is not used again in that *lai*, lies dormant until energized in this new context. Men or women of great *pris*, says Marie, attract envious slanderers, backbiters who "comencent le mestier / Del malveis chien coart, felun, / Ki mort la gent par traïsun." (*Guigemar* 7–14, "Thus they act like / vicious, cowardly dogs / who bite people treacherously").

Werewolves are not common, but there are more ordinary ways in which people behave like beasts, and worse, to other people by turning them into the prey of feral imaginings. It is Marie's particular gift to identify and extract from the dreams and nightmares of the folk imagination their more mundane, more persistent (and therefore more terrifying) sources in everyday experience. The most existentially powerful sequence in the tale is the initial conversation between husband and wife as they try to negotiate their need for, and fear of, each other. Marie's telling, with its pervasive structure of conspicuous displacements, identifies the *lai*, as she has it from *li Bretun*, as itself a defensive displacement into romance and magic of such needs and such fears. Her conclusion identifies, as well, how much easier it is to make women rather than men the scapegoats of the process—and to keep on doing it.

V

Among the many services that Hanning and Ferrante have done the criticism of the *Lais,* an important one is their identification of the level of conspicuous fantasy in *Lanval.* I want to begin by emphasizing two things about it. The first is that certain details of the fairy lady and her entourage mark the fantasy she embodies as gendered male, the most important being the slightly prurient edge imparted by brief but pointed references to their revealing costumes. This begins with the handmaids who first greet Lanval, wearing purple tunics "laciees mut estreitment" (*Lanv.* 58, "tightly laced"); continues with the Playmate-of-the-Month pose of the lady herself (*Lanv.* 97–106); and is perhaps most amusingly noted near the end of the *lai,* when the handmaids appear to announce their mistress's approach, once again dressed in purple, "*tut senglement* a lur chars nues. / Cil les esgardent volentiers" (*Lanv.* 476–77, "*and nothing else* over their bare skin. / The men looked at them with pleasure"; translation altered and emphasis added). When the lady grants "sun amur e sun cors" (*Lanv.* 133, "her love and her body") to Lanval, the term she uses, "de mun cors seisine aveir" (*Lanv.* 150, "to have seisin of my body"), would, in a *lai* that is centrally concerned with female power, seem to stress her independence, since what she grants is a feudal term of *usufruct,* the possession in the sense of enjoyment, plainly extending here to the *jouissance, of* herself, but reserving *to* herself her ownership and final disposal. Nonetheless, what that use gives is the ideal life of a courtly male, satisfying not only his needs for erotic satisfaction and sustenance appropriate to a nobleman,[25] but allowing him to fulfill his chivalric spirit in generosity of a public, indeed kingly sort, giving hospitality, patronage, and rich gifts to all (*Lanv.* 203–15).

The second thing that might be noticed about the ideal quality of Lanval's dream lady is that she not only (no doubt) deserves and gets his undivided attention, but that she makes it possible precisely *because* she takes such good care of everything else. It is true that he remains faithful to her in adversity, of which more anon; but some odd details at the beginning of the poem work to bring out the way her care obviates a certain heedlessness on the hero's part. When Lanval rides into the woods to brood on his neglect by the king and court, he ignores the steed's trembling (presumably at the proximity of the Other World and its fairy mistress), unsaddles it, and leaves it to roll in the meadow (*Lanv.* 45–48). When the lady's maidens summon him to her, Marie takes time to mention that "Li chevaliers od eles vait, / De sun cheval ne tient nul plait, / Ki devant lui pesseit el pré" (*Lanv.* 77–79. "The knight went with them; giving no thought to his horse / who was feeding before him in the meadow"). After he has reached his accommodation with the lady, this bit of minor neglect is pointedly repaired at her unsolicited behest: "Quant del mangier furent levé, / Sun cheval li unt amené; / Bien li eurent la sele mise" (*Lanv.* 189–91, "When they finished dinner, / his horse was brought to him. / The horse had been well saddled").

The poem's pause to notice here is itself noticeable, but it would mean little if it did not connect to other places in the text. *Lanval* is the only one of the *Lais* set overtly and specifically at the court of King Arthur, and this move has several functions. To begin with, it allows Marie the use of a world that is the quintessence of Romance: it is discursively presupposed as the idealized and exemplary space of the celebration of chivalric virtue and the noble life, as Auerbach's analysis of Chrétien's *Yvain* in *Mimesis* long ago demonstrated. Everybody knows that Arthur's court was the gathering-place of the best, the bravest, and the most courtly knights who had ever been. In keeping with the demythologizing thrust of the *Lais*, however, Marie's opening description of Arthur's court identifies a conspicuous neglect that parallels Lanval's:

> A Kardoel surjurnot li reis
> Artur, li pruz e li curteis,
> Pur les Escoz e pur lis Pis,
> Ki destrueient le païs;
> En la tere de Logre entroent
> Et mut suvent la damagoent.
> A la Pentecuste en esté
> I aveit li reis sujurné;
> Asez I duna riches duns. . . .
>   (*Lanv.* 5–15)

> Arthur, the brave and courtly king
> was staying at Cardoel,
> because the Scots and the Picts
> were destroying the land.
> They invaded Logres
> and laid it waste.
> At Pentecost, in summer

the king stayed there.
He gave out many rich gifts. . . .

Despite the conventional formula in the second line, there is not much *proece* showing just now at this court. This framing helps to identify it as a place of *escape* from feudal/national politics and war, a retreat from such concerns to more relaxed and courtly pursuits that, for the moment, pointedly ignores the things it is escaping. The word *esbanier*, which Marie uses repeatedly to characterize the leisure of the inhabitants of the world of the *lai*,[26] catches the overall effect nicely. It refers to the condition of being unbound from *ban*, its cognates and extensions, whether that be taken to mean the feudal levy, the banner under which men fight, or the worlds of public proclamation and public order.[27] Marie's presentation focuses from the beginning on the attempted exclusion of real-world concerns that threaten the courtly ideal and identifies the knights and ladies of King Arthur less as exemplars of those ideals than as imperfect aspirants to them. As in the other *lais*, stories of the Other World and of Ideal Chivalry, like those of Arthur's Court, do not form the stable backdrop of these poems but occupy their foreground as social technologies that the characters use for evading whatever would trammel their comfort and self-esteem. Especially, given the other difficulties that emerge in the course of the *lai*, the characters are best seen as Camelot wannabees who *aspire* to their station as Arthurians, and the plot of the poem can be seen as a study in the art of covering up.

There is thus a metonymic relationship between Lanval and the Arthurian court: both turn away from the problems of the everyday world to fantasy. The *surplus* of human conflict that remains in the court—even after it has escaped from epic strenuousness to the re-*lax*ation of romance, exemplified in just such things as the unworthy treatment of Lanval by Arthur that is the hero's initial impetus—is further refined and repressed by and for him into the ideal love of a perfect mate who makes the trammels of social existence unnecessary while surreptitiously mastering them. He lives a purified core of ideal individual courtly existence (right at the edge of making that phrase an oxymoron), whose structure of displacement reveals what it has in common with the court he flees.[28] In both cases, the remainder of the Real that disturbs and questions the evasive fantasy is concentrated in the antitype and dark sister of the fairy mistress, perhaps the most articulate and powerful bearer of the voice of the hind in the *Lais*, Queen Guenevere.

As with the wife in *Bisclavret*, the queen's function as a voice for the suppressed of the system emerges best when her speeches and actions are given their full intertextual force, which here includes the wider Arthurian context as well as the other poems in Marie's collection. This context is pointedly evoked as the poem shifts from Lanval's private joys to the court scene at line 219: the famous knights are named (Gawain, Yvain), thirty of them gathered in the orchard beneath the tower[29] to amuse themselves. They invite Lanval to join them, at which the queen enters with thirty of her maidens, sees Lanval standing alone to one side, and propositions him with the offer of her *amur* and *druërie* (237–68).[30] The advantage Marie derives from the Arthurian setting in this case comes from our knowledge of the queen's erotic history. It is not clear from the text of *Lanval* whether Lancelot is already the queen's lover. In either case, however, his presence in the background of the story enforces the persistence of the queen's discontent and of her determination to find a lover: if not Lanval, then Lancelot; if Lancelot already, then Lanval as well; in either case, not Arthur.[31] Some sense of the precise bearing of this discontent is also conveyed in a remark Marie makes about Lanval immediately prior to the queen's approach, as an explanation for the way he holds himself apart from the festivities even when he has at last been invited to them: "L'autrui joie prise petit, / Si il nen ad le suen delit" (*Lanv.* 257–58, "he thought little of others' joys / If he could not have his pleasure"). In line with the metonymic relationship suggested above, the remark applies not just to Lanval but much more broadly to the men of the world of this *lai*, and indeed to all the other absent male lovers in Marie's larger poem. It applies with particular force here to Arthur, especially when, after Lanval has refused the queen and she has left him, "Li reis fu del bois repeiriez; / Mut out le jur esté haitiez" (*Lanv.* 311–12, "The king returned from the woods, / he'd had a very good day"). Arthur joins the ranks of Guigemar, Equitan, and Bisclavret in a context in which the impact of male absence on women's pleasure is given its full sexual force. Everything about the situation stresses its specific relation to female rage and resentment at the deeply embedded social denial of women's right even to *legal* orgasms.[32]

That anger also drives the queen's explicit sexualization of the equivocal aura that surrounds male bonding. She begins with an accusation that reflects back upon (and brings out a tacit possibility in) a common situation in earlier *lais*, marking the turn that social disapproval of a man who shows no interest in women can take if the observer is angry or malicious enough to make it:

Vallez avez bien afeitiez,
Ensemble od eus vus deduiez.
Vileins cüarz, mauveis failliz,
Mut est mis sires maubailliz,
Ki pres de lui vus ad suffert,
Mun escïent que Deu en pert.
(*Lanv.* 281–86)

You have fine-looking boys
with whom you enjoy yourself.
Base coward, lousy cripple,
My lord made a bad mistake
When he let you stay with him.
For all I know, he'll lose God because of it.

The language of the passage allows a slippage in its last three lines from Lanval to Arthur in particular and the wider world of masculinity in general. The condemnation of Arthur for "countenancing" Lanval's behavior implicates the king in Lanval's putative sin to a degree hard to specify,[33] since its apparent hyperbole invites the question of just what would put Arthur's soul in such danger. It is a question appropriately voiced in the shadow realm of social disapproval, whose protean perils Marie is so good at evoking: the world of "asez le m'ad hum dit sovent." Once this sexual reading of homosocial behavior is broached, the run of its reference is hard to contain; and though the other *lais* have no one who will quite broach it in the way the queen does here, her anger—echoing the hind's "a plague on your desire!"— adds a certain bite to the question of how the women in these poems may be feeling about the behavior of their men. That it is this imputation that stings Lanval to his near-fatal revelation of the existence of his mistress suggests that he feels that bite too.[34]

When the queen carries her dealings with Lanval into the public sphere by complaining of him to Arthur, the subsequent action of the poem gives us the most fully developed picture in the *Lais* so far of the complex behind-the-scenes negotiations, improvisations, and contestations that are involved in the increasingly precarious maintenance of the male *status quo*. To begin with, it is interesting that her complaint is two-pronged, comprising accusations of sexual harassment on the one hand and *lèse majesté* on the other (*Lanv.* 315–24). Whatever her motives for this, the reactions of Arthur and

the court are more interesting still. If the first accusation of an indecent proposal to his wife is true, one supposes that Arthur would be within his rights,
or at any rate within his power and its justification, to simply have Lanval
killed. From the beginning, however, the king's response is a curious blend of
expressed emotions proper to the first accusation and actions more appropriate to the second. In the presence of the queen,

> Li reis s'en curuçat forment;
> Juré en ad sun serement,
> S'il ne s'en peot in curt defendre,
> Il le ferat ardeir u pendre
> > (*Lanv.* 325–28)

> The king got very angry;
> he swore an oath:
> if Lanval could not defend himself in court
> he would have him burned or hanged.

Though the slight weaseling in the third line mars the effect a bit, the
pattern of strong talk and cautious action is only fully established when the
king leaves the presence of his wife ("Fors de la chambre eissi li reis," *Lanv.*
329. "The king left her chamber"), calls three of his barons, and summons
Lanval. When the latter appears, the king maintains his vehemence ("'Vassal, vus m'avez mut mesfait,'" *Lanv.* 363. "'Vassal, you have done me a great
wrong!'"); but his statement of the charge does not mention the more serious crime at all.[35]

When the king passes the problem on to his feudatories ("ses humes,"
382), he does so in part to get a verdict that will silence the affair, something
no one can question.[36] Though part of this aim requires that the judgment
not come too directly or too personally from the king (which is presumably
one reason the formal and legal language of feudal duties—for example,
the interpellation of Lanval as "Vassal!"—comes to dominate the situation
so quickly), the feudatories are equally reluctant to commit themselves. Their
first council results in a decision to postpone Lanval's day in court until the
full baronage is assembled, since only the king's household is currently present at court (394). As the matter snowballs, the roles of the participants become more clearly established. The king continues to press for justice and
a resolution (the queen's agency is always mentioned in this, stressing the

extent to which Arthur's hand is forced here), but in such a way as to continue to avoid taking direct action himself. The barons continue to stall, seeking excuses to postpone a verdict five times, by my count, before the matter is at last resolved. Most of them are at pains to indicate that their sympathies lie with Lanval. Gawain and his companions offer themselves as pledges for the hero, since he has no kin or friends at court (395–405); and Marie notes, "Jeo quid k'il en i ot teus cent / Ki feïssent tut lur poeir / Pur lui sanz pleit delivre aveir" (*Lanv.* 420–23, "I think there were a hundred / who would have done all they could / to set him free without a trial"). A bit later, the Count of Cornwall, who is apparently newly arrived and a stranger to the case, since he does not know Lanval (436), articulates what the reader as well as the participants may well have felt: that the case for *lèse majesté* is a flimsy one.[37] He goes on to declare the conditions of trial—that Lanval shall provide proof that his mistress and her entourage are superior in beauty and worth to the queen.

To take a larger view of these events in the light of the rest of the *Lais* is to see that we are dealing here with another instance of the way, by now familiar, that male interests close ranks to protect their own. But what are they protecting? It may well be that the maneuvering here arises from knowledge or suspicion of the injustice of the queen's complaint, but what such a reading ignores is the striking fact that, by the time the beauty issue is made the basis of the legal decision, the sexual charge has been read out of the situation. Part of what the long delay accomplishes is precisely the burying of this issue, which is kept marginally alive only by the increasingly tacit presence of the queen and by Arthur's increasingly *pro forma* exhortations to speedy justice. The fact that the delay and the maneuvering are so extensively portrayed marks the difference between the situation in this *lai* and previous ones, because it puts a new spin on the kind of casual and confident male solidarity we see in, say, *Bisclavret,* which here appears more defensively motivated. The same is true of Lanval's exemplary loyalty to his mistress. Once the magnificently, if scantily, attired maidens have started to appear, Lanval may well suppose his fairy lady cannot be far behind; and, in any case, claiming the wrong lady patently opens him to easy denunciation if, as he hopes for many reasons, the right one appears. His persistent, steadfast refusal to take the suggestion of the other knights, "Ici vienent deus dameisles, / Mut acemees et mut beles: / C'est vostre amie veirement!" (*Lanv.* 521–23, "Here come two maidens, / well adorned and very beautiful; one must certainly be your love.") says less about him than about the eagerness of the barons to jump on any plausible excuse to acquit him and, beyond that and more importantly, to do so on the issue of *lèse majesté* alone, now further refined into the issue of comparative beauty and worth; that is, into a matter not of fact but of consensus. What needs attention is not that the participants figure out how to get Lanval off, but that they work so hard to avoid having him tried for trying to seduce the queen. They do so because admitting the question of his desire cannot avoid raising the question of hers; and this is what the whole performance is dedicated to covering up.

On the surface, the story of this *lai* is a tale of the defeat of the queen's unjust abuse of her power by the superior power of true love, as embodied in the uncoerced generosity of the fairy mistress and her willingness to break her earlier behest for Lanval's sake. The queen is silenced and her desire suppressed, for the last hundred lines of the poem, in favor of the celebration of an ideal love too good for this world. But the framing of this happy ending, as I have tried to show, continually stresses the continuing power of what is being evaded in the pressure it exerts on the evasion; and the queen's last appearance as the voice of the hind makes that power and its continuance echo with devastating force:

[Li reis] ad tuz ses baruns mandez,
Que li jugemenz seit renduz:
Trop ad le jur esté tenuz;
La reïne s'en curuçot,
Que trop lungement jeünot
   (*Lanv.* 542–45, emphasis added)

[The king] summoned all his barons
to render their judgment;
it had already dragged out too much.
The queen was getting angry
because she had already fasted so long.

Hanning and Ferrante, in a note to this passage, report Ewert's emendation of *jeünot* to *atendeit*, "waited," "which is not as callously selfish" (p. 120, note 6).[38] I take the editorial fuss here to reflect the editors' sense of the *surplus*, the excess of the line, which they demonstrate by trying to mitigate it rather in the manner of the knights of the court. They want to edit it into decorum (those who do) because they can sense that she is not just talking about missing brunch.

In fact, the power of the line arises as much from its metaphorical in-direction, which allows it to function as a metonymy for the whole cumu-lative portrayal in the *Lais* of the blockage of feminine desire, as it does from its immediate context in *Lanval.* An intertextual reading of the kind of al-legorical figure or personification of love the *queen* (as opposed to the fairy lady) makes, enforces the general and persistent character of what it is the men don't want to have come out—what they don't want to know. To sup-pose that giving the queen a day in court over the issue of her desire would reveal something of the order that she is an adulteress and/or that Arthur is impotent, is a misplaced concretion—not only because there is no real evi-dence for such things in the text, but because it would confine the trouble the queen *is* and the trouble she *has* to the merely individual, and therefore genuinely marginal, case. What *Lanval* shows is not the queen's marginality but the laborious and conspicuous (and therefore unsuccessful) attempted *marginalization* of a character who carries the entire structure of gender re-lations and the gendered organization of desire, which the *Lais* as a whole has developed, into the center of the poem. Insofar as the queen speaks for the silenced, in trying to silence her the men in this *lai,* like those in the oth-ers before it, are trying to keep the voice of the hind from being heard, are trying not to hear it.

The complex of feminine discontents that I have been calling the voice of the hind emerges gradually through the first half of the *Lais.* I have ar-gued for its prominence in *Lanval;* and its emergence has a further conse-quence for the reading of the representation of feminine power in the poem as a whole. I have suggested that the cover story of the *lai* is the victory through love of a powerful, independent "good" woman over the attack on the proprieties, and on love itself, by a "bad" one. The latter's attempt to abuse her own position of power by working behind the scenes, through the men she coerces and deceives, is brought to naught in open court by un-forced public recognition of the gifts and virtues, as Lanval has it, "de cors, de vis e de beauté, / D'enseignement, e de bunté" (*Lanv.* 301–2: "in body, face, and beauty, / in breeding and in goodness") of the former. But if, as I have argued, the queen represents the deeper truth of women's situation in the poem, then the allegorical pretensions of the figure of the fairy lady are revealed as what they are—a fiction, a male fantasy—and this origin is manifested and played out in practical form in the *lai*'s conclusion. There is no real question of a decision on the "merits" of the case; it has been made fully clear by the time the fairy mistress appears that the barons were ready to declare any reasonable-looking woman the winner, and they were only blocked from doing so by Lanval's refusal to be acquitted too quickly.[39]

In these circumstances, the extended description of the procession of ladies leading up to the final one becomes a legal *surplus*, a description of what amounts to the bodily rhetoric that can be used to justify (in later accounts like this *lai*, for instance) the decision the barons were going to make anyway. This understanding of the situation gives a further twist to the bearing, and especially the dress (or lack of it) of the fairy and her servants. Besides giving a summary of the case that gets all parties except the queen off the hook (*Lanv*. 615–24), Lanval's lady also appears dressed "De chainse blanc e de chemise, / Que tuit li costé li pareient" (*Lanv*. 560–61, "in a white linen shift that revealed both her sides").[40] This, and the fact that, just before speaking her defense of Lanval, "Sun mantel ad laissié cheeir, / Que mieuz la peüssent veeir" (*Lanv*. 605–6, "she let her cloak fall so they could see her better"), focus us on the *kind of persuasion* that is being brought to bear here. What it stresses is that the fairy herself recognizes, at least in practical terms, the extent to which her apparent independence and power are, like the queen's, dependent on men and on her ability to appeal to their desire. The point is perhaps clearer if we reflect that, in order to clinch the win, these women put themselves in the position of promising, with the stipulation that they will not give it,[41] what the queen started the trouble by offering to give in deed. The good girls and the bad ones are closer together than might have been imagined.

The final outcome of the *lai*, in which Lanval exits the court—and, with it, what Sharon Kinoshita, following Roberta Krueger, calls "the project of primogeniture"[42]—shows the same structure of similarity underlying apparent difference. On the surface it appears that Lanval quits a world too corrupt to sustain the ideals of love and faithfulness he embodies; but at the very end there is a teasing detail, the hero's place of escape: "Od li s'en vait en Avalun, / Ceo nus recuntent li Bretun, / En un isle ki ut est beaus" (*Lanv*. 641–43, "With her he went to Avalun, / so the Bretons tell us, / to a very beautiful island"). Once again there is a convergence: Arthur too, after all the trouble the queen's adultery with Lancelot brings on internally, and after all the political/feudal strife, whose marker in this text might well be the almost-excluded Picts and Scots, will end up in dreamtime on the island of Avalon. "Pur," says the *Brut*, "ses plaies médiciner": to heal his wounds, whence the *Bretun* still await his return.[43] If this is a rejection of conventional masculine values, it is one, it seems to me, in the service of those values. The metonymy I argue earlier still holds: what the hyper-idealized image of love, fidelity, and a guaranteed income achieves now, the merely idealized though equally fictional Arthur will reach later; which is to say that the Arthurian world is constituted over a desire to escape itself. Given what it takes in the effort of domination and its cost in guilt, to be a "man" in these poems—a Bisclavret or Equitan, to say nothing of a Yonec or Eliduc—might well be something that the subjects in men's bodies on whom that masculinity is laid might want to escape. The *Bretun* built that escape into the limits of their favorite fantasy. They did so, moreover, in a way that insures—is meant to insure—that the healing they dream of is entrusted to a woman of a certain sort, one whose image blocks that of the woman they are always going hunting to avoid.

VI

Thus, a retrospect, from the vantage of *Lanval* back to the *lais* of the first half of the collection, brings out the extent to which the distinction between "good" and "bad"—in general, but, for starters, in women—has been progressively redefined as a distinction between "successful and unsuccessful in the generation and control of the future anterior"; that is, in the management of self-presentation and reputation. The effect of morality depends on the ability to influence the definition of what will have been, through control of the stories that will be told about oneself and one's actions. The poem has further established the ongoing practices of the gendering that structure this struggle for one's history: good girls are the ones who have submerged their own desire in order to create socially effective simulacra of the desires of men. In doing so, they have produced (or been forced to produce) a *surplus* of feminine discontent that shadows and whispers—the voice of the hind—to men and women alike. This is perhaps another reading of the hind's androgyny as a surrogate for the poetess: she must don male drag, the chivalric values that shape the stories the *Bretun* have left her, in order to be heard at all, though she also gains the option of telling those stories with a difference.

I do not wish to make the poet sound too polemical here; that is not her tone. In common with her mentor Ovid and his blank-faced dissection of the *mores* of the Roman singles-bar scene (and the mythological stories of the rapes and revenges of goddesses and heroines that are told in it), and along with her closest modern kinswoman Angela Carter, the mistress of

X-rated fairy tales for grown-ups,[44] Marie shares what I think of (following William Burroughs) as the cold eye that registers the nakedness of lunch—what's on the end of the fork. It is her ability to see and show that this is what people *do*, without giving way too quickly or too often to the rage and sorrow that may well be appropriate to the perception, that allows her to trace the *workings* of the generation and perpetuation of stories as richly and as deftly as she does. What she sees, in fact, is not simply that men oppress women and that women fight back by turning the instruments of their oppression to their own purposes. One of the things that makes *Lanval* a culmination, but also a turning point in the *Lais*, is the clarity and tenacity with which it portrays the ongoing *politics* of representation in courtly life and especially the way that politics is *persistently* shaped as much by what the actors try to escape as by what they try to affirm. This is why the *lais* in the second half of the collection become more fragmented, their endings less apparently conclusive, their meanings more evidently contested within the poems themselves. *Laüstic* is everybody's favorite instance of this, a *lai* in which what is remembered is not the meaning of the nightingale but the struggle of the three characters to give it one; but the double-named *lais, Chaitivel/Quatre Deuls*, and *Eliduc/Guildeluëc ha Guilliadun*, which Marie also passes on to us as not-yet-finished because not yet securely titled, turn in their different ways on the same interest in the ongoing processes of storymaking.

   Another of the meanings of the androgyny of the hind and her voice is that it speaks to the cultural/social/anthropological situation in which both sexes find themselves and with which, in their various ways, they have to do and be done by. Neither the hind nor Marie seems much taken with the choices and opportunities offered to men *or* women, though Marie at least is clearly fascinated by the variety, deviousness, and skill with which they make and take them. Though the playing field is scarcely level for both sexes, everyone can—must—play, and Marie is above all the poet of that game.

Notes

As the reader will discover, I do not follow the practice in this essay of citing published criticism in support of points I make or to acknowledge specific anticipations of my formulations. Though I have done my homework, I felt on reflection that for good or ill, the perspective developed here was sufficiently different, especially in its systematic nature, from what I found elsewhere to justify proceeding as I do.

Nonetheless—indeed, precisely for that reason—I ought here to declare my indebt-ednesses; and it is a pleasure to begin with the one that is both deepest and most appropriate to the occasion. That Bob Hanning is a close friend and Joan Ferrante a friendly acquaintance is much to me. But, in thinking about the *Lais* of Marie de France, what counts is my sense, developed over years of teaching the poems in most of the available translations, that their translation and commentary is the single best assemblage of criticism of the work in English or French, both because I find the translation itself continually rewarding and suggestive, a coherent act of criticism as a good translation should be, and because the commentary is one of the few (and in my estimation easily the best) attempts to deal with all the *lais,* both individu-ally and as a group. If I have quibbled with a translation or disagreed with a reading in what follows (and if such things did not happen there would be nothing to write or think about in literature), I have done so because they made it possible. The old saw about the shoulders of giants may seem grandiose in such a context, but it has its point here too. Therefore I have made *The Lais of Marie de France,* translated and with an introduction and notes by Robert Hanning and Joan Ferrante (New York: E. P. Dutton, 1978), the translation of reference in this essay. I cite it in the text, after the Old French, not only in aid of readers who may find it useful linguistically, but to keep the voices of these excellent critics, in the detail of critical choice that a translation is, constantly before us. I have, of course, also consulted Ferrante's *Woman as Image in Medieval Literature, from the Twelfth Century to Dante* (New York and London: Columbia University Press, 1975), and Hanning's other critical writings on the *Lais,* especially "The Talking Wounded: Desire, Truth Telling and Pain in the *Lais* of Marie de France," in *Desiring Discourse, The Literature of Love, Ovid through Chaucer,* ed. James J. Paxson and Cynthia A. Gravlee (Selinsgrove, Pa.: Susquehanna University Press, 1998), 140–61. For the original text I have used the edition of Jean Rychner, *Les lais de Marie de France* (Paris: Champion, 1969). I cite each *lai,* by an abbreviated title with line numbers, parenthetically in the text. In thinking about the poem over the years and again recently, I have drawn special benefit from the following. The discourse on Marie's work in the light of feminist theory and inter-pretation has been consistently illuminating, first in conversations with my former colleagues, Linda Lomperis, Kristine Brightenback, and Cécile Schreiber, and in the work and talk of my friend Roberta Krueger, and then in other published writ-ings, especially E. Jane Burns, *Bodytalk, When Women Speak in Old French Litera-ture* (Philadelphia: University of Pennsylvania Press, 1993); Michelle A. Freeman, "Marie de France's Poetics of Silence: The Implications for a Feminine Translation, *PMLA* 99 (1984): 860–83; and, most recently, in the article by my present colleague, Sharon Kinoshita, "Cherchez la Femme: Feminist Criticism and Marie de France's *Lai de Lanval,*" *Romance Notes* 34 (1994): 263–73, whose project is close to my own. I have also used the articles of Rupert T. Pickens, "Marie de France and the Body Poetic," in *Gender and Text in the Later Middle Ages,* ed. Jane Chance (Gainesville:

University Press of Florida, 1996), 135–71; and "The Poetics of Androgyny in the *Lais* of Marie de France: Yonec, Milon, and the General Prologue," in *Literary Aspects of Courtly Culture*, ed. Donald Maddox (Rochester, N.Y.: Boydell and Brewer, 1994), 211–19. Many of the articles in Chantal A. Maréchal, *In Quest of Marie de France, A Twelfth-Century Poet* (Lewiston, N.Y.: Edwin Mellen, 1992) have aided me; the most suggestive were concerned with *Yonec*, and so escape citation here. However, I must single out for special mention Robert M. Stein's "Desire, Social Reproduction, and Marie's *Guigemar*," 280–94 in that volume. Like many others, I have learned from R. Howard Bloch, both in his work on the treatment of misogyny in the *Lais* in *Medieval Misogyny and the Invention of Western Romantic Love* (Chicago: University of Chicago Press, 1991) and in the more deconstructively oriented articles: "The Lay and the Law: Sexual/Textual Transgression in *La Chastelaine de Vergi*, the *Lai d'Ignaure*, and the *Lais* of Marie de France," *Stanford French Review* 14, (1990): 181–210, and "The Voice of the Dead Nightingale: Orality in the Tomb of Old French Literature," *Culture and History* 3, (1990): 63–78. (Yet I am bound to say that Bloch is less willing to consider the texts as themselves deconstructive than I am.) Finally, I have tried to keep myself, probably in vain, from missing important recent work by consulting the valuable review article by Chantal A. Maréchal, "Marie de France Studies: Past, Present, Future," *Envoi* 8 (1999): 105–25.

1. Guigemar's lover might be supposed to feel something like this at times, perhaps especially when Meriaduc summons "el païs chevalier" to essay the belt she wears next to her skin (*G.* 741–42), but in this *lai* she does not speak at such times.

2. Her first sight of Guigemar tends to stress the extent to which she takes him as an occasion of emotional indulgence at the expense of more precise observation: "Le chevalier ad esgardé, / Mut pleint sun cors et sa beauté, / Pur lui esteit triste e dolente / E dit que mar fu sa juvente" (*G.* 295–98). Only then does she check more closely: "Desur le piz li met sa main: / Chaut le senti e le quor sein" (*G.* 299–300). That she is not a close observer and tends to prefer romance, the more dramatic the better, to other styles of interpretation is later confirmed by her ability to mourn her desperate situation for two years after Guigemar's departure before trying the door (*G.* 655–77).

3. This issue is a persistent one in the collection, at least as a device to drive plots. It is raised as a concern of the anxious subjects of lords who are too content with their mistresses in *Le Fresne* and *Equitan*, and again as the husband's motive for immuring his wife in *Yonec*, to mention only the most explicit instances. See the discussion of *Lanval* below.

4. I specify Francophone because such writers—for instance Marcabru, whom she may not have known, and Chrétien, whom she surely did—form Marie's extended literary community, the vernacular texts and discourses of reference,

imitation, criticism, and competition for her work. Of course Italian, German, and English writers notice, too, to say nothing of Ovid.

5. Hanning and Ferrante's translation here does not quite register the likelihood that the distinction between "dame" and "pucele" is one of marital status as well as age and sexual experience. This characterization of the contestants takes on even greater interest when the happy ending of the *lai* neglects to inform us that Guigemar married his lover: "A grant joie s'amie en meine" (*G.* 881), which they translate in a way that catches the implication of "amie" admirably: "Guigemar led away his mistress with great rejoicing" (54).

6. The lady herself is the first to be put in the position of displaying her body; she presumably further incites Meriaduc to lust in the attempt to fend him off: "Il la requiert, el n'en ad cure, / Ainz li mustre de la ceinture" (*G*, 721–22). This is complicated, because it eventually leads to Guigemar getting wind of her presence; but whatever her motives, the lady has literally to expose herself in a way he does not.

7. Marie's line, "but he could not come to the head of the matter," is a little rawer than the translation.

8. "Pur *deduire* fu fors alez" (*Eq.* 278), which suggests that there is something at work in the room, even before the wife enters, from which he feels the need for relief, literal "diversion."

9. The use of *tenir* here is interesting because it is a feudal term for the usufruct (or *jouissance*) of land, thus echoing the similar use of it by Meriaduc against Guigemar's claim to his lady: "Jeo la trovai, si la tendrai / E cuntre vus la defendrai!" (*G.* 851–52).

10. Perhaps the most striking instance of this theme in the poem is our belated discovery that the lovers' final embrace is being watched over by a servant girl *from inside the chamber* where they are making love: "L'us firent tenir e garder; / Une meschine i dut ester. / Li senescals hastis revint; / A l'hus buta, cele le tint. / Icil le fiert par tel haïr, / Par force li estut ovrir." (*Eq.* 285–90). How long has this practice been going on? *Somebody* must have brought in the boiling water ("L'ewe buillant feit [the wife] aporter," 275). Who *else* (the king's physician, or whoever bleeds him?) has been privy to the affair?

11. I'd like to press the possibility that this phrase means "and coming with him," in the light of my reading of Guenevere in *Lanval.*

12. Billy Wilder's 1944 film of *Double Indemnity,* by the way, responds well to a similar line of analysis. When Phyllis tells Walter of the unexpected love for him that renders her unable to carry out, to the *coup de grace,* the role of *femme fatale* he has assigned her throughout the movie ("I just couldn't fire that second shot"), she is rewarded by having him shoot her—twice.

13. Equitan seems to be one of the first to sexualize the representation of this particular form of *accedia,* prefiguring, if perhaps not influencing, the importance of the theme in Jean de Meun's Fals Semblant and in Chaucer's Pardoner.

14. See Marcel Mauss, *The Gift*, trans. Ian Cunnison (New York: Norton, 1967), especially the section on potlatch, 31–45; and Harry Berger, Jr., and H. Marshall Leicester, Jr., "Social Structure as Doom: The Limits of Heroism in *Beowulf*," in *Old English and Norse Studies in Honor of John C. Pope*, ed. Robert B. Burlin and Edward B. Irving, Jr. (Toronto: University of Toronto Press, 1974), 37–79.

15. The clearest example is the tacit bargain Gurun makes with the abbess who is the girl's warden: endowment of the abbey with lands in return for access to Fresne (*LeF.* 250–70); but this is just the tip of the iceberg. A more interesting, because better-covered, instance is the mother's horrifying decision at the end of her lament, "Pur mei defendre de hunir, / Un des enfanz m'estuet murdrir (*LeF.* 91–92). It is only after the lament is over that we are told it was made in the presence of the servants, "Celes ki en la chambre esteient" (*LeF.* 94), converting what looked like a despairing private resolve into the opening bid of a request to the Noblewomen's Network for help in solving the problem—which is at once forthcoming.

16. Since it is common knowledge that Fresne has been Gurun's mistress up to now, this message, with a few additional twists, might also reach both Codre and her mother, whether they discover who Fresne is or not. The servants, after all, at least know where the cloth came from; and Fresne's mother has reason to know what such folk are capable of.

17. That tone will have to wait for Chaucer's depiction of Le Fresne's descendent Griselde in the Clerk's Tale:

"My lord, ye woot that in my fadres place
Ye dide me streepe out of my povre weed,
And richely me cladden, of youre grace.
To yow broghte I noghte elles, out of drede,
But feith, and nakednesse, and maydenhede;
And heere agayn youre clothing I restoore,
And eek youre weddyng ryng, for everemoore

". . . But yet I hope it be nat youre entente
That I smokelees out of youre paleys wente.

Ye koude nat doon so dishonest a thyng,
That thilke wombe in which youre children leye
Sholde biforn the peple in my walkynge,
Be seyn al bare; wherfore I yow preye,
Lat me nat lyk a worm go by the weye. . . .

"Wherfore, in gerdon of my maydenhede,
Which that I broghte, and noght agayn I bere
As voucheth sauf to yeve me, to my meede,
But swich a smok as I was wont to were,

That I therwith may wrye the wombe of here
That was youre wyf. And heere take I my leeve
Of yow, myn owene lord, lest I yow greve."
(*CT* IV.862–68, 874–80, 883–89)

I cite from *The Riverside Chaucer,* 3rd ed., gen. ed., Larry D. Benson (Boston: Houghton Mifflin, 1987).

18. The ethnic joke that begins the *lai* sets out the conditions of the Norman *garwaf,* or EC horror-comic reading of the plot, The Return of the Thing in the Woods (which the the rest of the poem mostly avoids) in order to contrast it, a touch bathetically, with the more everyday Breton *bisclavret* world of noble pursuits that will occupy it thereafter: "Garvalf, ceo est beste salvage; / Tant cum il est en cele rage, / Humes devure, grant mal fait, . . . Del Bisclavret vus voil cunter" (*Bisc.* 9–11, 14).

19. From this point of view, the language used to describe the *bisclavret*'s downfall is significant—"Issi fu Bisclavret trahiz / E per sa femme maubailiz" (*Bisc.* 125–26)—because "maubailiz," ("badly served, in the way a bailiff would mismanage an estate") suggests the caretaker role the wife was left in before she found out why.

20. It should be noted that Guildeluëc in *Eliduc* is one of the few women in the *Lais* who may be thought to manage this.

21. "La dame ad cil dunc espusee / Que lungement aveit amee" (*Bisc.* 133–34). Hanning and Ferrante translate "The wife later married the other knight," but Marie's "dunc," "thereupon" adds stress to the aspect of conditional exchange of value for service in a matter whose aspects of mutual blackmail, sustained by public commitment, are evident enough.

22. Hanning and Ferrante translate the following line, "Deus feiz le vout mordre le jour!" as "twice that day he tried to bite the knight"; but it seems to me that the French must mean "twice *a* day," which also seems to me to increase the bathetic and comic effect by further stressing the futility of the werewolf's behavior.

23. Marie is careful to note that, even under torture, the most the wife can confess is "l'aventure qu'il [*scil.* her husband] li cunta" (*Bisc.* 269)—she has not seen him change.

24. Why did she keep them?—or did she? He might be supposed to have more than one set, if indeed he really needs clothing with a personal stamp to transform. Many of the casual details of the *lai* have the quality, when examined closely, of what Pooh Bah in *The Mikado* calls lending an air of verisimilitude to an otherwise bald and unconvincing narrative, of which more below.

25. Hence the magical transformation of his retinue, "Il est a sun ostel venuz, / Ses humes treve bien vestuz" (*Lanv.* 201–2)."

26. Of Lanval in the meadow, "Si s'est alez esbaneier," 42; of the knights of the court: "s'ierent alé esbanier," 222; of the queen and her entourage in the same scene, "li s'irrunt esbaniër," 245.

27. See the Larousse *Dictionnaire de l'ancien français,* s.v. *ban.*

28. Kinoshita, "*Cherchez la Femme,*" 269–70, following Bloch, *Medieval Misogyny,* sees Lanval as feminized, and there is a lot to this idea. For the reasons given in the text, however, the move seems best viewed as a strategic or *faux* femininity, playing a female role in order to gain male ends. It should be clear that a phrase like "false femininity" does not entail the possibility of a "real" one, if that is construed as some sort of female essence. It ought to be evident by now, from situations like the one described here, that Marie understands "male" and "female" as discourses and roles that can be played by anyone with a motive, conscious or unconscious, for doing so, and that they can be mixed and matched as well. This is one reflection of the hind's androgyny: that "she," "Marie, elle" can write as s/he does, with an understanding of the different *functions* of the same fantasies in the plural collocations of "masculinities" and "femininities." None of this, by the way, precludes noticing how the subjects who are forced or persuaded to be "women" are treated, the *political* logic of the structure called "femininity." I develop some of this further at the end of this section.

29. I take this tower, for reasons given immediately below, to be a slightly displaced allusion to Chretien's *Chevalier au charette,*

30. The language and the situation here are sufficiently parallel to the similar proposition made to Lanval by the fairy mistress to suggest that the queen again fills in the real-life effort, the labor and preparation women have to take in order to play the game of eros—the alertness to opportunities, the attention to the work of self-staging (for example, the deployment of the thirty ladies)—of which only the on-stage effect is manifest with the former lady.

31. See Rychner, *Le lais,* 256, note to line 259.

32. Lines 257–58 just cited, about Lanval's attitude to the pleasure of others, thus also describe in inverted form the queen's feelings as well.

33. The range of "Ki prez de lui vus ad suffert" is uncertain, but it might be glossed by the wife in *Bisclavret,* whose fear of her husband manifested itself as a desire not to lie "lez lui" any more. It is at least interesting that Marie uses the same word, "maubailliz," to describe Lanval's relation to Arthur (or the queen's version of it) and the werewolf's wife to her husband in *Bisclavret.* See note 19 above.

34. I do not wish to be understood as maintaining that the queen is accusing Lanval and the king of sleeping together, or even of sharing a taste for boys, much less that they or anyone else in the poem actually does these things. She is implying *something* about the two of them that carries resonances with other places in the *Lais.* The precise reference, if there is one, is almost certainly irrecoverable historically, and she herself may well be uncertain of it. If so, though, the men involved are more than likely to be equally uncertain of the precise justice of the imputation. One is reminded of Eve Kosofsky Sedgewick's marvellous analysis of the "coercive double bind" of male homosocial desire: "the tendency toward important correspondences

and similarities between the most sanctioned forms of male-homosocial bonding, and the most reprobated expressions of male homosexual sociality. . . . To put it in twentieth-century American terms, the fact that what goes on at football games, in fraternities, at the Bohemian Grove, and at climactic moments in war novels, can look, with only a slight shift of optic, quite startlingly 'homosexual,' is not most importantly an expression of the psychic origin of these institutions in repressed or sublimated homosexual genitality. . . . For a man to be a man's man is separated only by an invisible, carefully blurred, always-already-crossed line from being 'interested in men.'" *Between Men: English Literature and Male Homosocial Desire* (New York: Columbia University Press, 1985), 89. Marie's poem offers a number of situations where the tension of the double bind might be invoked, and she here offers a kind of *point de capiton* to organize a certain reading of them in the person of a woman with a reason for shifting the optic. At the very least, she shows that this possibility is present in the text as an option for its characters: and Lanval's response suggests further that the characters have to take it seriously even when it is not true, precisely because its social reality is discursive, independent of individual psyches and sexualities.

35. This puts Lanval, a few lines later, in the curious position of denying an accusation that has not been made: "Que la reïne ne requist" (*Lanv.* 374). The fact that he seems to expect it foregrounds the extent to which Arthur is conspicuously avoiding something that is common knowledge.

36. "C'um ne li puisse a mal retraire" (384). The verb is from Latin *retractare,* perhaps "so no one could *reconsider* it in a bad light," though "a mal" might carry the sense "maliciously."

37. Contextually it is not hard to remember here that in this culture, any man is entitled by convention to insist, in poetic public performance before the court, that his lady is the fairest in the land. There is something conspicuously wrongheaded or deliberately obtuse from the beginning about the queen's insistence on pulling rank over this question, which makes the court's hustling to address it look more awkward and adds force to the count's comment.

38. Rychner, *Le lais,* 259–60, *ad loc.,* similarly reports a like emendation suggested by Burger.

39. This is the point of their reaction to the second pair of ladies: "Mut les loërent li plusur / De cors, de vis e de colur: / N'i ad cele mieuz ne vausist / Qu'unkes la reïne ne fist" (*Lanv.* 529–32).

40. The lines preface a more conventional romance-courtly *blason* of her face (563–74), ending with the information that she has a cloak, "les pans en ot entur li mis" (572). To ask the question, "In that case, how do we know you could see her sides?" is to see the particular range of courtly voyeurism this passage is working, consistent with the general trope of the not-quite-covered-up that pervades the *lai.*

41. "Look but don't touch.—or you will blow the cover story that we are just talking about facts here by revealing the facts we are actually talking about." The

extent to which this *lai* and the *Playboy* cultural phenomenon continually illuminate one another is a source of continual inspiration and bemusement.

42. Kinoshita, "*Cherchez la Femme*," 270 and 272.

43. Cited in Rychner, *Les lais*, 261, note to line 641.

44. For Ovid I have in mind, of course, the itinerary that runs from the *Amores* through the *Ars amatoria* to the *Remedia amoris;* for Angela Carter, the short tales, especially those collected in *The Bloody Chamber.*

7

CHRISTOPHER BASWELL

Troy, Arthur, and the Languages of "Brutis Albyoun"

*Sed fortassis mos est cuique nationi aliquem de suis laudibus attollere
excessivis, ut quemadmodum Graeci suum Alexandrum, Romani suum
Octavianum, Angli suum Ricardum, Franci suum Karolum, sic Britones
suum Arthurum praeconantur.*

*But on cas it is the manere of everiche nacioun to overe preyse som oon
of the same nacioun, as the Grees preyseth here Alisaundre, and the
Romayns here Octavianus, and Englisshe men here Richard, and
Frensche men here Charles, and Britouns here Arthur.*

—Ranulph Higden, *Polychronicon*, translation of John Trevisa

Neither Great Britain nor America has any institution comparable
to that linguistic gatekeeper of respectable French, the Académie
française. This is a point often made, with a puzzlement border-
ing on despair, by entrepreneurs of Standard English as they bemoan the
decline and mongrelization of "our"—for which, read "their"—written lan-

guage. Such an absence merits no real surprise, though: in the nations in-
accurately called Anglophone, a mixed and shifting pool of tongues has always lapped along fractured and mobile borders of ethnicity, class, and even
gender. In America today we can witness a Latina student (already fluent
in the longest-used European tongue in this hemisphere), with an African-
American teacher instructing her in what is for that teacher an acquired dialect, Standard English; they live in a territory, further, whose truly native
languages have been virtually erased. And we can easily imagine a twelfth-
century boy of aristocratic birth with a nursemaid crooning in Anglo-Saxon,
a mother speaking in Anglo-Norman, and a clerical tutor of peasant Briton
stock eager to begin whipping Latin into him. In England and America both,
the multiplicity of languages, the conflicts and mobility of power and race,
and the frequent violence and repression that have characterized negotiations among them all, together make an authoritative language too touchy
a point to invite rational institutionalization. The improbability and illogic of
a single, authoritative tongue lie too close to the surface; and its real instability is too plain, even on cursory examination.

Again, consider twelfth-century England. Some fluid versions of the
Anglo-Saxon languages continued in wide use. Anglo-Norman speakers
controlled most political power and a lot of land. Latin was the language of
education (taught via French), the language still of most public and historical record, and the language of the sacred. This might suggest a fairly stable
linguistic hierarchy at the level of usage; but if a hierarchy, it was very unstable indeed. In fact, written Anglo-Saxon retained real prestige in some settings, as registered by the continuations of the *Anglo-Saxon Chronicle;* there
was also respect, though little real use, for the old Anglo-Saxon law codes.[1]
Whatever form of Latin may have made up the bulk of their written records,
Anglo-Norman was the active language of the royal court and of law, in contrast with the real hegemony of Latin in the ecclesiastical world. Yet even
sacred Latin was known to be just the translated (though divinely guided)
substitute for original biblical Greek and Hebrew, both of them virtually un-
available languages.[2]

Subtending these complicated facts of usage and power, there exist
equally influential if incoherent systems of belief about language and its roles
in cultural identity. These beliefs are inscribed within deeply held myths
of history and nationhood, and they equally resist any final settlement of
authority upon a single language. Operating within this field of practice
and belief, the hugely popular historical myth constructed by Geoffrey of

Monmouth proposed a native British imperial hero, Arthur, recorded in "quendam Britannici sermonis librum uetustissimum."[3] Geoffrey thus uses Latin only as a vulgar, secondary medium for disseminating that older and more authoritative (if imaginary) "very ancient book in the British tongue," provided to him alone by Archdeacon Walter of Oxford. As with the languages of the holy book, as with the Word of God itself, the language most ancient and hovering almost beyond human access held greatest prestige and authority. Latin in such a setting is made a mere, and late, vernacular. A claim to control such a privileged (if variable) language of authority could lend important prestige to competing ideologies and their efforts to manipulate contemporary insular historical myth. As Kellie Robertson has nicely put it, "The Trojan vernacular was the most influential language never spoken in the British Isles during the Middle Ages."[4]

This article looks at the enfolding of two key narratives of British imperial foundation—Brutus and his Trojans, Arthur and his Britons—into the emergent vernacular writing of English history from the later fourteenth century (Trevisa's *Polychronicon*, finished 1387) to the turn of the fifteenth century (the *Brut* or *Chronicles of England*), both contextualized by their backgrounds in Latin (especially Geoffrey of Monmouth) and Anglo-Norman (the earlier *Brut* versions). Given the extremely anxious position of a rising Middle English situated between royal ambitions (dynastic as well as newly imperial) and insurgent Wycliffite writing, I want to think about how an increasingly common language set about maintaining or reenacting the (always unstable but real) hierarchical linguistic authorities of the past.[5] To investigate this, I propose Trevisa's translation of the *Polychronicon*, commissioned and owned by aristocrats, as one pole; and the *Brut*, with no known commissioning origin and owned by a very wide range of readers, as another. I consider their respective efforts (or absence of effort) to "authorize" their foundational myths through such gestures as textual citation and argument by narrative voices. I also consider the very different classes of manuscripts in which they appear: the *Brut* typically in more mid-level books, efficiently produced and little decorated; Trevisa in books whose grandeur and scale suggest an almost fetishistic status. In the latter group, moreover, I describe a kind of page format, decoration, and rubrication (largely in Latin) all calculated to generate awe in the reader as much as they facilitate textual access.

There is a deep paradox here. The texts I will discuss revisit and help to extend a myth of international, continental origin and empire, but they do so in an insular tongue that excludes the continental objects of their imperial dreams. Nonetheless, the dreams themselves persist, formulated upon Geoffrey of Monmouth's now ancient mythic models of ethnic and political translation: a westwardly mobile empire (Brutus and the Trojans) reversible into eastwardly mobile conquest (Arthur and the Britons crossing the Continent toward Rome), both movements justified by and resolvable into a single genealogical line, yet simultaneously divided along fractures of ethnicity and language. The instance of Geoffrey of Monmouth, then, crystallizes several notions of *translatio* in the later medieval examples that I explore below. First, translation of language and *translatio imperii* are intriguingly linked in English national myth. The authorities of Mediterranean antiquity and its language, Latin, always have a destabilizing counterpart and competitor in Britain, in a native myth originally accessible (it is claimed) only through a native tongue.[6] Second, Arthurian tradition in England, from Geoffrey onward, nevertheless persistently arranges itself—translates itself—into some analogy of Mediterranean imperial antiquity, especially that of Troy and Rome, by means of narrative parallels, narrative inversions, and such evocative names as "Troynovaunt." And third, the claims and resources of what we call (however problematically) history and literature, or fact and marvel, play back and forth with one another in this tradition, especially at moments of translation, mutually constructing and drawing upon each other's authority, or just as often mutually subverting and deconstructing those authorities.

That is, to the categories of *translatio imperii* and *translatio sermonis*, I would add a category we might call *translatio fabulae*, by which events are variously retold, reparsed, or challenged as carrying a weight of fact or spurious fantasy. This third point perhaps demands a little elaboration. Within the great multilingual stew of classical story in the later Middle Ages, claims of historical authority and even linguistic prestige seem to have had less and less to do with mere textual antiquity (such as Geoffrey of Monmouth's "very ancient book") or the claims of eyewitness report (as with Dares or Dictys). Virgil's fictions, for example, though revered from late antiquity onward, were now increasingly alleged against him, for instance by Guido delle Colonne and his translators.[7] Historicity was generated more on the basis of commonly accepted story, narrative verisimilitude, and the canons of euhemerism and related modes of the analysis of fable, as will be seen in the *Polychronicon*. This was particularly the case as broadscale histories like the *Brut* and the Middle English *Polychronicon* moved away from their more learned points of origin and into the hands of users less acquainted with notions of archival documentation or even the historiographical debates around characters like Aeneas or Arthur.

As suggested above, Geoffrey of Monmouth lays double claim to his authority in *Historia regum Britanniae,* first through his exclusive access to an ancient book provided by Walter Archdeacon of Oxford, and second through the inaccessible language of that book, a native British tongue fairly few of his readers would have known. By contrast with this authorizing fiction of inaccessibility, the *Brut* translates an already popular Anglo-Norman text into a Middle English narrative whose huge popularity appears to have been second only to the Wycliffite Bible.[8] Over one hundred eighty manuscripts of the Middle English *Brut* survive, and fifty of its Anglo-Norman source.[9] The *Brut* thus became "the nearest equivalent to a national chronicle written in late medieval England,"[10] although my discussion of the *Brut* and *Polychronicon* manuscripts, below, undertakes to make problematic what we mean by "national" in these chronicles.

The great achievement of the Anglo-Norman and Middle English *Brut* texts is to marry Geoffrey of Monmouth's historical myths of Brutus and Arthur yet more firmly to a much extended and increasingly documentable narrative of the English kings, up to the death of Henry III (1272) in the earliest versions, and variously continued (as late as 1461) in versions in both languages.[11] This creates a single connected narrative that yokes the earliest myths of national foundation to the ongoing fortunes of the royal dynasties and provides the kind of shared national narrative on which more focused ideological projects can later depend. The Middle English *Brut* tells its story in a straightforward narrative style, little burdened with details of dates or parallel events (especially in the earlier sections), and with emphatically oral emphasis, despite its wide manuscript distribution: "as ye shul here afterwarde," and "as after ye shul here."[12]

By extending Geoffrey's history to the end of the thirteenth century and beyond, the *Brut* recasts Brutus and Arthur as justificatory prehistories for the feudal and imperial pretensions of later English royal dynasties.[13] Further, the *Brut*'s considerably abbreviated narrative of this British prehistory serves to emphasize analogies between the careers of Brutus and Arthur. Brutus and Arthur are both children of transgressive unions, Brutus of incest and Arthur of adultery.[14] After his banishment from Rome, Brutus receives the prophecy of "Diane the Goddesse," predicting his kingship in Albyon after he traverses "Fraunce, toward the west."[15] Similarly, Arthur demands a prophecy from Merlyn regarding the last kings of England.[16] Following the instructions of Diane's prophecy, Brutus sails for England, passing through "Gascoign," where he conquers its king, Goffar, and both founds and names Tours.[17] After this triumph, though, Brutus retreats from the French, whose superior numbers threaten to overwhelm him. Brutus's passage toward England thus creates a model of prophetically inspired but incomplete conquest in France. This is repeated, reversed, and completed (if only temporarily) by Arthur when he sets out eastward "to conquere al Fraunce."[18]

After a challenge from the emperor of Rome, who claims to be Arthur's overlord, Arthur undertakes a second campaign on the Continent, again triumphantly, although interrupted by Mordred's usurpation of the English throne.[19] Far from fleeing Latium as Brutus had, Arthur, in a letter to the emperor, lays genealogical claim to be Rome's overlord and threatens to march on the city to demand tribute:

> Uunderstondes amonges yow of Rome, that I am Kyng Arthure of Britaigne, and frely hit holde, and shal holde; and at Rome hastely y shal be, nought to geve yow truage, but forto axen truage; ffor Constantyne, that was Elynus sone, that was Emperour of Rome and of al the honour that thereto bilongede; ffor Maxinian conquerede al Fraunce and Almaigne, & mount Ioye passede, & conquerede al Lumbardye; and thise ij were myn ancestres; and that thai hade and helde, I shulde have, through Godes wille.[20]

The geography of Arthurian empire is thus mapped upon the earlier Roman empire, but also inverts it: England becomes the point of origin (and retreat) for militant empire, and Rome the far-flung (and unachieved) border of Arthurian ambition. Analogously, Britain by Arthur's time has become the source of the Roman imperial line, rather than *vice versa*. Arthur's second campaign on the Continent thus pits him against his own post-Trojan doubles, the Romans, and traces the split of Briton-Roman ethnicity and political ambition against the myth of their unified genealogical and geographical origin. Both these imperial models and the ideological fractures they display would have rung loudly in the ears of fourteenth- and fifteenth-century English readers, with their complex claims to empire in France and their frustrated efforts to execute those ambitions.

Despite the kind of dense analogies between Brutus and Arthur discussed above, concentrated by the relative brevity of their narratives in the *Brut,* the Middle English version of that text remained strikingly open, both accessible and permeable. Its very narrative ease and relative lack of documentary apparatus allows (though it does not require) a correspondingly loose range of reader responses. Especially in the Middle English extensions beyond 1333, urban preoccupations and details of urban history begin to compete with the earlier focus on foundation, empire, and royal lives. Textually, too, the *Brut* has a protean quality, sometimes abbreviated, repeatedly (and variously) extended into ever later periods, and full of interpolated texts such as Queen Isabella's letter to the commons of London.[21] The *Brut* appears to have been translated into Middle English toward the end of the fourteenth century, that is, close to the time of Trevisa's Middle English *Polychronicon* (1385–87) and Chaucer's pseudo-translation, *Troilus and Criseyde* (ca. 1381–85).[22] But its very wide dissemination, as noted above, was by no means limited to English. Its circulation in Anglo-Norman French, English, and versions retranslated into Latin also records the open movement of the text, serving varied purposes and varied readerships.

Interpolations, extensions, and multiple redactions were, of course, widespread features of medieval historiography. Higden's Latin *Polychronicon* was frequently and variously extended as it became the dominant world history in English monasteries. However, the *Polychronicon* became much more consistent and contained—a more closed text—when John Trevisa translated it into English under the patronage of Sir Thomas Berkeley. Ranulph Higden finished the most widely disseminated version of his *Polychronicon,* represented by nearly seventy manuscripts, in the later 1340s.[23] By contrast with the limited circulation of most fourteenth-century monastic chronicles, Higden's achieved a very wide readership and influence.[24] It was translated into English by Trevisa and again anonymously in the fifteenth century, while its influence beyond historiography can be traced in Chaucer, Usk, and Lydgate.[25] Part of the popularity of Higden's *Polychronicon* must result from its simple usefulness: the universal range, the very broad learning and variety of sources (ancient, patristic, and medieval), the careful chronology. But its special appeal in England is probably related to a canny paradox that Higden plays upon throughout his chronicle: the geographical marginality ("Anglia is i-cleped the other world") and increasing narrative centrality of the British Isles ("By cause of Bretayne alle the travaile of this storie was bygonne").[26] The *Polychronicon* thus translates England across categories of geographical eccentricity and historical centrality, although it never replicates the emphatic and quasi-mythic gestures of genealogy and imperial foundation we witness in the *Brut.*

The *Brut*, especially in its earlier sections, is straightforwardly narrative in style, mentioning little by way of sources or historical context beyond the British Isles. By contrast, using and often naming earlier universal histories, Higden synchronizes events in ancient, biblical, and later European history. So in the time of Deborah, he tells us, "began the kingdom of Laurentynes in Italy"; "And Ilus, Appolyn his sone, bulde Ilium in Troye." When "Abessa of Bethlehem" ruled in Israel, Priam was king in Troy.[27] The story of Brutus and his exile ending in Britain is placed, a bit more vaguely, after the time of Ruth.[28] These carefully constructed parallels situate, and thus validate, classical legend and myth through textual citation and the unchallenged veracity of the Bible, by contrast with the simpler assertive narrative of the *Brut*. Moreover, in the broad structure of his chronicle, Higden organizes history in seven books on the analogy of the seven days of creation.[29] Higden aims further to specify time in terms of numbered years organized along numerous, sometimes overlapping chronologies that draw from the "eyghte dyuerse manere of acountynge of yeres."[30] He begins numbering years from Abraham, then starts a new sequence with David. Marginal notes make reference to the regnal years of Jewish judges or kings, and then years from the foundation of Rome. Beginning with the Christian era, Higden numbers by *anno Domini* and the regnal year of the emperor of Rome, down to Charlemagne, after whom he records the regnal year of the king of any nation being discussed, which increasingly means England.[31]

Such care over chronology, as well as the context of simultaneous and irrefutable biblical events, contributes an air of documentary veracity to Higden's versions of Troy and the Brutus story. They serve to translate legendary and mythic narratives into the discourse of undisputed history, largely under the protection of the authority of the Bible. The overlapping systems of parallel events and chronologies become dense at moments crucial to the prehistory and early history of Britain. The foundation of Troy was mentioned above; its cataclysmic fall is elaborately located in terms of Old Testament history (in the third year of Abdon, 844 years after the birth of Abraham, 340 after the Israelites leave Egypt) and of Roman history (432 years before the founding of Rome).[32] The first arrival of "Bretouns" on the isles is aligned with the rulers of Israel and Latium, and the number of years that arrival occurred after the fall of Troy and before the foundation of Rome. That is to say, the foundation narrative of England draws together datings from the most important aspects of its prehistory—religious, colonial, and genealogical. This has intriguing analogies to geographical and genealogical remappings of British foundation myths upon ancient empires, as we see in the *Brut* tradition.

In a second gesture of authentication, drawing from but manipulating classical sources, Higden further translates myth—especially Trojan myth—into historicized versions by a subtle but aggressive use of inherited theories of fable, especially those that encourage euhemerist explanations. Dionysus, for instance, is euhemerized as a military leader, and the Bacchantes in his train are explained by his having a mixed-gender fighting force.[33] Hercules, who enters the narrative partly because of his role in Troy, is subjected to an elaborate critique and an artillery of ancient and patristic opinions, all deployed to divide his labors among several characters named Hercules and to reject some outright.[34] This in turn sparks a long digression offering a theory of euhemerist and allegorical fable that draws on Isidore, Augustine, Macrobius, and the third Vatican Mythographer.[35] Yet Higden also slices away from the Troy story any myth that resists such rationalizing, like that of Ganymede: "Than the fable of Iupiter is i-feyned; and so the rauyschynge of an egle is i-feyned and idul."[36] Higden's dual strategies of elaborate chronology and euhemerist exegesis of ancient myth, together, provide another instance of what I have called *translatio fabulae*. Higden historicizes ancient myth simply by placing it so carefully in parallel with the unchallengeable veracity of Old Testament history. And he uses euhemerism to shift the narrative register of ancient myth to a level coherent with that of the Bible or later documented history.

Higden's was "the first chronicle in England to treat world history in a serious and sustained manner that could appeal to the general reader."[37] His enormously wide range of sources, his selective but persistent absorption of ancient myth into British prehistory, and the growing focus on Britain as his chronicle progressed, all combined to create a uniquely popular work among insular readers of Latin history. As an expanding audience for vernacular English emerged in the late fourteenth century, then, it is not surprising that the *Polychronicon* became an attractive project for translation.[38] Trevisa prefaced his translation with the well-known dialogue between a "Dominus," a modestly educated baronial patron with only a little Latin, and a "Clericus," the more traditionally learned cleric who is asked to translate the *Polychronicon*. This dialogue revisits many of the questions of linguistic hierarchy and class that I raised at the start of this article. Clericus initially resists the commission, in a rather transparent fiction, but the arguments on each side are nonetheless intriguing: issues of linguistic access versus interpretative control, and of English insularity versus Latin internationalism. These themes are especially noteworthy in this context, screened as they are across the ragged and asymmetrical class ambitions of cleric and aristocrat, Latin reader and Middle English reader, international and insular affiliation.

The dialogue posits a kind of readership in which limited (but not absent) Latin is a register of higher rather than lower class, and the clerk's better Latin marks him as part of a service industry. Dominus frames his commission in terms of the multiplicity of languages after Babel. But Latin, while international, is socially restricted, known only to clerks and (less well) to some nobles. [39] Dominus therefore wants chronicles like Higden's "translated out of Latyn ynto Englysch, for the mo men scholde hem understonde...."[40] ("Mo men," we should note, is not the same as *all* men; and this expanded readership is *only* men.) "Clericus" argues for Latin internationalism as against translation into a narrow insular vernacular; besides, men can learn Latin if they want to read such texts.

Here Dominus moves the argument into the social realities of class and income: men may lack time, wit, and money enough to study Latin. Clericus stands fast on the privileges of his cohort: these books touch on philosophy and theology; they are appropriate only to clerks, and "scholde noght be translated ynto Englysch."[41] All his arguments in this section echo the current clerical anxieties over biblical translation and unmediated lay access to the Gospels and Catholic theology. The anxious resistance to broad lay access here moves well past the Bible and theology, though, and into knowledge of secular history. The issue raised within the dialogue, then, seems increasingly to skirt (and hence describe) the dangers of vernacular history falling into the wrong hands.

Dominus answers that such books have long been translated from Hebrew into Greek, Latin, and French. For what trespass has his national tongue been denied these works?[42] This sequence of tongues traces Biblical translation, but also begins to parallel post-Trojan *translatio imperii;* implicitly, English is the next imperial tongue. Here again national and political prestige tries to edge past the claims of an international ecclesiastical class and puts aside concerns about access beyond the class of empire builders. Clericus finally begins to give in and asks what kind of translation he is to supply, particularly whether it should be prose or verse. Dominus prefers prose, since it is "more cleer ..., more esy and more pleyn."[43]

This is a highly artificial dialogue, of course, and both interlocutors take somewhat disingenuous and self-contradictory positions. Dominus's interest in wider access to the text would in fact seem mostly pointed toward access for his own class, given his simultaneous concern with advancing the international political prestige of English and given the actual production of manuscripts of the resulting translation. And Clericus, while he does accede to Dominus, begins his translation in a way that nonetheless slyly resists his instructions and implicitly asserts the viewpoint of his ecclesiastical class: "Thanne God graunte grace greithlyche to gynne, wyt and wysdom wysly to wyrche, myght and muynde of ryght menyng to make translacion trysty and truwe, plesyng to the Trynyte, thre persones and o god in maieste, that ever was and evere schal be, and made hevene and erthe and lyght vor to schyne, and departed lyght and derknes."[44] Far from "more esy and more pleyn" prose, this syntactically dense sentence comes very close to alliterative verse.[45] Moreover, its content centers for the moment on divine creation and Biblical language (the domain of the church) rather than the human history to which it will turn. And further, as we will see, textual anxieties about control and interpretation consistently characterize Trevisa's version.

Trevisa is much noted, and rightly, for his skill in resolving Latin periods and absolute clauses into coherent but briefer sequences of Middle English independent clauses.[46] Consider the wanderings of Aeneas after Troy:

Post Trojae excidium Aeneas cum Anchise patre suo Ascanioque filio in navibus duodecim venerunt in Siciliam, ubi Anchise mortuo, cum vellet Aeneas navigare Italiam, tempestate pulsus venit in Africam; ubi a Didone regina nimium est adamatus. Sed post aliquantulae morae spatium relicta Didone devenit Italiam.

After the destroyenge of Troye, Eneas with his fader Anchises and his sone Ascanius with twelue schippes come to Sicil. There Anchises deide. And whanne Eneas wolde seille into Itali, tempest drof hym in to Affrica. There he was hugeliche i-loued of Dido the queene; but after a schort tyme he lefte Dido and come in to Italy.[47]

Higden opens this passage rather elegantly with two temporal clauses, divided by an ablative phrase ("ubi Anchise mortuo"); and he shifts nicely between clauses of time ("Post . . . cum . . .") and place ("ubi . . . ubi . . ."). Trevisa observes the narrative order of Higden's Latin and retains the emphasis on place, but splits the passage into four independent sentences, rendering the absolute clauses about Anchises and Dido ("relicta Didone") as simple active verbs. He also chooses to leave aside Higden's slightly reproach-ful note of Aeneas's delay ("aliquantulae morae spatium"), calling it just "a schort tyme."

The Latinity of Trevisa's source, however, and thus the authoritative tone of Latin historical writing, remains close to the surface of the trans-lated version; not in the sense of controlling its diction or syntax, but rather by moving Latin literally into the Middle English text itself. This is appar-ent in a number of Trevisa's habits. In passages where sense is etymological, Trevisa must import Latin terms into his English, as where he derives "fable" from the Latin "fando."[48] Quite frequently, he gives names in their Latin form, then pauses to explain their sense or pronunciation.[49] Similarly, Tre-visa imports reference to Latin to explain the acrostic of Christ's name in a Sibylline prophetic verse: "The heed lettres of these thre vers, and of the othere as they beeth i-write in Latyn, speleth this menynge: Ihesus Crist, Goddes sone, Savyour."[50] Such references not only emphasize the Latin source, but also imply the incompleteness of the translation, deprived of the visual play possible in the original, to which only the translator and his cleri-cal cohort have full access.

Latin enters the translation much more persistently in topic headings, presumably Trevisa's own, which gain still more prominence from their usual rubrication in the manuscripts: "De quibusdam Romanorum institutis et observantiis" or "De schiris Angliae, siue prouinciis."[51] Their simple Latin would suggest a readership that can negotiate a little Latin but needs assis-tance in English for the bulk of the text itself; and indeed such a reader has already appeared—"Dominus" in his description of his own level of Latin: "for they [Ich] cunne speke and rede and understonde Latyn ther ys moche Latyn in theus bokes of cronyks that Y can noght understonde."[52] Even more frequently, Trevisa uses Latin to identify source authors, texts, and the names of rulers and other important figures in his history. We read in the transla-tion, then, not of Virgil but Virgilius, not Isidore but Isidorus, not Horace but Horacius; and when Isidorus's book is cited, it appears as "Eth. libro decimo," not as the tenth book of the *Etymologies*.[53] So the authenticating gesture of citation is intensified by the authority of Latin, imported into an English text. The same impact is created when names and places are given, frequently, in Latin: "at the laste that lond highte Italia of Italus, rege Siculo-rum, kyng of Sicilia, and is the noblest prouince of al Europa."[54]

Far from creating the "more esy and more pleyn" Middle English trans-lation explicitly requested by "Dominus" in the prefatory dialogue, then,

Trevisa also often exploits English and traces of Latin toward a rather exclusive and elevated linguistic register. Together with the multiple importations of Latin into the translation, this at times creates almost a mixed-language text. Latin is not necessary for navigating it (though helpful), but an authorizing Latin original and an even less accessible system of Latin sources and learning behind that original are always emphatically present to the reader. While Trevisa may obey the commission of his patron, he nonetheless perpetuates in his very translation an awareness of the privileges and interpretative control of his class; even in English, "Clericus" is ever-present. At the same time, Trevisa's English translation is in fact carefully suited in its tone and linguistic demands to the specific education of his baronial patron and others of his rank, rather than to the generalized "mo men" for whom "Dominus" initially demanded the work. Trevisa's translation of the *Polychronicon* thus negotiates across boundaries of language, though in a complex and unresolved fashion; and that in turn contributes to a still more complex and unresolved negotiation across the lines of class.

Trevisa's impact on the tone and address of the *Polychronicon*, however, goes well past these local verbal strategies. Occasionally, he also pulls content toward the interests and political outlook of his patron's class. In one of his more extended personal interventions in the translation, Trevisa pauses to argue for the inclusion of that greatest insular and imperial hero, Arthur, whom Higden had rejected largely because his story was not consonant with most of the international tradition of Latin history.[55] Higden steps delicately around the question of the Arthurian story. He begins by citing the reliable and respected William of Malmesbury, "Willelmus de Regibus," who admits that Arthur fought some good battles while England was in decline, but otherwise dismisses him as "that Arthur about whom the silly tales of the Britons rave."[56] Higden then enters in his own voice and adds further details from at least four sources. From unidentified chronicles ("In quibusdam chronicis"), he reports Arthur's long struggle with Cerdicus. Then, from Chronicles of the English ("chronicis Anglorum"), he tells of Mordred's treacherous deal with the same Cerdicus. The story of Arthur's final combat with Mordred and Arthur's ensuing death, Higden takes from "the storie of the Britons" ("secundum historiam Britonum").[57] And finally, he cites the discovery of Arthur's and Guenevere's corpses, in the time of Henry II, from Gerald of Wales.[58] Higden's sequence of sources is intriguing, moving along ever more specific and increasingly Celtic-based reports and distinguishing histories of the English and the Britons. Yet he immediately begins to register doubts. Why does Geoffrey of Monmouth ("Gaufri-dus") alone so praise Arthur, when the other ethnic histories are silent about him? Higden goes on to allege several other inconsistencies between Geof-frey's story and that of the Romans, French, and Saxons. Nonetheless, in the passage with which this article began, he acknowledges the myth-making habits of all peoples and lists foreign heroes who are, implicitly, no more be-lievable than Arthur.[59]

In all this, Higden is very far from the *Brut*'s calm acceptance and sum-mary of Geoffrey of Monmouth's Arthur. And given his particular patron, Trevisa's response to Arthur has yet more at stake. As he translates this pas-sage, Trevisa has ratcheted up his English syntax.[60] Despite the general para-taxis and frequent colloquialism of his English, at certain moments of spe-cial importance, Trevisa will switch into a more challenging hypotactic syntax, appropriate to ambitious deductive argument and echoing, to an ex-tent, the sentence structure of sophisticated Latin. Trevisa now interrupts his source text with some asperity and inserts a series of counterarguments, using an English that continues to display syntactic and argumentative com-plexity in contest with the Latin: "Here William telleth a magel tale with oute evidence; and Ranulphus his resouns, that he meveth ayenst Gaufridus and Arthur, schulde non clerke moove that can knowe an argument, for it followeth it nought." Trevisa takes Higden's objection, and speaks as if in Higden's logic, but cleverly shifts the argument to the analogous situation of narrative inconsistencies in the Gospels. "Seint Iohn in his gospel telleth meny thinges and doynges that Mark, Luk, and Matheu speketh nought of in here gospelles, ergo, Iohn is nought to trowynge in his gospel." He then shifts back to his own voice and a dismissive colloquial tone: "He were of false byleve that trowede that that argument were worth a bene."[61] Further, Trevisa says, some history writers who do not mention Arthur were his ene-mies; and confusion about Arthur's opponents may result from the diversity of names in the past. Finally, Trevisa returns to William of Malmesbury and cites Higden's own earlier point that William is unreliable because he never read the "British book" that had been available to Geoffrey of Monmouth.[62]

Trevisa's interpolation is particularly important in the context of his ear-lier linguistic negotiation with a baronial readership. Such readers had a real if indirect stake in English territorial ambitions, which were supported by myths of Arthurian empire. And, as we have seen, their reading—through Geoffrey of Monmouth himself or through the widely distributed Brut narratives—included stories that linked the imperial movements of Brutus (whom Higden has included) and Arthur (whom Higden would largely exclude). It is not surprising, then, that Trevisa finds a way to reintroduce a heroic figure so important and widely known among the class of his patrons. To some degree, as international players in England's ongoing imperial ambitions, the class of Trevisa's patronage needed a controlled return to the imperial foundation narratives of Geoffrey and the *Brut*.

That same baronial class, though, equally had a stake in English territorial dominance in the Celtic areas of the British Isles. This would particularly be true of Trevisa's patron Thomas Berkeley, whose lands lay largely in Gloucestershire near the Welsh borderlands, as well as in Cornwall.[63] So while the legend of Arthurian conquest was an important precedent for both their insular and continental territorial ambitions, the further legend of his return from Avalon to redeem the Briton remnants could have been far from comfortable to readers like Berkeley. This is one reason that the remains of Arthur had already been "rediscovered," definitively dead, late in the reign of Henry II.[64] And it is surely one reason that Trevisa goes on to reject the story "that Arthur schal come aghe, and be eft kyng here of Britayne," calling it "a ful magel tale," a mangled story.[65] "Magel" is an interesting and rare term that Trevisa uses twice in rejecting the tale of Arthur's return; it means something bungled or botched, hacked, cut up.[66] It is the same term Trevisa had used earlier when arguing against William of Malmesbury (quoted above). So the notion of a bungled tale hedges in the Arthurian narrative on both sides here. It is a "magel tale" either to reject Arthur outright or preserve him as a redeemer of the Britons. Either version cuts into the imperial sentiments or local land tenure of Trevisa's baronial patron and his class.[67]

Trevisa thus argues forcefully for wholesale access to a "historical" Arthur whom he then anxiously delimits in the interests of a specific readership. This is another occasion when Trevisa asserts his own learned power and position, yet simultaneously negotiates around and accommodates the needs of his patron. It is a narrative gesture with analogies to the linguistic strategy for which I have argued above: a putatively easy and plain English, access to which is in fact qualified by its persistent registers of Latinity. And this contrasts, I have also suggested, with the rather more open, less controlled linguistic register of the *Brut* and its looser narration of the Arthurian story. I would like, now, to suggest an even more intense, if less controlled, version of such negotiations in the manuscripts of both works.

In 1305 Guy Beauchamp, earl of Warwick, gave away a French Brut text.[68] About a hundred years later, his descendant Richard, also earl of Warwick, owned a splendid copy of Trevisa's *Polychronicon*.[69] These two books exemplify a century's changes in the language of aristocratic reading and in some of its textual preferences. In the same decades that Richard Beauchamp had his Trevisa manuscript, further, we find evidence for growing mercantile ownership of the Middle English *Brut* chronicle. The surviving manuscripts of both works reflect, even enhance, the contrasting yet overlapping systems of access, prestige, and anxious control for which I have argued above.

Trevisa's *Polychronicon* survives in fourteen medieval manuscripts, of which thirteen are remarkably coherent in general style and grandeur of scale, consistent with their origin in high baronial patronage and (where known) their later ownership.[70] These are manuscripts of "folio" proportions, ambitiously produced in regard to page layout, handwriting, and often decoration.[71] Two have been located, on dialectal grounds, to the area of Berkeley Castle; on scribal or decorative grounds, five appear to be London productions; and three of those are linked by one scribe to the copying of such prestigious poets as John Gower.[72] They are grand books for grand owners.

Richard Beauchamp's copy exemplifies many of these points. It is carefully written in *Anglicana formata*—the formal English bookhand of the period—on good quality membrane, with a rather complex two-column page ruling that leaves generous blank margins.[73] In school texts, such marginal space is typically intended for the addition of annotations, even full commentaries. Here, and in other Trevisa *Polychronicon* manuscripts, its very blankness serves as a conspicuous display, especially when deployed (as here) with selective but elegant decoration.[74] The manuscript has two inhabited initials, beautifully executed decorated borders at the beginning of each work in the manuscript (and each book of the *Polychronicon*), and secondary capitals alternating blue and gold with contrasting infill.[75] In all these ways, it asserts its value and bespeaks the wealth and status of its owner.

If the costliness and display qualities of this manuscript establish its value as "cultural capital," removed both from the more practical aims of pedagogy and annotation and from access to less wealthy users, Additional 24194 and its cohort books nonetheless retain much of the practical learned apparatus of their Latin source. It is not unique, further, but it is worthy of comment that much of this apparatus is retained in Latin; and the presence of that language is emphasized by such means as rubrication and the hierarchy of hands. The English *Polychronicon* opens with a Latin index to topics and names in the text, cited by book and chapter; this is given precedence (in order, though not in decoration or writing) to an independent English index that immediately follows.[76] Latin chapter headings, in a larger hand,

and many Latin sources stand out in red within the columns; so do the multiple systems of dating, chapter numbers, and occasional topic headings—also in Latin—in the margins. The visual emphasis on Latin learning is most emphatic in the list of Latin authors and texts used as sources, entirely written in red.[77]

I have written elsewhere about Latin manuscripts, especially psalters and books of hours, whose images and vernacular headings provide "supported access" to the central text for users with limited Latin.[78] The presentation of Richard Beauchamp's *Polychronicon,* and others like it, I might call a system of "restrained access" to a vernacular text. Additional 24194 constantly reminds less educated viewers—if they came near so valuable an object—of what they do not know and of the Latin-oriented learned format that persists around Trevisa's translation. At the same time, the book reminds its aristocratic owners of the prestigious if limited Latin learning they do possess (as "Dominus" had noted in the "Dialogue") and of their ability to maneuver within the traditional learned page. Beauchamp's book stands in more than an ironical relationship to the Dialogue's claim of producing a history for the common run of English-speaking men. Rather, it encapsulates that offer of opening the textual restrictions of class (money, time, good will) within a book and page layout where many of those restraints are silently but clearly still in place.

When we turn to the enormous tradition of the *Brut,* the situation is far more diverse and less studied. Nonetheless, some broad observations can be made, largely in contrast to the English *Polychronicon* manuscripts. As noted earlier, at least forty-nine manuscripts of the Anglo-Norman *Brut* chronicle survive, another one hundred eighty-one of its Middle English translation and various extensions, and yet nineteen more of the Latin translation that was based on the Middle English.[79] Produced across the same decades, the Middle English *Brut* manuscripts, with few exceptions, are far more modest in scale and decoration than the *Polychronicon* manuscripts discussed above.[80] Many are copied in the more economical cursive bookhands of the period; most have a simple single-column page layout.[81] Their decoration, typically scribal, consists predominantly of enlarged capitals in red or red and blue, with rubricated English chapter titles either in the text frame or in the margins. There is generally less sense, then, of prestige production or the codex itself as a mediating, even controlling agent in access to the text. And at the same time, the simple listing of chapter headings and numbers in many manuscripts, along with their rubricated presence in the text, provide for easy access and navigation within the *Brut* narrative.[82]

While Middle English *Brut* manuscripts are owned by clergy and many gentry, neither in production nor ownership do they have the kind of high aristocratic setting traced above in the *Polychronicon* manuscripts. Rather, among lay persons, they circulate in the hands of modest provincial gentry and wealthy commoners (including a number of women) across England, including the growing urban merchant class, especially in London.[83] The later additions in Middle English, Matheson notes, "often reveal a marked interest in metropolitan affairs."[84]

This mixed, but notably urban and mercantile ownership is reflected in the *Brut*'s sources for later additions, which include London chronicles, and sometimes in the *Brut*'s companions within a single manuscript. In London, B. L. Egerton 650, for instance, the *Brut* (in the "Common Version" to 1419) is followed by a brief extension in the form of a London chronicle.[85] A colophon between the earlier *Brut* text and its extension in Egerton 650, further, helps suggest the speculative bookshop production of some of these manuscripts. The text breaks off incomplete, the colophon explains, "and that is be cause we wanted the trewe copy therof bot who so ever owys this boke may wryte it oute in the henderend of this boke or in the further end of it whene he gettes the trew copy."[86] This implies multiple people at work on the book and an owner who is as yet unknown. National history is being reshaped and repositioned in service to a changing and, to a large extent, new kind of audience; it participates thereby in an emerging urban identity.

I began this essay by proposing to trace some shifting, fractured, and ever-negotiated borders of identity, language, and class; and I proposed to do so through two historical texts whose versions of "English" (as language and as identity) strongly contrasted one another. To offer an argument based on such neatly polar categories (of text or class) is to ignore, inevitably, the denser complexity of the borderlands where these identities are negotiated and recreated. I close by glancing briefly at a few instances where, I think, we can see the borders in the process of shifting. I begin with Sir Thomas Berkeley himself. As Trevisa's patron and as a great landowner, Berkeley has repeatedly been my key instance of the aristocratic values buttressed and performed in the English *Polychronicon* and its manuscripts. But, as Ralph Hanna has shown in admirable detail, a good bit of Sir Thomas's wealth, hence his very ability to patronize translation, came from converting his land tenure into cash rental and from more direct involvement in shipping and urban trade.[87] The patrician qualities of his son-in-law's own copy might well be viewed as a costly but anxious assertion of a style of aristocratic identity that was under considerable pressure and transformation. At the same time, certain merchants were becoming very wealthy and aspiring to aristocratic titles and some of their appurtenances. In the later fifteenth century, the mercer William Purchas (chamberlain, alderman, and in 1497–98 mayor of London) may have owned one of the rare extensively illustrated copies of the *Brut*, Lambeth Palace 6, which includes his family's coat of arms.[88]

Just as owners can bump up against unstable borders of class, manuscripts too can shift across learned registers. Among the earliest *Polychronicon* manuscripts, Cotton Tiberius D.vii has an uncommon number of somewhat later English-language marginalia, some of which suggest a setting of English-language pedagogy.[89] This is intriguingly at odds with the sort of linguistic and codicological "restrained access" that I have outlined above. A reverse border-crossing, however, is suggested by the Middle English *Brut* manuscript, Huntington Library HM 136, whose margins are well filled with Latin notes and some Latin topic headings, in at least two fifteenth-century hands. The annotation includes a copy of the Latin "Bridlington Prophecy," distributed in the margins between folios 81v and 130r, as well as historical notes citing Geoffrey "the chronicler" and "Policronicam" [*sic*].[90]

Finally, another sort of aristocratic boundary—a financial one—seems to have been met by the mid- or late-fifteenth-century English *Polychronicon* manuscript, Huntington Library HM 28561.[91] A book of generous proportions (380 x 275 mm.), it is still not among the largest of Trevisa's translation; but its frame ruling and handwriting show a high level of discipline, as does the careful provision of catchwords, quire signatures, and numbered leaves within quires; there is, once again, a lavish display of blank space. More important, HM 28651 has among the most ambitious decorative programs of all the surviving copies, involving elaborate borders with gilding and many colors, coats of arms, as well as gold secondary initials on colored grounds. In large part, however, this is only a *program* of decoration. The earlier borders are completed, but increasingly they are only partly decorated, lacking gilding or colors; and, on later folios, they are merely sketched in.[92] Further, at folio 79r, either the scribe or his writing style changes markedly, from the earlier *Anglicana formata* to a more hurried cursive Secretary. Although it can be taken as no more than an emblem, this manuscript exemplifies a kind of aristocratic ambition that, if only in the form of a particular patron, has run out of steam—or cash. Its codicological gestures of wealth and prestige trickle away as the manuscript progresses; and the later, sporadic efforts to supply some of them are transparently ineffectual.

The idea of a national language sets up a boundary that is highly artificial and constructed, especially in the Middle Ages, as we have seen. Because it tries to yoke together ethnic, class, and political interests that are neither symmetrical nor neatly convergent, such a boundary is inherently unstable. Translation serves to import ideologically and culturally powerful texts into the national tongue; yet translation simultaneously emphasizes the existence of the constructed boundaries—of class, of learning, of prior and still influential languages—within that tongue. The translations and manuscripts I have examined here serve at once to occlude, display, and fragment the kind of contradictory but totalizing arguments we saw in the "Dialogue" between Trevisa and Sir Thomas Berkeley. They both police and trespass the borders they help draw. Nevertheless, even as they build and transgress social and linguistic borders, manuscripts like these are drawn into service to help create yet new social lines, new and emergent linguistic and historical identities.

Notes

This essay has been long in taking its current form. For early responses and suggestions I am grateful to Judith Ferster, Frank Brady, Judith Bennett, and Maíre Cruise O'Brien. More recently, I am indebted to participants at the Harlaxton Symposium of 2003, to my colleague Gordon Kipling, my student Margaret Lamont, and above all to the suggestions of Robert Stein.

　　1. For a general discussion, see Seth Lerer, "Old English and Its Afterlife" in *The Cambridge History of Medieval English Literature,* ed. David Wallace (Cambridge: Cambridge University Press, 1999), 7–34.
　　2. For the institutional roles of Latin, and competing languages of authority, see Christopher Baswell, "Latinitas," in Wallace, *The Cambridge History,* 122–42.
　　3. *The "Historia Regum Britanniae" of Geoffrey of Monmouth* I: Bern, Burgerbibliothek MS. 568, ed. Neil Wright (Cambridge: D. S. Brewer, 1985), 1. Translated by Lewis Thorpe, *The History of the Kings of Britain* (Harmondsworth: Penguin, 1966), 51. Any consideration of Geoffrey of Monmouth must acknowledge the fundamental influence of the superb discussion by Robert W. Hanning in *The Vision of History in Early Britain from Gildas to Geoffrey of Monmouth* (New York: Columbia University Press, 1966), 121–76.
　　4. Kellie Robertson, "Geoffrey of Monmouth and the Translation of Insular Historiography," *Arthuriana* 8 (1998): 42. Her article offers a probing argument for the ecclesiastical and political context of Geoffrey's linguistic and rhetorical strategies. Geoffrey's cunning claim to a doubly exclusive access to the past through an arcane language and a unique book may help explain the virulence with which some historians received his *Historia.* William of Newburgh's response in his *Historia rerum*

Anglicarum is probably the most famous; he calls Geoffrey's history "ridicula . . . fig-menta." *Chronicles of the Reigns of Stephen, Henry II, and Richard I,* ed. Richard How-lett (London: Rolls Series, 1884), 1:11–15.

5. Developments during the reign of Edward III are surveyed by W. M. Ormrod, "The Use of English: Language, Law, and Political Culture in Fourteenth-Century England," *Speculum* 78 (2003): 750–87. The Wycliffite context is ex-plored (among many other places) in Anne Hudson, *The Premature Reformation: Wycliffite Texts and Lollard History* (Oxford: Clarendon Press, 1988), chap. 9, "The Context of Vernacular Wycliffism," 390–445; and in Fiona Somerset, *Clerical Dis-course and Lay Audience in Late Medieval England* (Cambridge: Cambridge Uni-versity Press, 1998).

6. For the particular implications of translation in Geoffrey of Monmouth, see Robertson's entire article, "Geoffrey of Monmouth," 42–57.

7. Of course the accuracy of Virgil's imperial narrative had detractors as early as the Augustan historians. The relative antiquity of texts, anyway, often got quite fuzzy in late medieval writers' minds, as in the *Laud Troy Book,* whose redac-tor seems to think that Guido lived soon after Dares and Dictys. See Christopher Baswell, *Virgil in Medieval England* (Cambridge: Cambridge University Press, 1995), 17–21.

8. *Brut or the Chronicles of England,* ed. F. W. D. Brie, E.E.T.S., o.s. 131, 136 (London: Early English Text Society, 1906, 1908). For the background and popu-larity of the work, see John Taylor, *English Historical Literature in the Fourteenth Cen-tury* (Oxford: Clarendon Press, 1987), 110–32. For a magisterial survey of the many redactions of the *Brut* and its manuscripts, see Lister M. Matheson, *The Prose Brut: The Development of a Middle English Chronicle* (Tempe, Ariz.: Medieval and Renais-sance Texts and Studies, 1998).

9. Matheson, *The Prose Brut,* pp. xvi–xxxii, 6–8. The Wycliffite Bible is rep-resented by more than 230 copies.

10. Taylor, *English Historical Literature,* 113.

11. Ibid., 113–19. Matheson, *The Prose Brut,* 1–16. Much of this project had been accomplished by later twelfth-century and thirteenth-century historiographers working in Latin. For this process and its backgrounds in a split between the histo-riographies of secular and monastic clerics, see the superb article by Francis Ingle-dew, "The Book of Troy and the Genealogical Construction of History: The Case of Geoffrey of Monmouth's *Historia regum Britanniae,*" *Speculum* 69 (1994): 665–704, esp. 681–700.

12. *Brut,* o.s. 131: 83, 88. All further *Brut* quotes are from this, the first volume of Brie's edition.

13. For the broader context of genealogy in the rise of medieval secular his-toriography, and the return of the Trojan story as mediated through Virgil, see Ingle-dew, "Book of Troy," 668–76.

14. As told in the *Brut,* Brutus is the child of Eneas's grandson, Sylveyn, who slept incestuously with "a damysell that was Cosyn to Lamane . . . that was Eneas wyf, and brought the damysell with Chylde" (5). Arthur is famously conceived when Uter, magically made to look like her husband the Earl of Cornwall, sleeps with Igerne (67). In all Middle English quotations that follow, I modernize thorn and yogh, and distinguish vocalic u and consonantal v.

15. *Brut,* 8.

16. *Brut,* 72–76.

17. *Brut,* 12. Here, as often, the geography of the *Brut* is rather muddled.

18. *Brut,* 78–80.

19. *Brut,* 82–89.

20. *Brut,* 82.

21. Matheson has provided an enormous service in untangling and classifying the enormously complex versions of the Middle English *Brut.* Even with his unstinting labors, however, many versions remain, as Matheson calls them, "peculiar" or unclassified. See Matheson, *Prose Brut,* 49–54, 256–338.

22. The precise date of the Middle English translation of the *Brut* remains uncertain. Matheson dates it 1380–1400 (ibid., 47–48). Taylor, *English Historical Literature,* 127, places it in the "middle years of the fourteenth century," perhaps depending on Brie.

23. A short version ends with 1327; and Higden was at work on the longest version at his death in the 1360s. John Taylor, *The Universal Chronicle of Ranulf Higden* (Oxford: Clarendon Press, 1966), chap. 6, "The Development of the Text," 89–109. Other hands, in various monastic centers, contributed further extensions for the rest of the fourteenth and the early fifteenth century (110–33). See also Taylor, *English Historical Literature,* 95–103

24. Taylor, *Universal Chronicle,* 140–44. A. S. G. Edwards, "The Influence and Audience of the *Polychronicon:* Some Observations," *Proceedings of the Leeds Philosophical and Literary Society* 17 (1980): 113–19. For records of some monastic owners in the third quarter of the fourteenth century, see A. B. Emden, *Donors of Books to S. Augustine's Abbey Canterbury,* Oxford Bibliographical Society, Occasional Papers no. 4 (Oxford: Oxford Bibliographical Society, 1968), 5, 6, 18. Particularly interesting among these is Thomas Arnold, active in the 1360s and 1370s, who also owned Guido delle Colonne's *Historia destructionis Troiae* and French Arthurian romances; that is to say, texts from all three of the major historical and legendary traditions dealt with in this paper.

25. Edwards, "Influence and Audience of the *Polychronicon,*" 114–15.

26. *Polychronicon,* book 1, chap. 39 (part 2, pages 7 and 3). *Polychronicon Ranulphi Higden,* ed. C. Babington and J. R. Lumby, 9 vols. (London: Rolls Series, 1865–86). I cite by book and chapter, then part and page number, hence the above reference reads 1:39 (2.7 and 2.3).

27. *Polychronicon* 2:19, and 2:24 (2.379, 381, 407).

28. *Polychronicon* 2:27 (2.440–43). The collocation is intriguing, though, since *Ruth* too is a narrative of exile, return, and shifting ethnic identity.

29. *Polychronicon* 1:3 (1.26–27).

30. *Polychronicon* 1:4 (1.35–36). For Higden's careful and informed discussion of varying year counts, see *Polychronicon* 1:4 (1.35–41).

31. See the editors' introduction, part 1, xiii. Higden really agonizes over problems of year counts, foundation dates, and repeated or skipped generations in antique genealogies; this gets him especially exercised in relation to the chronological difficulty of Aeneas ever meeting Dido (2.432–33) or the generations between Aeneas and Brutus (2.442–43). This hesitation and concern add to the impression of documentary accuracy.

32. *Polychronicon* 2:25 (2.418–19).

33. *Polychronicon* 2:17 (2.357).

34. *Polychronicon* 2:17 (2.356–63).

35. *Polychronicon* 2:18 (2.362–79).

36. *Polychronicon* 2:17 (2.355). We will see related distinctions applied to Arthurian story by Trevisa, below.

37. Taylor, *English Historical Literature*, 97.

38. While there is no immediate parallel for so ambitious a translation of Latin history into Middle English, it was around the same time, as noted above, that the Anglo-Norman *Brut* became available in English and began its enormous popularity in that form. And, in the same general time, Nicholas Trevet's Anglo-Norman *Chronicles* appeared in a Middle English version that survives in only one manuscript; see Taylor, *English Historical Literature*, 94–95. For the socioeconomic setting of Trevisa's translation, see the excellent article by Ralph Hanna III, "Sir Thomas Berkeley and His Patronage," *Speculum* 64 (1989): 878–916.

39. Ronald Waldron, "Trevisa's Original Prefaces on Translation: A Critical Edition," *Medieval English Studies Presented to George Kane*, eds. E. D. Kennedy, R. Waldron, and J. S. Wittig (Woodbridge, Suffolk: Brewer, 1988), 285–99; see 289. The dialogue is also partly available, with helpful introduction and bibliography, in *The Idea of the Vernacular: an Anthology of Middle English Literary Theory, 1280–1520*, ed. Jocelyn Wogan-Browne et al. (University Park: Pennsylvania State University Press, 1999), 130–34. See also Hanna, "Sir Thomas Berkeley," 895–96.

40. Waldron, "Prefaces," 290.

41. Ibid., 292. The *persona* of Clericus should be distinguished from Trevisa himself, who associated with Wyclif at Oxford and may, David Fowler suggests, have had some hand in the Wycliffite Bible; see *The Life and Times of John Trevisa, Medieval Scholar* (Seattle and London: University of Washington Press, 1995), 227–29.

42. "Thanne what hath Englysch trespassed that hyt myght noght be translated into Englysch?" Waldron, "Prefaces," 292.

43. Ibid., 293.

44. Ibid.

45. See also Ronald Waldron, "John Trevisa and the Use of English," *Proceedings of the British Academy* 74 (1988): 177.

46. For an excellent discussion, see Traugott Lawler, "On the Properties of John Trevisa's Major Translations" *Viator* 14 (1983): 267–88. See also Waldron, "John Trevisa," 189–99.

47. *Polychronicon* 2:26 (2.433).

48. *Polychronicon* 2:18 (2.371; see another Latin etymology at 2.387).

49. He explains the sense and syllables in Iulus's name, *Polychronicon* 2:26 (2.437). He also adds information about Latin regarding the name of Silvius Postumus (2.439).

50. *Polychronicon* 2:23 (2.400–401).

51. *Polychronicon* 1:25 (1.239); 1:49 (2.85).

52. Waldron, "Prefaces," 290.

53. For example, *Polychronicon* 1:1 (1.11–13).

54. *Polychronicon* 1:23 (1.199).

55. For a survey of the Arthurian debate in Higden and Trevisa, see John E. Housman, "Higden, Trevisa, Caxton, and the Beginnings of Arthurian Criticism," *Review of English Studies* 23 (1947): 209–17. Housman suggests that Trevisa's enthusiasm for Arthur may result from his own connections to his Cornish birthplace and the Celtic world (214). Ronald Waldron, "Trevisa's 'Celtic Complex' Revisited," *Notes and Queries* 36 (234) (1989): 303–7, rejects this notion, since Trevisa "belonged to an English-speaking ascendancy in a county where, in any case, the Celtic language was extinct in the east and declining even in the west" (304). But given the national quality Arthur had taken on by this time, Waldron's objection seems overstated. Further, the very colonialist status of Trevisa and his Welsh marcher patron might encourage an "all-Britain" cooptation of the Arthurian legend. Certainly a fourteenth-century reader needed no command of Celtic tongues to gain access to Arthurian legend.

56. "Hic est Arthurus de quo nugae Britonum delirant." Trevisa's translation: "This [is] Arthur, of whom the Britoun that goth out of the weye telleth many idel tales." *Polychronicon* 5:6 (5.330–31).

57. Higden does not give an author, but this text is clearly Geoffrey of Monmouth, or one of the Brut narratives closely based on Geoffrey.

58. *Polychronicon* 5:6 (5.330–33). For a fascinating discussion of the "discovery" of the remains of Arthur and its swift entry into Latin narratives, see Antonia Gransden, "The Growth of the Glastonbury Traditions and Legends in the Twelfth Century," in *Legends, Traditions, and History in Medieval England* (London and Rio Grande: Hambledon, 1992), 153–74, esp. 165–74.

59. *Polychronicon* 5:6 (5.336–37).

60. *Polychronicon* 5:6 (5.336–37).

61. *Polychronicon* 5:6 (5.337).

62. *Polychronicon* 5:6 (5.339).

63. See Hanna, "Sir Thomas Berkeley," 880–82.

64. See Gransden, "Glastonbury Traditions."

65. *Polychronicon* 5:6 (5.339).

66. See *Middle English Dictionary:* "magel" and "maglen."

67. In Trevisa's discussion of Arthur, moreover, we may be witnessing yet further negotiation (stemming from Geoffrey of Monmouth and by now ancient) across divisions of ethnicity. This is a debated point, but Trevisa's probable Cornish birthplace could link him sympathetically to Celtic peoples and themes, even if he himself were of Anglo-Norman stock. See Fowler, *John Trevisa,* 11–23; Housman, "Higden"; and Waldron "Celtic Complex." As we have seen, Trevisa uses the issue of access to "the Brittische book" to weaken William of Malmesbury's authority regarding Arthurian history. But Trevisa is also careful to limit the impact of Celtic Arthurianism, to make it merely nostalgic, by rejecting the idea of Arthur's return.

68. It was perhaps the Anglo-Norman *Brut,* perhaps Wace's *Roman de Brut,* or a similar narrative. In 1310 Henry de Lacy, earl of Lincoln, commissioned from Rauf de Boun a short *Brut* whose sources remain unclear; Isabella of France (d. 1358) left a *Brut* to her son Edward III. See Matheson, *Prose Brut,* 9–11; Rauf de Boun, *Le Petit Bruit,* ed. Diana B. Tyson (London: Anglo-Norman Text Society, 1987).

69. MS London, B. L. Additional 24194. For a full description, see Kathleen L. Scott, *Later Gothic Manuscripts 1390–1490* (London: Harvey Miller, 1996), vol. 2, no. 19: 82–83; and vol. 1: illust. 81, 84. Scott dates the manuscript 1401–8. Also Ronald Waldron, "The Manuscripts of Trevisa's Translation of the *Polychronicon:* Towards a New Edition," *Modern Language Quarterly* 51 (1990): 281–317, esp. 286–87 and 309. Richard Beauchamp may also have owned Digby 233, the unique manuscript of Trevisa's translation of Giles of Rome's *De regimine principum;* see Hanna, "Sir Thomas Berkeley," 897–98.

70. They represent two divergent text traditions, however. Waldron, "Manuscripts." The anomalous manuscript (Cambridge, Corpus Christi College 354) is later (15/16c.) and much smaller than the others; Waldron speculates it may have been a hasty copy-text intended for better manuscripts (288).

71. Nine range 340–95 x 240–85 mm.; four are larger still, 395–450 x 290–320 mm. (the grouping is loose, as margins have certainly been trimmed in rebinding.). Of the latter group, two (BL Addit. 24194 and Oxford, St. John's H 1 = 204) and probably a third (Princeton Garrett 151) are copied by the London "scribe Delta" who also copied Gower manuscripts; for the scribe, see the classic essay by A. I. Doyle and Malcolm Parkes, "The Production of Copies of the *Canterbury Tales* and the *Confessio Amantis* in the Early Fifteenth Century," in *Medieval Scribes, Manuscripts, and Libraries: Essays Presented to N. R. Ker,* ed. Malcolm Parkes and Andrew G. Wat-

son (London: Scolar, 1978), 163–210; also Hanna, "Sir Thomas Berkeley," 909–10. The one surviving manuscript certainly owned by Thomas Berkeley himself (Bodley 953) is of the same proportions; see Hanna, "Sir Thomas Berkeley," 883–84.

72. Berkeley area: London, B. L. Cotton Tiberius D.vii and Manchester, Chetham's Library 11379; Waldron, "Manuscripts," 310, 314. London scribe Delta, see note 71. London decoration: St. John's H 1 = 204 (by scribe Delta); Aberdeen, University Library 21; Oslo and London, Schøyen 194; Scott, *Later Gothic Manuscripts*, vol. 2: 82. For further discussion of the Berkeley area manuscripts, dating, and facsimiles from four manuscripts, see Ronald Waldron, "Dialect Aspects of Manuscripts of Trevisa's Translation of the *Polychronicon*," in *Regionalism in Late Medieval Manuscripts and Texts*, ed. Felicity Riddy (Cambridge: D. S. Brewer, 1991), 67–87, esp. 68–75.

73. Ralph Hanna comments on a similar "display of tasteful magnificence" in a manuscript of Richard Rolle's English Psalter produced for Thomas Berkeley, Bodley 953; see "Sir Thomas Berkeley," 883–84. There are occasional marginal notes in Additional 24194, some roughly contemporary but rather more of later date. Of the fourteen known manuscripts, ten are in two-column format. Of the remaining four, one is the late Corpus Christi College 354; two are the early manuscripts linked to the Berkeley Castle area (Cot. Tib. D.vii and Chetham's Library 11379); the fourth is the (relatively) modest Harley 1900. See Waldron, "Manuscripts," 309–17.

74. The margins of London, B. L. Cotton Tiberius D.vii are an exception; see below.

75. For a full description, see Scott, *Later Gothic Manuscripts*, vol. 2, no. 19: 82–83. Both initials are reproduced at vol. 1: illust. 81 and 84. Folios 214r and 214v are reproduced in Waldron, "Manuscripts," plates 4 and 5. The inhabited initial at the start of the *Polychronicon* shows Higden at his desk, a frequent motif both in Latin and English copies.

76. Among the manuscripts with extant indices, eight include both Latin and English, always in that order; three have the English index alone.

77. Folio 37r. The early Cotton Tiberius D.vii shows a similar visual emphasis on Latin, as does Huntington Library HM 28561. Not all manuscripts are equally emphatic in these matters. The generally more modest Harley 1900 provides Latin topic headings in the margins, but not consistently in red. It gives the list of Latin authorities (beginning folio 45r) but in the ink of the main text, with only the first entry underlined in red; the rest are picked out only with a standard red paraph mark, frequent throughout the manuscript.

78. Baswell, "Latinitas," 142–44.

79. Matheson, *Prose Brut*, xvii–xx, 4–7. While Matheson's primary attention is to the textual tradition, not the codicology of the *Brut*, his catalog nonetheless greatly expands our knowledge of ownership and production of these books. Our

understanding of the manuscripts and their impact will take an enormous leap with the cooperative project based at Queen's University Belfast under the direction of Professor John Thompson, "Imagining History: medieval texts, contexts, and communities in the English *Brut* tradition"; for a prospectus, see http://www.qub.ac.uk/imagining-history.

80. They are mostly in the "quarto" range. Some typical sizes are San Marino, Huntington Library, HM 113 (257 x 172 mm.), HM 131 (199 x 165 mm.), HM 133 (284 x 185 mm.), and Ann Arbor, University of Michigan, Hatcher Library MS 225 (288 x 205 mm.)

81. There are of course exceptions. In San Marino, Huntington Library HM 113, the text is carefully written within a very consistent, fairly elaborate, indeed almost decorative frame ruling in red ink.

82. I owe this point to my student, Margaret Lamont.

83. See Matheson, *Prose Brut*, 12 – 14; again, such comments can be far more nuanced as the interim results of the "Imagining History" project begin to appear.

84. Ibid., 48.

85. Ibid., 100 – 101, 311 – 12. Matheson lists another five manuscripts where "appended material is left in the typical annalistic civic chronicle format," 13. See also Taylor, *English Historical Literature*, 123, 146. To these, I would add London, B. L. Egerton 2885, with an intriguing Latin summary of the Brut included in a collection of documents (mostly also in Latin, some French) relating to the London Fishmongers, about 1395.

86. Folio 111r; Matheson, *Prose Brut*, 101.

87. Hanna, "Sir Thomas Berkeley," 886 – 87, 906 – 9.

88. Matheson, *Prose Brut*, 298 – 99. The *Brut* could also be drawn into more traditionally aristocratic contexts, as in the case of Oxford, Bodleian, Laud. Misc. 733. This illustrated manuscript begins with the *De arte heraldica* of Johannes de Bado Aureo, followed by a Middle English *Brut*. See Scott, *Later Gothic Manuscripts*, vol. 1: illust. 373, 374; vol. 2, no. 97: 271 – 73; and Matheson, 266 – 67. The decoration at folio 1, with a coat of arms, suggests to Scott "that this book was ordered by a patron of considerable social status" (2:271).

89. The marginalia have often been trimmed in rebinding. One marginal list in English (folio 44v, at book 1, chap. 48) offers simple explanations of the pagan gods: "[M]ars godde of battell," "[Ve]nus godde of love," etc. Pointing hands with English notes draw attention to the arrival of new races, folio 50r. More telling, the English annotator (who can also use Latin), often puts his notes in the form of a question: folio 58r, "Who was Abraha[| ffader."

90. See the description by Consuelo Dutschke, *Guide to Medieval and Renaissance Manuscripts in the Huntington Library* (San Marino, Calif.: Huntington Library, 1989), 1:181 – 83; also Matheson, *Prose Brut*, 123 – 24, 163 – 64; and for later ownership by "Mistress Dorothy Helbartun," see Josephine K. Tarvers, "'Thys ys my

mystrys boke': English Women as Readers and Writers in Late Medieval England," in *The Uses of Manuscripts in Literary Studies: Essays in Memory of Judson Boyce Allen,* ed. Charlotte Morse, Penelope R. Doob, Marjorie C. Woods (Kalamazoo, Mich.: Medieval Institute Publications, 1992), 319–20.

91. For a full description, see Dutschke, *Guide,* 2:683–87.

92. Some were finished later in a coarse, almost amateur style, e.g., folio 82r, 85r, 88r (notably, following the change of hands). See Dutschke, *Guide,* 2:686 for details.

8

SUZANNE CONKLIN AKBARI

The Hunger for National Identity in *Richard Coer de Lion*

The hero of the *Romaunce of Richard Coer de Lion* is an aggressively English king: he leads men "of Englysshe blode," wields an axe "wroughte in Ynglande," and falls ill while on Crusade because he longs for a taste of the pork he ate at home.[1] He is almost supernaturally strong, a strength that shades over into a strangeness that the romance grounds firmly in Richard's maternal heritage: this English king is born of a woman who appears almost magically on the becalmed seas and who disappears by flying up and away from the chapel where her English husband, Henry, hears mass. Richard's identity, then, is founded on a paradox: this most English of English kings is a monstrous half-breed (half human and half faery), in the tradition of Merlin and Alexander.[2] The stress on English identity found in this romance has recently elicited readings that suggest that *Richard Coer de Lion* participates in the "discourse" of nationalism as it was manifested during the later Middle Ages. For Alan Ambrisco, the intersection of English, French, and Saracen national identities is what gives rise to the expression of English nationalism; for Geraldine Heng, who builds on the work of Diane Speed, *Richard Coer de Lion* is the most fully developed manifestation of a tendency, in medieval romance, to identify the hero with the nation he leads, so that his origin and destiny come to stand for that of the people as a whole.[3] Romance is presented as one of the main vehicles through which medieval English nationalism is expressed.

Yet both Ambrisco and Heng underestimate the importance of one crucial aspect of the expression of nationalism in *Richard Coer de Lion:* that is, the theological language and symbolism used to depict the nature of Richard's link to the nation he represents and the manner in which his actions and his very being serve to unite the community of the English. To argue that the romance participates in a "discourse" of nationalism is to invoke a Foucauldian paradigm that leaves little room for the involvement of religious modes of thought.[4] That is not to say that Heng or Ambrisco ignores the role of religion in the romance: for Heng, religion functions as "an expressly national resource," while Ambrisco suggests that the text includes "discursive strategies based alternately on Christian and nationalist propaganda."[5] Yet to characterize religion in this way is to assume that it is simply a tool of the nation, a mode of discourse that can be adapted to other, secular ends. I will argue instead that the discourse of nation in the *Romaunce of Richard Coer de Lion* relies upon eucharistic symbolism in which the community is united through a sacrificial act, performed by one of its members on behalf of the group as a whole. Far from being a mere embellishment of a fundamentally secular paradigm, eucharistic symbolism is the framework out of which the discourse of nation emerges, with the king located at the same liminal point inhabited by the priest who celebrates the mass.

In the following pages, I will first outline the presentation of English national identity in *Richard Coer de Lion,* both as it is presented directly and as it is delineated indirectly by contrast with French and Saracen identity. Second, I will go on to illustrate how several acts of eating in the romance function as public performances in which the bonds of community are either reaffirmed or broken, depending upon whether or not the feast is completed. The assimilation of the food consumed, a process in which matter is absorbed to become part of the body, alters the identity of both him who consumes the food and of the community on whose behalf he consumes it. Richard's hunger for English food is what impels him to eat Saracen flesh, assimilate to himself Saracen identity, and thus give rise to a reformulated English identity in which all his followers can partake. Finally, I will describe how religion functions in the constitution of national identity, both in scholarly accounts of modern nationalism and in the context of early fifteenth-century England, where Lancastrian efforts to promote a distinctively English national identity through the official use of the English language came into conflict with

Lollard efforts to employ the vernacular in preaching, at trial, and in study of the Bible. The eucharistic symbolism of *Richard Coer de Lion* proves to exemplify the intertwining of religious and royal authority promoted by Henry IV and his chancellor, Archbishop Arundel.

English National Identity

Diane Speed has argued that national identity, in medieval romance, is predicated on the identity of the hero. This is certainly true in *Richard Coer de Lion*, in which Richard's English identity, paradoxically based on heterogeneous and mysterious origins, gives rise to an English national identity that is comparably composite and that is fully realized only far away from England itself, in the encounter with Saracen enemies and French (false) friends. The *Romaunce of Richard Coer de Lion*, which was one of the most popular romances of its time,[6] survives in two versions, although the manuscript evidence overlaps somewhat: a number of fantastic embellishments, which overshadow the essentially historically accurate base narrative, appear in some (but not all) of the fifteenth-century manuscript witnesses.[7] In some of the fifteenth-century manuscripts, such as British Museum Harley 4690 and College of Arms Arundel 58, the historical content of the romance is clearly emphasized by the surrounding context, and the fabulous embellishments are absent; in others, however, such as Cambridge Gonville and Caius 175 and the London Thornton manuscript, the legendary elements are emphasized. These include Richard's maternal origins, his superhuman chivalric skills, and the dramatic scenes of cannibalism.

Alan Ambrisco locates the origins of Richard's extreme fierceness and strength in his "barbarity," a kind of "subhuman" quality that derives from his maternal genealogy: he is a "demon." Yet to identify this aspect of Richard as barbaric or subhuman is to tell only part of the story, for Richard is not subhuman, but superhuman; not simply barbaric, but ultra-English. Before considering the elements in Richard that constitute his English identity, let us consider the supernatural elements. The romance opens with a brief description of the unmarried king of England, Henry; meanwhile, in a faraway kingdom, a king named Corbaryng has a dream that he should bring his beautiful daughter Cassodorien to England. The daughter marries the English king and bears him three children: Richard, John, and a daughter named Topyas. But the queen has a problem: if she is present in the church at the elevation of the Host, she faints. As a result, the queen soon develops the habit of withdrawing before that point in the mass. The king's nobles object to this behavior and demand that the queen be forcibly kept in the church for the duration of the mass. What they evidently suspected turns out to be true: just before the elevation of the Host, the queen flies out of the church, taking her younger son John and daughter Topyas with her, and is never seen again. Richard's fierceness, then, can be explained by his parentage. His mother is some kind of unnatural being, and Richard's deviation from the norm must therefore come from her. Yet the mother's magical powers are only one aspect of the legacy she leaves her son; for the faraway country she comes from is in the Near East: Cassodorien's father, Corbaryng, is the king of Antioch, the last great stronghold besieged by the crusaders en route to Jerusalem. This suggests that, paradoxically, Richard's ability to be a western conqueror comes from his eastern origin. The territory he seeks to conquer, in a sense, already belongs to him. For its account of the origins of Richard's mother in Antioch, along with the scenes of cannibalism to be discussed in the second section of this essay, the late medieval redactor of the expanded version of *Richard Coer de Lion* drew upon the *Chanson d'Antioche*, taking the name of Cassodorien's father from the name "Corbarans," leader of the Saracens (the historical Kerbogha). This adaptation would have seemed natural in view of the fact that Corbarans was said to have ultimately converted to Christianity and fought on the side of the crusaders, a story recounted in the thirteenth-century *Chrétienté Corbaran*, one of the continuations of the Jerusalem cycle.[8] Through his maternal lineage, then, Richard lays claim to both supernatural powers and legitimate descent from the former Saracen rulers of Antioch and its region.

From the opening lines of the romance, Richard is presented as an English king: the poet laments the lack of "jestes" devoted to the "doughty knyghtes off Yngelonde," and offers as a remedy the present narrative "Off a kyng, doughty in dede: / Kyng Rychard, the werryour beste / that men fynde in ony jeste" (27–32). While Richard's claim to the English throne comes through his father, "Kyng Henry" receives only cursory attention in the romance. That this romance is based in the reign of the Plantagenet kings is made clear by the reference to this being the time when "Seynt Thomas was islawe / At Cauntyrbury" (40–41), although the description of "Kyng Henry" as a weak ruler, led by his nobles both to take a wife and subsequently to disown her, accords poorly with the historical Henry II. It is Richard's deeds, however, more than his genealogy that make manifest his English identity, an identity that is expressed in the romance in four different modes: language, place, blood, and goods. The importance of the English language is apparent both in the telling of the romance itself and in the language used within the narrative. In the opening lines, the poet states that "Lewede men cune Ffrensch non" (23), which creates a need for romances written in English. Subsequently in the narrative, the use of English is pointed out explicitly, as when a knight approaches Richard and tells him "Tales in Englyssh, stoute and bolde" (1916). Englishness is also manifest in the narrative with regard to place, conceived in regional as well as national terms: the knights who will go on crusade with Richard are initially marshaled at "Londoun, that cite" (named three times in seventeen lines [1247–63]), and are feasted at "Westemynstyr" (1343). Once the crusaders face Saladin and his armies, they welcome reinforcements "comen ffro Yngelonde" (2963). England appears in the romance not just as temporal homeland, but as counterpart to that spiritual homeland represented by Palestine. In preparation for the crusade, Richard and two of his most trusted men, disguised as pilgrims, secretly visit Jerusalem and its surrounding territory. An account of their itinerary ends: "Thus they vysytyd the Holy Land, / How they myght wynne it to here hand; / And seththen homward they hem dyght, / To Yngelond with al here myght" (647–50). Here, the "Holy Land" and "Yngelond" are the two end points of a journey, each of them both beginning and end: the journey from England to the Holy Land spurs the journey from the Holy Land to England (to marshal the crusade), which in turn spurs the subsequent journey of crusade from England to the Holy Land.

Far more than language or territory, however, blood or lineal descent is the most common way of defining Englishness in *Richard Coer de Lion*. The romance refers repeatedly to the "Englysshe" and "Englysshmen," as well as "Englysshe peple" (1660), "the ffolk Englysch" (3057), and so on. Often these are specified as "our Englyssh" (2069) or, of Richard, "hys Englyssh" (6035, 6479). These men are "Iborn of Ynglyssche nacyoun" (3930), in the fundamental sense of "nation" as denoting birth, whether the territory in which one is born or one's parentage. They are of "Englysshe blode" (1953), set against the "hethene blood" (4675) they seek to destroy. English identity, based in language, territory, and blood, is further affirmed in the romance by the goods and objects one uses. This is evident in the weapons used by Richard in his effort to take Jerusalem: the axe and the "Mate-Gryffon," a small tower or "castell" used to attack fortified cities in siege warfare. Even before the major engagements in the crusade against the Saracen enemy, the English become involved in a preliminary skirmish against those who should rightly be their allies, the French and the Griffons (Greeks). Richard, outraged against those who "haue dyspysed our nacyons," proposes the use of a "castell . . . made of tembre of Englonde," henceforth to be known as the "Mate-Gryffon" (1848–50, 1856). The use of English materials in the weapon both guarantees its efficacy (one is reminded of early twentieth-century paeans to "good British steel") and makes the weapon into a metonymic representative of the warrior himself. This is evident in Richard's weapon of choice, not the more usual chivalric sword but rather an axe "that was wroughte in Ynglande" (6802). It is a superhuman weapon, with a head weighing "twenty pounde of stele," commissioned by Richard "Or [before] he wente out of Englonde . . . To breke therwith the Sarasyns bones" (2210–14). Like the Mate-Gryffon, the axe is as English as the man who wields it.

Richard's preferred weapon is an odd choice for a king: the axe is a plebeian tool, used by foot-soldiers and (according to Giraldus Cambrensis) Irish guerrillas.[9] In the romances, giants use axes while knights use swords; the only knight to use an axe is the Saracen prince Ferumbras (and even that in only one of the Middle English versions of *Ferumbras*).[10] In the *Chanson de Roland,* Roland rebukes Oliver at great length for striking the enemy with his "bastun" (the broken shaft of his spear) and neglecting his sword.[11] In spite of the base nature of his weapon, Richard destroys his enemy with the efficacy of Roland and Oliver: he "Schede[s] the Sarazynes blood and brayn" (272), eviscerating and even cutting his enemies' bodies in half (2569–78, 3129–36, 7049–52). The unconventional nature of Richard's preferred weapon is clearly important in the romance, for it is referred to frequently and even merits prominent illustration in the Auchinleck manuscript.[12] To be English thus means more than simply being born of English parents: it is to display certain behaviors different from those of other nations—to use a battle-ax made in "Englonde" (2212), to long for the "mete and drynk" that one finds "in Yngelonde" (3046–48). The use of and desire for English materials is, in large measure, constitutive of Richard's English identity.

While Englishness is directly evoked in *Richard Coer de Lion*—English men, English blood, the English nation, English goods, and so on—it is also indirectly evoked through comparison with other peoples, most notably the Saracens and the French. Several critics have noted the extent to which French identity is the necessary counterpart to the expression of English identity in the romance. Alan Ambrisco argues that, in the poem, France is an "other who is too close for comfort," so that English "ambivalence" regarding the French identity of the historical Richard I requires that the French be condemned in no uncertain terms.[13] Geraldine Heng suggests the romance engages in "a strategic act of forgetting," in which the French ties of the royal family are erased and an English heritage substituted.[14] The conflict of the English and the French in the romance is largely centered on the personal conflict between their two kings, one full of virtue, the other full of vice. From the outset, the intentions of the French king are clearly duplicitous, a fact Richard himself recognizes: "Richard sawe and vnderstode / the King of Fraunce wolde hym no gode" (1747–48). Philip repeatedly shows himself to be morally weak relative to Richard, willing to accept payment from the Saracens in exchange for abandoning the siege of their position. Like Richard, Philip falls ill while on crusade; but while Richard pursues his aims, even strengthened by the nourishment he takes to combat his illness (to be described further in the next section), the French king abandons the fight when he falls ill. The poet relates that, "he myght nought hool ben" (5915), a state of being that reflects Philip's inadequacy. Like Richard, Philip is representative of his people. An account of Philip's deception of Richard (3833–40) concludes by summarizing the French national character: "Ffrenssche men arn arwe and ffeynte, / And Sarezynys be war, and queynte, / And off here dedes engynous; / the Ffrenssche men be couaytous" (3849–52). This comparison of the "Ffrenssche" and "Sarezynys" suggests that the two are similar; the English must therefore be as different from the French as they are from the Saracens. If anything, they are more similar to the Saracens than to the French, for the qualities attributed to the Saracens—who are "war," "queynte," and "engynous"—are also qualities attributed to Richard himself, and which he increasingly shares with his men.[15] The comparison of the French and the Saracens implicitly distinguishes English identity more sharply from that of the French than that of the Saracens. In this context, it makes sense that the poem locates Richard's maternal origin not in France but in the East: Eleanor of Aquitaine, the Provençal mother of the historical Richard, former wife of the king of France, is replaced by the eastern princess Cassodorien. The choice of Antioch as the place of Cassodorien's origin may have its source in the abundant invective directed against Eleanor, some of which centers on her ties to the East. William of Tyre and John of Salisbury imply that Eleanor had an incestuous relationship with her uncle, Raymond of Antioch,[16] while the Minstrel of Rheims more fancifully suggests that the queen had an affair with Saladin himself.[17] The replacement of Eleanor with Cassodorien, Aquitaine with Antioch, produces a Richard whose alien nature is not French, but Oriental.

It is worth pointing out, however, that English identity is not defined in the romance only with reference to Saracen and French identity: other national groups, including the Germans and the Griffons (Greeks), provide foils for the constitution of English identity. As Linda Colley has demonstrated with regard to the emergence of British (as distinct from English) national identity, the nation is "an invention forged above all by war."[18] Comparably, in *Richard Coer de Lion*, the encounter with the enemy—be it German, Griffon, French, or Saracen—ends in the reassertion of the fundamental rightness of the English side and the increasingly complex definition of English identity. Richard's conflict with Modard, the king of "Almayne" (Germany), results not only in Modard conferring upon Richard the name by which he comes to be commonly known ("He may be callyd, be ryght skylle, / Kyng jcrystenyd off most renoun, / Stronge Rychard Coer de Lyoun!" [1116–18]), but also in an accord sealed by a shared feast: "That ylke day Kyng Modard / Eet, jwis, with Kyng Rychard" (1615–16). Initially, the military threat posed by the Griffons is treated together with that posed by the French: the two groups are united in their assault on the English and are repeatedly referred to as a joint enemy.[19] Thereafter, the encounter of the English with the Griffons takes a course similar to that taken with the Germans: although the traitorous "emperour" never comes to accept Richard's authority as Modard does, his lords reject his call to fight the English, while the chief of the barons declares "With such a lorde kepe j not holde / To fyght ayenst Rycharde the kynge, / The best vnder the sonne shynynge" (2422–24). Here too, a shared feast in which all "were at one accorde" and "ete at one borde" (2389–90) cements the union of the English with an alien culture.

Far from being the unique focus of the clash of national cultures, then, the conflict of the French and the English is one of a series of encounters that result in the definition of English national identity and the recognition of its superiority. This is not to deny that the French identity of the historical Richard I is suppressed in the romance's construction of a purely English king, but to assert that English identity is constructed in the romance in a dynamic way, through the repeated encounter with a series of other nations, each of which differs from that of the English and comes to acknowledge its own inferiority. Each alien nation is in turn absorbed into the crusading force led by Richard, so that even the French (after the departure of Philip from the field) join with the English to drive three thousand Saracens into a huge mire outside Jaffa: "And thoo that wolden haue come vppe, / They drank of Kyng Richardis cuppe" (7023–24). In a parody of the reconciliation of former enemies that takes place in a series of feasts described earlier in the poem, these enemies (and only these enemies) are drowned by the draught from Richard's "cuppe": they can never be members of the community united by the ritual feast.

Eating and Assimilation

While the most famous (infamous?) scene of eating in the *Romaunce of Richard Coer de Lion* is the shocking episode of cannibalism in which the king consumes the flesh of his Saracen enemies, food, hunger, and shared meals appear repeatedly during the course of the poem. Richard shares meals with a variety of companions, ranging from the English barons he hopes to persuade to accompany him on crusade to rulers of foreign lands. These meals mark occasions of social accord: for example, the "ryal ffeste" in England ends with the barons declaring "We ben at on acord" with Richard (1343, 1377); while the meal with the German king, Modard, ends with a kiss of peace and declaration of mutual friendship (1612–14). Richard's shared meal with the emperor of the Griffons results in concord, but only after some complications: the emperor swears friendship as they "ete at one borde," but truthfully "In herte hym was nothynge well" (2390, 2396). He soon attempts to turn on Richard, but the lords among the Griffons refuse to participate in the betrayal: all of them "sayd at one worde / That Rycharde was theyr kynde lorde" (2426–27). In each of these cases, unity is emphasized—the men, "at on acord," gather at "one table," speaking "one worde" in agreement. The converse of these scenes of social concord appears as well, when a celebratory feast is abruptly broken in response to an external stimulus. This takes place early in the venture of the crusaders, when Richard has gathered with them to celebrate the "grete feste" of Christmas. All the barons are gathered, served with "grete plente / Of mete and drynke," when suddenly a messenger bursts in to report the treasonous attacks of the French and the Griffons against the English. Richard responds by furiously kicking over the table, so that "it wente on the flore fote-hote"; he is "wrothe, and egre of mode, / And loked as he were wode" (1784–1810). Here, the disruption of social concord resulting from the behavior of the supposed allies of the English is reflected in the disruption of the feast. A similar dynamic is evident on another occasion when Richard is gathered with his barons for an ordinary "soupere," and is disturbed by the appearance of two Saracen messengers who deliver Saladin's request that Richard "'Tourne agayne to thyn owne land . . . Home to thi contree by the see'" (6887, 6924–26). Once again, Richard is outraged at a suggestion that is so manifestly wrong, for (in the view of the poem) his "owne land" is precisely the Holy Land itself. He reacts with fury: "In anger Rycharde toke a lofe, / the croste in his hondes all torofe, / And sayde . . . The deuyll hange yow with a corde!" (6927–29, 6932). The fragmented bread reflects the utter division between the position conveyed by the messengers and that held by the English king. Shared meals thus reflect social concord, while their disruption reflects disorder in the surrounding world.

Shared meals are a powerful symbol of unity which generally take place in public in order to make manifest the interpersonal liaisons forged at the feast. Yet meals have another function as well, one which is not invariably dependent upon the presence of an audience: the matter consumed in a meal can have a transformative effect on the person who consumes it. This phenomenon appears twice in *Richard Coer de Lion*, first in the episode concerning the lion which results in Richard receiving his new surname, and second in the scenes in which Richard eats Saracen flesh. In the first episode, Richard is on his way to the Holy Land, disguised as a pilgrim, determined to learn information that will prove useful on his later crusade. While in Germany, he is captured; he rapidly makes the German king into an implacable enemy by killing his son in a fight and having an affair with his daughter. When the German king wants to punish Richard, however, he faces a dilemma: because Richard is royal, he cannot be hanged or drawn and quartered. The king comes up with an ingenious solution, arranging to have a hungry lion released in Richard's cell; the lion, the German king assumes, will eat Richard. The king's daughter, however, warns Richard of her father's plans, and Richard is able to prepare by wrapping his forearm with layers of cloth. When the lion is released into his cell, Richard reaches into the lion's mouth and pulls out its heart. Holding the heart which is "al so warme" (1100), Richard coolly walks to the hall where the German king is eating dinner. Richard squeezes the blood out of the heart he still holds, dips it into a salt cellar, and "Withouten bred the herte he eet" (1109). This rather shocking episode establishes Richard's fierceness and his ability to do things other men cannot do; it also gives him a new name to suit the new character he has just displayed. The German king says,

This is a devyl and no man,
That has my stronge lyoun slawe,
The herte out of hys body drawe,
And has it eeten with good wylle!
He may be callyd . . . Stronge Rychard Coer de Lyoun! (1112–18).

By eating the lion's heart, Richard becomes lion-hearted, earning an altered name to suit his altered identity: the lion's strength becomes his own.
Richard is subsequently said to be "in dede lyon, in thought lybarde" (2194)
and is likened to a "wood lyoun" (3610). This quality rubs off onto his men,
who late in the romance are themselves characterized as "lyouns" in battle
(6856).

The nature of this process is familiar: there are many rituals in which,
by eating some substance, one absorbs or assimilates its qualities. For example, the pagans depicted in the *Sowdone of Babylone* "drinke wilde beestes
bloode, / Of tigre, antilope and of camalyon [giraffe]" in order to "egre her
mode" ["impassion their spirits"].[20] Richard's eating of the lion's heart is a
similar ritual process, for eating the heart gives Richard the qualities of the
lion: its fierceness, its savagery, its lack of humanity. For a modern reader—
and for a medieval reader as well—the most familiar ritual of this sort is the
eating of the wafer of Christ's body in the communion of the mass, an act
which, as Caroline Bynum notes, the early Church father Tertullian characterized as "a paradoxical redemption of that most horrible of consumptions:
cannibalism."[21] Cannibalism is practiced in order to incorporate qualities of
the person whose body is consumed, whether that person be an enemy or a
beloved relative. The anthropologist Peggy Sanday has argued that different
types of ritual cannibalism can be distinguished: in substitution cannibalism, for example, another kind of food takes the place of human flesh in the
ritual, as in the case of the bread used in the sacrifice of the mass. In projection cannibalism, enemy groups are imagined to be themselves cannibals;
this justifies their torture, murder, and the eating of their flesh. In Sanday's
words, projection cannibalism enables a "group's power and dominance [to
be] affirmed by consuming and digesting the power harbored by the flesh of
the enemy."[22] This phenomenon is dramatized in the encounter of the English with the Saracens in *Richard Coer de Lion*.

Richard's assimilation of the lion's nature in the earlier episode is a fore-
taste of the assimilation of Saracen nature found in the subsequent scenes
of Richard's cannibalism, a practice which Richard falls into unknowingly,
but which he embraces wholeheartedly. When his troops are besieging Acre,

Richard falls ill; nothing will restore his health, it seems, but a taste of English food. What he longs for in particular is pork, but even though his men hunt high and low, no pigs can be found in this Muslim country. As Richard's condition worsens, his men become more and more concerned; at last an "old knyght" proposes a solution:

> Takes a Sarezyn yonge and ffat;
> In haste that the theff be slayn,
> Openyd, and hys hyde off fflayn,
> And soden fful hastely,
> With powdyr, and with spysory,
> And with saffron off good colour.
> . . . .
> Whenne he has a good tast,
> And eeten weel a good repast,
> And soupyd off the brouwys a sope,
> Slept afftyr, and swet a drope,
> Thorwgh Goddes myght, and my counsayl,
> Sone he schal be ffresch and hayl.
> (3088–102)

Richard's cook prepares the food, but presents it as pork; he fears Richard's reaction when the king finds out what he has eaten. The concern, however, proves to be groundless. Richard eats heartily, and his health is so restored by the meal that he becomes "hool and sounde" (3118). In fact, Richard enjoys his meal so much that he soon requests some more of the delicious pork. When the trembling cook presents the leftovers, Richard's reaction is not one of horror. On the contrary, when he sees the head and how its "lyppes grennyd wyde," the king "laughe as he were wood" (3213, 3215), and eats some more. The Saracen identity already latent in Richard, received from his grandfather Corbaryng of Antioch, becomes heightened by his assimilation of Saracen flesh in the Holy Land: this flesh makes Richard not less than he was, but "hool." What Richard has eaten is, paradoxically, food from home. This is evident in the narrator's description of the cause of Richard's illness and the necessary remedy: he fell ill because of the

> strong eyr off that cuntree,
> And vnkynde cold and hete,
> And mete and drynk that is nought sete

To hys body, that he there ffonde,
As he dede here in Yngelonde
(3044–48)

What made him fall ill was the climate, which is "unkynde" or unnatural to an Englishman, and the strange food, which is unsuited to his body;[23] his cure can only be found in food that is "sete / To hys body," that is, Saracen flesh.

This episode, however, is only the first of two cannibalistic feasts recounted in the romance. The first takes place in private, a meal that has an effect only on the one who consumes the transformative matter. In the second, however, Richard displays his cannibalism in a more public setting, which extends the effects of the cannibalism into the larger community. Like Richard's public consumption of the raw lion's heart, standing calmly in the German king's great hall, the public consumption of Saracen flesh causes change not just in Richard himself, but in how he appears to others. When envoys come from Saladin to carry on negotiations with Richard, he invites them to a celebratory feast: a covered dish is placed before each guest and, when the tops are removed, each guest discovers the head of a fellow Saracen, boiled, and carefully labeled with the victim's name. Richard mocks his guests for their unwillingness to eat and suggests that perhaps the meat is not to their liking; he himself eats from his dish with gusto, but thoughtfully has other food brought out for his guests. Richard's act of eating Saracen flesh has a dramatic effect on those who witness the act. The envoys sent by Saladin are so terrified by being served with plates bearing the severed heads of their kinsmen that "the teres ran out of here eyen" (3466). Upon seeing Richard eating the flesh "with herte good," they poke one another and whisper, " 'This is the deuelys brothir, / That slees oure men and thus hem eetes!' " (3484–85). The effect of the horror is preserved in Richard's subsequent speech to the messengers, in which he instructs them to tell Saladin that besieging the English will do no good, because "We schal neuer dye ffor hungyr" as long as there are Saracens remaining to be eaten. A single Saracen, says Richard, will feed nine or ten "Off my goode Crystenemen . . . Ther is no fflesch so norysschaunt / Vnto an Ynglissche Cristenmen . . . As is the flesshe of a Sarezyn." Richard concludes by promising that this cannibalism will continue indefinitely, not just as a defensive measure against siege, but as an offensive measure designed to consume the Saracens entirely: "Into Yngelond wol we nought gon, / Tyl thay be eeten eueryl-kon" (3540–62). The envoys obediently relay this message to Saladin, telling him that Richard will "slee alle that he may fynde, / Sethe the fflesch, and with teeth grynde. / Hungyr schal hem neuere eyle." The English king will not return "Into Yngelond . . . Tyl he haue maad al playn werk" (3651–55). They conclude by reiterating the fear caused by Richard's insatiable hunger for Saracens: "He has ment, yiff he may, go fforth / To wynne est, west, south, and north, / And eete oure chyldren and vs" (3667–69). At this point, the effect of the spectacle—Richard's public feast on Saracen flesh—has spread out beyond the confines of the English camp, permeating "east, west, south, and north" in a harbinger of the English conquest to come.

Because the account of cannibalism in *Richard Coer de Lion* is so bizarre, one might assume that it is a fanciful invention on the part of the romance's author. Although it is true that no episodes of cannibalism are associated with the Third Crusade, several medieval chronicles state that such incidents did take place during the First Crusade. Both the anonymous author of the *Gesta Francorum* and Fulcher of Chartres report that Christian crusaders near Antioch were driven by hunger to eat the flesh of dead Muslims.[24] In the ninth book of his *Ecclesiastical History*, Orderic Vitalis reports the same episode of cannibalism. Like Fulcher, he acknowledges the grisly nature of the event, but makes a greater effort to justify the act and prepare the reader for it. Before describing the episode of cannibalism, Orderic notes that "everything edible was very dear. The spectre of famine walked abroad." Shortly afterward, he again mentions the crusaders' "lack of bread," explaining that great hunger caused the Christians "to eat horses and asses and any other unclean things available." This consumption of "unclean things" culminates in their devouring of "things that were filthy, strange, disagreeable, and even forbidden. Some even ate the flesh of Turks." Though he acknowledges the horror of the event he describes, Orderic maintains that the Christians' behavior was understandable under the circumstances: "It is true that they acted unlawfully, but overriding necessity forced them to violate the law."[25] The eating of Muslims' bodies is seen simply as the last step in a process of eating gradually less and less pure foodstuffs: the Christians are driven first to eat animals that are "unclean," then things that are "filthy" and "strange," and finally human flesh. In spite of the rationalizations offered by Orderic, western Christians' revulsion regarding cannibalism is evident in the manner in which the chronicle accounts were altered in their literary adaptations.[26] In the *Chanson d'Antioche*, for example, cannibalism during the First Crusade is said to have been practiced not by the Christians but by the Tafurs, itinerant beggars who follow the Crusaders.[27] The Christians merely tolerate the cannibalism practiced by others; they do not participate in it. In *Richard Coer de Lion,* on the other hand, cannibalism is practiced not only by a Christian, but by the king himself; and the act is not furtive, but open and even celebratory. The many correspondences between the two texts make the differing treatment of cannibalism—shameful in one case, exuberant in the other—all the more remarkable.[28]

By eating unclean things, Richard assimilates that which is outside the boundaries of ordinary life, becoming a liminal figure. He performs the ritual feast on behalf of his people, but the price he pays for doing so is that he can never be completely reintegrated among them; appropriately, within the confines of the romance, Richard's return "homward to Yngeland" (7204) is followed immediately by his death ("he was schot, allas" [7207]). Hunger is the engine, as it were, that drives the formation of the community. It causes the members to draw together, united by their common want. Descriptions of the experience of hunger appear repeatedly in *Richard Coer de Lion;* each time, the English king is the mediator who resolves the state of hunger and satisfies the longings of his people. Upon approaching the Holy Land by sea, the crusaders are faced by a seemingly impassable chain across the harbor at Acre, a barrier that has caused the Christians there to suffer "gret hongyr" and "payne" (2619). Richard, however, lifts up his mighty axe and "smot it on twayne" (2636), relieving the want of the Christians at Acre. Richard subsequently learns from the Archbishop just how much they had suffered, in an evocative passage that recalls the chronicles of the First Crusade:

> For hungyr we loste, and colde wyndes,
> Off oure ffolk syxty thousyndes!
> Thenne oure goode hors we slowe,
> Dede sethe, and eete the guttys towe.
> The fflesch was delyd with grete deynte:
> Theroffe hadde no man plente.
> Al to peses we carf the hede,
> And on the coles we gan it brede,
> In watyr we boylyd the blood:
> That us thoughte mete fful good!
> (2843–52)

The passage goes on to describe the inflated prices of all foods—an ox for forty pounds, a hen for fifteen shillings, an apple for sixpence, and so on.

Yet nothing matches the terrible hunger implied in the description of how the little stores of meat were divided up "with grete deynte," each bit carefully apportioned; they ate any kind of flesh for "they myghte haue non othir thyng" (2875).

In this extended description of a population suffering unspeakable hunger, the relief of the hungry is not explicitly shown, and no scene of feasting follows the end of the period of want. Instead, hunger re-emerges almost immediately as a constraining factor: this time, however, the hunger is not suffered by the community at large but by the king himself. Richard's hunger is not a generalized want, but rather a specific craving: he is "alongyd" after pork (3071). Unlike the earlier scenes in which hunger is described but its satisfaction is left implicit, the satisfaction of Richard's hunger is repeatedly described: first in Richard's hearty repast of the meat he thinks is pork, and which restores him to health; second in the meal he enjoys on the following day, when he asks the cook for more of the meat he had eaten before; third at the communal banquet with the Saracen envoys as spectators; and finally in the envoys' vivid description of Richard's feast. With each episode, the description of Richard's pleasure in eating—and intention to consume still more—becomes more extravagantly detailed. His gustatory satisfaction remains unique to him, in spite of the fact that it is repeatedly suggested in the text that his men might also partake in a similar feast. After enjoying Saracen flesh for the second time, Richard suggests that his men may want to imitate him: "Now i haue it prouyd ones, / Ffor hungyr ar i be woo, / I and my ffolk schole eete moo!" (3224–26). At the communal feast, he tells the Saracen envoy that the food he has just eaten is the most nourishing of all for "an Ynglyssche Cristen-man" and promises that "we"—that is, he and his men—will not return to England until every last Saracen has been consumed (3549, 3561). Finally, the envoys repeat Richard's message to their lord, affirming that hunger will never affect the English ("Hungyr schal hem neuere eyle" [3653]) as long as a supply of Saracen victims remains. They too are aware of the potential that Richard's cannibalism can extend to become a characteristic of the English at large: something practiced by "I and my folk."

This potential, however, is never realized: even though Saracen flesh might be the most nourishing to "an English Christian-man," no one in the romance other than Richard himself ever partakes in acts of cannibalism. Instead, Richard's men, at least at the outset, seem to regard cannibalism with the same horror experienced by their Saracen counterparts: the cook is so afraid when he reveals what Richard had eaten earlier that he falls to his knees and begs for mercy (3209–10), and Richard's soldiers never touch the unnatural food their king devours. He alone eats this meat, consumes it in place of his men, on behalf of the whole community. It does not matter that the English soldiers do not eat the meat of their Saracen prisoners, for Richard has done it for them. Here, a comparison to the sacrifice of the mass is appropriate: just as the priest consumes the Host on behalf of the spiritual community, so Richard as king consumes the flesh on behalf of the national community. Through Richard, the English become empowered to consume the world of the Saracens, if only in a metaphorical sense. Richard's promise to "eete / Al so manye as we may gete," not departing until the Saracens are "eeten everylkon" (3559–62), is indicative of a ravenous hunger for conquest, one that will extend out not only geographically but temporally, on into the future. This fear is reflected in the Saracens' response to Richard's threat, their recognition that the English intend to "eete oure chyldren and us" (3669). Here, the threat is of a kind of perpetual cannibalism, in which the Saracens (or, at least, their territory) will not cease to be "eaten up" by the English until their hunger for the Holy Land is sated.

Nation and Religion

The use of eucharistic symbolism to characterize the role of the English king is not unique to *Richard Coer de Lion*. It is also found in the parliament rolls of Henry IV, which were produced in that tense period of initial consolidation of Lancastrian authority after the deposition of Richard II in 1399. Although Richard had already died in prison, rumors that he still lived were in circulation during the winter and spring of 1401–2, and were harshly repressed.[29] During that time, Archbishop Arundel used the ceremonial opening of Parliament and other state occasions as opportunities to proclaim the unity of secular and spiritual authority in the person of the king, a unity that would be reflected in his own combination of the ecclesiastical role of Archbishop of Canterbury and (after 1406) the secular role of chancellor. Peter McNiven has pointed out the extraordinary character of Arundel's addresses to the two assemblies preceding Henry's coronation ceremony, "in which political and religious concepts were blended with a thoroughness which bordered on the blasphemous."[30] Arundel took as the text of one of his sermons a passage from 1 Samuel 9:17: "And when

Samuel saw Saul, the Lord said to him: Behold the man, of whom I spoke to thee. This man shall reign over my people."[31] Here, Arundel inhabits the role of the prophet Samuel, Henry the role of Saul, God's anointed; appropriately, the verse quoted is followed, in the biblical account, by a description of Saul being anointed by Samuel, just as Arundel would shortly proceed to anoint Henry in the coronation ceremony. Arundel's agenda is reflected in the conduct of subsequent parliaments: for example, the parliament rolls for 2 Henry IV include appeals from the Commons asking that their king work to resolve the papal schism—speeches designed to cast Henry in the role not of a treasonous usurper, but of a force for "Union et Concorde."[32]

The most striking conflation of secular and spiritual authority in the person of the king, however, appears in the record of the closing assembly of Parliament on 15 March, in which an extended analogy is made between the Parliament and the mass:

> The said Commons put forth to the king that it seemed to them that the Parliament could be likened to a Mass, for in the opening of this Parliament, the Archbishop of Canterbury began with the Office, and read the Epistle, and explained the Gospel. And in the middle of the Mass, when the sacrifice is offered to God on behalf of all Christians, the King (to accomplish this goal [*mesne*, lit. "middle"]) has, at this Parliament, many times declared plainly to all his liegemen, that his will be that the faith of Holy Church should be sustained and governed just as it was in the time of his noble progenitors; and, as he has sworn by Holy Church, that the laws would be maintained and guarded in all ways, with regard to the poor as to the rich; which fact gives great pleasure to God and comfort and consolation to his liegemen. And, moreover, at the end of each Mass it is necessary to say, "Ite missa est, et Deo gratias"; similarly, it is performed by the Commons [on leaving Parliament].[33]

Arundel's effort to shore up Henry's claims to legitimacy with the union of secular and spiritual authority in the person of the anointed king is mirrored in the words of the Speaker of the Commons. The "mesne," or middle of the mass (that is, the central moment in which the eucharistic sacrifice is made and the Host is consumed by the priest on behalf of the community), has its counterpart in the Parliament: namely, the expression of the king's will, which is that things should be just as they were in the past. (An ironic wish, given the drastic break with precedent seen in the Lancastrian usurpation.) The passage goes on to explicate the three reasons why the Commons say "Thanks be to God," all of which center on the accomplishments of their king: because he is so well endowed with wisdom and "Humanite"; because, under his rule, the "evil doctrine" of Lollardy is "on the point of being annihilated"; and, finally, because the hearts of the Lords and Commons are "faithfully connected into one" ["en une fiablement connexez"] with the heart of their Lord the King.[34] This union is the secular equivalent of the union of the Christian community in the sacrifice of the mass.

I would not argue that the use of eucharistic symbolism to characterize Henry IV's relationship to his subjects is the source for the use of similar symbolism in *Richard Coer de Lion;* I do suggest, however, that in the years around 1400 it had become possible to conceive of the king in terms of the priest's role in the sacrifice of the mass, and that this new perspective is apparent both in the parliament rolls of 2 Henry IV and in *Richard Coer de Lion.*

It is significant that the closest romance analogue to the figure of Richard is not a knight or king but rather an archbishop: Turpin, a character familiar from the *Chanson de Roland* as well as the numerous Middle English adaptations of the Charlemagne legend, is depicted similarly to Richard in the late fourteenth-century *Siege of Melayne.* Both romances feature a Christian hero who assimilates eastern power in the service of the West and who displays a bloodthirstiness and abandon more typical of a Saracen than a Christian knight. Turpin exerts himself so passionately in battle that his own men cannot recognize him because he is so completely covered in pagan blood (1465–67).[35] Within the romance, Turpin repeatedly displays behaviors typical not of Christians, but of Saracens. When he hears of a French defeat in battle, for example, Turpin heaps abuse on the Virgin Mary, telling her "the wyte [blame] is all in the[e]" (555). This behavior is typical of the *chansons de geste,* in which Saracen sultans tumble down their pagan idols in disgust after a military defeat.[36] Throughout the romance, Turpin is described in terms applied to the pagan sultan Arabas; both of them display both passionate woe and passionate joy: after witnessing a miracle, "Than wexe the sowdan woo" (450); upon a Christian setback in battle, "The Bischoppe was so woo" (559). When the sultan hears the captive Christian knights describe their faith, "Thane loughe the sowdane withe eghne full smale" (415). Turpin similarly responds to his enemy with laughter: "For egernesse he loughe" (912; cf. 1104). The disruptive laughter of the sultan and Turpin, which both attests to the *sang-froid* of the one who laughs and generates fear in those who hear it, also appears in the *Richard Coer de Lion:* when he learns the true nature of what he has eaten as "pork," Richard "laughe as he were wood" (3215). This "wood" laughter of Richard finds its counterpart in Turpin's "egernesse"; their transgressive passion acts as the rallying point for the Christian host, enabling victory.

Finally, both Richard and Turpin unite their communities through performance; in each case, the body is the stage. Richard consumes matter which transforms him and consequently alters his people as well: eating the lion's heart makes him lion-hearted, but it also makes the English into "lyouns," as "woode" and "egre" as Richard himself (5105–8, 6856). Yet while Richard's performance is based on what he takes into his body, Turpin's performance is based on what he excludes from it: "There sall no salve my wonde come nere . . . Ne mete ne drynke my hede come in, / The Cite of Melayne or we it wyn" (1190–93; cf. 1349–51). By refusing medicine to soothe his wounds, food to relieve his hunger, Turpin focuses his community on the task at hand. Although Charlemagne repeatedly asks if he can "see" the bishop's wounds (1187, 1342), Turpin refuses, because the wound must remain, paradoxically, both hidden and open in imitation of the suffering of Christ, to which Turpin refers repeatedly. Turpin vows to keep his body in a state of openness—his wounds unstitched, his hunger unfilled, his eyes wide open (1352)—in mute witness to the divine will in action at the siege of Milan. He does all this, says Turpin, because "The sothe is noghte to hyde" (1356). This open truth is simply Christian "right," as evident here as in the declaration of Christian "dreit" in the *Chanson de Roland.* Theological language supports the formation of the community as both Turpin and Richard enact rituals of communion on behalf of their people. Turpin celebrates the mass itself, explicitly unifying the body of Christian believers: the "fayre oste of brede," (893) which miraculously appears on the altar, is a metonym for the military "hoste" (904) who partake in the ritual.[37] Moreover, Turpin unifies the community in other respects, dividing the food he himself refuses among the wounded (1195–96) and allowing the men to share spiritually in his wounds: when Turpin's hidden "wondes" are referred to for the third and last time in the poem, the "oste" is united in their sorrow and resolve to take the besieged city (1594–96). In *Richard Coer de Lion,* the ritual of communion is echoed as Richard eats the lion's heart and, later, the Saracen's head in place of his men, on behalf of the whole community.

The *Romaunce of Richard Coer de Lion* and the *Siege of Melayne* are not unique in their incorporation of religious symbolism and imagery into the conventions of the romance. Diana Childress and others have noted the presence of a curious hybridity in Middle English romance, where the essentially chivalric content of the narrative is coupled with a kind of "secular hagiography" in the characterization of the hero of the romance.[38] Some such religious component can be found in several medieval romances, especially when one examines the variant versions of a single narrative: the version of *Ferumbras* found in the Fillingham manuscript, for example, considerably shortens the overall text of the romance even while it amplifies the descriptions of the holy relics stolen by the Saracens and the devotion displayed by the Christian knights who retrieve them. The romance concludes with a spiritual exhortation to the reader which seems to run counter to the conventional aims of the romance genre:

> Nowe endyth thys gest nowe here
> Off firumbras de Alisavndre and syr Olyuer
> and al-so of Charlemayn, that gode, holy kyng.
> By-seke whe to god, that he yeve vs hys blessyng!
> God for the Rode loue yeue hem hys benysoun,
> that hauen herd thys gest with gode deuocyoun
> of the spere & the naylys and of the crovn!
> Schullen [thay] haue an . C. dayes vnto pardoun!
> Our lord graunt that it so be,
> seyth all amen pur Charite!
>
> (1831–40)

I have argued elsewhere that texts such as the *Siege of Melayne* and the Fillingham version of *Ferumbras* can be described as "devotional romances," texts whose function is as much spiritual edification as festive diversion.[39] They are testimony to the desire on the part of laypeople for works that could offer spiritual consolation in the vernacular language they could read independently. The audience for such devotional romances must surely have overlapped with the audience for the Wycliffite translation of the Bible and other heterodox writings in English. It is all the more striking, then, that they display an extremely orthodox theology with regard to the role of images in worship, the veneration due to relics, and the efficacy of indulgences.

Such orthodox theology also underlies the eucharistic symbolism employed in *Richard Coer de Lion*. The presence of theological content creates a dilemma, however, if we continue to see this romance as representative of the emergence of English national identity in the late Middle Ages: if nationalism is conceived of as a fundamentally secular knowledge, what do we make of the presence of devotional elements and theological symbolism not only in the romance, but in official documents of Lancastrian rule such as the parliament rolls? To answer this question, it is helpful to consider the role of religion in national identity as theorized in modern studies of nationalism, both in order to understand the comparative context and to illuminate the peculiar relationship of religion and nation in Reformation and pre-Reformation England. In contradistinction to the modernist approach (typified by Gellner, Hobsbawm, Nairn, and Anderson), in which nations are thought to fill the void left by "the dusk of religious modes of thought,"[40] the ethno-symbolic approach to theorizing national identity (developed largely by Anthony Smith) explicitly considers what role religion might play in the self-definition of the nation, both in modern and pre-modern societies.[41] Smith's approach takes into account the substantial development of nationalism in the late eighteenth century so strongly emphasized in the modernist approach, yet acknowledges the continuity of earlier ethnic identities with these later, more explicitly articulated manifestations of nationalism.

Adrian Hastings has argued, however, that Smith does not go far enough in pursuing the medieval antecedents of later expressions of nationalism, especially in England, and points out the crucial role that religion played in premodern articulations of national identity.[42] Following the influential work of Liah Greenfeld, Hastings suggests that some of the most powerful expressions of English national identity took place in the context of the Protestant Reformation.[43] Strangely, however, Hastings largely overlooks the role of religion in fourteenth- and fifteenth-century expressions of nationalism, perhaps because of the awkward fit of the "premature Reformation"—that is, Lollardy[44]—into the expression of English national identity, especially with regard to the status and use of the English vernacular.[45] Hastings's treatment of the relationship of religion and nationalism is paradoxical: how could the Reformation itself be an essential element in the expression of English nationalism in the sixteenth century, but the "premature Reformation" be divorced from English nationalism in the early fifteenth century? The English Reformers themselves clearly saw Lollardy as a harbinger of their own efforts, as can be seen (for example) by the inclusion of Wyclif and others in Foxe's *Book of Martyrs*.[46] This disjunction is perhaps the reason why Hastings, in spite of his extended treatment of the role of the Wycliffite translation of the Bible in medieval conceptions of the "nation," is forced to insist that "there was nothing inherently nationalist about Protestantism."[47] Following Hastings, one would have to conclude that the overwhelming popularity of the English vernacular in the years following 1400 was a universal phenomenon, embracing both the Lollard translators and fierce opponents of Lollardy.

I would suggest instead that Lollardy played a more specific role in the late medieval expression of English national identity. English nationalism during the early fifteenth century was largely defined in the terms set by the Lancastrian regime,[48] which pursued Lollardy as both heretical enemy of the Church and treasonous enemy of the Crown.[49] As seen in examples from the parliament rolls quoted above, secular and spiritual authority were integrated in Lancastrian documents to an extraordinary degree, to the extent that the declaration of the king's judgment was likened to the sacrifice of the mass. Lollardy played a pivotal role in the formation and expression of fifteenth-century English nationalism, not as a source of English nationalism in itself[50] but as a rival to Lancastrian claims of English authenticity: a rival that would go on to be mercilessly stamped out. Within the crucible that produced fifteenth-century English nationalism, the late versions of the *Romaunce of Richard Coer de Lion* play a special role. They illustrate how popular romances both participated in the forging of an idea of the nation that emerged from a framework of religious symbolism, and disseminated it across a broad reading community. Richard's hunger is the English hunger for territory, the pressure to expand at the borders that consolidates the nation. Conquest both sates the hunger for expansion and whets the appetite for more.

Notes

An earlier version of this essay was presented at the annual meeting of the Medieval Academy of America, Kansas City, Kansas, April 11–13, 1996. Thanks to Fiona Somerset for her helpful suggestions; special thanks to Bob Hanning for sharing with me his unpublished work on *Richard Coer de Lion,* and for many years of friendship.

1. The romance of *Richard Coer de Lion* survives in seven manuscripts dating from the early fourteenth to the late fifteenth century, as well as two printed editions of the early sixteenth century. The existence of an Anglo-Norman original is often assumed, following the argument of Gaston Paris ("Le Roman de Richard

Coeur de Lion," *Romania* 26 [1897]: 353 – 93). For description of the surviving manuscripts, see Gisela Guddat-Figge, *Catalogue of Manuscripts Containing Middle English Romances*, Münchener Universitäts-Schriften 4 (Munich: Wilhelm Fink, 1976). On the manuscript tradition, see Karl Brunner's introduction to his edition of the text, *Der mittelenglische Versroman über Richard Löwenherz*, Wiener Beiträge zur Englischer Philologie 42 (Wien, 1913). All quotations of *Richard Coer de Lion* are from Brunner's edition and are cited in the text by line number.

2. On Alexander's parentage, see George Cary, *The Medieval Alexander*, ed. D. J. A. Ross, 2nd ed. (Cambridge: Cambridge University Press, 1967), 232 – 36, 254 – 56 and *passim;* Christine Chism, "Too Close for Comfort: Dis-Orienting Chivalry in the *Wars of Alexander*," in *Text and Territory: Geographical Imagination in the European Middle Ages*, ed. Sylvia Tomasch and Sealy Gilles (Philadelphia: University of Pennsylvania Press, 1998), 116 – 42, esp. 127 – 28. On Merlin's, see R. Howard Bloch, "Merlin and the Modes of Medieval Legal Meaning," in *Archéologie du signe*, ed. Lucie Brind'Amour and Eugene Vance, Papers in Mediaeval Studies 3 (Toronto: Pontifical Institute of Mediaeval Studies, 1982), 127 – 44, esp. 129.

3. On the "national discourse" of *Richard Coer de Lion*, see Alan S. Ambrisco, "Cannibalism and Cultural Encounters in *Richard Coeur de Lion*," *Journal of Medieval and Early Modern Studies* 29 (1999): 499 – 528, esp. 522. On *Richard* as a text "exercising the discourse of the nation," see Geraldine Heng, "The Romance of England: *Richard Coer de Lyon*, Saracens, Jews, and the Politics of Race and Nation," in *The Postcolonial Middle Ages*, ed. Jeffrey Jerome Cohen (New York: St. Martins, 2000), 135 – 71, esp. 158, 151. On the relationship of hero and nation, see Diane Speed, "The Construction of the Nation in Medieval English Romance," in *Readings in Medieval English Romance*, ed. Carol M. Meale (Cambridge: D. S. Brewer, 1994), 135 – 57, esp. 146 – 47.

4. On the totalizing Foucauldian framework of Heng's argument, see Michael Calabrese's 2001 review of Jeffrey Jerome Cohen, ed., *The Postcolonial Middle Ages*, in *The Medieval Review*, http://www.hti.umich.edu/t/tmr. On the applicability of the Foucauldian notion of discourse to medieval cultures, see Suzanne Conklin Akbari, "Orientation and Nation in Chaucer's *Canterbury Tales*," in *Chaucer's Cultural Geography*, ed. Kathryn L. Lynch (London and New York: Routledge, 2002), 102 – 34, esp. 102 – 3 and 124.

5. Heng, *Romance of England*, 154; Ambrisco, "Cannibalism and Cultural Encounters," 522. Ambrisco also presents theological symbolism and secular nationalism as alternative rhetorical modes in his dissertation, "Medieval Man-eaters: Cannibalism and Community in Middle English Literature (John Gower, Geoffrey Chaucer)" (Ph.D. diss., Indiana University, 1999).

6. Pearsall identifies it as one of the eight most popular romances read during the fifteenth century (58 note 2). Derek Pearsall, "The English Romance in the Fifteenth Century," *Essays and Studies* n.s. 29 (1976): 56 – 83.

7. Most scholars follow Karl Brunner, the text's early twentieth-century editor, in assigning the manuscripts to two groups: the basic version (b), found in five manuscripts; and the expanded version (a), found in two. This neat division is complicated by the fact that one fourteenth-century manuscript (British Museum Egerton 2862), ascribed by Brunner to the b-group on sound philological grounds, includes some of the marvelous material. Ambrisco, in my view, wrongly dismisses the significance of this anomaly, suggesting that Brunner's designation of the manuscript must be in error (Ambrisco, "Medieval Man-eaters," 524 note 3).

8. *La Chanson d'Antioche*, ed. Suzanne Duparc-Quoic, 2 vols., Documents relatifs à l'histoire des croisades II (Paris: Paul Geuthner, 1976). *La Chrétienté Corbaran*, ed. Peter R. Grillo, in *The Old French Crusade Cycle*, vol. 7: *The Jérusalem Continuations*, part I (University: University of Alabama Press, 1984).

9. "From an old and evil custom, they always carry an axe in their hand as if it were a staff. In this way, if they have a feeling for any evil, they can the more quickly give it effect. Wherever they go they drag this along with them. When they see the opportunity, and the occasion presents itself, this weapon has not to be unsheathed as a sword, or bent as a bow, or poised as a spear. Without further preparation, being raised a little, it inflicts a mortal blow. At hand, or rather, in the hand and ever ready is that which is enough to cause death." Giraldus Cambrensis, *The History and Topography of Ireland (Topographica Hiberniae)*, trans. John J. O'Meara, rev. ed.(Mountrath, Ireland: Dolmen Press, 1982), 107. Thanks to Jesse Polhemus for this reference.

10. *The Romaunce of the Sowdone of Babylone*, ed. Emil Hausknecht, E.E.T.S., e.s. 38 (Oxford: Oxford University Press, 1881; reprint, 1969), line 2995; the text can also be found in *Three Middle English Charlemagne Romances*, ed. Alan Lupack (Kalamazoo, Mich.: Medieval Institute, 1990).

11. *The Song of Roland*, ed. and trans. Gerard J. Brault, 2 vols. (University Park: Pennsylvania State University Press, 1978), 2:84–87 laisses 106–7, lines 1351–78.

12. Richard's axe is described at 2209–24, 2634, 3140, 6801–2, 6866, 6942, and 7005–6. For the manuscript illustration, see the facsimile of *The Auchinleck Manuscript*, ed. Derek Pearsall and I. C. Cunningham (London: Scolar Press, 1977), folio 326; noted in Roger S. Loomis, "*Richard Coeur de Lion* and the *Pas Saladin* in Medieval Art," *PMLA* 30 (1915): 509–28, esp. 523.

13. Ambrisco, "Cannibalism and Cultural Encounters," 520–22.

14. Heng, *Romance of England*, 156.

15. Richard disguises himself "In a full stronge queyntyse" (268), devises a tower for use in battle "that queynteyly engynours made" (1395), and summons his men to do battle "With queyntyse and with strength of honde" (1846). This quality is also seen in his attack on the lion, which is undertaken "with sum gyle" (1070; cf. 4002, 4008); see also the many references to Richard's "thoght" in moments of crisis (e.g., 592, 1032, 1069, 1090, 6373, 6381).

16. William of Tyre states that Eleanor "disregarded her marriage vows and was unfaithful to her husband." William of Tyre, *A History of Deeds Done Beyond*

the Sea, trans. Emily Atwater Babcock and A. C. Krey, 2 vols., Records of Civilization 35 (New York: Columbia University Press, 1943) 2:181. See also *John of Salisbury's Historiae Pontificalis Quae Supersunt* (Oxford: Clarendon Press, 1927), 53.

17. "Et quant la roine Elienor vit la deffaute que li rois avoit menee avec li, et elle oi parleir de la bontei et de la prouesce et dou sens et de la largesce Solehadin, si l'en ama durement en son cuer; et li manda salut par un sien druguement; et bien seust il, se il pouoit tant faire que il l'en peust meneir, elle le penroit a seigneur et relanquiroit sa loi." *Récits d'un ménestrel de Reims au treizième siècle*, ed. Natalis de Wailly (Paris, 1876), 4 – 5 ; translation in Edward N. Stone, *Three Old French Chronicles of the Crusades*, University of Washington Publications in the Social Sciences 10 (Seattle: University of Washington Press, 1939).

18. Linda Colley, *Britons: Forging the Nation, 1707–1837* (New Haven: Yale University Press, 1992), 5; cf. 367 – 68.

19. On the pairing of the French and Griffons, see (for example) lines 1771, 1793, 1822, 1847, 1854 – 56, 1892, and 1942. On the historical accuracy of this portion of the romance, see John Finlayson, "*Richard, Coer de Lyon:* Romance, History, or Something in Between?" *Studies in Philology* 87 (1990): 171.

20. Hausknecht, *Sowdone of Babylone*, lines 1007 – 9.

21. Tertullian, *De resurrectione mortuorum*, ed. J. G. P. Borleffs, in *Tertulliani Opera*, pt. 2: *Opera Montanistica*, Corpus christianorum: Series latina (Turnhout: Brepols, 1954), chap. 8, 931 – 32; cited in Caroline Walker Bynum, *The Resurrection of the Body in Western Christianity, 200–1336*, Lectures on the History of Religions, A.C.L.S., n.s. 15 (New York: Columbia University Press, 1995), 41. On the function of the Eucharist in the ritual of the mass, see Mary Douglas, *Natural Symbols: Explorations in Cosmology*, 2d ed. (London: Barrie and Jenkins, 1973), 69, 70; also P. J. Fitzpatrick, *In Breaking of Bread: The Eucharist and Ritual* (Cambridge: Cambridge University Press, 1993), 198 – 208.

22. Peggy Reeves Sanday, *Divine Hunger: Cannibalism as a Cultural System* (Cambridge: Cambridge University Press, 1986), 51.

23. Interestingly, these are the very same causes to which illness is attributed in eighteenth- and nineteenth-century colonial narratives; see Alan Bewell, *Romanticism and Colonial Disease* (Baltimore: Johns Hopkins University Press, 1999).

24. ". . . famem nimiam gens nostra pertulit. dicere perhorreo, quod plerique nostrum famis rabie nimis vexati abscidebant de natibus Saracenorum iam ibi mortuorum frusta, quae coquebant et mandebant et parum ad ignem assata ore truci devorabant. itaque plus obsessores quam obsessi angebantur." *Fulcheri Carnotensis Historia Hierosolymitana (1095–1127)*, ed. Heinrich Hagenmeyer (Heidelberg: Carl Winter, 1913), 266 – 67 (1.25.2); translation in Fulcher of Chartres, *A History of the Expedition to Jerusalem, 1095–1127*, trans. Frances Rita Ryan (Knoxville: University of Tennessee Press, 1969), 112 – 13. See also *Anonymi Gesta Francorum et aliorum hierosolymitanorum / The Deeds of the Franks and the other Pilgrims to Jerusalem*, ed. and trans. Rosalind Hill (London: Thomas Nelson, 1962), 80.

25. *The Ecclesiastical History of Orderic Vitalis,* ed. and trans. Marjorie Chibnall (Oxford: Oxford University Press, 1975), 5:72–75, 98–99, 140–41.

26. Geraldine Heng goes so far as to argue that the historical episode of cannibalism during the First Crusade served as the stimulus for broad trends in twelfth-century romance; see "Cannibalism, the First Crusade, and the Genesis of Medieval Romance," *Differences* 10 (1998): 98–174.

27. *La Chanson d'Antioche,* ed. Suzanne Duparc-Quoic, 2 vols. (Paris: P. Geuthner, 1976) 1:169–223, chant 5, laisses 138–77.

28. The *Chanson d'Antioche* includes many elements found in the later Middle English poem, including the name of Richard's maternal grandfather, Corbaryng of Antioch; the single scene of Saracen idolatry (compare *Antioche,* lines 4891–909 [laisse 202] with *Richard,* lines 6241–90); and the terrible hunger suffered by the Christian crusaders, which leads them to eat unclean things, including their own horses.

29. On the rumors of Richard's survival and plan to reclaim his throne, see Peter McNiven, *Heresy and Politics in the Reign of Henry IV: The Burning of John Badby* (Woodbridge: Boydell, 1987), 95–99; Paul Strohm, *England's Empty Throne: Usurpation and the Language of Legitimation, 1399–1422* (New Haven: Yale University Press, 1998), 106–8.

30. McNiven, *Heresy and Politics,* 68; on the intertwining of Arundel's career with Lancastrian ambitions, see 63–78.

31. "Et mox dictus Archiepiscopus Cantuariensis, vix facto silentio propter gaudium omnium circumstantium, Collationem modicam fecit et protulit in hec verba: Vir Dominabitur populi. . . . Populum quando petebat sibi dari Regem Populus ille: Et non inepte de Domino nostro Rege moderno dici possunt." *Rotuli parliamentorum* 3:423.

32. "[L]a Scisme de seinte Esglise se avoit endurrez tres longement, a tres grand dolour et desolation de seinte Esglise, et des toutes Cristiens, par ont mesmes les Communes prierent a mesme nostre Seigneur le Roi, q'al reverence de Dieu, et pur sustenance de seinte Esglise et de la Foie Catholike, luy pleust mettre et faire ses entiers diligence et labour, pur reformer et faire Union et Concorde celle partie." *Rotuli parliamentorum* 3:465 (10 March 1400/1).

33. "[L]es dites Communes monstrerent au Roy, Coment leur sembloit, que le fait de Parlement purroit estre bien resemblez a une Messe dont a comencement de mesme cest Parlement l'Erchevesque de Canterbirs comencea l'Office, et list la Epistle, et exposa l'Evaungile. Et a la mesne de la Messe, qe feust la sacrifice d'estre offertz a Dieux pur toutz Cristiens, le Roi mesmes a cest Parlement pur acomplir celle mesne, pleuseurs foitz avoit declarez pleinement as toutz ses lieges, Coment sa volunte feust, que la Foie de Seinte Esglise serroit sustenuz et governez en manere come il ad este en temps de ses nobles progenitours, et come il est affirme par seinte Esglise, et que les Loies serroient tenuz et gardez des toutz partz, si bien as povres

come as riches: quele chose feust grand pleisir a Dieu et comfort et consolation de ses lieges. Et auxint au fyne de chescun Messe y covient de dire, Ite missa est, et Deo gratias. Semblement y feust monstrez par mesmes les Communes." *Rotuli parliamentorum* 3:466 (15 March 1400/01). Unless otherwise noted, all translations from the French are mine.

34. "Et ceo par trois causes; l'une, de ceoque Dieux de sa benigne grace leur avoit ottroiez un Roi gracious, qi vorroit faire Justice des toutz partz, et auxint de Seen graciousement endowez, et de Humanite, en sa propre persone, come notoirement est conuz al greindre partie du mond, pur resistence de ses Enemys, honorablement adressez. Par ont ils sont bien tenuz de dire cel parol, Deo gratias. La seconde cause, pur ceo que la ou la Foie de Seinte Esglise, par malvoise Doctrine feust en point d'avoir este anientz, en grand subversion du Roi et du Roialme, mesme nostre Seigneur le Roy ent ad fait et ordeignez bon et joust remede, en destruction de tiele Doctrine et de la Secte d'icelle, par ont ils sont ensement bien tenuz de dire cet parol, Deo gratias. La tierce cause, pur ceo que les Seigneurs et Communes du Roiaulme considerantz le bon et entier Coer de nostre dit Seigneur le Roi envers les ditz Seigneurs et Communes, et auxi les bones Coers des ditz Seigneurs et Communes envers nostre dit Seigneur le Roi, et Coment q'ils sont par la grace de Dieux tout en une fiablement connexez, ils puissent entierment dire cel parol, Deo gratias." *Rotuli parliamentorum* 3:466 (15 March 1400/01).

35. *The Sege of Melayne*, ed. Sidney J. Herrtage, E.E.T.S., e.s. 35 (London: N. Trübner, 1880); also available in *Three Middle English Charlemagne Romances*, ed. Alan Lupack, TEAMS (Kalamazoo, Mich.: Medieval Institute Publications, 1990); cited by line number in the text.

36. Suzanne Conklin Akbari, "Imagining Islam: The Role of Images in Medieval Depictions of Muslims," *Scripta Mediterranea* 19/20 (1998–99): 9–27, esp. 10–18.

37. This play on words is evident also in the description of the soldiers, drenched in blood from their own wounds, with nothing to drink "Bot blody water of a slade [stream] / That thurghe the oste ran" (1208–9). On the eucharistic symbolism, see Suzanne Conklin Akbari, "Incorporation in the *Siege of Melayne*," in *Pulp Fictions of Medieval England: Essays in Popular Romance*, ed. Nicola McDonald (Manchester: Manchester University Press, 2003), 22–44.

38. Diana T. Childress, "Between Romance and Legend: 'Secular Hagiography' in Middle English Literature," *Philological Quarterly* 57 (1978): 311–22; Jocelyn Wogan-Browne, "'Bet . . . to . . . rede . . . on holy seyntes lyves': Romance and Hagiography Again," in *Readings in Middle English Romance*, ed. Carol M. Meale (Cambridge: D. S. Brewer, 1994), 83–97; Andrea Hopkins, *The Sinful Knights: A Study of Middle English Penitential Romances* (Oxford: Clarendon, 1990).

39. On the usefulness of the term "devotional romance," see Akbari, "Incorporation." For a broader survey of the devotional content of popular romances, see

Roger Dalrymple, *Language and Piety in Middle English Romance* (Cambridge: D. S. Brewer, 2000).

40. Benedict Anderson, *Imagined Communities: Reflections on the Origin and Spread of Nationalism,* rev. ed. (London: Verso, 1991), 11.

41. Anthony D. Smith's work is the foundation of much recent work on religion and nation. On Islam and Arab nationalism, see Fred Halliday, *Nation and Religion in the Middle East* (Boulder, Colo.: Lynne Rienner, 2000), 31–54; on Hinduism and Indian nationalism, see Harnik Deol, *Religion and Nationalism in India: The Case of the Punjab* (London: Routledge, 2000), 8–29.

42. As Hastings puts it, Smith has "abandon[ed] the full orthodoxy of late eighteenth-century origins but . . . refuses quite to grasp the nettle of medieval nations." Adrian Hastings, *The Construction of Nationhood: Ethnicity, Religion, and Nationalism* (Cambridge: Cambridge University Press, 1997), 54. Smith has responded by identifying Hastings's insistence on the continuity of English nationhood (extending from the Anglo-Saxon realm of King Alfred on into the modern period) as a manifestation of the perennialist approach, which both defines the concept of the nation too broadly and neglects the specific details of the historical context of each given expression of nationalism. Anthony D. Smith, *The Nation in History: Historiographical Debates about Ethnicity and Nationalism* (Cambridge: Polity Press, 2000), 36–40, 50–51.

43. According to Hastings, religious identity has often served to coalesce or strengthen English national identity: for example, the "early English nation owed a very great debt indeed to Catholic Christianity and the papacy in particular" (51). Hastings concurs with Greenfeld that the Reformation served to "heat up English nationalism . . . while reshaping it as a thoroughly militant and Protestant force," and he agrees with Linda Colley that, by 1707, "Britishness seemed almost intrinsically bound up with Protestantism" (55, 65). On the role of English nationalism within early modern British colonialism, see David Armitage, *Ideological Origins of the British Empire* (Cambridge: Cambridge University Press, 2000).

44. Anne Hudson, *The Premature Reformation: Wycliffite Texts and Lollard History* (Oxford: Clarendon Press, 1988).

45. Hastings refers to Lollardy in a very circumspect way, suggesting that if Shakespeare had wished to lend a Protestant cast to the expression of English nationalism in his history plays, "he could well have brought Wyclif or some later Lollard in" (57). He adds that "the requirements of their work" led clergymen "to think in local, vernacular and, increasingly, national terms"; this was true not only during the Reformation but also "much earlier," with the need to provide instruction in the vernacular being "one of the factors pushing priests into Lollardy or the like" (192). For a more coherent assessment of how the use of English in preaching became politicized as a result of Lollards' advocacy of the use of the vernacular, see H. Leith Spencer, *English Preaching in the Late Middle Ages* (Oxford: Clarendon Press, 1993).

46. On the revival of Lollard texts, see Anne Hudson, "'No Newe Thyng': The Printing of Medieval Texts in the Early Reformation Period," in *Lollards and Their Books* (London: Hambledon Press, 1985), 227–48.

47. Hastings, *The Construction of Nationhood*, 15–17, 23–24, 55.

48. On the linguistic aspects of the Lancastrian program, see John H. Fisher, "Chancery and the Emergence of Standard Written English in the Fifteenth Century," *Speculum* 52 (1977): 870–99, and "A Language Policy for Lancastrian England," *PMLA* 107 (1992): 1168–80; Malcolm Richardson, "Henry V, the English Chancery, and Chancery English," *Speculum* 55 (1980): 726–50.

49. Margaret Aston, "Lollardy and Sedition, 1381–1431," *Past and Present* 17 (1960): 1–44, reprinted in *Lollards and Reformers: Images and Literacy in Late Medieval Religion* (London: Hambledon, 1984), 1–47.

50. As Anne Hudson points out, it does not "seem right to discern nationalism as a major force in the origin of lollardy [sic] or in its continuance. . . . [W]hilst Hussitism did become identified with the incipient movement towards a recognition of national identity, Lollardy did not" (143). "Lollardy: The English Heresy?" in *Lollards and Their Books*, 141–63.

II. CHAUCER'S TEXTS AND CHAUCER'S READERS

9

PETER W. TRAVIS

The Body of the Nun's Priest, or, Chaucer's Disseminal Genius

F ragment VII of the *Canterbury Tales*, a linked sequence of six quite radically different narratives, has for a long time been appreciated as a sustained metapoetic interrogation of the aesthetic ramifications and linguistic dimensions of Chaucer's own literary art. In 1967, Alan Gaylord argued that Fragment VII was Chaucer's "literary fragment," whose premier subject is "the art of story telling" itself.[1] In 1984, Helen Cooper maintained that the "basic question" of "the status of language" is so much its focus that Fragment VII could be known as Chaucer's linguistic fragment.[2] More recently, the fragment has been explored as an experiment in the genres of partial, or parodic, failure: the ice-cold uncomedy of the Shipman's fabliau; the spiritual ferocities of the Prioress's boy martyrology; the narrative and prosodic pratfalls of Chaucer's *Sir Thopas;* the monitory confusion of a thousand proverbs running amok in the *Melibee;* the anti-cathartic effect of a hundred tragedies promised by the Monk. While each of these five tales can simultaneously be read straight as well as askew, an artistic success as well as a parodic near miss, as a literary collocation they appear to be seeking some form and vision that would unify or transcend their partialities and imperfections.

I believe Fragment VII's metapoetic quest for a fully realized supreme fiction is recoded and parodied by Harry Bailly's quest for the supremely masculine male. Most dramatically, nearing the end of the fragment, Harry thinks he has finally discovered in the person of the Monk the sexual super-man of his dreams. We "borel men," he confesses unabashedly to the Monk, we ordinary men are nothing but puny "shrimpes": we are incapable of sat-isfying our wives in bed, just as we are unable to generate heirs who are anything but "sklendere" and "feble" (VII.1955–58).[3] By contrast, Harry can see that the Monk is a sexual champion, big of "brawnes and bones," who would be and should be a "tredefowel aright," copulating with such inde-fatigable vigor that he would beget "ful many a creature" (VII.1941–48). But the Monk fails to live up to Harry's supermanly vision, the only appar-ent reason being his perceived failure at the art of storytelling. Interrupted by the Knight after his sixteenth straight "tragedie," the Monk has now been deflated, in Harry's eye, into less than a shrimp, his superhuman tes-ticular potencies as teensy as those Canterbury bells tinkling and "clynkynge" on his horse's bridle. So it is only at the end of the fragment that Harry fi-nally turns, with little apparent optimism, to the Nun's Priest, hoping for a full "murie" tale (VII.2815). But if the Nun's Priest's unimposing horse, a "jade" both "foul" and "lene" (VII.2813), is a metonym of its owner's person, then this priest's artistic and sexual powers may prove to be just as disap-pointing as the Monk's.

A broad consensus in Chaucer studies has maintained for generations that the beast fable told by the Nun's Priest about Chauntecleer, Pertelote, and Reynard the fox is a brilliant success, a signature masterpiece providing many a resolution to the queries implicitly asked in the fragment's preceding tales. In this essay I do not wish to add to an analysis of the tale itself, but rather to stay with Harry, Chaucer's inscribed reader and critic, by moving beyond the tale to its end link. In lines repeating some of the terms of his earlier hyperbolic praise of the Monk, Harry, at fragment's end, finally pro-vides a physical portrait of the Priest, a portrait—I wish to emphasize—pointedly lacking in the *General Prologue* itself:

"Sire Nonnes Preest," oure Hooste seide anoon,
"I-blessed be thy breche, and every stoon!
This was a murie tale of Chauntecleer.
But by my trouthe, if thou were seculer,
Thou woldest ben a trede-foul aright.
For if thou have corage as thou hast myght,
Thee were nede of hennes, as I wene,

Ya, moo than seven tymes seventene.
See, whiche braunes hath this gentil preest,
So gret a nekke, and swich a large breest!
He loketh as a sperhauk with his yen;
Him nedeth nat his colour for to dyen
With brasile ne with greyn of Portyngale.
Now, sire, faire falle yow for youre tale!"
                              (VII.3447–61)

As seen through Harry Bailly's scopophilic imagination, the Nun's Priest
has morphed from an indeterminate former state into a mightily impressive
physical personage; even before checking out his great neck, his large breast,
and his brawny physique, Harry's netherward gaze remarks upon the quality
of the Priest's "breche, and every stoon" (that is, his undershorts and his
[many?] testicles). Here, finally, stands Harry's macho man in all his somatic
glory; were it not for his spiritual calling, Harry allows, the Priest would
prove to be, like his beast fable hero, a "tredefoul aright" able to service hens
"moo than sevene tymes seventene." In addition to the Priest's hypermasculinity and hypersexuality, two more significant physical aspects catch Harry's
attention: the Priest's penetrating eyesight ("He loketh as a sperhauke with
his eyen") and his undyed ruddy complexion ("Him nedeth nat his colour
for to dyghen / With brasile ne with greyn of Portyngale").

No doubt Harry's quest for a manly alter ego reveals a great deal about
his personal identity anxieties as well as ongoing marital tensions with his
wife Goodelief, whom he represents as an emasculating, henpecking spouse
threatening to give up her distaff, take up Harry's knife, and do with it as
she will.[4] And no doubt this unusual epilogue—unusual in part because
several of its lines appear in slightly modified form and with greater textual
authority in Harry's earlier praise of the Monk—reveals something about
Chaucer's personal interests in the problematics of manliness, whatever
manliness may mean and be.[5] In addition, however, I wish to suggest in this
essay that the physical realization of Harry's sexual ideal at the end of Fragment VII contains a quite specific aesthetic and hermeneutic agenda. To be
precise, the epilogue to the *Nun's Priest's Tale* is Chaucer's complex statement about the power, medium, and appropriate style of his own literary art.
And each of the Nun's Priest's attributes—his spiritual calling, his manly
physique, his X-ray vision, his homely breeches, his ruddy complexion, his
refusing any dyes, his seminal potencies, and his "every stoon"—each of these

attributes engages themes and tropes found in Western aesthetic debates ranging from classical treatises on style to those found in the Middle Ages and the Renaissance. Thus, understanding the major stylistic norms embodied in the Nun's Priest's masculine person means, first, tracing their articulation in the works of various classical, medieval, and Renaissance authorities. And, second, it means tracing the masculine figure of Genius-as-Priest, developing from the *genii* of Bernardus Silvestris's *De Cosmographia* and provided full human form in the Genius figures of Alain de Lille and Jean de Meun. Although Alice Miskimin asserts that "the archetypal image of Natura's Priest, Genius, never appears directly in Chaucer's poems,"[6] I believe that, with only the slightest amount of indirection, Genius does in fact appear in the physical person of Chaucer's Nun's Priest; and that, through the priest's genial mix of hypermasculinity, priesthood, celibacy, and sexual potency, Chaucer is invoking and then critiquing the artistic ideologies his priest embodies.

The ambition of this essay is to ascertain Chaucer's assessment of the stylistic precepts, linguistic themes, and artistic principles he invokes through Harry's hypermasculine vision of literary genius. But because the ultimate task is to define Chaucer's aesthetic position (and not merely Harry's), we need in fact to acknowledge the puzzling absence of the Nun's Priest's body, as well as its presence. We must address, that is, that manuscript issue already briefly alluded to: of all the pilgrims, it is only the Nun's Priest's body that is marked by a pure absence from the reifying ground of the *General Prologue*. Corresponding, I suggest, to Derrida's "affirmation of the nonorigin" of all linguistic signifiers, this manuscript aporia helps to configure the Nun's Priest's body as Chaucer's sign of linguistic dissemination. In addition, as a projection of Harry's symptomatic homoerotic desires and his fears of castration, this absent/present body exposes the "disseminal" anxieties at the core of the very traditions that have made its formation possible. Harry's unintentional parody of these aesthetic ideals, in other words, contains Chaucer's own critique of these traditional celebrations of language's potency and of literature's hypermasculine valence.

In her essay "Virile Style," Patricia Parker focuses on the anxiety of many classical and neoclassical poets that their literary language is forever on the verge of succumbing to effeminacy.[7] In an epistle written in 1527, for example, Erasmus takes aim at an "effeminate" Ciceronian style to which he feels his fellow humanists are ever in danger of losing their manhood. We need a language "more genuine," he writes, "more concise, more forceful, less

ornate, and more masculine."[8] In *Timber; or Discoveries,* Ben Jonson similarly calls for literary styles that *ossa habent, et nervos* (that would have "bones
and sinews") as against a style that is "fleshy . . . fat and corpulent . . . full of
suet and tallow."[9] In these and other contributions to the Renaissance debates
on style, the keyword is *nervus,* denoting sinews, but also the sexual male
member, and, by extension, force, energy, and manly strength.[10] Only its opposite, *enervis,* appears with greater critical frequency, marking the omni-
present danger of slipping into an effeminate writing style of unmanly excess
and weakness, a literary style that is again translated into "the metaphorics of
the male body."[11]

We see the same sexual anxieties in these texts' Roman originals. In one
of his *Epistles,* for instance, Seneca excoriates "a degenerate style of speech"
that has the "mincing" (*infracta*) and womanish (*effeminatus*) gait of the *cin-
aedus:* that is, the penetrated partner in sexual relations between men.[12] Tacitus, mixing misogyny and orientalism, records his hostility to the more co-
pious "Asiatic" and "effeminate" style of Cicero, consistently using *enervis*
(weak, effeminate) as well as *fractum* (broken, impotent) as pejoratives.[13] Not
to be outdone, Horace plays on his own name, Quintus Horatius Flaccus,
by characterizing a flaccid style as akin to a slack and useless member, as opposed to a "firm" (*constans*) male virility.[14] These fears of paralyzing impotence invariably extend into an aggressive denigration of the female and, even
more fiercely, of the passive male homosexual. Quintilian, for example, while
praising the good circulation, healthy complexion, firm flesh, and shapely
thews of the writer whose style is properly virile, condemns that man who
would seek to enhance his literary graces by the use of depilatories and cos-
metics and the wearing of dress effeminate and luxurious, rather than tasteful and dignified. In fact, Quintilian discusses a whole range of such unmanly behavior: "the plucked body, the broken walk, the female attire," all
signs of "one who is *mollis* and not a real man" but rather a womanish, passive male.[15]

Staunchly opposing this overdressed effeminacy is the Spartan style and
physical frame of the real man. "It is with eloquence as with the human
frame," writes Tacitus. "There can be no beauty of form where the veins are
prominent, or where one can count the bones: sound healthful blood must
fill out the limbs, and riot over the muscles, concealing the sinews in turn
under a ruddy complexion and a graceful exterior."[16] While policing proper
male sexual identity is clearly a core concern in all of these aesthetic prot-
estations, what is equally, and perhaps even more fundamentally at issue is

the nature of language itself and the need to monitor the proper relationship between words and things.[17] In the *Institutes*, to take one example, Quintilian admonishes his readers to hold in highest regard "the things [i.e., the content] that are the sinews of any speech [rather than] devote themselves to the futile and crippling study of words in a vain desire to acquire the gift of eloquence."[18] This privileging of the masculinity of the signified over the effeminacy of the free-floating signifier is, of course, a recurring trope in the history of Western thought and one to which we shall return.

In the Middle Ages, the precepts of literary style, sexual desire, regulated language, and the male body were bound together in ways powerfully indebted to the classical Latin tradition, yet their articulation was positioned within an ethical, religious, and educational context distinctive to their time. In the twelfth and thirteenth centuries, for example, the classroom study of the Latin language and the literary arts served as an ongoing object lesson in proper masculine attitudes and behavior. Matthew of Vendôme's *Ars versificatoria*, to take one mainstream case study, combines sexually transparent *exempla* in order to illustrate to its schoolboy readers the attractions of proper schemes and tropes and the barbarity of improper ones. Apocope, Matthew explains without skipping a beat, is the name for the dropping of a letter in writing, while it is also the name for the act of penile castration;[19] syncopation, which leaves out certain sounds in a line of verse, Matthew analogizes to "the thick penis [that] cuts off the sounds of intercourse."[20] It is not surprising that Matthew's program of grammatical and sexual instruction finds room to lambaste effeminate poetasters, whom he calls, relying upon Quintilian, "the category of vicious and decadent rhetoricians," those "hypocrites who while speaking about virtue wiggle their buttocks."[21] At the same time, as Garret Epp's reading of the *Ars versificatoria* illustrates, Matthew's instruction in grammatical solecism and prosodic transgression often leads him into a potentially promiscuous undoing of his own heteronormative mandates.[22] And this is not surprising, since many standard classroom texts, such as the *Ars amatoria*, the *Achilleid*, and *Pamphilus*, profile the male body as an object of admiration even while instructing "young boys . . . about sexual violence as a method of defining their manhood and controlling their own lives."[23]

Thus, in order to define a new, fourteenth-century style of literary manliness, Chaucer reassembles a large number of conventional signifiers and fashions them into the Nun's Priest's distinctive personal attributes—his ruddy complexion, his heavy-weight testicles, his refusal to apply dyes to his person, his classical bearing, and his athletic physique. And he has been able to do so successfully by integrating these signifiers inside a second tradition, the topos of masculine Genius, a concept deriving from Plato's *Timaeus* and explored before Chaucer by Bernardus Sylvestris, Alain de Lille, and Jean de Meun. This aesthetic tradition, while also male-centered, does not simply reiterate the anti-effeminacy of the virile style. In striking contrast, the ideology of Genius often celebrates the feminine, especially the gift of natural procreation. At the same time, since the figure of Genius is ultimately a stand-in for the male artist, even while the poet may admire and emulate Nature's gifts, more often than not he is intent on appropriating and displacing her powers of natural procreation with his own powers of literary production.

Bernardus Silvestris's mid-twelfth-century *Cosmographia*, a cosmogenic myth about creation itself, paralleling the world's creation with the creation of humankind, is a case in point. The only absolutely masculine forces in Bernard's universe are the four orders of genius. The "highest" and "lowest" *genii* are most relevant: Pantomorphus, a deity of the highest regions who is "devoted to the art and office of delineating and giving shape to the forms of things";[24] and the *genii* of the male sexual organs, those "twin brothers" who, along with the "crafty penis," are assigned the task of perpetuating mankind.[25] While this deity and these organs are masculine, the remaining powers in Bernardus's vision of creation are all impressively feminine. Coterminous and nearly coequal with God are the three neo-Platonic Forms: Silva, Natura, and Noys. These sisterly goddesses, shaping and informing the act of creation, suggest in their contiguity with each other and with the divine that God may be ambiguously transgendered. If Bernard's God has a penis, in other words, it remains invisible and immobile. Instead, as Claire Fanger argues, it is God's capacious "womb" that figures as a "generative aspect of the divine—an aspect that often seems to be represented as ontologically prior to the masculinity that it forms or engenders."[26] In this way, and despite its enormous indebtedness to the *Timaeus* and to Plato's well-known womb-envy complex,[27] Bernard's *Cosmographia* is unusually generous in its celebrations of the ontological priorities of the feminine. Yet the tensions found in Plato between form and matter, spirit and flesh, the masculine and the feminine, the phallus and the womb, are found here as well. Even in Bernard's seemingly holistic universe, a major power struggle between the sexes is dramatized; and ultimately the site of this struggle is the mind of the poet himself, a creator who needs to counter the natural gifts of the feminine with his own phallic fantasies of auto-genesis and artistic creation.

Alain de Lille's *Complaint of Nature* takes this gender struggle a step further by allegorizing the sexual identity and erotic desires of language itself. The most important figure in the *Complaint* is Nature, vicar and vice-regent of God, *genetrix rerum* of the natural world, whose creative function is to stamp on matter the appropriate form, copying the divine ideas so as to insure an uninterrupted continuance of impermanent entities. Venus, the goddess of Love, is in turn Nature's vicegerent; for in obedience to Nature, and thus to God, she performs the same divinely approved function of assisting all creatures in being fruitful and multiplying. The male figure of Genius, a priest who appears only at the end of the *Complaint*, is also fashioned in Nature's image, and, at a further remove, in the image of God. Like Nature, he wears magnificent robes that are continually changing their colors, displaying images of natural objects that appear and disappear. Unlike Nature, but very like the male literary artist for whom he stands, Genius brings things into being by means of his phallic pen. With this he writes upon "the pelt of a dead animal," thus "endow[ing] with the life of their species images of things that kept changing from the shadowy outline of a picture to the realism of their actual being."[28] But in addition to serving as Nature's priest, Genius is also her Platonic lover: by means of a kiss he and Nature have begotten a daughter, Truth. Unfortunately, Truth is attended by a shadow sibling of unnamed parentage, the dark and ugly Falsitas, who secretly lies "in wait" in order to disgrace "by deformity" whatever Truth has "graced by conformity."[29]

In exercising his priestly powers, Genius's primary assignment is to excommunicate mankind because of its sexual and linguistic perversions. Having rampantly abused Nature's laws of grammatical copulation, having recklessly changed "he's" into "she's," having converted the active sex into the passive sex, having attempted to be both subject and predicate at once, modern man, Nature complains, no longer is charmed by "the little cleft of Venus" and thus deserves to "be excommunicated from the temple of Genius."[30] Even among "those men who subscribe to Venus' procedures in grammar," Nature laments, "some closely embrace those of masculine gender only, others those of feminine gender, others, those of common, epicene gender."[31] And then there are those heteroclite auto-eroticists, "disdaining to enter Venus' hall, [who] practice a deplorable game in the vestibule of her house."[32] While Nature asserts that she "bring[s] no charge of dishonourable conduct against the basic nature of Desire, if it restrains itself with the bridle of moderation," she does bring a charge against it "if its little fountain grows into a torrent, if its luxurious growth calls for the pruning-hook to shorten it, if its excessive swelling needs treatment to heal it."[33] In other words, in the *Complaint*, the wildness of erotic desire is so powerful and in need of such aggressive pruning that its husbandry would appear at times to border on sexual/linguistic castration.

It is obvious from just this abbreviated summary that much insecurity surrounds Alain's fantastic celebrations of heteronormative poetry and literary paternity. Is it possible that Truth is solely Nature's child, and that Genius's only offspring is a fraudulent figure named Falsehood? Is Genius's language in fact capable of spawning any form of being? Is it perhaps the case that erotic promiscuity is an inherent condition of language itself? To some degree, Alain acknowledges that Nature's standards of proper coition and art's standards of orthodox writing are both subject to inventive experimentation. Venus herself eventually grows bored with the duplicative process of orthodox sex. Forsaking her husband Hymnaeus, she takes up a life of "fornication and concubinage" with Antigenius, with whom she produces a child called Jocus, or Sport, a churlish buffoon whose lifestyle inspires all manner of linguistic and sexual free play. Yet, as many scholars have noted, Alain, like his master Matthew of Vendôme before him, cannot himself resist indulging in the onanistic arts of those linguistic perverts he calls "falsigraphers."[34] Looking aghast at "sodomites of style" who take "immeasurable pleasure" in embracing grammatical defects, Alain nevertheless finds himself falling prey to "barbarolexis," sporting, like his enemies, in the "jubilant fount of his own poetics."[35] Indeed, the extreme floribundence of Alain's rococo style itself indicates that the effete sins of language he seeks to condemn are only slightly distorted images of his own poetic vocation.

Thus a basic issue addressed throughout *The Complaint of Nature* concerns the transgressive nature of poetry itself: could it be that all tropes are a form of "fornication" and linguistic "concubinage," or, even more dangerously, that all poetry, in fact, is "queer"? Alain heightens the sexual valence of poetic tropes by equating language's proper hue with the desires of robust innocence and by defining all that is rhetorically "foreign" as tainted with illicit concupiscence, arguing that false grammarians are guilty of "discolour[ing] the colours of beauty by the meretricious dye of desire."[36] But he leaves unresolved the difficulty of distinguishing chaste colors from meretricious ones, or of discriminating between poetry's natural pigmentation and its application of artificial dyes. Even more, as Andrew Cowell has shown, the medieval "dye of desire" topos serves, both here and in a variety of other texts, as "a key medieval site for considering the relation between the literal and the figural, and between the 'natural' body of meaning and the rhetoric in which it was expressed."[37] As we shall see, all of these linguistic, sexual, and poetological issues are encoded in the signature attributes of the Nun's Priest's body.

But before returning to Chaucer's Priest, we need to consider one final literary progenitor: Jean de Meun's figure of Genius. Perhaps more than even *The Complaint of Nature*, *The Romance of the Rose* is a text about "the process of 'becoming male.'"[38] By stripping away the "stylistic equivocation and polite euphemism" of his forebears, Jean lays bare "the insistent demands of male desire and men's preoccupation with their sexual potency."[39] The powers of the phallus, the duties of the testicles, the fears of castration, the abhorrence of the homosexual, the conquest of the female beloved, the insemination of the Rose, and the allure of the human body (be it naked or fully clothed): these preoccupations, as Alastair Minnis argues in *Magister Amoris*, participate in a "phallocentric demythologization" of earlier works that had been much more explicitly about poetry, language, creation, form, and style.[40] Yet each of the sexual preoccupations in the *Rose* remains a literary preoccupation as well, especially the preoccupation with nakedness and dress. The human body in or out of dress, Minnis suggests, is likely to involve an "integumental hermeneutics," where the "rude and nude" embodies a plain or satiric style, and the elaborately dressed body represents the value of one of the "higher" literary registers.[41] Thus Jean's Genius removes his sacerdotal vestments as Nature's priest to put on secular clothing, leaving "his limbs / More free, as if he would attend a dance,"[42] and later dons the robes of Cupid in order to preach his sermon on the virtues of fleshly copulation: "we should all scriveners / Become!"[43] Genius's change of habiliment suggests the ever-shifting relationship between the spiritual, the literal, and the figural, whereas his refusal to practice sexually what he preaches spiritually bespeaks another complex reading of the role of the poet's art. A servant of a servant of God, Genius as Nature's "Venerean" priest is expected to practice total sexual restraint even though complete genital functionality is requisite to his vocation.[44] A sexual enthusiast who nevertheless has taken vows of celibacy,[45] Jean's figure of Genius appears self-conflicting and self-conflicted. But these inconsistencies are apparently symbolic elements essential to defining the vocation of the poet and the powers of his literary craft.

Given these classical and medieval traditions of linking the ideal male form and the ideal poetic function, what precisely is the "meaning" of the Nun's Priest's masculine body as it suddenly comes into view at the very end of Fragment VII? This body I think we can now decode as constituting a template of recognizable attributes, all of which focus on defining the principles of a new, fourteenth-century virile style. In accordance with the dictates of the classical ideal, the brawny power and handsome girth of Chaucer's priest represent the sinewy and muscular qualities of a manly literary aesthetic. His "gret . . . nekke," "large breest," and impressive physique articulate a straightforward, reality-based literary language where the signifieds of *res* are firmly embodied in *verba* as signs. The priest's undyed flesh argues for a rhetorical style that eschews elaborate tropes, preferring the unadorned and natural. The natural colors of the Priest's healthy complexion mandate that the *significatio* of poetry be seen to reside in the literal rather than in the spiritual. And even the Priest's homely underpants, his "breech," can be understood as supporting a low-mimetic poetics. In contrast to the well-attired Genius figures in *The Complaint of Nature* and in *The Romance of the Rose*, Harry's priest is visualized as fully naked except for one functional, nondescript covering that just barely hides from sight the potent genitals we are assured it contains. Of course it is the prowess of the Priest's "every stoon" that is the cynosure of Harry's intense admiration. Developing from symbolic and literal genitalia inscribed in various cosmogenic treatises, preceptive grammars, and courtly allegories, the Nun's Priest's "every stoon" demonstrates that the artistic instruments of the male poet are superabundantly potent, capable of generating life as well as satisfying the erotic needs of many women, "Ya, moo than seven tymes seventene."

As an aesthetic pronouncement, the Nun's Priest *effictio* thus seems to stand secure in its masculine semiotics. In this regard it differs markedly from its classical and medieval predecessors, most of which implement stratagems of misogyny and homophobia in order to elevate the heterosexual virtues of the virile style and to celebrate the powers of male procreation. By contrast, Chaucer's portrait notably omits all explicit denigrations of the effeminate, of the feminine, or of the queer. Any latent womb envy or anxiety about literary paternity is camouflaged, so to speak, by this priest being a nun's priest rather than Nature's priest and by our understanding that his generative potency is held (just barely) in check by his vows of professional celibacy. Thus does Chaucer's compressed integration of the classical mandates of the virile style and of the traditional medieval ideals of masculine genius appear—at least on first reading—to be complete and unproblematic. And unproblematic it might remain were it not for the fact that Fragment VII's concluding vision of the Priest's hypermasculine body is nothing more nor less than an ungrounded figment of Harry's testerical imagination.

Radically different in design from the *effictiones* of the *General Prologue* and clearly the personal projection of its creator, this free-floating somatic vision reveals much about Harry himself: his class prejudices, his over-the-top enthusiasms, his homoerotic fantasies, and his sexual uncertainties. But in addition to being "in character," these personal markers, for Chaucer, work more fundamentally as a complex parody of the need for a hypermasculine literary aesthetic. That is, Chaucer uses Harry's abject relationship to the ideal male body as a way of foregrounding, dramatizing, and parodying the obsessions and fantasies that lurk just beneath the surface of the aesthetic tradition that culminates in the Nun's Priest himself. In dramatically counterpointing the figure of the Priest and the figure of Harry, Chaucer has cleanly split apart the ideological economy of his inherited masculinist culture in order to scrutinize its underlying pathology as well as to honor its enduring strengths. What this means is that the Nun's Priest's body provides a satisfying, if *de trop*, celebration of medieval literary masculinity; at the same time, Harry's affective relationship to that exaggerated ideal acts out the fears and fantasies that necessitate its existence. Thus, Harry's intense admiration of the Nun's Priest's genitals can be seen as "outing" the homoerotic fascinations found in almost all the aesthetic treatises we have reviewed. As in these classical and medieval treatises, so with Harry: it is difficult to determine if the viewer's ultimate desire is to possess or to become the poetic ideal of male virility. Harry's castration anxieties work in a similar fashion. The priest's raptor vision ("He loketh as a sperhauk with his yen"), which is his only aspect not developed from earlier tropes, jibes with Harry's self-doubts as well as with the sexual insecurities that permeate the heritage of virile stylistics. As Freud has famously argued, "there is a substitutive relation between the eye and the male organ," such that "anxiety about one's eyes . . . is often enough a substitute for the dread of being castrated."[46] In a preemptive maneuver, Harry here converts his fears of being unmanned into the penetrating powers of his oedipal authority, the emasculating gaze of the priestly father. Thus Harry's castration complex, foregrounding the male insecurities that underlie so many medieval paeans to poetic virility, serves as an additional element in Chaucer's critique of the traditions embedded in the Nun's Priest sources.

At the core of these medieval celebrations of artistic genius lurks an urgent need to give credence to the poet's auctorial mastery over language and to language's capacity to inseminate the signifieds of his desire. However, as we have seen in *The Complaint of Nature*, language's polymorphous desire appears to originate somewhere other than in the author's controlling will. Further, as we have noted while discussing the medieval Genius topos, assertions of literary paternity inadvertently reveal their authors' deep fear that language may itself be impotent and barren. Perhaps in some way the poet is always and already castrated; perhaps language is a discourse of *dis*-semination rather than *in*semination. Such medieval apprehensions anticipate a modern critique offered in *Dissemination*, where Jacques Derrida argues that language—an unauthored, ungrounded, and ungenerative play of unending lexical substitutions—is equivalent both to "dissemination" and to "castration":

> No more than can castration, dissemination . . . can never become an originary, central, or ultimate signified, the place proper to truth. On the contrary, dissemination represents the affirmation of this nonorigin, the remarkable empty locus of a hundred blanks no meaning can be ascribed to. . . . Castration is that nonsecret of seminal division that breaks into substitution.[47]

In light of Derrida's critique of language's impotence, and in light of the recurring medieval alignment of language with castration, it is imperative, I believe, that the Nun's Priest's celibacy be understood as something more than merely a requisite part of his religious vocation. In terms of the linguistic and artistic ideologies the Priest embodies, I suggest his celibacy is ultimately a sign of the caponized poet's "castrated" and "disseminal" relationship to the realm of the signified, to the "place proper to truth."

Chaucer's most telling parodic maneuver in destabilizing the authority of this masculinist aesthetic program is sited in a place where the Nun's Priest's body is not to be found. In *The Canterbury Tales*, the "origin," the place of the "ultimate signified," is the portrait gallery of the *General Prologue*. Yet within this fictionalized ground of the real, there is already apparently an absence, a gap. That is, of the thirty pilgrims Chaucer tells us are on the pilgrimage, only twenty-nine are accounted for. More precisely, the Second Nun appears in one-and-a-half lines, after which there follows a puzzling, line-filling phrase, "and preestes three" (I.164). After an expert review of the possible explanations of this strange state of affairs, Leger Brosnahan concludes that, in all extant *General Prologue* manuscripts, there is a "hole"; this hole, he speculates, was once filled by a completed portrait of the Second Nun and by a full portrait, "if it were ever written," of her one priest.[48]

While I find Brosnahan's "admission of a hole" entirely persuasive, rather than attempt to fill that manhole with an imaginary lost presence, I think it is important that it remain a meaningful absence, serving as an "affirmation of the nonorigin" of the Nun's Priest's body.[49] This powerful gesture, Chaucer's "pre-erasure" of the Nun's Priest's material existence, would thus seem to "castrate" the entire tradition he embodies. For what it means is that everything that the Nun's Priest stands for—centuries' worth of argument in defense of the virile style and of the potent art of the male genius—has been cut away from its putative foundation in reality and in truth. As a consequence, these masculinist precepts are now represented by Chaucer as being no more (and no less) valid than any other constructs of our free-floating imaginations.

But does this mean that Chaucer's intent, from the outset, has been ultimately to destroy these medieval masculinist aesthetic ideals? My answer to this question is a qualified "no." In the figure of one fantastic body (the Nun's Priest) and in the figure of one slightly neurotic fan (Harry Bailly), Chaucer has managed to diagnose and decenter the phallocentric presuppositions of a complex European aesthetic tradition. But ultimately he has chosen to do so by employing the double-voiced poetics of parody rather than the cutting-edge aggressivity of satire. In his critical diagnosis, in other words, it has been his preference to counterbalance the celebratory and the dysfunctional, the positive and the problematic, the enabling and disenabling elements of this tradition. While Chaucer may well be unique among his peers in his commitment to pruning back the tradition, there is no evidence that he is committed to killing it off *tout court*. Indeed, were he intent on completely undoing the medieval precepts of the virile style and of masculine literary Genius, even as an unusually evolved poet he would be in grave danger of cutting himself with his own knife.

Notes

1. Alan T. Gaylord, "*Sentence* and *Solaas* in Fragment VII of the *Canterbury Tales*: Harry Bailly as Horseback Editor," *PMLA* 82 (1967): 226–35.

2. Helen Cooper, *The Structure of the Canterbury Tales* (Athens: University of Georgia Press, 1984), 162.

3. Quotations from the *Canterbury Tales* are from *The Riverside Chaucer*, 3rd ed., gen. ed., Larry D. Benson (Boston: Houghton Mifflin, 1987), with fragment and line numbers in parentheses.

4. See VII.1907 and, more generally, 1893–1933, where Harry reveals that Goodelief considers him a "milksop" and a "coward ape."

5. While including these lines in brackets in its master text, the *Riverside* edition explains: "These lines occur in a group of nine MSS generally taken to be of inferior authority and may have been cancelled by Chaucer when he wrote lines 1941–62 of the Monk's Prologue, where the same ideas are repeated" (*Riverside Chaucer*, 941; see also 1133). For Harry's earlier and similar praise of the Monk, see VII.1941–62; and for the Chaucerian narrator's praise of the Monk as a "manly man" in the *General Prologue*, see I.167.

6. Alice S. Miskimin, *The Renaissance Chaucer* (New Haven: Yale University Press, 1975), 78.

7. Patricia Parker, "Virile Style," in *Premodern Sexualities*, ed. Louise Fradenburg and Carla Freccero (New York: Routledge, 1996), 201–22.

8. *Epistle 899*, quoted by Parker, ibid., 201.

9. Quoted by Parker, ibid., 202.

10. See ibid., 201–22.

11. Ibid., 202.

12. Quoted by Parker, ibid., 204.

13. Quoted by Parker, ibid., 202.

14. Quoted by Parker, ibid., 204.

15. Quoted by Parker, ibid., 205.

16. Quoted by Parker, ibid., 204.

17. For an application of these ideas to Boccaccio's linguistic predilections, see Teodolinda Barolini, "'Le Parole Son Femmine e I Fatti Sono Maschi': Toward a Sexual Poetics of the *Decameron* (*Decameron* II, 10)," *Studii sul Boccaccio* 21 (1993): 175–97. As noted by Parker (214), the Old Italian proverb "Fatti maschi, parole femmine" (Men are Deeds, Women are Words) still serves as the motto on the Great Seal of Maryland.

18. Quoted by Parker, "Virile Style," 203.

19. Matthew of Vendôme, *Ars Versificatoria*, trans. Roger P. Parr (Milwaukee: Marquette University Press, 1981), 75 (translation modified slightly by Epp, see note 22).

20. *Ars Versificatoria*, 74 (translation modified slightly by Epp, see note 22).

21. *Ars Versificatoria*, 75 (translation modified slightly by Epp, see note 22).

22. Garret P. J. Epp, "Learning to Write with Venus's Pen: Sexual Regulation in Matthew of Vendôme's *Ars versificatoria*," in *Desire and Discipline: Sex and Sexuality in the Premodern West*, ed. Jacqueline Murray and Konrad Eisenbichle (Toronto: University of Toronto Press, 1996), 265–79.

23. Marjorie Curry Woods, "Rape and the Pedagogical Rhetoric of Sexual Violence," in *Criticism and Dissent in the Middle Ages*, ed. Rita Copeland (Cambridge: Cambridge University Press, 1996), 73.

24. *The Cosmographia of Bernardus Silvestris,* ed. and trans. Winthrop Wetherbee (New York: Columbia University Press, 1973), 96.

25. Ibid., 126.

26. Claire Fanger, "The Formative Feminine and the Immobility of God: Gender and Cosmogony in Bernard Silvestris's *Cosmographia,*" in *The Tongue of the Fathers,* ed. David Townsend and Andrew Taylor (Philadelphia: University of Pennsylvania Press, 1998), 81.

27. In their studies of Bernard's primary source, Plato's *Timaeus,* Luce Irigaray and Judith Butler both focus upon Plato's patriarchal valorizing of *hyle,* that is, the nature of feminine matter. Matter for Plato is "sterile," writes Irigaray, "female in receptivity, not in pregnancy . . . castrated of that impregnating power which belongs only to the unchangeably masculine." Luce Irigaray, *Speculum of the Other Woman,* trans. Gillian C. Gill (Ithaca, N.Y.: Cornell University Press, 1985), 244. Butler expands upon Irigaray's analysis, arguing that the cosmogony of Forms in the *Timeaus* is "a phallic phantasy of a fully self-constituted patrilineality, and this fantasy of autogenesis or self-constitution is effected through a denial and cooptation of the female capacity for reproduction." Judith Butler, *Bodies That Matter: On the Discursive Limits of "Sex"* (New York: Routledge, 1993), 43.

28. Alanus de Insulis, *The Plaint of Nature,* trans. James J. Sheridan (Toronto: Pontifical Institute of Mediaeval Studies, 1980), 216.

29. Ibid., 218.

30. Ibid., 71–72.

31. Ibid., 136.

32. Ibid., 137.

33. Ibid., 154–55.

34. See especially Jan Ziolkowski, *Alan of Lille's Grammar of Sex: The Meaning of Grammar to a Twelfth-Century Intellectual* (Cambridge, Mass.: Medieval Academy of America, 1985); Alexandre Leupin, *Barbarolexis: Medieval Writing and Sexuality,* trans. Kate M. Cooper (Cambridge, Mass.: Harvard University Press, 1989), 59–78; Winthrop Wetherbee, *Platonism and Poetry in the Twelfth Century: The Literary Influence of the School of Chartres* (Princeton: Princeton University Press, 1972), 188–211; Winthrop Wetherbee, "The Function of Poetry in the *de Planctu Naturae,*" *Traditio* 25 (1969): 87–125; Miskimin, *The Renaissance Chaucer;* Hugh White, *Nature, Sex, and Goodness in a Medieval Literary Tradition* (Oxford: Oxford University Press, 2000), 84–95; and Larry Scanlon, "Unspeakable Pleasures: Alain de Lille, Sexual Regulation, and the Priesthood of Genius," *Romanic Review* 86 (1995): 213–42.

35. Leupin, *Barbarolexis,* 67.

36. Alanus, *The Plaint of Nature,* 135.

37. Andrew Cowell, "The Dye of Desire: The Colors of Rhetoric in the Middles Ages," *Exemplaria* 11 (1999): 116.

38. Alastair Minnis, *Magister Amoris: The Roman de La Rose and Vernacular Hermeneutics* (Oxford: Oxford University Press, 2001), 201.

39. Ibid., 169.

40. Ibid.

41. Shedding light on the semiotics of nakedness and of clothing in medieval poetry and aesthetics, Minnis connects Chaucer's opposition in the Prologue to the *Legend of Good Women* between "the naked text" and "glosyng" to "the crucial importance of the *sensus literalis*" in relation to the "fabulous garments of style which had adorned the *integumenta poetarum*" (*Magister Amoris*, 137).

42. Guillaume de Lorris and Jean de Meun, *The Romance of the Rose*, trans. Harry W. Robbins (New York: Dutton, 1962), 411 (ll. 19436–37).

43. Ibid., 415, lines 19610–11.

44. Minnis discusses the expectation in the Middle Ages that a priest should be sexually intact (*Magister Amoris*, 195).

45. Jean never makes these vows explicit. In fact, Nature, as she sends her priest to Cupid, allows that "Of Forced Abstinence / I've much suspicion": *The Romance of the Rose*, 410, lines 19347–48.

46. Sigmund Freud, "The Uncanny," in *Literary Theory: An Anthology*, ed. Julie Rivkin and Michael Ryan (Malden, Mass.: Blackwell, 1998), 160.

47. Jacques Derrida, *Dissemination*, trans. Barbara Johnson (London: Athlone, 1981), 268 note 67.

48. Leger Brosnahan, "The Authenticity of *And Preestes Thre*," *Chaucer Review* 16 (1982): 306.

49. For an interesting interpretation of the "'blank' persona" of the Nun's Priest, see Richard Neuse, *Chaucer's Dante: Allegory and Epic Theater in the Canterbury Tales* (Berkeley: University of California, 1991), 119.

10

MARGARET AZIZA PAPPANO

"Leve Brother"

*Fraternalism and Craft Identity in
the Miller's Prologue and Tale*

"Leve brother Osewold," the Miller begins in a conciliatory tone as he responds to the choleric Reeve's protest over his projected tale. But the ensuing speech is rather ambiguous, failing to address the Reeve's concerns about character defamation or to heed his advice that "thou mayst ynough of othere thynges seyn" (3149).[1] This speech, constituting sixteen lines of the Miller's Prologue, represents a peculiar logic that deserves closer study than it has hitherto received, despite the preeminence that the Prologue itself has achieved in Chaucerian scholarship. Frequently, discussions of the Miller's Prologue have focused on the Miller's "interruption" of the Host and the tale-telling process, configuring relations between Knight and Miller in terms of a confrontation between value systems—feudal or courtly on the one side and peasant or "popular" on the other.[2] This essay proposes that the "values" etched out in Robyn's response to the Reeve may be seen in a more specific context: in his striving to propound a theory of male relations in an economy of exchange, the Miller's speech draws upon, even as it reformulates, a discourse of fraternalism that was associated with the late medieval craft guilds.[3] The Miller has been often interpreted as a peasant rather than an artisan, but an examination of the theory of brotherhood that

subtends his Prologue and Tale aligns him more closely with the organizations of late medieval craftworkers. What is at stake in this argument is both
a new way of understanding the "masculine rivalries" of Fragment I and also
a suggestion that we reconsider Chaucer's literary engagement with the urban
politics that played such a large part in his extraliterary life.

"Leve brother" is therefore not simply an empty rhetorical term deployed
in a gesture of appeasement; it also represents Robyn's address to the Reeve
as his fellow in the same collective enterprise, albeit laden with complex
and multiple motivations. "Leeve brother" is also the term by which the
clerks address each other in their shared merriment over John the Carpenter's misfortunes at the end of the Miller's Tale, where it represents a term
of group identity constituted over and against the "wood" woodworker. Indeed, throughout the *Canterbury Tales*, Chaucer deploys the phrase in contexts that are highly charged, signaling the often subjective and strategic motivations through which men claim relations of brotherhood. Most strikingly,
in the Miller's Prologue itself, the Host attempts to parry the Miller's drunken
interruption with the identical term: "Abyd, Robyn, my leeve brother; / Som
better man shal telle us first another" (3129–30). Twenty lines later, Robyn
uses the same phrase with the Reeve, seemingly transforming it from a context of patronizing authority exercised by Harry Bailly to argue on a basis of
shared identity. As a tavern keeper, Harry aligns himself with the Miller in
opposition to the "better" degree of the Monk, and thus "leeve brother" may
be understood here as a sign of shared class (artisanal) identity.[4] Yet even while
Chaucer invokes this sense of shared interests on one hand, on another, his
doubling of the phrase signals his concern with the multiple and highly artificial constructions of "brotherhood," which in the late fourteenth century
most notably included the "brotherhood" of the craft guilds.

Given their ubiquity and influence in medieval Europe, it is striking
how little philosophical discussion of craft guilds there was in the Middle
Ages; according to Antony Black, it is not a topic to which many medieval
writers, with the exception of jurists, turned their attention.[5] Chaucerians
have likewise noted the author's lack of engagement with the discourses of
craft guilds, despite his concern in the *Canterbury Tales* with occupational
identities and despite the marked expansion and influence of the guilds and
companies in London and, more generally, in England in his lifetime.[6] This
is all the more surprising given his twelve-year position as a controller in the
customs' house, which necessitated constant contact with the tradesmen of
the city and which coincided with his work on the *Canterbury Tales*. Even

if Chaucer was more directly involved with merchants than artisans in this work, the overlaps and tensions between these two groups was an inescapable part of London life in the late fourteenth century.[7]

Chaucer's relation to *religious* guilds has been explored by Carl Lindahl and David Wallace, among others;[8] indeed, for Wallace, it is precisely the "voluntary and exclusionary" and "dynamic" nature of these guilds that makes them such resonant models for Chaucer's pilgrimage *compaignye*. Certainly the difference between craft and religious guilds could be so murky as to be indistinguishable sometimes: a single guild could serve a dual purpose, salvational and occupational; and a guild might alter focus in the course of its lifetime.[9] But the difference could also be quite marked, in terms of its "voluntary" nature (usually, master artisans were required to join their designated occupational guilds); in terms of its role in town governances (the craft guilds often formed a recognized body that had a defined political role in the civic structure); and in terms of membership, especially gender composition (women could be members of craft guilds, but with very few exceptions, did not participate in their polity).[10] Religious guilds, as Wallace points out, could incorporate a diverse group of people, similar to the broad variety of types that characterizes the Chaucerian pilgrims: women, men, religious, seculars, a range of occupational affiliations and social "degrees." The majority of local religious guilds actually tended to associate people of similar social status;[11] such diverse groupings as Wallace outlines are found, however, in the largest, most well-known religious guilds that drew their membership from across the nation, such as the Corpus Christi Gild of York. Even there, it is important to note that "servants" were excluded from membership.[12]

In opposition to the "collective, mixed-gender behavior" that Wallace attributes to (religious) guilds, the craft guilds strove for homogeneity and tended to be composed solely of married male householders who practiced the same occupation. Since the craft guild was the venue for guarding the "secrets of the craft," membership was closely monitored and sameness was a constituent feature of association. The presumption of sameness underlies the Miller's notion of male identity and forms the basis of his story-telling dynamic. The corporate ideology of the craft guild provides the framework within which the artisan can stake his place in relation to the Knight and Monk, figures whose difference of "degree" would usually proscribe such direct address; this mode of group identity produced its own myth-making apparatus, as I discuss below, which elevated the social status of the artisan. However, even as Chaucer associates the Miller with this discourse, he points out its limitations as a model of fellowship. The language of "fair exchange" upon which craft guilds predicated their membership and vied for political power is exposed, in the *Canterbury Tales*, for its dependence upon an impossible and fantastical notion of masculinity.

Craft Guilds and Corporate Masculinity

From the 1319 royal charter of Edward II, all inhabitants of a town admitted to its freedom had to be "of some mystery"; this rendered guild membership essential to recognition of citizenship and the guilds themselves the medium of such rights. As the *Canterbury Tales* adumbrates, occupation and identity were more closely linked in premodernity than they are now. Guild membership, in fact, created artisanal identity, for it was only through such membership that an artisan's skill was recognized: "Only the possession of membership allowed for individual empowerment and the meaningful exercise of rights," Margaret Somers observes.[13] Knowledge and value rest with the collectivity, and the artisan's individual identity is thus bound up with the prosperity and political viability of the guild; he was nothing outside of it—a "foreigner," as one former haberdasher was classified when ejected from his guild for violating the terms of membership.[14] An errant member might be reinstated, not by the decision of the guild's "wardens" (elected leaders), but by "the assente and consente of al the hool feleshepe of the sayd fraternite beynge togydres."[15] The sense of identity as collectively determined meant that, for those of the artisanal class, masculinity was also tied into group experience—fully achieved, at least ostensibly, when admitted to the craft fraternity, which often coincided with marriage. "There was . . . a very real sense," Charles Phythian-Adams writes, "in which the transitory structure of each household was subsumed into the more enduring organization of the fellowship."[16]

Guild activities and legislation were designed to promote a discourse of "eternal brotherhood."[17] Ordinances enforced a commitment to the collective, imposing fines for slandering or "meddling in the craft" of brothers and for refusing fraternal duties, like participation in offices, assemblies, processions, funerals, and feasts.[18] Civic ceremonial was important to the production and display of guild identity: in venues such as Corpus Christi plays and processions, the brothers publicly identified themselves as a "body corporate" and vied to mark their guild's centrality to town life.[19] Guild membership theoretically guaranteed a "rough equality."[20] No single guild member was supposed to expand at the expense of another; members were expected to, with the same constraints on production and exchange, produce the same goods for the same money and make the same profit on them. Regulations stipulated against taking on extra apprentices (a cheap form of labor) or luring away journeymen and servants from a brother, against using manufacturing processes that constituted shortcuts or substituting sub-par or cheaper raw materials, against working extra hours or retailing in new venues—all of these practices constituted forms of "deceit" by which a member sought personal profit rather than attending to the greater "honor of the craft." Hence, an individual innovation in production was shared with the whole and became group property, one of the "secrets" of the craft.[21] An ordinance of the Bowers stipulates that "if any one of the same mistery shall buy more than 300 bow staves he shall divide them among the men of the said mystery";[22] a similar ordinance for the Carpenters and Joiners of Worcester insisted on an equitable sharing of timber.[23] An unexpected windfall was, at least theoretically, to be shared amongst all of the craft. Likewise, a failure of one member was expected to be borne by the whole. Many guilds included legislation that, if a member fell into misfortune by means other than his own negligence, he would receive support from the guild coffers.[24] However, as Black points out, "outsiders did not count."[25]

Increasingly, in the course of the fourteenth century, the craft guild was constituted as a self-regulating brotherhood, and as such, ever more concerned with the maintenance of individual group identity, especially the monitoring of membership. While the apprenticeship system continued to function as the chief means of exercising control over membership for the guilds, masters sought to install ever greater obstacles between the completion of apprenticeship and accession to master craftsmanship to maintain a small, elite community. In order to preserve the integrity of its self-definition and governance, the guild also stressed that conflicts should, if possible, be resolved within the confines of the brotherhood. The London Cordwainers ordinances of 1375 states that, "If anyone of the trade shall be found offending touching the trade, or rebellious against the wardens thereof, such persons shall not make complaint to anyone of another trade . . . but he shall be ruled by the good folks of his own trade." The ordinances of the London Cuttlers reflect this important change in emphasis between 1344 and 1380.[26] The earlier set of ordinances permits members to seek redress from the Mayor and aldermen in case of conflict, while the later insists upon the internal settlement of disputes, reinforcing the firm boundaries of guild: "No one shall be permitted to follow the said trade . . . within the city, if he will not stand by the rule of the overseers, sworn and chosen by the said trade."[27]

The Miller's attempt to appease the Reeve, "leve brother Osewold," in terms similar to the Host's—here the authority in charge of the storytelling— reflects a similar movement away from a higher, external authority towards a fraternal negotiation of differences. Significantly, the Host does not intervene in the dispute between the Miller and Reeve, as he does between the Friar and Summoner; nor does the Knight, another figure of higher authority, step in, as he does between the Pardoner and Host. The Miller, Reeve, and Cook—artisan narrators concerned with the artisanal subjects of carpenter, miller, and victualler, respectively—are represented as (temporarily) freed from external regulation, as their verbal forays constitute the type of idealized structure of collective governance propounded by the guilds. Although often intercraft disputes were mediated by a town's mayor and aldermen, Chaucer's grouping together of his artisanal narrators in Fragment I, each responding to the others as if in a circumscribed dialogue, explores the prevailing fictions of guild fellowship. But there is no fair and equal exchange in the Canterbury universe, and the Miller's complicated cajoling of the Reeve with a language of shared fraternalism exposes the myths of fellowship and fairness upon which craft guilds depended for their political viability.

Craft petitions and charters typically represent the men of the craft as upholding the public good. By demanding that production and trade be mediated by guilds, members claimed to ensure that the commonality receive high quality goods, not "false work," adulterated or underweight products that cause, in that endlessly repeated phrase, "deceit of the people." In 1350, the Glovers successfully complained about foreign gloves and girdles that were "of false fashion and vamped up of false materials, in deceit of all the people and to the great scandal of the whole trade."[28] The trade here represents its public repute at stake by the circulation of poor quality products; guarding their reputation is equated with protecting the people from faulty foreign wares. It is not only that the artisans, like "all" the people, are hurt by bad products, but that by ensuring the guild control of products, they will likewise be protecting the people. The argument by the Bowstringers capitalizes on this theme of civic protectorate. In 1385, Alan Birchore was convicted of selling false and deceptive bowstrings, "in deceit of the common people and to their manifest peril." It was argued that "because through such . . . strings, so falsely and deceitfully made, the greatest damage might easily ensue unto our Lord the King and his realm," Birchore should be sentenced to the pillory and the strings burnt beneath him.[29] Guilds repeatedly found ways to link their goods to the benefit of the commons and the realm, thus seeking to justify and perpetuate their claims to product monopolies and to elevate their own place in the social order. Their sense of corporate brotherhood, the good of the entire craft, is hence projected onto their privileged understanding of the good of the entire city and/or realm—and in a reverse logic, protecting the realm means protecting the guild.[30]

The craft guilds thus provided a means of linking the artisan into the larger project of maintaining the stability of the realm, a quintessential masculine activity traditionally associated with the Knight. The corporate body of the guild is imagined in microcosmic relation to the larger corporate bodies of city and nation; the boundedness of these bodies, united against the corrosive influence of aliens (those "false" citizens who manufacture and sell "false" goods) provides an ostensible discursive structure for this relationship; but, in fact, notions of masculine identity are deeply implicated in these claims as well. D. Vance Smith argues that in medieval thought a dual relationship exists between the *corpus politicum* and the male body: "it [the male body] stands, in many ways, for the larger world; but is also responsible, in part, for producing and maintaining that world."[31] According to Smith, male production, often imagined as labor, is a critical element of masculine identity, suggesting that, while the *corpus* may be bounded, it needs to be constantly remade, its boundaries produced and reproduced. Through this model, one can understand how the male artisan imagines that his work, however minute and specific, is essential to the integrity of the whole. A bowstringer can save England as well as a knight can, and indeed, to guard the integrity of the realm, the bowstringers need to continue to work, which means maintaining their guild's monopoly over the manufacture and sale of their products. Guilds thus provided the necessary language to situate the individual male body in the body politic, to link labor to meaning. It is perhaps for this reason that guild ordinances will occasionally stipulate that no master may enroll apprentices with physical deformities. The issue is not one of whether the deformity will hinder the apprentice's work but rather about the impossibility of a deformed body representing the civic wholeness that was basic to the guild's imaginary.

In a similar way, women's bodies are alienated from popular images of work and its corporate community. Although women continued to participate in the workforce, the organization of guilds as units of "eternal brotherhood," effectively elided women's representation in the official domains of craft identity.[32] By having no voice in guild politics and no place in the brotherhoods' public ceremonial, women's work was liable to be constructed as trivial, secondary, and even open to censure. Craft ordinances from the fourteenth century repeatedly limit or prohibit altogether the employment of women, such as the 1355 ordinance of the Braelers, which warns that "no one of the said trade shall be so daring as to set any women to work in his trade, other than his wedded wife or daughter."[33] While acknowledging the fact of women's work in the household, such ordinances seek to locate women's labor within the male authority of the family structure rather than as contractual employment. The wife of an artisan is represented chiefly as "wife" rather than as coworker in craft guild discourse, a configuration that served to magnify the association of productivity with masculinity. The subordination of the wife is, as Robyn explains, the key feature of masculine corporate identity, associating artisan status with masculine sexual and domestic dominance, a model whose limitations are rendered glaringly apparent in the character of the aged and decrepit Reeve.

The Bonds of Cuckoldry

Robyn's declaration that he intends to "telle a legende and a lyf / Bothe of a carpenter and of hys wife, / How that a clerk hath set the wrights cappe" (3141–43) is immediately challenged by Osewold the Reeve, a former member "of carpenteris craft" to whom this subject represents a direct affront. The Carpenters' Ordinances from the town of Coventry assess severe fines on anyone who "sclanders or telles eny tale be ony of hys bredryn . . . wheche he can make no profe by."[34] The Reeve's objections must be seen not only in reference to his individual identity but also in relation to the legislation of contemporaneous craft guilds that emphasizes the supreme importance of preserving fellowship through proscribing such tale-telling: "It is a synne and eek a greet folye / To apeyren any man, or hym defame, / And eek to bryngen wyves in swich fame" (3146–48), he cautions the Miller. The Reeve here notably includes women in a category separate from men, as individuals for whom defamation also represents serious injury. When Robyn responds, it is to deflect the charge by triangulating the relations: by making the women, the wife, into an object, a sort of commodity, the rivalry between the men is transformed into a bond of shared position, of "brothers." In fact, he argues, relations between men are possible precisely by the process of subordinating the wife, of making her instrumental and accessory to brotherhood. Karma Lochrie observes that this process of subordination was achieved in medieval marital practice as the legal term *femme covert* implies: "women *become* covered in marriage, thereby losing their agency."[35] The notion of triangulation is articulated by Eve Sedgwick, in her now classic *Between Men*, where she discusses the processes in which male "homosocial" relations can take the form of "a desire to consolidate partnership with authoritative males in and through the bodies of females."[36] The asymmetry of power in the gender formations that subtend the erotic triangle has important historical correspondences. In medieval artisanal culture, male partnerships required women (wives) as crucial to their formation and functioning, and yet wives' agency needed to be effaced to sustain the myths of masculine productivity.

In response to Osewold's objections, Robyn assures him:

Who hath no wyf, he is no cokewold.
But I sey nat therefore that thou art oon;
Ther been ful goode wyves many oon,
And evere a thousand goode ayeyns oon bade.
That knowestow wel thyself, but if thou madde.
Why artow angry with my tale now?
I have a wyf, pardee, as wel as thow;
Yet nolde I, for the oxen in my plogh,
Take upon me moore than ynough,
As demen of myself that I were oon;
I wol bileve wel that I am noon.

(3152 – 62)

Rather than address Osewold's concerns about character defamation—for both men and women—Robyn replies with a gesture of male corporateness: we're all cuckolds, he says. His strategem is not to assault Osewold directly but to imply that they are in the same situation (brothers), since they are both married men, with wives. He thus casts his tale as a collective address rather than an individual assault. Male relations are achieved through coming to a mutual understanding of women, which entails understanding them categorically and structurally, not in terms of an individual wife in relation to a husband, but in terms of "wives" who, as feminine beings, constitute objects of sexual investment (or cukoldry) for men's relationship with each other. Lochrie writes of this passage, "Cuckoldry is, in a sense, every husband's secret"[37]—a formulation that I would extend to saying that it is the secret of the group, even, indeed, the constitutive element of the group, like the "secret of the craft." Robyn insists that he is not saying that Osewold is a cuckold. He himself prefers to *believe* that he is not a cuckold, although he too is married. But belief is not certainty, and it is this small but significant possibility—perhaps one in a thousand—that represents the essence of masculine corporate identity to Robyn, the small nick in identity that is the shared secret and the basis of the bond.

Joseph A. Dane's close study of the syntax of lines 3159–61 of the Miller's Prologue proposes one meaning for the complicated sentence. In his reading, an accurate modern rendition would be, "I would not take on myself more than what the oxen in my plow can handle, that is, I would not deem myself a cuckold."[38] As Dane among others has pointed out, the plow is a metaphor for the penis in medieval culture; this serves to call attention to the brawny Miller's genital endowment, which he also appears to accentuate in his dress, wearing (as described in the General Prologue) "a swerd and a bokeler . . . by his syde" (558). Hence, while ascribing the state of cuckoldry to all married men *ipso facto*, the Miller assures the Reeve that his public masculine identity is intact. Robyn's reference to his own genitals very specifically points to his sexual powers, and this is significant for an understanding of his notion of cuckoldry. The Miller seems to say that he would not consider himself a cuckold without being able to cuckold in turn—it would be "moore than ynogh" (too much) to be in the position of simply being a cuckold, implying that being cuckolded is acceptable only if one may cuckold back. Robyn assures Osewold that cuckoldry does not necessarily involve an injury to masculine identity or "defamation"; for one can, in turn, cuckold another: cuckoldry is thus defined as relational. It forms the basis of a circulating system, a system in which knowledge and value are never absolutely fixed but depend upon one's position and perception.

Thus, although Robyn *wants* to believe that he is not a cuckold, he advises the Reeve that it is better not to know for sure:

An housbonde shal nat been inquisityf
Of Goddes pryvetee, nor of his wyf.
So he may fynde Goddes foyson there,
Of the remenant nedeth nat enquere.
(3163–66)

Indeed, the circulation of values in this system necessitates blindness.[39] A husband believes that he is not being cuckolded as he cuckolds another, increasing his sense of gain ("Goddes foyson"). To "enquere" after the "remenant" is to seek to know the whole truth, to ascertain if one is a cuckold, and therefore to exercise control over one's wife. Under such circumstances, as the ensuing tale describes, the system would fail and circulation would stop. The "wyf" provides the necessary mediating object through which rivalry and desire among men is simultaneously enabled and deflected in Robyn's model. Although gain in this model involves a risk (being cuckolded), it is a shared risk, something common to every man who has a wife. Hence, one's participation in the system involves a subordination of the self to the group. It preserves masculine identity by not naming oneself as a cuckold; rather, it is construed as a shared characteristic of working men.

Although cuckoldry obviously was not a requirement for guild membership, Robyn's system draws upon the guild mentality of shared risks and gains and subordination of household to brotherhood, pushing the notion of corporateness to its extreme and absurd articulation. Robyn's model of corporate cuckoldry is based, moreover, upon a fantasy of fair exchange among equals, one that is circumscribed and available only to the limited members of the brotherhood, who usually constituted the married householders of a town with burgess status. Therefore, when Osewold objects to the contents of his tale, the Miller's response is not to change or curtail his story but to cast it as one of modulated competition among equals, designed to enter into circulation with other stories: "I have a wyf pardee, as wel as thou," he says, suggesting that a similar story could be told about him. Osewold may return the *quite*, as language (storytelling), consumer goods, and women are all constructed as objects to be exchanged among men. Like Robyn, Osewold can tell a tale, trade his goods for profit, "swyve" a "wyf." They both exist in the same semistable economy of circulating values and are both subject to the same constraints on production and retail that entail both gains and losses, gives and takes. The "foyson" is available to all, as long as its partiality is accepted, as long as one does not go after the "remenant."

The model of fellowship that Robyn described in his prologue is challenged by the ensuing tales, and indeed all of Fragment I, exposing the prejudices upon which fraternalism is based and its inadequacy as a corporate structure. Indeed, the irony escapes no one that Robyn proposes such a masculinist model of fellowship to the aging Reeve, whose ability to participate in the game of cuckolding is curtailed by his limited sexual abilities:

"by his side he baar a rusty blade," we are told in the General Prologue (618). Much of his own prologue is taken up with the lament that he may "not pley for age; / Gras tyme is doon" (3868). Yet, it is important to note that the Reeve's departure from artisanal production to a position in estate management, a step up in class status, is specifically linked with his sexual deficits. The General Prologue informs us that "In youthe he hadde lerned a good myster: / He was a wel good wright, a carpenter" (613–14). The positive value judgments appended to artisanal work, his "good myster," suggest a loss inherent in his present position as Reeve. In these terms, which are closely aligned with those of the Miller, loss of handicraft production is bound up with loss of sexual prowess, and this loss threatens masculine identity: the Reeve is, notably, twice described in terms of clergy, with hair like a priest and clothing like a friar. Osewold presents a very suspicious picture to an artisan: decked out like a cleric and working as a manager in the interests of a lord, he is feared "as of the deeth" by the locals (605). Clearly, he has left his artisan affiliations behind, forsaking fraternity for individual profit, productive labor for the "sleight[s]" and "covyne[s]" of management, masculine identity for a celibate appearance (604). His material success has been won at the costs of fraternal and craft identity, which the narrator of the General Prologue suggests is a bad compromise: he is a failed artisan and a failed man.

The Miller's Tale appears to be constructed in close relation to the Prologue, enacting its very terms. In the tale, John the Carpenter, who functions as the Reeve's *fabliau doppelganger*, immediately defies the very precepts of Robyn's cuckoldry system by guarding Alisoun, his wife, rather than letting her circulate around town: "Jalous he was, and heeld hire narwe in cage / For she was wylde and yong, and he was old / And demed himself been like a cokewold" (3224–26). Cuckoldry indeed means something different to an old man than to a "stout carl" like the Miller. One way of reading the tale is to see John guilty of privileging the couple over the company; in this way, it functions as an artisanal exemplum designed to encourage male relations and punish offenders by demonstrating the pitfalls of uxorious behavior. When informed by Nicholas of the impending flood that threatens all mankind, John's response shows marked lack of care for his fellows, as his sole concern is with the fate of his wife: "Allas, my wyf! / And shal she drenche? Allas, myn Alisoun!" (3522–23).

As Sandra Pierson Prior has pointed out, the contemporaneous mystery cycles provided an important intertext for the Miller's Tale.[40] John the Carpenter represents the figure of Noah, charged with the tasks of

constructing the ark. The analogy between John and Noah serves to emphasize John's position as artisan since the cycle plays were often associated with
the town craftsmen, who financed, produced, and acted in them; and John is
charged by Nicholas the clerk with physically constructing and enacting the
elements of the "play," much as an artisan-actor would be. The Noah plays
were particularly important venues for the articulation of male craft identity, since the scene in which God instructs Noah in shipbuilding was often
staged as the divine authorization of artisanal production itself. The extant
cycles associated with craft guild production sought to represent the skilled
labor that is involved in shipbuilding as received directly from God.[41] In the
Newcastle play of "Noah's Ark," God says:

> Although he be not a wright,
> Therfore bid him not lett;
> He shall have wit at will,
> Be that he come therto;
> All things I him fulfill,
> Pitch, tar, seam and rowe.[42]

The link between the Noah story and the carpenter's trade is cogently represented in a sixteenth-century mural in the London Carpenters' Hall, where
the theme of divinely authorized craftwork is also depicted.[43] God is shown
in the upper lefthand corner imparting instructions to Noah, which he thus
carries out with his sons in the image of building the ark to the right, emphasizing both the divine foundations of carpenters' skills and the importance
of the skilled wrights to God's salvational plan.

Concomitantly, the exclusion of Noah's wife from artisan work is specifically thematized in the plays as she complains about her husband's absence and even, in the York play, about being left at home and out of the
ark-building process. The Noah plays are important public sites for the production of gendered craft identity: in these plays, artisan work becomes syn-
onymous with *male* artisan work, and women are shown as split off from
men's important labor and represented as having limited intellectual and
spiritual capacities to understand its meaning. In the Newcastle "Noah" play,
at Noah's announcement of the ark's completion, his wife's scornful response
is "Who, devil, made thee a wright?"[44] In the York cycle, Noah reprimands
his wife in Christ-like terms, "O woman, arte thou woode? / Of my workis
thou not wotte" (93–94).[45] Failure to believe in her husband's capacities for

skilled labor becomes equated with failure to understand the spiritual enterprise of God's salvation represented by the ark. The christological associations of Noah's speech and the typological associations of the ark with cross exemplify the dualistic claims of masculine identity: Noah's body is the world and is responsible for making the world. The productive and reproductive facets of masculine identity converge here through Noah's association with Christ (who is both the world and redeemer of the world), physical production of the ark (which is also the world in miniature), and the repopulation of the world through his sons.

In his tale, however, the Miller represents the uxorious John as failing to live up to the example of the patriarchal craftsman Noah, the old man whose body and soul are remade and reinvigorated through the divine infusion of artisan work. In the York play, Noah comments how his body is made youthful again through building the ark:

> Fyfe hundreth wyntres I am of elde—
> Methynk ther yeris as yesterday.
> Ful wayke I was and all unwelde,
> My werynes is wente away.[46]

In the Noah plays, this new work identity typically transforms the old husband into authoritative patriarch of the new world order, now capable of ruling over family and earth. In most mystery play versions, this new identity, as it "rights" the domestic hierarchy, strains marital relations in the family. Noah's wife is commonly represented as the stock figure of a "scold" or "unruly woman" as she resists Noah's newly acquired authority.[47] This is the version that the Miller evokes as Nicholas explains to John:

> Hastou nat herd, quod Nicholas, also
> The sorwe of Noe with his felaweshipe,
> Er that he myghte gete his wyf to shipe?
> Hym hadde levere, I dar wel undertake,
> At thilke tyme, than alle his wetheres blake
> That she hadde had a ship hirself alone.
>
> (3538–43)

Nicholas' description summons the quarrelsome couple to the reader's mind; as the clerk tells it, Noah would have given up all of his valuable black sheep rather than be cooped up in the same boat with his wife for forty days. In this context, John's uxoriousness, keeping his wife "narwe in cage," runs counter to the Noah story, raising the question of his difference, of his failure of masculine artisanal identity and its concomitant mastery of household relations. Neither John's authority nor aged body is remade by the work of shipbuilding, as is the legendary Noah's; John, in fact, breaks his arm and, through the machinations of Nicholas and Alisoun, becomes the laughing stock of the town by the end of the tale.

In the Miller's terms, John's excessive concern with his wife represents a regressive privileging of household over guild, leaving him open to manipulation by the well-organized fellowship of clerks. In his response to Osewold, Robyn proleptically delineates the cautionary message of his tale in his prologue when he warns "An housbonde shal nat been inquisityf / Of Goddes pryvetee, nor of hys wyf" (3163–64). Husbands, in possession of wives, are defined in contradistinction to clerks, those who do not have wives and hence, by definition, cannot be cuckolded (which also excludes them from the artisanal economy as Robyn has outlined it). The Miller warns that husbands should seek neither clerical knowledge, which is figured as absolute knowledge, nor absolute knowledge of their wives, by guarding them. Clerks and wives, celibates and women, represent two poles against which masculine artisanal identity is constituted. Therefore, in seeking information about the flood ("Goddes pyvytee"), John dangerously aligns himself with Nicholas the clerk. When the flood has receded, Nicholas promises, "thanne shul we be lordes al oure lyf / Of al the world, as Noe and hys wyf" (3581–82). The rewards that Nicholas promises him are at odds with artisanal identity by their emphasis on the couple and by the use of the term "lord," pointing to a striving above and beyond the egalitarian identity represented by craft brotherhood. "Lord" is, significantly, the term associated with Theseus' form of governance in the Knight's Tale. Moreover, the impossibility of this formulation fails to strike John, but it should strike the reader: if there are three implied in the "we," there will be an uncomfortable lordship after the flood with two men sharing Alisoun; if there are two, it may not include John (or perhaps not with Alisoun), since "we" necessarily includes the speaker, Nicholas himself. Who the "lords" will be and who exactly is referred to in the phrase "Noah and his wife" is highly ambiguous here; but in any combination, it is compromising to the position of "husband."

In many ways, the craft guild represented an alternative to the organizational structure of clerical culture, and this was particularly true in medieval Oxford, the setting for the Miller's Tale. Composed of "husbands" rather than celibate men, the structure of "eternal brotherhood" bound the brothers together in a powerful organization of horizontal male bonds, predicated on the exclusion of women. For working men, "men who swink," the guild's collectivity provided a shared means of gaining access to power and privileges. But John's refusal of guild ties in favor of the couple puts him at a disadvantage, leaving him subject to the ridicule of the town without any protection from his brotherhood. Robyn's opening address to Osewold, "Leve brother," takes on a particularly ironic twist at the end, as John's fate is determined collectively—not by his "brothers" but by the fellowship of the clerks who, through sheer group strength, are able to promulgate their interpretation of events throughout the town:

> . . . he was holde wood in al the toun;
> For every clerk anonright heeld with oother.
> They seyde, "The man is wood, my leeve brother"
> And every wight gan laughen at this stryf.
> (3846–49)

As they "hold with" Nicholas, their fellow clerk, the clerks perform the very cohesive fellowship that is supposed to be characteristic of guild brothers. The clerks of the tale constitute their identity in categorical terms, much like Robyn's wishful concept of the "housband" in his prologue. Their affiliation to each other, when threatened by the outsider, the craftsman, transcends their manifold differences to form a collective voice of derisive laughter.

The Carpenter is in fact beaten by both clerk and wife, a point that is structurally significant for the framework of the tale. It is not simply that John the Carpenter fails to "hold with" his fellow artisans, but that the fraternal system itself fails to hold. Alisoun's refusal, or rather clever use, of the subordinate identity assigned to the "wyf" is something that Robyn's fraternalism precludes; as has been frequently argued, she is the only figure who goes unpunished as male rivalries and desires collide and are exercised upon each other's bodies.[48] Thus she looks forward to the figure of Alisoun of Bath, another woman who utilizes, towards her own ends, the position of passivity that cuckoldry assigns to her. Like Robyn, the Wife of Bath advocates the law of blindness in cuckoldry, but for reasons that further her own profit:

We love no man that taketh kep or charge
Wher that we goon; we wol ben at oure large.
Of alle men yblessed moot he be,
The wise astrologien, Daun Ptholome,
That seith this proverbe in his Almageste:
"Of alle men his wysdom is the hyeste
That rekketh nevere who hath the world in honde."
(321–27)

As long as her husband has "queynte right ynogh at eve" (332), the Wife asks, why should he complain or seek to know more? The Wife of Bath's Prologue reveals that the commodity form that is assigned to wives by the artisanal structure allows them to effectively enter into exchange for their own purposes. Never suspected of being agents themselves, women may in fact treat husbands as commodities, as the Wife exchanges one for another at the same time that she accumulates their goods; they, in turn, believe that they are getting "[her] body and [her] good" (314). As Mary Carruthers observes, "Alisoun is no modest artisan," but a trader of international caliber, a "capitalist entrepreneur."[49] In this capacity, the Wife exerts control over a workforce of weavers and wool-producers, perhaps, in her obvious material success, manipulating the workers as effectively as she does her husbands, about whom she claims, "How pitously a-nyght I made hem swynke!" (202).

In the *Canterbury Tales,* productive labor is figured as a masculine attribute, much as Robyn depicts it: although artisans are well represented in the tales, secular women are rarely shown in any situation other than wife, widow, or daughter. (The "compeer" of Perkyn Revelour, who has a wife who "swyved for hir sustenance" (4422), constitutes one of the only exceptions to this pattern.) This characteristic is all the more striking for its collusion with contemporaneous guild representations, which as I noted above, effectively elided evidence of women's labor. While Chaucer seems to reproduce the masculinist biases of Robyn's system, he also subjects it to the destabilizing power of its very constituent others—women, clerics, and apprentices. This is especially apparent in Fragment I, in which the artisan protagonists are successfully challenged in each tale by these very categories of individuals. The essence of the power of the artisan is revealed to be predicated on practices of exclusion. In this way, it represents association of the most limited and precarious sort, association that is precisely opposite to that of the international trading world represented by the Wife of Bath and the Man of Law.[50]

No Priests, Bakers, or Unaccompanied Wives Allowed

The Ordinances of the Cambridge Guild of the Annunciation include the curious rule that "nullus capellanus, pistor, aut uxor, in dicta gilda recipiatur, nisi vir uxoris ante eam in eadem gilda fuerit receptus" [no chaplain or baker or wife will be received into the said guild, unless the husband of the wife will have been admitted before her].[51] Although religious guilds in contradistinction to craft guilds usually admitted women as freely as men, the restriction on wives without husbands here points out some of the prejudices that also demonstrate a continuity with craft organizations. The middling values of these associations reinforced the hierarchy of the family, deeming women without husbands a potential source of conflict. However, I want to conjecture that there is something more at stake in this rule that illuminates the culture Chaucer explores in the Miller's Prologue and Tale. While the exclusion of priests and wives, the oppositional categories of male artisan identity, is understandable in the terms of guild culture, the exclusion of the baker, however, points to the fantasy of communal identity through which these organizations sustained themselves. Perhaps more often than any other trade, bakers are cited in town governance and contemporary literature as infringers of the common good. Their widespread reputation as cheats and liars likely proceeds, at least partly, from the centrality that their product, bread, occupied in the daily diet of medieval people; their crimes were escalated in the eyes of medieval people, since it was thought that they profited from cheating their own neighbors. In the fifteenth century, John Lydgate wrote, "Let mellerys and bakerys gadre hem a gilde / And alle of assent make a fraternite; / Undir the pillory a litil chapel bylde" (17–19),[52] pointing to the ubiquity with which bakers (and millers) were cast into the pillory for violating civic laws; the poem suggests that such cheats should form their own fraternity, distinctly marked and separate from the associations of others.

By excluding bakers, the Cambridge Gild of the Annunciation seeks to establish itself as an organization of reputable men all commonly invested in the public good, which artisans associated with the sense of shared loss and gain that they enshrined in guild discourse. Bakers, like priests and women, were considered unreliable members, since it was thought that they failed to accept the ideals of brotherhood, pursuing individual over common gain. It is not surprising that Lydgate associates bakers and millers, since the two trades were often conflated in practice and thus might occupy the same craft guild; there is evidence, for instance, that bakers commonly leased mills.[53] Chaucer's attribution to the Miller of a language of fraternalism is thus suspect from the outset, since it comes from one of the notorious cheats of the craft world, as his portrait in the General Prologue clearly emphasizes.[54] In these terms, the Miller's discourse of brotherhood, and by extension, craft fraternalism, reveals not only the impossible fiction of egalitarianism upon which it is predicated but also the way that such an egalitarian fiction can be strategically and deviously employed for personal profit. Despite his rhetoric of accepted gains and losses, the Miller hopes to gain more than he loses in his contest with Osewold; at the same time, he needs Osewold to face the Knight. The supposed enduring and natural relations of brotherhood become transparently provisional and contingent in the Canterbury context. However, Chaucer's critique of craft fraternalism as a model of fellowship may not so much signify his championing of its constituent others (women, priests, apprentices), though he gives these groups a voice, as it does his interest in the dynamics of international exchange that runs counter to the small-time, local interests of these fraternal organizations. Perhaps, as much as anything else, it is the artisanal commitment to provincial experience as the domain of English identity that accounts for the termination of Fragment I and speaks to Chaucer's grander ambitions for his work.

Notes

1. All citations of Chaucer's work are from *The Riverside Chaucer*, 3rd ed., gen. ed., Larry D. Benson (Boston: Houghton Mifflin, 1987). Line numbers will be cited parenthetically in the text.

2. There are too many occurrences of this topos in recent scholarly literature to cite them adequately, but critics who use a Bakhtinian framework have exploited this opposition particularly productively. See, for instance, John Ganim, *Chaucerian Theatricality* (Princeton: Princeton University Press, 1990).

3. Critics have tended to speak of Chaucer's Miller as a peasant, mostly in contrast to the courtly Knight, but many towns included millers' guilds, and millers were frequently classified as artisans. Lee Patterson discusses the ambiguity of the Miller's vocational status in *Chaucer and the Subject of History* (Madison: University of Wisconsin Press, 1991), 255–58.

4. For a discussion of artisans as a class, see Heather Swanson, *Medieval Artisans: An Urban Class in Late Medieval England* (Oxford: Basil Blackwell, 1989).

5. Antony Black, *Guilds and Civil Society in European Political Thought from the Twelfth Century to the Present* (Ithaca, N.Y.: Cornell University Press, 1984), 29.

6. Chaucer's interest in the countryside and rural production, rather than in the urban politics of the city, has been explored by Patterson in *Chaucer and the Subject of History*, and by David Wallace in *Chaucerian Polity: Absolutist Lineages and Associational Forms in England and Italy* (Stanford, Calif.: Stanford University Press, 1997). Recently, James H. Landman has discussed the *Canon's Yeoman's Tale* in terms of the "special discourse" associated with the "urban guilds of merchants and artisans," suggesting that the Yeoman's belated meeting with the Canterbury pilgrims stages a confrontation between two different forms of community with different rules of collective behavior—that of "craft guilds" and that of the pilgrimage, the former concerned with guarding secrets and the latter with tale-telling. "The Laws of Community, Margery Kempe, and the 'Canon's Yeoman's Tale,'" *Journal of Medieval and Early Modern Studies* 28.2 (1998): 389–425.

7. In 1383 the commercial and artisan interests came to a head in the clash between Nicholas Brembre and John de Northhampton for the mayoral office. See Pamela Nightingale's detailed discussion, "Capitalists, Crafts and Constitutional Change in Late Fourteenth-Century London," *Past and Present* 124 (1989): 3–35.

8. Carl Lindahl, *Earnest Games: Folkloric Patterns in the Canterbury Tales* (Bloomington: Indiana University Press, 1987), esp. 25–31; and Wallace, *Chaucerian Polity*, esp. 65–103.

9. For a discussion of such shifts in guild affiliations, see Gervase Rosser, "Workers' Associations in English Medieval Towns," in *Les métiers au moyen âge: Aspects economiques et sociaux*, ed. Pascale Lambrechts and Jean-Pierre Sosson (Louvain-la-Neuve: Publications de l'Institute d'Études Médiévales, 1994), 283–306.

10. I am taking explicit issue here with Wallace's criticism of tendencies to draw a "simplistic distinction between craft guilds and religious confraternities." While I agree with him that sometimes the two did merge and a "religious" fraternity might even become the governing body of a town (for example, Norwich's Guild of St. George and Lichfield's Guild of St. Mary), or a guild with economic functions might have an elaborate pious component (like the Mercers and Merchants Guild of York), craft guilds did play an important structural role in economic organization that religious guilds *usually* did not. Moreover, women's roles, even the frequency and terms in which "sisters" were referred to, reveal important distinctions in gendered participation in the types of guilds. A person did often belong to two different guild organizations. The 1389 returns, the basis of Wallace's argument, tend to portray greater similarities between types of guilds than those ordinances preserved in civic and parish records; it may be that in accentuating their pious activities in the returns, the craft guilds were attempting to downplay their role as labor organizations.

11. Miri Rubin, "Small Groups: Identity and Solidarity in the Late Middle Ages," in *Enterprise and Individuals in Fifteenth-Century England*, ed. Jennifer Kermode (Wolfboro Falls, N.H.: Allan Sutton, 1991), 132–50; Ben R. McRee, "Religious Gilds and Regulation of Behavior in *Late Medieval Towns*, in *People, Politics,*

and Community in the Later Middle Ages, ed. Joel Rosenthal and Colin Richmond (New York: St. Martin's, 1987), 108–22.

12. This, of course, does replicate the organization of the pilgrimage *compaignye* itself, with the ambiguous exception of the Cook, whose truncated tale appears to represent his anomalous status between artisan and servant.

13. Margaret R. Somers, "The 'Misteries' of Property: Relationality, Rural Industrialization, and Community in Chartist Narratives of Political Rights," in *Early Modern Conceptions of Property,* ed. John Brewer and Susan Staves (New York: Routledge, 1996), 75.

14. *Liber Albus,* ed. Henry Thomas Riley (London: Longman, Brown, 1859), 258–59.

15. From the "Ordinance and Memorandum Book of the Grocers' Company," Corporation of the City of London, Appendix A to Landman, "The Laws of Community," 421.

16. Charles Phythian-Adams, *Desolation of a City: Coventry and the Urban Crisis of the Late Middle Ages* (Cambridge: Cambridge University Press, 1979), 98.

17. For a discussion of this language, see Black, *Guilds and Civil Society,* chapter 1, "The Guild: Ethos and Doctrine," 12–31.

18. Many of these ideals of association can be found today in labor unions, including the union's responsibility for funeral arrangements. See, for instance, *The Constitution and Laws of the United Brotherhood of Carpenters and Joiners of America* (as amended 1987).

19. See, for example, the ordinances of the Tailors of Exeter, who declare that "the gild shall be a body corporate," in *English Gilds,* ed. Toulmin Smith (London: Early English Text Society, 1870), 301.

20. A. B. Hibbert, "The Economic Policies of Towns," in *The Cambridge Economic History of Europe,* ed. M. M. Postan, E. E. Rich, and Edward Miller (Cambridge: Cambridge University Press, 1952), 3:213.

21. Sylvia Thrupp, "The Gilds," in *The Cambridge Economic History of Europe,* 230–80.

22. From Letter Book H, reprinted in *Memorials of London and London Life in the XIIIth, XIVth, and XVth Centuries,* ed. and trans. Henry Thomas Riley, 2 vols. (London: Longmans, Green, and Co., 1868), 2:414.

23. Smith, *English Gilds,* 210.

24. Rosser, "Workers' Associations," 302–4.

25. Black, *Guilds and Civil Society,* 16.

26. George Unwin, *The Gilds and Companies of London* (London: Frank Cass, 1963), 89.

27. "Ordinances of the Cutlers" from Letter Book H, reprinted in Riley, *Memorials of London,* 2:440.

28. Letter Book F, reprinted in Riley, *Memorials of London,* 1:250

29. Letter Book H, reprinted in ibid., 2:486.

30. Landman notes a similar mechanism operating in an ordinance of the London Horners' guild, which claimed to bolster the fortunes of all "englissh chaffare" by preserving the Horners control over local horn production; he writes, "[t]his ordinance not only reconciles craft confidentiality and city-wide common profit—it asserts their interdependence," Landman, "The Laws of Community," 16.

31. D. Vance Smith, "Body Doubles: Producing the Masculine Corpus," in *Becoming Male in the Middle Ages*, ed. Jeffrey Jerome Cohen and Bonnie Wheeler (New York: Garland, 1997), 5.

32. Martha C. Howell, in *Women, Production, and Patriarchy in Late Medieval Cities* (Chicago: University of Chicago Press, 1986), provides an excellent analysis of the repercussion of guild organization on women's work and role in the civic and family structure. See also her "Citizenship and Gender: Women's Political Status in Northern Medieval Cities," in *Women and Power in the Middle Ages*, ed. Mary Erler and Maryanne Kowaleski (Athens: University of Georgia Press, 1988), 37–60.

33. Letter Book G, reprinted in Riley, *Memorials of London*, 1:278.

34. Quoted in Phythian-Adams, *Desolation of a City*, 110.

35. Karma Lochrie, *Covert Operations: The Medieval Uses of Secrecy* (Philadelphia: University of Pennsylvania Press, 1999), 142. See Lochrie's analysis of the "Miller's Tale" for similar concerns about women's work, 164–76.

36. Eve Kosofsky Sedgwick, *Between Men: English Literature and Male Homosocial Desire* (New York: Columbia University Press, 1985), 38.

37. Lochrie, *Covert Operations*, 166.

38. Joseph A. Dane, "The *Syntaxis Recepta* of Chaucer's 'Prologue to the Miller's Tale,' Lines 3159–61," *English Language Notes* 31.4 (1994): 10–19, 11.

39. As Sedgwick writes of cuckoldry, "most characteristically, the difference of power occurs in the form of a difference of knowledge: the cuckold is not even supposed to know that he is in such a relationship." Sedgwick, *Between Men*, 50.

40. Sandra Pierson Prior, "Parodying Typology and the Mystery Plays in the Miller's Tale," *Journal of Medieval and Renaissance Studies* 16.1 (1986): 57–73.

41. The image of representing details of shipbuilding technique and thus highlighting skilled craft knowledge in the Noah's Ark plays is prevalent in all of the extant cycle plays except for N-Town, which in all likelihood is not produced by urban artisans.

42. *The Non-Cycle Mystery Plays*, ed. Osborn Waterhouse (London: Early English Text Society, 1909), 19–25, lines 21–26.

43. See B. W. E. Alford and T. C. Barker, *A History of the Carpenters Company* (London: George Allen and Unwin, 1968), 225–28, for an illustration and discussion of the dating of the murals in the Carpenter's Hall.

44. Waterhouse, *The Non-Cycle Mystery Plays*, 24, line 172.

45. "The Flood," in *The York Plays*, ed. Richard Beadle (London: Edward Arnold, 1982), 85, lines 93–94.

46. "The Building of the Ark," in Beadle, *The York Plays*, 81, lines 91–94.

47. For a reading of the figure of Noah's wife that locates feminine resistance in her character, see Ruth Evans, "Feminist Re-Enactments: Gender and the Towneley *Uxor Noe,*" in *A Wyf Ther Was: Essays in Honour of Paule Mertens-Fonck,* ed. Juliet Dor (Liège: Université de Liège, 1992), 141–54.

48. See, for instance, the analysis by Elaine Tuttle Hansen, "Women-as-the-Same in Fragment I," in *Chaucer and the Fictions of Gender* (Berkeley: University of California Press, 1992), 223–44.

49. Mary Carruthers, "The Wife of Bath and the Painting of Lions," *PMLA* 94 (1979): 210.

50. For a discussion of the role of international commerce in the Man of Law's Tale, see Robert W. Hanning's essay, "Custance and Ciappelletto in the Middle of It All: Problems of Mediation in the *Man of Law's Tale* and *Decameron* 1.1," in *"The Decameron" and "The Canterbury Tales": New Essays on an Old Question,* ed. Leonard Michael Koff and Brenda Deen Schildgen (Madison, N.J.: Farleigh Dickinson University Press, 2000), 177–211.

51. Smith, *English Gilds,* 271.

52. "Against Millers and Bakers," in *Minor Poems of John Lydgate,* ed. H. N. MacCracken, part 2 (London: Early English Text Society, 1934), 448–49.

53. Swanson, *Medieval Artisans,* 13.

54. See George Fenwick Jones, "Chaucer and the Medieval Miller," *Modern Language Quarterly* 16 (1955): 3–15, for a discussion of the deceitful occupational habits attributed to millers in the Middle Ages.

11

WILLIAM ASKINS

All That Glisters

The Historical Setting of the Tale of Sir Thopas

Though the Tale of Sir Thopas is perhaps the last of the *Canterbury Tales* still read in essentially literary terms, the traditional view that it is simply a parody of contemporary literary practice has itself met with occasional resistance. This dissent was initiated by Lilian Winstanley, who thought that the tale ridiculed Philip van Artevelde, one of the leaders of Flemish opposition to the earl of Flanders, Louis de Male. Readings that have suggested other historical contexts for this piece have been offered since by John Matthews Manly, George Williams, V. J. Scattergood, and most recently David Wallace.[1] Though the interpretations offered by Winstanley, Manly, and Williams no longer find subscribers, the assumptions that underlie these readings still merit consideration. Those assumptions are the sense that the Flemish setting of the tale matters, that the tale offers comment about contemporary Anglo-Flemish relations, and that it has been shaped by developments associated with the Hundred Years War. What follows is an exploration of details within this tale that continue to point in these directions.

Anglo-Flemish relations were primarily defined by the wool trade— or, if one looks at it from the Flemish point of view, the cloth trade—and Chaucer, controller of the Wool Custom, Wool Subsidy, and Petty Custom, knew a great deal about this traffic. Though these markets were shaped and reshaped by the vicissitudes of the Hundred Years War, what remained constant was that the English provided the Flemish with wool they could not obtain elsewhere, and the Flemish in their turn provided the English with cloth woven on their looms (as well as other goods that passed through their fairs).

It is to this context, I think, that some of the gags in "Thopas" clearly refer. There is, for example, the matter of its hero's attraction to wrestling (VII.740–41). The usual view is that the humor here depends upon class distinctions; that a knight like Thopas has no business engaging in sport more appropriate to a yeoman or some farmer on a Saturday night. The joke, however, seems to turn on the remark about the prize that the winning wrestler receives: that is to say, the ram — nothing less than a reference to the wool trade at what can only be described at its point of origin. (One can have neither wool without sheep, of course, nor, as ewes know, sheep without rams — recent scientific novelties aside.) To have said in the fourteenth century that a Flemish knight wrestled for the ram in a country where a good ram was hard to find would have been inherently ludicrous.

The reference to wrestling is itself a sign that Chaucer is toying with the idea of national identities and national types. In both French romance and French satirical literature, it is the *Englishman,* the English knight in particular, who is stereotyped as the gifted and perhaps devious wrestler; and Chaucer carefully prepares the reader for this wisecrack by noting in the previous line (739) that Thopas was also adept at archery. Archery, however, was again the *English* national sport, responsible for much of the nation's success in the Hundred Years War.[2] Skilled Flemish archers were as scarce as prize Flemish rams; and, as the historical record to which I later refer indicates, when the Flemish allies of England required the services of persons who knew how to use bow and arrow, they relied on the legion of English archers stationed at Calais. The athletic aspirations of Sir Thopas are not unlike his romantic desires: his longing for the elf-queen he has never seen rather than the bevy of real women, maidens all, who want to share his bed. What matters most, however, is that the humor in the passage in question is contingent upon national types rather than class distinctions and that this is but one of a number of signs in the text suggesting that its readers might consider the social, economic, and political histories that shaped the relationship between England and Flanders in the late fourteenth century.

The warrant for reading Thopas in terms of these histories is provided by the text itself and provided, I believe, at precisely the moment when the text refers to the literary tradition it is supposed to burlesque. The stanza in which the poet seems to link Thopas with the heroes of popular romances is one case in point.

> Men speken of romances of pris
> Of Hornchild and of Ypotys
> Of Beves and sire Gy
> Of sire Lybeus and Pleyn damour
> But sire Thopas he bereth the flour
> Of real chiualry (897–902)

I cite the text provided by Manly and Rickert here, rather than *The Riverside Chaucer,* largely because of its use of *real* in the final line, a spelling drawn from the Hengwrt manuscript (among others).[3] *The Riverside Chaucer* follows the Ellesmere manuscript and offers *roiale* instead. As the *Middle English Dictionary* attests, Middle English *real* also signifies Modern English *real,* in the sense of *true* or *actual;* and the possibility that Chaucer is exploiting the multiple meanings of *real* seems reasonable.[4] What finally determines the meaning of this word (or wordplay) is a sense of what this stanza means. As its syntax indicates, the poet is not simply likening Thopas to the other characters he mentions, but playfully indicating that Thopas is different in some fundamental way. Nor does that difference seem to be a matter of social class: Thopas is a *royal* specimen of chivalry, the others perhaps run-of-the mill knights. Horn, for one, was the son of an English king; Beves, the son of the earl of Southampton and the king of Scotland's daughter; Sir Guy, the son of pretenders to the throne. The thrust of the stanza seems to be, rather, that while the heroes of "romances of pris" are fictions, creatures of the spoken word, Sir Thopas is, as they say, the *real* thing; and this notion is delivered with the sort of cheap swagger that marks Chaucer's approximation of the minstrel voice.

Similar considerations are raised by the other stanza in the tale that refers to the romance: the account of the sort of literature Thopas likes to hear while he dresses, perhaps, to kill.

> Do come he seyde my mynstrales
> And gestours for to tellen tales
> Anon in my armynge

> Of romances that been reales
> Of popes and cardynales
> And eek of love likynge
> (845–50)

Though it is possible that the last three lines of this stanza refer to three different kinds of tale, the usual view is that they refer to "real" romances that deal with popes and cardinals, and presumably, their desires. I find it impossible to understand what kind of fare Thopas has in mind here, and I am not willing to suggest that it is appropriate for a knight from a textile-producing country to want to hear tales about heroes who are, well, men of the cloth. Though scholars have gone to some length to suggest that such texts exist, this description of these "romances" seems hopelessly muddled and a signal that something beyond literature is at issue here—that, again, Chaucer wants us to think about the "real" world through which he moved.[5]

Reading this piece along these lines requires a reconsideration of the poem's details, about which there is widespread critical agreement. The commonplace that Sir Thopas is named after a gemstone is a case in point. In the most thorough examination of this issue, John Conley ransacked medieval lapidaries in the course of establishing, first, that Chaucer probably had the yellow versions of this stone in mind rather than the green; and, second, that the virtues attributed to the topaz in these lapidaries are so various that it is not possible to reduce the significance of the gem to a single coherent idea.[6] Conley, however, chose not to pursue the line of inquiry suggested by the secondary meaning of *topaz,* this drawn from heraldic manuals in which the word refers not to the stone itself but to its color, or, as the *Oxford English Dictionary* puts it, to "the designation of the tincture *Or.*" In the course of describing the color or "tincture" of a coat of arms, heralds resorted to a variety of vocabularies; they might employ the appropriate French terminology or refer to the color of precious stones or, in some cases, to the "color" of the planets. Thus the color red might be indicated by *Gules* or Ruby or Mars, and, again, the color gold might be represented by *Or* or Topaz or Sol.[7] The heraldic meaning of *topaz* is consistent with a second apparent reference to a gemstone in the poem: the mention of the charbocle "byside" the boar's head on the hero's shield. As John Burrow notes in *The Riverside Chaucer,* the word likely refers not to a gemstone but to "the heraldic escarbuncle, a rayed bearing held to represent the precious stone carbuncle."[8] The notion, then, that Thopas is named after a gemstone may have inspired Skeat's witty and much repeated remark that it is "an excellent name for a gem of a knight"; but it is just as clear that, in this instance, Skeat took refuge in the modern vernacular and that he nodded. The use of things to represent color occurs elsewhere in "Thopas," for example, when Chaucer mentions that the hero's beard was "lyk saffron"—the point being of course that it is like the *color* of saffron. Thopas is associated with both gold and yellow throughout the poem, and his name is meant to suggest, among other things, the color of money. This is corroborated by an examination of the "heraldic" images the poet locates on the crest of his hero's helmet and, perhaps, his shield.

The image on the crest is that of a lily protruding from the top of a tower. John Burrow takes this heraldic reference seriously and, after noting that towers frequently figure in crests, claims that "the lily stuck in the tower is unparalleled and probably, like Thopas's escutcheon, fanciful."[9] The problem is that this image is not drawn from heraldry at all and that Chaucer's humor here depends on his switching contexts, decorating his hero's helmet with a well-known image that appeared on both gold and silver coins issued at the outset of the Hundred Years War, first by Philip VI, then John II of France. The coin, the *gros tournais,* is the specific issue marked with the lily in the tower, the *gros d'or au châtel fleurdilisé.* Widely distributed (and widely counterfeited), these coins have surfaced in hoards unearthed from Dover to the Middle East.[10]

Chaucer also toys with this mix of heraldic and numismatic contexts when he describes the "shield" of Thopas. The shield is said to be pure gold, "al of gold so reed." This is frequently compared to the shield of another hero of a tail-rhyme romance, the Fair Unknown, whose "scheld was of gold fyn."[11] In that instance, however, it would seem that that poet is indicating that the shield of the Fair Unknown is plated with gold. Chaucer, all seriousness aside, arms his hero with a shield that is useless, solid gold, too heavy to lift, the metal too soft to resist any missiles Sir Oliphant might toss in its owner's direction. Small wonder that, later in the poem, Chaucer the minstrel invokes divine assistance when it comes to the shielding of Thopas (908). In this passage, however, Chaucer the poet deliberately muddles the primary meaning of "shield" with its secondary meaning: the French gold coin, the *florin d'escu.*[12] Given these numismatic references, one appropriate context for this tale might be the tradition of medieval poems in Latin, French, and English that personify money; Thopas, brother to Queen Money, Mother Purse, Sir Penny, and Lady Meed.[13] References to coins are commonplace in the *Canterbury Tales*. The Pardoner, for example, refers to virtually every form of gold and silver currency issued by Edward III and Richard II, references that underscore his avarice.[14] In "Thopas," however, the money on the table is French rather than English, the issues more complicated than greed pure and simple, and the remark that "ful many a mayde" is smitten by Thopas is contingent upon the usual misogynistic humor about women and money—humor of the kind in which Chaucer was deeply versed.

Beneath the droll remark that the "shield" of Thopas was pure gold lies a second reality about Anglo-Flemish trade in the late fourteenth century: the problem of debased and counterfeit currency. Though the weight of precious metals in English coinage was regulated by statute, in Flanders the minting of both debased and counterfeit coins was a matter of state policy, the work of both Louis de Male, the earl of Flanders (1346–84), and his son-in-law and successor, Philip the Bold, duke of Burgundy. As David Nicholas indicates, during the reign of Louis de Male, "Flemish silver coinage was debased eighteen times and the gold twenty-two."[15] Philip the Bold continued what another scholar has called these "aggressive debasement policies" and by 1388 actually counterfeited "the much prized English gold *noble*," the coin commonly known as the *real* (if I may invoke that word one more time). This was decorated on its obverse with the stylized rose—the flower twice mentioned in the opening lines of "Thopas," first to describe the color of the hero's lips (726) and then his virtue—his purity, as it were (746–47).[16] The prospect of receiving debased or counterfeited foreign moneys for their exports and then paying for imports with unalloyed English gold created difficulties for English merchants and the nation at large. The English gold that English merchants paid for imports was transported to Flanders and used as bullion, turned by the earls of Flanders into debased currency, which was then paid to English merchants for their exports. This created both a shortage of the bullion upon which English currency was based and such a dearth of hard currency that modern numismatists complain about the rarity of coins issued under Richard II, and Chaucer's contemporaries complained about being unable to find small change to buy a quart of beer or to give to the poor. The parliamentary rolls and the statutes enacted during the reign of Richard II make continual reference to these difficulties, difficulties that exacerbated a depressed market on both sides of the English channel.[17]

Apart from these national concerns, Chaucer had an immediate professional interest in the circulation of debased and counterfeit currency. Though

Chaucer's position at the port of London is sometimes regarded as a sinecure, the searchers he supervised were under considerable pressure to seize counterfeited moneys before they entered the country. A statute of 1382, for example, required that "wardens and searchers of the ports and passages of England" take every measure to confiscate debased and counterfeit currency from abroad or face the possibility of forfeiting their office, their goods, and having their bodies "committed to prison, there to remain a whole year without redemption."[18] Measures like this would have had to shape the consciousness at play in the Tale of Sir Thopas, to have fed the poet's imagination. Indeed, as a second line of defense, English innkeepers like Harry Bailly were authorized by statute to search their guests for such currency in the event that it had been smuggled past port authorities.[19] Bailly's backhanded compliment to the Monk in the prologue to the latter's tale (VII.1960-62), the quip that the Monk does not pay Venus with "lussheburghes," is not only a reference to a notorious example of debased currency from the Low Countries but also a sign of an occupational twitch the innkeeper and the poet shared.[20]

Another element in the poem associated with Anglo-Flemish trade is the birthplace of Sir Thopas. It is usually said that Poperinghe was selected for this honor because it was a backwater town with an amusing name. However, as David Nicholas points out, apart from the so-called Three Cities — Ghent, Bruges, and Ypres — Poperinghe housed the largest textile industry in Flanders.[21] Furthermore, merchants from Poperinghe had been members of the London Hanse since the twelfth century, and it is not unlikely that Chaucer and his colleagues at the Wool Quay would have known such merchants by name.[22] By the fourteenth century, Poperinghe was the most advanced of what textile historians have come to call "the new draperies," to distinguish them from the traditional drapery centers: Ghent, Bruges, and Ypres. Though the weavers in these "new draperies" produced what J. H. Munro calls "costly, luxury oriented woolens," they were continually accused by the weavers of Ghent, Bruges, and Ypres of "deliberately counterfeiting their own fine woolens" and marking their woolens with selvages and seals in imitation of those found on the fabric loomed in the older draperies. In 1373, Ypres was involved in a protracted and well-documented lawsuit over the right of Poperinghe to produce these "counterfeit woolens," which Munro describes as "good quality imitations of traditional luxury woolens" that the merchants of Poperinghe could offer at a cheaper price because they used less expensive wool than did the weavers of Ypres and because they paid their own weavers lower salaries.[23] There is a long history of this kind of competition in the textile industry, and Chaucer's contemporaries would have associated Poperinghe with ideas more complex than silliness or insignificance. Among those associations would have been the cutthroat competition of the marketplace and the trade in counterfeited goods that appear elegant but bespeak deceit on the part of the seller and pretension on the part of the buyer, party to the deception. This is the cloth from which "Thopas" is cut.

As controller of the Petty Custom, Chaucer had firsthand knowledge of the kinds of luxury goods, genuine and counterfeit, that entered England through the port of London. It is not, I think, a coincidence that "Thopas" is laced with references to such items: expensive textiles (scarlet in grayn, sylkatoun, linen); clothing of the kind that might be imported to England (shoes of Spanish leather and hosiery from Bruges); metalwork and armor; spices or "herbs" (saffron, zedoary, cloves, nutmeg, and licorice); and drink and food that might be imported or made with imported ingredients (sweet wine, sugar, gingerbread, and payndemayne). The notion that all these references were culled from tail-rhyme romances is one that will not, I think, withstand close scrutiny; a more likely source, the kinds of documents Chaucer would have seen day in and day out, would be the bills of particulars or bills of lading submitted to the controller of the Petty Custom. Compiled by the collectors or their clerks, these manifests list the names of the merchants, the amount of customs they paid, the names of the ships and shipmasters in their employ, and, most importantly, the details of the cargoes these ships contained.[24] Recently the subject of a study by Vanessa Harding, these documents indicate that the majority of luxury imports, whatever their country of origin, passed through Flemish markets before they arrived at English ports in the holds of Flemish boats and that they included not only woolens from Poperinghe and the other "new draperies" in Flanders but also napery, linens, cloth of Arras, fine armor, metalwares, small manufactured items, exotic spices, and foodstuffs—in short, precisely the kinds of goods with which Thopas is associated.[25]

Other catalogues in the tale may seem closer to those found in the tail-rhyme romances, but they too admit to multiple readings. Consider the description of Thopas pricking across the plain:

> He priketh thurgh a fair forest
> Ther inne is many a wilde best,
> Ye bothe bukke and hare;

And as he priketh north and est
I telle it yow hym hadde almest
   Bitid a sory care.

Ther spryngen herbes grete and smale
The lycorys and the cetewale
   And many a clove-gylofre
And notemuge to putte in ale
Wheither it be moste or stale
   Or for to leye in cofre

The briddes synge it is no nay
The sparhauk and the popyniay
   That ioye it was to here
The thrustlecok made eek his lay
The wodedowve upon the spray
   She sang ful loude and cleere
       (754–71)

One indication that these lines are not quite what they seem is the odd reference to the practical uses of nutmeg at the end of the catalogue of herbs and spices, a note never struck in the "literary" analogues. The use of nutmeg to disguise stale ale underscores the idea of deception, one of the tale's running themes; and the idea that it is placed in coffers perhaps to scent stale clothing reminds the reader of the references to textiles in the work and may hint at the habits of dandies like Absolon in the *Miller's Tale*. Now, in his notes to the "herbs" or spices mentioned in these lines, John Burrow mentions that none of them are indigenous to Flanders.[26] However, if nutmeg and clove did not grow in Flanders' fields, they grew nonetheless in the drapery towns of Flanders where English wool was turned to, among other things, Flemish tapestry or "arras." Chaucer's account of the landscape through which Thopas pricks reads like the description of the background of "millefleur" or "verdure" tapestries. Though the most accessible examples of this kind of work (the Unicorn tapestries housed in the Cloisters Museum in New York, for example) date from the fifteenth century; tapestries with a "millefleur" or "verdure" ground were common by the late fourteenth century; and among the surviving examples from this period are armorial tapestries in which a solitary knight bearing armor sits on horseback against these backgrounds of exotic plant life, song birds, and small animals or "bestelettes."[27] The image of Thopas in these stylized woods is, then, not simply "literary" and may suggest that he is quite literally a carpet knight— and that the degree to which his very name approximates French "tapis" is not coincidence.

The late fourteenth-century market for Flemish tapestry was created and manipulated by the same person who manipulated Flemish currency, the earl of Flanders and duke of Burgundy, Philip the Bold. This is hardly surprising. As one scholar has noted, continental tapestries served "as a medium for investment and a stimulus for economic activity" and offered "along with gold plate, a tangible sign of the rank, wealth, and, consequently, power of a prince."[28] Before he took title to Flanders, Philip helped his father-in-law, Louis de Male, to defeat Ghent at Westrozebeke in 1382 and to consolidate the power he would shortly inherit; and, in the aftermath of that battle, he demanded that the weavers from Ghent who had survived the slaughter turn out a 200–foot-long tapestry commemorating the defeat of their city. Between 1388 and 1393, Philip led the negotiations for a truce with England and rewarded English diplomats with cartloads of tapestries; the recipients of these gifts included Richard II and the dukes of Lancaster, Gloucester, and York.[29] Uncommon in England before this date, these tapestries seem to have a profound impact on tastes of English aristocrats, who had heretofore decorated their chambers with wall paintings or English embroidery, *Opus Anglicanum.* According to Gervase Matthew, who offers no explanation for these developments, "the taste for elaborate tapestry work was one of the marks of the continuous court culture between 1389 and 1429."[30] Between 1394 and 1398, Richard II may have "purchased no fewer than twenty-four pieces of arras," some worked with gold thread and some more than thirty feet long, but he was not the only English aristocrat to acquire them.[31] By the 1430s, Chaucer's monkey, John Lydgate, was actually composing what have been called "tapestry poems," stanzas perhaps meant to serve as captions for the images that graced these hangings.[32] As one scholar has recently said, the subject matter of this work was usually secular, "especially romances and scenes of courtly love and hunting." A number of them depicted the heroes of the *roman courtois:* Beves of Hampton, Charlemagne, Sir Perceval, and Octavian of Rome, the last two being the subject of tapestries given by Philip the Bold to the duke of York in 1390.[33] These, of course, are the same heroes celebrated in the tail-rhyme romances preserved in the Auchinleck and Thornton manuscripts, the texts to which readers of

"Thopas" have so frequently turned. If these tapestries had survived, scholars might be able to list and to display visual analogues for virtually every scene in "Thopas" and to explain that tale with material that is more contemporaneous with its composition. It is worth noting, too, that these tapestries were sometimes described in contemporary documents as "counterfeit arras," an indication that they had been loomed not in Arras but elsewhere, usually by the weavers of Flanders.[34]

Whatever the response of Richard II and his immediate circle to these pretty woolen images threaded with gold—these gifts they received from the earl of Flanders in the 1390s—the English property owners who sat in the House of Commons regarded luxury goods produced abroad with suspicion. In the parliament of 1378, they demanded that those who imported "cloth of gold, silk, handkerchiefs, precious stones, jewels and furs" take measures to prevent gold bullion from leaving the country. In the parliament of 1381, they again requested that those who imported "grocery, mercery, furs, ivory, and precious stones" take the same steps. In the parliament of 1379, the Commons asked that individuals be allowed to spend no more than forty pounds per annum on "perree, pellure, drap d'or, ribane d'ore et drap de soye," this but one of many examples of their sense that their economy was being drained by the spending habits of the wealthy.[35] But, if these petitions were designed to curb the enthusiasms of the English aristocracy, they also indicate that the Commons pinned the responsibility for the nation's economic difficulties on the Flemish aristocrats who manipulated this marketplace. A petition of 1397, for example, specifically points the finger at Philip the Bold and his officers in Flanders.[36] Since Chaucer himself sat with the Commons in the parliament of 1386, the point of view that these documents represent might not be far from his own; and, though it is commonly said that "Thopas" ridicules the values of the bourgeoisie, I would suggest that it is actually pitched towards the aristocratic mentalities at issue in these petitions.[37]

The details I have mentioned so far are, of course, bound together by the narrative framework of "Thopas," and, however fragmented that narrative might be, it too suggests that the satire targets the earls of Flanders. Though elements of the plot of "Thopas" may surface in a dozen or so tail-rhyme romances, they also appear in contemporary historical narratives, the most significant of which are accounts of the Ghent war (1379–84).

During the Ghent war, the English crown supported the attempts of the Gentalars to overthrow their feudal overlord, Louis de Male.[38] The Gentalars

enjoyed a number of victories in the early stages of this war, the most spectacular being the battle at Bevershoutsveld in May of 1382, where they routed
the army of the earl of Flanders.[39] As Jean Froissart indicates, the Gentalars
entered their battles carrying a banner that bore three crowned heads and
shouting their war-cry "Ghent! Ghent! Ghent!," a cry that might have suggested the adversary of Thopas, the three-headed *giant*. The sound of the
word "geaunt" is emphasized by his oath, "by Termagaunt"; and the name of
the city gave courage to urban dissidents in the streets of Amiens, Rouen,
and Paris, who shouted "Long live Ghent" at the news of the commune's
victory at Bevershoutsveld.[40] In the aftermath of the battle, the Gentalars
overran Flanders, cornered the remnants of the army of Louis de Male at
Oudenaarde, and besieged the city with the help of 200 English archers from
Calais, sent by order of Richard II. It was here, too, that the Gentalars constructed extravagant siege-engines, which Froissart, who had no sympathy
for their cause, describes with a sense of wonder and horror.[41] The "giant"
in Chaucer's tale, we recall, repulses Thopas with a *staf-slynge* (829), which,
as John Burrow notes in *The Riverside Chaucer*, "does not figure in the armory of ME giants" and appears to be "a kind of siege-engine" rather than
a sling shot.[42]

At the battle of Bevershoutsveld, Louis de Male lost his horse, then
wandered about the country on foot clad in "a miserable jerkin" and hid himself underneath "a huge thorn-bush" until he was rescued by the husband
of one of his illegitimate daughters. At this point, he turned to the French
crown for help, just as Thopas turns to the French oath, *par ma fay*, in response to the threat posed by the giant (820). Louis, presumably clad in a
new outfit and reinforced by the armies of his heir, the Duke of Burgundy,
and Charles VI, then crushed Ghent and its Flemish allies at the battle of
Westrozebeke, 27 November 1382, at daybreak—or, as Thopas puts it when
he threatens the giant with peculiar specificity, "er it be fully pryme of day"
(825). As Froissart tells the tale, the English court ("the king of England,
his uncles and the nobility") greeted news of the defeat of the Gentalars
with utter contempt, pledged to invade Flanders in retaliation, and were especially distressed at the prospect that Louis de Male would "banish from
Bruges and Flanders our English merchants who have resided there up-
wards of thirty years."[43] In fact, the agreement that Louis's successor, Philip
the Bold, reached with the defeated Flemish communes in 1385 prohibited
trade with England, and it was not until 1396–98 that Philip was willing to
relax the restrictions he had placed on Anglo-Flemish commerce.[44] This

last development helps to explain why a tale like "Thopas," composed in the late 1380s or early 1390s, might call on memories of a war that took place in the early 1380s.

Because the Ghent war continued on the commercial front, it gave rise to a series of diplomatic exchanges between Philip the Bold and representatives of the English crown well into the 1390s. Chaucer himself may have played some role in these exchanges. In 1387, he was scheduled to journey to Calais with William Beauchamp, a practiced diplomat in this arena, as well as with a representative of the English textile industry, London draper John Wawe.[45] Whether he made the journey or not, the assignment suggests the poet was engaged with the kinds of issues that I believe are woven into the fabric of the Tale of Sir Thopas.

Beyond questions of commercial policy, the tale also suggests that the character of Flemish chivalry is at issue in "Thopas," much the way an assessment of Chaucer's character by Harry Bailly comes into play in the vignettes that bracket the tale. Both Louis de Male and Philip the Bold had been prisoners of war in England, and the English, in an attempt to cement their relation with Flanders, had offered both men English brides: to Louis, a daughter of Edward III, and to Philip, a daughter of John of Gaunt. Both men rejected these marriages, and Louis did so in an especially deceitful way, abandoning his bride while she was being readied for the altar. Both earls of Flanders were furthermore notoriously pretentious and given to the kind of luxury to which Chaucer's tale refers. Both too were especially inept on the battlefield—the failure of Philip the Bold to invade England with a massive army in 1386, the most striking example of this failing. The problem with reading "Thopas" exclusively in terms of its literary analogues is that, as many scholars have demonstrated, the *roman courtois,* the chivalric romance, the tail-rhyme romance, and even comic appropriations of the genre eventually validate chivalric values. The Tale of Thopas, on the other hand, seems much more subversive—so much so that Harry Bailly suggests that it is immoral and that Chaucer should correct that impression with another performance. It is only by stepping outside of boundaries of traditional literary inquiry that the reader can, I think, discover the prompts for this subversion and begin to understand why a world driven by a bankrupt chivalric ethos—a world like Chaucer's—led the poet to imagine a world where artists themselves counterfeit, where they play the fawning hack, where the poet is a puppet, and the poet's work, as Harry Bailly would have it, is not worth shit.

Notes

1. See Lilian Winstanley, ed., introduction to *The Prioress's Tale and the Tale of Sir Thopas* (Cambridge: Cambridge University Press, 1922). Winstanley's interpretation was extensively cited and glossed by John Matthews Manly, "Sir Thopas: A Satire," *Essays and Studies by Members of the English Association* 13 (1928): 52–73. Decisive objections to both of these studies were offered by W. W. Lawrence, "Satire in Sir Thopas," *PMLA* 50 (1935): 81–91. Though details within the poem continued to attract the attention of historians, the next attempt to look at this piece within a strictly historical context was the work of George Williams, *A New View of Chaucer* (Durham, N.C.: Duke University Press, 1965), 145–51. More recent readings along these lines include V. J. Scattergood, "Chaucer and the French War: Sir Thopas and Melibee," in *Court and Poet*, ed. Glyn S. Burgess (Liverpool: Cairns, 1981), 287–96; and the valuable essay by David Wallace, "In Flaundres," *Studies in the Age of Chaucer* 19 (1997): 63–91.

2. On wrestling, see the evidence collected by P. Rickard, *Britain in Medieval French Literature* (Cambridge: Cambridge University Press, 1956), 163–65; see also Elaine C. Block, "Rural and Urban Occupations on Medieval Misericords," http://tell.fil. purdue.edu/RLA-Archive/1991/French-html. Professor Block has examined about 18,000 misericords in Europe and England and found that only English choir-stalls depict wrestlers.

Among the many discussions of the role of archery in the Hundred Years War, see May McKisack, *The Fourteenth Century* (Oxford: Oxford University Press, 1959), 240–41. According to Henry Knighton, the French king John the Good turned to Edward III on his death-bed and confessed that he had spent his captivity in England collecting English gold, which he had hidden in steel chests, as well as a thousand English long-bows concealed within sacks of wool; see *Knighton's Chronicle: 1337–1396*, ed. and trans. G. H. Martin (Oxford: Clarendon Press, 1995), 190.

3. I make frequent reference to the notes composed by John Burrow that accompany the text of "Sir Thopas" in *The Riverside Chaucer*, 3rd ed., gen. ed., Larry Benson (Boston: Houghton, Mifflin, 1987), 917–23. However, I cite the text of this tale in *The Text of the Canterbury Tales*, ed. John M. Manly and Edith Rickert (Chicago: University of Chicago Press, 1940), 4:141–47; and, because it offers information about variants not found in Manly and Rickert, I have also taken note of the text (and variants) offered in *The Canterbury Tales: A Fascimile and Transcription of the Hengwrt Manuscript*, ed. Paul G. Ruggiers (Norman: University of Oklahoma Press, 1979), 213v–15r.

4. The value of reading the variants in the text of "Thopas" in the light of the information provided by the *MED* has recently been illustrated by Mechthild Gretsch, "Mittelenglische Lexikographie und Literarische Parodie: Zu einigen Wörtern in Chaucers Sir Thopas," *Anglia* 108 (1990): 113–32.

5. For what I think are similar anxieties about this stanza, see the remarks of John Burrow, in Benson, *The Riverside Chaucer,* 921, note to lines 848–50.

6. John Conley, "The Peculiar Name Thopas," *Studies in Philology* 73 (1976): 42–61. Conley's view that Chaucer refers to the yellow gemstone has since been corroborated by the appropriate entries in the *MED.*

7. For more on this, see Conley, ibid.; Charles Fox-Davies, *The Art of Heraldry: An Encyclopedia of Armory* (New York: Benjamin Blom, 1968), 48; or the entry for *or* in James Parker, *A Glossary of Terms Used in Heraldry* (London: Parker, 1847).

8. *The Riverside Chaucer,* 921, note to lines 869–71.

9. Ibid., 922, note to line 907.

10. For illustrations of this coin in gold, see the many plates appended to *The Gros Tournois: Proceedings of the Fourteenth Oxford Symposium on Coinage and Monetary History,* ed. N. J. Mayhew (Oxford: Ashmolean Museum, 1997), 551 ff. Several of the essays in this collection are devoted to counterfeit versions of this coin. For issues in silver, see James N. Roberts, *The Silver Coins of Medieval France: 476–1610 AD* (South Salem, N.Y.: Attic Books, 1996), 133. Some earlier versions of this image appear on the *denier* issued in various parts of France in the late thirteenth and early fourteenth centuries. Examples of these are housed in the collection of the American Numismatic Society and are conveniently catalogued and described in their electronic database: www.amnumsoc.org.

11. Laura Hibbard Loomis, "Sir Thopas," in *Sources and Analogues of Chaucer's Canterbury Tales,* ed. W. F. Bryan and Germaine Dempster (New York: Humanities Press, 1958), 530.

12. As the MED attests, the word commonly refers to this gold coin. This definition is contested by Kenneth S. Cahn, "Chaucer's Merchants and the Foreign Exchange: An Introduction to Medieval Finance," *Studies in the Age of Chaucer* 2 (1980): 85. This discussion of the Bruges money market makes no reference whatsoever to the economic and political problems that plagued English merchants trading in Flanders in the late fourteenth century.

13. The classic work of scholarship on this tradition is John A. Yunck, *The Lineage of Lady Meed: The Development of Medieval Venality Satire* (Notre Dame, Ind.: University of Notre Dame Press, 1963); equally useful, the same scholar's earlier articles: "Medieval French Money Satire," *Modern Language Quarterly* 21 (1960): 73–82; "Dan Denarius: The Almighty Penny and the Fifteenth Century Poets," *American Journal of Economics and Society* 20 (1961): 207–22. For Middle English versions of such poems (including one in the tail-rhyme stanza), see "Sir Penny I" and "Sir Penny II" (or "Narracio de Domino Denarii") in *Secular Lyrics of the XIVth and XVth Centuries,* 2nd ed., ed. Rossell Hope Robbins (Oxford: Clarendon Press, 1961), 50–55.

14. Walter Scheps, "Chaucer's Numismatic Pardoner and the Personification of Avarice," *Acta* 4 (1977): 107–23.

15. David Nicholas, *Medieval Flanders* (London: Longman, 1992), 233.

16. J. H. Munro, *Wool, Cloth and Gold: The Struggle for Bullion in Anglo-Burgundian Trade, 1340–1478* (Toronto: University of Toronto Press, 1973), 43–63.

17. For a list of exact references to the standard editions of the *Rotuli Parliamentorum* and *The Statutes of the Realm* that address the problem of counterfeit and debased currency during the reign of Richard II, see Rogers Ruding, *Annals of the Coinage of Great Britain and Its Dependencies* (London: John Hearne, 1840), 1:236–48. Ruding translates and paraphrases many of these documents. For an excellent summary of currency problems during the reign of Richard II as well as comment on the scarcity of Ricardian coinage, see C. H. V. Sutherland, *English Coinage: 600–1900* (London: Batsford, 1973), 81–84. The problem is explained in detail by John Munro in his classic study, *Wool, Cloth and Gold: The Struggle for Bullion in Anglo-Burgundian Trade*, by which Munro means, actually, Anglo-Flemish trade. On depression and contracting markets on both sides of the channel, see John H. Munro, "Monetary Contraction and Industrial Change in the Late Medieval Low Countries: 1335–1500," in *Coinage of the Low Countries (880–1500)*, ed. N. J. Mayhew (Oxford: B. A. R., 1979), 95–161; Harry A. Miskimin, "Monetary Movements and Market Structures: Forces for Contraction in Fourteenth and Fifteenth Century England," *Journal of Economic History*, 24 (1964): 470–90.

18. For a full translation of this statute, see Ruding, *Annals* 1:242–43.

19. On the duties of searchers at the port on London, see *Chaucer Life-Records*, ed. Martin M. Crow and Clair C. Olson (Oxford: Clarendon Press, 1966), 175; on innkeepers, Alice Beardwood, "Royal Mints and Exchanges," in *The English Government at Work, 1327–1336*, ed. James Willard, William Morris, and William Dunham (Cambridge, Mass.: Medieval Academy of America, 1950), 3:54.

20. I am grateful to Bob Hanning for reminding me of this exchange.

21. Nicholas, *Medieval Flanders*, 280.

22. Richards Lyons, who both farmed the customs and served as a collector, lived next door to the Hanse at the Steelyard at Cosin Lane and Thames Street and was murdered there in 1381. Fishmonger and mayor of London, William Walworth, also a customs collector, was elected alderman of the Hanse in the same year. There has been some debate about whether or not Flemish and German merchants shared the same London Hanse. For a summary of this debate, see Alice Beardwood, *Alien Merchants in England* (Cambridge, Mass.: Medieval Academy of America, 1931), 15, note 4. The question, however, seems settled by the recent work of Stuart Jenks, *England, die Hanse und Preussen: Handel and Diplomatie, 1377–1474*, 3 vols. (Köln: Böhlau, 1992). In the third volume of this remarkable work, Jenks lists the name of every Hanse merchant who did business in England during this period and includes Flemish merchants among them (847–982). These names have been gathered from the manifests discussed below, note 25.

23. For a recent, detailed discussion of these matters, see J. H. Munro, "The Origin of the English 'New Draperies': The Resurrection of an Old Flemish Indus-

try, 1270–1570," in *The New Draperies in the Low Countries and England*, ed. N. B. Harte (Oxford: Oxford University Press, 1997), 35–127, especially the material on 38. The lawsuit filed by the weavers of Ypres against the weavers of Poperinghe is discussed in Nicholas, *Medieval Flanders*, 284.

24. *Chaucer Life-Records*, 208. Crow and Olson suggest that they have excluded bills of particulars submitted to the Petty Custom because such records do not exist for the years when Chaucer was its controller. Such records, however, are included with documents related to the Wool Custom, since merchants who exported wool also imported goods subject to the Petty Custom. See Harding, below.

25. Vanessa Harding, "Cross-Channel Trade and Cultural Contacts: London and the Low Countries in the Late Fourteenth Century," in *England and The Low Countries in the Late Middle Ages*, ed. Caroline Barron and Nigel Saul (New York: St. Martin's Press, 1995), 153–68. By way of exploring Harding's account of these documents and resolving differences between her study and the material offered by Crow and Olson, I have examined the following documents in the Public Records Office (PRO) (reference to the file numbers are followed by dates for the documents they contain): E122/71/2 (1379–80); E122/71/3 and E122/71/4(1380–81); E122/71/5 (1380–82); E122/71/9 (1384–86); E122/71/10 (1386–87); E122/71/11 (1388–90). There are at least another eight files containing bills of particulars from the 1390s, which might repay study for those interested in knowing more about Chaucer's experience as controller of the Petty Custom; these are recorded in the typewritten finding lists available at the PRO.

26. *The Riverside Chaucer*, 919, note to lines 760–65.

27. For a number of specimens of this kind of work, see, for example, the catalogue prepared by Geneviève Souchal, *Masterpieces of Tapestry from the Fourteenth to the Sixteenth Century* (New York: Metropolitan Museum of Art, 1973).

28. Francis Salet, "Introduction," in ibid., 17–18; many of my remarks about late fourteenth-century tapestries are indebted to the notes in this catalogue.

29. Richard Vaughn, *Philip the Bold: The Formation of the Burgundian State* (London: Longman, 1962), 50. See also Scot McKendrick, "Tapestries from the Low Countries in England during the Fifteenth Century," in Barron and Saul, *England and the Low Countries in the Late Middle Ages*, 45.

30. Gervase Matthew, *The Court of Richard II* (London: John Murray, 1968), 50.

31. McKendrick, "Tapestries," 49.

32. On these "tapestry poems," see Derek Pearsall, *John Lydgate* (Charlottesville: University Press of Virginia, 1970), 180.

33. McKendrick, "Tapestries," 49; and, on the gifts of Burgundy to York, 54, note 15.

34. For a discussion of the term "counterfeit arras," see ibid., 48; the phrase seems analogous to "counterfeit woolens," discussed above. Among the useful information collected in McKendrick's essay are his remarks about the weaving of tapestry

in England, remarks that suggest the "tapicer" among the Five Guildsmen mentioned in the prologue to the *Canterbury Tales* was quite different from his contemporaries in the Low Countries, did not manufacture tapestries on the scale of the Flemish or French, and was involved primarily in the repair of imported pieces or the production of small pieces of "counterfeit arras."

35. *Rotuli Parliamentorum*, ed. J. Strachey et al. (London: Records Commission, 1767), 3:369–70, item 80.

36. For the parliament of 1378, see ibid., 3:66, item 54; for that of 1381, 3:126, item 2. For the proposal that there be a limit to the amount of money spent by individuals on luxury imports, see 3:66, item 55.

37. For more evidence that the behavior of Thopas is in keeping with aristocratic practice, see S. J. Herben, "Arms and Armor in Chaucer," *Speculum* 12 (1937): 475–87.

38. English support for the Gentalars has been the subject of some dispute. See David Nicholas, *The van Arteveldes of Ghent: The Varieties of Vendetta and the Hero in History* (Ithaca, N.Y.: Cornell University Press, 1988), 182–83. Nicholas remarks that a pension of 100 marks and the dispatch of those 200 English archers from Calais to help at the siege of Oudenaarde was "the only assistance that Philip van Artevelde ever received from the English" and that "when significant English aid for Flanders finally did arrive, in the spring of 1383, it came not from the royal government but from the Bishop of Norwich." However, Bishop Despenser's attempt to aid the Gentalars after the battle of Westrozebeke was endorsed by both Richard II and his parliament; and it was extremely popular among the English citizenry, who enthusiastically provided Despenser with both the funds and manpower he required for his "crusade." After his initial successes, the last of which was the sack of Poperinghe, Despenser was stopped at the gates of Ypres, forced to withdraw from Flanders, and faced disgrace on his return to England. That disgrace was, however, short-lived. Finally, after the dust had settled, Richard II also granted a pension to Philip van Artevelde's co-conspirator, Peter van den Bosche of Ghent. Chaucer was familiar with this arrangement, since this pension was drawn on the wool custom and van den Bosche's name appears on the accounts the poet audited. See *Chaucer Life-Records*, 203 and 241. For a recent account of the Despenser crusade that takes some of these issues into consideration, see Nigel Saul, *Richard II* (New Haven: Yale University Press, 1997), 102–5.

39. For the account of the Ghent war that follows, I have relied primarily on that offered by Jean Froissart, *Chronicles of England, France, Spain and the Adjoining Countries*, trans. Thomas Johnes (London: Bohn, 1857). For a description of the humiliation of Louis de Male, see Froissart, *Chronicles*, 1: 704–6.

40. Ibid., 1:643 and 703; and on the chant of French urban rebels, Nicholas, *Medieval Flanders*, 230.

41. Froissart, *Chronicles*, 1:710.

42. *The Riverside Chaucer,* 920, note to line 829.

43. For the entire account, see Froissart, *Chronicles,* 1:756. Several modern historians, including David Nicholas, have taken note of another passage in Froissart, which seems to suggest that the English were pleased with the defeat of the Flemings at Westrozebeke. But this text indicates only that a few unspecified nobles were relieved that Flemish "peasants" had not vanquished French noblemen, a view that betrays recent memories of the Peasant's Revolt rather than a considered position regarding the Ghent war. For this passage, see Froissart, *Chronicles,* 1:740.

44. For a discussion of these developments, see John Matthews Manly, *Some New Light on Chaucer* (New York: Holt, 1926), 189–93; and more recently, Nicholas, *Medieval Flanders,* 319–22.

45. *Chaucer Life-Records,* 61–62.

12

GEORGE D. ECONOMOU

Chaucer and Langland

A Fellowship of Makers

I f it had prevailed, John Matthews Manly's theory of multiple authorship of *Piers Plowman*[1]—since its assertion at the beginning of this
century, the single most dominant issue to possess the field of that
poem's study—would not only have radically altered our ways of addressing the poem(s), it also would have enabled us to link it, in an unexpected
way, with what seems to be shaping up as one of the foremost issues to challenge the field in recent years. I refer to the double-barreled proposition that
William Langland and Geoffrey Chaucer knew each other's work and possibly knew one another personally. Chaucer, whose reading of Dante inspired
him to insinuate himself into a company of five ancient poets in the envoi
to *Troilus and Criseyde* (V.1786–92);[2] whose sense of self-irony enabled him
to associate himself with the five churls portrayed last in the *Canterbury
Tales* General Prologue (I.542–44); and whose subtle, sometimes teasing
stance toward his audience led him to ask them to fill in the blank space—
perhaps with his name—of the Wife of Bath's awaited, welcome sixth husband (III.45), could then, by virtue of an autonomous reader's act, have joined
Manly's putative five authors of *Piers Plowman* to constitute still one more
set of significant sixes.

   Responsibility for this hypothetical act of linkage to what is a very real
series of critical observations must be mine, of course; and I would temper

its obvious playfulness by explaining that it is also offered as an expression of confidence in the ongoing energy and ingenuity of today's medieval English studies, particularly the concentration on Chaucer and Langland. So intensely focused is the present convergence of scholarly activity on coupling the two poets, I think I could talk myself into risking the prediction that even if Manly's theory of multiple authors of *Piers Plowman* had ruled the day, we would still be trying, despite the considerably different conditions, to read them and Chaucer in closer comparative terms than ever before; we would still be trying to figure out their relationship, not only as we see it but also through the ways they themselves and their contemporaries and near contemporaries saw it. But that is a complication that the question of Chaucer's and Langland's fellowship, demanding and exciting enough as we now have it with the fairly stable standing of Manly's "mythical author of all these poems,"[3] need not reckon with at any great length for the moment: not, that is, until the newly mutating advocates of a more-than-one author theory out there among us—"shope" for the time being, perhaps in the same "shroudes" as the rest of us—reemerge. That this is not merely a bit of *Piers Plowman* paranoia can be seen from the recent revival of arguments for a change from the ABC order of the versions of the poem.[4] The proposal that A was composed last, as a kind of condensation or abridgement of B in the spirit of the *Readers' Digest*—is there any major poet in the language other than Langland about whom such a suggestion would be made? Even when offered with a strong claim for Langland's having written it, this necessarily leaves the door open to the possibility of another redactor. But then we have always coexisted and worked under such conditions: *Piers Plowman* waters have never been still, though they have always run deep.

So, referring to Chaucer and Langland in terms of a fellowship may suggest several different things, given the wide range of the word's meanings in Modern as well as in Middle English. They could be fellows in the sense of being contemporaries, or by virtue of sharing a common interest, or by being companions, part of a company or society, or complementary individuals of a pair, counterparts of a kind of match. These, I believe, cover the present variety of perspectives on the relationship between Chaucer and Langland as poets and persons, though I would coin the word "followship" to describe the exclusively one-way direction that the case for literary influence has taken, from Langland to Chaucer. The intensity of the pursuit to demonstrate that reading, if not knowing, Langland had what has been called a "massive" effect on Chaucer may be measured by the application lately of terms like "nervous" "and "anxious," which have usually been reserved for Langland, in analyses of Chaucer's sense of his writing ambitions and performance.[5] The implication that Chaucer's misgivings about his *Canterbury Tales* enterprise fall just short of "full-blown Langlandian neurosis" demonstrates how extensive the interaction between them has been perceived to be.[6] To the contemplation of the possibility of shared texts, shared scribes, and shared readers, add a shared existential condition: the fellowship of artistic angst, with a new refrain, "*Timor makyng conturbat me.*"

By representing their fellowship as one of makers, I merely wish to stress its priority over all other considerations of how they and what they made can be connected. Both Chaucer and Langland used the words "make" and "making" to refer to their own writing and compositions, and both would have recognized its bond, despite the notable differences in their craft and art. Though each of them in the course of his career tried to stretch the idea of making into something superior, Langland by striving for identity as one of God's minstrels and Chaucer by reaching for standing among the poets of Europe,[7] they both might have taken some comfort in knowing, if they could have, that in Greek poet *is* maker, as man and as creator, just as it is in English. God the Father in the Nicene Creed is ὀυρανοῦ καί γῆς, Maker of heaven and earth. The word, it turns out, was always worthy of their best efforts.

What Chaucer and Langland made—that is, the authorial materials most of us take, on an act of faith, as having essentially survived their manuscript transmission in the form of a series of assiduously (though, at times, contentiously) edited texts from the late nineteenth century to this very day—has always presented us with grounds for the discernment of fascinating and telling resemblances as well as pronounced differences between them, and even for some limited speculation about their having known each other's makings. But recent scholarship and criticism have been much more insistent about the probability of a Chaucer-Langland interaction. For example, the assumption that Chaucer had to have been aware of the invocation of Piers Plowman, the figure, as an ally by John Ball and others involved in the Peasants' Revolt of 1381 is just a small step away from the further assumption that Chaucer must have read the poem—a conviction that owes as much, however, to textual interpretation as it does to the application of historical evidence.[8] The comparative study of the *Piers Plowman* Prologue and the *Canterbury Tales* General Prologue has long been the bellwether of Chaucer-Langland literary relations; but for the last two or three decades, the argument for that relationship being contingent upon some form of poetic or personal exchange has been building. Several eminent medievalists, using a variety of approaches, have suggested, proposed, or unequivocally declared that Chaucer read Langland's Prologue (and more of the poem, in some cases) and was directly influenced by it in writing his own General Prologue and, possibly, in shaping the rest of his poem.[9] The combined effect of these studies of the two poems has been the gradual construction of a compelling, virtually unquestioned, case for Chaucer having been inspired by Langland. There is not one shred of "hard evidence" that this actually occurred, yet the mounting conviction behind the critical inference that it did occur makes it increasingly difficult to convince or even to suggest that it did not.

This is not necessarily an undesirable state of affairs, for it recommends, as directly as possible, the likelihood that such a literary transaction did take place; though the supposition that that transaction actually happened is, to use one of George Kane's favorite words in his essay on autobiographical fallacy in Chaucer and Langland studies, unverifiable.[10] Still, it demonstrates the primacy and power of the critical, interpretive approach as it functions in concert with bibliographical and historical information. The critical approach to Chaucer and Langland connections, however, cannot avoid inheriting the enormously complex, almost murky, textual history of *Piers Plowman,* a manuscript tradition that is far more problematic and vexing than that of any of Chaucer's poems—or, for that matter, of any other poem of the English Middle Ages. Unlike Piers, who, in the famous scene unique to the B version (7.115) tears the problematic pardon "for pure tene,"[11] itself a major example of the countless authorial revisions that mingle with the ineluctable parade of scribal variants that attend the poem's manuscript transmission, critics cannot escape confronting the palimpsest-like nature of the piece of paper that has been put into their hand. To complicate things even more, the contents of that piece of paper include not only the authorial/scribal aggregate poem, but also all efforts to sort it out. In other words, wherever critical interpretation leads on the fellowship of Chaucer and Langland, it cannot avoid the mediation of ongoing bibliographical bulletins. Its steps into new pastures will always be dogged or herded, so to speak, by concomitant movements concerning the poems'—mainly Langland's—provenance and dispersal. For example, a recent authoritative argument that Chaucer based his General Prologue on Langland's Prologue specifies, following the conventional ordering and dating of the traditional three versions, and taking into account the version known as the Z-text as well, that it was the A version of *Piers Plowman* that Chaucer had read.[12]

In just a few years—a relatively short period in the time-scheme of scholarly criticism—two proposals concerning the order and circulation of A have been made that might present some significant, though I suspect not insurmountable, problems for this case.[13] The previously mentioned theory that A was the final revision of the poem, along with a more recent argument that what we regard as A derived from a draft in progress that circulated in Langland's immediate group of readers and was then generally released—perhaps as long as a decade—later than B, would have to be taken into account if the presumption that Chaucer read Langland in the A version during the 1370s is indispensable to the comparative interpretation of the two prologues. Certainly, if this latter explanation of A's transmission is correct, Chaucer could still have read A as a member of that inner London group. But even this possibility reassures us that the critic's dance must always keep in step with that of the textual scholar. It also announces a new approach in our consideration of this fellowship of makers.

Would it be fair to refer to the very latest turn that Chaucer-Langland studies has taken as avant-garde? If by avant-garde, we mean—I slap down the impulse to say "cutting edge"—the vanguard, what is out front, a pointing toward a redefinition of the configuration and order of an artistic movement or, as in this instance, of an intellectual enterprise, then the current, rapidly growing interest in exploring questions of scribal connections, audience, patronage, book ownership, and reading circles as they might pertain to a conjunction of Chaucer and Langland, clearly qualifies. As an effort to draft a new context in which to view the production, dissemination, and intertextuality of later fourteenth-century poetry in its own day and during the following century, this direction raises the possibility of many new elements to be added to the equation. From the possibilities that certain scribes made copies of both *The Canterbury Tales* and *Piers Plowman;* that Langland himself might have been a scrivener with close ties to bureaucratic, legal London; to the chance that the imitations of Langland's poem came out of a social group of readers and writers that included Chaucer; this approach seeks to tie together speculations, suspicions, and educated guesses about a rich body of historical and bibliographical evidence. In the midst of this diversity of explorations is the central and unifying notion of a special group of individuals with a strong common interest in poetry, a group that at some time or other, and perhaps at the same time, Chaucer and Langland called home.[14] Since "coterie" is the term that is used almost exclusively by those who are writing about this subject, I shall have to put aside my aversion for this word, which, despite its etymological suitability to the consideration of a poem with a peasant hero, connotes an exclusivity I find hard to take, probably because of my experience of it as a deliberately elitist (unintentionally effetist) term in the other world of contemporary poetry.

That the theory of a late fourteenth-century coterie is still in an early, formative state may be seen not only from the frequency of conditional verbs in its discourse, but also from the appropriately cautious and tentative expression of its primary concern by two of its most effective advocates:

> We still do not know enough about the early London transmission of *Piers* (and we know even less about its Dublin readers), but even what we have presented here shows that it was not so utterly removed from the Continental urbanity of Chaucer's metropolitan readership as it sometimes has been thought. Indeed, the two poets seem generally to have shared a readership—shared it with each other, and with Gower and (later) Hoccleve, and with all those scribes who propagated and sometimes elaborated their texts.[15]

Given our collective's track record on anything even approaching unanimity, closure on a definition and depiction of this coterie that would achieve general acceptance may be a very long-term, if not an illusory, goal. There are numerous uncertainties that cling tenaciously to a representation of this coterie. For example, what is the incidental effect on it of the complicated matter of the presumed expansion of Langland's audience just before 1381? Did a coterie audience, once it had dilated to include the rebel leaders and their following—became, in other words, a vernacular literary public—then contract or reform, after the rebellion was suppressed, into one to which Langland could address his exculpatory revisions and deletions in C, the most prominent of which is, of course, the omission of the tearing of Truth's pardon? Or did it just continue, basically unaffected by the expansion? And what are the implications of the supposition that the rebels (who use the phrase "do welle and better" and call upon Piers, not the poem, unless by synecdoche), knew the work imperfectly or depended on second-hand oral accounts of it? That they did not, in other words, constitute a truly new literary public? Or what is to be inferred from the fact that most manuscripts of C strongly reflect the dialectal properties of southwestern Worcestershire, including Malvern: that Langland left London and returned to his "opeland" (C5.44) home to begin C? Or that he stayed and kept on remaking where he was—supposedly in Cornhill—because of the strong possibility that scribal practice in London tolerated and accommodated provincial language?[16] Despite the likelihood that these and other questions relevant to the idea of a London coterie, in which Chaucer and Langland occupy prime positions, will be taken up in ways that will be better and best, one wonders what the chances are for consensus in an often divided, not just diverse, field of scholars, two of whose leading figures can simultaneously aver that medieval scribes should be regarded as our first literary critics and that we would be in bad shape indeed if we relied on scribes for any kind of literary insight.[17]

Like all avant-gardes, which are inevitably absorbed into the present,[18] this one, its layers of scholarly difficulties notwithstanding, is being comfortably drawn into the prior Chaucer-Langland movement. The concept of the coterie, no matter where it may take us in the future, has become for the moment yet one more type of "evidence" to be marshaled in behalf of the *a priori* likelihood that Chaucer had read Langland. From Kane to Cooper, from Bennett to Pearsall to Kerby-Fulton, almost all of us can agree about this one thing; and, whatever our individual interpretations of the form and magnitude of its consequences, it seems we do not just assume but that we believe this happened.

It is no surprise that we believe more deeply, as we ought to, in the literary interaction than in the personal one, no matter how appealingly and imaginatively the latter has been described: with Chaucer headed home in the evening to Aldgate, perhaps with a copy of *Piers Plowman* under his arm,[19] whose author he was bound to meet if he had not already. The parallels between the two prologues, especially the assertions that Chaucer's Parson and Plowman are based on Langland, have been noted for some time and have been recently reinforced. Chaucer's line in the Parson's portrait, "A shame it is, if a prest take keep, / A shiten shepherde and a clene sheepe" (I.503–4), has been attractively described as "a virtuoso compassing of Langlandian style and vocabulary."[20] Still I would ask that this reception be considered, as well, in the context of Chaucer's general use of alliterating phrases—and particularly the heavily alliterative passage in the fourth part of the Knight's Tale, epitomized by the line, "Ther shyveren shaftes upon sheeldes thikke" (I.2605). Though Chaucer may well have had Langland in mind when he wrote the line for the Parson's portrait, he may also have had other alliterative poems in mind. Either way, Chaucer meets "the genre-specific" demands of their verse form in these passages in a manner that is, at

best, a cut below, even as first-rate decasyllabic parody, of Langland's "sophisticated modulation" of alliteration and meter.[21] Chaucer's choice of the
Plowman as chief representative of the peasantry, and his positive treatment
of him as the Parson's brother, has been traced to Langland; and more recently a persuasive claim has been made for Langland's originality in bringing about a significant shift in the conception of the ideal and central figure
of the Christian hero from shepherd to plowman.[22] If it is true that Chaucer's
portrayal of the Plowman was impossible without Langland's innovative
creation of Piers, it also strikes me as true that this is one of the most unusual instances of Chaucer's literary appropriation. Considering the powerful
role that Piers plays in Langland's poem—here I suppose knowing which
version (or versions?) Chaucer might have read would be especially helpful—
Chaucer's use of his source material, a process generally acknowledged to
be highly creative in its own right, is in this case notably restrained, even
uncharacteristically uncreative. Perhaps the proximity and recognition factor
of the unnamed poet-source, unlike Boccaccio, contributed to what might
have been an uncomfortable situation for Chaucer as he worked on *The Canterbury Tales*, a possibility about which speculation, as mentioned earlier, has
already begun.

At the same time, the exploration of similarities and possible indebtedness has extended beyond the General Prologue to other parts of *The
Canterbury Tales* and to other poems as well. Prominent among these are
two examples, both inspired by the intensifying interest in the opening
104 lines of *Piers Plowman* C5, the extremely important waking episode between the first and second visions commonly referred to as "the autobiographical passage" or the "poet's *apologia*."[23] Because this interlude, which
is unique to the C version, constitutes one of Langland's most significant
revisions and involves a self-examination of his activity as a maker, as well
as an assessment of the merits of what he has spent his life making, it has
been profitably compared with the Prologue to *The Legend of Good Women*
and with Chaucer's Retractions. Due to its having two distinct versions,
the Prologue to the *Legend* offers a singular opportunity to study Chaucer's
otherwise rather unclear and critically controversial revising process, which
invites comparison with the more substantial information we have acquired
about Langland's revising; moreover, the Prologue contains a defense of
Chaucer's making, which provides further grounds for juxtaposing it with the
C5 *apologia*.[24] Though the C5 passage and the Retractions have been viewed
for some time as comparable in various ways, criticism of late has reflected

an urgency for a more searching reading of them. The possibility that this waking episode was the last addition Langland made to his life-long poem has strengthened the conviction that the *apologia* and the Retractions should be regarded as close counterparts.[25]

If the C5 passage represents the last lines that Langland made for his *Piers,* there is also a good chance that the last lines of verse that Chaucer ever made as he closed out *The Canterbury Tales* show that he might have—must have?—had Langland in mind. The last line of the Parson's Prologue according to the manuscripts—if not most of the editions we use—in which the Host invites the Parson to tell his "meditacoun," resonates richly with *Piers Plowman:* "And to do wel God sende yow his grace!" (X.72). Noting the "do well," compare the last line of Langland's B and C versions—"And sethe he [Conscience] gradde aftur Grace tyl y gan awake" (C22.386)—and try to resist the urge to allege a connection, whether the Chaucerian line arrives in the ultimate or in the antepenultimate position at the end of the Parson's Prologue.[26] I will not speculate here on how the question of the order of the last lines of poetry in Chaucer's work may reflect the games that scribes and editors play, or on future games that critics, including myself, may play. Instead, in closing, I would like to turn to the couplet, some thirty lines above this ending, in which the Parson makes his famous southern man's disclaimer, "I kan nat geeste 'rum, ram, ruf' by lettre" (X.43): a line that, despite its illustrating that Chaucer retained his humorous edge to the end, has been often overplayed as evidence of his disdain for Langland's choice of verse form. But let us not emulate Lady Meed's decontextualization of scripture at the end of B and C3 and fail to read on. "Ne, God woot, rym holde I but litel better" (X.44). Let us not overlook that it is the Parson speaking, and that in holding both our makers' kinds of versifying in low esteem, he seconds the skeptical attitudes toward Will's making of Imaginative in B12 and Reason and Conscience in C5. Could it be that Chaucer, retaining a last indirect work through the judgment of the Parson, has anticipated us all by reserving a place for himself and Langland in the special and, alas, sometimes suspect fellowship of makers?

Notes

This essay is a revised version of a paper given at the Eleventh International Congress of the New Chaucer Society at the Sorbonne, Paris, July 19, 1998.

1. J. M. Manly, "*Piers Plowman* and Its Sequence," in *The Cambridge History of English Literature*, vol. 2, *The End of the Middle Ages*, ed. Sir A. W. Ward and A. R. Waller (Cambridge: Cambridge University Press, 1963), 1–42.

2. All quotations from and references to the works of Chaucer are from *The Riverside Chaucer*, 3rd ed., gen. ed., Larry D. Benson (Boston: Houghton Mifflin, 1987).

3. Manly, "*Piers Plowman* and Its Sequence," 1.

4. See Jill Mann, "The Power of the Alphabet: A Reassessment of the Relation between the A and the B Versions of *Piers Plowman*," *Yearbook of Langland Studies* 8 (1994): 21–50. For responses to Mann's proposal, see Traugott Lawler, "A Reply to Jill Mann, Reaffirming the Traditional Relation between the A and B Versions of *Piers Plowman*," *Yearbook of Langland Studies* 10 (1996): 145–80; and George Kane, "An Open Letter to Jill Mann about the Sequence of the Versions of *Piers Plowman*," *Yearbook of Langland Studies* 13 (1999): 7–33.

5. See David Wallace, *Chaucerian Polity: Absolutist Lineages and Associational Forms in England and Italy* (Stanford, Calif.: Stanford University Press, 1997), 240; and Steven Justice, *Writing and Rebellion, England in 1381* (Berkeley: University of California Press, 1994), 239 and 239 note 142, where the author writes, "Anne Middleton is preparing work on the importance of Langland in redirecting, and finally stalling, the *Canterbury Tales*." This arresting sentence exemplifies the virtually unqualified acceptance of the notion that prevails at this time that Chaucer read Langland. It also nicely illustrates the position that Chaucer must have paid a heavy artistic price for that reading. But, perhaps even more provocatively, the presentation of this statement as documentary support for a critical position typically suggests that the scholars who promote the theory of a "coterie" of late fourteenth-century writers, which will be discussed later, run the risk of becoming a "coterie" of sorts themselves.

6. Wallace, *Chaucerian Polity*, 81.

7. Much has been written on this subject. My own view of Langland's artistic self-consciousness may be found in "Self-Consciousness of Poetic Activity in Dante and Langland," in *Vernacular Poetics in the Middle Ages*, ed. Lois Ebin, Studies in Medieval Culture 16 (Kalamazoo: Medieval Institute Publications, Western Michigan University, 1984), 187–98. Helen Cooper has recently discussed Chaucer's "self-consciousness" of his poetic mission in "Four Last Things in Dante and Chaucer," *New Medieval Literatures* 3 (1999): 59–60.

8. See Helen Cooper, "Langland's and Chaucer's Prologues," *Yearbook in Langland Studies* 1 (1987): 73–74.

9. See Nevill Coghill, "Chaucer's Debt to Langland," *Medium Aevum* 4 (1935): 89–94; J. A. W. Bennett, "Chaucer's Contemporary," in *Piers Plowman: Critical Approaches*, ed. S. S. Hussey (London: Methuen, 1969), 310–24; Jill Mann, *Chaucer and Medieval Estates Satire: The Literature of Social Classes and the General Prologue to the*

"Canterbury Tales" (Cambridge: Cambridge University Press, 1973), 208–12; Cooper, "Langland's and Chaucer's Prologues," 71–81; George Kane, *Chaucer and Langland, Historical and Textual Approaches* (Berkeley: University of California Press, 1989), 121–33, especially 128; and Derek Pearsall, *The Life of Chaucer* (Oxford and Cambridge, Mass.: Blackwell, 1992), 98, 124. Speculation about the Chaucer and Langland fellowship has yielded some beguiling and graphic images of the poets, especially of Chaucer, as in Bennett's well-known depiction of him heading home to Aldgate with copies of Macrobius and *Piers Plowman* under his arm (322); but none are so curious as Pearsall's representation of a London scene in which "one can imagine that street corners frequented by William Langland might well have seen some excitement" (162). The projection of Langland out of his poetic voice into an embodiment of it as a fourteenth-century London version of a Hyde Park Speakers' Corner (perhaps in the vicinity of Paul's Cross?)—if that is the kind of excitement Pearsall has in mind—comes as something of a surprise from one who has reproved Donald Howard for the "speculative grammar" of his biography of Chaucer (2). On Paul's Cross as a point of homiletic and forensic activity, see D. W. Robertson, Jr., *Chaucer's London* (New York: John Wiley & Sons, 1968), 29, 68, 111, 119, 189, 198, 218. Oddly, Robertson mentions the poem *Piers Plowman* five times in this book (189, 191, 192, 193, 205) but never names its maker. That may help explain why he can say, "London was a city in which everyone knew everyone else; the impersonal atmosphere of our large metropolitan centers and the faceless masses that inhabit them had not yet come into being" (52), without the possibility of a Chaucer and Langland encounter there crossing his mind. If this, in its modest way, does not illustrate the transformation of literary historicist thinking during the last three decades, it certainly indicates that Robertson never lived in a great city for a significant period of time.

10. George Kane, *The Autobiographical Fallacy in Chaucer and Langland Studies*, The R. W. Chambers Memorial Lecture (London: University College, 1965); reprint in *Chaucer and Langland*, 1–14.

11. This quotation and further references to B are from *Piers Plowman: The B Version—Will's Visions of Piers Plowman, Do-Well, Do-Better, and Do-Best*, ed. George Kane and E. Talbot Donaldson (London: Athlone Press, and Berkeley: University of California Press, 1988). Quotations and references to the C version are from *Piers Plowman by William Langland: An Edition of the C-Text*, ed. Derek Pearsall (Exeter: Exeter University Press, 1994).

12. Cooper, "Langland's and Chaucer's Prologues," 71–81.

13. Mann, "The Power of the Alphabet," 21–50; and Ralph Hanna III, *Pursuing History, Middle English Manuscripts and Their Texts* (Stanford, Calif.: Stanford University Press, 1996), 203–43; Hanna rejects Mann's argument for a BCA order, 230–32. Also see A. I. Doyle, "Remarks on Surviving Manuscripts of *Piers Plowman*," in *Medieval English Religious and Ethical Literature: Essays in Honour of G. H.*

Russell, ed. Gregory Kratzmann and James Simpson (Cambridge: D. S. Brewer, 1986), 35–48.

14. See Kathryn Kerby-Fulton, "Langland and the Bibliographic Ego," in *Written Work: Langland, Labor, and Authorship*, ed. Steven Justice and Kathryn Kerby-Fulton (Philadelphia: University of Pennsylvania Press, 1997), 110–22.

15. Kathryn Kerby-Fulton and Steven Justice, "Langlandian Reading Circles and the Civil Service in London and Dublin, 1380–1427," *New Medieval Literatures* 1 (1997): 83. For further information on this subject, see Kathryn Kerby-Fulton and Denise L. Despres, *Iconography and the Professional Reader: The Politics of Book Production in the Douce "Piers Plowman"* (Minneapolis: University of Minnesota Press, 1999); and the spirited "Review Article and Response" between Ralph Hanna, III, "*Piers Plowman* and the Radically Chic," and the authors, "Fabricating Failure: The Professional Reader as Textual Terrorist," *Yearbook in Langland Studies* 13 (1999): 179–206.

16. See M. L. Samuels, "Langland's Dialect," *Medium Aevum* 54 (1985): 232–47; and "Dialect and Grammar," in *A Companion to Piers Plowman*, ed. John Alford (Berkeley: University of California Press, 1988), 201–21, especially 207–8.

17. See Derek Pearsall, "Editing Medieval Texts: Some Developments and Some Problems," in *Textual Criticism and Literary Interpretation*, ed. Jerome J. McGann (Chicago: University of Chicago Press, 1985), 103; and Kane, *Chaucer and Langland*, 208, respectively.

18. See Frederick R. Karl, *Modern and Modernism, The Sovereignty of the Artist, 1885–1925* (New York: Atheneum, 1988), 13–14.

19. See Bennett, "Chaucer's Contemporary."

20. Justice, *Writing and Rebellion*, 239 note 142.

21. Kane, *Chaucer and Langland*, 84 and 77–89.

22. See Christopher Dyer, "Piers Plowman and Plowmen: A Historical Perspective," *Yearbook in Langland Studies* 10 (1994): 155–76.

23. All of the essays in Justice and Kerby-Fulton, *Written Work*, explore the significance of this passage. Also see Kane, *Chaucer and Langland*, 121–33, especially 130–32; and, most recently, David C. Fowler, "*Piers Plowman:* Will's 'Apologia pro vita sua,'" *Yearbook in Langland Studies* 13 (1999): 35–47.

24. See, for example, Hanna, *Pursuing History*, 240–41; Kerby-Fulton, "Langland and the Bibliographic Ego," 80; and Pearsall, *The Life of Chaucer*, 192.

25. See Anne Middleton, "Acts of Vagrancy: The C Version 'Autobiography' and the Statute of 1388," in Justice and Kerby-Fulton, *Written Work*, 213.

26. See the textual note on X.73–74 in *The Riverside Chaucer*, 1134.

13

ELIZABETH ROBERTSON

"Raptus" and the Poetics of Married Love in Chaucer's Wife of Bath's Tale and James I's *Kingis Quair*

Both rape and marriage figure prominently in two late medieval literary works that have yet to be considered in relationship to one another: Geoffrey Chaucer's Wife of Bath's Tale, written in the 1390s, which begins with rape and ends with marriage; and James I of Scotland's *The Kingis Quair*, written in the 1420s, in which the narrator recalls his own "rape" or abduction as a child and, while constructing a poem in honor of his forthcoming marriage to Joan Beaufort, meditates on the classical story of the rape of Philomel.[1] In both works, representations of rape, I shall argue here, are pivotal events that initiate critiques of late medieval social formations governing the relationships between men and women (for example, theological, ecclesiastical, and legal constructions of both rape and marriage). They also allow us to examine assumptions about subjectivity, free will, agency, and desire that these social formations encode. The nature of sexual violence against women, a subject raised by the works' portrayals of rape, is ultimately subordinated to a more general concern with male and female agency. At the heart of both works lies a developmental process whereby the protagonist, by perpetrating or contemplating rape and by learning the contingency of all human action, comes to acknowledge the legitimacy of female desire. Such an awareness is shown to be a prerequisite for success in love and marriage. These representations thus make manifest the late medieval understandings of the nature of the female subject at the same time that they offer visionary possibilities of new social formations. Furthermore, the visionary possibilities expressed in these works result in a critique of both poets' inherited traditional poetic forms, the courtly romance and the courtly love lyric. Throughout his career, Robert W. Hanning has been committed to illuminating Chaucer's social imagination; in this spirit, I wish to show the paradoxical socially transformative function of representations by Chaucer and his later followers of one of society's most dysfunctional events: rape.[2]

In order to comprehend the way their authors and their audiences understood their representations of, and meditations upon, sexual violence against women, we need to contextualize these literary works within late medieval English legal and cultural constructions of rape and marriage. It should be noted that, although James I is known as a Scottish poet and was himself Scottish, from age twelve until the time of the composition of his poem, he lived in England; thus, the theory and practices of rape and marriage that he would have known at that stage of his life would have been English. Rape and marriage in late medieval England have recently garnered attention from legal, historical, and literary critics alike; but critics have yet to highlight the implications these cultural practices have for our understanding of medieval subjectivity and agency—that is the capacity of the individual to be a discerning person who can act on his or her own behalf.[3]

What we are able to reconstruct about medieval relationships between the sexes tells us that apparently very different interactions such as rape and marriage were actually quite closely related to one another.[4] Instances of rape, either as involuntary abduction for the purposes of forced coitus or willing abduction for the purposes of marriage against the wishes of the parent or guardian, are often indistinguishable in the medieval record. All forms were called *raptus* and were viewed first and foremost as violations of the proprietorship of the lord: that is, the husband, father, local lord, or king. The ambiguity between rape as forced coitus and rape as abduction contributes to the difficulty critics have experienced in trying to determine exactly what charge was invoked when, in 1380, Cecily Chaumpaigne released Geoffrey Chaucer from "all manner of actions as they relate to my rape or any other thing or cause" ("omnimodas acciones tam de raptu meo tam de aliqua re vel causa").[5]

Raptus, in both its meanings, was considered a serious crime throughout the later middle ages and was nominally punishable in most decades by death or dismemberment, though such punishments were rarely meted out. According to the records remaining in the plea rolls, many cases of "raptus" were settled by material compensation; but, and this is a point of some significance in a consideration of the legal background of the Wife of Bath's Tale, other cases were resolved by the appellant marrying the defendant.[6] And, of relevance to *The Kingis Quair,* men are represented as often as women in cases of rape where abduction has taken place; for the practice of abduction for the sake of marriage involved a wealthy male child ward almost as often as it did a wealthy female child ward.[7]

The underlying principle about identity that links these apparently different kinds of sexual relationships is the assumption that individuals may be less significant than the property they represent. In the case of aristocratic women, there is often no legal distinction between their status as persons and the property with which they are associated. This is certainly true of the Westminster Statutes against rape from 1275 to 1382, with their increasing concern to protect the family or guardian seeking material compensation for rape.[8] Because concerns for property dominated both rape and marriage, the marriages and abductions of those of lower social status were of less concern than those of upper social status. Perhaps surprisingly, those of lower social status seem to have been able to enact a greater degree of choice in marriage than members of the aristocracy.

According to Church doctrine, all marriages of whatever social status and circumstances required the consent of each partner.[9] Present consent was understood to be the use of words such as, "I take you as wife/husband," and was considered sufficient to make a marriage valid; whereas future consent, which used words such as, "I promise to take you as wife/husband," made a valid marriage if that consent was followed by sexual intercourse. Although the consent of both partners was required to make a valid marriage, consent was in some cases just a formality. In most late medieval English marriages of those of upper social status, in practice, a woman was married to a man according to the wishes of her guardian, whether her father, the local lord, or the king. Medieval marriage practices thus often share with rape the subordination of individual desires, especially those of women, to the larger claims of the family or lord, whose primary concerns were the property transfers that resulted from marriage.

Where consent actually came to the fore was in a marriage practice that often conflicted with the desires of the family or guardian, known as clandestine marriage. Clandestine marriages, that is, marriages that took place privately between two individuals who exchanged words of consent with no witnesses, were often described legally as instances of "raptus," that is, rape or abduction for the purposes of marriage. This practice is of particular importance for an investigation of the legitimacy of female desire in late medieval England; for, upheld by canon law, clandestine marriage allowed women and men of upper social status much more freedom and autonomy in marriage choice than is usually associated with such marriages. The courts validated clandestine marriages on the basis of those same decretals that validated the voiced desire of the individual in any marriage.

Clandestine marriage disputes most readily illustrate the social significance of the doctrine of consent, for it is in these cases that words of consent were most thoroughly scrutinized. Furthermore, once the court had determined that a mutual exchange of present consent had taken place, individual desire and choice, whatever the desires of guardians or lords, were legally upheld. Although the participants might have to pay the parent or guardian a compensation fee if their marriage went against the wishes of that male figure, the ecclesiastical court nonetheless chose to support the claims of the individual over and above those of the guardian. It was, of course, difficult to determine exactly what words constituted present consent and, interestingly from the point of view of questions of agency, the word "volo" ("I wish") was highly ambiguous, and even phrases such as "volo habere te in uxorem" ("I wish to marry you") might not constitute present consent.[10] Court cases often turned on disagreements about the precise words exchanged. While it was often difficult to determine legally what constituted consent, the theological requirement of mutual consent to marriage assumes the agency and subjectivity of both marriage partners, an assumption that at times had significant consequences in the secular world.

The principle of choice that allowed clandestine marriages to be validated was under particular stress in the fourteenth century, as seen in the large number of cases that went to court.[11] A spectacular example of the conflict between clandestine marriage and the court's control of marriage, undoubtedly well known both to Chaucer and to James I of Scotland, is that of Joan of Kent who clandestinely married twice; and in both cases, the personal choices of the individuals prevailed over the wishes of the family and even the king.[12]

Both the Wife of Bath's Tale and *The Kingis Quair* in different ways reflect and respond to the tension that existed in fourteenth-century England between these two practices and definitions: the acknowledgment of individual desire in opposition to the desires of the family or lord in the ecclesiastical courts' recognition of clandestine marriage; and the frequent denial of individual subjectivity and agency in late medieval English secular practices regarding rape, abduction, and marriage. Both include representations of violent acts of sexual coercion and one includes a meditation on abduction. Both also explore the nature of female desire and offer a celebration of companionate marriage. Beyond simply upholding the principles of consent that underlies clandestine marriage, both works develop the implications of this validation of individual choice for new visions of sexual relationships based not on force and denial of subjectivity (rape), but on sexual pleasure and mutuality. In each of these works, the occasions of rape in the text are easily overlooked by the reader; they seem almost incidental. Those events are, however, crucial occasions in the text that initiate complex studies of the relationship between men and women, of the nature of female desire, of the power of language, and, finally, of the responsibility and/or potential of the poet to imagine new social structures and even new poetic forms based on mutual acknowledgment.

The Wife of Bath's Tale begins with an account of a knight's gratuitous rape of a maid of unspecified social standing:

> He saugh a mayde walkynge hym biforn,
> Of which mayde anon, maugree hir heed
> By verray force, he rafte hire maydenhed;
> For which oppressioun was swich clamour
> And swich pursute unto the kyng Arthour
> That dampned was this knight for to be deed,
> By cours of lawe, and sholde han lost his heed—
> Peravanture swich was the statut tho—
> But that the queene and othere ladyes mo
> So longe preyeden the kyng of grace
> Til he his lif hym graunted in the place.[13]

This event recalls numerous literary precedents of the rapes of peasant maids that occur in the pastourelle so importantly analyzed by Kathryn Gravdal.[14] Not only does this account recall literary convention, but also, as Robert Blanch and Corinne Saunders have so carefully demonstrated, medieval rape law permeates this passage.[15] This swift account of rape, which includes the rape, the pursuit of the rapist, the trial of the rapist, his punishment, and the deferral of his punishment by the intercession of the queen and her ladies, neatly captures a number of crucial aspects of the theory and practice of rape in late medieval England. Rather than echo specific fourteenth-century legal practices, it hearkens back to a somewhat earlier time, since it refers to a statute "tho" in which rape was clearly punishable by death.[16] The language that describes the rape and its aftermath mimics the language of the courts where "verray force" is necessary for rape to have occurred. The "clamor and pursute unto the kyng" echoes the early medieval requirement that the rape victim cry out publicly immediately after being raped, and the punishment of death meted to the knight by King Arthur reflects the severity of the punishments assigned, although not often enforced, by law. Finally, as in some historical court cases of rape, this one is resolved through the rapist's marriage, although in this story it is not clear that the hag who becomes the bride is also the maid victimized earlier in the tale.

Unlike many legal instances of "raptus," this account is striking for the clarity of the event being described; there is no confusion between rape and abduction here. The act is unambiguously a case of forced coitus against the will of a maiden. The fourteenth-century legal ambiguity about rape and marriage is engaged, however, as the tale shifts from rape to marriage. Furthermore, the tale goes on to explore what medieval rape and marriage share: the fundamental fourteenth-century legal assumption that women's desires are less significant than property concerns.

Blanch objects that the tale finally distorts reality by allowing women to manipulate the law; he condemns the tale for its "fragmented social structure in which women illegitimately employ the coercive power of law in order to reinforce the concept of female sovereignty."[17] He concludes that Chaucer intends to ridicule a "misrule" invented by the Wife of Bath, objecting, for example, that "Guenevere's attempt to assume Arthur's powers by gaining sovereignty over the knight . . . violates the very notion of jurisdiction."[18] Blanch here has failed to acknowledge first of all the significant influence women did, in practice, have on mitigating the severity of punishments.[19] More importantly, Blanch has missed the fact that the treatment of the law by women allows Chaucer to bring to the fore another realm of the law: the assumptions about female subjectivity that govern legal conceptions of marriage.

Others object that this tale can hardly be about rape, since the victim disappears from the tale entirely.[20] Nonetheless, the concerns of the maid resurface in the confrontation between the knight and the hag, and the tale as it unfolds explores the nature of victimization from both a male and a female perspective. The rape that begins the tale asserts woman's status as property, since the maiden's desires are irrelevant to the act. The knight violates the maiden "maugree hir hed" (880), a phrase that echoes French formulations of rape law such as that of Westminster Statute I, in which the rapist is condemned if he has violated a woman "maugre soun."[21] Although the violation is condemned by the representative of patriarchal law, King Arthur, the maiden demonstrates no agency of her own in bringing forward a case. Indeed, the maiden is curiously absent from all the events that occur to her and about her. It takes a woman's rule, Guenevere's, to teach the knight that the act of rape denies women both agency and subjectivity.

The knight learns that it is wrong to construct women as voiceless property, in part through his progressive feminization in the tale. Forced to consider what women most desire for a year and a day, the knight must come to acknowledge what he had failed to consider in the act of rape, women's desire itself. Furthermore, he is put into the position of the rape victim in being forced to have intercourse with someone he does not choose. The gross inequity of women's status as property is reinforced when the knight begs the hag to release him from his promise. He asks her to "chees a newe requeste! / Taak al my good, and lat my body go" (1060–61). The knight, in the position of male privilege, is able to separate his body from his goods in a way that is not open to the maiden. Denied choice, the knight is forced to begin to experience what it means to be a woman in his culture.

In many ways the tale is not only about an inequitable social system, but also about the ways in which language itself, when controlled by men, reinforces that inequity, a point that has been made by critics in studies of the Wife's prologue.[22] Like the prologue, the tale explores the way language can be used to exert power over others, particularly women; but, as we shall see, in redefining words such as "sovereignty" as one that implies mutuality rather than hierarchy, the tale suggests a use of language that frees the user from binary oppositions. The tale's representation of the patriarchal system of justice, law as defined and set in operation by men, in opposition to a new female rule—one based on Christian values of mercy, tolerance, and release of power—challenges what Lacan would call the hierarchy of the Law: that is, the phallic realm of the symbolic.

The opening of the tale, in its contrast of the world of fairydom with the present world, highlights the relationship between those who control the realm of language and those who control women's bodies. "In th'olde dayes

of Kyng Arthour" (857): a fairy-tale past in which men and women have control of the law, women might fear rape by an "incubus" (880); now that world
has been replaced by a world of friars who are busy "Blessynge halles, cham-
bres, kichenes, boures, / Citees, burghes, castels, hye toures, / Thropes, bernes,
shipnes, dayereyes" (869 – 71). In this present, "Wommen may go saufly up
and doun. / In every bussh or under every tree / Ther is noon oother incubus
but he, / And he ne wol doon hem but dishonour" (878 – 81). Although the
passage initially suggests that the exorcism of fairies by friars should be good
for women, it actually asserts the opposite, or at least suggests that women's
vulnerability to rape in the old days has not changed much, though the perpetrator may have changed names. Furthermore, the description here underscores a notion of the female body as property, since the friars not only
claim the world through language—blessing places (or naming them) and
making those places (cities, towns, dairies) part of their domain—but also
lay claim to the bodies of women. By criticizing the friars for this appro-
priative behavior, Chaucer not only satirizes the acquisitiveness and un-
chaste behavior of friars, but also hints that the Church itself is the source
of many oppressive ideas about women. In moving from the world of fairydom to a Christian world, we discover that the world of patriarchal Christian ideology has claimed all property, even the landscape, leaving no space
free for women. The end of the passage reverts to the past, because, while the
past and present both share the threat of rape, what the past world of fairy
does offer is the possibility of envisioning a legal system that educates and re-
forms the rapist.

The interrelationship among sexuality, power, and language is explored
in a variety of ways in the tale, including in the Midas digression, but perhaps the most significant revisioning takes place in the hag's "gentilesse"
speech. This speech, also sometimes viewed as a digression, is actually central to the utopian vision of the tale as it unfolds. Clearly, as Lee Patterson
notes, the "gentilesse" speech, "challenges the patriarchal ideology of property and inheritance."[23] And such a challenge, furthermore, disturbs the very
social structures that support rape. Patterson concludes that the speech is ultimately conventional, thus underestimating the degree to which it reinforces the entire tale's attack on the system—both legal and verbal—that
produces rape. The hag justifies her concept of "gentilesse" by turning to
Christ as the model of true nobility and by claiming that "gentilesse" comes
from grace rather than privilege. By redefining "gentilesse," the hag thus
paves the way for the utopian relationship described at the end of the tale

in which sovereignty and mutuality stem from their interdependence rather than from hierarchy, an ideal relationship formulated in theory in Church doctrine, though only imperfectly realized in secular practice. This speech brings to the fore the central issue that permeates and unites many rape and marriage cases in late medieval England; that is, relationships between aristocratic and royal men and women in late medieval England were preeminently determined by concerns about property.

The apparently subservient model of women in the happy ending of the tale troubles feminist readers. The ending has several steps. It begins with the hag's offer to be either old, ugly, and faithful or young, beautiful, and faithless. Surrendering decision making to the hag, the knight says, "I put me in youre wise governance; / Cheseth yourself which may be moost plesance / And moost honour to yow and me also" (1231–33). The hag specifically confirms that the knight intends to give her "maistrie" before turning into the beautiful, young, and faithful wife he desires. She then, we are told, "obeyed hym in every thyng / That myghte doon hym plesance or likyng" (1255–56). Those who object to this ending argue that, having first reversed power hierarchies by allowing women to have power over men, the tale now returns to the status quo. Further, they complain that the knight-rapist unfairly receives a reward of a subservient and beautiful young wife—in other words, as Patterson puts it, the knight's surrender of "maistrie" only results in a reinscription of male wish-fulfillment.[24]

But, if we assume that the wife has reverted to subservience here, then we miss the point of the tale's questioning of the very idea of hierarchy as the basis of sexual relationship. A fuller understanding of the ending of the tale depends on recognizing its persistent defamiliarization to the meaning of words; for this ending redefines the meaning of the word obedience. As Jill Mann writes, the tale "strips obedience of its oppression by making it an emotional response which matches and balances male surrender."[25] In the light of this definition and of the mutuality of the relationship described here, the word "sovereignty"—what women most desire—also takes on a new meaning. Both the knight and the hag maintain their sovereignty at the end, in the sense that the OED defines "sovereign" to mean "preeminent in respect of excellence or efficacy." Thus, such relationships are redefined to be those that respect the right of each individual to make choices, even the choice of obedience. In this reimagined society, obedience does not necessarily imply subordination, women are no longer the property of men, and sexuality is no longer an aspect of a power hierarchy, but rather part of a realm of mutual give and take. The tale ends as it begins, with a representation of a sexual relationship; but this one is based on mutual "plesance" rather than on violation or hierarchical domination.

This realm of pleasure depends on the knight's willingness to give up power. It is possible that, up to the moment that he releases power, the knight has learned nothing from his quest. But, by receiving his desire because of this release, the knight learns another power, that of surrender. The hag confirms his submission, not because she wants mastery herself, but rather because she desires that he learn the lesson of giving up mastery. The youth and beauty of the transformed hag is thus necessary to confirm that submission leads to the fulfillment of one's own desire. Chaucer's vision of marital harmony here is not simply a visionary fiction, however; for Chaucer draws here on an ideal of companionate marriage formulated in Christian commentaries that argue that the relationship between man and wife is analogous to that of Christ and the soul or of the Church and the individual.[26] The end of the tale in its celebration of companionate marriage thus illuminates understandings of relationships between the sexes possible in Christian theory, but only partially realized in secular practice. By exposing the equation of women and property in both marriage and rape, Chaucer has shattered the received understandings of hierarchical relationships that are at the heart of courtly lyrics and romance. His Christian idealism thus challenges the assumptions of the traditional secular genre of the courtly romance he utilizes. In its concerns with the social significance of the doctrine of consent and with the important role mutuality has in marriage, both ideas fundamental to Christian commentary, the tale finally has more in common with a religious tale than with a courtly romance.[27]

The fifteenth-century *Kingis Quair* by James I of Scotland, to which we now turn, explores further the theme of the Wife of Bath's Tale: that acknowledging subjectivity must be the basis for love, and hence, love poetry. This poem does not narrate an account of a rape as part of the action of the story; rather, the poet first of all recalls obliquely his own biographical experience of *raptus*, then cites a mythological story of rape—the story of Philomel—as part of his musings on the nature of song. As in the Wife of Bath's Tale, the protagonist of the poem, because of his own experience of being denied agency and choice, comes to realize the limits of relationships based on coercion and of the forms of poetry that implicitly accept inequitable relationships. The poetics the narrator develops, what one might call a poetics of married love, is one that acknowledges, in order to reject, the violence against women that is hidden within the tradition of the courtly love poetry he has inherited.

In contrast to Chaucer, who possibly perpetrated *raptus*, James was himself a victim of *raptus*—that is, he was abducted. In 1406, when sent to France to escape the vicissitudes of an unstable court at home, James, at the age of twelve, was abducted by the English and imprisoned by Henry IV until he was released eighteen years later in 1423. His experience of confinement was not entirely one of deprivation: he was well fed and clothed, and he received a superb education, possibly from the royal tutors—an education that contributed markedly to his development as a poet and as a leader. At this period, he studied English law and read widely in literature including Chaucer and Lydgate. Upon his release, he married Joan Beaufort, and they returned to Scotland, where he ruled according to the political principles he had learned while confined. In the course of his reign, James granted Joan unusual property rights and authority in the court. Factionalism continued to rage in Scotland, however; and in 1437, at the age of 43, James was murdered.[28]

I summarize this biography because the poem James I is believed to have written shortly after his release and marriage is semiautobiographical.[29] Indeed, a consideration of his own biography is a crucial step in the poet's development of his theme, which, in addition to being a love poem and a philosophical inquiry, is a self-conscious analysis of poetic vocation. The poet explores the role his own personal experience of suffering plays in his understanding of the value and social responsibilities of poetry. Crucial to his development as a poet is a recognition of the difference between his own recollected experience of *raptus*, in which he was put in a passive female role as an abductee, and the experience of the *raptus* recalled by the female nightingale later in the poem, one that focuses particularly on the brutality of an act that violates the female body. By distinguishing his suffering from that of others, the poet—like the knight in the Wife of Bath's Tale—learns not to appropriate the suffering of women. This process initiates the dream that furthers his exploration of poetic vocation as he comes to espouse a poetics of fulfillment and marriage rather than of aggressive desire. At the beginning of the poem, he explores the ways in which his childhood experience of *raptus* indelibly marked him; by the end of the poem, he acknowledges male privilege and his desire to transcend a poetics that reinscribes female suffering.

Let me summarize this relatively unknown poem. The narrator opens the poem with an allegorical meditation on the difficulties of writing, in which he compares his task to that of a navigator on a storm-tossed sea (99–133). He then turns to an account of his childhood experience of *raptus*, in which he again describes an experience in a storm-tossed sea, although here the account is biographical rather than allegorical (148–75). After completing his consideration of his writing task and his past, the narrator, who is imprisoned, turns to the present and celebrates the beginnings of spring that he observes in the garden outside his window. He puzzles over a group of nightingales singing, for no apparent reason, of the joys of love. He is then arrested by the sight of a beautiful maiden. After praising her ideal form and recognizing the beginnings of love in himself, he then notices that the nightingales have stopped singing. Contemplating a now single nightingale, he urges her to sing. Eventually all the nightingales resume singing. The lady leaves the garden, and, disconsolate, the narrator dreams a dream in which the goddesses Venus, Minerva, and Fortune advise him on how to achieve happiness. Told finally by Fortune that, in order to win the fruits of the world, he must enter it by climbing on Fortune's wheel, he awakes, whereupon a turtledove bears a message of promise and fulfillment to him in his cell. In an epilogue to the poem, the poet begs the reader for a generous reading of his poem and commends his work to Chaucer and Gower.

The opening of the poem, seen by some as disconnected from the dream vision itself, actually sets the question of the nature of poetic vocation to be investigated by the poem as a whole. In his recollection of his past experience on a stormy sea, the poet blends the fictional and the biographical in what A. C. Spearing calls a "symbolic and generalizing account of the poet's real experience."[30] Set next to his allegory of writing, this opening sequence suggests the poet's inability to separate the biographical from the fictional and raises the question of how one's own experience of personal violation shapes one's poetry. His various experiences on the sea, including the dangers of being becalmed, now metaphorically disturb his ability to write. For example, he complains: "The lak of wynd is the deficultee / In enditing of this lytill trety small."[31] Literally imprisoned, he seeks not only release, but also a poetic form that will free rather than bind him.

The poet contemplates a different kind of *raptus* in the nightingale sequence of the poem. This meditation begins in stanza 33, where the narrator contemplates first one, then a group of nightingales singing "hymns of love," as a prelude to mating:

And on the small[e] grene twistis sat
The lytill suete nyghtingale, and song
So loud and clere the ympnis consecrat

Of lufis use, now soft, now loud among,
That all the gardyng and the wallis rong
Ryght of thair song and o[f] the copill next
Of thair suete armony;—and lo the text. . . .
(225–31)

At this stage in the poem, the narrator scoffs at their frivolity and queries the motivation of their singing. He asks, "Quhat life is this, that makes birdis dote?" (248), and concludes, "It is nothing, trowe I, bot feynit chere, / And that men list to countrefeten chere" (252). The narrator wants to know "Quahat makis folk to iangill" (266) so of love. He is drawn to the song of the birds because it suggests freedom to him. He wants to know if love can unbind him and concludes by embracing a paradox, arguing that if love can make thralls free, then he wants to become a servant (267–73). At this stage, the poet can only imperfectly grasp the meaning of communal celebrations of mating primarily because he has not yet experienced desire. The song of the nightingales inspires a longing to participate, but not until he, too, is in love can he join in.

It is at this point that the poet sees the maiden and falls in love. After an extensive meditation on her virtues, the narrator notices that the nightingale has stopped singing. Why does the poet here turn his attention to a single female nightingale rather than to the group, and why does the nightingale become silent at the precise moment that desire is awakened in the narrator? The narrator here identifies the source of singing as suffering, for he urges the nightingale to sing for the sake of her experience of *raptus*,

And eke, I pray, for all the paynes grete
That for the love of Proigne, thy sister dere,
Thou sufferit quhilom, quhen thy brestis wete
Were, with the teres of thyne eyen clere
All bludy ronne—that pitee was to here
The crueltee of that unknyghtly dede
Quhare was fro thee bereft thy maidenhede.
(379–85)

He has shifted from identifying himself with a collective group of nightingales of unspecified gender singing a song of mating to identifying himself with a single female nightingale, who is supposed to sing a song of lament.

Although the narrator says he wishes the nightingale to sing a song to cheer his lady, the song he asks her to sing is one of rape. Kathryn Gravdal, Nancy Jones, and others have illuminated for us the history of violence against women that is hidden in the courtly love lyric, and the poem here draws our attention to the history of violation that could be expressed in the lament of the nightingale.[32] By recalling the rape that resulted from the gaze of Tereus on his wife's sister, the poem here signals the potential violence embodied in the gaze of the narrator as he looks upon his beloved. At this point in the poem we do not know what kind of love he holds for his beloved: will it be the love of the courtly love lyric—that is, an illicit love of force and one that focuses first and foremost on the nature and fulfillment of male desire; or will it be one that recognizes the subjectivity of the other? The nightingale's song is historically ambiguous, however; for while it often is associated directly with a grim story of rape and betrayal, it also is traditionally associated more positively with love and desire. The nightingale refuses to sing either song. Her silence, here, perhaps more eloquently than song, can be said to act both as a warning to the maiden of the potentially threatening gaze that has been turned upon her and as an encouragement to the narrator to meditate on the nature of his desire.

Because the narrator here has become a lover, the poem has complicated the narrator's exploration into the nature of his vocation as a love poet. Here the writerly narrator has discovered a desire not only for the beloved, but a desire to ally himself with female song. Furthermore, the issues of freedom and mastery raised by the evocation of the Philomel story are linked closely to the poet's own life—to his own condition as abducted and imprisoned and to his search for a form and meter that will free rather than bind him. Initially, this stage of his poetic development is one of identification. He sees himself as like the female nightingale in his desire to sing a song of love. Yet, as we shall see, to become a poet the narrator must move beyond identification to an acknowledgment of the subjectivity of the other, then back again to a notion of collectivity. At this point, the narrator has learned one step in this process: to acknowledge not only the role his own personal history of *raptus* plays in his poetry, but also the collective history of *raptus* or violence against women that is found in love songs. Yet the narrator unexpectedly shifts his attention, in the next stanza, away from the violence of *raptus* to a different subject—disloyalty in marriage. He urges the nightingale:

Lift up thyne hert and sing with gude entent,
And in thy notis suete the tresoun telle
That to thy sister trewe and innocent
Was kythit by hir husband false and fell;
For quhois gilt (as it is worthy wel)
Chide thir husbandis that ar false, I say,
And bid thame mend, in the twenty devil way.
(386–92)

This stanza suggests that the function of love poetry should not be to valorize rape, nor simply to recount suffering, but more precisely to warn against betrayal and treachery, "tresoun" in marriage. As it is summarized here, this is not the sad story of Philomel raped by Tereus, but of Procne betrayed by her husband. This stanza therefore suggests that the proper function of poetry is as a different kind of social regulator, one that enhances commitment in love.

The narrator nonetheless expresses frustration that the nightingale still refuses to sing, and he shifts his focus from sympathy for the victim of violence to threatening violence himself. He calls her a "lytill wrecche" (393) and commands her to "opyn thy throte" (396) to sing. This petition has overtones of a sexual threat, given that the poem has just evoked the sexual violence endured by Philomel—and given that medieval commentary traditionally associated the female mouth with female genitalia and female verbal activity with female sexual activity. The narrator cannot understand the nightingale's lack of desire to sing at the moment of his recognition of his own desire for love. He contemplates possible motivations for the bird's silence: "Hastow no mind of lufe? quhare is thy make / Or artow seke or smyt with ielousye? / Or is sche dede, or hath sche thee forsake?" (400–403).[33] Although the narrator can, of course, understand silence in one who is without a mate—since he, too, had no desire to sing until he had found a mate— he nonetheless begins here to acknowledge the subjectivity of the nightingale, allowing it motivations for song that are not his own. He asks "Quhat is the cause of thy malancolye / That thou no more list maken melodye?" (404–5). Counter to the tradition in which melancholy produces song in the nightingale, in this poem, the narrator believes that melancholy is the cause of silence in the nightingale. He resumes and complicates his earlier investigation of the origins of song by considering whether or not song emanates from the single suffering figure or from group celebration. Does the song of love originate from violation, betrayal, or union?

The narrator finally succeeds in forcing the nightingale to sing by sing-ing a song of nature: "blawe wynd, blawe, and do the levis schake" (419). The reason why this song inspires the nightingale to sing is obscure, but what-ever the motivation, the nightingale does take up her song at this moment and is, significantly, joined by others. The nightingale who had refused to sing a lament of the solitary victim does sing as part of a communal celebra-tion of mating. In stanzas 61 and 62, the narrator represents himself for the first time as a composer of verse. Upon hearing their song, he identifies with the birds as he says "I flawe for ioye" (426); and, recalling the earlier im-agery of freedom found in constraint, he says his "wittis " are "boundin all to fest" (427). He is not only bound to love, but he is also bound to meter, the strict meter of rhyme royal. We are told that he here *adds* his song to that of Philomel: "And to the notis of the philomene / Quhilkis sche sang, the ditee there I maid" (428 – 29). His song therefore is not a replacement of the nightingale's song, but is one that is added to the song of lament and betrayal of the female voice. Masculine words are added to feminine song. The poet narrator has learned, therefore, that love songs, before expressing personal de-sire, must acknowledge the history of violence against women that has been encoded in love poetry. The nightingale's potential song of lament and be-trayal is transformed into a male song of desire in which he asks for mercy from his beloved in stanza 63: "Quhen sall your merci rew upon your man / Quhois seruice is yit uncouth unto yow?" (435 – 36). After he sings his "ditee" (429), the birds take up "anothir sang" (443) celebrating sexuality, mating, and the spring that allows them the freedom to fulfill their desires. The narrator has thus moved from considering a song of mating to an unsung song of rape to a song of his own desire and back again to a song of mating. This final song is, in effect, a duet.

These passages raise a variety of questions about the poet's conception of poetry. The poem asks whether poetry can, or should be, an expression of personal suffering and a projection of selfish desire, and whether the voice can be singular or communal—that is, self-consciously part of a social group. The nightingales sing collectively and not out of single melancholy. The history of melancholy is projected onto that silent nightingale who rejects this history as the basis for song, since she will sing only as a part of a col-lective voice. The subject of song then is not the single, historical person, nor the subject alienated from the social through violence, but rather an in-tegrated social being. History, the personal experience of *raptus,* is relegated to the sphere of the private and individual, whereas the proper sphere of poetry is deemed to be the public and the collective. The poem points towards marriage as a subject suitable for celebration and song. Yet, since the narrator has nonetheless considered the potential violence against women that can be found in the lyric, we might argue that the poet has learned to recognize the feminine as a subject who has a history. His recognition that the object of his desire has the right to be a subject with her own desires prepares him both to enter into marriage and to become a poet. The narrator has undergone a process necessary to the development of poetry: a process that first involves identification and empathy, and then separation. Crucial to his development as a poet, then, is his full understanding of the meaning of "pitee," meaning here the sympathetic acknowledgment of the other.

The narrator's encounter with the nightingales leads into his dream, thus taking the narrator even further into his exploration of the nature of poetic vocation. Through his encounter with Venus, Minerva, and finally, Fortune, the narrator learns how love, wisdom, and experience intersect in the development of poetry. The poem as a whole thus develops a complex poetics, not of personal desire, but of the problems of fulfillment in love.

In the Wife of Bath's Tale, through the voice of the wife, Chaucer creates a gender inversion that acknowledges the social construction of gender and the neglected subjectivity of women in medieval culture. The tale questions women's status as property and asks whether not only female, but also male desires can be fulfilled under a system that reduces women to voiceless property. It goes on to suggest another way of conceptualizing sexual relationships without hierarchy and domination. James I creates a "feminized" narrator who similarly recognizes the importance of acknowledging the subjectivity of the feminine. James thus identifies a cultural problem that Chaucer also sees. Unlike Chaucer, however, James identifies the source of this problem in poetics, not in social structures. Offering critiques of the forms of love poetry that deny equality between men and women, both poets dramatize visionary protagonists who, through suffering the poverty of identity when an individual is denied agency, come to value companionate, non-hierarchical relationships between the sexes based on mutual recognition.

Notes

I am grateful to William Askins, Christopher Cannon, Bruce Holsinger, Karen Palmer, Marjorie McIntosh, Jeffrey Robinson, and the editors for their helpful comments on this essay.

1. I am assuming that the dating argued by John Norton-Smith is accurate and that the poem is both in fact by James I and written just after his release from captivity and marriage to Joan Beaufort and just before his return to Scotland in 1424. See John Norton-Smith, ed., *James I of Scotland: The Kingis Quair* (Oxford: Clarendon Press, 1971), xix–xxv.

2. See, for example, Robert W. Hanning's biennial lecture for the New Chaucer Society, "'And countrefete the speche of every man / He koude, whan he sholde telle a tale': Toward a Lapsarian Poetics for *The Canterbury Tales,*" *Studies in the Age of Chaucer* 21 (1999): 27–58.

3. For recent discussions by literary critics about rape, see Christopher Cannon, "*Raptus* in the Chaumpaigne Release and a Newly Discovered Document Concerning the Life of Geoffrey Chaucer," *Speculum* 68 (1993): 74–94, and H. A. Kelly, "Meanings and Uses of *Raptus* in Chaucer's Time," *Studies in the Age of Chaucer* 20 (1998): 101–66. More recently Cannon has broadened his study of medieval rape to consider the meaning of consent in his essay "Chaucer's Rapes: Uncertainties' Certainties," in *Representing Rape in Medieval and Early Modern Literature,* ed. Elizabeth Robertson and Christine Rose (New York: Palgrave, 2000), 255–80; first printed in *Studies in the Age of Chaucer* 22 (2000): 67–92. For two book-length literary analyses that take into account the history of rape law, see H. A. Kelly, *Love and Marriage in the Age of Chaucer* (Ithaca, N.Y.: Cornell University Press, 1975), and Corinne Saunders, *Rape and Ravishment in Medieval England* (Cambridge: D. S. Brewer, 2001). The standard historical overview of the law and sexual relationships is James A. Brundage, *Law, Sex, and Christian Society in Medieval Europe* (Chicago: University of Chicago Press, 1987), and that of marriage in England is R. H. Helmholz, *Marriage Litigation in Medieval England* (Cambridge: Cambridge University Press, 1974). See also M. M. Sheehan, "The Formation and Stability of Marriage in Medieval England: Evidence of an Ely Register," *Mediaeval Studies* 33 (1971): 228–63, reprinted in his *Marriage, Family and Law in Medieval Europe: Collected Studies,* ed. James K. Farge (Toronto: University of Toronto Press, 1996), 38–76. This collection also includes several other useful chapters on marriage and law. I am following the definitions of subjectivity and agency as discussed by Paul Smith in his *Discerning the Subject* (Minneapolis: University of Minnesota Press, 1988).

4. The interconnection between rape and marriage revealed in the history of rape law furthers Catherine McKinnon's provocative argument that rape and marriage are linked today. See her *Toward a Feminist Theory of the State* (Cambridge, Mass.: Harvard University Press, 1989). Andrea Dworkin makes a similar case in her book *Intercourse* (New York: Free Press, Macmillan, 1987).

5. See Cannon, "*Raptus*" and "Chaucer's Rapes," and Kelly, "Meanings and Users of *Raptus,*" for discussions of this case.

6. See J. B. Post's discussion of the various punishments meted out for *raptus* in his "Ravishment of Women and the Statutes of Westminster," in *Legal Records and the Historian,* ed. J. H. Baker (London: Royal Historical Society, 1978), 152.

7. See Sue Sheridan Walker, "Free Consent and Marriage of Feudal Wards in Medieval England," *Journal of Medieval History* 8 (1982): 123–34.

8. See Post's summary of the Westminster statutes in "Ravishment," and also his "Sir Thomas West and the Statute of Rapes, 1382," *Bulletin of the Institute of Historical Research* 53 (1980): 25–26. See also Christopher Cannon's important discussion of property and female identity in his "The Rights of Medieval Women: Crime and the Issue of Representation," in *Medieval Crime and Social Control*, ed. Barbara Hanawalt and David Wallace (Minneapolis: University of Minnesota Press, 1999), 156–85.

9. The predominant view of marriage in the Middle Ages was set forth in 1140 by Gratian, who set out to consolidate the, at times, conflicting canonical understandings of marriage to that date. For a marriage to be legal, so Gratian asserted, the partners could not be related within certain set degrees of blood ties, could not have been previously married, and could not have made final religious vows. Furthermore, the marriage was to be the result of an informed decision (usually age 12 for girls, age 14 for boys), and each party to the union had to consent freely to the marriage. Gratian emphasized that a marriage was initiated by the consent of both parties, but it was only rendered indissoluble by sexual union. Peter Lombard argued that present consent alone and not coitus made a marriage and an indissoluble bond; an unconsummated match by present consent was valid, but an unconsummated match by future consent was not. Views of the nature of consent were clarified in numerous discussions of marriage cases in papal letters of Alexander III (1159–1181) and Innocent III (1198–1216), who further refined rules of consent by arguing that the expression of interior consent alone determined a marriage. For summaries of marriage law and doctrine, see Helmholz, *Marriage Litigation;* Saunders, *Rape and Ravishment;* Kelly, *Love and Marriage;* M. M. Sheehan and Charles Donahue, Jr., "The Canon Law and the Formation of Marriage and Social Practice in the Later Middle Ages," *Journal of Family History* 8 (1983): 144–58; and Frederick Pedersen's *Marriage Disputes in Medieval England* (London: Hambledon Press, 2000).

10. For a discussion of the ambiguities of words of consent, see Helmholz, *Marriage Litigation,* 33–40. And, as Pedersen points out, at times even a marriage that most recognized as intended might be invalidated based on misstatement. For example, when, in the 1340s, Agnes of Huntingdon's husband Simon proved to be abusive, she sought an annulment by claiming the words they had exchanged were not words of present consent. See Pedersen, "Romeo and Juliet of Stonegate," in *Marriage Disputes,* 25–28.

11. See Kelly, "Meanings," 101–65.

12. See Karl P. Wentersdorf, "The Clandestine Marriages of the Fair Maid of Kent," *Journal of Medieval History* 5 (1979): 203–31.

13. *The Riverside Chaucer,* 3rd ed., gen. ed., Larry D. Benson (Boston: Houghton Mifflin, 1987) lines 886–96. All further quotations from Chaucer will be taken from this edition, and line numbers will be cited in the body of my text.

14. Kathryn Gravdal, *Ravishing Maidens: Writing Rape in Medieval French Literature and Law* (Philadelphia: University of Pennsylvania Press, 1991). It should be noted, however, that there is no specific evidence here that the victim is a peasant or that this event takes place in the country, although it would be unlikely for her to be alone in a town.

15. Robert J. Blanch, "'Al was this land fulfild of fayerye': The Thematic Employment of Force, Willfulness, and Legal Conventions in Chaucer's *Wife of Bath's Tale*," *Studia Neophilologica* 57 (1985): 41–51.

16. Hornsby suggests that Chaucer might not be referring to a particular statute here, but rather to a phrase he would have heard, since it was common in ravishment cases to include a formulaic statement that the rape and abduction had occurred in violation of the statute ("contra formam statuti"). Chaucer may have known of the phrase from his own brush with a rape case or because of serving as a justice of the peace in the case of Isabella Hull's abduction, or he simply may have been aware of the existence of statutes of rape. See Joseph Allen Hornsby, *Chaucer and the Law* (Norman, Okla.: Pilgrim Books, 1988), 119.

17. Blanch, "'Al was this land,'" 41.

18. Ibid., 44.

19. As Paul Strohm has shown, women—and most notably Queen Anne— often effectively interceded on behalf of criminals. See his "Queens as Intercessor," in *Hochon's Arrow: The Social Imagination of Fourteenth-Century Texts* (Princeton: Princeton University Press, 1992), 95–119. Indeed, a glance at the plea rolls shows several instances of women's successful intercession on behalf of a criminal.

20. For a recent objection of this kind, see Saunders, *Rape and Ravishment*, 309, as well as her fuller discussion of this issue in "Woman Displaced: Rape and Romance in Chaucer's *Wife of Bath's Tale*," *Arthurian Literature* 13 (1995): 41–51.

21. See Post's citations of the statutes in "Ravishment," 162–64. This phrase appears in Westminster I, c. 13.

22. Robert W. Hanning was one of the first to explore the relationship between gender and language in the Wife's prologue. See Hanning's "From Eva and Ave to Eglentyne and Alisoun: Chaucer's Insight into the Roles Women Play," *Signs* 2 (1977): 580–99. See also his "Roasting a Friar, Mis-Taking a Wife, and Other Acts of Textual Harassment in Chaucer's *Canterbury Tales*," *Studies in the Age of Chaucer* 7 (1985): 3–21. Since then, this topic has been explored extensively by feminist readers, including Carolyn Dinshaw, "'Glose / bele chose': The Wife of Bath and Her Glossators," in *Chaucer's Sexual Poetics* (Madison: University of Wisconsin Press, 1989), 113–31, and Elaine Tuttle Hansen, "The Wife of Bath and the Mark of Adam," in *Chaucer and the Fictions of Gender* (Berkeley: University of California Press, 1992), 26–57.

23. Lee Patterson, "The Wife of Bath and the Triumph of the Subject," in his *Chaucer and the Subject of History* (Madison: University of Wisconsin Press, 1991), 313. For an excellent discussion of the prologue and tale in relationship to medieval

marriage practices that comes to rather different conclusions than my own, see also his "'Experience woot well it is noght so': Marriage and the Pursuit of Happiness in the *Wife of Bath's Prologue and Tale*," in *Geoffrey Chaucer, The Wife of Bath*, ed. Peter G. Beidler (New York: Bedford Books of St. Martin's, 1996). Louise Fradenburg, who makes similar points, also suggests that the hag, in her argument that social position should be determined by deeds rather than inheritance, underscores the relationship between class and gender oppression. See her "The Wife of Bath's Passing Fancy," *Studies in the Age of Chaucer* 8 (1986): 31–58.

24. See Patterson, *Chaucer and the Subject of History*, 314.

25. Jill Mann, *Feminist Readings: Geoffrey Chaucer* (Atlantic Highlands, N.J.: Humanities Press International, 1991), 93.

26. For summaries of the history of notions of marital affection and mutual pleasure in marriage see the essays in Glenn W. Olsen, ed., *Christian Marriage: A Historical Study* (New York: Crossroads, 2001), and in Robert. R. Edwards and Stephen Spector, eds., *The Olde Daunce: Love, Friendship, Sex, and Marriage in the Medieval World* (Albany: State University of New York Press, 1991).

27. I disagree here with Saunders, who concludes in her discussion of the end of the tale in *Rape and Ravishment:* "The tale affirms patriarchal values: we hear no more of the victim, the knight is punished, but finally rewarded through otherworldly adventure, and the male fantasy of the young, beautiful and obedient wife is upheld; rape finally assists in the writing of romance" (309). One might argue further that the courtly romance as a genre, in fact, turns on the very ambiguous status of female consent that I have outlined in this essay. Chrétien's *Yvain*, for example, which begins with a marriage enacted by force but ends with a marriage made by consent, seems a case in point.

28. This biography is based on that provided by Norton-Smith, *James I,* xxi–xxv, and by E. W. M. Balfour-Melville, *James I, King of Scots* (London: Methuen, 1936).

29. The manuscript in which the poem appears, Selden B24, is dated no earlier than 1488, on paleographical grounds, and is believed to have been copied in Scotland. The poem, which celebrates a marriage in lines 1264–1351, is believed to have been composed just after James's release from prison and his marriage to Joan, but before his return to England. See Norton-Smith, *James I,* xi and xxxi, and A. S. G. Edwards and Julia Boffey, eds., *Bodleian Library Ms. Arch. Selden. B24: A Facsimile* (Cambridge: Boydell and Brewer, 1997).

30. A. C. Spearing, *Medieval Dream Poetry* (Cambridge: Cambridge University Press, 1976), 184.

31. Norton-Smith, *James I,* lines 122–23. All quotations from the Middle English will be taken from the Norton-Smith edition, and line numbers will be given within parentheses in the body of my text. I have silently altered the text's v's to u's where appropriate.

32. See Kathryn Gravdal and Nancy Jones, "The Rape of the Rural Muse: Wordsworth's 'The Solitary Reaper,' as a Version of Pastourelle," in *Rape and Representation*, ed. Lynn A. Higgins and Brenda Silver (New York: Columbia University Press, 1991), 263–77. See also Higgins and Silver's introduction, 1–14.

33. Notice that the gender of the nightingale here shifts from female to male. This gender confusion may simply be the result of the poor quality of the manuscript, or it may be the result of the narrator's shifting concerns as his meditation progresses. For a brief discussion of the manuscript issues, see A. S. G. Edwards and Elizabeth Robertson, "The Kingis Quair: 402," *Notes and Queries*, n.s. 41, no. 3 (1994): 307.

14

LAURA L. HOWES

Chaucer's Criseyde

The Betrayer Betrayed

O f course Criseyde betrays Troilus. The poem says as much at the outset, and Criseyde's actions late in the poem simply seem to confirm that early characterization. But Criseyde is also a victim in the poem in a complex series of betrayals by men. These betrayals begin with the treason of her father, continue through the decision by the Trojan parliament to trade her, are evident in Pandarus's abandonment of his role as her helpmate once the trade has been set, and culminate in the narrator's neglect in telling her side of the story in the later books. In short, every man in her life—save Troilus, unless one believes he could have prevented the trade,[1] and Diomedes—betray Criseyde's trust. Why, then, is *she* painted with an unforgiving negative brush by readers? How has Chaucer managed to turn the fascinating character we come to know in books two and three, full of nuance and humor and life, into the kind of female character we see represented practically everywhere else in late medieval literature: an inconstant woman who seduces men, tricks them, and leads them unfailingly into a state of sorrow and woe?

I will begin with the fairly straightforward betrayals by Calchas, the Trojan Parliament, and Pandarus, before moving to what I see as a betrayal of Criseyde by the narrator of the poem. Finally, I will turn to a discussion of how expectations of genre and generic conventions serve to form readers' impressions of Criseyde and to shape our negative assessment of her. This constitutes the final betrayal, and one in which, I will argue, Chaucer is fully complicit. And yet, Chaucer's designs extend beyond this series of betrayals to provoke a concern for Criseyde among readers, a concern generated by the conflict of social and literary conventions embedded in this poem, a concern that in turn interrogates audience distaste for Criseyde.

The Betrayal of Criseyde

The first instance of betrayal comes within the first one hundred lines of the poem. Calchas, knowing by foresight that Troy will fall, leaves town "softely," "ful pryvely," and "anon" (I.78, 80, 81),[2] after which we learn that he has left his daughter behind in the doomed city, bereft of friends, herself a widow. As a result of his secretive departure from Troy, his daughter fears for her life. Left "in this meschaunce" (I.92), she "of hire life . . . was ful sore in drede" (I.95). Indeed, her fears are acknowledged within the world of the poem when Hector grants her amnesty within Troy. He will not hold her responsible for her father's acts; he promises her "al th'onour that men may don yow have" (I.120) when her father was in town, and he personally vouches for her physical safety: "and youre body shal men save, / As fer as I may ought enquere or here" (I.122–23).

Hector's reassurance, of course, sets Criseyde up for a second betrayal, when her father's claim on her is reasserted, and she is handed over to the enemy camp by popular demand. Within the first one hundred lines of book four, Calchas regrets that he had left his daughter in Troy, "slepyng at home" (IV.93), and begins to fret about the fate of his Criseyde as the end of Troy draws near. Hector, to his enormous credit, responds to the Greek request with: "Syres, she nys no prisonere. . . . We usen here no wommen for to selle" (IV.179, 182). But the majority wins out, pleading with King Priam in unison: "thus sygge we, / That al oure vois is to forgon Criseyde" (IV.194–95). And so, Criseyde is "forgon" a second time: forfeited, given up, cast out—her trust in the Trojans, and Hector personally, misplaced.

And what of her surrogate father in Troy, Uncle Pandarus? Upon hearing the news of Criseyde's trade, Pandarus goes straight to Troilus's house:

Pandare, which that in the parlement
Hadde herd what every lord and burgeys seyde,
And how ful graunted was by oon assent

For Antenor to yelden so Criseyde,
Gan wel nigh wood out of his wit to breyde,
So that for wo he nyste what he mente,
But in a rees to Troilus he wente.
(IV.343–50)

And, if there is any doubt as to his allegiance in this matter, he proceeds to try to convince Troilus that another lover can be found: "Forthi be glad, myn owen deere brother! / If she be lost, we shal recovere an other" (IV.405–6).

Later, when Pandarus arrives at Criseyde's house, sent there by Troilus, he uncharacteristically lacks a plan of action. After listening to her sorrowful complaint for several lines, he asks: "what thynkestow to do? / Whi ne hastow to thyselven som resport? / Whi wiltow thus thiself, allas, fordo?" (IV.849–51), suggesting that if she cannot come up with a plan, she will "fordo"—destroy—herself. In the same meeting, Pandarus urges her to plot with Troilus:

So shapeth how destourbe your goynge,
Or come ayeyn soon after ye be went.
Women ben wise in short avysement;
And lat sen how youre wit shal now availle,
And that that I may helpe, it shal nat faille.
(IV.934–38)

While Pandarus offers his help in some unspecified way, the onus for coming up with a plan sits squarely with Criseyde. Her womanly "wit" is somehow considered equal to this task. Or is it? Perhaps Pandarus understands it as an impossible task and, wishing to wash his hands of the whole affair, delegates the responsibility for it to Criseyde. He can then claim that he allowed her to do just as she thought best and, unfortunately, her plan did not work out. If Pandarus had never hatched a plan before this time, then I might be more willing to trust in his trust in Criseyde. But he has never left the planning to her before this, and famously so; the clear abnegation of his normal role as panderer here signals his forfeiting of Criseyde: Let her go. Let her plan whatever she wants, in order to placate herself and Troilus, his actions say here. But I, Pandarus, will not even attempt to plot her return or to hinder her going.

Finally, as though these three betrayals were not enough, the narrator himself betrays Criseyde in a well-calculated series of narrative maneuvers that are played out in the last three books of the poem. While we may not agree with the critic who wrote that the narrator is in love with Criseyde, it is hard to quibble with E. Talbot Donaldson's attendant claim that, despite the narrator's best intentions, his difficulty in admitting Criseyde's guilt in the later books often "suggest[s] . . . reasons for us to distrust and hate her."[3] The narrator skews his readers' perceptions of Criseyde and is therefore involved in the defamation of her character. He would like to defend her, but at the same time he leaves her open to suspicion: did she fall in love with Troilus too quickly? Does she have any children? He does not know; and by telling us he does not know, he raises potentially damaging questions.[4]

In fact, Criseyde disappears from the poem even before she is forced to leave Troy.[5] From line 1582 of book three, after Pandarus "hath fully his entente" in the bedroom with Criseyde, until line 743 of book four, she is not present.[6] That is nearly 1,000 lines, which is over half the length of any book in the poem. I emphasize this because it is the striking and unambiguous start of Criseyde's absence from the poem while she is still present in Troy. On one level, this absence, coinciding with her father's request and the parliament's decision to trade her for Antenor, may be taken as evidence of her helplessness.[7] Although her future is at stake, no one consults her; and by treating her as Antenor's equivalent, the parliament makes it clear that they consider her a prisoner, though she never sees herself in this way. On another level—the level of narrative structure rather than plot—Criseyde's absence from the poem prefigures her betrayal of Troilus. It is as though she intentionally withholds herself from us during these thousand lines, just as we begin to imagine her withholding herself from Troilus. The narrator duplicates and anticipates Troilus's experience of Criseyde's absence from Troy in our experience of Criseyde's absence from the poem, subtly allying readers with Troilus.

Another example of narrative sabotage, and of Criseyde's voice being submerged in the poem, can be found in the description of Criseyde as she meets her father for the first time since he committed treason. We have already overheard her rail at him in book four when she learns she is to be traded: "O Calkas, father, thyn by al this synne!" (IV.761). But when she meets Calchas in the Greek camp, we do not know what she says as her father kisses her twenty times:

And twenty tyme he kiste his doughter sweete,
And seyde, "O deere doughter myn, welcome!"

> She seyde ek she was fayne with hym to mete,
> And stood forth muwet, milde, and mansuete.
>
> (V.191–94)

Her action, or inaction, is probably socially determined here, as is discussed below; but at a moment when what Criseyde actually might say or be thinking is crucial to our understanding of her character, we get nothing except the narrator's blandest verse.

Criseyde's interaction with Diomedes is similarly veiled. Again, during the exchange of prisoners, Diomedes speaks to Criseyde for fifty-seven lines on their way to the Greek camp, but Criseyde is silent. Then, when she does speak, we do not get direct speech, but only what the narrator says she said:

> But natheles she thonked Diomede
> Of al his travaile and his goode cheere,
> And that hym list his frendshipe hire to bede;
> And she accepteth it in good manere,
> And wol do fayne that is hym lief and dere,
> And tristen hym she wolde, and wel she myghte,
> As seyde she; and from hire hors sh'alighte.
>
> (V.183–89)

The narrator has just told us she was beside herself with sorrow during the exchange ("Hire thoughte hire sorwful herte brast a-two" [V.180]), but he tells us nothing about her inner reaction to Diomedes. When Criseyde accepts Diomede's friendship, does she do it just to be polite? Is she genuinely grateful? Is she afraid of what might happen to her if she did not accept it? There is no way of knowing. Not only does the narrator filter her voice— by not giving us her direct speech—but he tells us nothing about what she may be feeling at this crucial juncture.

In fact, it is only in the third meeting between Criseyde and Diomedes that Criseyde speaks for herself. When Diomedes tells her she might as well give up her feelings for Troy and everyone in it because they are all doomed, Criseyde says she doubts that Troy will fall. She then speaks of love:

> "But as to speke of love, ywis," she seyde,
> "I hadde a lord, to whom I wedded was,
> The whos myn herte al was, til that he deyde;

And other love, as help me now Pallas,
Ther in myn herte nys, ne nevere was."
(V.974–77)

We may wonder here, since Criseyde recalls only her late husband and not
her lover Troilus, whether she ever really loved Troilus or whether she has
completely forgotten him. And these thoughts add to our growing sense of
Criseyde's instability. Still, we should not automatically read these lines as
a denial of Troilus, since she is speaking to Diomedes here, and may have
reasons for not mentioning her illicit love affair with Troilus. In any case,
Criseyde's direct speech in this instance serves not to clarify her feelings
for Troilus, but to muddy the waters. Her experience with Troilus is veiled
by means of her speech. The narrator does *not* step in to explain or to allow
Criseyde to muse in private. All we have is her puzzling response to Diomedes, which becomes an opportunity for us to exercise our interpretive
powers. As Donaldson has written: "Even in the clearest, most straightforward accounts of Criseyde's behavior, ambiguity intrudes."[8]

When we are not told the whole story, we tend to invent it. Clearly,
Criseyde has begun to warm up to Diomedes, but still we do not know what
led to her softening stance, and we are quick to fill in the blanks: she is fickle
by nature; she is morally flawed; she is too afraid to take action and return
to Troilus; she cannot escape the patriarchal role of object to be traded among
men. These explanations are all possible, but are all impossible to prove as the
single explanation. We simply do not have sufficient evidence for the crucial
period during which Criseyde decides, finally, to make the best of a bad situation.[9] In her words:

"But syn I se ther is no bettre way,
And that to late is now for me to rewe,
To Diomede algate I wol be trewe."
(V.1069–71)

In addition, Criseyde's final speeches—soliloquies in which we might
expect her to make a firm bid for our sympathy—are all immediately undercut by the narrator's remarks. In book five, Criseyde speaks about her
plans to escape from the Greek camp; she does not know which direction to
take, and she plans to escape in some still-to-be-determined way (V.689).
Nevertheless, her speech concludes: "'For which, withouten any wordes mo, /

To Troi I wole, as for conclusioun'" (V.764–65). But then the narrator continues the stanza: "But God it wot, er fully monthes two, / She was ful fer
fro that entencioun!" (V.766–67). Startlingly, in the space of two lines, two
months elapse. The narrator gets ahead of his story, entirely skipping over the
events of the night in which Criseyde says she will escape. Her plan is dismissed out of hand by not being discussed at all. The rhyme of Criseyde's
"conclusioun" with the narrator's "entencioun" emphasizes the discrepancy:
what Criseyde would have as the end of her story, the narrator shows to be
only her desire. Further, the narrator finishes the stanza in the future tense:

> For both Troilus and Troie town
> Shal knotteles thorughout hire herte slide;
> For she wol take a purpos for t'abide.
> (V.768–70)

Nothing could undercut our perception of Criseyde's resolve as forcefully
as these lines. Like "before" and "after" snapshots, they leave out the middle—
the process by which "before" becomes "after"—and they thus omit entirely
the process by which Criseyde, the woman we love, becomes Criseyde, the
woman we love to hate.

The next, and last, time Criseyde speaks directly to us, Diomedes has
found his way into her heart. She has given him Troilus's bay steed and
brooch. She laments her certain negative future reputation and, addressing
much of her speech to the absent Troilus, she takes her formal leave of us:

> "And trewely I wolde sory be
> For to seen yow in adversitee;
> And gilteles, I woot wel, I yow leve.
> But al shal passe; and thus take I my leve."
> (V.1082–85)

The narrator then overtly seeks to excuse Criseyde. He says she has suffered
enough already. Besides, she is clearly sorry for what she did:

> And if I myghte excuse hire any wise
> For she so sory was for hire untrouthe,
> Iwis, I wolde excuse hire yet for routhe.
> (V.1097–99)

But immediately following this, the narrative returns to Troilus who is—amazingly—still languishing on the ninth night after Criseyde's departure! How can we excuse her in the event while Troilus—at least two months behind her, given the narrator's comment at V.766, quoted above, and possibly two years behind her[10]—still expects Criseyde to keep her word and return on the tenth day? He of course knows nothing of her future acts. Arthur Mizener has written extremely well about the odd timing of book five: "Chaucer has arranged the sequence of the events in the narrative in the order which will give the maximum effectiveness to the tragic scene. This arrangement hopelessly muddles in the reader's mind any possible chronology, so necessary if we are to follow the development of Criseyde's character."[11] Indeed, Criseyde's character is so veiled from us at this point as to be at best inscrutable and at worst morally repugnant.

Finally, Criseyde's two letters to Troilus are the last we hear from her. Their placement near the close of book five is highly strategic. Criseyde grows fainter, less real to us, and this distancing reinforces her image as the absent and ultimately unfaithful woman. Her voice is not only surrounded by a narrative that undercuts it in a variety of ways, as I have tried to show, but her voice is present by the end only in the letters, words written on paper—a disembodied voice, divided from the complex character we feel we once knew well.[12] When all is said and done, Criseyde is most often defined in terms of the lover she betrays.[13] While this narrative strategy is extremely effective,[14] Chaucer's intention vis-à-vis Criseyde is more complex than many critics have admitted.

Chaucer's Criseyde and Conventional Imperatives

Indeed, the last betrayal I would like to outline here is the one performed by many readers of the poem, with Chaucer's full knowledge. In addition to emphasizing the betrayals of Calchas, the Trojan parliament, Pandarus, and the narrator, Chaucer complicates our responses to Criseyde's character significantly by setting her at the intersection of two sets of conventions governing female behavior: romance literary convention on the one hand, and a set of social expectations for obedient daughters on the other.

In the middle of book four, as the young lovers privately discuss what the upcoming trade of Criseyde to the Greeks will mean for them, Criseyde faints, and for eight and a half stanzas Troilus believes her to be dead

(IV.1150–1212). In many ways, the death of Criseyde would better satisfy audience expectations for courtly literature than her ongoing and eventually traitorous life does, as she herself seems to know when, earlier in the book (IV.771–77), she contemplates suicide by starvation.[15] This false-death scene invokes Ovid's version of the story of Pyramus and Thisbe as an alternate narrative, as well as the double-death model of Tristan and Isolde; clearly it is one that would leave Criseyde's reputation as a courtly lover intact. But if Chaucer's narrator really does mean to defend, and even rescue, Criseyde from the accusations of generations of readers, as he so often claims, then why does he bring this scene to the fore? Why even hint at the fact that Criseyde could have remained untarnished if only she had died before she forsook Troilus? Not only does this event contribute to the narrator's own betrayal of Criseyde, no matter that he claims to want to rescue and protect her. But, further, it highlights the conflict between Criseyde the romance heroine and Criseyde the dutiful daughter. This conflict in expectations confuses readers and may contribute to a covert defense of Criseyde, engineered by Chaucer.

The scene in question opens the lovers' last night together. This is the night during which Criseyde convinces Troilus that they should not run off together, as he proposes, defying social convention and tarnishing their good names, but that she will return to Troy in ten days' time either by tricking her father, or by luck—should the war end soon—or by some other unspecified means. But before this discussion, the two meet, weep uncontrollably for a time without speaking, and then, with few words, Criseyde faints:

> With broken vois, al hoors forshright, Criseyde
> To Troilus thise ilke wordes seyde:
>
> "O Jove, I deye, and mercy I beseche!
> Help Troilus!" and therwithal hire face
> Upon his brest she leyde and lost speche—
> Hire woful spirit from his propre place,
> Right with the word, alwey o poynt to pace.
> And thus she lith with hewes pale and grene,
> That whilom fressh and fairest was to sene.
>   (IV.1147–55)

Her spirit is said to leave its own right and proper, usual place and to pass continually by its one standard point or position. This unusual hovering-like activity of her spirit not only causes Criseyde to turn pale and greenish, but also makes her limbs, which Troilus touches, cold, and makes her eyes roll back in her head: "Hire eyen throwen upward to hire hed" (IV.1159). Troilus "ofte tyme" kisses her cold mouth (IV.1161); and two stanzas later he feels for her breath and finds none:

> She cold was, and withouten sentement
> For aught he woot, for breth ne felte he non,
> And this was hym a pregnant argument
> That she was forth out of this world agon.
> (IV.1177–80)

None of the usual signs of life are present in Criseyde, and Troilus then "gan hire lymes dresse" (IV.1182), preparing her body as a corpse. Four more stanzas have him melodramatically making his own death speech, blaming Jove and Fortune for killing Criseyde (IV.1192) and declaring that he must accompany his lover in death. With his sword at his heart, ready to die, Criseyde comes out of her swoon (IV.1212), and the scene then proceeds with their lengthy conversation.

Boccaccio's Cressida also faints at this point in *Il Filostrato*, but Chaucer emphasizes Criseyde's death-like state, having Criseyde uniquely exclaim "I deye" (IV.1149) before she faints; having Troilus notice three times how very cold her body is (to Troilo's once); and having Troilus kiss Criseyde's cold lips, recalling the kiss Thisbe gives her dying Pyramus in Ovid's *Metamorphoses*.[16]

Like Troilus and Criseyde, Pyramus and Thisbe discuss running off together to defy their parents' prohibition. But unlike Chaucer's lovers, the Ovidian lovers carry out their plan, meeting in a prearranged spot outdoors at night, and both are dead at tale's end.[17] While these Ovidian lovers are not mentioned by name in *Troilus and Criseyde*, the situation is so similar that the echo cannot be mistaken. It lends substance to the fears Criseyde has about running away, as well as suggesting a better romance ending for Chaucer's heroine.

What sort of a romance heroine is Chaucer's Criseyde, anyway? Gretchen Mieszkowski argues that "romance conventions do not account for Chaucer's substanceless Criseyde" and that "nothing in the genre requires the heroine's inaction." Mieszkowski finds that Chaucer re-created his Criseyde to be "superlatively attractive to male readers" by subtracting all traces of independent thought and action.[18] While I might argue that Criseyde does display isolated instances of independence, and that one of the tragedies of this poem is that Criseyde believes she has free will when in fact she does not, still, Mieszkowski's generalizations about Criseyde's *un*romantic character provide plenty of evidence for Criseyde's failure as a romance heroine.

In addition, Susan Crane's study of insular romance argues that Middle English romances "endorse . . . the fundamental premises that love improves lovers and that [knightly] prowess can fruitfully serve love"; and further, that love "improves lovers not so much by refining their sensibilities as by encouraging their progress toward a full, varied experience of life."[19] In this sense as well, and perhaps most obviously, Criseyde falls miserably short of the conventional romance ideal. Instead of using their forced separation as an opportunity to prove her undying love for Troilus by refusing all new offers of love, Criseyde succumbs, at some undisclosed point, to the advances of Diomedes.

Finally, a dead romance heroine is always better than a live one who misbehaves. Thomas of Britain's Ysolt:

> Sun espirit a itant rent,
> E murt dejuste lui issi
> Pur la dolur de sun ami.
> Tristrans murut pur sun desir,
> Ysolt, qu'a tens n'i pout venir.
> Tristrans murut pur sue amur,
> E la bele Ysolt pur tendrur.
> (3118 – 24)[20]

> (Ysolt) . . . rendered up her spirit completely
> And suffered death there at his side
> Out of her sorrow for her true love.
> Tristan perished because of his love,
> And Isolde because she did not come in time;
> Tristan perished from his deep passion
> And Isolde from her compassionate love.[21]

Criseyde's faint points up the potential for such a "compassionate" love ("tendrur"), a love that would kill Criseyde through grief. Thus, when Criseyde faints and Troilus prepares to kill himself over her seemingly dead body, Chaucer signals the possibilities for another outcome to this story, one that is impossible, given the traditional nature of the tale he has set himself to tell, but one which, nevertheless, is invoked to suggest the potential for other endings.

It is not that Criseyde is, or even tries to be, a model romance heroine. But this scene suggests how she might have been one, and how she could have answered audience expectations for the genre. As Angela Jane Weisl has put it so succinctly and well, "because Criseyde has defied the [romance] genre's expectations by failing to remain faithful to Troilus, the poem cannot remain faithful to romance's narrative conventions.... Because gender roles have been upset, the genre itself is upset, and the poem can no longer support a romance conclusion."[22] Gayle Margherita has similarly argued that "Criseyde betrays romance as surely as her father betrayed Troy," locating this genre-based betrayal where romance meets history.[23] Chaucer signals here his aversion to the romances of his predecessors in England and on the continent. They were perceived as "outmoded" in Susan Crane's analysis; they border on the melodramatic in Donaldson's still-fresh reading.[24] But they are nevertheless invoked by Chaucer—gestured at—when Criseyde faints and Troilus prepares for suicide. And then the tragedy is sidestepped; the moment passes, as if to say, I could have given you that story, but I have not. This one is different. Keep reading, and you will see.

The melodrama of a lover's potential suicide colors Dorigen's speeches in the Franklin's Tale, a tale Chaucer also took from Boccaccio. Confronted by Aurelius with the promise she had made him, in her husband's absence, Dorigen spends a day or two weeping and wailing (V.1348). Feeling trapped by circumstances she never anticipated, Dorigen complains against "Fortune . . . / That unwar wrapped hast me in thy cheyne" (V.1355–56), a trap from which she can only see two ways out: "deeth or elles dishonour" (V.1358). Like Criseyde, Dorigen is fully aware that she stands to lose her good name. Dorigen sees it as a fate worse than death, and she muses upon several examples of wives and maidens who chose death over defilement. Indeed, at two points in her lengthy speech, she determines to commit suicide (V.1363 and 1423), but the list of examples continues on. Dorigen's stock of stories about worthy women keeps her alive until the return of Arveragus, her husband.

The humor of a death delayed—the way in which language about suicide can put off what one claims is a clear purpose to die—informs both Dorigen's tribulation in the Franklin's Tale and Troilus and Criseyde's potential double suicide. In both, the moment passes, to the apparent relief of the speaker who was not so intent on suicide that he or she actually achieves it.

In conflict with the conventions that would dictate Criseyde's unflagging loyalty to her lover stand fourteenth-century British social conventions dictating obedience to a father, a husband, or other male relative acting as a surrogate parent. Another fertile strain of Criseyde scholarship demonstrates quite convincingly, I think, that Criseyde's social, or sociopolitical, situation influences much of her behavior in Chaucer's poem. Indeed, Chaucer highlights the historical context of the love story at particular junctures in the narrative, most notably for us at the opening to book four; and this serves in part to illuminate the political context Criseyde inhabits.[25]

As David Aers writes, "when we come to the now famous phrase describing aspects of [Criseyde's] being as 'slydynge of corage' (V.825), we have been given ample grounds for grasping this in the full light Chaucer has cast on the crippling social reality and ideology which constitute her circumstances."[26] Carolyn Dinshaw has investigated the "trafficking in women" that goes on in this poem and its effects on Criseyde;[27] while Diane Vanner Steinberg has explored the commodification of Criseyde in the martial economies of both Troy and the Greek camp, demonstrating that Criseyde herself seems aware "of the fragility of a single woman's power and place in Troy."[28]

That Criseyde acts appropriately, given medieval social expectations for female behavior, can be seen in her obedience both to her uncle and to her father. Criseyde's obedience to Pandarus is a factor in her first all-night rendezvous with Troilus. She agrees to stay the night at Pandarus's house after dinner because it is raining so heavily, and also "sith he hire that bisoughte, / And, as his nece, obeyed as hire oughte" (III.580–81). Similarly, when delivered to her father in the Greek camp, she stands "forth muwet, milde, and mansuete" (V.194)—the picture of filial obedience.

The trajectory of this argument extends as well to the scene in book three that finds Pandarus prying under the sheets of the bed where his niece lies, following the first night of sexual intimacy between the two young lovers. The narrator concludes the short, but contested, passage with the assertion that Pandarus "hath fully his entente" (III.1582), an intent which many critics now agree is incestuous.[29] Whether Uncle Pandarus actually rapes Criseyde here is far less apparent to most critics of the poem; but in light of her role as obedient niece, and her new situation as Troilus's secret lover, it would seem obvious that Criseyde has no choice but to submit to Pandarus's *entente,* whatever that may be. Criseyde's helplessness is further emphasized by our awareness that Pandarus *can* do with her whatever he wants. She is powerless to complain about his behavior to anyone, for if she were to threaten

Pandarus with public exposure, he can now do the same with her: blackmail her with his knowledge of her secret affair.

It may seem odd to us that Criseyde, a widow, does not enjoy more independence than she does in this poem. But she is clearly still considered "chattel" to her father, who can demand her in trade from Troy. Indeed, Criseyde's returning to her father's house as a widow confirms her status as an upper-class, rather than merchant, woman, and may also suggest that she does not have sufficient dower income to secure her own independent household.[30] If she had had children by her first husband, they have gone off to be raised by others, perhaps by her late husband's extended family. And so she *has* resumed her place as a marriageable daughter, albeit once widowed, with none of the independence that we might expect.

These two sets of conventional expectations—the romance convention that would have Criseyde defy social norms to persevere in her love affair with Troilus, on the one hand; and fourteenth-century social conventions that dictate filial obedience, and which Criseyde appears to have internalized, on the other hand[31]—produce in the reader an uncomfortable impasse regarding Criseyde, an impasse which can either be elided, as when Pandarus says: "I hate, ywys, Criseyde" (V.1732), or acknowledged and investigated.

If we demand that Criseyde remain "true" to Troilus, in the tradition of romance heroines, then we are also asking her to defy her upbringing, to become a kind of social revolutionary in thought and action, a *dis*obedient woman in a world that values obedient women. If we applaud, or at the least seek to understand, Criseyde's obedience to her father and to the patriarchal culture that surrounds and defines her, then we have no business deriding her for accepting Diomedes. Imagine Chaucer's original audience in this situation, at this impasse—not modern women and men who may have become more comfortable with nontraditional social ideals and less accepting of blind obedience than a medieval audience may have been. If we can imagine a medieval parent who may demand of her or his daughter strict filial obedience, then the force of conflicting conventions in this poem gains potency.

One of Chaucer's experiments in *Troilus and Criseyde*, it seems to me, is to cast the accepted social practice of his own contemporaries into an odd and unsettling light. If there is a parent in his audience who wants Criseyde to disobey her father and escape with Troilus, as Ovid's Thisbe does, then Chaucer has initiated a revolutionary thought. If there is a daughter in Chaucer's extended audience who understands Criseyde's dilemma and resolves that she will never allow herself to be trapped as Criseyde is, by her own obedience, then Chaucer has planted the seed of filial disobedience. In fact, there are many examples of female characters in medieval literature who are punished for their *dis*obedience—punished in the literary sense of, for example, being made a mock of, or being made to seem trivial. But Criseyde is one of a few in court literature who is punished in this way for her *obedience*.

We may compare her to Chrétien de Troyes' Enide, who so pointedly disobeys her husband only to be—surprisingly—praised for this action.[32] Criseyde fills out the other side of this equation, if you will: not praised for her disobedience but vilified for her obedience. We may also compare her fruitfully with female saints—girls and women who obey their heavenly father and are punished for their obedience. St. Cecile, in Chaucer's Second Nun's Tale, described before her forced wedding to Valerian as "ful devout and humble in hir corage" (VIII.131), devotes herself, body and soul, to Christ: "O Lord, my soule and eek my body gyne / Unwemmed, lest that I confounded be" (VIII.136–37). She then proceeds to keep her body pure by convincing her new husband to forgo the usual intimacies with her. Her devotion and obedience to God never shaken, she dies at tale's end, first tortured and then murdered. Still, the point of difference is instructive: the saints routinely defy earthly and pragmatic expectations, while Chaucer's Criseyde conforms to her earthly role as daughter.

Thus, while Chaucer may not be able to rescue Criseyde herself from the negative assessments that fill the tradition about her, he nevertheless has created a narrative that is potentially destabilizing for its original audience. In Criseyde—as in the Wyf of Bath—Chaucer poses questions about stereotypical responses to female disobedience and independence; and in so doing, he clears a path along which countless others have since traveled.

Indeed, the narrator's overt and disruptive defenses of Criseyde throughout the poem work on at least two levels. First, they raise questions about her intentions that seem better left unraised. An example, mentioned above and discussed by Donaldson,[33] comes when Criseyde falls in love, seemingly at first sight. The narrator interrupts the story to defend her action, presumably because a woman who falls in love quickly may be expected to fall out of love quickly:

Now myghte som envious jangle thus:
"This was a sodeyn love; how myght it be
That she so lightly loved Troilus

Right for the first syghte, ye, parde?"
Now whoso seith so, mote he nevere ythe!
For every thyng a gynnyng hath it nede
Er al be wrought, withowten any drede.
(II.666–72)

Readers of the poem have not necessarily thought to themselves that Criseyde has fallen in love too quickly, especially since she does so more slowly than Troilus himself did in the previous book, and the act did not seem at all suspicious there. Here, the unexpected and outsized attack on anyone who would question Criseyde's motives—"may he never thrive!"—also suggests the narrator's great concern for this character. He means to protect her. His overt defenses of her may call up doubts about her motives, but they also enact his paternalistic care of her and, in so doing, contribute to a covert defense of Criseyde's actions. By performing here the parental relationship that is otherwise broken (in the case of Calchas and Criseyde) and abused (in the case of Pandarus and Criseyde), Chaucer suggests a continuing narrative for her, which is not followed in this poem but which is nonetheless potentially fruitful: her ongoing life among the Greeks, reunited with her (negligent) father and her new love, Diomedes. What, one may ask, is so bad about that? Unless, of course, that one is Troilus.

Chaucer has gone to great lengths in this poem to ally readers with Troilus, and this necessarily colors our perceptions of Criseyde. But he has also embedded in this poem the trace of another poem, a poem of Criseyde's post-Troilian life that is not, on the face of it, tragic at all. If Troilus represents, to some readers, idealism in love to Criseyde's pragmatism, so be it. Is idealism automatically to be preferred? Why is it better than a pragmatic approach to love? The issue has two sides, Chaucer's poem whispers, and in another tale, told in another voice, the other side will finds its due: "Experience, though non auctoritee / Were in this world, is right ynogh for me / To speke of wo that is in mariage."[34]

Notes

The first section of this essay was originally written for a graduate seminar taught by Robert W. Hanning at Columbia University in the mid-1980s. My ongoing fascination with Chaucer's Criseyde has everything to do with Bob's teaching, mentoring, and friendship, for which I am immensely grateful. The second section of the essay has benefited especially from the insightful comments of Robert W. Hanning, R. Allen Shoaf, and Joseph Wittig. Thanks are also due Susan Ridyard, for the opportunity to present this work at the Sewanee Mediaeval Colloquium in March 2000, and to Susann Samples for inviting me to present an earlier version to the International Courtly Love Society's session at the MLA in December 1999.

1. See Catherine S. Cox on Troilus's betrayal of Criseyde, in *Gender and Language in Chaucer* (Gainesville: University Press of Florida, 1997): "But while Criseyde's professed fidelity to Troilus is compromised once she belongs to the Greeks, it is Troilus who betrays Crisedye first" (47). Cox also argues, as I do, that Criseyde is a victim of several betrayals, though she points to somewhat different scenes and acts in several cases (48). See also Victoria Warren on Troilus's inability to "read the text of Criseyde" (1), which constitutes a betrayal of her as well, in "[Mis]Reading the 'Text' of Criseyde: Context and Identity in Chaucer's *Troilus and Criseyde*," *The Chaucer Review* 36 (2001): 1–15. Louise O. Fradenburg discusses the feminine "subject position" in chivalric culture and its "renunciation of all desire" in her "'Our owen wo to drynke': Loss, Gender and Chivalry in *Troilus and Criseyde*," in *Chaucer's Troilus and Criseyde: "Subgit to all Poesye*," ed. R. A. Shoaf (Binghamton, N.Y.: MRTS, 1992), 105.

2. All quotations from Chaucer's works are taken from *The Riverside Chaucer*, 3rd ed., gen. ed. Larry D. Benson (Boston: Houghton Mifflin, 1987).

3. E. Talbot Donaldson, *Speaking of Chaucer* (New York: Norton, 1970), 83.

4. On falling in love quickly, see II.666–72; on whether or not Criseyde has children, see I.132–33.

5. Catherine Sanok writes, in "Criseyde, Cassandre, and the *Thebaid:* Women and the Theban Subtext of Chaucer's *Troilus and Criseyde*," *Studies in the Age of Chaucer* 20 (1998): 41–71, that "[y]anked from the narrative Pandarus had constructed to one that Diomede will orchestrate, Criseyde drops not only out of Troilus's life but out of Chaucer's poem as well" (54).

6. See Elizabeth Archibald for a consideration of the word "entente" in the poem and its sexual connotations, in "Declarations of 'Entente' in *Troilus and Criseyde*," *Chaucer Review* 25.3 (1991): 190–231, esp. 202–3. Criseyde's absence accompanies the exclusion of Pandarus from the private sphere as well, according to Sarah Stanbury, "The Voyeur and the Private Life in *Troilus and Criseyde*," *Studies in the Age of Chaucer* 13 (1991): 141–58, esp. 153.

7. On Criseyde's helplessness, see David Aers, "Criseyde: Woman in Medieval Society," *Chaucer Review* 13 (1979): 177–200; reprint in *Critical Essays on Chaucer's "Troilus and Criseyde" and His Major Early Poems*, ed. C. David Benson (Toronto: University of Toronto Press, 1991), 128–48.

8. E. Talbot Donaldson, *The Swan at the Well: Shakespeare Reading Chaucer* (New Haven: Yale University Press, 1985), 84. See also Susan Yager, "'As she that':

Syntactical Ambiguity in Chaucer's *Troilus and Criseyde,*" *Philological Quarterly* 73 (1994): 151–68.

9. See Susan Yager for a discussion of syntactical ambiguity in books four and five which "make the reader's judgments of motive more difficult" ("'As she that,'" 158).

10. Arthur Mizener, in "Character and Action in the Case of Criseyde," *PMLA* 54 (1939): 65–81, maintains that Criseyde's last letter could have arrived in Troy two months after she had left, and that Criseyde does not yield to Diomedes until two years have passed.

11. Ibid., 77.

12. John McKinnell, in "Letters as a Type of the Formal Level in *Troilus and Criseyde,*" in *Essays on Troilus and Criseyde,* ed. Mary Salu (Cambridge: D. S. Brewer, 1979; reprint 1982), 73–89, argues: "This distancing is also inherent in the use of the letter form itself; we see the letter as received by Troilus, not as Criseyde is writing it (whereas we are shown Troilus writing his letter, V.1303–16)" (88).

13. See, for example, Mark Lambert, "*Troilus,* Books I–III: A Criseydan Reading," in *Essays on Troilus and Criseyde,* ibid., 105–25. He argues that Criseyde's world, represented in the early books, is "attractive, warm," and that "we, like Chaucer's timid widow, are seduced into forgetting the limitations of the quiet life" (107). In the last two books, Lambert claims that the heroic mode of the poem emerges, not only shutting out the domestic but acting as an implicit critique of the domesticity and comfort of the early books. Lambert goes so far in his "Criseydan" reading to say that "finally it matters that Criseyde's is a smaller soul than Troilus's. He can bear pressures that she cannot; he thinks more important thoughts than she does" (122).

14. For a discussion of narrative structure and the audience's role in the poem, particularly as it affects our reading of Troilus, see John Ganim, *Style and Consciousness in Middle English Narrative* (Princeton: Princeton University Press, 1983), 79–102.

15. As Gayle Margherita writes, the poem's first mention of Criseyde suggests "that had Criseyde died in a more timely fashion, she might not have betrayed Troilus at all": "Criseyde's Remains: Romance and the Question of Justice," *Exemplaria* 12.2 (2000): 258. E. Talbot Donaldson locates in this scene Chaucer's break with the convention of love tragedy: "The poem would have been a much more satisfactory tragedy if the lovers had died bloodily in this scene, but it would not have been the great poem it is" (*Swan at the Well,* 25).

16. *Metamorphoses,* ed. W. S. Anderson (Leipzig: Teubner, 1977), IV.141. I am indebted to B. A. Windeatt's notes on this scene in his edition of the poem *Troilus and Criseyde* (London: Longman, 1984), 415–17.

17. John Gower included the tale of Pyramus and Thisbe in his *Confessio Amantis,* ed. Russell A. Peck (Toronto: University of Toronto Press, 1980). While it is unlikely that Chaucer could have read Gower's version of the tale, since Chaucer finished *Troilus and Criseyde* just as Gower was starting work on *Confessio Amantis* sometime around 1386–88, the tale might have been discussed between the two

men. Chaucer did, of course, include it in his *Legend of Good Women* just a short time after completing the *Troilus*. Gower too has Thisbe kiss the dead Pyramus, although he does not specify exactly where:

And with this word, where as he lay,
Hire love in armes sche embraseth,
Hire oghne deth and so pourchaseth
That now sche wepte and nou sche kiste,
Til ate laste, er sche it wiste,
So gret a sorwe is to hire falle,
Which overgoth hire wittes alle.

(482–88)

This kiss contributes to the loss of Thisbe's "wittes," and her act of suicide follows in just three lines. "Moral Gower," as Chaucer calls him at the end of *Troilus and Criseyde* (V.1856), uses this story as an example of how foolhardy love can make a man and to warn his audience of the very real dangers of love.

18. Gretchen Mieszkowski, "Chaucer's Much Loved Criseyde," *Chaucer Review* 26 (1991): 109–32, quotation at 129–30.

19. Susan Crane, *Insular Romance: Politics, Faith, and Culture in Anglo-Norman and Middle English Literature* (Berkeley: University of California Press, 1986), 209. In her *Gender and Romance in Chaucer's Canterbury Tales* (Princeton: Princeton University Press, 1994), Crane begins with the premise that by the late fourteenth century "romance is not only [perceived as] feminine, but [is] outmoded in Chaucer's milieu" (11), a fact that helps explain Chaucer's aversion to the romance genre here.

20. *Le Roman de Tristan de Thomas [of Britain]*, ed. Joseph Bédier (Paris: Firmin Didot, 1902).

21. From Thomas of Britain, "Tristan," trans. Bartina H. Wind, reprint in *The Romance of Arthur*, ed. James J. Wilhelm (New York: Garland, 1994), 293.

22. Angela Jane Weisl, *Conquering the Reign of Femeny: Gender and Genre in Chaucer's Romance* (Suffolk: D. S. Brewer, 1995), 3. See also Cox, *Gender and Language in Chaucer*, esp. 48.

23. Margherita, "Criseyde's Remains," 257–92. See also her *Romance of Origins: Language and Sexual Difference in Middle English Literature* (Philadelphia: University of Pennsylvania Press, 1994), esp. 108–28.

24. Crane, *Gender and Romance*, 11; Donaldson, *Swan at the Well*, 25.

25. See Aers, "Criseyde: Woman in Medieval Society" reprint, esp. 138–39; and Barry Windeatt, *Oxford Guides to Chaucer: Troilus and Criseyde* (Oxford: Oxford University Press, 1992), esp. 284–85.

26. Aers, "Criseyde," 143.

27. Carolyn Dinshaw, *Chaucer's Sexual Poetics* (Madison: University of Wisconsin Press, 1989), 58.

28. Diane Vanner Steinberg, "'We do usen here no wommen for to selle': Embodiment of Social Practices in *Troilus and Criseyde*," *Chaucer Review* 29.3 (1995): 259–73, at 260. See also Elizabeth Robertson, "Public Bodies and Psychic Domains: Rape, Consent, and Female Subjectivity in Geoffrey Chaucer's *Troilus and Criseyde*," in *Representing Rape in Medieval and Early Modern Literature*, ed. E. Robertson and Christine Rose (New York: Palgrave, 2001), 281–310. She writes that "Book Five shows the tragic plight of an emergent female subject who is granted no social role outside of a sexual one" (304). See also Warren on the "precarious" position of medieval court women, in "[Mis]Reading the 'Text' of Criseyde," 12.

29. See Richard W. Fehrenbacher, "'Al that which chargeth nought to seye': The Theme of Incest in *Troilus and Criseyde*," *Exemplaria* 9.2 [1997]: 341–69, for a full discussion of the incest issue here and a review of previous scholarship. See Michael Calabrese, *Chaucer's Ovidian Arts of Love* (Gainesville: University Press of Florida, 1994), for the reference to Myrrha in IV.1139, another Ovidian tale of incest, and its relevance to the last books of *Troilus and Criseyde* (55–58). For a discussion of "mediated desire" and the "erotics of translation" in this poem, see Robert W. Hanning, "The Crisis of Mediation in Chaucer's *Troilus and Criseyde*," in *The Performance of Middle English Culture: Essays on Chaucer and the Drama*, ed. James J. Paxon, Lawrence M. Clopper, and Sylvia Tomasch (Cambridge: D. S. Brewer, 1998), 143–59, esp. 151.

30. For considerations of the options available to late-medieval widows, see Janet Senderowitz Loengard, "'Legal History and the Medieval Englishwoman' Revisited: Some New Directions," in *Medieval Women and the Sources of Medieval History*, ed. J. T. Rosenthal (Athens: University of Georgia Press, 1990), 210–36; Joel T. Rosenthal, *Patriarchy and Families of Privilege in Fifteenth-Century England* (Philadelphia: University of Pennsylvania Press, 1991); and Sue Sheridan Walker, "Widow and Ward: The Feudal Law of Child Custody in Medieval England," in *Women in Medieval Society*, ed. Susan Mosher Stuard (Philadelphia: University of Pennsylvania Press, 1976), 159–72.

31. Aers, "Criseyde," 140–41.

32. Chrétien de Troyes, *Erec et Enide*, ed. Mario Roques (Paris: Honoré Champion, 1973), esp. lines 4856–97.

33. Chaucer "occasionally allow[s] his narrator to engender suspicion of Criseyde in attempting to quell it." Donaldson, *The Swan at the Well*, 82.

34. Chaucer, "Wife of Bath's Prologue," III.1–3.

15

JOHN M. GANIM

Chaucer and Free Love

F
or the past few years, there has been a great deal of important work on what might be called the politics of medievalism and medieval schol-arship, the complicated ways in which interpretations of the medi-eval past are implicated in the symbolic imagination of the eighteenth, nine-teenth, and twentieth centuries, and the ways in which these interpretations predict modern critical quandaries.[1] This essay takes a byway from this study of public medievalism to pursue the psychological history of a medieval-ism employed for private rather than public purposes. My topic is an un-derground history of Chaucer as he is imagined in the period between Ar-noldian condescension and modern canonization. My subjects are William Morris and Virginia Woolf, because these are writers, and people, for whom the distinction between the public and the private, the literary and the so-cial, is not always clear, and who therefore represent an interesting test case for how modernity privatizes the premodern.

My specific argument is that Chaucer and Woolf's greatest contributions to Chauceriana, Woolf's widely reprinted essay on "The Pastons and Chau-cer," and the Kelmscott *Chaucer* by Morris and Burne-Jones, are linked by an autobiographic or biographic impulse. To predict my argument in relatively broad outline, I will suggest that the tone and topics of Woolf's essay are in-formed by her developing relationship with Vita Sackville-West and by the related writing of *Orlando*, and that the Kelmscott *Chaucer* is in some fashion a visual record of the informing crises of Morris's own personal life. While much of my evidence is circumstantial, it is consistent with both writers' self-reflections; and, if Richard Ellmann's biographical speculations in *Golden Codgers* can be taken as a model, this biographical and autobiographical turn in late-Victorian, Edwardian, and early-modernist productions is one that we have ignored in our struggles with formal and period influences.[2]

"The Pastons and Chaucer" begins with the romantically elegaic image of Sir John Falstof's Caister castle in ruins and, nearby, the unstoned tomb of the elder Paston. In the spare and harsh landscape of East Anglia, Margaret Paston, handicapped by her sex, attempts to maintain order and protect the Paston holdings against threats, lawsuits, and raids. At the death of her husband, her son takes title, but he is not temperamentally suited to this world, preferring London and the court, hawking, and books. His generation, suspiciously like Woolf's own, is distant from the stern values of his mother's generation. He seems temperamentally incapable of engaging the constant struggle against decline, with the responsibilities of land and manor that primogeniture has placed upon him. Delaying attention to the drudgery of business, including the business of building his father's headstone, he turns to his books—particularly, according to Woolf, to his Chaucer, where he finds the world he knows in brighter colors and more manageable forms.

Woolf's Chaucer also turns from the harshness of nature. His poetry is a poetry of things as they are, and his characters, even in different tales, are in some fashion expressions of a few, recognizable personality types. He offers his readers a way of making sense of the world, a way of facing it, a way of wanting to know what happens next. But the next world, which for Margaret Paston explained this one, is in Chaucer accepted but not explored. Chaucer's confluence of the everyday and the courtly explained to John Paston his own situation, offering both justification and escape.

"The Pastons and Chaucer" appeared in Woolf's volume of literary essays, *The Common Reader* of 1925.[3] While most of the essays appearing in that volume had been previously published in *The Times Literary Supplement* or elsewhere, this essay was previously unpublished, and forms a sort of beginning for the very loose literary history that the volume projects. It is one of the great essays of criticism of the last century, reflecting the complex use of the literary past in general, while also offering solace and privacy and conversation against and in the face of a fear of obliteration: a way of holding together against both self- and social contradictions. From this relatively early essay through her last novel, *Between the Acts,* where Chaucer's characters are enacted as part of a local pageant and appear now and again through the action, Chaucer stands as a point of origin and difference for Woolf. According to her letters and diaries, Chaucer forms part of Virginia Woolf's reading program throughout her life, though he is always mentioned as someone she plans to get through. On January 13, 1932: "And I want to write 4 more novels: Waves, I mean; & the Tap on the Door; & to go through English literature, like a string through cheese, or rather like some industrious insect, eating its way from book to book, from Chaucer to Lawrence."[4] Woolf's canon here already predicts that of Leavis. On Sunday, October 30, 1938, she writes in her diary, "I should like to be quit of all this: am more & more dissatisfied with modern lit: & the criticism thereof . . . yet suspect that I must grate myself upon people to get my sense of 'words' dried up. . . . I think I shall read Chaucer . . . concurrently with French prose."[5] But her dissatisfaction is with more than modern literature. The entry begins with a "little sensation" that morning, which is collocated with an apparently depressing birthday party for Mrs. Woolf, but also with Vita's new poem. "Does it jab at my nerves?"[6] On Tuesday, November 15, 1938, "My one quiet evening since Thursday. Read Chaucer: began Lytton Q. E. and Essex [Strachey's *Elizabeth and Essex,* 1928] for my article. Ideas popped up, but I want to write fiction, my weeks off, not more hard highroad prose. . . . I shall read Sevigné & Chaucer."[7] In an intimate letter to Vita Sackville-West on 29 December 1928, she says that she has been reading *Troilus and Criseyde* and claims that "long poems are the only things I want to read."[8] On 14 March 1939, she writes a witty little letter in the form of a play to Vita:

> Scene, sitting room after tea. V. W. hoping to read Chaucer.
> Telephone rings.
> *V.* Oh my God why do we live in London? (Tosses Chaucer on the floor).[9]

A few weeks earlier, on 2 February, she had written a letter to the poet May Sarton, complaining about having to read so much modern poetry and claiming that "I am reading Chaucer and hope in a year to have recovered my palate."[10] Throughout Woolf's life, Chaucer is both solace and inspiration for fiction.

Her classic contribution to Chaucer criticism has much earlier origins, coinciding with her most productive years as a novelist and following upon years of writing reviews and essays. Beginning in late 1921, she begins reading the Paston letters, and her essay, written over the next two years, "The Pastons and Chaucer," appears in *The Common Reader* in 1925. Woolf first records writing about the Pastons on January 3, 1922; by August 4, 1922, she says that she has already written "4 thousand words," which seems to refer to the notebooks she compiled while working on *The Common Reader*.[11] During this time, Woolf is also rereading a good deal of Chaucer himself, and her reading notebooks include a number of items suggesting that she is working through various *Canterbury Tales*. The Paston essay remains of interest to us partly because of its focus on the fifteenth century, in many ways evolving as the crucial period for late twentieth-century medievalists and its way of reading Chaucer, a subject of recent scholarly interest. After all, there is no real reason why Woolf should have chosen Chaucer as an organizing theme of the essay. There is plenty to talk about, as historians have proven, above and beyond the literariness of the Pastons.

The Chaucer that Woolf turns to throughout her life is one shaped relatively early in her career. The Chaucer described in Woolf's essay is not the Chaucer of modern irony, or even the Ibsenian Chaucer of Kittredge. It is the Chaucer flooded with light and clear of vision, who sees things and presents them as they are—a Chaucer surprisingly (given Woolf's own writing) not as different as one would expect from the Chaucer of late Victorian and Edwardian sensibility, a Chaucer who produces the stained-glass images he himself was attracted to as an avenue of imagination. Indeed, "Chaucer," for Woolf, is not so much an influence as an icon. Woolf discusses Chaucer's poetry only occasionally. It is as if his image is laden with symbolic and psychological significance. An idea of Chaucer refracted through a certain surprisingly romantic construction of his age is finally as important as what he wrote, or so one would imagine from Woolf's reading notebooks or from *The Common Reader*.[12] We now perceive the loosely aesthetic portrait of Chaucer as a largely lay or amateur assumption, replaced by a more complex and socially striated Chaucer of academic study. But as Steve Ellis observes, "in the late nineteenth century and the earlier part of the twentieth century there is some difficulty in distinguishing between an academic interest in Chaucer and that represented by a more general readership, whereas such a distinction becomes entrenched as the century progresses."[13]

For a writer whose place in the canon depends partly on highly self-conscious and experimental techniques, Woolf's portrait of Chaucer as read by Sir John Paston is surprisingly, even determinedly, uncomplex. Woolf's

Chaucer is akin to Benjamin's "storyteller" with a direct and unmediated connection to his social community. Elsewhere in her writings, Woolf distinguishes Chaucer's unself-conscious to Spenser's highly self-conscious art, almost recreating Schiller's famous distinction between "naive" and "sentimental" poetry.[14] For Woolf, and significantly, for Sir John Paston, Chaucer represents an alternative to a complex and ambiguous present, even if that present is only the fifteenth century. Chaucer ends up stripped of the very irony that will mark his place in later twentieth-century academic criticism by a writer whose own position is as an ironic writer in a movement dominated by irony.

This almost populist version of Chaucer is, in fact, not unsophisticated or unintentional. Throughout *The Common Reader* and Woolf's own critical writings, there is a consistent effort to rescue literature from academic straitjackets, to validate "the common reader" in his or her responses. Moreover, the emphasis on a tactile and sensual response to literary worlds is not unrelated to the beginnings of what, in retrospect, is one of the bridges between novelistic recreations of the historical past in romantic historiography and the beginnings of the new social history. Interestingly, on June 13, 1925, the Woolfs invited Eileen Power to dinner. Power's *Medieval People*, still consulted by students today, was published in 1924, probably too late to influence "The Pastons and Chaucer" in print form.[15] By that time, *The Common Reader* was in press, but the Woolfs probably had some earlier contact with Power, who was then at the London School of Economics. Indeed, in a letter to her sister Vanessa Bell on 12 May 1926, Woolf notes another dinner party with Power and relates Power's pessimistic opinion on the outcome of the general strike of that year.[16] Power's interest in how things were in the Middle Ages, forging a social history that was equal parts economics and phenomenology, would have been of great interest to Woolf, as would Power's interest in the works and days of medieval women. In her last reading notebook, dating from 1940 until her death, she lists "Medieval English Nunneries/Eileen Power" in a list of sources, but she certainly could have read that study much earlier.[17]

There is an agenda behind the Paston essay, and it is an agenda that is simultaneously literary and personal, as is virtually everything about Virginia Woolf. For the way the rebellious Paston son—book collector and bon vivant, obsessed with his standing and court politics, to the ruin of his property and his father's grave—turns to Chaucer is indicative of Woolf's sense of the danger and the value of literature, of the perils of imagination itself, at least as it is being imagined in Bloomsbury: "So Sir John read his Chaucer in the comfortless room with the wind blowing and the smoke stinging, and left his father's tombstone unmade. . . . He was one of those ambiguous characters who haunt the boundary line where one age merges into another and are not able to inhabit either."[18]

There is another character, not in Chaucer, but in Virginia Woolf herself, who is also "ambiguous" and who haunts "the boundary line where one age merges into another"—and other boundary lines, as well. This is, of course, the title character of *Orlando: A Biography*, which appeared in 1928.[19] In the substantial source literature on *Orlando*, it is something of a surprise that Woolf's portrait of the early modern past has not been mentioned as in some ways a brief draft for the novel that was to take shape several years later. This oversight is partly because of the time lag between the two works, and also because of the difference in genre. Yet the fact is that *Orlando*'s early publication history was controversial not only because of the subject matter of the novel, but because of uncertainty as to whether it was a novel at all, or, as its subtitle suggests, a biography; this caused conflict between its publisher and booksellers. In no other of Woolf's fictional writings is the demarcation between fiction and nonfiction so thin, though such a demarcation is always thin in the genre of historical fiction that *Orlando* parodies. None of the other essays in *The Common Reader* indulge in quite the same narrative and fictionalizing excess as "The Pastons and Chaucer," even when they describe works from early historical periods.

Orlando was, in fact, written quickly, and it seems motivated by the personal events of the years surrounding it, especially Woolf's increasing worry that Vita Sackville-West, the model for Orlando, had turned her affections elsewhere. As a result, scholarship has focused on these events and this immediate context. Indeed, the preface to *Orlando* reads like a greeting to all of Bloomsbury in the late 1920s. Yet it must be remembered that the romance between Sackville-West and Woolf began shortly after they met in mid-December of 1922. Woolf wrote an enthusiastic description of Vita in her diary entry for that evening; and a week later, on December 19, 1922, Vita wrote to her husband Harold Nicholson of Woolf, "Darling, I have quite lost my heart."[20] Throughout 1922, Woolf is conducting research in preparation for "The Pastons and Chaucer," and may have already written a draft, since she has been reading the Paston letters since November of 1921. She notes in her diary for October 4 of 1922 that she is "reading" Chaucer and the Pastons, though "reading" in her diary sometimes alludes to preparation for what will become *The Common Reader.*[21] Her entry for May 11, 1923 suggests she is still writing, or perhaps revising, the essay.[22] What I want to suggest is that her vision of the life of the Pastons, and particularly her portrait of the character of Sir John, is as much personal as it is historical. Her Sir John is a type of a fantasy character that will soon take on a flesh-and-blood shape in her life, either because she has drawn Sir John as a portrait, or because her particular writing of Vita is, in fact, implicated in this earlier fantasy. Of course, Orlando is explicitly planned by Woolf as a portrait of Vita (literally so in the photographs of Vita that "illustrate" the "biography"), but Orlando contains within his/her character as much of Woolf herself as of Vita. The mysterious seven-days' sleep after the departure of the Russian princess resembles nothing so much as depression, and Orlando's alternate embrace of and rejection of court society mirrors Woolf's own involvement in the social world of London. His obsessive writings resemble Woolf's own discipline.

Both *Orlando* and "The Pastons and Chaucer" share an interest in the architectural. Houses, castles, and manors play as important a part in the novel and the essay as characters or texts. The almost haunted Paston manor recalls the Edwardian fascination with the Tudor style, which replaced an earlier medieval revival fashion. At the 1900 Paris exhibition, England is controversially represented by a Tudor-styled manor designed by Sir Edward Lutyens, the great architect of the Empire and the hero of contemporary postmodern historicism. Lutyens based details of the building loosely on Knole, the Sackville estate, and Vita herself wrote an account of Knole.[23] By the war years, Lutyens had developed a relationship with Lady Sackville, Vita's mother, for whom he built many projects. Lutyens's own wife had become a fanatic follower of theosophy, and it consumed her whole life. Lutyens's relation with Lady Sackville continued until that lady's eventual mental deterioration.[24] The brooding presence of the Paston manor and the struggles to keep it echo the legal struggles over Knole, the ownership of which was being challenged on the basis of the question of male inheritance, an issue which is made explicit in *Orlando,* who loses legal stature with her gender transformation.[25] Again, however, the architectural theme of both *Orlando* and "The Pastons and Chaucer" has overdetermined resonances. The Woolfs were themselves deeply concerned with and influenced by buildings and settings; and Leonard's autobiography, *Downhill All the Way: An Autobiography of the Years 1919 to 1939,* opens with an account of how the houses they lived in changed Virginia and Leonard: "In each case the most powerful moulder of them and of their lives was the house in which they lived."[26] Both *Orlando* and "The Pastons and Chaucer" may be read as a quiet debate with Leonard's assertion. The portrait of the brooding John Paston is an elegy for the modern self, just as Orlando marks the dawn of the performed postmodern subject. In a way similar to what she imputes to Chaucer, Woolf's characters often seem coterminous with each other from novel to novel. "The Pastons and Chaucer" is a dry run for *Orlando* in its imagining of a subversive past. Its "Chaucer" is figured as a kind of conservative haven in a complex personal and political world, on the one hand, and as a license for personal and literary experimentation, on the other.

Behind Woolf's essay is another Chaucer, whom Woolf would inevitably have engaged—the Chaucer of William Morris. Morris, I want to argue, had also employed Chaucer, both as a kind of fetish that wards off the confusions of the sexual and political present and as a muse that simultaneously offers an inspiration for innovation and experiment. For Morris, and as opposed to his use of Malory, where sacrifice and redemption are underlined, Chaucer offered a way of combining innocence and fatalism. The Kelmscott Chaucer, which Morris worked on during the last years of his life, is shaped by this concern. More strikingly, Burne-Jones, Morris's confidant and associate for his entire life, seems to have understood this, and the illustrations of the volume sketch a kind of visual biography of Morris's life and of his troubled marriage to Jane.

By the 1890s, Morris had turned almost all of his considerable energies to the Kelmscott Press, his effort to return bookmaking to the aesthetic and the aura of medieval manuscript production. In so doing, he initiated and completed yet another phase in his various roles in and against Victorian culture. By his twenties, in the 1850s, he had already made a mark as a nationally significant poet and had apprenticed under the charismatic Dante Gabriel Rossetti as a painter (helping to paint the domed frescoes on the ceiling of the Oxford Union). This was after working for a year as an architectural assistant in the offices of G. E. Street, one of the chief architects of the Gothic revival. Morris then, in 1861, regrouped his loose brotherhood of artist acquaintances into a production association, soon to become one of the chief decoration and design firms in Britain—especially after Morris reorganized and took over the firm in 1875 as Morris and Company, by which time he was recognized as one of the founders of the arts and crafts movement. His own house, "Red House," designed by Philip Webb and completed in 1860, was one of the signal buildings in the architectural development of the arts and crafts style. The communal Ruskinian politics of these enterprises soon advanced to an identification with radical socialism. By the early 1880s, Morris was one of the founders of the Socialist League and the editor of *Commonweal.*

Morris was no less significant in terms of the unconventional nature of his personal life. The Pre-Raphaelite Brotherhood was fascinated with their German precursors, the Nazareans, who experimented with a monastic style of life. Throughout his life, Morris shared living arrangements with close friends: both Burne-Jones at times and, in 1871, at Kelmscott Manor with Rossetti, after the suicide of Rossetti's wife. Rossetti had famously discovered Jane Burden Morris at a theater and convinced her to serve as a model. Her languorous beauty became the hallmark of Pre-Raphaelite femininity, and it attracted Morris powerfully. Morris and Jane Burden were married in 1861, but Rossetti and Jane carried on an affair for many years, and it was not to be Jane's last affair. Triangles multiplied throughout the Morris circle. Despite his devotion to his wife, Burne-Jones carried on an affair with Mary Zambaco, ending with his mental breakdown in 1869. Morris's daughter, May, left her husband, Henry Halliday Sparling, as she continued to be George Bernard Shaw's mistress. Yet the emotional and psychic resonances of these chaotic arrangements can hardly be traced in Morris's writings or conversations, despite his powerful and explosive personality, and must be gleaned from Burne-Jones, Jane Morris, and others. Morris must have negotiated this personal chaos by a manic absorption in his work, and in the 1890s, that meant the Kelmscott *Chaucer* and the other productions of the Kelmscott Press.

Morris was indeed famously private about his inner life, though he could be exuberant or enraged about business, art, or politics. Even his daughter, May Morris, wrote in her biography of him, "no glimpse of his inner life . . . was ever vouchsafed even to his closest friends."[27] One has the sense that Burne-Jones intuited, rather than shared, Morris's feelings. Several of his poems, however, have traditionally been understood as autobiographical, however obliquely. The lyrics of *The Earthly Paradise,* a framed fiction inspired by Chaucer's story collections, are often read as an expression of his sense of longing, loss, and regret for Jane: "Can we regain what we have lost meanwhile?"[28] While *The Defence of Guinevere* predates Morris's marriage (and even his acquaintance with Jane), it projects a strangely sympathetic and prophetic understanding of the romantic triangle and its compromises, so much so that Guinevere seems to speak almost as much for the betrayed as for the betrayer. Morris's vocalization of the plight, even the justification, of the adulterous woman is nowhere more striking than in the "Helen and Menelaus" section of the early dramatic poem, *Scenes from the Fall of Troy*. Awake at three in the morning, now married to Deiphobus, Helen is musing over her own aging and is remembering her affair with Paris:

> In these old days whereof this is the last,
> Yea I shall live sometimes with sweet Paris
> In that old happiness 'twixt mirth and tears?
> The fitting on of arms and going forth,
> The dreadful quiet sitting while they fought,
> The kissing when he came back to my arms.[29]

Suddenly, she hears a noise, and she starts as if waking from a dream. Menelaus appears and orders her to help slay the sleeping Deiphobus: "I am the Menelaus that you know / Come back to fetch a thing I left behind."[30] The complex scene takes a sadistic and punitive vengeance as Deiphobus forces her on the bloodied bed, as Troy is sacked outside the window. The narrative of Morris's personal history is prefigured in the dramatic tensions of his early writing. A certain autobiographical note can be traced in the works of Morris and his circle, and there is an uncanny way in which his art predicts the circumstances of an emotional life about which he is otherwise famously silent.[31]

Despite the enormous iconic importance of the Kelmscott *Chaucer*, Morris, like Woolf, took a surprisingly distant tone in his statements about Chaucer. Morris and Burne-Jones were fervent admirers of Chaucer for their entire lives, though according to the official biography by Mackail, Morris came to Chaucer rather late in his education.[32] At the same time, despite their fascination with visualizing Chaucer, Morris seems to distance himself from any conscious imitation. In 1895, for instance, he writes to Hans Ey, a German student who had reported the negative results of a thesis exploring Chaucer's influence on Morris, "I quite agree with your friend as to the resemblance of my work to Chaucer; it only comes of our both using the narrative method: and even then my turn is decidedly more to Romance than was Chaucer's. I admit that I have been a great admirer of Chaucer, and that his work has had, especially in early years much influence on me; but I think not much on my style."[33] Chaucer remains, throughout Morris's life, somewhat distinct from both Morris's politics and his literary achievements, however much he might inspire his work in the visual and decorative arts.

Morris founded the Kelmscott Press in 1890, shortly after splits within the Socialist movement began to develop. This was also during the time when he distanced himself from the Anarchists and from the gradualist path that he had argued against. The radical political scene in the next few years would resemble Conrad's *Under Western Eyes,* with agent provocateurs, spies, and informers abounding. Morris had rented the cottage where much of the business of the Press would be conducted; but almost immediately, in 1891, his health began to fail, probably as the first indications of the serious diabetes which was to claim his life five years later. Although Morris attended to the details of the Press with the characteristic involvement he brought to everything else in his life, except perhaps to Janie, that involvement was less messianic than pastoral, or even elegaic. The affair between Rossetti and Jane had died out in the 1870s, but in the later years of her marriage to Morris, probably continuing into the Press years, Janie had an affair with the poet Wilfrid Blunt (whose letters show some of the most remarkably accurate estimations of Morris himself).

Morris was failing in his health when the Chaucer volume finally came out, after several delays. "It has been a wretched sight all this year to see him dwindling away," wrote Burne-Jones to Swinburne on August 8, 1896. Burne-Jones explained to Swinburne that he had avoided illustrating the Miller's Tale despite Morris's enthusiasm, for "he ever had more robust and daring parts than I could assume."[34] The illustrations, however, I would want to argue, are in some fashion illustrations as much of Morris's vision as they are of Chaucer, and they are both Burne-Jones's tribute and his visual biography of his friend. According to some accounts, the artist's hand at this time may have been increasingly unsteady, and much of the line drawing may have been done by Robert Catterson-Smith, who himself gave credit to Burne-Jones when a controversy erupted over the authorship of the drawings. Whatever the actual sharing of responsibilities, the Burne-Jones pencil drawings were insufficiently linear to be successfully transferred onto wood blocks and were eventually transferred to photographic prints, which were retraced to emphasize their linearity. Nevertheless, the various stages of the drawings demonstrate how completely the conception and planning of them were in the hands of Burne-Jones and Morris.

One of the eerie qualities of Pre-Raphaelite portraiture is its masquerade quality: the group used each other as models, the most famous being Jane Morris herself. Here, however, in the portrait of Chaucer (fig. 1), Burne-Jones merges the qualities of known illustrations of the poet with a biographical note. The resemblance of Morris to Chaucer was noted by his

FIGURE 1. Illustration from William Morris, *Kelmscott Chaucer*, 1896. Reproduced by permission of The Huntington Library, San Marino, California.

friends, and it is famously enshrined in the official biography by J. W. Mackail, who observes that "The resemblance even extended to physical features: the corpulent person, the demure smile, the 'close, silent eye.'"[35] Steve Ellis, commenting on this supposed resemblance, shrewdly notes that "Chaucer seems to have resembled a good many people in the nineteenth century."[36] In fact, Mackail was observing Morris's place in a long pantheon of middle-class London writers, including Dr. Johnson and Isaac Walton. But it is also true that Burne-Jones's portraits of Chaucer in the Kelmscott *Chaucer* are strangely solitary and detached and even seem to age as the volume progresses.

As Diana Archibald notes, "all the illustrated tales have in common the subject of chivalry or of women in distress. Almost every instance of a woman in dire straits or a knight in shining armor is illustrated in the texts."[37] In good neo-romantic fashion, the illustration of the beginning of the Knight's Tale emphasizes the triangle (fig. 2). While the scene seems prescient of our own recent concern with spectatorship, voyeurism, and masochism, it also echoes the historical origins of the Morrises' quandary: one woman being

FIGURE 2. Illustration from William Morris, *Kelmscott Chaucer*, 1896. Reproduced by permission of The Huntington Library, San Marino, California.

virtually invented by two men, who require her to be a certain something in order to be themselves. At times, Burne-Jones departs from the text in front of him to create images more appropriate to Lancelot and Guinevere or Tristan and Iseult, overlaying Chaucer with the Arthurian triangle that Morris himself used to filter his experience (fig. 3). Interestingly, one of Morris's few known paintings is variously called "Queen Guinevere" or "La Belle Iseult" and portrays a woman, obviously modeled on Jane, standing next to an unmade bed. A small dog sleeps where the covers are pulled back. Her hairbrush and jewelry lie on a table next to the bed, and she is apparently buckling a belt or girdle around her dress. As in the Kelmscott illustrations, the Tristan myth overlays or underlies other narratives. The Wife of Bath's Tale (fig. 4) is envisioned as a depiction of male rather than female fantasy, of imagination turning shame and loathing into innocence. During a time when it is Morris's own body that is deteriorating, the female is pictured in the familiar wasting of momento mori—rather than carpe diem—imagery (fig. 5). Even the dilation of narrative in their choice of scenes emphasizes the love triangle. The highly Arthurian-inflected scene of Arcite's

FIGURE 3. Illustration from William Morris, *Kelmscott Chaucer*, 1896. Reproduced by permission of The Huntington Library, San Marino, California.

FIGURE 4. Illustration from William Morris, *Kelmscott Chaucer*, 1896. Reproduced by permission of The Huntington Library, San Marino, California.

FIGURE 5.   Illustration from William Morris, *Kelmscott Chaucer*, 1896. Reproduced by permission of The Huntington Library, San Marino, California.

funeral, for instance (fig. 3), has Palamon and Emilye holding hands and grieving together in front of a strangely pacific reclining body of Arcite, which looks as much like a sculpted tomb as a body ready for cremation. Here the illustrations leave the textual basis and conflate deathbed, funeral, and cremation.

Contemporary Chaucer criticism has valorized the great scene of Criseyde looking down upon Troilus because of its interiorization of erotic psychology, its reverse voyeurism, its meditation on agency and female spectatorship. But Burne-Jones shifts everything to ground level, and includes two men and one woman, recreating the by-now mythic meeting of Jane, Rossetti, and Morris on the street (fig. 6). And in scene after scene, the image of the woman led by or torn between two men is underlined again and again (figs. 7 and 8). Interestingly, in the illustrations of *Troilus and Criseyde*, Diomede is presented more neutrally than the text would allow. Criseyde sometimes seems modeled on Jane, as were so many Pre-Raphaelite female figures, but at other times seems to be rendered generically. This is also true of the other female figures in Kelmscott.

FIGURE 6. Illustration from William Morris, *Kelmscott Chaucer*, 1896. Reproduced by permission of The Huntington Library, San Marino, California.

FIGURE 7. Illustration from William Morris, *Kelmscott Chaucer*, 1896. Reproduced by permission of The Huntington Library, San Marino, California.

FIGURE 8. Illustration from William Morris, *Kelmscott Chaucer*, 1896. Reproduced by permission of The Huntington Library, San Marino, California.

Steve Ellis, in an important chapter on the Kelmscott *Chaucer* in his *Chaucer at Large*, comments on the paradoxical sense of stillness and order-liness that the Kelmscott designs impose on Chaucer. He is expanding on Elizabeth Archibald's important thesis that the Kelmscott *Chaucer* imposes an uncanny unity on the variety of Chaucer's voices and texts. Ellis relates this to an earlier Pre-Raphaelite treatment of Chaucer, often by Burne-Jones him-self, that read him as a poet of nature. In the reinterpretations of Chaucer by Morris and Burne-Jones, Chaucer's poetry provides an occasion for a cer-tain Romantic classicism. Ellis adds to this observation of stillness a quality of timelessness in the Kelmscott figures:

> the illustrations to the beginning and end of the "Clerk's Tale" (127, 139) portray a Griselda as maidenly and youthful at the time of her final rec-onciliation as she was before he married her . . . where a figure is in-eluctably marked by time, as in the case of the old hag in the "Wife of

Bath's Tale," she yet maintains a statuesque body arranged in elegant *contraposto* in keeping with many of the other Burne-Jones figures.[38]

It is possible that Catterson-Smith emphasized a slight downturn in Griselda's head and attempted to indicate sadness around her eyes in 139, but this only goes to prove Ellis's point. Ellis also interestingly observes some distinctions between Woolf's and Morris's Chaucer, notably the tendency of Morris and Burne-Jones to see Chaucer as a nature poet, with a heavy stress on the dream visions and continental literary traditions; while Woolf's Chaucer is much more "English" and almost exclusively the Chaucer of the *Canterbury Tales*.

There is a visual link between Morris and Woolf, specifically in the medieval masquerade photographs of Julia Cameron (a relative of Woolf), which both capture Morris's own fantasies of longing, desire, and distance embodied in an imaginary Middle Ages and which also provide one of the sources for Woolf's own use of photography and historical and sexual masquerade in *Orlando*.[39] But what links Morris's and Woolf's historical imaginations here with their use of Chaucer is more than a specific chain of connections. Despite their experimentation in literature and politics, Morris and Woolf nurtured a surprisingly therapeutic and pacific view of Chaucer, one that contrasts strikingly with the conflict model of much recent academic scholarship.[40] For both turn to Chaucer for permission to carry on the great romantic and modern agenda to live one's life as a work of art—and also as a retreat from the damage wreaked by such an effort. From Mary Shelley's *Frankenstein* on, Romanticism had articulated and criticized this very desire, and this dual impulse towards experimentation and awareness of the dangers of moving beyond the limits continues through high modernism, where everywhere in the imagery of its canonical texts and figures—from T. S. Eliot's *Wasteland* onwards, is a record of the costs both of repression and experimentation. The versions of Chaucer we find in Morris and Woolf are part of this larger struggle to invent and reinvent the modern self, simultaneously authorizing and consoling us as agents of and victims of art.

Notes

1. See, for instance, R. Howard Bloch and Stephen Nichols, eds., *Medievalism and the Modernist Temper* (Baltimore: Johns Hopkins University Press, 1996);

Lee Patterson, *Negotiating the Past* (Madison: University of Wisconsin Press, 1987); Carolyn Dinshaw, *Getting Medieval: Sexualities and Communities, Medieval and Postmodern* (Durham, N.C.: Duke University Press, 1999); Kathleen Biddick, *The Shock of Medievalism* (Durham, N.C.: Duke University Press, 1998); and the series *Studies in Medievalism*, (Cambridge: D. S. Brewer).

2. Richard Ellmann, *Golden Codgers: Biographical Speculations* (Oxford: Oxford University Press, 1973).

3. Virginia Woolf, *The Common Reader* (London: Hogarth, 1925).

4. Virginia Woolf, *The Diary of Virginia Woolf, 1882–1941*, ed. Anne Olivier Bell, 5 vols. (London: Hogarth, 1977–84), 4:63.

5. Woolf, *Diary*, 5:183.

6. Woolf, *Diary*, 5:182.

7. Woolf, *Diary*, 5:186–87. See also 5:193, 207, 209, 214, and 217.

8. Virginia Woolf, *A Change of Perspective: The Letters of Virginia Woolf*, ed. Nigel Nicholson, 6 vols. (London: Hogarth, 1977), 3:569.

9. Woolf, *Letters*, 6:322.

10. Woolf, *Letters*, 6:314.

11. Woolf, *Diary*, vol. 2: *1920–1924*.

12. See Brenda R. Silver, ed., *Virginia Woolf's Reading Notebooks* (Princeton: Princeton University Press, 1983) for a complete catalogue of the notebooks.

13. Steve Ellis, *Chaucer at Large: The Poet in the Modern Imagination* (Minneapolis: University of Minnesota Press, 2000), 17.

14. See "Anon" in Brenda R. Silver, "'Anon' and 'The Reader': Virginia Woolf's Last Essays," *Twentieth Century Literature* 25 (1979): 356–441. These essays would have comprised part of Woolf's last project, *Reading at Random*.

15. Eileen Power, *Medieval People* (London: Methuen, 1924).

16. Woolf, *Letters*, 3:261–62.

17. Silver, ed., *Reading Notebooks*, 187.

18. Woolf, *Common Reader*, 20.

19. Virginia Woolf, *Orlando: A Biography* (London: Hogarth, 1928).

20. Nigel Nicolson, ed., *Vita and Harold: The Letters of Vita-Sackville West and Harold Nicholson* (London: Weidenfeld and Nicolson, 1992).

21. Woolf, *Diary*, 2:205.

22. Woolf, *Diary*, 2:242.

23. V. Sackville-West, *Knole and the Sackvilles* (London: Heinemann, 1922).

24. See the excellent study by Jane Brown, *Lutyens and the Edwardians: An English Architect and His Clients* (New York: Viking, 1996).

25. Woolf, *Orlando*, 118.

26. Leonard Woolf, *Downhill All the Way: An Autobiography of the Years 1919 to 1939* (London: Hogarth, 1967), 14.

27. May Morris, *William Morris: Artist, Writer, Socialist* (Oxford: Blackwell, 1936), 1:441.

28. "The Earthly Paradise," vols. 3–6 of William Morris, *The Collected Works of William Morris*, 24 vols. (London: Longmans Green, 1910–15); quotation from book 2, line 143 (vol. 4).

29. "Scenes from the Fall of Troy," in Morris, *Collected Works*, 24:45.

30. Ibid., 47.

31. The most elaborate psychobiographical study of Morris is Frederick Kirchhoff's *William Morris: The Construction of a Male Self 1856–1872* (Athens: Ohio University Press, 1990), which employs Harry Stack Sullivan's ego psychology to trace Morris's gradual coming to terms with himself.

32. J. W. Mackail, *The Life of William Morris* (London: Longmans, 1901), 1:61.

33. Letter 2427 "To Hans Ey" in William Morris, *The Collected Letters of William Morris*, ed. Norman Kelvin (Princeton: Princeton University Press, 1996), vol. 4: *1893–1896*, p. 338.

34. Quoted in Duncan Robinson, *William Morris, Edward Burne-Jones and the Kelmscott Chaucer* (London: G. Fraser, 1982), 27.

35. Mackail, *The Life of William Morris*, 1:214.

36. Ellis, *Chaucer at Large*, 170 note 37. Morris himself thought that Rossetti resembled Chaucer and used Rossetti as a model for "Geoffrey Chaucer Reading," a painted earthenware ceramic of 1864 that shows the head of Chaucer in profile, reading a book, with a flower taking up the upper left section of the circle.

37. Diana C. Archibald, "Beauty, Unity, and the Ideal: Wholeness and Heterogeneity in the Kelmscott *Chaucer*," *Studies in Medievalism* 7 (1995): 175. Archibald notes "a strict program of choice" throughout the series of illustrations.

38. Ellis, *Chaucer at Large*, 10.

39. *Idylls of the King and Other Poems Photographically Illustrated by Julia Margaret Cameron* (New York: Janet Lehr, 1985).

40. Ellis, *Chaucer at Large*, notes, for instance, how far late nineteenth-century and early twentieth-century academic and popular understandings of Chaucer are from the widely accepted contemporary view of Paul Strohm, for whom Chaucer juxtaposes unresolved social and cultural positions.

16

SEALY GILLES AND SYLVIA TOMASCH

Professionalizing Chaucer

John Matthews Manly, Edith Rickert, and the Canterbury Tales *as Cultural Capital*

I n many ways, John Matthews Manly and Edith Rickert's three great Chaucer projects can be thought of as the last of the great nineteenth-century philological endeavors. The projects that constitute the bulk of Manly and Rickert's later collaborations—the editing of the eight-volume *Text of the Canterbury Tales* and the publication of the complete *Life-Records*, as well as its companion volume, *Chaucer's World*—are modeled upon and meant to update F. J. Furnivall's six-text Canterbury Tales and the "old" Chaucer Society *Life-Records*.[1] But the story of Manly and Rickert's construction of Geoffrey Chaucer is very much an American story. While Manly and Rickert were too scrupulous as scholars ever to mistake a fourteenth-century English poet for a twentieth-century American, they nonetheless remade him according to their own ideals. The Chaucer they found in contemporary records and in his own works was democratic, plain-spoken, honest, efficient, entrepreneurial, and thoroughly professional: in a phrase, an ideal bourgeois.

This bourgeois ideal emerged from Manly and Rickert's own investment in the intellectual and professional issues of their own time and place. Beginning at the turn of the century, they worked to foster professional values and innovations, actively participating in some of the most important trends in American intellectual life, from the rational organization of research universities and the professionalization of military intelligence to the specialization of academic departments and the supersession of ancient texts by modern ones. In other words, Manly and Rickert created the Chaucer they knew and loved out of the new universities, the new English departments, and the new American century. More specifically, they consistently employed the protocols of a growing professionalism and the methods of evolutionary science in the service of a romantic ideal: the recovery of a beloved author and his original text. The best qualities of the Chaucer thus conceived—romantic and entrepreneurial, visionary and pragmatic, traditional and forward-thinking—resemble nothing so much as the best qualities of the American ideal embodied in their own characters and careers.

Early in the twentieth century, this ideal guaranteed for Chaucer (and for the projects intended to recover the author and his text) a secure place in the cultural economy of an increasingly professionalized academy. However, in the years leading up to the Second World War, shifts in American educational and cultural values compelled a reassessment of the author, his text, and the processes by which that text is reconstructed. In tracing the careers of Manly and Rickert, therefore, we are also, more broadly, tracing the fortunes of medieval studies in twentieth-century America. For the story of their partnership is also the story of science in the service of the humanities, of technology's role in literary discovery, of the search for ever-elusive origins, and of the rise and fall of Chaucer as cultural capital.

The New University

Although Manly and Rickert's early twentieth-century version of Chaucer is rooted in the traditions of editing that flourished in the 1800s, their sense of the man and of their own work was profoundly shaped by the academic world whose contours were changing rapidly around the turn of the century. As David R. Shumway and Gerald Graff have described, American universities during the late nineteenth and early twentieth centuries remade themselves as research institutions along the "scientific" lines of German institutions of higher education.[2] The University of Chicago, established in 1882, is a particularly strong example of the move away from a liberal arts emphasis in higher education. Using as models the newly reorganized Harvard,

Johns Hopkins, and Clark, William Rainey Harper founded the University of Chicago "to be primarily if not exclusively a center of advanced scholarship and scientific research."[3] This fundamental reconceptualization of the university was premised on the replacement of the classical curriculum with "curricula that would permit more specialized training and better use of specialized faculty."[4] Two important consequences of such changes are familiar to us more than a century later: specialists gained control over academic appointments within their fields, and universities established learned journals and societies.[5] Throughout his career John Manly actively promoted these hallmarks of professionalization.[6]

In 1898, at Harper's request, Manly moved from Brown University along with a number of other eminent academicians who came "to Chicago not to found a college but to embody the University Spirit in a new institution. The prospect of combining the 'desire and ability to participate in the advancement of knowledge' in a center of graduate research and study made it worth their while to leave eminent and comfortable positions elsewhere."[7] During his early years at Chicago, not only did Manly create an English curriculum organized "in six period courses each occupying a quarter, running from the sixteenth century to the nineteenth,"[8] but he also actively worked to shape the future of the institution. His involvement in the university's growth ranged from drawing up plans to construct an "English building"[9] to evaluating the qualifications of librarians for their "businesslike spirit," "progressiveness," and "thorough knowledge of library methods."[10] These qualities of practicality, forward-looking competence, and scrupulous professionalism are the very traits that Manly and his later collaborator, Edith Rickert, would subsequently discover in Geoffrey Chaucer.

During this early period, Manly's work in the humanities was imbued with a profound interest in the substance and methodology of contemporary scientific advances that later also informed his work on the *Canterbury Tales*. As his professional interests stretched beyond the precincts of the University of Chicago to the academy as a whole, his enthusiasm for the methods of contemporary science was translated into a disciplining of his own profession. In November of 1900, for instance, Manly spoke to the Bibliographical Society of Chicago, arguing for "a really scientific bibliography of sources, texts, and discussions" to enhance "the study and teaching of English literature."[11] In this address, he posited a taxonomy modeled on the natural sciences, categorizing literature by species and emphasizing context and chronology. Five years later, in a speech before the English Club of

Princeton University, Manly seized upon the new science of evolution, in particular Hugo De Vries's theory of mutations, to explain the sudden appearance of new dramatic forms in the medieval period.[12] Here, the biological paradigm promised to provide incontrovertible evidence of literary origins. In these addresses a number of themes emerged that would be echoed in the next several decades in Manly's correspondence and publications: the primacy of the natural sciences, the appropriation of scientific method for the study of literature, the importance of specialization and collaboration, and the particular aptitude of American scholars and institutions for such work. These themes, of course, were not Manly's alone. Rather, as Lee Patterson notes, Manly was one of a group of early twentieth-century American medievalists whose aim was to transform "the study of medieval literature from uncritical amateurism into a scientific profession."[13] And he could do this because he believed that scientific investigation and classification would yield a greater and more reliable truth.

Cryptography

In the fall of 1917, Manly was given the opportunity to test his blend of science and textual analysis in the service of his nation. Five months after the United States declared war on Germany, Manly offered his services as a cryptographer. He wrote as a patriot, a specialist, and an administrator: "I shall . . . be glad if the Government can use me in any way. I know something about ciphers and have had some experience in administrative work."[14] When he was offered "a commission as a captain for work . . . in the Military Intelligence Section in cipher decoding,"[15] Manly "accept[ed] gladly."[16] His administrative experience and his decrypting skills served him well when he was later asked to head the American Black Chamber (MI-8), established by Herbert O. Yardley and devoted to cracking enemy codes. As the leader of Yardley's team, Manly enlisted a number of his junior colleagues to decipher the letters, telegrams, and diplomatic memoranda that poured into the office.[17] Among his recruits was Edith Rickert, a former doctoral student at Chicago and, at this time, a part-time instructor there.[18] The medievalist training of Manly and Rickert, Manly's early schooling in mathematics, and their shared commitment to the scientific method conjoined to make them ideal candidates for cryptographic work, as David Kahn admiringly describes:

The cast of mind that can thus sort out, retain, and then organize innumerable details into a cohesive whole was just what was needed for the Gothic complexity of the 424-letter Witze cryptogram. In a three-day marathon of cryptanalysis, Manly, aided by Miss Rickert, perceived the pattern of this 12-step official transposition cipher, with its multiple horizontal shiftings of three- and four-letter plaintext groups ripped apart by a final vertical transcription.[19]

Their success in this instance led directly to the conviction and imprisonment of an important German spy.[20]

Although the *Canterbury Tales* project would not even begin for another seven years, Manly and Rickert's experience in wartime intelligence had a profound impact on their subsequent scholarship. In the introduction to *New Methods for the Study of Literature,* Rickert credits cryptography with shaping a new scientific approach to literary analysis. Of the genesis of her textbook, she writes:

> Its root lies, strangely enough, in the methods of code analysis used in the Code and Cipher Section of the Military Intelligence in Washington, during the war. In the belief that processes which served to bring content out of series of numbers and other meaningless symbols might also be applied to the analysis of literature, an attempt was made in 1922, in a graduate course at the University of Chicago, to work out scientifically some of the phenomena of tone color and rhythm. Later, methods were found for the study of imagery, of words, of sentences, and of visual devices.[21]

Manly himself continued to be involved in projects, such as the Voynich controversy, that brought together his knowledge of medieval culture, manuscript traditions, textual editing, and cryptography.[22] In fact, despite his later denial,[23] editing and cryptography remained closely linked throughout his and Rickert's careers. The connection between them, moreover, went well beyond Kahn's "cast of mind." Manly and Rickert's involvement in the war effort introduced them to the new technologies of the photostat and the ultraviolet light, then known as the "blue light cabinet," which they later used to manage the increasing numbers of manuscripts discovered in their search through the British Isles for all extant *Canterbury Tales* collections and fragments.[24] A decade after their military service, the use of ultraviolet light would allow the editors to illuminate obscure features of manuscripts and expose the original script, while photostating would make possible the collation of vast numbers of variants in circumstances "when a MS can be examined only occasionally."[25] Those collations, in turn, were the groundwork for the evolutionary framework that promised the recovery of the original archetype. But, as they later came to acknowledge, that promise was one that could not be fulfilled.

The Scientific Method

In 1920, however, in Manly's presidential address to the Modern Language Association, his faith in the recoverability of origins by means of science and technology resonated strongly. In this speech, Manly applied goals that had governed the reorganization of the University of Chicago English Department twenty years earlier to a restructuring of the MLA's annual meeting. Manly successfully proposed to reorganize the conference from a single forum in which all members gathered to hear and discuss papers of general interest by eminent scholars into a series of smaller, concurrent meetings in which "small groups of members actively devot[e] a whole session . . . to different phases or parts of some topic in which all of them [a]re keenly interested."[26] His goal was not only to make the MLA "more influential" but to "aid in the promotion of research."[27] As yet, he lamented, "there are no great outstanding accomplishments in the field of scholarship that can be placed to the credit of the Association. No one great author has been fully studied; no great text or body of related texts has been edited; no problem of literary history has been made the object of concentrated or consistent study."[28] In an "age [that] is increasingly one of specialization and of organization for the accomplishment of purposes too large for a single investigator," the study of literature should be conducted along the lines of "chemistry or physics or botany or astronomy."[29]

Seven years after Manly's presidential address, Rickert wrote in very similar terms:

The methods of study which in the past have been confined largely to the materials of science are the only known methods by which even an approximation to the truth can be reached. In the nineteenth century these methods were almost exclusively used for the interpretation of the external world; for the understanding of literature, there was only the formal rhetoric of classical and medieval theorists, and when this was abandoned, nothing was found to take its place. As a result of this situation, science progressed as never before and the study of literature lagged far behind. Is it not, then, reasonable to believe that the methods which have carried us so far toward an understanding of our external environment may help us to interpret the reflection of our inner life in literature?[30]

By recasting literary studies in a scientific mold, both Manly and Rickert held out the hope that the projects of literary scholars would be seen as possessing the value needed to secure a position atop the cultural hierarchy. Key to this revaluing of literary studies was the foregrounding of data collection, but Manly in particular coupled this pragmatic aim with a visionary argument: "no doubt astronomy has many practical uses, but it is not these which have enabled it to obtain the funds it needed; it has won by its appeal to the imagination of men."[31] In rhetoric rarely heard in academic discourse today, Manly exhorted humanists to be more like scientists in celebrating the progressive disciplining of originary chaos:

We too have stars in our firmament, systems as mysterious and fascinating as comets or double suns, but we have too seldom invited the public to look through our telescopes and share our visions of the strange and interesting processes by which the chaotic chatter of anthropoid apes has been organized in the wonderful fabric of human speech or their formless outbursts of emotion have after many centuries issued in lyric and drama.[32]

This marvelous burst of scientific enthusiasm strove to validate the rigorous search for and study of origins—in particular, medieval literary origins—but its progressivist mythology ultimately rendered those origins inferior to later, more rational, and more fully developed forms of life: the ancestor to organized poetic expression is mere sound and fury. Inherent in a scientific model that reads texts in evolutionary terms is the relegation of medieval literature to the primitive shape of an early ancestor.

Although he seemed unaware of the danger, by privileging medieval studies as an origin of civilized discourse, Manly also set the stage for the triumph of American literature, the most recent twig on the literary tree.

During this postwar period, the shift from a focus on (ancient) British to (modern) American literature was linked to a burgeoning nationalism, which in turn sometimes embraced an agenda of racial hegemony. For example, Charles Mills Gayley, professor of English at the University of California, Berkeley, worked to define the United States as a purified Anglo-Saxon nation rooted in a mythical English Renaissance: "[o]ur American heritage is that of the revolutionary fathers, of the colonial fathers, of the English founders of colonial liberty—the contemporaries and friends of the poet and prophet of the race"[33]—that is, William Shakespeare. For Gayley, the connection between modern and early modern times was incontrovertible: "Their ventures and failures, their faults and virtues, are our history, Anglo-Saxon and American, as well as theirs."[34] Closing his paean to American liberty with a diatribe against an open-door immigration policy, he called "for exercise of American discipline; for maintenance of American prerogatives . . . in one historic and moral consciousness and one national ideal of democracy finding its soul."[35]

Manly also saw himself as a patriot, and he too was committed to promoting English and American linguistic traditions as well as medieval literature. In his 1920 address, he argued that a survey of American English was justified "since the war has made clear to the Government and to every public spirited citizen the fundamental importance to our institutions and our civilization of the English language"[36] He vigorously supported Sir William Craigie's *Dictionary of American English*[37] and advocated funding such projects as "a series of American historical manuscripts" and "a dictionary of American plays," even though they would compete with the Chaucer projects.[38] For Manly and Rickert, however, the privileging of the Anglo-American tradition did not authorize anachronistic historical conflations. Scrupulous adherence to their version of scientific scholarship enabled them to avoid racialist conclusions. In an early lecture entitled "Narrative Writing in Anglo Saxon Times," Manly was careful to place Old English literature within the larger context of all early literatures and not characterize it as inherently racially unique.[39] In another instance, Manly insisted that the "'Americanization' of Chaucer is the last thing we should wish to accomplish. We hope rather to throw as much light as we can upon the life and work of an Englishman of the fourteenth century."[40] Committed as he was to the necessity of accurate historical contextualization, Manly never indulged in the explicitly political transmutation of a founding figure that lay at the heart of Gayley's cooptation of Shakespeare. At the same time, however, neither he nor Rickert was completely immune to the shaping force of class and the privileging of a particular cultural vision. Even as they recognized and respected the historical specificity of their iconic author, they nonetheless ended by constructing a Geoffrey Chaucer who conformed closely to their own personal and professional ideals.

The Author and the Text

By 1924, John Manly and Edith Rickert began to raise money for an ambitious project to gather all extant manuscripts of the *Canterbury Tales*, to collate all the variants, and to use Lachmannian stemmatics to attempt to establish the definitive text of the *Tales*, based on O^1, the earliest scribal archetype.[41] The lure of scientific methodology and technology proved to be a powerful fundraising tool in this endeavor,[42] but the editors themselves were inspired by less tangible goals as well. For their project attempted to reconstruct not only the original text of the *Tales* but also the character of its author. And just as their initial belief in an ur-text governed the protocols of their manuscript editing, their vision of the ideal author, a middle-class poet of democratic values, shaped their biographical research.

Manly and Rickert's construction of the author, begun in the *Life-Records* two years after the beginning of work on the *Text*, both stemmed from and competed with their editing endeavors. As primary supervisor of the *Life-Records* project, Edith Rickert published letters in the *(London) Times Literary Supplement* recounting newly discovered evidence about Chaucer's life, evidence that supported the construction of Chaucer as an ideal bourgeois. On numerous occasions from 1927 through 1933, Rickert praised Chaucer for his honest record-keeping, his successful balancing of disparate careers, his respectable accounting practices, and his forthright admission and satisfaction of debt—all of which, she suggested, were family traits. For instance, of Chaucer fulfilling his duties as customs officer, she wrote: "All the records we are finding of Chaucer's business career tend to the conclusion that he was both honest and efficient and that the diplomatic talent which caused him to be sent on missions served also to keep him out of trouble in difficult positions." [43] Of Chaucer fulfilling his duties as Clerk of the Works, she stated: "it is pleasant to read that when in 1391 Chaucer was called upon for an accounting of his clerkship, he did so promptly . . . in propria persona sua to settle his accounts."[44] And of Chaucer successfully balancing a dual career, she wrote that he was "a heavily burdened and successful business man, whose poetry was written in odd hours and times of leisure for his own pleasure and entertainment of his friends."[45] None of this should surprise us, given that he was born and bred, as Rickert saw it, within the best bourgeois tradition. Of his grandfather, she asserted, Robert Chaucer was "an efficient man of business of the type of his famous grandson."[46] In other words, what is revealed in these and other records is a Chaucer who came from good stock and whose practices perpetuated the virtues of his ancestors. As a businessman, Chaucer was, Rickert believed, meticulous in his practices, open in his dealings, and scrupulous in his rendering of accounts.

In the *Life-Records*, then, Rickert discovered a Geoffrey Chaucer whose personal, business, and poetic practices conformed to an early twentieth-century American sense of middle-class rectitude. Just as, according to Stephanie Trigg, Chaucer's "own biography and family connections with royalty and the aristocracy played an increasingly important role in sixteenth-century editions of his work,"[47] so too the traces of Chaucer as a London businessman played a crucial role in the Manly-Rickert edition of the *Canterbury Tales* four hundred years later. In their view, the "poet of courtly love" in *Troilus and Criseyde* was supplanted in the *Canterbury Tales* by the poet as bourgeois hero. In his 1926 *Chaucer and the Rhetoricians*, Manly valued the plain speaking of the later Chaucer over the "astonishingly artificial and sophisticated art with which he began," and celebrated "the gradual replacement of formal rhetorical devices by methods of composition based on close observation of life."[48] In the same year, in *Some New Light on Chaucer*, he argued that in Chaucer's fourteenth century "[t]he elaborate and splendid structure of feudalism . . . was crumbling to decay and was being rapidly replaced by the new forces of commercialism and the powerful, though as yet chaotic, stirrings of the common people."[49] So, too, Rickert might well have included the *Tales* in her 1910 description of late medieval carols as "part of the great fourteenth-century movement of the middle classes in England, of the stir towards democracy, of the conquest of the people's English over the Latin of the clergy, over the French of the court."[50]

Rickert's rendering of the plain-speaking, honest professional who takes pleasure in his avocation was intertwined with the search for the scribal archetype of the text that most thoroughly represented its author's virtues. The painstaking reconstruction of the *Canterbury Tales* relied not only on a sense of its author as satisfying a bourgeois ideal but also on the professional talents and dedication of his modern editors. Fundamental to their efforts was a belief in the elusive archetype, the retrievable origin—in cryptographic terms, the plaintext[51]—as susceptible to the ministrations of skilled and dedicated workers employing scientific techniques. As the *Canterbury Tales* project moved forward, Rickert organized the workers into research teams along the lines of those employed in scientific investigations. In their "Chaucer laboratory"[52] at the University of Chicago, as well as in their London rooms, small cohorts of graduate students and assistants utilized the elaborate system of collation cards developed by Rickert to track manuscript variants and reduce human error.[53] Because Manly too believed that the "authoritative" text "must be based on a scientific study of all the early manuscripts," he planned "to bring together here at the University photostatic copies of all the manuscripts and from them to construct, according to the best scientific principles the authoritative" text. Through scientific means, the text so "established would never be displaced, and would form the basis, not only of all future editions of the *Canterbury Tales,* but of all the numberless volumes of selections studied throughout the English-speaking world in high schools and colleges."[54]

Of course this never happened; the text Manly and Rickert established for the *Canterbury Tales* was never widely used. On one level, however, in terms of data collection and analysis, the *Canterbury Tales* project was a huge success. The number of known manuscripts doubled; indeed not one additional manuscript has been unearthed since Edith Rickert's and Sir William McCormick's exhaustive searches through the libraries and manor houses of the British Isles and Europe. Rickert's collation system generated 60,000 cards documenting variants and errata for every line of Chaucer's tales. Numerous stemmata were traced back through the fifteenth century in a determined search for the scribal archetype, the hypothetical basis for Manly's "authoritative text."[55] In the end, however, this plethora of material defeated the very end it was supposed to serve, and Manly and Rickert realized that their ambition was unachievable. In a very real sense, the author himself had failed them. As Manly wrote J. S. P. Tatlock in 1934:

There can be no possible doubt, I think, that Chaucer in his lifetime never arranged the *Canterbury Tales* or had a MS which was a copy of the Tales as a whole. The arrangements we have were, I am confident, all made after his death by persons who were attempting to collect the *Canterbury Tales.* . . . In some cases extant copies seemed to derive ultimately from Chaucer's own rough drafts; in some cases from fair copies made probably by his scribe and not always thoroughly corrected by him. In still other cases, some texts seem to represent earlier versions of tales which were circulated separately as they were written.

Although he began by stating "there can be no possible doubt," Manly ended by expressing his very real concerns: "With regard to some of these conclusions it is very difficult to be entirely positive on account of the enormous amount of contamination which exists even in some of the earliest extant MSS." In fact, he acknowledged their inability to resolve their quandaries: "We cannot hope to solve all the problems of the text before we publish."[56]

Thus, despite the scientific model upon which Manly and Rickert structured their work—the teams of investigators working in laboratories, the use of modern technologies learned in the war, the careful construction of phylogenetic stemmata—the archetype remained irretrievable. The very methodology that promised to yield the textual origin had shown that it did not exist. Nevertheless, they continued to work as if the archetype existed, while freely confessing that their evidence pointed in precisely the opposite direction: "We have therefore proceeded as if all MSS were from the same archetype, being on the watch, however, for indications of separate origin and separate lines of descent."[57] The author so carefully inferred from court rolls and civic registers—the "efficient man of business"—had proven unreliable. Faced with evidence of various stages of production, Manly and Rickert were compelled to conclude not only that "[a]pparently Chaucer did not read carefully the copies from which his MSS have descended,"[58] but also that "the major inconsistencies [in the manuscript tradition] are due to Chaucer himself."[59] Nonetheless, Rickert spent the day before she died in 1938 heroically working on her theory that the "inferior" Fitzwilliam manuscript was in fact representative of Chaucer's own early, undeveloped drafts.[60] Although Manly very much doubted the validity of such a radical revaluation of the Fitzwilliam manuscript, he also could not resist the lure of a more orderly stemma. Even as the final typescript was being prepared for publication, he wrote Mabel Dean, the project's specialist on dialect: "I think I have found a way of training the branches of the genealogical tree so as to reduce the number of separate lines from 12 to 4, as Miss Rickert intended. . . . This is so important that I must reconsider the problems. Please therefore return to me all the materials on FkT."[61] It is not clear from the correspondence whether Dean, who (along with Manly's sister, Mrs. H. M. Patrick) had taken over many of Rickert's duties after her death, returned

"The Franklin's Tale" materials to Manly. What we do know is that *The Text* was published without Manly and Rickert ever achieving their goal of delineating the evolutionary tree.

Cultural Capital

Even as recension denied Manly and Rickert their desired textual origin, so too the careful exercise of scientific method failed to guarantee for Chaucer the cultural capital dreamed of by Manly in his 1920 MLA address. Ten years after that address, as discoveries by orientalists and archaeologists filled the newspapers with the romance of a more distant past, he spoke to the Medieval Academy of America, lamenting that "[u]nfortunately for the mediaevalist, his treasures have lost their publicity value."[62] In this presidential address, he argued valiantly for the importance of the medieval past as not only a good in its own right but as an instance of cultural continuity. The medieval period, he asserted,

> lies close to us. In it arose many of our most important institutions. Our social life—our customs, our ideals, our superstitions and fears and hopes—came to us directly from this period; and no present-day analysis can give a complete account of our civilization unless it is supplemented by a profound study of the forces and forms of life, good and evil, which we have inherited from it."[63]

But in the new, professionalized American era, an era which Manly himself helped shape, such arguments from history had little currency.

Even at their home institution, even during the period of greatest productivity in the *Canterbury Tales* project, the field of medieval studies was in trouble. Soon after Robert Maynard Hutchins was inaugurated as the president of the University of Chicago in 1929, he began promoting the Great Books curriculum, a deracinated version of origins far removed from the data collection, textual study, and historical contextualization that characterized the Chaucer projects. As part of his belief in metaphysics as the true foundation of all education,[64] Hutchins objected to "the practice of accumulating items about the lives of authors, the influences to which they were exposed, and the dates of their labors without regard to the contribution which such studies may make to the understanding of their works."[65]

No wonder then that, almost immediately upon Hutchins's arrival, Manly confessed his anxiety about trends at the university. In an April 1930 letter to David H. Stevens, head of the General Education Board, Manly reiterated his philosophical position that the "laws" of "human action" are fertile ground for scientific investigation:

> The whole field of human action—present and past—is one of those in which the laws, that is, the regular sequences of causes and effects, remain to be discovered. Many persons contend that the factor of human volition makes all these fields impervious to law and therefore no fit subject of scientific investigation. Five or six years ago in a lecture at Northwestern University I tried to show the absurdity of this view, and in my address to the Mediaeval Academy, without going deeply into the argument, I try to point out the conditions under which human actions are proper subjects of scientific inquiry.[66]

This visionary statement was, of course, couched in precisely those terms to which Hutchins would be impervious.

Hutchins was hardly the only American intellectual to turn away from the Middle Ages. In hindsight, it is not surprising to learn that in March of 1934 Manly was informed that the General Education Board, or GEB (in 1934 recently incorporated into the Rockefeller Foundation), which had supported the Chaucer projects from their inception, no longer intended to "make a special appropriation for the Chaucer work . . . because the Foundation is now especially interested in American culture and the Dictionary of American English suits its program very well."[67] While Manly and Rickert managed to eke out the necessary funding from a variety of sources in order to bring *The Text* to print, every year the struggle became greater.[68] Such diminishment of interest was inevitable, however, once the University of Chicago and the GEB decided to follow the general trends of university education by focusing more on the American present and less on the medieval past.

Although *The Text of the Canterbury Tales* was published in 1940 to generally favorable reviews and the work received the Haskins Medal of the Medieval Academy of America in 1942,[69] the praise seems almost perfunctory, perhaps because the world's attention was turning to war. Reviewers seemed both awed and baffled by the "enormously complicated classification" [70] of manuscripts and warned that the "casual reader will pass these four [sic] volumes [of variants] by with a shudder."[71] So it is that *The Text of the Canterbury Tales* as constructed by Manly and Rickert out of eighty-four manuscripts with thousands upon thousands of collated variants—the *Text* for which they had such high hopes and to the publication of which they devoted the last fifteen years of their lives—this text, as it turns out, has been little used by either students or scholars. In fact, when in 1984 it was seriously reconsidered, George Kane roundly lambasted the editors' Lachmannian methodology, their editorial decisions, and their artificial text as failures, "obscure" and "incomprehensible."[72] More recently, Peter Robinson, director of the electronic Chaucer Project, recounts the multiple reasons for Manly and Rickert's "failure":

> they worked under conditions of great difficulty (Rickert died before it was finished, and Manly was ill in the latter stages); no later editor has accepted their text; the presentation of their conclusions is so obscure that it is difficult to determine how far they achieved their stated aim, of uncovering the textual relations of all the witnesses. It is clear that they left vital questions unanswered.[73]

Rare among late twentieth-century Chaucerians, Roy Vance Ramsay argues that "the textual evidence in [the *Canterbury Tales* manuscripts] represents such overwhelming bulk and complexity that no current study of the text can dispense with—or even make much of a start without—Manly-Rickert."[74] But, in fact, few Chaucer studies attend to *The Text of the Canterbury Tales* at all. In spite of Ramsay's claim, until very recently the eight volumes of *The Text* moldered on library shelves, little consulted and rarely read, their methodology discredited and their hard-won technology superseded.[75]

Yet in other ways the scientific humanism of John Matthews Manly and Edith Rickert continues to shape our work as medievalists today. Like them, we undertake to ground our work in scrupulous data collection, disciplinary specialization, service to the profession, innovative technology, and collaborative scholarship. We too struggle to remain true to what we understand of history and philology. Our Chaucers are also meant to stand forever. Nevertheless, Manly and Rickert's story teaches us that shifts in medieval studies, English departments, the academy, and American culture will inevitably locate our own work firmly within its own time. Like Manly and Rickert, in other words, we too are caught between the paradigms we acknowledge and those that, hidden from us, nonetheless shape our work and our lives.

Notes

This article seems especially appropriate for a festschrift honoring Robert Hanning. Manly and Rickert's generosity and erudition, shared with friends, colleagues, and students throughout their lives, are mirrored in Hanning's own. This research was supported by a grant from the PSC-CUNY Research Foundation. We wish to thank Jay Satterfield and the staff of the University of Chicago's Regenstein Library Special Collections for their help.

1. John Matthews Manly and Edith Rickert, eds., *The Text of the Canterbury Tales, Studied on the Basis of All Known Manuscripts*, 8 vols. (Chicago: University of Chicago Press, 1940); *Chaucer Life-Records*, ed. Martin C. Crow and Clair C. Olson, from materials compiled by John M. Manly and Edith Rickert, with the assistance of Lilian J. Redstone and others (Austin: University of Texas Press, 1966); *Chaucer's World*, comp. Edith Rickert, ed. Clair C. Olson and Martin M. Crow, illustrations selected by Margaret Rickert (1948; reprint, New York: Columbia University Press, 1968).

2. David R. Shumway, *Creating American Civilization: A Genealogy of American Literature as an Academic Discipline* (Minneapolis: University of Minnesota Press, 1994), esp. 97–103; Gerald Graff, *Professing Literature: An Institutional History* (Chicago: University of Chicago Press, 1987), 55–80.

3. David E. Orlinsky, "Not Very Simple, but Overflowing: A Historical Perspective on General Education at the University of Chicago," in *General Education in the Social Sciences: Centennial Reflections on the College of the University of Chicago*, ed. John J. MacAloon (Chicago: University of Chicago Press, 1992), 33.

4. Shumway, *Creating American Civilization*, 98.

5. Ibid.

6. For example, Manly himself was instrumental in the founding of *Poetry*, according to David H. Stevens, *The Changing Humanities: An Appraisal of Old Values and New Uses* (New York: Harper, 1953), 127. Also see Elizabeth Scala, "John Matthews Manly, 1865–1940. Edith Rickert, 1871–1938," in *Medieval Scholarship: Biographical Studies on the Formation of a Discipline*, ed. Helen Damico (New York: Garland, 1998), 2:300.

7. Orlinsky, "Not Very Simple," 36–37; he quotes from a 1927 statement by a University of Chicago faculty committee (quoted also on 33 but nowhere cited).

8. Robert Morss Lovett, *All Our Years: The Autobiography of Robert Morss Lovett* (New York: Viking, 1948), 92.

9. John M. Manly to W. R. Harper, 25 November 1901, University of Chicago Library, President's Papers 1889–1925, box 45, folder 22.

10. Manly to W. R. Harper, 30 March 1901, ibid.

11. See Aksel G. S. Josephson, minutes of The Bibliographical Society of Chicago meeting on November 1, 1900. *The Library Journal* 25 (1900): offprint, University of Chicago Library, John M. Manly Papers, box 6, folder 19, 1.

12. Later published as John M. Manly, "Literary Forms and the New Theory of Origin of the Species," *Modern Philology* 4 (1907), 577–95.

13. Lee Patterson, *Negotiating the Past: The Historical Understanding of Medieval Literature* (Madison: University of Wisconsin Press, 1987), 15; Patterson groups Manly with "Root, Kittredge, . . . Lowes, Hammond, Tatlock, Patch, Dempster, and Malone" (14).

14. Manly to Lieut. Col. G. H. Macdonald, 11 September 1917, National Archives at College Park, Maryland. Correspondence of the Military Intelligence Division of the War Department General Staff 1917–41, RG 165, file 10020–68.

15. Lt. Col. R. H. Van Deman to Manly, 15 September 1917, ibid.

16. Telegram repeated in a follow-up note from Manly to Van Deman, 24 September 1917, ibid.

17. David H. Stevens, *The Changing Humanities: An Appraisal of Old Values and New Uses* (New York: Harper, 1953), 127.

18. On Rickert's credentials for this work, see Edith Rickert, Personal History Statement, 22 April, 1918, National Archives at College Park, Maryland, Correspondence of the Military Intelligence, RG 165, file 8930–354, 2. In the prewar years, Edith Rickert's work was twofold: she was an active scholar, editing medieval carols, romances, and other texts; she was also a prolific novelist in her own right. We are working on an article about this period in Rickert's life, tentatively entitled "Edith Rickert, Romancer." On Rickert, Manly, and their relationship, see Elizabeth Scala, "Scandalous Assumptions: Edith Rickert and the Chicago Chaucer Project," *Medieval Feminist Forum* 30 (2000): 27–37; also Scala, "John Matthews Manly."

19. David Kahn, *The Codebreakers: The Story of Secret Writing*, rev. ed. (New York: Scribner, 1996), 354.

20. Ibid.

21. Edith Rickert, "To Skeptics," *New Methods for the Study of Literature* (Chicago: University of Chicago Press, 1927), v.

22. Box 6 of the Manly Papers at the University of Chicago Library contains a wealth of cryptographic materials, both military and literary: lists for German codes; cipher wheels; word frequency lists for English, Spanish, and German; Elizabethan ciphers; photostats of Shakespeare texts; philological notes. For Manly's contributions to the Voynich manuscript discussion, see Wilfrid M. Voynich to Manly, 2 July 1917, Manly Papers, box 2, folder 8; Manly to William Romaine Newbold, 26 June–17 July 1922, Manly Papers, box 2, folder 1. Manly publishes an extensive description of

the manuscript and a refutation of Newbold's solution to the cipher in "Roger Bacon and the Voynich MS," *Speculum* 6 (1931): 345–91.

23. Manly to James M. Stifler, 27 July 1932, University of Chicago Library, English Department Papers, box 18, folder 5, 2. Manly is writing in response to a proposed article (never published due to Manly's disapproval) by Rollin Lynde Hartt, entitled "The Americanization of Geoffrey Chaucer."

24. See Manly's inquiry to E. K. Carver, 21 December 1925, ibid., box 17, folder 17, concerning the value of the "violet light process" for "reading ancient manuscripts." Carver was a former colleague in MI8. These technologies are also discussed in Roy Vance Ramsay, *The Manly-Rickert Text of the* Canterbury Tales (Lewiston, N.Y.: Edwin Mellen Press, 1994), 71.

25. Manly and Rickert, *The Text of the Canterbury Tales*, 1:1.

26. John M. Manly, "The President's Address: New Bottles," *PMLA* 35, issue appendix (1920): lv.

27. Ibid., lv–lvi.

28. Ibid., xlviii.

29. Ibid., xlix.

30. Rickert, *New Methods for the Study of Literature*, 22.

31. Manly, "New Bottles," lii.

32. Ibid.

33. Charles Mills Gayley, *Shakespeare and the Founders of Liberty in America* (New York: Macmillan, 1917), 224.

34. Ibid., 1.

35. Ibid., 224. On Anglo-Saxonism and American nationalism, see Shumway, *Creating American Civilization*, 70–72.

36. Manly, "New Bottles," l.

37. Manly to E. D. Burton, 8 April 1925, University of Chicago Library, English Department Papers, box 17, folder 17.

38. Manly to Professor D. H. Stevens, 8 October 1931, ibid., box 18, folder 4, 2.

39. Manly's handwritten draft is undated; "Narrative Writing in Anglo Saxon Times," University of Chicago Library, John M. Manly Papers, box 3, folder 20 .

40. Manly to James M. Stifler, 27 July 1932, University of Chicago Library, English Department Papers, box 18, folder 5.

41. Manly to Emil C. Wotten, 26 November 1924, ibid., box 17, folder 17; Manly to George A. Plimpton, 20 December 1924, ibid.

42. Manly to Frederic Carpenter, 19 July 1926, ibid.; also Manly to Mrs. F. I. Carpenter, 3, 24 August; 26 September 1927, ibid., box 17, folder 18. The Carpenter bequest of $10,000 to the Department of English at Chicago funded most of the photostat copying.

43. Edith Rickert, "Chaucer Called to Account," *Times (London) Literary Supplement*, 8 December 1932, 943.

44. Edith Rickert, "New Life Records of Chaucer—I," *Times (London) Literary Supplement,* 27 September 1928, 684.

45. Edith Rickert, "Chaucer and the Treasures of Calais," *Times (London) Literary Supplement,* 17 November 1933, 859.

46. Edith Rickert, "Chaucer's Grandfather in Action," *Times (London) Literary Supplement,* 6 April 1933, 248.

47. Stephanie Trigg, "Discourses of Affinity in the Reading Communities of Geoffrey Chaucer," in *Rewriting Chaucer: Culture, Authority, and the Idea of the Authentic Text, 1400–1602,* ed. Thomas A. Prendergast and Barbara Kline (Columbus: Ohio State University Press, 1999), 276.

48. John Matthews Manly, *Chaucer and the Rhetoricians* (London: British Academy, 1926), 5.

49. John Matthews Manly, *Some New Light on Chaucer: Lectures Delivered at the Lowell Institute* (1926; reprint, New York: Peter Smith, 1951), 268.

50. Edith Rickert, Introduction, *Ancient English Christmas Carols, MCCCC to MDCC, collected and arranged by Edith Rickert* (1910; reprint, London: Chatto and Windus, 1914), xvi.

51. On the definition of plaintext, see Kahn, *The Codebreakers,* xv–xvi.

52. Manly to David H. Stevens, 16 August 1929, University of Chicago Library, English Department Papers, box 18, folder 2.

53. See Manly and Rickert, *The Text of the Canterbury Tales,* 2.1–12, for a description of their collation methodology.

54. Manly to Emil C. Wotten, 26 November 1924, University of Chicago Library, English Department Papers, box 17, folder 17.

55. For an account of this process, see Ramsay, *The Manly-Rickert Text,* 99.

56. Manly to J. S. P. Tatlock, 9 August 1934, University of Chicago Library, English Department Papers, box 18, folder 8, 1.

57. Manly and Rickert, *The Text of the Canterbury Tales,* 2:39.

58. Ibid., 1:xii.

59. Manly, unlabeled typescript, n.d., University of Chicago Library, John M. Manly Papers, box 3, folder 17, 5–6.

60. Manly and Rickert, *The Text of the Canterbury Tales,* 2:xii and 2:495–518. We discuss Manly's (and others') reactions to Rickert's death in greater detail in a forthcoming article, "Editing as Palinode: *The Invention of Love* and *The Text of the Canterbury Tales.*"

61. Manly to Mabel Dean, 23 March n.d., University of Chicago Library, John M. Manly Papers, box 2, folder 4.

62. John M. Manly, "Humanistic Studies and Science," *Speculum* 5 (1930): 249.

63. Ibid., 250.

64. Robert Maynard Hutchins, *The Higher Learning in America* (New Haven: Yale University Press, 1936), 97–98: "The aim of higher education is wisdom. Wis-

dom is knowledge of principles and causes. Therefore, metaphysics is the highest wisdom."

65. Robert Maynard Hutchins, "A Reply to Professor Whitehead," *The Atlantic Monthly* 143 (1936): 584.

66. Manly to David H. Stevens, 21 April 1930, University of Chicago Library, English Department Papers, box 18, folder 3.

67. Gordon J. Laing to Manly, 23 March 1934. ibid., box 18, folder 7.

68. See Manly to David H. Stevens, 1935 or 1936, ibid., box 18, folder 9, for one account of the struggle to finish *The Text*.

69. C. H. Beeson, George La Piana, and J. S. P. Tatlock, "Report of the Committee on Award of the Haskins Medal," *Speculum* 17 (1942): 453–54.

70. Robert K. Root, Review of *The Text of the Canterbury Tales, Studies in Philology* 38 (1941): 7.

71. Carleton Brown, Review of *The Text of the Canterbury Tales, Modern Language Notes* 55 (1940): 621. Other reviewers include Kurt Rydland, "The Meaning of 'Variant Readings' in the Manly-Rickert *Canterbury Tales:* A Note on the Limitations of the Corpus of Variants," *Neuphilologische Mitteilungen* 73 (1972): 805–14; and Dorothy Everett in *Review of English Studies* 18 (1942): 93–109.

72. George Kane, "John M. Manly and Edith Rickert," in *Editing Chaucer: The Great Tradition,* ed. Paul Ruggiers (Norman, Okla.: Pilgrim Books, 1984).

73. Peter Robinson and Kevin Taylor, "Publishing an Electronic Textual Edition: The Case of *The Wife of Bath's Prologue* on CD-ROM," *Computers and the Humanities* 32 (1998): 274.

74. Ramsay, *The Manly-Rickert Text,* vii.

75. On the possibilities for editing medieval texts afforded by new technologies, see Peter Robinson and Elizabeth Solopova, "The *Canterbury Tales* Project," http://www.ucalgary.ca/~scriptor/chaucer/rob.html.

III. ITALIAN CONTEXTS

17

WARREN GINSBERG

"Gli scogli neri e il niente che c'è"

Dorigen's Black Rocks and
Chaucer's Translation of Italy

For the listener, who listens in the snow,
And, nothing himself, beholds
Nothing that is not there and the nothing that is.

—Wallace Stevens, "The Snow Man"

C ritics have long thought that the Franklin's tale of Dorigen, Arveragus, and Aurelius was influenced by Menedon's *quistione d'amore*
in the *Filocolo;* more recently, scholars who believe Chaucer knew
the *Decameron* have examined the parallel story of Dianora, Gilberto, and
Ansaldo (10.5) as a possible source.[1] These readings are each haunted by one
central fact: no phrase or sentence in Chaucer's narrative directly translates a
sentence or phrase in either of Boccaccio's. In most cases, Chaucerians have
explained this lack of verbal correspondence by trying to explain it away. I believe that we should instead acknowledge the absence of textual contact and
make it the basis of new understanding of cross-cultural translation.

In this essay I will argue that both the obstacle the lady places before her would-be lover in the *Filocolo* and the manner in which he overcomes it reveal a mode of meaning that is peculiarly Italian. "Mode of meaning" is a phrase I am adopting from Walter Benjamin's "The Task of the Translator";[2] I will use it to indicate those literary, cultural, and linguistic schemes that shape the events a text records and that make them understandable to its audience. These interpretive schemes were only partially available to Chaucer, as they would be only partially available to any English poet who had spent limited time in Florence, none in Naples, and knew little, it would seem, of Provençal poetry or the *stil novo*. The different task and different resolution of "The Franklin's Tale" might therefore lead one to suspect they bespeak a different mode of meaning. The thesis I want to begin to explore here is that, whether or not Chaucer knew Boccaccio's romance, their versions of the story do indeed become translations when we see each simultaneously following and disarticulating the other's signifying mode as the result of alternate forces of production, distinct literary traditions, and diverse social formations in England and Italy.

In order to give some sense of the models of reading this kind of translation solicits, I will, as I have said, enlist ideas that Walter Benjamin introduced in his essay "*Die Aufgabe des Übersetzers.*"[3] For Benjamin, the translator's task is to express "the central reciprocal relationship between languages."[4] This relationship resides "in the intention underlying each language as a whole—an intention, however, which no single language can attain by itself but which is realized only by the totality of their intentions supplementing each other: pure language."[5]

What a language as a whole intends, the end it aims at, is never contained within the language itself. Its intention becomes apparent only when a language is seen in relation to other languages, such as happens when it is translated. But in supplementing the original, a translation displaces its language from any proprietary claim to be the final word. *Brot* and *pain* "intend the same object," Benjamin explains, but disparities in sound and affinity make the way each means "bread" entirely distinct. Because the German and the French words excite different chains of associations, the one cannot be exchanged for the other without disclosing the intention of each language as a whole—the direction in which it is pointed, as it were, the particular cultural arc along which it moves.[6] The aggregation of such disclosures, which are revelations of discrepancies between the intent to name and the words themselves as conglomerations of consonants and vowels, is what Benjamin calls *"reine Sprache."* For him, "pure language" does not denote some anagogic fullness of meaning that a transcendent consciousness can encompass, but the basic, material elements of sound and letter in a state completely prior to and unfettered from signification, out of whose differences all languages are comprised.[7] The relation of any given language to this pure speech is the mode or manner in which it expresses its intention, and it is a language's mode of intention that translations should seek to translate:

> Instead of making itself similar to the meaning, to the *Sinn* of the original, the translation must rather, lovingly and in detail, in its own language, form itself according to the manner of meaning [*Art des Meinens*] of the original, to make both recognizable as the broken parts of the greater [pure] language, just as fragments are the broken parts of a vessel.[8]

In finding a manner of meaning that forms itself according to that of the original, the translation disarticulates the source, estranges it to itself, by exposing the fact that the languages of both texts, by virtue of their derivation from "pure language," have always been fragments. A coalescing of parts that remain fractured, the translation and translated texts disenchant the fantasy that there ever was a whole vessel that the one or the other constituted, separately or together. Instead of projecting an image of that wholeness, the unassimilable materiality of *reine Sprache* makes evident "a permanent disjunction which inhabits all languages," a disjunction that, for Paul de Man, frustrates the inclination to see hermeneutics and poetics as complementary, grammar and significance as compatible, the symbol and what is being symbolized as adequate to each other.[9] In impeding these correlations, translation opens the possibility, as Tom Cohen has said, of "passing from one system of manufacturing history and meaning (passive, reactive, mimetic, 'humanist' . . .)" to another, "at war with the first, yet inhabiting it . . . a pro-active mimesis without model or copy."[10] That is to say, translation for Benjamin is a mode of writing that disrupts the ways mimetic narratives make meaning by installing alternative itineraries of signification next to one another; it suspends received constructions of the past and sets other ways of managing time and memory alongside them.

In the fourth book of the *Filocolo,* a raging storm has caused Boccaccio's hero to delay his quest for Biancafiore in Naples. On the way to visit the tomb of

Virgil, he meets a group of courtly men and women; they all retire to a garden where they debate thirteen questions of love. Menedon's is the fourth; he introduces the noble knight and lady of his *quistione* by saying:

Nella terra lá dov'io nacque, mi ricordo essere un ricchissimo e nobile cavaliere, il quale di perfettissimo amore amando una donna nobile della terra, per isposa la prese (4.31.2).[11]

In the land where I was born, I remember there was a very rich and noble knight who loved a noble lady of that land with a perfect love and took her as wife.

In the next sentence, however, Menedon tells us that Tarolfo, another noble knight, struck by the lady's beauty, fell in love with her, "and loved her with such love that he saw nothing beyond her, nor did he desire anyone more" ("di tanto amore l'amava, che oltre a lei non vedeva, né niuna cosa più disiava," 31.3). Because the knight and lady at the start and throughout the tale remain anonymous, the fact that Tarolfo is named takes on a prominence that pricks the reader's curiosity. Perhaps Menedon's silence reflects his belief that the couple's marriage has submerged the individuality each had prior to their union; whoever they were before, "husband" and "wife" tell us what they are now. If so, Tarolfo differs from his fellow knight precisely because he still bears his name. Yet the proper noun that secures his distinction is troubling, not least because Tarolfo would seem to owe his *nome* to the impropriety of his desire. The husband, Menedon has said, loved his lady with a perfect love ("di perfettissimo amore amando"); Tarolfo, he tells us, also loved her greatly: "e di tanto amore l'amava." The parallel wording suggests that there must be some imperfection in his ardor that distinguishes Tarolfo from the husband. So we search for a fault and do not have to go far before we find one: Tarolfo may indeed have eyes for no one else and desire no one more, but these indications of his affection hardly testify that the lady is his Beatrice, the pattern of womanhood who has become the animating marrow of his being. He has neither ceased to notice that there are other women to look at nor has he stopped longing for them; he simply has come to focus all his attention on this one because he thinks she is beyond compare. Something calculating and narcissistic resides in the way Tarolfo idealizes his love, something that, even more than his coveting another man's wife, makes him Tarolfo.

At the same time, however, the passion both men share for the same woman makes it hard to tell them apart. If marriage has canceled the noble knight's name, Tarolfo retains his as the precipitate of lack. The husband, we have been told, won his wife because his love is "perfettissimo," but in the absence of any description of his doting devotion, perfection seems less to denote the quality of his affection than to signify that the knight has brought his love to completion, has reduced it, as the scholastics would say, from potency to act, by taking the lady as wife ("per isposa la prese").[12] Tarolfo equally wants to possess the wife; if he does, though, the implication runs, he too will lose his name, certainly because he will have behaved dishonorably; but also because, by sleeping with her, he and the husband will have become interchangeable.

From the start, then, a contradictory logic of chivalric and gendered identity seems to be at work in Menedon's story: "perfettissimo amore" makes the first knight a husband by erasing his name as knight; Tarolfo will preserve his name only so long as he does not "make perfect" the passion from which his distinctiveness derives. At this point, one could still reasonably suppose the opposing directions in which these inferences move, if not entirely an invention on my part, might be the adventitious outgrowth of Boccaccio's "mise en scène"; it turns out, however, that the characters' subsequent actions continue to distinguish and merge husband and lover.

This simultaneous drawing and blurring of distinctions is especially brought about by the wife, who, although nameless herself, is both agent and object through whom each knight establishes and endangers the name he has. After Tarolfo makes his intentions known, the lady "keeps them and her response to herself" ("celatamente sostenea, sanza dare o segno o buona risposta al cavaliere," 31.4). She reasons that if she gives Tarolfo "neither sign nor favorable answer," he will cease wooing her. When he persists, she fears her husband may hear about it; she therefore considers telling him herself, but finally decides silence is the better course, since she suspects her husband might believe she was encouraging Tarolfo and is convinced that revealing his attentions could so "provoke both men she would never be able to live happily" ("Io potrei, s'io il dicessi, commettere tra costoro cosa che io mai non viverei lieta," 31.6). So she determines to take matters into her own hands: she sends Tarolfo a message in which she asks for a gift as an earnest of his love; if he should not wish to give what she requests, he should "entice her no further, except to the extent that he would be willing she reveal to her husband" ("non stimolarla più avanti, se non per quanto egli non volesse che essa questo manifestasse al marito," 31.7).[13]

In each of these deliberations, the lady manages to confirm her loyalty as wife and avoid putting a stop to Tarolfo's pursuit of her as his *donna*. She is sure Tarolfo will read her silence as she undoubtedly intends: an unambiguous sign that she rejects his advances. Yet her decision not to tell her husband about those glances, messages, and gifts also suggests she perhaps would not altogether object if they continued. At the very least, her musings reveal a mind oddly at odds with itself: in choosing muteness first as her means of refusing Tarolfo and then of remaining faithful to her husband, she equates the men who love her. Even though she would establish antithetical relations with each of them, she deals with both the same way. Of course we can sympathize with the lady's concern that her husband might mistakenly assume she has encouraged Tarolfo's admiration, though one wonders why she would think someone whose love was perfect would entertain such a doubt. Beyond this worry, however, the second reason she discovers for keeping silent seems of even greater moment: her happiness depends on her husband and Tarolfo not coming into conflict with one another. Once again she plainly has her spouse's well-being in mind; the violent vendettas noble families in Italy often waged to prosecute their rivalries certainly justify her anxiety. But once again she has equated the knights, this time by setting alongside the care she anticipates as a consequence of her husband's suspicions the care she foresees besetting her if he and Tarolfo quarrel. When she finally concludes that she must respond to Tarolfo, the message she sends him perfectly captures her ambivalent feelings. She informs him he should woo her no more than he would be willing for her to tell her husband; to preserve her happiness she would require Tarolfo not to eliminate but to legitimate his regard, to allow her to speak its name to her husband, even as she now is speaking to him.[14]

These divided impulses are epitomized in the gift she asks for: "in the month of January, in that land, a large and beautiful garden, filled with grass and flowers and trees and fruit, as if it were the month of May" (31.8). Interestingly, just before he reports it, Menedon calls this demand "una sottile malizia" ("a clever trick"), as if he would begrudge in advance the appreciation her subtlety and guile will perforce elicit from him. Perhaps we should consider the aversion his phrase fuses with his admiration the unwarranted reflex of an underlying antifeminism. The task the lady imposes, after all, may be shrewd and a trick, but politic circumvention is precisely what the situation calls for: by means of her ploy she tells Tarolfo, who wants to supplant her husband, that she will be his when he supplants winter's cold with springtime fruitfulness. Since this is impossible ("cosa impossibile"), she is quite right to think she has hit upon a tactful way to rid herself of Tarolfo's pursuit. To the misogynist, however, her "malizia" is evidence that supports the canard that, from Eve on, women are creatures who have put their wily intelligence at the service of their desire, whether or not they intend to. For all her cageyness, it never occurs to the lady that her stratagem already tilts toward the displacing suitor because it is itself a displacement of her fear that Tarolfo will brawl with her husband. Rather than face the prospect of having her happiness impaired by one man casting out the other, she includes both: she asks for a spring garden in winter, an Eden of concinnity where May and January harmoniously cohabit with one another.[15]

On his part, Tarolfo also realizes the lady has bid him do a thing that cannot be done; despite his certainty that his efforts will be futile, he does not waver from trying. One wonders why. No doubt the thought never crosses his mind that his mistress, by obliging him to violate the order of nature to win her, wants him to consider the ineluctability of succession. Had it occurred to him that winter always precedes spring, so that even were he to conjure up a garden, it would still be January and he would be the lady's second, not her sole lover, he might well have cut his losses then and there. On the contrary, he is able to press on because he deliberately ignores the lady's intent, which he perfectly comprehends, so that he can latch on to her words; instead of accepting the impossibility of the undertaking as a sign of her unconditional refusal, he focuses exclusively on the fact that she has given him a promise. Nor is he entirely unjustified to take her pledge as grounds to disregard the fact that fulfilling it is hopeless: to his ears, the vow she gives to him must seem not merely to counterbalance the vows she gave in marriage but to replace them, for how could she suggest more clearly her desire to possess his May in the midst of her husband's January?

Still, however self-serving Tarolfo is to seize on the lady's promise and dismiss her motivation in making it, a strange idealism seems to spur his readiness to persevere in his labors and live by and for her word alone. Perhaps he truly believes undeterred devotion in the face of outright rejection is the surest proof he can give that his love is perfect. If so, this is a perfection, as we have seen, that Tarolfo, if he is to remain Tarolfo, can achieve only by not achieving the end for which he exerts himself. In order to win the lady's love, he must create the garden; but if, having created it, he requires her to keep her word and go to bed with him, the very act through which he believes he will assert himself fully as a man will also entail the surrender of his identity to her. For unless Tarolfo, who has already subjugated himself to the terms of her promise, foregoes executing it, he will become, at the moment of its execution, not the knight who has vanquished her husband in love but his doppelgänger, a second man with whom she has slept because she has sworn to love him. On hearing the lady plight her troth, Tarolfo placed all his hope in it, and none in the likelihood that his pains would bear fruit; once he has produced the garden, he will discover that her promise, rather than offering an escape clause from the impossible, somehow has bound him both to honor her intent in asking for it and to ignore his purpose in creating it. Tarolfo will have to be content to discover himself, as a good knight should, entirely in the deed he has done—a fitting lesson for someone who was so bent on separating task from vow. But even his deed, he is about to learn, is less his own than the lady's, because the garden he has had made will not be the scene where he perfects his quest to call himself her lover but the place where he promises to continue to deny himself as lover. Once he has entered the woman's world of words and vows, Tarolfo finds it impossible to break free from their power to determine who Tarolfo is.

Because Menedon's *quistione* turns out to be about gendered, aristocratic identity at least as much as it is about *liberalità*, I think it is important to italicize the misogyny that underwrites his story. The lady exists within the confines of silence and speech; moreover, what she says or chooses not to say exerts a control over men that endangers their authority to define themselves as men. Boccaccio sought to contain this threat in a number of ways, the most obvious of which, of course, was to put antifeminist sentiments in the mouth of Fiammetta, the *donna* who decides this and the other *quistioni d'amore*. A more subtle transposition of the tale's distrust of womanly influence can be found in the specific circumstances that inspire Tarolfo to release his mistress from her vow.

After the lady visits the garden, which she thinks delightful, she returns home heavy-hearted. She repeatedly deflects her husband's questions about what has dispirited her until finally she breaks her silence and reveals her pact and the reasons she made it. The husband acknowledges her purity of heart and directs her to go to her admirer:

Va, e copertamente serva il tuo giuramento, e a Tarolfo ciò che tu promettisti liberamente attieni: egli l'ha ragionevolmente e con grande affanno guadagnato. (31.44)

> Go, and keep your oath in secret, and hold to what you promised to
> Tarolfo freely; he has rightfully earned it with great toil.

The husband's generosity in according rights to those who have no true claim
to them is remarkable. He grants contractual weight to his wife's "giuramento" even though it has no legal traction: as Fiammetta will soon affirm,
a wife is part of her husband and therefore cannot enter into a binding
agreement without his consent; furthermore, a second oath cannot vacate
the obligations of a previous one. Since the wife had sworn fidelity with her
marriage vows, she could not validly bind herself to any venture that would
compromise her chastity (34.2). Presumably the husband is aware of these
points as well; he is prepared to ignore them because he feels pressed by a
more urgent necessity—the need to reestablish the proper order of language
in his household. His wife's promise, after all, has put his name as husband
at risk, if only because it has limited his response to "go" or "stay." By com-
manding her to go and do what she vowed to do, he counters in kind; he
gives his consent the form of an imperative that allows him to ratify what she
has sworn at the same time that he disavows her license to swear it. By si-
lencing the protests she goes on to make, he does more than repay his wife's
previous silences to him; his charge proves him her husband because his word
controls her as sexual body.

    Only someone supremely confident of his standing as husband would
direct his spouse to commit adultery "liberamente"—"liberally, freely, openly,
willingly." Yet in the same sentence he enjoins her to act secretly ("copertamente"). One doubts he would so quickly contradict himself unless he were
equally eager to cover in silence the disgrace he knows the name of cuckold would bring him. The conjunction is strange; it suggests that the shame
he risks by sending his wife, rather than being at odds with his husbandly as-
surance, is somehow part of it. By affirming that Tarolfo's hard-won success
has entitled him to the reward he was promised, the husband openly endorses
the idea of interchangeability that his wife's silences, her promise, and her
request for a May garden in January hinted at: Tarolfo, he feels, should gain
her love because he has shown that his love is as perfect as his own. The husband seems actually to want to see Tarolfo as a version of himself, and for
good reason; by doing so, he domesticates his wife's ambiguous wishes by
casting himself as their object, no matter which man they tend toward. But
there is, one senses, a deeper, more equivocal insecurity that drives his willingness to command his own cuckolding; he wants to reclaim the chivalric
masculinity he lost when he married. In Tarolfo he sees a stand-in for his

former self, the self he was when he still bore his name as knight. The husband orders his wife to go to Tarolfo, it appears, both as a consequence of his perfect love for her and to reimburse himself for what it has cost him.

When the wife understood what her husband wanted, she adorned and made herself beautiful and went with her retinue ("e presa compagnia," 31.46) to Tarolfo's dwelling. She tells her happy but startled lover that she has come to place herself totally at his pleasure. He responds, "You astonish me to no end, considering the hour you have come and the company with you; this could not be unless something unheard-of has occurred ('sanza novità stata' 31.48) between you and your husband. Tell me what it is." She then unfolds the entire story to Tarolfo "tutta per ordine." On hearing it, Tarolfo is moved to release her from her vow:

> Gentil donna, lealmente e come valorosa donna avete il vostro dovere servato, per la qual cosa io ho per ricevuto ciò che io di voi desiderava." (31.50)

> Gentle lady, you have kept your "devoir" loyally and like a woman of valor, for which reason I hold as received that which I desired of you.

Tarolfo's quitclaim is as curious as the husband's fiat. He begins by recognizing the lady's loyalty and worthiness. The adverbs he uses imply that he in fact takes her dutifulness as directed to himself as much as to her husband: "lealmente" refers to the fidelity with which she will discharge her promise to him in addition to the steadfastness of her love for her spouse; "come valorosa donna" describes the way she honors her commitments even as it identifies her with the woman of valor of Proverbs. But in the second part of the phrase, where Tarolfo would acknowledge her virtues as the cause ("per la qual cosa") of the handsome act he is about to perform, he, like the husband whose generosity he imitates, all but erases her presence. Instead of saying "I consider you to have done what you gave your word to do," he emphasizes that it was his love that furnished the occasion for her to fulfill her pledge, and that he alone has the authority to declare she has redeemed it. At the moment he agrees to check his desires, Tarolfo feels compelled to assert his authenticity, not only as paramour—by implying that his passion, instead of enthralling him to the lady's demand, has invented it—but also as the co-husband he fancies himself, by forgetting how long he was debtor to her promise and accentuating that he now has the power to call it paid. In each instance, like the husband, he reestablishes his selfhood by denying her agency. And, like her husband, in each instance he denies her agency by ascribing to himself control over the binding force of the vow she has taken.

The inconsistency in Tarolfo's explanation is a signal that his liberality is an attempt to compensate for having twice subjected himself, first to the impossible task of satisfying the wife's wish, then to the impossibility of satisfying his own. He tries to negotiate a way out of this crisis of selfhood by confessing that her story has made him appreciate her husband's great munificence; then, after thinking to himself that "anyone who thought of behaving like a churl ('pensasse villania') to so generous a man would deserve the gravest reproach" (31.49), he tells the wife that she should return to her husband, thank him for acting so graciously, and excuse his folly, which he will never repeat (31.50). These courtesies will allow Tarolfo to keep his name, but they are hardly the first fruits of a new-found virtue; Tarolfo acts as he does to save face. He cannot sleep with the wife either as knight or as lover because neither the garden, which he commissioned but did not make, nor her promise, has brought her to him. She appears at his "ostiere" because her husband has ordered her to go there; her coming, by day one assumes, and the retinue that accompanies her, alert Tarolfo that she is not the prize his vigor and enterprise have won but a *gift* the husband is presenting to him. His self-pride will not let him take her under these terms; but the terms themselves show yet again that masculinity in this story is constituted less through the possession and domination of women than through the knights' anxious attempts to recover prerogatives they consider their birthright but which wives and mistresses, by subtlety or trick, have somehow dispossessed them of. The garden that Tarolfo travels the globe seeking knowledge to create is a paradise where he can imagine himself an unalienated Adam.

To this point I have said nothing of Tebano, the magician who does fabricate this fantastic projection of male and male-imagined female desire. Like the other characters in Menedon's story, he is a compound of contrary tendencies. As with Tarolfo, the very fact that he has a name is noteworthy. "Io sono di Tebe, e Tebano è il mio nome" ("I come from Thebes and Tebano is my name," 31.13), he informs the knight, as if to say "I am ocular proof of Dante's dictum that words are the consequence of things:[16] one knows who I am as soon as one learns where I come from." Yet on first seeing him, Tarolfo is unsure whether he can call him a man at all. Tebano is simple and utterly without contrivance, yet he instructs Tarolfo that surface appearances may bear no relation to inner worth. He wears the vilest garments but harbors precious knowledge within his soul. He makes a virtue of his poverty, yet is eager to be freed from want. He wanders in Thessaly on the plains of Pharsalia, yet instead of Erichtho's monstrous necromancy and internecine combat, which the setting is patently meant to recall, his magic conjures up prodigies of generosity. He dominates the story—the description of his Medea-like flight revels in its eye-catching virtuosity and is far longer than the accounts of the events that frame it—yet he plainly is not the focal point of attention.[17]

No doubt Tebano is Boccaccio's surrogate in the tale, the spokesman through whom he articulates his own qualities and those of his fiction. In Tebano we see both the romancer, whose *alta fantasia* delights in its capacity to make consorts of May and January, and the ethical proto-humanist, whose erudition invites readers to set chivalric economies of selfhood and gendered relations against their dark, classical counterparts, the autochthony and incest of Thebes and the atrocious depravities of Roman civil war. In Tebano we also see Boccaccio in Naples, quietly sure of himself and his art, but impoverished and not entirely embraced by an Acciaiuoli he fully expected would be his great patron. Certainly the alacrity with which Tebano accepts Tarolfo's pledge of half his castles and their treasures would seem to bespeak a hope that Niccolò, himself a newly named aristocrat, will prove his soul as lofty as his station by rewarding the poor poet for the enchanting works he has created. And certainly the generosity Tebano shows in releasing Tarolfo from his promise should remind Acciaiuoli, like Boccaccio the illegitimate son of a merchant father, of the princely magnanimity he ought now to exemplify.[18] Indeed, the liberality Tarolfo and Tebano both exhibit provides Boccaccio the opportunity to champion the *stilnovists'* conviction that a man is ennobled by his comportment, not his birth. But Tarolfo's readiness to pawn his patrimony also reveals Boccaccio already in the process of trying to accommodate mercantile conduct and aristocratic refinement. As social commentary, of course, the *Filocolo* is not the *Decameron;* Emilia's retelling of Menedon's tale is much more rooted in the details of daily life. In the *quistione,* the balancing of promises—the lady's to Tarolfo, Tarolfo's to Tebano—still hedges its bets on the union of commerce and culture it foresees by suggesting their compatibility is a (garden-variety) reverie, as improbable a combination of incompatible things as spring flowers in the dead of winter. But for my purposes, the values Boccaccio assigns the different registers he juxtaposes is not as important as the juxtaposition itself. For the admixture of forwardness and modesty in Boccaccio's manner enacts his tale's mode of meaning, and it is this mode of meaning, I will claim, that the Franklin's Tale translates.

Artistic works always comment on the personal history, social ideologies, economic and cultural conditions that shape them; the habits and modes of production of *trecento* Italy, however, were sufficiently foreign to Londoners of Chaucer's day to make one doubt an English reader would have noticed or understood the ways in which Boccaccio's tale addresses them or is their outgrowth. Perhaps, though, thematic correspondences would have caught his eye; it takes no knowledge of Angevin Naples or time spent in communal Florence to see, for instance, that the lady, her husband, Tarolfo, and Tebano are all drawn so that they recapitulate the purpose for which Menedon tells the story. As befits a *quistione d'amore*, in which the same action elicits opposing judgments, each character behaves in a decidedly equivocal manner. Every unselfish deed in the tale serves some self-serving end. Fiammetta's arguments for the superiority of the husband's generosity may eventually silence Menedon's for Tarolfo and Tebano, but her judgment, conclusive though it seems to those who hear it, cannot settle the matter.

Chaucer's poems often foreground a like-minded resistance to definitive pronouncements; Chaucerians often point to this proclivity as a sign of Boccaccio's influence. The Franklin's version of Menedon's story appears to be a case in point: it ends, after all, with a question, not a verdict. But the distinguishing feature of the *quistioni* in the *Filocolo* is that they do end with verdicts; even when—as in the tale of the husband, wife, and Tarolfo—"pro" and "con" can look to the same evidence for support, Fiammetta still arbitrates the issue at hand.[19] Precisely because the Franklin refrains from offering arguments, his query distances Chaucer from Boccaccio at the same time that it establishes a connection with him.

In the *Filocolo*, as in the *Filostrato*, the love debates are self-conscious interventions in Italian literary history; both are part of Boccaccio's ongoing project to submit the high-minded psychologism of the *stil novo* to rhetorical scrutiny. In place of lyrical self-absorption in the metaphysical beauty of the beloved, Boccaccio substituted a more instrumental passion in which idealism always collides and colludes with self-interest. Instead of fixing the soul's eye on a perfection of being against which all things are measured, love in Boccaccio moves people in ways no single standard of valuation can assess. Guinizzelli and Cavalcanti, with very different effect, had shifted the location of Amor's court from aristocratic romance to the sessions of an enthralled mind in conversation with itself; Dante had transported it to the visionary consistory of the heavenly rose. Boccaccio returned it to earth, to a more forensic and ultimately a more urban arena where love's properties were debated *in utramque partem*.[20] When he called on circumstance and motive to elucidate the ways and means of *fin amour,* Boccaccio invented a new mode of meaning by having older "fourme[s] of speche ... to wynnen love" (II.22–28), as the narrator of the *Troilus* calls them, and the probative protocols of civic alliance interrogate and supplement one another in unexpected ways.

Chaucer was equally aware of the importance of motive and circumstance, but he culled their operations from different literary traditions and conceptualized their influence in different ways. The Franklin ends his tale with a *demande d'amour* because he associates it with French, aristocratic romance. He has heard the Knight conclude the first part of his tale with such a *demande;* he now presents his own, at least in part to show his wayward heir, so unlike the Squire, that his father is indeed a man from whom he can learn the fair forms of courtly discourse. At the same time, though, the Franklin directs his question not exclusively to "yow loveres," as the Knight had (I.1347), but to "Lordynges" (V.1621), by whom he clearly means all the men on the pilgrimage.[21] In keeping with his earlier exchange with Harry Bailly, the Franklin feels every man-child's blood is blue enough to warrant cultivation of those graceful manners that are the mark of good breeding.[22]

Like the lady and Tarolfo in Menedon's tale, the Franklin's predilections run in opposite directions; like the debate in the *Filocolo,* the fact that he asks a question is freighted with literary and social import. Unlike Boccaccio's characters, however, whose words, whether inside or outside his tale, disclose the ways in which gender ironically destabilizes sexual identity, the Franklin's *demande* betrays the precariousness of identity based on rank. As an *arriviste* to the gentility he is so eager to propagate, the Franklin would want to shy away from rating one character's generosity over another's, because to discriminate between their deeds would be to acknowledge that benevolence has its degrees. And if the virtues have their distinctions, then truly noble acts can be differentiated from those merely accounted noble. By forbearing to say who "was the mooste fre" (V.1622), the Franklin keeps at a safe distance the anxieties that grading might cause a prosperous man still accustoming himself to the attitudes of personages of note.

At the same time, the Franklin's circumspection allows him to display the "fredom" he possesses in abundance. By favoring neither Arveragus nor Aurelius nor the clerk of Orleans, Chaucer's worthy "vavasour" proves himself untouched by that narrowness of empathy he believes is incommensurate with the open-armed hospitality of a gentleman. Throughout his tale, the Franklin has maintained a liberal impartiality by bestowing on each character a plentiful portion of his own values and enthusiasms; he is therefore quite content to have the pilgrims appraise the height of their generosity because no matter whom they choose, they will choose the Franklin as well. He may not be able to respond to his *demande* without discomfiting his sense of who he is, but he can eagerly pose the question to others because he has already established himself as its answer.

In relation to Boccaccio's novella, the Franklin's closing query is thus part of the *"niente che c'è"* that makes his tale a translation, whether or not Chaucer read the fourth book of the *Filocolo*. The absence of any verbal parry in the English version highlights the incongruity of its presence in the Italian. Whatever we may think of his idea of nobility, the Franklin does make us suspect that there is something ungenerous in making generosity the subject of debate.[23] But even if we decide, as I think we should, that it is not outside the spirit of liberality to calibrate its amplitude, the fact that Boccaccio's knights and ladies insist on doing so will suggest, now more than before, that the matter truly at issue for them is one in which making and maintaining distinctions is crucial. For Menedon, that issue, as we have seen, concerns the subtle tricks of women that induce men to lose their name to love. Against the backdrop of the Franklin's uncharacteristic reluctance to speak his mind at the end of his tale, Menedon's *quistione* no longer seems innocent or neutral; he has aligned his story with a form of argument whose power to enforce differences has a history of having adjudicated other differences, such as the prerogatives claimed by men and women, in men's favor. The *domanda*, we begin to understand, is already prejudiced towards Menedon's wish to preserve and justify masculine predominance over the maidens and wives who threaten it.

By silhouetting Menedon's deeper fears, in other words, the Franklin's reticence exposes the give and take of seemingly disinterested debate as an agent of Menedon's unexpressed desires. The Franklin's reticence, that is to say, disarticulates the mode of meaning of the *quistione* in the *Filocolo* by revealing the antagonism between the scholastic and the rhetorical analysis of love that the story marries together. Fiammetta's arguments carry the day because they appeal to abstract principles. At the same time, the actions those abstract principles are meant to explain are sufficiently motivated by masculine anxiety to make us aware that ulterior intentions, whether premeditated or unacknowledged, can always conscript a discussion before it takes place.

More specifically, Chaucer's tale makes visible Boccaccio's need to remain loyal to *stilnovism* even when he is most skeptical. With the Franklin, ideas and motives comprise the man; they do not float free from the figure who enacts them but are embedded as his ruling disposition. In the *Filocolo*, motives and ideas tend to be considered as such; at least in the debate between Menedon and Fiammetta, generosity has its own discrete qualities against which the characters' behavior is judged. Yet the more rationally Fiammetta makes her case (for the husband), the more, Boccaccio and his audience would agree, she contends like a man. The same habit of mind, one realizes, that has labeled the lady's request a "sottile malizia" grants Fiammetta her triumphs. In the tale, the cleverness of the gift the unnamed wife asks for corroborates misogynistic stereotypes; in the disputation that follows, Fiammetta's intelligence divorces her from her supposed nature as woman. By cloaking her judgments in the heightened idiom of the *stil novo,* Boccaccio thus gilds the ungenerous conceit that permits him to endow her with such "virile" authority. Especially in the case of Menedon's tale, he had to; otherwise his readers might too readily notice that Boccaccio circumscribes the efficacy of Fiammetta's ruling in precisely the same manner that Tarolfo and the husband circumscribed the force of the wife's vow.

If the Franklin's smudging the borders of social distinction translates Menedon's longing to prosper in a world where the hierarchies that order the sexes are clear, Boccaccio's *quistione* in turn exposes how class subsumes gender in Chaucer's tale. The Franklin's epicureanism and Dorigen's complaint have not often been considered in tandem. From the perspective of the *Filocolo,* however, their conjunction seems an extraordinary transposition of Boccaccio's classicism. Like Cavalcante de' Cavalcanti in the *Inferno,* the denial of the immortality of the soul, which Dante made the hallmark of "Epicurio" and "tutti suoi seguaci" (*Inf.*10:14), has caused the Franklin to focus all his attention and hope on his son: the repressed unease that inevitably attends the absence of belief in an afterlife emerges as his all-too-evident obsession to live his life again through his child. The Franklin's consternation over his heir's profligacy is undoubtedly a version of aristocratic anxieties about succession; the "gentilesse" that would reincarnate him in his son, however, is not something his scion was born with and is squandering but something his father thinks he can acquire by "communing" with "gentil wight[s]." The Franklin wants to bequeath his nobility, yet he cannot express this desire by appealing to the vocabulary of lineage, since to do so would be to declare himself a late-come sir. In the *Filocolo*, the husband embodied the paradox that marriage, the institution by which well-born families preserved their names, was also the institution that deprived the knight of his. In the Franklin's exchange with the Squire, the elision of genealogy, which itself at heart is an elision of women, permits Chaucer to exhibit the paradox of the new man whose name and status seem at once consubstantial and adopted, fitting and misfitted to each other.

It is Dorigen's lament, however, that brings to the surface the suppressed gender relations on which the Franklin has founded his social identity. To steel her resolution to kill herself rather than compromise her chastity, Dorigen invokes virgins like Phidon's daughters; only later does she turn to wives like Lucretia. Because she cites so many suicides of each kind, one feels that Dorigen needs to see herself as both maiden and spouse. Like the lady in Menedon's story, she is desperately seeking a way to accommodate conflicting roles; however, instead of doubling as faithful paramour and bride, as the *donna* in the *Filocolo* tries to do, Dorigen's fidelity requires her to believe she must first merge the self she is as Arveragus's wife with the self she was when she was unmarried and then annihilate both. In the *Filocolo*, the lady asked Tarolfo to create an impossible space in which she could simultaneously honor and sidestep the bonds of her marriage vows; by affiliating herself with virgin martyrs, Dorigen identifies her own impossible place of escape, a past in which she was intact and whole and a future in which she will remain unblemished and faultless as a loyal wife who preferred death to breaching her chastity. If the terrain Boccaccio gave women to express their selfhood was limited, the room they can call their own in the Franklin's Tale has shrunk to the size of a tomb.

The slant of light Menedon's tale casts on the Franklin's illuminates the underpinnings of his "fredom." In the *quistione*, Tebano is medium as well as magician; through him Boccaccio summons the classical loci of personal and political identity. From this vantage point, it becomes easier to see the identity politics that connect the Franklin's being "Epicurus owene sone" (I.335) and Dorigen's learned invocation of chaste pagans. The Franklin is able to dine with the gentry because the boundary lines of nobility in England have become negotiable; Boccaccio's tale leads us to suspect that their negotiability depended on a redoubled effort to tighten the stays on feminine liberty.

The Franklin will therefore call for reciprocity in marriage in order to remain faithful to his idea of himself; in the event, however, the "lordshipe and servage" (V.794) that he counsels husbands and wives to hold over one another, which is a marital version of his vision of a nobility that excludes no one who can afford it, is an invitation to mutuality in word alone. For all Arveragus's and Dorigen's promises, his lordship proves to be as absolute as Walter's, her submissiveness as unconditional as Griselda's in the Clerk's Tale. Consider Dorigen's other moment of self-expression, her meditation on the black rocks. Ostensibly she is so alarmed that the rocks will destroy Arveragus on his return to Brittany, she is ready to question God's wisdom in creating them. Yet she never expresses this fear directly. She does commend her lord's safety to the same God who made the wind blow, then leaves His purposes to clerks to divine and wishes the rocks "were sonken into helle for his sake" (V.892). Even if we take "his" as referring to Arveragus rather than to God (the closest antecedent), Dorigen still does not explicitly say that she hates the rocks because they could kill her husband. Her circuitousness makes her vexation more conspicuous; what is there about those rocks besides their menace that has stirred her angry dislike of them? Arveragus has abandoned her so he can joust in England; since his departure, she has been desolate. Her great anguish may well have fed an understandable resentment; the displeasure she felt, but could not blame him for causing, she here transfers to the rocks. It is, one suspects, less the rocks themselves than their stability that provokes Dorigen, for their staying power is precisely what she has learned her marriage lacks, despite Arveragus's vows. The black rocks disenchant her own and the Franklin's illusions that she is an equal in her relationship; when she asks Aurelius to make the rocks disappear, she is asking him to restore this fantasy.

Ultimately, reading Menedon's tale as a translation of the Franklin's, which in a sense is what I have tried to do these last few paragraphs, seems to me as warranted and as fruitful as reading Chaucer's tale as a version of Boccaccio's *quistione*. As I said at the start, the manner of translation I have elaborated in this essay cannot tell us whether Chaucer knew the *Filocolo* or what he did to it if he did. I have written instead about the conditions that can enable us to read two parallel texts from different cultures as translations. Wallace Stevens seems to me to have caught the essence of these conditions in the lines that I have taken as my epigraph. But rather than close this brief investigation into the "nothing that is not there, and the nothing that is" of "The Snowman," I would like to end with the words of another Italian author who has pondered the task of translation. In *Se una notte d'inverno un viaggiatore,* Italo Calvino's narrator describes his reaction as he listens to Uzzi-Tuzzi, a professor of Bothno-Ugaric Languages and Literatures, render a Cimmerian novel, *Sporgendosi dalla costa scoscesa* (Leaning out from the steep slope):

> Ascoltare poi uno che sta traducendo da un'altra lingua implica un fluttuare d'esitazione intorno alle parole, un margine d'indeterminatezza e di provvisorietà. Il testo, che quando sei tu che lo leggi è qualcosa che è lí, contro cui sei obbligato a scontrarti, quando te lo traducono a voce è qualcosa che c'è e non c'è, che non riesci a toccare. (67)[24]

> Listening to someone who is translating from another language involves a fluctuation, a hesitation over the words, a margin of indecisiveness and of the provisional. The text, when you are the reader, is something that is there, against which you are obliged to crash yourself. When someone translates it aloud to you, it is something that is there and is not there, that you are not able to touch.

To acknowledge, if not touch, the something / nothing that is there and the nothing / something that is not, is a goal I think all cross-cultural translations should intend.

Notes

1. See, for instance, Robert R. Edwards, "Rewriting Menedon's Story: *Decameron* 10.5 and the *Franklin's Tale,*" in *Chaucer and Boccaccio: Antiquity and Modernity* (New York: Palgrave, 2002), 153–72. Edwards cogently discusses the differences between Boccaccio's tales; I have therefore not discussed the story in the *Decameron* here.

2. Walter Benjamin, "The Task of the Translator," in *Illuminations,* trans. Harry Zohn (New York: Schocken, 1969), 69–82. I have silently altered some of Zohn's renderings to make them more literal.

3. I draw the following paragraphs from *Chaucer's Italian Tradition* (Ann Arbor: University of Michigan Press, 2002), in which I discuss at greater length the ideas presented here in telegraphed fashion.

4. Benjamin, "The Task of the Translator," 72.

5. Ibid., 74.

6. Here I am following the elaboration of Benjamin's point in Paul de Man's essay "Conclusions: Walter Benjamin's 'The Task of the Translator,'" in *The Resistance to Theory* (Minneapolis: University of Minnesota Press, 1986), 87–91. When *Brot* is translated as *pain*, a fundamental discrepancy is revealed between the intent to name *Brot* and the word *Brot* itself as a conglomeration of sounds and letters. In the context of Benjamin's essay, de Man notes that the word *Brot* causes him to hear *Wein* with it because Holderlin's *Brot und Wein* seems everywhere present in Benjamin's meditation. *Pain et vin*, the French equivalent, moves in an entirely different direction; if one translates the one phrase with the other, one has translated meaning but ignored the materiality of *Brot*, the mode by which the word means.

7. See further Tom Cohen, *Ideology and Inscription* (Cambridge: Cambridge University Press, 1998), 13.

8. I give here de Man's translation of this sentence, "Conclusions," 91. Benjamin's *"Art des Meinens"* is itself difficult to translate: I have used "mode" and "manner," "meaning" and "intention" interchangeably to suggest the range of choice a reader faces each time the phrase appears.

9. De Man explains the first of these disjunctions in his discussion of *Brot* and *pain:* "Conclusions," 87–91.

10. Cohen, *Ideology and Inscription*, 11.

11. All citations are from Giovanni Boccaccio, *Il Filocolo*, in *Tutte le opere di Giovanni Boccaccio*, ed. V. Branca, vol. 1 (Milan: Mondadori, 1964). Book, chapter, and sentence numbers are given in the text. Unless otherwise noted, all translations are mine.

12. Boccaccio's use of perfection in its scholastic sense, the reduction of potency to act, is I think very much in keeping with his manner of couching the *quistioni d'amore* in the elevated language of the *stil novo*. For an analysis of the way Boccaccio invokes and scrutinizes the philosophic pretensions of this language in a different *quistione*, see my "'Medium autem, et extrema sunt eiusdem generis': Boccaccio and the Shape of Writing," *Exemplaria* 5 (1993): 185–206, now rewritten and expanded in *Chaucer's Italian Tradition*, 148–89.

13. The meaning of the final clause of the lady's sentence, "se non per quanto egli non volesse che essa questo manfestasse al marito," is hard to determine: there seem to be too many negatives. Donald Cheney translates it "unless he wanted her to tell her husband about it" (Giovanni Boccaccio, *Il Filocolo*, trans. Donald Cheney with the collaboration of Thomas Bergin [New York: Garland, 1985], 255). This reading is possible, but there are two problems with it. It does not account for the "per quanto," which makes the lady's ultimatum that he no longer entice her seem somewhat less than absolute, and it contradicts the fear she has just expressed that her happiness would be compromised by the quarrel she foresees if her husband hears about Tarolfo's courtship. I think the clause is better rendered as "except to the ex-

tent that he would be willing she reveal to her husband." The difficulty with this translation is the "non" of "non volesse." I take it as pleonastic, triggered by the comparison that is implied in "per quanto"—a common Italian usage. The important point for my analysis, however, is that in either version the lady qualifies her discouragement enough for Tarolfo to find reason to continue his pursuit.

14. By sending an intermediary to Tarolfo, the lady continues to distinguish and equate him and her husband. She distinguishes him by speaking to him, but through a messenger, which enables her, at least in a technical sense, to remain silent, and thus by extension, faithful to herself and her husband. A corresponding moment with her husband occurs later in the tale. After Tarolfo has created the garden, she resists telling her husband her dilemma, again fearing he might think she was wicked; finally she yields to his constant questioning. She here confirms her fidelity by revealing everything to her husband; but the way he obtained her confession, by constantly importuning her, makes him another Tarolfo, whose relentless entreaties had caused the lady to speak to him unwillingly in the first place.

15. The copresence of January and May is underscored by the repetition of phrases in the lady's request: ". . . volea del mese di gennaio. . . . come se del mese di maggio fosse . . ." (31, 8).

16. I am referring, of course, to the famous statement (itself a scholastic commonplace), in the *Vita nuova:* "nomina sunt consequentia rerum" (13.4) .

17. On all these aspects, see the sensitive comments of Steven Grossvogel, *Ambiguity and Allusion in Boccaccio's Filocolo* (Florence: Olschki, 1992), 212–29.

18. In later life, Boccaccio would definitely look back with disappointment at how pusillanimous Acciaiuoli proved to be. See his bitter letter to Francesco Nelli (XII), which Vittore Branca discusses in *Boccaccio: The Man and His Works,* trans. R. Monges (New York: New York University Press, 1976), 135–37.

19. Even in the *Decameron,* where Emilia closes her narrative by asking "amorevoli donne" for their opinions ("che direm qui?"), she immediately begs the question by declaring Ansaldo's liberality so great, she thinks it makes any comparison ridiculous.

20. I discuss the importance of the *argumentum in utramque partem* for Boccaccio in *The Cast of Character* (Toronto: University of Toronto Press, 1983), 98–133. In the *Filocolo,* Boccaccio's *quistioni,* of course, take French *demandes d'amour* as their model. But Boccaccio stages his debates differently from the way, say, Machaut conducts his; already in the *Filocolo* and the *Filostrato* he has, I would argue, laid claim to the informing principles of Roman rhetoric.

21. All quotations of *The Canterbury Tales* are from *The Riverside Chaucer,* 3rd ed., gen. ed., Larry D. Benson (Boston: Houghton Mifflin, 1987), and are given their fragment number and line number within the text. That the Franklin's "Lordynges" seems naturally to elide the women in the company forecasts, for me, the way Arveragus subsumes Dorigen's wishes in his own.

22. For the Franklin, as for Chaucer, the pedigree of these marks of good breeding, of course, is French. Perhaps this "vavasour" wants to exhibit this aspect of his "curteisie" when he identifies his tale as a Breton lay. If he does, Chaucer wittily causes his display of polish to tarnish itself in the showing.

23. One might compare here *Decameron* 10.3, the story of the competition between Nathan and Mithridanes.

24. Italo Calvino, *Se una notte d'inverno un viaggiatore* (Turin: Einaudi, 1979). I have slightly altered the translation of William Weaver, *If on a Winter's Night a Traveller* (Toronto: Key Porter Books, 1995).

18

JOAN M. FERRANTE

Women in the Shadows of the *Divine Comedy*

Towards the end of his canto-long speech on the history of the Roman empire, the emperor Justinian praises another soul in the heaven of Mercury, Romeo de Villeneuve, whose work was "grande e bella." That work was to arrange the marriages of the four daughters of Count Raymond Berengar of Provence to four kings:

> Quattro figlie ebbe, e ciascuna reina,
> Ramondo Beringhiere, e ciò li fece
> Romeo, persona umile e peregrina (Par.6.133–35).[1]

> Four daughters he had, and each a queen,
> Raymond Berengar, and that was accomplished for him
> by Romeo, a humble pilgrim.

Dante focuses on the legendary aspect of the humble servant who was believed to have been, like him, falsely accused and exiled. He makes little in this passage of the striking fact that the four daughters of a count all became queens, except that by including it with the history of the empire, he seems to suggest that those marriages uniting different lands into one family might serve the cause of empire. Though alliance by marriage may seem a passive peace-weaving role for women, the women in this extraordinary family were far from passive in contemporary affairs, while many of the men in the family were more passive than they should have been, as their appearance among the negligent princes in Purgatory 7 indicates. There is good reason to think that Dante knew a good deal about the history of the family of Savoy—Beatrice of Savoy was the mother of the four queens—from the attention he gives it in the *Comedy* (in Purgatory 7 as well as Paradise 6). If Dante is indeed using this family, which was deeply involved in contemporary European politics, to make political points, he may also be assuming his audience's awareness of women in the family to give added dimension to his treatment of a woman who is not in the shadows of the *Comedy:* Beatrice. Beatrice is a name with powerful political resonances in Italian history, and Dante may well be evoking many of those resonances in the figure of his guide and personal savior.

I will suggest what Dante and his contemporaries might have known about the women he alludes to, drawing on contemporary documents, primarily letters to (or from) them. Letters are more likely to reveal what women were actually involved in than historic accounts, which may only reveal what the author wants his audience to think.[2] I have suggested elsewhere that, while he may speak as a misogynist moralist in Hell, Dante shows women in positive roles in Purgatory and Paradise, as examples of virtue, as counterbalances to the violence and corruption of men, and as models and guides.[3] His God has a female side, male souls are described in the feminine or identified by their wives, men identify with female relatives. Family is the important unit in Purgatory, where the queens' male relatives appear, and women represent family.

In order to set the stage for what Dante does with the family of Savoy in the *Comedy*, I want to say something about two other historic women, not members of that family but women whose roles in history and in the *Comedy* are well known to the audience. Clare of Assisi and Matelda of Tuscany stand on their own as striking examples of good lives in the *Comedy*, and their positions in the poem make it more likely that Dante and his audience were aware of the women in the family of Savoy. The only human being who is said to have lived a perfect life in the *Comedy* is St. Clare: "Perfetta vita e alto merto inciela / donna più sù," "perfect life and high merit enheavens a lady higher up" (Par.3.97–98). Clare is another woman who does not appear in person, but Dante knew her as a follower of Francis, and probably knew that she struggled with the papacy to remain true to Francis's teachings and encouraged others to do the same. She exchanged letters with Agnes of Prague (daughter of Ottokar/Otakar I, king of Bohemia, and aunt of the Ottokar II who appears in Purg.7). Agnes, who might have married the emperor Frederick II but chose to found a monastery and bring Clare's rule to eastern Europe, looked to Clare not only as a model, but as a source for the authentic teaching of St. Francis on poverty and fasting (ep.3). Clare, who had her own struggles with the pope, found support in the princess's unswerving devotion to the ideal of poverty.[4] Clare praises Agnes for having chosen Christ rather than the emperor as her spouse (ep.1) and encourages her to remain true to the propertiless status of her house, despite the pope's interference: "Indeed, if someone tells you something else or suggests anything to you that may hinder your perfection and that seems contrary to your divine vocation, even though you must respect him, still, do not follow his advice (ep.2.17)."[5] Dante certainly sympathized with Clare's stand against the pope and her devotion to poverty, which he describes as Francis's lover in Paradise 11.74.

Matelda, the figure who presides over Dante's earthly paradise, is another woman who stands on her own both in the poem and in history. First seen quite literally "in the perpetual shade" on the other side of the stream "sotto l'ombra perpetüa" (Purg.28.32), Matelda remains figuratively in the shadows, nameless through most of her time on stage.[6] But when the name comes (from Beatrice in Purg.33.119), it carries great significance. Dante's earliest commentators (for example, his son Pietro di Dante, Jacopo della Lana, the Ottimo, Benvenuto da Imola) identified her without hesitation as Countess Matelda of Tuscany, the major imperial feudatory emperor in Italy, a cousin of Emperor Henry IV, and the major secular supporter of the reform papacy. The role Dante assigns Matelda is appropriate to the historic countess. He argues in the *Monarchy* that man has two goals with a guide appointed for each: the emperor is needed to lead mankind to temporal happiness, figured in the earthly paradise; the pope to eternal happiness in heaven (Par.3.16). Matelda was an effective ruler who not only provided moral, political, military, and financial support to the reform papacy and fought corruption in the church in her territory, but who also firmly exercised her secular powers by presiding over courts, making judgments in cases involving laymen and religious, and putting down rebellions. And she mediated between the popes she supported and her cousin, the emperor.[7] She is a most suitable figure to represent secular power in harmony with religious teaching.

Matelda seriously considered giving up the world, but at the strong encouragement of Pope Gregory VII, Anselm of Canterbury, and John of

Mantua—who all told her that her work in the world was too important for her to leave it—she continued to rule until her death in 1115 at age 69. In his commentary on the Song of Songs, which she had asked him to write, John of Mantua encourages her to action as well as contemplation, emphasizing her role as a secular ruler. He tells her that earthly powers are established to protect men from the devil's agents, that their love of justice and their power comes from God. As a most prudent "virago" who terrifies her subjects, she must not be distressed that she has to bear arms as well as to contemplate, to supply with her sword when the word does not prevail. The sword of Peter must be employed in the cause of justice but exercised in concert with the authority of Peter, since the pope fights heresy with the sword of heaven, Matelda with the sword of the world.[8]

In Dante's poem, Matelda introduces him to the earthly paradise, the place meant to be home for the human race ("questo luogo eletto / all'umana natura per suo nido" [Purg.28.77–78]), describing it as free from the [weather] disturbances that make "war" on man below, because in the earthly paradise all is in harmony with God's will (Purg.28.100). She leads Dante to, and focuses his attention on, the procession of Bible authors (Purg.29) preceding Beatrice, who is heralded as the bride of the Canticles, as Christ, and as emperor (Purg.30.11, 19, 21). Beatrice confesses Dante; Matelda supports Dante when he faints, bathes him in Lethe to forget his sins, and brings him to the cardinal virtues. She also leads Dante and his fellow poet Statius—the countess was a patron of letters—to the tree of justice to watch the drama of church-state relations (Purg.32), to see the monster the church becomes when it is corrupted by secular power, and to hear the prophecy of an imperial heir destined to destroy that corruption. Finally, at Beatrice's request, she takes Dante to drink the waters of Eunoe, to remember good done so he can act in the world. Her words, the last spoken by a character in Purgatory, are addressed to Statius, but they are presumably an invitation to all Dante's audience, all potential inhabitants of the restored earthly paradise: "Vien con lui" (Purg.33.135).

Beatrice's role in this long episode is even more important, suggesting Christ in history, through his bride, the uncorrupt church, and his chosen governor, the Roman emperor; and Matelda is her vicar. It is an interesting coincidence, but surely more than coincidence to Dante, that the historic Matelda ruled with her mother, "Duke" Beatrice, 1069–76, until her mother's death.[9] In the poem, Matelda's realm, like the emperor's, is the earthly paradise; Beatrice, like the pope, will guide Dante to the heavenly paradise, functioning as priest, confessing Dante, teaching him theology. She may represent theology and the reformed papacy, and she is certainly a woman who inspired his love and poetry, but she also has a political function, perhaps less obvious than her other roles. Her first appearance to Dante in the earthly paradise culminates in her prediction about an emperor and the corrupt papacy, the eagle's heir who will kill the whore (Purg.33.38–45); and her last words in the poem point out the place in the rose that awaits an emperor, Henry VII, and the hole in hell that awaits a pope, Boniface VIII (Par.30.133–48).

The political aspect of Dante's Beatrice may be enhanced by the historic Beatrices the name evokes: one of them Matelda's mother, another the empress of Frederick I and mother of Henry VI, who brought the empire into southern Italy when he married Constance, heiress of Sicily. Constance appears in Dante's Paradise and she too was the daughter of a Beatrice. But it is the more contemporary Beatrice of Savoy, mother of the four queens, and a number of her relatives also named Beatrice, who are likely to have fired Dante's imagination. Beatrice of Savoy was the daughter of Thomas of Savoy, named imperial vicar of all Italy by Frederick II in 1226, and Marguerite of Geneva, from whom she inherited lands she would rule in the Alps. (See genealogy of the Savoy family for the various members of the family mentioned in this discussion.) Many of her relatives, male and female, were involved in the affairs of northern Italy. Beatrice became countess of Provence by marriage to Raymond Berengar V, with whom she had the four daughter-queens: Marguerite married Louis IX, king of France; Eleanor, Henry III, king of England; Sanchia, Henry's brother Richard of Cornwall, later king of the Romans; and Beatrice (her father's heir in Provence), Louis's brother, Charles of Anjou, later king of Sicily. Meanwhile, Beatrice's brothers became counts or archbishops, or both—Philip who had been named archbishop of Lyon left the church to be count of Savoy and marry a countess-palatine. One brother, Boniface, became archbishop of Canterbury while his niece was queen of England; another, Thomas, married first Countess Joan of Flanders, then Beatrice dei Fieschi, niece of Pope Innocent IV and sister of Pope Hadrian V, the soul who dominates Purgatory 19.[10] All of them, male and female, were deeply involved and skilled in European politics and diplomacy.

Beatrice dei Fieschi, second wife of the younger Thomas of Savoy and mother of the count of Savoy Amadeo V (1285–1323), who ruled for most of Dante's lifetime, had to deal with the difficult situation in Piedmont while her husband was held prisoner for nineteen months and, after he died, when

Extended Family of the House of Savoy

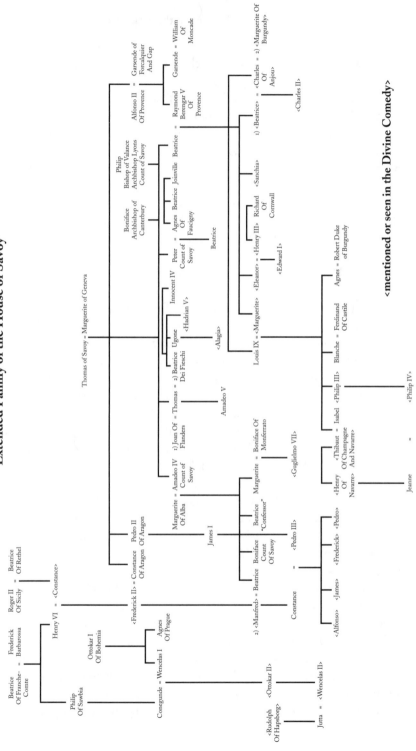

<mentioned or seen in the Divine Comedy>

her sons were still held hostage. When Pope Clement IV tried to claim some of their possessions for the bishop of Torino, she ignored a long series of papal summonses—in some cases, the bearers were afraid to deliver them directly to her—as well as the threat of excommunication, until the pope died. Dante would have approved that kind of opposition to secular claims by the church. She is the last of the women in the family who, as Cox puts it, by their "energy and intelligence did much to keep enemies in the Alps at bay" while the men were occupied elsewhere.[11]

Other Beatrices in the family include nieces: Beatrice, "Contesson," daughter of Amadeo IV, a nun; and her sister, Beatrice of Saluzzo (by her first marriage), who married Manfredi, the illegitimate son of Frederick II and his heir in Sicily. Manfredi, who appears in Purgatory 3, sends a message to their daughter Constance. Yet another Beatrice, daughter of Peter and Agnes of Faucigny, inherited Faucigny from her mother but was challenged by one of her father's brothers and by her mother's sister. She fought indefatigably if only partly successfully for her inheritance on a large European stage throughout the 1270s and 1280s.[12] The youngest of the four queens was also a Beatrice. She was her father's designated heir to Provence, but her story is overshadowed by the actions of her husband, Charles of Anjou, who alienated her sisters and their mother by refusing to recognize their claims in Provence.

The claims of the mother, Beatrice of Savoy, were based on her husband's will. Raymond Berengar, count of Provence, had left her the usufruct of the county for her lifetime, though he left the county itself to their daughter. The struggle continued for many years, with Beatrice forming "the nucleus of a powerful anti-Angevin party"[13] from her base in lands her husband had left her, Forcalquier and Gap, which had been his mother's. Those lands Beatrice ruled directly from 1245 to 1256. The conflict over the usufruct of Provence was settled finally by arbitration; the decision acknowledged the legitimacy of her claim but awarded two-thirds of the income to Charles, the de facto ruler.[14] It was only after Beatrice had spent some time in the French court with her daughter and son-in-law, Marguerite and Louis IX, that she agreed to a large payment (of 5,000 Turin pounds) in return for surrendering her territories in Provence. But not trusting Charles, she insisted the money be paid through his brother, Louis.

Beatrice, who was skilled in financial matters as well as diplomacy, did not have such problems with her other sons-in-law. She persuaded Henry III to lend her husband 4,000 marks on the security of five castles in

Provence, which she controlled after Raymond's death, refusing to release them to Charles until Henry did so in 1257. While she was in England for the marriage of her daughter Sanchia to Richard of Cornwall, she persuaded Henry to grant his sister's husband, Simon de Montfort, a yearly stipend of 500 marks, since there had been no marriage portion. Henry also endowed Beatrice with an annual stipend of 400 pounds and grants of property. In the lands her mother left her, Beatrice worked to improve travel conditions in the Alps, repairing and building roads and bridges. But in 1255, when her brother Thomas was captured by citizens of Asti, her loyalty to him made her close the Piedmont routes through her territory and arrest the "Lombards" who came through.[15] The importance of family concerns for Beatrice is clear from provisions in her will that leave sums to a number of nieces, including a nun, to be paid when they married.[16]

How much of her history Dante knew, I cannot say, but he probably had some idea of the struggle she and her daughters had with Charles over Provence. He may allude to that in the remarks Hugh Capet makes about the "gran dote provenzale," the great Provençal dowry that was the beginning of rapine by force and fraud (Purg.20.61–65). He must have known some of the compliments paid her by Provençal poets.

Attributed to Giraut de Borneil:

Pro contess'es qui Proenza mante
Et tot lo mal i fai tornar en be,
Caps es de pretz e caps de cortesia,
Per q'en val mais Savoia e Lombardia![17]

An excellent countess is she who is the mainstay of Provence
and who turns all evil there to good;
supreme is she in renown and supreme in courtliness,
so that Savoy and Lombardy increase in worth.

Sordello:

"En Sordell, e qe'us es semblan
de la pro comtessa prezan? . . ."

. . . .

"Peire Gilhem, per far mon dan,
mes Dieus en leis tot son afan

e las beutatz qe autras an
son nientz, e'l pretz es menutz"

"Sir Sordello, what do you think
About the good, highly thought of countess? . . ."

. . . .

"Peter William, God put all his care
Into fashioning her for my loss,
And the beauties that other women have
Are nil, and their worth minute."[18]

Aimeric de Belenoi:

Venjes las en la pros comtessa fina
De Proensa, on a tota valor[19]

Let her avenge them on him, the worthy and noble countess
of Provence, where all merit lies.

And another by Aimeric de Belenoi:

De la comtessa Beatris non poiria
Tan de ben dir, que mais en lieis no'sia:
Qu'en lieis ha Dieus tan de ben ajustat,
Com per part n'a a las autras donat.[20]

Of the countess Beatrice, one could not
say so much good that it would not be surpassed in her;
for in her God has brought together so much good
that he has only divided among others.

Elias de Barjols who had been at the court of Provence in the time of Raymond's father Alfonso, wrote poems for both countesses of Provence, Raymond's mother Garsenda, herself a poet,[21] and Beatrice, as well as one for Beatrice's mother.[22] He calls Beatrice "the noblest lady that can be seen," whom worth chooses for best,[23] the most beautiful of the ladies seen in the world,[24] and he praises her good sense and lovely bearing.[25]

Dante certainly knew about Beatrice's daughters, the four queens. He mentions the youngest, Beatrice, by name to identify her husband Charles

418 JOAN M. FERRANTE

(Purg.7.128). The two oldest, Marguerite, queen of France, and Eleanor, queen of England, who died in the 1290s, were still active during Dante's lifetime. How much he knew is again a question, but the roles they played in the history of their countries is notable enough to have reached his ears.[26] Marguerite managed to make her presence felt in public life despite two potential disadvantages: she was overshadowed early in her married life by her extraordinary and unsupportive mother-in-law, Blanche of Castile—Louis was only nineteen when they married in 1234—and she was married to a "saint"—Louis was later canonized. Marguerite ruled directly for only a few months in Damietta during a crusade in 1250. Louis had left the city, troops, and the royal fleet in Marguerite's hands when he set out for Cairo, was captured, and held for ransom. During the crisis, Marguerite gave birth to a child but managed both to hold on to the troops who wanted to desert and to negotiate the terms of Louis's release.

Otherwise, her political activity was as a mediator, particularly in English matters: she mediated between her brother-in-law, Henry III, and Simon de Montfort;[27] she negotiated for her husband Louis with Henry and Eleanor during a rebellion against Henry in England while Louis's counsellors were opposing Henry; and she pressured her husband's brother, Alphonse of Poitiers, to lend a fleet to transport the army her sister was raising for Henry. Marguerite did not always favor her sister; in a long dispute between a Gascon couple and the English crown, which was given to Marguerite to settle, she found for the couple, and Eleanor, then acting as regent in Gascony, honored her decision, a testament to the political acumen of both sisters. Marguerite wrote to Henry III about disputed possessions of an English monastery whose mother-house was in France; and about loans, suggesting terms and acknowledging receipt of royal jewels deposited as surety. He asked her to negotiate for him with her husband for restitution of lands he had seized and to persuade her son-in-law, the king of Navarre, to assign lands he had promised to Henry's future son-in-law, so as not to delay the marriage which Marguerite had arranged. She also pressed her own claims in Provence, seeking support from Henry, from his son Edward I, from her own son, Philip III; she attempted to prevent marriages that would strengthen the Angevin cause and to arrange others that would weaken it; and she raised an army to oppose her brother-in-law, Charles of Anjou.[28] She remained active as dowager queen, presiding in 1283 with the duke of Burgundy over a Savoy family conference about the succession, and being named an arbiter of the opposing claims.[29]

Marguerite worked closely with her sister Eleanor, the queen of England, not only on their mutual claims to Provence, but also to restore royal sovereignty in England. Eleanor was equally active and more visible on the public scene. Eleanor was about thirteen when she and Henry married in 1236, but she was involved in public matters early on: there were grants or sales of custody of lands and people to her from the early 1240s, as well as pardons, exemptions, quittance of debts, and grants of land at her instance; and she was caught in a struggle between the archbishop of Canterbury, her uncle Boniface, and her husband, over a disputed election of a bishop in 1244. Though normally Boniface and her other Savoy uncles were strong and crucial supporters of the English monarchy, in this case Henry's candidate was not appropriate. Eleanor was able to avert a falling out between her husband and the archbishop by convincing Henry first that she supported *him,* and then that his man was more useful in his current position—a move that impressed Matthew Paris, who was not a fan of the foreign queen or her family.[30]

Henry relied on Eleanor's abilities. When he left England to deal with a rebellion in Gascony, he appointed her regent, with the counsel (not co-regency) of his brother Richard, leaving the care of his heir, other children, and all his territories to her.[31] There are letters from Henry instructing her to transfer holdings, assign escheats (even to Richard), to receive money in the king's name, and to oversee various government operations, including forests and ships. She or Richard or both together witness every act in the patent rolls during the period of the regency, her name appearing ten times as often as his. Eleanor was able to work with her enemies when it was in the interests of her husband and son, and she was highly effective at gaining diplomatic and military support for their cause from her friends on the continent. Her success was admired even by her enemies. After she raised an army, she wrote to Alphonse of Poitou asking for ships; when he said he had none available, she asked him to detain any British ships within his territory, claiming that in a national emergency the king has a right to them. When he refused again, she asked him only to encourage captains and sailors to receive her messengers favorably, and that he agreed to. Meanwhile, in Gascony, which she controlled, Eleanor had English ships seized. The queen kept royal authority alive in Gascony during the rebellion in England by going there and asserting it herself, while her husband and son were in Simon de Montfort's hands.[32] The Gascons and the French king Louis IX accepted Eleanor's right to act for Henry, even in defiance of writs that were issued in his name at Simon's instance.

Eleanor's talents were financial as well as diplomatic. She managed to increase her holdings by buying debts and taking or leasing land given in surety for them, and she held profitable wardships—there are many documents among patent rolls on debts that she held.[33] She dealt with Jewish and Florentine financiers—was this talked about in Florentine financial circles?—and she negotiated debts for the kings of England and Scotland and for princes Edward and Edmund. Her credit was good because she paid her debts.

Eleanor and Marguerite are not named in the *Comedy*, as their sister Beatrice is, but Eleanor's husband and Marguerite's son both appear in Purgatory 7, in the valley of negligent princes, which is populated by men connected to their family. Beatrice is named in that same canto, to identify her husband, Charles of Anjou (Purg.7.128), and she is named with his second wife Marguerite [of Burgundy].[34] This Marguerite is not a member of the family; the name has resonances within the family and within the poem, which may be connected. The maternal grandmother of the four queens, who left their mother Beatrice her possessions in the Alps, was Margaret of Geneva. Beatrice named the eldest of her four daughters, the one who became queen of France, Marguerite. The last man Dante sees in Purgatory 7, Guglielmo, marchese of Monferrato, is the son of another Marguerite (daughter of Count Amadeo IV and first cousin of the four queens), perhaps named for the same grandmother as the queen of France (although her mother was also a Marguerite).[35]

The name is not attached to an important woman in the *Comedy*, but it does figure symbolically in interesting ways in Paradise. In Italian, Margarita means pearl, and Dante describes one of the heavens and several souls as "margherite," pearls. Indeed he introduces the passage that mentions the four queens thus:

E dentro a la presente margarita
luce la luce di Romeo, di cui
fu l'ovra grande e bella mal gradita. (Par.6.127–29)

Inside this pearl [the heaven of Mercury]
lights the light of Romeo, whose
great and beautiful work [the four marriages] was badly rewarded.

Might the *margarita* here be a hidden reference to the mother of the Savoy dynasty, the Margarita from whom they all descend? The first heaven, the moon, which receives Dante and Beatrice into itself, is also a *margarita* (Par.2.34); it is the heaven in which Dante meets women who wanted to give themselves to God but were forced by male relatives into serving bad worldly purposes, innocent if compliant victims of male ambitions—a sharp contrast to the forceful women, like countess Matelda, and the various women connected to Savoy.

Dante sees only two souls in this heaven, Piccarda whom he knew and who speaks to him, and the empress Constance, the heir to Sicily, who gave the Hohenstaufen their base in southern Italy when she married Henry VI. Piccarda points her out as "la gran Costanza," who engendered the third and last power from the second wind of Swabia: the mother, in other words, of the last Hohenstaufen emperor, Frederick II. Frederick's son, Manfred, married to one of the Savoy Beatrices, identifies himself in Purgatory 3 as the grandson of this Constance: "Io son Manfredi / nepote di Costanza imperadrice" (Purg.3.112–13). He also asks Dante to take the message that he is saved to his "lovely daughter," Costanza, a Savoy descendant, "bella figlia, genitrice / de l'onor di Cicilia e d'Aragona" ["mother of the honor of Sicily and Aragon"] (Purg.3.115–16). This Constance is named in Purgatory 7 to identify her husband, Pedro III, who is himself related to the four queens on their father's side. It is not an accident that Manfred, the Hohenstaufen heir to Sicily and the last to rule there, should identify himself with the two women at the beginning and end of the Hohenstaufen line in Sicily, whose name is "constancy," the virtue that characterizes the imperial cause in Italy by its absence. It is no more an accident that when Dante names Constance in Purgatory 7, it is to point out that her husband (Manfred) is superior to the husband of Beatrice (Charles of Anjou) who became king of Sicily but was succeeded on the throne by two of Constance's sons, James and Frederick.

Purgatory 7 is where most of the men related to the four queens appear, and all of the men in Purgatory 7 are in some way related to them, by marriage or birth, through their wives or mothers (see genealogy). Sordello, the poet who points out the princes in the valley to Dante and Virgil, spent time in Provence at the courts of both Raymond Berengar V, the father of the four queens, and Charles of Anjou, husband of the youngest.[36] The first pair named, Rudolph of Hapsburg and his rival and enemy Ottokar II, are only distantly related: Ottokar is the son of Wenceslas I and a Hohenstaufen princess, Cunegunde, daughter of Philip of Swabia. Since she was a first cousin of Frederick II, her son is second cousin to Manfred and her grandson third cousin to Manfred's daughter Constance, a direct Savoy descendant. The others, in order of appearance are:

Philip III of France, son of Marguerite of Provence, one of the four queens;

Henry of Navarre, father of Jeanne who married Philip IV, thus a father-in-law of Marguerite's grandson, but also a brother-in-law of her daughter Isabel, who married Henry's brother, Thibaut of Champagne;[37]

Pedro III of Aragon, a second cousin of the four queens on their father's side, who married Constance, daughter of Manfred and Beatrice of Saluzzo, a first cousin on the Savoy side;

Charles of Anjou, husband of the fourth sister, Beatrice, who is named in line 128, and paternal uncle of Philip III;

Henry III, king of England, husband of the second sister, Eleanor, brother-in-law of Charles of Anjou and maternal uncle of Philip III;

Guglielmo di Monferrato, an imperial vicar and head of a Ghibelline league, the son of a first cousin of the four queens, Marguerite of Savoy, sister of Beatrice of Saluzzo, making Guglielmo the first cousin of Constance, Manfred's daughter.

The importance of family in this episode is underlined in a number of ways: Dante emphasizes fathers and sons, often to the detriment of the sons (e.g., Ottokar and Wenceslas, 100–102; Pedro and Alfonso or Pedro, 115–16;[38] not to mention James and Frederick, 119; Charles of Anjou and Charles II, 124–25), and only in one case to the son's advantage (Henry III of England and Edward I, 131–32). He pairs fathers and fathers-in-law (Rudolph and Ottokar II,[39] Henry of Navarre and Philip IV, 109). Dante's identification of two of the men by their noses, "nasetto," ("little nose," Philip III), "maschio naso," and "nasuto" ("masculine nose" and "big nose," Charles of Anjou), may in part be a humorous suggestion of family by physical resemblance, since Charles is the brother of Philip's father, Louis IX.[40] Finally, the reminder of the wives by whom the men are connected, and by whom they are connected also to Manfred, underscores the importance of their family to the European political scene.

But the fact that all these princes are presented in the valley of negligent princes tells us that, despite the great respect Dante has for the Savoy family, he thinks they should have done more to unify Europe, particularly given the extraordinary opportunity afforded them by those four marriages in addition to their already considerable talents and connections. We are reminded of the potential of those marriages as a force for peace in Europe and support of the empire when they are inserted into Justinian's history of the empire in Paradise 6: "quattro figlie ebbe e ciascuna reina," queens of France, England, Sicily, and empress/queen of the Romans. The connections between the family and the empire are many, not only political alliances but also the marriage of Manfred, the imperial vicars from Thomas of Savoy to William of Monferrato, and the election of Richard of Cornwall as King of the Romans. The opportunities were not realized. Justinian is speaking from the heaven of Mercury, the sphere of those who were active for honor and fame—limited motivations that enabled them to serve, if not to achieve, the higher purpose. But by naming the men in Purgatory and the women in Paradise, Dante may be suggesting that the women did work for the cause of peace and empire, while the men undermined their efforts or failed to carry them through.

Notes

1. The citations are from *"La Commedia" secondo l'antica vulgata*, ed. Giorgio Petrocchi, (Milan: Mondadori, 1966–67), reprinted in the *Enciclopedia Dantesca*. The translations are mine. I am grateful to Russell Peck and the University of Rochester for giving me the opportunity to present the first version of this paper as a Russell Hope Robbins lecture in 2001.

2. I have been collecting letters to and from medieval women, to be made available with translations in a database called *Epistolae* (http://www/db/ccnmtl. columbia.edu). Letters of many of the women mentioned here are either available on the database or in process.

3. See *Woman as Image in Medieval Literature* (New York: Columbia University, 1975) and *Dante's Beatrice, Priest of an Androgynous God* (Binghamton, N.Y.: MRTS, 1992). That Dante values active over passive is indicated even by his presentation of Francesca. Barolini has argued persuasively that by giving Francesca a voice and an active role in her own life, Dante counters both her treatment as a passive pawn by her family and the silence of historic accounts. Teodolinda Barolini, "Dante and Francesca da Rimini: Realpolitik, Romance, Gender," *Speculum* 75 (2000): 1–28.

4. For the letters from Clare to Agnes, see Joan Mueller, *Clare's Letters to Agnes: Texts and Sources* (Great Falls, Mont.: St. Bonaventure Press, 2001). Prof. Mueller has generously contributed her texts and translations, which I cite here, to *Epistolae*. Cf. Jo Ann McNamara, *Sisters in Arms, Catholic Nuns through Two Millennia* (Cambridge, Mass.: Harvard University Press), 309: "In 1245, Innocent IV tried to subject the Clarisses to the Benedictine rule but withdrew in the face of Clara's and Agnes

of Bohemia's protests." McNamara notes (311) that few houses had the resources to defy the pope, as Agnes's did.

5. These words recall Francis's words in a letter to Clare and her sisters, counseling them to live always in the most holy life and in poverty and not to allow the teaching or counsel of anyone to move them from it. *Opuscoli del Serafico Patriarca San Francesco d'Assisi* (Florence: SS Concezione di Raffaello Ricci, 1880), Ep.5.

6. Matelda is called "la donna," which may simply denote her sex and rank, but which may also be a translation of *domina*, ruling lady, the masculine equivalent of *dominus*. She was the ruler of Reggio, Modena, Mantua, Brescia, Verona, Ferrara, Tuscany, and Upper and Lower Lorraine. She is still a presence in fourteenth-century Italian history. See Giovanni Villani, *Istorie Fiorentine* (Milan: Società Tipografica dei Classici Italiani, 1802), book 4, chapters 18, 20, 22, 27, 29.

7. For 139 historic documents of Matelda's rule, see *Die Urkunden und Briefe der Markgräfin Mathilde von Tuszien,* ed. Elke Goez and Werner Goez, MGH Laienfürsten und Dynasten Urkunden der Kaiserzeit (Hanover: Hahn, 1998). For texts and translations of letters to and from Matelda, see *Epistolae.*

8. *Iohannis Mantuani In Cantica Canticorum et De Sancta Maria Tractatus ad Comitissam Matildam,* ed. Bernhard Bischoff and Burkhard Taeger (Freiburg: Universitätsverlag, 1973), Spicilegium Friburgense 19, Tractatus in Cantica Canticorum ad Semper Felicem Matildam, 28r–v. Cf. Register *Gregors VII,* MGH, EpSel, ed. Erich Caspar, ep.1.50: "If . . . there were one who might assist the miserable and oppressed churches in your place, and serve the universal church, I would take pains to advise you to leave the world with all its cares." And *Sancti Anselmi Cantuariensis Archiepiscopi, Opera Omnia,* ed. F. S. Schmitt (Edinburgh: T. Nelson, 1946–63), ep.325, 5.256–57; Anselm thanks Matelda for saving him "not once but many times from the power of my enemies"; he recalls her desire to leave the world, from which she is restrained by her love for the church.

9. Matelda's husband died the same year as her mother, and Matelda inherited his lands as well as her father's; but contemporary writers sympathetic to Matelda, including her biographer Donizo, treat her as a "virgin queen," and that may be Dante's view as well: "una donna soletta," Purg.28.40. Her mother, first cousin of Emperor Henry III, was a formidable woman in her own right, an effective regent, and recognized as a powerful supporter of the papacy by both friends and enemies. Gregory VII openly relied on her support, and Peter Damian (incidentally, one of the few churchmen who is featured in Dante's Paradise) exchanged letters with her.

10. Hadrian was thus a brother-in-law of Beatrice's brother and was uncle of several Savoy children, cousins of the four queens. His last words in the poem describe a niece on the dei Fieschi side, Alagia: all that is left to him and good in herself, unless she is corrupted by the example of that house (Purg.19.142–45). Hadrian's uncle, Innocent IV, wrote a letter of consolation to Beatrice of Savoy when her husband died and also sent a letter of protection. See Francisque Viard, *Béatrice de Savoye*

(Lyon: L'Echo de Savoie, 1942), documents 4 and 5. A lawyer, he is probably the Innocent Dante refers to in his letter to the Italian cardinals; see entry on Innocent IV by Simonetta Bernardi in *Enciclopedia Dantesca* and *Dantis Alagherii Epistolae*, ed. Paget Toynbee (London: Oxford University, 1920; reprint 1966), ep.8.

11. Eugene L. Cox, *The Eagles of Savoy, The House of Savoy in Thirteenth Century Europe* (Princeton: Princeton University Press, 1974), 250. Much of what I know of the larger Savoy family comes from Cox.

12. Ibid., 374 ff. An earlier Beatrice in a family closely related to the Savoys, Beatrice of Monferrato, was celebrated in a poem by Raimbaut de Vaqueiras as the leader of an army of ladies out to build their own city, *The Poems of the Troubadour Raimbaut de Vaqueiras*, ed. Joseph Linskill (The Hague: Mouton, 1964). In the poem, the ladies choose as their podestà the lady of Savoy, Marguerite of Geneva, maternal grandmother of the four queens: "poestat fan de midons de Savoia" (18.75).

13. Cox, *The Eagles of Savoy*, 160.

14. Ibid., 160 ff., and Viard, *Béatrice de Savoye*, documents 6, 7, 9.

15. Cox, *The Eagles of Savoy*, 257.

16. Viard, *Béatrice de Savoye*, documents 16, 17.

17. *The cansos and sirventes of the troubadour Giraut de Borneil: a critical edition*, ed. Ruth Verity Sharman (Cambridge: Cambridge University Press, 1989), 52.45–48, with translations. Sharman describes the poem as "of doubtful attribution," and indeed it is unlikely that Giraut was still alive and composing by the time Beatrice was countess of Provence. But since the only manuscript it is found in, P (Florence, Biblioteca Laurenziana), attributes it to Giraut, Dante presumably knew it as Giraut's. Dante mentions Giraut in *De vulgari eloquentia* and alludes to him in Purgatory.

18. *The Poetry of Sordello*, ed. and trans. James J. Wilhelm (New York: Garland, 1987), 14.1–2, 7–10. The identification is not absolute, but the fact that Sordello is coming to serve the lady whom Blacatz has long served makes the countess of Provence a likely candidate. Sordello spent about fifteen years, from 1230 to 1245, at Raymond Berengar's court (Wilhelm, xviii), where he probably wrote his lament for Blacatz, on which Dante modeled the litany of princes in Purgatory 7 (see below). After Raymond Berengar's death, Sordello was retained by his successor, Charles of Anjou.

19. *Poésies du Troubadour Aimeric de Belenoi*, ed. Maria Dumitrescu (Paris: SATF, 1935), 15.27–32. The translations are mine. Dumitrescu identifies the countess in 15.27 and 19.46 as Beatrice of Savoy, countess of Provence. Aimeric also mentions two cousins of the countess: another Beatrice and Agnes of Saluzzo, 15.29–32. Dante mentions Aimeric in *De vulgari eloquentia*.

20. *Poésies du Troubadour Aimeric*, ed. Dumitrescu, 19.46–49.

21. We have only one stanza extant in an exchange with Gui de Cavaillon from Garsenda de Forcalquier, Beatrice's mother-in-law and paternal grandmother of the four queens. See Angelica Rieger, *Trobairitz* (Tübingen: Max Niemeyer, 1991), 5.

22. *Le Troubadour Elias de Barjols,* ed. Stanislas Stronski (Toulouse: Edouard Privat, 1906), poems 5 to 8 for Garsenda, 10 to 13 for Beatrice, 9 for her mother. I can find no direct evidence that Dante knew Elias.

23. Ibid., 11.43-44.

24. Ibid., 12.41-44.

25. Ibid., 13.47-48.

26. For Marguerite, see Gérard Sivéry, *Marguerite de Provence, Une reine au temps des cathédrales* (Paris: Fayard, 1987). For Eleanor, see Margaret Howell, *Eleanor of Provence, Queenship in thirteenth-Century England* (Oxford: Blackwell, 1998). Howell also provides very useful and detailed material about Marguerite and others in the family.

27. Howell, *Eleanor of Provence,* 186.

28. Edward had tried peaceful means to settle the Provence claims for his mother and aunt, but could not move his intransigent uncle Charles any more than his grandmother could. Marguerite's son, Philip III, supported her claims in Provence to the extent of not interfering with her attempts to raise the army, perhaps using Marguerite for his own diplomatic purposes, to do what he could not do directly.

29. Cox, *The Eagles of Savoy,* 447.

30. *Chronica Majora,* 4.509-10. When Eleanor's sister, Sanchia, married Henry's brother, Richard of Cornwall, in 1243, Matthew Paris worried that "the whole business of the kingdom would be disposed of at the will of the queen and her sister . . . who would be as it were a second queen" (*Chronica Majora* 4.190, cited by Howell, *Eleanor of Provence,* 38). Certainly the marriage strengthened Savoyard influence in the court, but Sanchia was not openly politically active. I have seen only records of some grants of wardship, joint approval of marriage with the queen and their uncles, occasional pardons and license at her instance, and a letter from Adam Marsh responding to her support for a request from the queen; whereas I have sixty letters for Marguerite so far, and over 150 for Eleanor.

31. See *Calendar of the Patent Rolls* for Henry III, vol. 4, 1247-1258 (London: Mackie and Co., 1908), July 1253, 4:206.

32. Howell, in *Eleanor of Provence,* says Eleanor helped to bring about the overthrow of Simon de Montfort and to rescue her husband and eldest son from his control (xviii).

33. For details on Eleanor's financial dealings, see Margaret Howell, "The Resources of Eleanor of Provence as Queen Consort," *EHR* 102 (1987): 372-93, from which the material in this passage is drawn.

34. "Più che Beatrice e Margherita, Costanza di marito ancor si vanta" ["Constance can boast still more of her husband than Beatrice and Marguerite"] (*Purg.*7.128-29). Constance is Beatrice's cousin; her superior husband is Manfred.

35. Another Marguerite whose name might well have had positive associations for Dante is the empress of Henry VII, Marguerite of Brabant. She does not appear in the *Comedy* and is not a member of the Savoy family; but Dante probably

wrote three letters to her for the countess of Battifolle, palatine countess of Tuscany, all of them in support of the emperor's cause in Italy—a clear instance of women on the right political side. Indeed, the countess expresses views, very dear to Dante, about the Roman prince designated by God to restore the family of mortals (VIIa), the single prince provided for human civilization/civilized humanity (VIIb), and the hope of a better world under the renewed empire (VIIc).

36. Raymond is the only prince mentioned in Sordello's lament for Blacatz, which Dante echoes in Purgatory 7, who does not lack courage to fight (Wilhelm, ed., *Sordello*, 26.37–40). While Sordello suggests that all the other princes, beginning with the emperor, be fed Blacatz's heart to give them the courage they lack, he says the count of Provence needs to eat it to help him carry his heavy burdens, "sitot ab esfors si defen ni's chapte, / ops l'es mange del cor pel greu fais qu'el soste" ["though he fights and defends himself with guts"] (Wilhelm, ed., *Sordello*, 26.37–40).

37. Thibaut is mentioned positively in Inf.22.52, "il buon re Tebaldo."

38. There is a difference of opinion on this reference, whether it is to Pedro's first son, Alfonso, who became king of Aragon but died young, or to his youngest son, Pedro, who never ruled. Whichever Dante had in mind, he would be a cousin of the four queens on both sides.

39. The son of Ottokar II, Wenceslas II, married Rudolph's daughter, Jutta, after the death of his father in battle against Rudolph; but Dante does not mention this connection.

40. I owe the connection of noses and family resemblance to Teodolinda Barolini.

19

JOSEPH A. DANE

Linear Perspective and
the Obliquities of Reception

T he perspective model discussed below, one known variously as *cos-truzione legittima,* linear perspective, single-point perspective, and, somewhat curiously, "three-point perspective," is familiar to art historians and has recently raised interest in general cultural studies. Histories of this model traditionally associate it with Leon Battista Alberti's *De Pictura* of 1434, and the model itself finds variants in artworks and in drawing manuals through the twentieth century. The geometry of the model is not difficult, given the assumption of the visual ray as a straight-line projection from the object in space to a viewpoint. But art historians, literary critics, and cultural historians have often misrepresented this rather simple geometry by interpreting it within larger contexts: aesthetics, artistic tradition, histories of representation, careers of individual artists, the physiology and psychology of vision. Problems associated with these higher levels of concern (for example, the curvature of space as defined by twentieth-century science) have been projected onto the model itself or used as its critique. In addition, the model has been analyzed in terms of value: if the model is characterized as progressive, "better" artworks must be seen as examples of it; if it is disparaged, "better" artists (Leonardo) must be seen as rejecting it. The model thus is modified according to the intellectual contexts in which it is discussed.

My focus in the following chapter will be on two problems: the phrase "three-point" perspective and its somewhat elusive referents, and the problem of curvilinearity as it is described in relation to the linear-perspective model. The first section deals with basic concepts in linear perspective—the models of Alberti and Viator and the rules of their production; the second concentrates on variants of the problem of curvilinearity.

Linear Perspective—Alberti and Viator

What is generally presented as the key text in most histories of linear perspective is Alberti's *De Pictura* (Latin and Italian), 1435.[1] Because of Alberti's centrality to this history traditionally (a centrality to which some scholars have objected), he has often been credited with quite contradictory theories: Norman Bryson claims that what Alberti "has in mind" is the *camera oscura*, whereas other scholars use the phrase "Albertian perspective" somewhat more loosely to refer to composite methods of perspective, common in Renaissance paintings, but quite different from the geometrical Albertian model.[2] J. V. Field has reacted against this, arguing that Alberti's treatise itself is not mathematically specific (which is clearly true), and further (and more problematically), that it did not function as a practical manual.[3] Alberti defines his method as a practical application of geometrical principles and asks to be considered "not as a mathematician but as a painter."[4] Alberti's principles were later embodied in genres other than purely aesthetic ones. They are found in many architectural manuals (for example, by Serlio), and are repeated in numerous seventeenth- and eighteenth-century drawing manuals (for example, by Desargues); they are also found, less coherently presented, in drawing manuals available in bookstores today.[5] As did many after him, Alberti defines the basic elements of his system—point, line, and plane—and defines a picture as a "cross-section of a visual pyramid," with the visual pyramid understood as a cone with its apex in the eye and its center at the line of sight.[6]

Alberti's formula produces as its fundamental figure the checkerboard floor illustrating foreshortening. For later artists and architects, this will also serve as a grid on which any patterns can be projected onto other plane surfaces or even onto curved and irregular surfaces. Alberti's diagram consists of a centric point from which lines are drawn to a line divided into equidistant segments at the base of the picture frame. Alberti constructs a vertical line

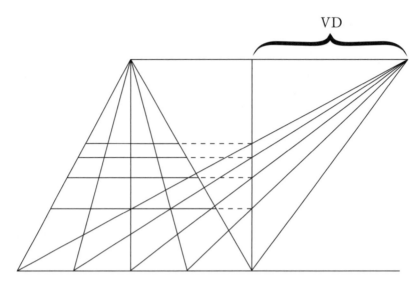

FIGURE I. Alberti's Method of Perspective

at the edge of the base. He then draws a second point level with the centric point, and from that point constructs a second set of lines to the segments on the base. At the points where these lines cross the vertical, lines parallel to the base line are drawn, and these give the correct foreshortening, with the viewing distance equal to the distance from the second point to the vertical (see fig. 1). Most of the early printed editions of Alberti (although not all of them) contain a version of this diagram.[7]

Alberti's description localizes the viewer as a point in space, fixed by the relation between the picture and the reality it depicts. The "correctness" (real and apparent) of Alberti's drawing depends on the proper placement of the viewer, at a distance VD. That Alberti's treatise is addressed to, say, an amateur rather than a mathematician or even a painter (a point emphasized by Field) is shown by placement of the centric point within the picture frame itself. This has to do with the conventions of picture placement in halls, where viewers studying a painting tend to place themselves directly in front of it. It is not required by mathematics nor even for purposes of composition.

Although it is fairly easy to construct a checkerboard floor in perspective using Alberti's method, a far more elegant practical method was developed by Viator in 1505. Here, no vertical line is drawn. Instead, lines drawn to the base line and their points of intersection serve to define the foreshortened squares.

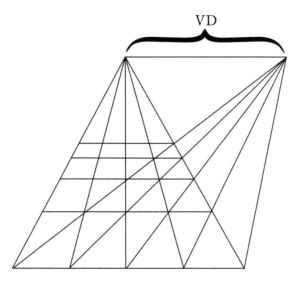

FIGURE 2. Viator's Method of Perspective

Their intersections with the lines from the centric line determine the foreshortened squares. The second set of lines in turn provides the real diagonals in the checkerboard, as they do not in the Alberti method.[8] Note that in the two constructions, the viewing distances are the same. (See fig. 2.) Alberti and Viator are now included in what has become a canon of perspectivists—Brunelleschi, Piero della Francesca, Manetti, Uccello, and Leonardo.[9] But these artists and writers are not consistent in their use of the model. Brunelleschi's often described views of the church of San Giovanni and the Palazzo dei Signori of Florence are real-world tests or practical applications of the mathematics of the model, but not practical exercises in artistic production. If standard interpretations of Manetti's contemporary description of this are accurate, the Brunelleschi constructions are not conventional paintings at all, but installations involving mirrors, peepholes, and even particular weather conditions (painted clouds merge with reflections of real ones). They are, in effect, parlor tricks collapsing nature, reality, art, and the viewing process.[10] Although there are no contemporary illustrations of Brunelleschi's constructions, in the seventeenth and eighteenth centuries there are many engravings of artistic peepholes, grid-frames, and other devices.[11]

Leonardo in his Notebooks rejects the strict application of this model, which involves not one but multiple perspectives: a viewer facing a picture painted in *costruzione legittima* interprets it through a mixture of "artificial perspective" (what is painted on the canvas) and "natural perspective" (how the eye sees what is there).[12] Leonardo opts instead for what he somewhat paradoxically calls "simple perspective"—the simplicity of which is belied by the various and contradictory interpretations of what he means by this: "Simple perspective is the perspective of art on a site equidistant from the eye in each of its parts; composite perspective is that involving a site for which no part is equidistant from the eye" (Frag. #90). If taken literally, this would make "simple perspective" the perspective of a spherical surface seen from its focal point.[13] Yet the fragment can only make sense if it is interpreted through fragments #107–8: simple perspective involves long implied viewing distances such that each part of a canvas is *effectively* equidistant from the eye, and lines of sight are parallel.[14] Simple perspective eliminates the constraints placed on the viewer that the model of strict linear perspective entails:

> This invention [the linear-perspective model] requires that the viewer stand with an eye at a peephole, and then everything looks correct from that peephole. But since many eyes are not able to see at the same time a work made with such art, and only one can see properly the effect of such perspective and the others remain confused, one should therefore reject such composite perspective and hold to simple perspective. (Frag. #108)

Principles of the Linear-Perspective Model

Most of the early histories and experiments in perspective are based on a series of fairly simple assumptions: that sight can be described in terms of rays—perfectly straight, unidimensional forces. The reception of light and its perception thus involves the transmission of light stimuli along straight lines, and the process of sight (the reception of these rays) involves the hypothesis of a real or virtual point of view. The theory is expressible through simple geometrical models and permits a wide variety of modifications. Sight could be produced on the surface of the eye, or anywhere within the eye. The point of view might be virtual; it might have different relations to the process of sight itself (for example, serving as the pinhole in a pinhole camera or camera oscura, or as the actual seat of vision itself).

The mathematics of the model are thus far less restrictive than is sometimes claimed, and radical changes in the science of optics do not overturn the model.[15] Despite revolutions in the field of optics, practical manuals produced in the nineteenth century (and even those sold today) are perfectly in accord with earlier manuals; they contain the same theories, the same contradictions, and the same increasingly obsolete descriptive theory of light. Since the theory can be expressed in terms of plane geometry, its dissemination on the two-dimensional printed page may be one factor in its durability.[16]

Brook Taylor makes one of the clearest statements on the principles of the model.[17] Taylor claims "to consider this Subject entirely anew, as if it had never been treated of before" (iv), although Taylor's principles are little more than a clarification of what is implied in other manuals. Taylor remains important in freeing the actual model from some of the extraneous conventions often seen as restrictions of the model (the notion of a central viewpoint; the privileging of the floorplane).[18] In Taylor, there is no difference between the horizon plane and any other plane, "since Planes, as Planes, are alike in Geometry" (iv). The fact that many perspective paintings have a checkerboard floor with the central row placed vertically on the picture frame is irrelevant to the general rules, as are such things as the rectilinear nature of picture frames, limitations on the natural focal distance of the human eye, the number of vanishing points, and so forth.

By drawing on Taylor, one can define the essential rules of the linear-perspective model as follows:

(1) Reality is depicted as the intersection of an infinite number of planes.

(2) Lines that are straight in one plane will be straight when projected onto any other (including the picture plane).

(3) Parallel lines in any one plane will intersect at points in a straight line that will be considered the "horizon" of that plane. All lines parallel to each other in any plane intersect at the same point. Taylor: "The vanishing point of all lines in any original plane are in the vanishing line of that plane; original planes that are parallel have the same vanishing line."

(4) A picture is the mapping of points from any of these planes onto a single viewing plane.

These principles are often confused with their practical implications. Taylor assumes, more radically than other theorists, that a painting constructed according to perfect perspective will be indistinguishable from the original: "A Picture drawn in the utmost degree of Perfection, and placed in a proper Position, ought so to appear to the Spectator, that he should not be able to distinguish what is there represented, from the real original Objects actually placed where they are represented to be" (11–12). Although a twentieth-century reader might construe Taylor's conditionals as a reflection of the inadequacy of the theory (a painter *could* produce a perfect painting this way *if* the theory were valid, which it is not), to the eighteenth-century reader, these simply reflect the known imperfection of human beings: no painter can produce the perfect painting. Thus: "A Figure in a Picture, which is not drawn according to the Rules of Perspective, does not represent what is intended, but something else" (vii).

The Logic of Three-Dimensionality and the Myth of Three-Point Perspective

One feature of discussions of perspective is the persistent notion that perspective is somehow progressive: that there is a hierarchy or series of perspectives, moving from the simple to the complex: thus "one-point" perspective moves through "two-point" perspective to a more complex "three-point" perspective.[19] The obvious and easily understood logic of such a formula leads to its projection onto history and onto particular texts (Viator's), which are then misread to accord with it.

In modern drawing manuals, the mythologized "three points" are occasionally used as the three vanishing points of the sides of a foreshortened cube, no side of which is parallel to the picture plane. I have seen references to this definition of "three-point perspective" as a nineteenth-century formulation, but I am not certain when this consensus developed. It is, however, quite at odds with the early history of perspective and completely falsifies some of the earliest documents and discussions.

B. A. R. Carter's often-cited article on perspective in the *Oxford Companion to Art* (1970) is a good example of how various understandings, practical and theoretical, collide in modern history. Carter defines the "Principle Types of Perspective" as follows:

(a) parallel perspective: "the representation of parallels as parallels. . . . The term may also refer to the case in scientific perspective when the picture plane is parallel to a principal surface of the object as is commonly found in Renaissance pictures."

(b) angular or oblique perspective: "A term of scientific perspective used when a rectangular form is represented at an angle to the plane of the picture such that its horizontal parallels recede into depth to the left and the right, thus requiring two vanishing points, but its verticals remain parallel to the picture plane."

(c) three-point or inclined picture plane perspective: "A term of scientific perspective used with regard to a rectangular form placed so that none of its sides is parallel to the picture plane."[20]

According to this discussion, the three types exist in an apparent progression. But all three are perfectly compatible with Alberti's theory. The different "forms" (a–c) only refer to the orientation of the object depicted. Carter then adds other forms; here the progression appears to be historical: (d) axial perspective (arguably a medieval form);[21] (e) inverted perspective (pre-Renaissance); and finally two forms of linear perspective: (f) negative perspective and (g) bifocal perspective.[22] The example of negative perspective is from Dürer's *Underweyssung der Messung* (1525) and shows a viewer staring at a large tablet. For letters to appear the same height to a viewer on the ground, the letters on the top need to be larger than those on the bottom. This should be a simple example of "lateral distortion" and will appear so when the diagram is turned on its side.[23] Carter describes "bifocal perspective" as follows: "A term for an empirical construction that uses two vanishing points placed symmetrically on the margins of the picture for the purpose of drawing a diagonal floor-grid." Carter correctly cites P. Guaricus and Uccello. But he misrepresents his diagram. It is Viator's, and the presumed "two vanishing points" are simply two of the infinite number of vanishing points that exist for all possible parallels in the plane.

Carter's table of perspectives, then, writes the history of perspective as two progressions: the first scientific (from one-point to three-point); the second, historical, from medieval axial perspective and negative perspective to two presumed Renaissance varieties, ending with what seems to be a description of Viator. Carter's following discussion of that history, however, cannot be mapped onto this. At one point, Carter defines Viator's method as follows: "The distance point or three-point construction. This is historically the most important construction after Alberti's costruzione legittima and is by far the best known."[24] Yet this is exactly the model described as "bifocal perspective" three pages earlier, and one that is also entirely adequate to construct any of the figures in the progressive series a–c.

The confusion is in part due to the language used by Viator, which misleads even the normally reliable Ivins: "Viator's book, the *De artificiali perspectiva* . . . contains the first statement of the familiar 'three point' or 'distance' method."[25] Ivins is translating Viator's own words: but note that the three points in Viator have nothing whatsoever to do with the three vanishing points of an obliquely oriented cube in space (Carter's perspective type c):

The principle point in perspective should be placed on the level of the eye. This point is called the fixed point or subject point. Afterwards, a line should be drawn through that line to each side. And in that line two other points should be marked equidistant from the subject point; and these are called "third points" (Lat.: *tertia puncta;* Fr.: *tiers points*). If you are representing a close viewing distance, place them close; if you are representing a distant viewing distance, place them far from the subject point. And on this line, can be made more points, for drawing edifices of various angles or in different orientations. That line is called the "pyramidal line" because angles or points of pyramids begin from there. It is also called the horizon line.[26]

Viator is talking about the practical problem of constructing a grid. He is not concerned with theoretical, mathematical, or optical problems. Viator's "pyramids" are simply lines on the drawing representing lines in space; they are not the familiar "visual pyramids" of light striking the eye. All Viator is saying is what most drawing manuals since have said: that the vanishing points of all pairs of parallel lines within a single defined plane will occur on a single line. One, two, three, or a thousand such points can exist and are determined only by the relative orientations of the parallels. This is better described as "third-point" perspective, not "three-point" perspective. These "third points" are equidistant from the "principal point."[27] Unless an artist wants to do no more than draw obliquely oriented cubes, the notion that each object must have three vanishing points will be useless.

Erwin Panofsky and Curvilinear Perspective

Closely associated with the history of linear perspective is the notion of curvilinear perspective, and it is this that will be the subject of the remaining sections of this chapter. The problem of curvilinear perspective has challenged the model of linear perspective almost throughout its history. Cartographers dealt with the problem practically—how does one project three-dimensional (and necessarily curved) courses onto a two-dimensional map.[28] Scientists of vision tested it on a theoretical level, rejecting the convenient geometrical fiction of a single point of reception and invoking physiological curves in the science of vision: both the lens surface (Leonardo) and the retina itself (Kepler).

The problem of what might be called the psychological analysis of curves as straight lines is classical. Vitruvius notes that columns must increase in width in proportion to height; Alberti himself dealt casually with the problem in "Delle Prospettiva," in a section entitled "On why the land and the sea appear flat."[29] The problem became central to discussion of linear perspective in the twentieth century through Erwin Panofsky, whose 1924 "Die Perspektive als 'symbolische Form'" largely determined the direction and the points of issue for all later discussions.[30] Nearly half this study, now a book, is devoted to the problem of curvilinear perspective, under which rubric Panofsky conflates several things: the lurking problem of curves always associated with the apparent linearity of the model; the curvature of the retina; the ill-defined notion of "marginal distortion" found in modern photographs; and finally the twentieth-century notion of curved space. Panofsky concludes that reality is curved, whether we mean by that real space or the perceived space represented on the retina. Straight lines are geometrical constructs, and the perception of straight lines is a matter of conditioning, a conditioning Panofsky somewhat illogically associates with the very camera he elsewhere credits with producing distortions.

Panofsky's conflation of these elements has been condemned.[31] But even some of the most vigorous condemnations quickly become defenses. Damisch criticizes Panofsky for claiming that the brain takes the geometrical images on the retina as a model of reality: "no one formulated the problem in terms of this absurd requirement before the end of the nineteenth century" (14). But Panofsky is immediately exonerated: his discussion is "erroneous" but historical; Panofsky's "naivete" is characteristic of an entire era.

Euclid's Eighth Theorem states that the apparent size of an object is a direct function of its visual angle. According to Panofsky, Renaissance translations of Euclid under the influence of the linear perspective model, modify this theorem to state that the apparent size of an object is directly proportional to the distance of that object from the viewer. Thus, the Renaissance acceptance of the theory of linear perspective (whereby "size" is a function of distance) replaces the classical theory, whereby apparent size is a function of viewing angle.[32] Panofsky finds these two versions of the theorem in conflict, and further finds the difference itself to be an index of the difference between curved images (retinal images) and the rectilinear images of linear painting.

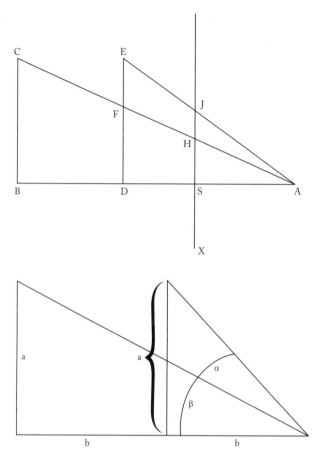

FIGURE 3.   From Panofsky, *Perspective,* p. 36 (264 German ed.)

Panofsky was committed to the historical development of two competing theories of perspective. In Panofsky's "classical" perspective, the size
of an object is a function of its viewing angle. In Albertian (or what Panofsky calls "Brunelleschian") perspective, "magnitudes objectively equal appear
inversely proportional to their distances from the eye."[33] But Panofsky's version of history has been questioned,[34] and his presentation of geometrical
evidence is misleading.

    Let us look at two figures in his 1924–25 "Perspektive," diagrams that will
be conflated in his 1953 study *Early Netherlandish Painting* (based on lectures
of 1947–48):

[Panofsky]: "Contrast between the 'linear perspectival' and 'angle-perspectival' constructions: in linear perspective [above], the apparent sizes (HS and JS) are inversely proportional to the distances (AB and AD); in angle perspective [below], the apparent sizes (β und α + β) are not inversely proportional to the distances (2b and b)."[35]

As a geometrical explanation, this statement is, I think, correct. But the two diagrams are not analogous, and Panofsky's term "not inversely proportional" is evasive and vague, obscuring the positive relation between the units which can be expressed in terms of the tangent function.[36] Furthermore, in terms of perception theory, there is a clear error in the language Panofsky applies, the same error that occurs in the later conflated drawing printed in *Early Nether-landish Painting*. In the first diagram, it is not the case that HS and JS are "apparent sizes" or (as translated in a typescript from the New York School of Fine Arts) "visual magnitudes" (*Sehgrößen*). They are projected sizes—what would appear on a vertical canvas; they are representations of what is seen, not what is seen or even models of what is seen.

In *Early Netherlandish Painting* (1953), the following diagram is given, a diagram which combines the two diagrams in the 1924 study. In and of itself, the diagram is extremely clear in pointing out the difference between "apparent size" (represented by angles) and "represented size" (projections onto the plane). But Panofsky misrepresents what the diagram shows.

"Modern" perspective . . . represents a central projection onto a plane surface, which means that magnitudes objectively equal appear inversely proportional to their distances from the eye; if, for instance, two equal vertical lines, a and b, are seen at the distances d and 2d, respectively, b will appear, in the perspective image, precisely half as long as a. According to classical optics, . . . the apparent magnitudes are not inversely proportional to the distances but directly proportional to the visual angles, α and β, so that the apparent magnitude of b will more or less considerably exceed one half of that of a.

What is portrayed in this diagram is again the difference between "represented" size and "apparent" size. The diagram shows two equal objects perpendicular to the line of sight (a and b). The apparent sizes of the images are of course the same as the apparent sizes of their projections onto the (unlabelled) plane surface, which I have marked x. The length of those projections is directly proportional to the relative distances from the eye.

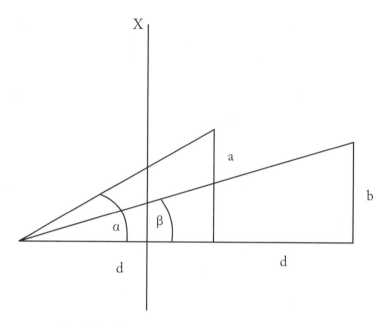

FIGURE 4. From Panofsky, *Early Netherlandish Painting*, p. 11

Panofsky is correct that the object at a distance 2d appears greater than half the size of the object at a distance d. But it is not the case that in Brunelleschian or Albertian perspective "b will appear, in the perspective image, precisely half as long as a." Rather b *is* half as long as a in the perspective image. Viewed from the view point, the linear projection of the two images a and b will appear *precisely* in the same proportion as the ratio of the visual angles.

Beyond this simple problem is another. Distance is only unambiguous when referring to two points, not to two-dimensional entities or to three-dimensional objects in space.[37] Even in the diagrams above, "distance" must be described as "perpendicular distance" or "distance to a base point." For three-dimensional objects, such as a sphere or column, doubling the distance to the center point does not double the distance to points on the surface. Thus, close viewing distances require lateral distortion on the canvas. Spheres distant from the viewing point should be drawn as ellipses (although they seldom are). For a row of columns parallel to the picture plane; the column directly in front of the implied viewing point must be drawn as more narrow than those at the margins.[38]

In Panofsky's discussion, curvatures of various kinds, geometrical, physiological, and perceptual, are associated:

A line is divided so that its three sections a, b and c subtend equal angles, these objectively unequal sections will be represented on a concave surface like the retina as approximately equal lengths; whereas if projected on a flat surface they will appear, as before, as unequal lengths. This is the source of those marginal distortions which are most familiar to us from photography, but which also distinguish the perspectivally constructed image from the retinal image. . . . A normal checkerboard pattern appears at close range to swell out in the form of a shield; an objectively curved checkerboard, by the same token, will straighten itself out. (31–33)

We will discuss the problem of the "swollen checkerboard" below in reference to Jean Fouquet. Panofsky has correctly analyzed the problem, but the notion of photographic "distortion" ("die sogenannten 'Randverzerrungen'") is misleading. The discussion involves the image produced in a pinhole camera; line segments projected onto a picture frame are not distorted at all, but are exact models of the real lines they depict. What Panofsky means is that the relation of the visual arcs are not the same as the relations of the projected line segments. Why has the notion of distortion migrated from the mythical retinal image to the precise and exact replicas that the geometrical model produces?

Let us examine Panofsky's logic here: first, the historical logic. If curvature is characteristic of the ordinary (naive) way of perception, then how does one explain the grim linearity of the model of perspective that is the subject of discussion, its popularity throughout the period of lens development, and its decline into "historical curiosity" at the very moment when lenses began to produce photographs (presumably "reinforcing" the linear system)? The historical progression is precisely the reverse of what Panofsky argues here. Second, the logic itself: according to the assumptions here, the objective world is curved (as described by of Einstein), and we "really" see it as curved (because of the curved retina). But camera images presumably pervert our perception, reinforcing linearity, and we *claim* to see lines as straight.

The villain in Panofsky's discussion is modern photography, which conditions us to misperceive the real distortions in reality. "And indeed, if even today only a very few of us have perceived these curvatures, that too is surely in part due to our habituation—further reinforced by looking at photographs—to linear perspectival construction" (34). But what kind of photographs is Panofsky thinking of? The only photographic machine that operates according to the linear perspective model is an ideal pinhole camera, with a flat photographic plate. Although most of us are familiar with photographic distortions, how many of Panofsky's readers of the past seventy-five years think of these as the distortions characteristic of pinhole camera images?—images perfectly focused in all details, where all straight lines are perfectly straight; but spheres, oddly, are elongated, and will only become round if viewed from the correct viewpoint?[39] No photograph taken with an ordinary lens meets these requirements, but rather it produces an image that is quite different from that of a perspective drawing: straight lines at the margins are curved (so-called "barrelling"); in its extreme form, this is the familiar "fish-eye" image characteristic of wide-angle lenses. Ordinary photographs, thus, reinforce the notion of curvilinear perspective, not linear perspective; that is, they train viewers to see pictures in precisely the opposite way that Panofsky claims.[40]

Medieval Curved Space

In *The Birth and Rebirth of Pictorial Space,* John White notes the checkerboard patterns found in fourteenth- and fifteenth-century French painting, in works of Jean Fouquet, Jean Pucelle, and in the manuscript painting of the des Limbourges. Succeeding horizontal rows are foreshortened in an increasing ratio; parallels seem to recede to a single vanishing point, but a curious phenomenon occurs: the diagonals of those checkerboards curve inward. In Fouquet, such curves seem to find their way onto the presumed horizontals nearest the picture frame. Carter implies that such patterns are in some sense primitive; they are one of the errors corrected by Alberti (*Oxford Companion to Art,* 843 and fig. 45). White, however, sees no progression here from Fouquet to Alberti; his discussion of these painters follows chapters devoted to the development of classical linear perspective. The Limbourgian perspective is an alternative to Albertian perspective, not a predecessor; it is "undertaken for the selfsame reasons" (231); that is, it is a naturalistic representation of visual foreshortening.

The dates support White, and many of the French paintings postdate both the Alberti treatise and the tradition of perspective it seems to foster. But White implies that the curving diagonals are neither accidental nor purely aesthetic. They are representational; furthermore, they reflect real

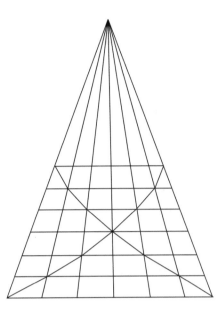

FIGURE 5. Checkerboard with inwardly-curving diagonals

curves in the actual world: "The subtly curving streets of the late medieval towns of France . . . are a further illustration of the union between visual experience and pictorial composition which was being forged by Fouquet" (228). In this appealing formulation, the "curving streets" of medieval towns and their artistic representation foreshadow the truth of real curves, even the curvature of space as understood by twentieth-century science.

But is this at all reasonable?

At first glance, there is nothing particularly shocking or even mannered about the checkerboard floor pattern in the French drawings. The squares are foreshortened—parallel lines parallel to the plane of the picture remain parallel to the picture; and parallel lines perpendicular to the plane of the picture converge toward a single point on the horizon. But the diagonal lines, implied by the points forming the tile pattern, curve inward (see fig. 5).[41]

Alberti's discussion of methods of constructing such checkerboard patterns shows that a number of his contemporary painters relied on arithmetic estimates—methods that might well account for what we see here; in one, each successive row is two-thirds the width of the preceding one.[42] The precise formula for linear foreshortening is trigonometric, and before the publication of trigonometric tables, this and other such methods would have been only approximations. Alberti's treatise, by contrast, shows artists how to construct this foreshortening mechanically, *without reference* to the mathematics of it. And this involved the simple assumption that the French miniaturists did not accept: that lines that are straight in any plane in space will be projected as straight lines on any other plane. Since the diagonals implied by the corners of a checkerboard are straight, these lines must be straight in the painting as well (the test Alberti recommends for determining the accuracy of the construction [57]). Constructing a foreshortened checkerboard according to the two-thirds formula can, in fact, lead to the kinds of checkerboards seen in the French illuminations, where the tiles were constructed in progressive foreshortening, but without regard to the straightness of implied diagonals. For short implied viewing distances, the two-thirds model produces inwardly curving diagonals; for long implied viewing distances, the diagonals produced by this model seem to curve outward. Note that the foreshortening of the near ranks of squares appears as accurate in the French model or in fig. 5 as in the models of Alberti and Viator (figs. 1 and 2). But the radical foreshortening required of distant squares according to the Albertian model may be more difficult to accept conceptually—and also more difficult to construct artistically.

In a representational drawing, it is less important that an object (a checkerboard) be accurately depicted than that it be identifiable. The Limbourg brothers, and those who constructed checkerboard patterns as they did, simply produced what most of us would produce if asked to draw a series of (foreshortened) parallel lines. The distant lines in space (those higher on the picture plane) are less foreshortened than the rules of perspective require. Those curving diagonals that result are in all likelihood accidents of construction, and, in most drawings, they are obscured by strategic placement of subject figures. The presumably "alternative" method of perspective is a perfectly predictable result of the mechanical application of two of the basic rules of linear perspective and can be reproduced by anyone today who attempts to draw checkerboards in accordance with a single vanishing point. The Fouquet miniatures neither anticipate theories of curved space nor produce a peculiarly medieval version of it.[43]

Modern Problems in Curvilinearity

Scholars of perspective have found much artistic and critical support for the notion of "curved artistic space," repeating in essence an argument developed between Wilhelm Schickhardt and Kepler. Such evidence appears to challenge the presumed rigidity of the model of linear perspective; but as pointed out even by Schickhardt, the model itself predicts absolutely the very phenomenon of perceived curvature that has been cited as its refutation.[44] The question is whether such perceived curves should be represented as curves on a plane surface (the rules of the linear perspective model claims they should not be). I imagine riding in a helicopter and facing a building with perfectly parallel sides. The sides of the building seem to converge toward the top floor. They seem to converge towards the base as well. Obviously, they cannot actually converge if they are actually straight; but more important, they cannot *seem* to converge if they *seem* to be straight. I am standing on a railroad track. I look straight down. In either direction, the railroad tracks *seem* to converge. They cannot do this if they *seem* straight.[45]

In terms of representational images, such anecdotes are irrelevant to the question "what is to be represented" (two things that Panofsky occasionally conflates in his words *Sehgrößen* and *Sehkurven*). Kepler's objection to Schickhardt deals precisely with this: if straight lines in the real world appear curved, that should not affect how the artist represents those straight lines on a canvas.[46] Whatever I may see, I construct the sides of the represented building as straight. I paint the railroad tracks as two straight parallel lines. When the viewer assumes the proper viewing point (which might be, say, ten feet away from a 100–foot–high canvas, or five feet from a canvas of several miles in width, or an inch from a canvas a mere five or six feet in height or width), that viewer will perceive the same lines (curved or straight) I *claim* to have perceived as curved before constructing them as straight.

A right angle is projected onto an oblique plane (one of the most basic exercises in perspective drawings); as the right angle recedes on that plane, it becomes measurably oblique. A square is inscribed within a circle. A viewer views this with the axis of sight at the center of the circle. As the viewer approaches the center, what is the behavior of the angles of the square? They obviously become increasingly oblique. And the only way that a four-sided object can consist of four oblique angles is for its sides to be convex. The perceived square is thus neither the real square nor the represented one (both of which obey basic geometric laws).

The model of linear perspective clearly predicts such perceived curves, which do not depend on specific theories of perception or on the physiology of vision. Those curves are predicted whether the eye is an ideal lens-less *camera oscura* (from the seventeenth century) or a more modern mathematically chaotic blob of jelly. Curvilinearity is no limitation on the model, nor is its artistic expression a challenge to the model. Constructions such as those of Schickhardt or Flocon are less representational (of objects in space) than descriptive (of geometrical facts).

Conclusion

The rules of linear perspective require that no distortion take place on the picture plane in representing shapes on any plane surface parallel to that picture plane. A row of two-dimensional discs on a plane in space will be represented as a row of perfectly circular disks on the picture plane and can be drawn with a compass. But three-dimensional objects do not behave in this way on the picture plane: a row of spheres will bulge, overlap; if viewed from the wrong viewpoint, they will become increasingly "monstrous" as they are placed away from the intended viewing axis. The paradox is that real discs, unless viewed from an axis perpendicular to the center, are *always* foreshortened into bulging ellipses; whereas real spheres in space never suffer from apparent foreshortening. Yet to represent this behavior of a sphere in a picture designed to be seen from a particular viewpoint requires that it be drawn as the very "bulging ellipse" it never appears to be, and most artists have refused to do this.

What is seen as "monstrous" in a painting depends on psychological factors involving our understanding of the objects in space, not on their visual appearance. When we examine an image of a row of spheres produced by a pinhole camera or by the strict application of the rules of linear perspective, we see lateral distortion and deformation, consequent on the geometry of the model; and we will generally perceive this even if we attempt to view such an image from the correct viewpoint. But other examples do not bother us. In a photograph reproduced by Pirenne, a political candidate stands before an oversized poster of himself, placed at an oblique angle to the camera. The poster, thus, appears on the photograph in radical foreshortening. Nonetheless, that radically foreshortened poster appears an accurate portrait of the candidate standing before it, even though we are forced to view it from the wrong viewpoint. Psychologically, we confront and somehow correct the same marginal distortion we find so unsettling in pinhole camera images of columns or spheres.[47]

Standard drawing manuals and standard discussions of the representation and construction of shadows, reflections, curves, winding roads, and hills are often in error; yet the errors in these histories seem to have remarkably little practical consequence. Artists trained in the basic principles of linear perspective can evade their paradoxes and perplexities through the infinite viewing distances implied by Leonardo's "simple perspective" or in Canelletto paintings. Or they can simply ignore such principles, just as the best students will ignore the dictates of their professors. Thus, even the most inarticulate of draftsmen can produce convincing drawings that I must labor over. And literary critics, cultural historians, and certain art historians can likewise see, through misreadings of Alberti, Viator, and even Panofsky, a coherence in a past that to me is remote, inaccessible, and tangled in contradictions.

I stare at the railroad tracks receding in each direction. They are straight, but I know they appear curved. I stare at a set of wall tiles. The central tile appears larger than the more distant tiles. I know the lines appear curved, converging toward distant vanishing points, above me, below me, to the right and left. But again I stare at those tracks and tiles. I allow myself to think differently. Parallel lines do not *actually* converge; they only *seem* to converge. The fact of the matter is that the recession is illusory. I think about that, staring at the row of tiles, and I now see those lines as *diverging,* with the smaller tiles at the center of my vision. The railroad tracks open wide, toward the horizon.

Albert Flocon and André Barre, along with their English translator, Robert Hansen, have proposed, as a supposed alternative to linear perspective, the loopy, strange drawings produced by the assumption of converging parallels and curved lines of horizon—an elaboration of the model proposed by Schickhardt.[48] The mathematics that is the basis of these drawings I can barely follow, but their demonization of linear perspective is curious. In the history constructed by Flocon and Hansen, the master villain is Alberti and the notion of the "single vanishing point" (a doctrine I am not certain is to be found in Alberti). Heroes include Jean Fouquet, Leonardo, and oddly, Uccello. Flocon himself praises the "metaphysical urban views of Giorgio di Chirico [which] bring before my eyes . . . Florence of Masaccio, Brunelleschi, and Uccello, the inventor of a silvery, luminous reborn world."[49] This is a strange history, to be sure, since to my eye, some of the more radical Uccello's are produced by following the implications of linear perspective to extremes, rather than by evading those implications, as Flocon implies. The rhetoric of Hansen is much more extravagant. Hansen imagines Flocon as anti-legislative; irregular, and one whose work constitutes "a revolutionary manifesto, a call to liberation from dogma."[50]

But is the tradition that Flocon reacts against a rule-bound one? Some of the strongest voices against the power of tradition have not been "anti-legislative" at all, but rather have rejected the vagaries of tradition in favor of alternative sets of rules: strict linear perspective, Flocon's mathematics, the rules of twelve-tone music. The power to fear is perhaps not one of articulable rules at all, but rather that of apparent "ruled-ness" with its inevitable and inexplicable exceptions—an art and scholarship that moves capriciously between rigor and whim, the unelongated perfect sphere resting comfortably at the edges of a Raphael painting, the uncritical and intellectually crippling notions of "realism," "accommodation," and "reasonableness." It is one of many ironies of the history sketched here that those who wished to break away from tradition, or who objected to its constraints, often lapsed into the belief that evil could somehow be defined or reduced to a set of easily understood, and thus easily rejected, rules. A better way to challenge such oppressive "ruled-ness" may be simply to follow the implications of particular rules, with all the comforting insulation of scholarship, to their amusing and often irritating conclusions.

Notes

1. John R. Spencer, *Leon Battista Alberti: On Painting* (New Haven: Yale University Press, 1966), 21, calls it the first theoretical statement of "one point perspective"; see also Cecil Grayson, "L. B. Alberti's 'construzione legittima,'" *Italian Studies* 19 (1964): 14–22. Italian text from Luigi Malle, ed., *Leon Battista Alberti: Della pittura* (Florence: Sansoni, 1950).

2. Norman Bryson, *Vision and Painting: The Logic of the Gaze* (New Haven: Yale University Press, 1983), 104. See, among recent studies, esp. Hubert Damisch, *The Origin of Perspective* (1987), trans. John Goodman (Cambridge, Mass.: MIT Press, 1994); M. J. Kemp, *The Science of Art: Optical Themes in Western Art from Brunelleschi to Seurat* (New Haven: Yale University Press, 1990); Thomas Frangenberg, "The Angle of Vision: Problems of Perspectival Representation in the Fifteenth and Sixteenth Centuries," *Renaissance Studies* 6 (1992): 1–45.

3. J. V. Field, "Alberti, the Abacus, and Piero della Francesca's Proof of Perspective," *Renaissance Studies* 11 (1997): 61–88, esp. 62. Whatever Alberti's original intentions, printed editions of his text are sufficiently rich in illustrations to enable it to be used as a practical manual, at least by amateurs. See note 6 below.

4. Spencer, *Leon Battista Alberti: On Painting*, 43.

5. Sebastiano Serlio, *The Five Books of Architecture* (1584; English trans. 1611; reprint, New York: Dover, 1982); A. Bosse, *Manière Universelle de Mr Desargues pour*

pratiquer la perspective par petit-pied (Paris: Deshayes, 1648); John Montague, *Basic Perspective Drawing: A Visual Approach*, 2d ed., (New York: Van Nostrand Reinhold, 1993). The work of Eakins shows a clear use of these techniques; see Michael Fried, *Realism, Writing, Disfiguration: On Thomas Eakins and Stephen Crane* (Chicago: University of Chicago Press, 1987), 46–53.

6. Spencer, *Leon Battista Alberti: On Painting*, 52. See esp. Martin Kemp, "Leonardo and the Visual Pyramid," *Journal of the Warburg and Courtauld Institutes* 40 (1977): 128–49.

7. Svetlana Alpers, *The Art of Describing: Dutch Art in the Seventeenth Century* (Chicago: University of Chicago Press, 1983), 53, states that Alberti is entirely unillustrated. This may be true of the original treatise, but nearly all sixteenth- and seventeenth-century printed editions I have seen are illustrated.

8. Jean Pèlerin (Viator), *De artificiali Perspectiva* (1505); the fundamental and most lucid study is William M. Ivins, Jr., *On the Rationalization of Sight* (1938; reprint, New York: Da Capo Press, 1973); see also Timothy K. Kitao, "Prejudice in Perspective: A Study of Vignola's Perspective Treatise," *The Art Bulletin* 44 (1962): 173–94.

9. See Martin Kemp, *Behind the Picture: Art and Evidence in the Italian Renaissance* (New Haven: Yale University Press, 1997), 83–117. For English readers, this canon is in part due to Elizabeth G. Holt, *A Documentary History of Art*, vol. 1: *The Middle Ages and the Renaissance* (Princeton: Princeton University Press, 1947).

10. Alberti, "Della Pittura," 57, characterizes his own productions in a similar way and claims his friends called them "miracles" when viewed from the correct viewpoint. On Brunelleschi's constructions, see the conjectural image by B. A. R. Carter, "Perspective," in Harold Osborne, *Oxford Companion to Art* (Oxford: Oxford University Press, 1970), 840–61; see further, discussion in Damisch, *Origin of Perspective*, 75–85; Martin Kemp, "Science, Non-science and Nonsense: The Interpretation of Brunelleschi's Perspective," *Art History* 1 (1978): 134–52.

11. In the engraved title page to the English translation of Jean Dubreuil, *Perspective Practical* (London, 1698), Goddess Perspectiva holds what is either a mirror, or an oval perspective drawing; putti have hand-held peepholes.

12. *The Notebooks of Leonardo da Vinci*, ed. Jean Paul Richter (1883; reprints New York: Dover, 1970), #107, #108 = Notebook E. 16a and b. My translations here correct the often maddeningly obscure translations by Mrs. R. C. Bell in Richter's edition. See further, diagrams in Richter, sections 77, 66: these show that the problem is a variant of other problems regarding the *camera oscura*, the representation of shadows, and even the description of eclipses.

13. So Frangenberg, "Angle of Vision," 19–22.

14. So James Elkins, "Did Leonardo Develop a Theory of Curvilinear Perspective, Together with Some Remarks on the 'Angle' and 'Distance' Axioms," *Journal of the Warburg and Courtauld Institutes* 51 (1988): 190–96. Cf. James S. Ackermann, "Leonardo's Eye," *Journal of the Warburg and Courtauld Institutes* 41 (1978): 108–13,

who considers simple perspective the same as *costruzione legittima*. All agree that what Leonardo calls *composta* involves a close viewpoint.

15. In most accounts, the most important figure in this history is Kepler and the theory of the retinal image. See David C. Lindberg, *Theories of Vision from Al-Kindi to Kepler* (Chicago: University of Chicago Press, 1976), esp. 178–208, and more recently, Adrian Johns, *The Nature of the Book: Print and Knowledge in the Making* (Chicago: University of Chicago Press, 1998), and Alpers, *Art of Describing*, chap. 2. In Kepler's model of the eye, the "point" is the entry point of rays into the eye. The image is reversed on the retina. According to the "pre-Keplerian" theory (from Alhazen), light rays were refracted in the eye, with vision seated at various locations.

16. When nonplane surfaces are involved, problems can be solved practically. In the painting of the Church at St. Ignazius, Pozzo seems to have used a mechanical means of projecting points of light onto the ceiling, using a net and string, essentially duplicating in the real world the perfectly usable theory of linear vision. See esp. M. H. Pirenne, *Optics, Painting, and Photography* (Cambridge: Cambridge University Press, 1970), 92; Pozzo (A. Putei), *Rules and examples of perspective proper for painters and architects* (1693, 1707). See further, Arthur K. Wheelock, Jr., *Perspective, Optics, and Delft Artists around 1650* (1973; New York: Garland, 1977), 70–72, 90–92.

17. Brook Taylor, *New Principles of Linear Perspective of the Art of Designing on a Plane*, 3rd ed., revised John Colson (London, 1749).

18. So Decio Gioseffi, "Perspective," in *Encyclopedia of World Art* 11 (1959), English trans. (New York: McGraw-Hill, 1966), who claims that Taylor "freed perspective from the tyranny of the ground plane" and that, with Taylor, perspective became mathematics (211).

19. An example involves misreadings of Vitruvius's distinctions *ichnographia*, *orthographia*, and *scenographia*; see *On Architecture*, I.2.2, ed. Frank Granger, 2 vols. (Cambridge, Mass.: Harvard University Press, 1931). The first two, which are simply "groundplan" and "elevation," are reinterpreted as a progression, the first two steps in a series of increasingly complex representations; in Danielle Barbaro, *La practica della perspettiva*, the series ends in the depiction of complex shapes such as dodecahedrons and "doughnuts." See also, Serlio, *Five Books of Architecture*, book two.

20. Carter, "Perspective," 843–45.

21. For axial perspective, see the clear discussion in Rudolf Arnheim, *Art and Visual Perception: A Psychology of the Creative Eye* (1954; rev. ed., Berkeley: University of California Press, 1974), 280 ff.

22. Carter, "Perspective," 845–47.

23. See further, Thomas Frangenberg, "Optical Correction in Sixteenth-Century Theory and Practice," *Renaissance Studies* 7 (1993): 214–15. That Dürer has to some extent misrepresented the problem is shown by the fact that the letters, despite where they are positioned, are the same shape.

24. Carter, "Perspective," 851.

25. Ivins, *Rationalization of Sight*, 14.

26. Both 1505 Latin text and 1509 French texts are reproduced in facsimile by Ivins, *Rationalization of Sight*; quotation at sig. A2v and sig. a2v. The French translation seems to have difficulty in this passage with several formulations describing the horizon line.

27. See also Jean Cousin's later 1560 manual. The "third points" are *any* points drawn on the horizon that are the vanishing points of parallels in the picture; Cousin, *Livre de Perspective* (Paris, 1560), sig. G1: "Icelles lignes & coings . . . sont renuoiez par lignes droittes iusques à la ligne Terre, comme est icy . . . depuis la ligne Terre, sont renuoyez au poinct Principal: puis de .b. tireres lignes aux deux Tiers poincts, merquez. 1. 2."

28. The most lucid discussion is in later editions of Nathaniel Bowditch's *American Practical Navigator* (Washington, D.C.: Department of Defense, 1977), e.g., chap. 3 "Chart Projections," 64–89.

29. *Opere volgari*, ed. Anicio Bonucci, 5 vols. (Florence: Tipografia Galileiana, 1847), 103. The sea does not in fact seem flat to sailors I know, but rather as the slight curve it actually is, one that causes objects to disappear over the horizon.

30. Erwin Panofsky, "Die Perspektive als symbolische Form," *Vorträge der Bibliothek Warburg*, 1924–25 (Leipzig, 1927), 258–330; or the English version, *Perspective as Symbolic Form*, trans. Christopher S. Wood (New York: Zone Books, 1991). Unless otherwise indicated, references below are to the English edition.

31. Samuel Y. Edgerton, Jr., *The Renaissance Rediscovery of Linear Perspective* (New York: Basic Books, 1975), 153–56, speaks of Panofsky's "egregious error." See also Joel Snyder, "Picturing Vision," *Critical Inquiry* 6 (1980): 515.

32. Panofsky, "Perspektive," notes 15–17. Panofsky cites the 1557 translation by Johannes Pena: "Aequales magnitudines inaequaliter ab oculo distantes, non servant eandem rationem angulorum quam distantiarum."

33. Erwin Panofsky, *Early Netherlandish Painting: Its Origins and Character*, 2 vols. (1953; New York: Harper and Row, 1971), 11.

34. Kim Veltman, "Panofsky's Perspective: A Half Century Later," in *La Prospettiva rinascimentale: codificazioni e trasgressioni*, ed. Marisa Dalai Emiliani, (Florence: Centro Di, 1980), 1:565–84.

35. "Textfig. 4 Gegensatz zwischen 'planperspektivischer' und 'winkelperspektivischer' Auffassung: bei der 'planperspektivischen' (oben) verhalten sich die Sehgrößen (HS und JS) umgekehrt proportional zu den Entfernungen (AB und AD); bei der 'winkelperspektivischen' (unten) verhalten sich die Sehgrößen (β und $\alpha + \beta$) nicht umgekehrt proportional zu den Entfernungen (2b und b)" (264).

36. So also John White, *The Birth and Rebirth of Pictorial Space* (1957; 3rd ed., Cambridge, Mass.: Harvard University Press, 1987), 250, on Euclid: "The dependence of apparent magnitude on the size of the visual angle is demonstrated, together with the corollary that the rate of apparent diminution is not proportional to the distance"

(250). The negative formulation is vague: for "not proportional" one should read "not *directly* proportional."

37. See Frangenberg, "Angle of Vision," 44–45. To speak of "distance to an object" in optical terms also requires that the object maintain the same orientation to the eye, a problem commonly misrepresented in drawing manuals; see for example, Montague, *Basic Perspective Drawing*, 7: a cube is shown at various distances from a viewer, but the viewer's eye is represented as above the plane along which the cube moves.

38. This is the classical three-column paradox; see the discussion and diagrams in Piero della Francesca, *De prospectiva pingendi*, ed. G. Nicco Fasola (1942; reprint, Florence: Le Lettere, 1984), concluding chapter of book 2. Such distortions are rejected by Leonardo, Frag. 109 (see *The Notebooks*, ed. Richter). Panofsky, "Perspective," note 8, calls Piero's rigorous insistence on such apparent distortions a privileging of perspective over reality.

39. See Snyder, "Picturing Vision," 507–11, on the problem of focus in camera images; the perfect focus characteristic of a painting is only achieved by pinhole camera images, not "ordinary" camera images. See further the pinhole-camera images in Pirenne, *Optics, Painting, and Photography*, 95–115. These often unnerving photographs show that Panofsky is quite wrong to claim that a camera (of any sort) reinforces a model of "untroubling" perspective.

40. So John H. Hammond, *The Camera Obscura: A Chronicle* (Bristol: Hilger, 1981), 64. By contrast, James S. Ackermann, "Alberti's Light," in *Studies ... in Honor of Millard Meiss*, ed. Irving Lavin and John Plummer (New York: New York University Press, 1977), 3, associates the rise of photography with the popularity of teaching of linear perspective.

41. In the *Tres Riches Heures* drawings, the diagonals are only implied by points on the checkerboard; the paintings of Fouquet contain drafted lines of such curves.

42. Alberti, *On Painting*, 56; Italian text, 37–38.

43. See also the often reproduced diagram of Jan Vredeman de Vries, *Perspective* (1604, 1605), intro. by Adolf K. Placzek (New York: Dover, 1968), fig. 1, called by Wheelock a "diagram of the eye's visual field" (170 and fig. 14); cf. Fragenberg, "Angle of Vision," 40–41, citing the same diagram as illustrating foreshortening in all directions, with reference to Kemp, *The Science of Art*, 109–10. Again, the diagram does not anticipate later theories of curvilinearity, but is a pure mechanical construction, based on constructing Viator's "horizon" line (so labeled) as a circle.

44. See discussion in Fragenberg, "Angle of Vision," 1–5, and diagrams from Schickhardt, fig. 1. Panofsky cites Guido Hauck and Schickhardt (33). White cites Ivon Hutchins (276). Pirenne notes that the notion of perceived curvature of straight lines is not a recent phenomenon and cites R. Smith, *A Compleat System of Opticks* (1738). Smith says a friend claims to perceive straight lines as curved (148). And most of us doubtless have friends like those of Smith.

45. For a historical example of the same problem, see Wheelock, *Perspective, Optics*, 80–81, and his discussion of Marolois. See also Panofsky, *Perspektive*, note 10 and Textfig. 10, on Wilhelm Schickhardt's proof of "Sehkurven," and Albert Flocon and André Barre, *Curvilinear Perspective: From Visual Space to the Constructed Image* (1968), trans. Robert Hansen (Berkeley: University of California Press, 1987), 58–59.

46. Fragenberg, "Angle of Vision," 2–4.

47. See Pirenne, *Optics, Painting, and Photography*, 95–115.

48. See Flocon and Barre, *Curvilinear Perspective*.

49. Ibid., 5.

50. Hansen, "Introduction," ibid., x.

20

DAVID ROSAND

Una linea sola non stentata

Castiglione, Raphael, and the Aesthetics of Grace

I send you this book as a portrait of the Court of Urbino, not by the hand of Raphael or Michelangelo, but by that of a lowly painter and one who only knows how to draw the main lines, without adorning the truth with pretty colors or making, by perspective art, that which is not seem to be.[1]

For all its conventional modesty, Baldesar Castiglione's authorial disclaimer affirms the pictorial ambition of his project. Beyond the literary portrayal of the ideal courtier, the ostensible aim of the game chosen by the courtiers and ladies at the court of Urbino, *Il Libro del Cortegiano* offers the richest image, remarkably nuanced and honest, of the culture we call the High Renaissance. Emblematic of that culture, defining it most clearly for us, as well as for Castiglione, were the achievements of its artists, Raphael and Michelangelo above all. He invokes the artists and their art to represent issues of style and self-representation, of comportment and physical appearance; they prove central to his discourse. The pages of the *Courtier* offer a sensitive articulation of High Renaissance aesthetic values, if not quite a systematically articulated theory of art.

In his dedicatory letter to Don Michel de Silva, Castiglione further qualifies his modest talent as a portraitist with confession of a double disability. He dare not attempt to portray the virtues of the Duchess herself "because not only is my style [*il mio stile*] incapable of expressing them, but my mind [*l'intelletto*] cannot even conceive them [*imaginarle*]." Then there is the question of language, his failure to imitate Boccaccio or to adopt the preferred Tuscan of his own day, which leads him to a series of observations that will find fuller elaboration later in the *Courtier:* the historical and critical relativism that allows that Boccaccio "had a fine talent by the standards of his time" and distinguishes between his writing "when he attempted with diligence and labor [*con diligenza e fatica*] to be more refined and correct" and his writing "when he let himself be guided solely by his natural genius and instinct [*dall'ingegno ed instinto suo naturale*]."

Regarding artists, undoubtedly the best known passage in the *Courtier* is that on critical judgment (I.37), which moves from comparison of Petrarch and Boccaccio through the varied harmonies and modes of music to visual pleasure and Castiglione's canonical list of painters. He names the most advanced masters in Italy about 1507, the putative year of the dialogues— which, presumably, would account for the absence of Titian:

> Consider that in painting Leonardo da Vinci, Mantegna, Raphael, Michelangelo, and Giorgio da Castelfranco are most excellent; and yet they are all unlike one another in their work: so that in his own manner no one of them appears to lack anything, since we recognize each to be perfect in his own style.[2]

And the ideal courtier will be sensitive to such distinctions of style, his judgment capable of responding to such diverse excellence. In order to exercise that judgment, according to Count Ludovico da Canossa, he should have "a knowledge of how to draw and an acquaintance with the art of painting itself [*il saper disegnare ed aver cognizion dell'arte propria del dipingere*]" (I.49).[3] Such a requirement of the courtier leads, *per forza*, to a defense of painting as a liberal art: "And do not marvel," continues the count,

> if I require this accomplishment, which perhaps nowadays may seem mechanical and ill-suited to a gentleman; for I recall reading that the ancients, especially throughout Greece, required boys of gentle birth to learn painting in school, as a decorous and necessary thing, and admitted it to first rank among the liberal arts; then by public edict they prohibited the teaching of it to slaves.[4]

A generation earlier, Leonardo da Vinci was strenuously protesting the exclusion, by the *letterati*, of painting from the liberal arts, for she is "a true daughter of nature, and performed by the most worthy sense [viz., sight]."[5]

Indeed, the count's defense of the art of painting continues a theme argued often by Leonardo himself: its universality as a microcosmic representation of the original Creator's world.

> For this universal fabric which we behold, with its vast heaven so resplendent with bright stars, with the earth at the center girdled by the seas, varied with mountains, valleys, rivers, adorned with such a variety of trees, pretty flowers, and grasses—can be said to be a great and noble picture painted by nature's hand and God's; and whoever can imitate it deserves great praise, in my opinion: nor is such imitation achieved without the knowledge of many things, as anyone knows who attempts it. (I.49)[6]

It is Castiglione himself, of course, who proves a most able spokesman on behalf of painting; indeed, aside from the projected treatise of Leonardo, it would be hard to find so considered a commentary on the art in the first decades of the Cinquecento, however apparently casual the presentation and scattered through the pages of the *Courtier*. It is clear that our author is *al corrente* with the discourse in pictorial aesthetics taking place in both the professional workshop and the humanist studio.

Speaking of the desirable balancing of opposing virtues—such as boldness and modesty—Federico Fregoso adduces the example of

> good painters who, by their use of shadow, manage to throw the light of objects into relief, and, likewise, by their use of light to deepen the shadows of planes and bring different colors together so that all are made more apparent through the contrast of one with another; and the placing of figures in opposition one to another helps them achieve their aim. (II.7)[7]

Such apposite invocation of the technical operations of *chiaroscuro* and *contrapposto* confirms the author's own visual literacy, his knowledge of the painter's art—indeed, even as that art was articulated in the notebooks of Leonardo.[8]

Turning to the *paragone* between painting and sculpture, Castiglione assumes as axiomatic that both arts "spring from the same source, namely, good design [*il bon disegno*]." *Disegno* was the complex concept, at once practical and theoretical, that was located at the core of artistic thinking from the very early Renaissance, in the handbook of Cennino Cennini and in the humanist treatise on painting of Leon Battista Alberti, in the commentaries of Lorenzo Ghiberti and the perspective treatise of Piero della Francesca; summarizing this tradition by the mid-sixteenth century, Giorgio Vasari will celebrate *disegno* as "the father" of the three visual arts: painting, sculpture, and architecture.[9] Castiglione's casual assumption of its foundational value, then, further certifies his aesthetic expertise.

And it is Castiglione who elevates the artistic politics of papal Rome to the level of principled aesthetic discourse, as the names of Raphael and Michelangelo are invoked to personify the *paragone* between their respective arts of painting and sculpture. The debate between Count Ludovico da Canossa and the sculptor Giancristoforo Romano begins with a rehearsal of issues already commonplace (I.50).[10] Sculpture "requires more labor and more skill and is of greater dignity than painting." That dignity, the count concedes, is because "statues are more durable" and because "they are made as memorials"; but it is only in "this service to memory" that sculpture can claim superiority to painting, which, "while it lasts," remains the more beautiful art. Both arts have as their goal the imitation of nature. Sculpture is more successful, for it exists in reality, in three dimensions, whereas painting deceives the eye by applying colors to a flat surface. In painting, mistakes are easily corrected; whereas a botched job of carving cannot be mended in marble. Therefore sculpture is the more difficult art.[11]

The name of Raphael is then introduced by Giancristoforo, who charges the count with defending painting "entirely for your Raphael's sake." And this, he declares, "is to praise an artist and not an art." Laughing, the count dismisses that objection, naming, in turn, the second personified representative: "I am not speaking for Raphael's sake, nor must you think me so ignorant as not to know Michelangelo's excellence in sculpture . . . " (I.51). Michelangelo is named in response to the claim of sculpture's greater difficulty, precisely the notion that will come to be associated with Michelangelo in subsequent literature on art. Insisting that he is indeed "speaking of the art and not of the artists," the count elevates the level of debate to one of higher aesthetic ontology: "it is not a matter of painting seeming and of sculpture being [*che la pittura appaia e la statuaria sia*]." And he proceeds to celebrate the universal range of painting, its imitation of light and dark, of the color of flesh and the colors of nature, of anatomy. Even more than the sculptor, the painter must possess an understanding of the human figure and, speaking of difficulty, "in this an even greater skill is needed to depict those members that are fore-shortened and that diminish in proportion to the distance, on the principle of perspective; which, by means of proportioned lines, colors, light, and shade, gives you foreground and distance on the surface of an upright wall, and as bold or as faint as he chooses." The count concludes this part of his discourse with an ekphrastic peroration of poetic enthusiasm:

And do you think it a trifle to imitate nature's colors in doing flesh, clothing, and all the other things that have color? This the sculptor can-not do; neither can he render the grace of black eyes or blue eyes, shin-ing with amorous rays. He cannot render the color of blond hair or the gleam of weapons, or the dark of night, or a storm at sea, or lightnings and thunderbolts, or the burning of a city, or the birth of rosy dawn with its rays of gold and red. In short, he cannot do sky, sea, land, mountains, woods, meadows, gardens, rivers, cities, or houses—all of which the painter can do. (I.51)

This litany of pictorial topoi draws upon an awareness of modern artistic achievement, especially, we may assume, Raphael's frescoes in the Vatican *stanze*, and a knowledge of ancient sources—in particular, Pliny the Elder.[12] And it leads to a celebration of the artistry of ancient painting, which "we can still see from certain slight remains, particularly in the grottoes of Rome, but we can know it much more clearly from the writings of the ancients in which there is such frequent and honored mention both of the works and of the masters, from which we learn how much the latter were always hon-ored by great lords and republics" (I.52). There then follows a rehearsal of well-worn Plinian anecdotes concerning the painters of antiquity—Apelles, Protogenes, Metrodorus, Zeuxis: "So let it be enough simply to say that it is fitting for our Courtier to have knowledge of painting also, since it is decorous and useful and was prized in those times when men were of greater worth than now."

Knowlege of painting, which "brings one to know the beauty of living bodies, not only in the delicacy of the face but in the proportions of the other parts," is thus a source of very great pleasure.

And let those consider this who are so enraptured when they contem-plate a woman's beauty that they believe themselves to be in paradise, and yet cannot paint; but if they could, they would gain much greater pleasure because they would more perfectly discern the beauty that engenders so much satisfaction in their hearts.[13]

Precisely because the painter is able to imitate beauty, he is better able to discern and appreciate it. Thus "Apelles must have taken more pleasure in contemplating the beauty of Campaspe than did Alexander," and therefore did Alexander give her to the painter, who had "the ability to discern [her beauty] more perfectly" (I.53). Finally, the account of Zeuxis' eclectic formation of "a figure of surpassing beauty"—the combinatorial selection by the ancient Greek painter of the best features of five individual models to create a more perfect female figure (Pliny, *Natural History*, XXXV.64)—is interrupted by the arrival of the Prefect, initiating the closing of book one of the *Courtier*.

The theme of beauty and its perception will of course be revived most expansively toward the end of book four, in Pietro Bembo's grand discourse on love, wherein the Zeuxian anecdote, depersonalized, is subject to a Platonizing drive to sublimity. Bembo's courtier, no longer young, will carry the image of his beloved "shut up in his heart, and will also, by the force of his own imagination, make her beauty much more beautiful than in reality it is [*chiuso nel core si porterà sempre seco il suo prezioso tesoro ed ancora per virtù della imaginazione si formerà dentro in se stesso quella bellezza molto più bella che in effetto non sarà*]" (IV.66). Urged toward ever higher levels of appreciation, "he will make use of this love as a step by which to mount to a love far more sublime" (IV.67), transcending the limits of "contemplating the beauty of one body only," and,

> in order to go beyond such a close limit, he will bring into his thought so many adornments that, by putting together all beauties, he will form a universal concept and will reduce the multitude of these to the unity of that single beauty which sheds itself on human nature generally. And thus he will no longer contemplate the particular beauty of one woman, but that universal beauty which adorns all bodies; and so, dazzled by this greater light, he will not concern himself with the lesser, and, burning with a better flame, he will feel little esteem for what at first he so greatly prized.[14]

In his dedicatory letter, Castiglione assumes a comparable Platonizing stance in addressing criticism that his enterprise is futile, for it is impossible "to find a man as perfect as I wish the Courtier to be" (3). "To such as these

I answer (without wishing to get into any dispute about the Intelligible World or the Ideas) that I am content to have erred with Plato, Xenophon, and Marcus Tullius; and just as, according to these authors, there is the Idea of the perfect Republic, the perfect King, and the perfect Orator, so likewise there is that of the perfect Courtier."

As conceived by Bembo, the perfect courtier will turn from this intelligible world to that of ideas in his contemplation of beauty, "and in his imagination give it a shape distinct from all matter [*e dentro nella imaginazione la formi astratta da ogni materia*]" (IV.66). This debate between the *mondo intelligibile* and that of *idee*, between *la bellezza particular d'una donna* and *quella universale*, necessarily implicates the visual arts and their mimetic goal, and Castiglione dramatizes it in another venue.

In 1554 Lodovico Dolce published a letter that has become one of the most resonant aesthetic documents of the High Renaissance: "Lettera di M. Rafaello da Urbino pittore et architetto . . . al Conte Baldasar Castiglione."[15] Referring to his recent appointment as architect of St. Peter's, the artist here speaks of his ambition to rise above the models of his predecessors ("io mi levo col pensiero piu alto"), of his search for "beautiful forms" in the buildings of antiquity, of the insufficiency of Vitruvius as a guide. He then turns to the fresco of Galatea in the Farnesina, the villa suburbana of Agostino Chigi. To paint such a beauty, the artist explains, he would have to study many beautiful models and (like Zeuxis) select the best features of each. However, given the dearth of such beauties and of good judges, he avails himself of an Idea of beauty that he has formed in his mind ("io mi servo di certa Idea, che mi viene nella mente").

In an impressive philological study of this text, John Shearman has explored its sources in Giovanni Francesco Pico della Mirandola (*De imitatione* [1512]) and in Cicero (*Orator*, ii, 9).[16] More significantly, he demonstrated that the author of the letter was not Raphael but was, in fact, the *Signor Conte* to whom it was addressed: Castligione himself.[17] Such authorial masking is precisely the sort of literary fiction to be found in the *Elegy* addressed to himself that Castiglione wrote in the voice of his wife Ippolita—and which reports their son's response to Raphael's portrait of the father (fig. 1).[18] Shearman concluded that the letter represents Castiglione's literary portrait of Raphael, a "portrait of the mind," written just after the artist's death in 1520.

Castiglione's Raphael letter succeeded in imposing a Platonic idealism on the painter's art. Such idealism seemed perfectly suited to the classicism of that art, for, its literary subterfuge notwithstanding, the letter speaks in a voice that we find consonant with the style we see in the paintings. We, like

FIGURE. I. Raphael, *Portrait of Baldesar Castiglione.* Musée du Louvre, Paris. Courtesy of Réunion des Musées Nationaux/Art Resource, NY.

Castiglione, feel compelled to idealize Raphael's figures, which seem to transcend the accidents of nature to approach a more perfect form. But the image of the artist rendered by Castiglione is fuller than the letter to himself from "Raphael"; the elements of its design, essential outlines as well as coloring, are to be found in the pages of his *Courtier.* Defining the qualities of the ideal courtier, Castiglione sets forth a vocabulary and set of values that will effectively determine the image of the artist for succeeding generations.

When, between 1523 and 1527, Paolo Giovio writes of Raphael that his art is characterized by "that particular beauty that we call grace," he is transposing to the criticism of art the language of courtesy, itself already informed by ineffable spiritual values.[19] This is the language that will be further broadcast in 1550 with the publication of the first edition of Giorgio Vasari's *Lives*, by now applied to the artist as well as to his art. Indeed the opening of Vasari's biography of Raphael exploits the full resonance of that key term, *grazia:*

How bountiful and benign heaven shows itself at times in blessing a single person with the infinite riches of its treasures, endowing him with all those graces [*ampie grazie*] and rare gifts that are usually spread over a long space of time and distributed among many individuals; this can clearly be seen in the case of Raphael Sanzio of Urbino, no less excellent than gracious [*grazioso*], who possessed all that modesty and goodness which is to be found in those whose special humanity and gentle nature is further adorned by a gracious courtesy [*graziata affabilità*], those, unique or rare, who generously share such gifts through their courteous behavior at all times toward persons of whatever station. Such was the gift that nature made to us, when, having already been satisfied by being vanquished by art through the hand of Michelangelo Buonarroti, wished now by Raphael to be vanquished by both art and character [*dall'arte e da i costumi*].[20]

In Vasari's aesthetic hagiography Raphael is brought into the world to shed the light of civility among the crowd of uncouth artisans, Raphael in whom there "so brilliantly shone all the finest qualities of mind, along with such grace, industry, beauty, modesty, and excellence of character [*chiarissimamente risplendevano tutte le egregie virtú dello animo, accompagnate da tanta grazia, studio, bellezza, modestia e costumi buoni*]." Overcoming vice by the virtue of such gifts, Raphael is more than just a man but must be counted among the mortal gods ["dèi mortali"].[21] Vasari concludes his biography with a celebration of the quasi Orphic effect of Raphael's graciousness, taming the baser instincts of those around him; those who worked directly in his company found themselves united in harmony, freed of bad humors and vile thoughts, influenced "dalla cortesia e dall'arte sua." And Raphael himself, always accompanied by a retinue of artists when he went to court, conducted himself as a prince: "Egli insomma non visse da pittore, ma da principe."[22]

In the "proemio" to the third part of his *Lives,* Vasari appropriates the vocabulary of courtesy to characterize the *maniera moderna,* that style initiated by Leonardo da Vinci and further refined by Raphael and Michelangelo. The preceding style, of the Quattrocento—which Vasari later characterized as labored, a "maniera secca, cruda e stentata"[23]—is criticized for its rigid concern with rule and measure, its lack of spontaneity and proper visual judgment. Missing from that art, and essential to the modern achievement, was a certain "grace beyond measure [*una grazia che eccedesse la misura*]."[24] Of all the early masters of the modern manner, "the most graceful" was Raphael ("il graziosissimo Raffaello"), whose creatures, reflecting the character of their creator, manifested "il dono della grazia."[25]

In faces painted by Raphael was to be found "quella grazia del volto" celebrated in the *Courtier* (I.19). It is Count Ludovico da Canossa, spokesman for painting (and for Raphael), who in fact introduces the concept of grace into the dialogue as an essential component of the ideal courtier:

I would wish the Courtier favored in this other respect, and endowed by nature not only with talent and with beauty of countenance and person, but with that certain grace which we call an "air" [*un sangue*], which shall make him at first sight pleasing and lovable to all who see him; and let this be an adornment informing and attending all his actions, giving the promise outwardly that such a one is worthy of the company and the favor of every great lord. (I.14)

And it is the count who, when pressed for clarification of this ineffable quality, this "gift of nature and the heavens" (I.24), carries the discourse to its most resonant conclusion. As Cesare Gonzaga observes, "by the very meaning of the word, it can be said that he who has grace finds grace." How then is one to acquire this gift? Although "it is almost proverbial that grace is not learned" (I.25), it is possible to acquire it through judicious imitation, imitation in a Zeuxian eclectic mode: "And even as in green meadows the bee flits about among grasses robbing the flowers, so our Courtier must steal this grace from those who seem to him to have it, taking from each the part that seems most worthy of praise" (I.26). Better still, however, the count offers his

universal rule . . . valid above all others, and in all human affairs whether in word or deed: and that is to avoid affectation in every way possible . . .

and (to pronounce a new word perhaps) to practice in all things a certain *sprezzatura*, so as to conceal all art and make whatever is done or said appear to be without effort and almost without any thought about it. And I believe much grace comes of this: because everyone knows the difficulty of things that are rare and well done; whereas facility in such things causes the greatest wonder.

Therefore, he concludes, "we may call that art true art which does not seem to be art" [*si po dir quella esser vera arte che non pare esser arte*].

Castiglione's formulations will enter the literature of art most directly through Lodovico Dolce's *Dialogo della pittura, intitolato l'Aretino*, published in Venice in 1557 in response to the first edition of Vasari's *Lives*, as a corrective to the Tuscan's teleological adulation of Michelangelo and his total neglect of Titian. Among the most active *poligrafi* in the hectic publishing world of Cinquecento Venice, Dolce was a particularly close reader of Castiglione's *Courtier*, of which he prepared an edition.[26] His own dialogue on painting—after Vasari's *Lives*, the most influential sixteenth-century publication on the art—even more deliberately and creatively adapted the language of the *Courtier* to the critical evaluation of painting.[27] In the *paragone* that opens the dialogue, against the acknowledged *disegno* and *terribilità* of Michelangelo's figures is set "la maniera leggiadra e gentile" of Raphael; against Michelangelo's *difficultà* Raphael's *facilità*, which is "the main criterion of excellence" in painting and "the hardest to attain."[28] And Dolce's Aretino concludes this part of his argument with the aesthetic dictum that art is the hiding of art: "è arte a nasconder l'arte." Dolce, the professional literary man, surely knew its ancient pedigree in Ovid's "Ars est celare artem" (*Ars amatoria*, II.313), but his appropriation of that literary commonplace for the painting of an artist possessing all the qualities and gentle manners befitting a gentleman ("ogni virtù, & ogni bel costume e gentil creanza, che conviene a gentil'huomo")[29] suggests the more immediate inspiration of Castiglione's *Courtier*.

That inspiration is overt in Dolce's boldest transposition of courtly virtue to the painter's studio, his appropriation of Castiglione's "new word," *sprezzatura*. Indeed, his own wording seems intent upon declaring the model that he emulates. The subject is the coloring of figures: "In questo mi pare che ci si voglia una certa convenevole sprezzatura," without which there is the danger of affectation, "which denies grace."[30] A certain sprezzatura, affectation, grace: the vocabulary is Castiglione's. As is the culminating anecdotal example of Apelles' criticism of Protogenes, who didn't know when to stop, when to take his hands from the painting. Too much diligence is to be avoided, for it is always harmful: "Bisogna sopra tutto," declares Aretino, "fuggire la troppa diligenza, che in tutte le cose nuoce."[31]

In the *Courtier*, this Plinian anecdote leads Castiglione's count to further examples of *facilità* in various human activities: in arms, in dancing, and in music—for instance, a singer who ends a phrase with an ornament casually tossed-off "with such facility that he appears to do it quite by chance," thus demonstrating that he is capable of much more.[32] From such vocal sprezzatura, the discourse returns to painting and to the most original and revealing passage on the subject in all of the *Courtier:*

> Spesso ancor nella pittura una linea sola non stentata, un sol colpo di penello tirato facilmente, di modo che paia che la mano, senza esser guidata da studio o arte alcuna, vada per se stessa al suo termine secondo la intenzion del pittore, scopre chiaramente la eccellenzia dell'artifice, circa la opinion della quale ognuno poi si estende secondo il suo giudicio; e 'l medesimo interviene quasi d'ogni altra cosa. (I.28)

> Often too in painting, a single line which is not labored, a single brush stroke made with ease in such a manner that the hand seems of itself to complete the line desired by the painter, without being directed by care or skill of any kind, clearly reveals that excellence of craftsmanship, which people will then proceed to judge, each by his own lights. And the same happens in almost every other thing.

The count's appreciation of a single unlabored line, a single inspired stroke of the brush, demonstrates this particular courtier's own aesthetic *virtù*. Beyond that personal validation of credentials, however, it is in itself a remarkable statement. Such a line, independently realizing its goal, testifies at once to its own sprezzatura, as a mark, as well as to that of its maker.[33] Perhaps the clearest articulation of sensitivity to the *art* of painting from the High Renaissance, the count's observation is a response to the painter's performance as well as to his product, an appreciation of the creative act itself.

Leonardo, reflecting on the creative act of drawing, had recognized in the sketch the very dynamics of imaginative projection; in his commentaries on the sketch, exploring the dialectical reciprocity between the drawing hand and the emerging image, between the creator and his creation, he had been

observing his own creative performance.[34] Castiglione extends that awareness from the practicing artist to the responsive viewer, the amateur whose
knowledge of the practice of art heightens his appreciation of the finished
work of art. As visual literacy assumed increasing importance in the education of a gentleman, whether in fact a man of letters, who has "never laid
hands on a paintbrush," was capable of judging painting was becoming
an issue of contention—to be addressed directly by Dolce.[35] In the count's
praise of that single stroke, Castiglione freed art criticism from its previous
dependence on rhetorical models and, in effect, took it back into the studio.[36]
His courtier's knowledge of painting was not to be purely theoretical but
based on the practical experience of knowing how to draw: "il saper disegnare." That, we may assume, is the kind of experience implicit in the count's
appreciation of the single line.

The hand that appears to move of its own volition, beyond studied professional control, offers a most graphic example of the art that hides art. In
isolating such a phenomenon, Castiglione refines, even as he epitomizes, assumptions about the mark that go back to the early Renaissance and find
their ultimate roots in classical antiquity. Already by about 1400, Cennino
Cennini had declared skill of hand (*operazione di mano*) along with imagination (*fantasia*) as essential to the painter's invention, his ability to find things
unknown (*di trovare cose non vedute*), to fix them with the hand (*fermarle con
la mano*), to make manifest that which does not exist (*a dimostrare quello che
non è, sia*).[37] And a generation later, Leon Battista Alberti, in isolating the
separate elements of the art, revealed a fuller appreciation of pure drawing:
"Nor is it unusual to see a good circumscription alone, that is, a good drawing
by itself be most pleasing [*uno buono disegno per sé essere gratissimo*]." Circumscription, indeed, should be of lines so fine that they are hardly visible: "di
linee sotilissime fatta, quasi tali che fuggano essere vedute."[38]

In defining *circonscrizione*, the foundational element of painting, the humanist Alberti invokes the example of Parrhasios, famous in antiquity for
the particular fineness of his lines. And he then cites the other celebrated
ancient master of the fine line, Apelles, with a glancing allusion to his line-
splitting competition with Protogenes (Pliny, *Natural History*, XXXV.81–83).
In that extraordinarily resonant anecdote of antiquity, Protogenes recognizes the presence of Apelles in a single line—recognizes, as the Renaissance
would have it, *la sua mano*. The mark of Apelles, his *linea summae tenuitatis*,
stands as both trace and index of the artist. A demonstration of skill tossed
off with inevitably self-referential *disinvoltura*, it is a declaration of profes-

sional self, at once work and signature. Thus professionally challenged, Protogenes drew a still finer line upon Apelles' line; Apelles, in turn, topped that performance with the finest imaginable line. The resulting panel, Pliny reports, appeared a blank surface with lines that were nearly invisible, but to those who know, especially to artists, it seemed a true marvel (*artificum praecipuo miraculo*). The exact nature of Apelles' line was to become a professional concern of painters in the Renaissance (and a problem to subsequent scholars); but, whatever their form, the lines of both competitors stood as models of virtuosity—and, to Castiglione's reading, certainly, of sprezzatura.[39]

But it was Parrhasios, as Alberti well knew, who was unrivalled in the rendering of outline, in creating contours that seem to follow the surfaces of the bounded figure, to enclose it so as to imply even the parts hidden from view (Pliny, *Natural History*, XXXV.67–68). The line of Parrhasios, a mimetic contour, will prove to be the more relevant challenge to artists: the single line that seems to disrupt the flatness of the surface, subtly inflecting itself into space, disappearing behind its own horizon. Representing the complex potential of line itself, a mark at once created and creating, this is what Leonardo was to call the *serpeggiare* of the line.[40]

Behind the count's celebration of the single unforced line, then, lies an ancient tradition of such critical appreciation. The more immediate inspiration, as his association with the artist in Castiglione's dialogue confirms, is the art of Raphael. That *linea sola non stentata* is in every sense the line of Raphael. In a drawing by Raphael, the flow of line and the flow of form identify with particular ease (fig. 2). Fluency of figural action depends as much on the mellifluous movement of the draftsman's hand as on the actual poses struck by the imagined bodies, on a concinnity between the two. The slow sinuosity of Raphael's line, its unforced course, matches that same quality in his figural conception, the easy strain of athletic grace: calligraphy and choreography in mutually expressive operation. This quiet but persuasive fulfillment of mimetic function by line epitomizes that *grazia* recognized as the special virtue of Raphael's art and person, a grace of comportment, manifesting itself in the movements of the artist and his creations. Like Apelles, Raphael possessed that "grace called *charis* in Greek," and his figures, like those of the ancient master, manifested that same rare quality of charm (*venustà*), which is so hard to define.[41] The easy transference of the term between artist and art, identifying one with the other, assumed a relationship that was to form a basic principle of connoisseurship. Ultimately, the count is indeed subject to the charge of confusing the artist and the art (I. 50).

FIGURE. 2. Raphael, *Study for the Figure of Melpomene.* Courtesy of the Ashmolean Museum, Oxford.

By his line shall the artist be known. An earlier Renaissance variant on that Plinian topos was the story of the "O" of Giotto, the artist's celebrated demonstration of his mastery. When asked to submit a sample of his work for papal consideration, Giotto, "che cortesissimo era," took up a brush and drew a perfect circle, telling the puzzled emissary to take that back to his holiness. The artist chose a circle to represent himself. His freehand rendering was indeed a display of virtuosity, and Vasari is careful to describe the mechanics of this performance—how Giotto transformed himself into a compass by steadying his arm against his body and, with his wrist as pivot, moving only his hand, turned a perfect circle: "Eccovi il disegno." Giotto's performance was a marvel to behold ("che fu a vederlo una maraviglia grandissima"). But the messenger, believing this a mockery of art, failed to appreciate such a manifestation of sprezzatura. It is what I have done, replies the artist; take it to Rome and see if it will be understood (". . . è quel che io fatto: mandatelo a Roma insieme con gli altri e vedrete se sarà conosciuto"). In Rome, of course, it was understood by the pope and by many *cortegiani intendenti*, who recognized in that freehand-drawn circle the excellence of Giotto.[42]

The scenes of incomprehension, protest, and final appreciation that make up the narrative of the Giotto story—proving the obtuseness of the pope's man (who thought the artist was joking) and, by contrast, the aesthetic infallibility of papal judgment (recognizing the rarity of the talent so manifest)—are socially revealing. The master painter tests the connoisseur. In Giotto's divinely controlled line could be seen all the virtue of his art—by those who could see. Returning to the classical source, and ostensibly quoting Michelangelo himself in a dialogue set in Rome in 1538, Francisco de Hollanda neatly summarized the situation: "in a mere straight line Apelles was recognized by Protogenes."[43] The line is recognized as the natural expression of the artist, an extension of his very person, and the means by which the viewer gets to know him. In this most elementary expressive sign, the artist reveals himself by demonstrating his art. Pliny's tale of the Apelles-Protogenes competition was cast in the most professional terms, of both technical virtuosity and sensitive connoisseurship. The story is recounted, yet again, by Paolo Pino to exemplify the necessity of the painter being possessed of a swift but steady hand, which can only be a natural gift: "La prontezza e sicurtà di mano è grazia concessa dalla natura."[44] From such grace flows a naturally graceful line, the virtue of which, its *facilità*, will be apparent to the eyes of those who understand, *cortegiani intendenti*.

Like Vasari, Pino too disparages the art of his Quattrocento predecessors, those masters who drew "con tanta istrema diligenza."[45] Above all, as the count admonished, one must avoid the "troppo diligenza" that Apelles criticized in Protogenes; it is facility in achieving the difficult that inspires "grandissima maraviglia," whereas the opposite, "il sforzare," yields only disgrace ("dà summa disgrazia").

Una linea sola non stentata, un sol colpo di penello tirato facilmente: Apparent effortlessness, ease and facility, the masking of application — this is the true art, which is at once the source and manifestation of grace. In the movements of the body it manifests itself as "quella sprezzata desinvoltura," that easy nonchalance of the naturally graceful figure. These are the qualities Castiglione and his contemporaries recognized in Raphael and his art, but no other humanist or courtier articulated that recognition with such critical precision. In comparison, Giovio's words sound as rhetorical as they are, part of a shared vocabulary of *venustas* and *gratia*, but without visual conviction. In isolating the single line, Castiglione brought to critical focus the essential element of Renaissance *disegno*. In appreciating its making, as well as its form, he acknowledged the intimate rapport between the artist and his mark, but also, by implication, between the figure of the artist and the figures of his creation. *Disegno,* as Dolce put it, "is the form given by the painter to the things he is imitating; and it is really a turning movement of lines in various ways, which give form to the figures."[46] That identity of drawing and form, of line and figure, will become something of a commonplace, but in the context of the *Courtier* it resonates with special reference to Raphael. In his drawing, a single unforced line, a naturally flowing contour, moves with ease across the paper, inflecting itself into space with the figure it defines. A study for one of the mothers in the fresco of the *Expulsion of Heliodorus from the Temple* epitomizes the essential conception of the figure in the graceful contour of her turning neck (fig. 3); studied again to the right as an isolated motif, that line summarizes the entire formal issue. As her neck is the pivot of dramatic action here, the critical moment of turn back into space, so its outline carries the full responsibility of spatialization — folding back, enclosing the object, and "clearly suggesting what it conceals": Parrhasios redivivus. Castiglione, who knew the artist so well, created the language of our appreciation of Raphael's line.

Giving modern critical voice to High Renaissance aesthetic ideals, Heinrich Wölfflin offered eloquent testimony to the continuing force of that critical tradition: "It now seems that a new sympathy has been aroused

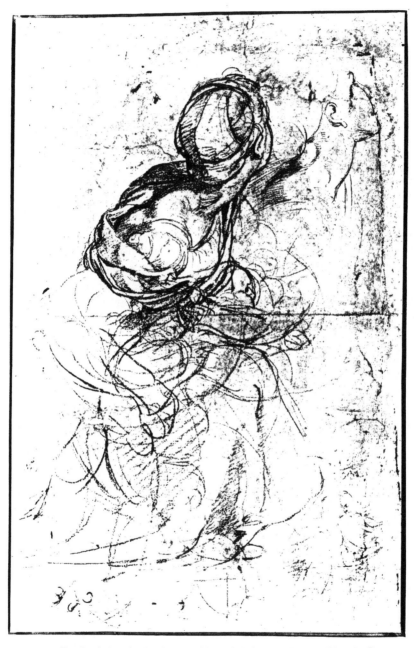

FIGURE. 3. Raphael, *Studies for the Expulsion of Heliodorus from the Temple.* Courtesy of the Ashmolean Museum, Oxford.

for the line in itself, as if it were now conceded that it has a right to live its own life."[47]

That Vasari and Dolce subsequently appropriated the language of the *Courtier* for commentary on the visual arts is clear, but, as I have suggested, Castiglione's contribution to art criticism goes beyond his offering a model of courtly behavior. "The fact that Vasari's grace derives from a book of manners," wrote Anthony Blunt, "shows the real significance of the idea in his works."[48] True, Vasari sought the painter's entry into the world of the court, and, equally true, Raphael seems to have offered the ideal model of such comportment and social accomplishment. We have learned, however, not to limit the achievement of the *Courtier* to its reception as a mere book of manners, as international as its influence was in that regard; its equivocal vision of both reality and ideality testifies to its greater complexity, to its *serio ludere* and to its genuine *pathos*.[49] So, too, must we avoid limiting the full achievement of Castiglione's commentary on art. More than serving as a social model, his *Courtier* gives voice to a truly visual sensibility, a profound appreciation of the art of painting and of the painter. In this regard, it speaks eloquently for its culture, a culture that had come to appreciate and admire both the formal creation and the act of the creator.

Notes

This clearly is the appropriate occasion to acknowledge my debt to a friend and colleague, who will recognize how much I owe to what has been, for me, the very best experience in teaching over many years: our Columbia College colloquium on themes in the art and literature of the Renaissance. Teaching with Bob Hanning, reading texts and images with him, has been an extension of my own education, a recall to the poetry of art and an exploration of its great resonance. I offer this essay in friendship and gratitude, a gesture of appreciation for his grace.

1. Baldesar Castiglione to Don Michel de Silva, Bishop of Viseu: ". . . mandovi questo libro come un ritratto di pittura della corte d'Urbino, non di mano di Rafaello o Michel Angelo, ma di pittor ignobile e che solamente sappia tirare le linee principali, senza adornar la verità de vaghi colori o far parer per arte di prospettiva quello che non è." *Il Libro del Cortegiano con una scelta delle opere minori di Baldesar Castiglione*, ed. Bruno Maier, 2d ed. (Turin: Unione Tipografico–Editrice Torinese, 1964), 71. Translation by Charles S. Singleton, *The Book of the Courtier* (Garden City, N.Y.: Doubleday Anchor Books, 1959), 3.

2. "Eccovi che nella pittura sono eccellentissimi Leonardo Vincio, il Mantegna, Rafaello, Michel Angelo, Georgio da Castel Franco: nientedimeno, tutti son tra sé nel far dissimili, di modo che ad alcun di loro non par che manchi cosa alcuna in quella maniera, perché si conosce ciascun nel suo stilo esser perfettissimo." Later in the dialogues (III.36) the count alludes to women who have excelled in painting and in sculpture, as well as in letters and in music, assuming that such instances are well known to his fellow players.

3. So too should the *donna di palazzo* share in such knowledge: "voglio che questa donna abbia notizie di lettere, di musica, di pittura," proclaims signor Gaspar Pallavicino (III.9).

4. "Né vi maravigliate s'io desidero questa parte, la qual oggidì forse par mecanica e poco conveniente a gentilomo; ché ricordomi aver letto che gli antichi, massimamente per tutta Grecia, voleano che i fanciulli nobili nelle scole alla pittura dessero opera come a cosa onesta e necessaria, a fu questa ricevuta nel primo grado dell'arti liberali; poi per publico editto veteto che ai servi non s'insegnasse." The recollected ancient readings were Aristotle, *Politics*, VIII.3, and Pliny the Elder, *Natural History*, XXXV.77. The argument had been made a century earlier, with some reluctance, by the humanist Pier Paolo Vergerio, who nonetheless maintained that "drawing has no place amongst our liberal studies; except in so far as it is identical with writing (which is in reality one side of the art of drawing), it belongs to the painter's profession" (*De ingenuis moribus*, trans. William Harrison Woodward in his *Vittorino da Feltre and Other Humanist Educators* [1897; reprint, New York: Teachers College Press, 1963]), 107.

5. Leonardo da Vinci, *Treatise on Painting [Codex Urbinas Latinus 1270]*, ed. A. Philip McMahon (Princeton, N.J.: Princeton University Press, 1956), I, 28; see also Claire J. Farago, *Leonardo da Vinci's 'Paragone': A Critical Interpretation with a New Edition of the Text in the Codex Urbinas* (Leiden: E.J. Brill, 1992), 237 (chap. 27). A measure of the continuing humanist prejudice is offered by Castiglione's contemporary, Mario Equicola, court humanist to Isabella d'Este at Mantua, in the *eruditissimo discorso della pittura* appended to his *Institutioni . . . al compore ogni sorte di rima della lingua volgare*, published posthumously in 1541 but written about 1510 – 15: "Quantunque adunque degna di laude sia la pittura, la plastice e la scultura, nondimeno inferiori assai alla poetica si giudicano di autorità e di degnità. E' la pittura opera e fatica più del corpo che dell'animo, dagli idiotici esercitata il più delle volte. . . ." Paola Barocchi, ed., *Scritti d'arte del Cinquecento* (Milan and Naples: Riccardo Ricciardi Editore, 1971 – 77), 259.

6. "E veramente chi non estima questa arte parmi che molto sia dalla ragione alieno; ché la machina del mondo, che noi veggiamo coll'amplo cielo di chiare stelle tanto splendido e nel mezzo la terra dai mari cinta, di monti, valli e fiumi variata e di sì diversi alberi e vaghi fiori e d'erbe ornata, dir si po che una nobile e gran pittura sia, per man della natura e di Dio composta; la qual chi po imitare parmi esser di

gran laude degno; né a questo pervenir si po senza la cognizion di molte cose, come ben sa chi lo prova."

7. "Però bisogna che sappia valersene, e per lo paragone e quasi contrarietà dell'una talor far che l'altra sia più chiaramente conosciuta, come i boni pittori, i quali con l'ombra fanno apparere e mostrano i lumi de' rilevi, e così col lume profundano l'ombre dei piani e compagnano i colori diversi insieme di modo, che per quella diversità l'uno e l'altro meglio si dimostra, e 'l posar delle figure contrario l'una all'altra le aiuta a far quello'officio che è intenzion del pittore."

8. Cf., e.g., Leonardo, *Treatise on Painting*, ¶845: "*Of giving aid by means of artificial lights and shadows to the simulation of relief in painting.* To increase relief in painting, interpose a beam of bright light, which separates the shape from the obscured object between the shape represented and the visual object which receives shadow. . . ." ¶271: "*Of varying the vigor, age, and complexion of bodies in narrative paintings.* I say also that in narrative paintings one ought to mingle direct contraries so that they may afford a great contrast to one another, and all the more when they are in close proximity. . . ." For fuller discussion of these issues, see David Summers, "Contrapposto: Style and Meaning in Renaissance Art," *Art Bulletin* 59 (1977): 336–61.

9. For the evolving notion of *disegno*, see David Rosand, *Drawing Acts: Studies in Graphic Expression and Representation* (Cambridge: Cambridge University Press, 2002), 24–60, with further bibliography.

10. The nomination of Raphael and Michelangelo as representative of their respective arts occurs as well in Pietro Bembo, *Prose della volgar lingua* (III.1), published in 1525: ". . . Michele Agnolo fiorentino e Rafaello da Urbino, l'uno dipintore e scultore e architetto parimente, l'altro e dipintore e architetto altresì" (Pietro Bembo, *Prose e rime*, ed. Carlo Dionisotti, 2d ed. [Turin: Classici UTET, 1966], 183–84). Raphael's name is first inserted into this passage in the *Courtier* in a manuscript datable to ca. 1516: see John Shearman, "Castiglione's Portrait of Raphael," *Mitteilungen des Kunsthistorischen Institutes in Florez* 38 (1994): 69–97, esp. 72–74.

11. Castiglione's presentation of the *paragone* anticipates many of the points that will later be argued rather more academically by Benedetto Varchi's *Lezzione nella quale si disputa della maggioranza delle arti e qual sia più nobile, la scultura o la pittura* (1546; ed. Paola Barocchi, in *Trattati d'arte del Cinquecento* [Bari: Gius. Laterza and Figli, 1960], 1:1–82), in which a number of contemporary artists, including Michelangelo, were invited to respond to the query. See Leatrice Mendelsohn, *Paragoni: Benedetto Varchi's Due Lezzioni and Cinquecento Art Theory* (Ann Arbor, Mich.: UMI Research Press, 1982).

12. As examples of appropriately monumental princely patronage, in addition to the "noble palace" of Urbino, which hosts the dialogues, Castiglione cites the great enterprises of Julius II in Rome, the rebuilding of St. Peter's and the Belevedere

(IV.36), both projects of Bramante. The count's inventory of landscape effects is typical of ekphrastic exercises, while the more ephemeral phenomena in particular recall Pliny's praise of ancient Apelles, who "painted the unpaintable, thunder, for example, lightning and thunderbolts" (*Natural History*, XXXV.96). Philostratus the Elder offers another relevant ancient celebration of painting's imitative range (*Imagines*, I, introduction).

13. With the Pygmalion legend as ultimate reference, the painter's ability to inflame the passion of the lover with an effigy of the beloved was a point in Leonardo's argument of the superiority of his art over that of the poet: *Treatise on Painting*, ¶33; Farago, *Leonardo da Vinci's 'Paragone'*, 231.

14. "Ma tra questi beni troveranne lo amante un altro ancor assai maggiore, se egli vorrà servirsi di questo amore come d'un grado per ascendere ad un altro molto più sublime: il che gli succederà, se tra sé anderà considerando come stretto legame sia il star sempre impedito nel contemplar la bellezza d'un corpo solo; e però, per uscire di questo così angusto termine, aggiungerà nel pensier suo a poco a poco tanti ornamenti, che cumulando insieme tutte le bellezze farà un concetto universale e ridurrà la moltitudine d'esse alla unità di quella sola che generalmente sopra la umana natura si spande; e così non più la bellezza particular d'una donna, ma quella universale, che tutti i corpi adorna, contemplarà; onde offuscato da questo maggior lume, non curerà il minore, ed ardendo in più eccellente fiamma, poco estimarà quello che prima avea tanto apprezzato."

15. Lodovico Dolce, *Lettere di diversi eccellentiss. Huomini, raccolte da diversi libri: tra le quali se ne leggono molte, non piu stampate* (Venice: Gabriel Giolito de Ferrari, 1554), 226–28. The letter was revised in subsequent editions of Dolce's book and in other publications. The original text, which I have used, is reprinted in the fundamental study by John Shearman, "Castiglione's Portrait of Raphael," 69–97, which contains a full bibliographic review.

16. Shearman, "Castiglione's Portrait of Raphael," 80–82. For more on the epistolary exchange between Pico della Mirandola and Bembo regarding the nature of imitation, see Clark Hulse, *The Rule of Art: Literature and Painting in the Renaissance* (Chicago: University of Chicago Press, 1990), 92–106.

17. Castiglione had collaborated with Raphael in the equally famous letter to Pope Leo X regarding the antiquities of Rome, a response to the pope's charge that the artist "ponessi in disegno Roma antica." For the text, see Barocchi, ed., *Scritti d'arte del Cinquecento* 3:2971–85; and Ettore Camesasca, *Raffaello: Gli scritti. Lettere, firme, sonetti, saggi tecnici e teorici* (Milan: Biblioteca Universale Rizzoli, 1993), 257–322, with a review of the relevant critical literature. For further discussion, see Roger Jones and Nicholas Penny, *Raphael* (New Haven: Yale University Press, 1983), 199–205.

18. "Balthassaris Castilionis elegia qua fingit Hippolyten suam ad se ipsum scribentem " (*Il Cortegiano, con una scelta delle opere minori*, ed. Maier, 596–604). For

the complicated bibliography on the poem, see Shearman, "Castiglione's Portrait of Raphael," 79, with further references. For the relationship of the elegy to Raphael's portrait of Castiglione, see David Rosand, "The Portrait, the Courtier, and Death," in *Castiglione: The Ideal and the Real in Renaissance Culture,* ed. Robert W. Hanning and David Rosand (New Haven: Yale University Press, 1983), 91–129; John Shearman, *Only Connect . . . : Art and the Spectator in the Italian Renaissance* (Princeton, N.J.: Princeton University Press, 1992), 135–37; and, setting the poem within the broader circle of Raphael, Hulse, *The Rule of Art,* 77–114, esp. 90–92. On Raphael's portrait of Castiglione, see John Shearman, "Le portrait de *Baldassare Castiglione* par Raphaël," *Revue du Louvre* 29 (1979): 261–70; and, with the most recent bibliography, the exhibition catalogue *Raphael: Grace and Beauty,* ed. Patrizia Nitti et al. (Milan: Skira Editore, 2001), cat. no. 7.

19. "Caeterum in toto picturae genere numquam eius operi venustas defuit, quam gratiam interpretantur." Giovio's *Raphaelis Urbinatis vita* is published in Barocchi, ed., *Scritti d'arte del Cinquecento,* 1:13–18; for the dating of the manuscript, see 1098–1101, with further references. On Giovio's biographies of Leonardo, Michelangelo, and Raphael, see T. C. Price Zimmerman, "Paolo Giovio and the Evolution of Renaissance Art Criticism," in *Cultural Aspects of the Italian Renaissance: Essays in Honour of Paul Oskar Kristeller,* ed. Cecil H. Clough (Manchester: University of Manchester Press, 1976), 406–24.

20. Giorgio Vasari, *Le vite de' più eccellenti architetti, pittori, et scultori italiani, da Cimabue insino a' tempi nostri (Nell'edizione per i tipi di Lorenzo Torrentino, Firenze 1550),* ed. Luciano Bellosi and Aldo Rossi (Turin: Giulio Einaudi Editore, 1986), 610: "Quanto largo e benigno si dimostri talora il cielo collocando, anzi per meglio dire, riponendo et accumulando in una persona sola le infinite ricchezze delle ampie grazie o tesori suoi, e tutti que' rari doni che fra lungo spazio di tempo suol compartire e molti individui, chiaramente poté vedersi nel non meno eccellente che grazioso Rafael Sanzio da Urbino; il quale con tutta quella modestia e bontà, che sogliono usar coloro che hanno una certa umanità di natura gentile, piena d'ornamento e di graziata affabilità, la quale in tutte le cose sempre si mostra, onoratamente spiegando i predetti doni con qualunche condizione di persone et in qualsivoglia maniera di cose, per unico od almeno molto raro universalmente si fé conosciere. Di costui fece dono la natura a noi, essendosi di già contentata d'essere vinta dall'arte per mano di Michele Agnolo Buonarroti, e volse ancora per Rafaello esser vinta dall'arte e da i costumi."

21. Ibid., 610–11.

22. Ibid., 640. For fuller discussion of Vasari's life of Raphael, see Patricia Lee Rubin, *Giorgio Vasari: Art and History* (New Haven: Yale University Press, 1995), 357–401.

23. Giorgio Vasari, *Le vite de' più eccellenti pittori, scultori ed architetti* (1568), ed. Gaetano Milanesi (Florence, 1878–85), 7:427.

24. Vasari, *Vite* (1550), ed. Bellosi and Rossi, 540.

25. Ibid., 542. Still a fine introduction to *grazia* in Vasari is Anthony Blunt, *Artistic Theory in Italy 1450–1600* (Oxford: Oxford University Press, 1940), 93–98

26. *Il libro del Cortegiano, nuovamente con diligenza rivisto per Ludovico Dolce* (in Vinegia, appresso Gabriel Giolito de' Ferrari, 1566). It is worth noting that the *editio princeps* of 1528 and the subsequent five editions of Castiglione's book were all published in Venice, "nelle case d'Aldo Romano e d'Andrea d'Asolo." See the bibliographic note in *Il libro del Cortegiano*, ed. Maier, 55–56.

27. On Dolce's book, its sources and its influence, see the introduction to Mark W. Roskill, *Dolce's "Aretino" and Venetian Art Theory of the Cinquecento* (New York: New York University Press, 1968), 5–82; and for its position in the development of a larger aesthetic tradition, see Rensselaer W. Lee, *Ut Pictura Poesis: The Humanistic Theory of Painting* (New York: W. W. Norton, 1967), originally published in *The Art Bulletin* 22 (1940): 197–269. For the possible influence of Dolce's *Dialogo* on Sidney's *Defense of Poesy*, see David Rosand, "Dialogues and Apologies: Sidney and Venice," *Studies in Philology* 88 (1991): 236–49.

28. Dolce, *Dialogo della pittura*, ed. Roskill, in *Dolce's "Aretino,"* 90–91, 176–77.

29. Ibid., 178–79.

30. Ibid., 156–57.

31. Ibid. Cf. Castiglione, *Cortegiano*, I.28: "Eccovi adunque,—rispose il Conte,—che in questo nòce l'affettazione, come nell'altre cose. Dicesi ancor esser stato proverbio presso ad alcuni eccellentissimi pittori antichi troppo diligenzia esser nociva, ed esser stato biasmato Protogene da Apelle, che non sapea levar le mani dalla tavola. . . . Voleva dire Apelle che Protogene nella pittura non conoscea qual che bastava; il che non era altro che riprenderlo d'esser affettato nelle opere sue. Questa virtù adunque contraria alla affettazione, la qual noi per ora chiamiamo sprezzatura, oltra che ella sia il vero fonte donde deriva la grazia, porta ancor seco un altro ornamento, il quale accompagnando qualsivoglia azione umana, per minima che ella sia, non solamente sùbito scopre il saper di chi la fa, ma spesso lo fa estimar molto maggior di quello che è in effetto; perché negli animi delli circunstanti imprime opinione, che chi così facilmente fa bene sappia molto più di quello che fa, e se in quello che fa ponesse studio e fatica, potesse farlo molto meglio." The source of the anecdote is Pliny, *Natural History*, XXXV.80.

32. "Un musico, se nel cantar pronunzia una sola voce terminata con suave accento in un groppetto duplicato, con tal facilità che paia che così gli venga fatto a caso, con quel punto solo fa conoscere che sa molto più di quello che fa." On music in the *Courtier*, see James Haar, "The Courtier as Musician: Castiglione's View of the Science and Art of Music," in Rosand and Hanning, *Castiglione: The Ideal and the Real*, 165–89. Cf., as well, Philip L. Sohm, "Affectation and *Sprezzatura* in 16th and Early 17th-Century Italian Painting, Prosody and Music," in *Kunst, Musik, Schauspiel* (Akten des XXV. Internationalen Kongresses für Kunstgeschichte), ed. Stefan Krenn (Vienna: Herman Böhlaus Nachf., 1985), 23–40, with further bibliography.

33. The modernity of such appreciation of linear will may be gauged against the observation of Matisse: "One must always search for the desire of the line, where it wishes to enter or where it wishes to die away." Alfred H. Barr, Jr., *Matisse: His Art and His Public* (New York: Museum of Modern Art, 1951), 551.

34. On Leonardo's discovery of the sketch, see Rosand, *Drawing Acts*, 50–54.

35. Dolce, *Dialogo della pittura*, ed. Roskill, in *Dolce's "Aretino,"* 100–101. Fabrini, the other interlocutor in the dialogue, addressing the question to Aretino, acknowledges that he is "giudiciosissimo in quest'arte." Aretino had indeed created a critical language appropriate to Titian's *pittura di macchia* and was articulately responsive to the "single brush stroke." Further on Aretino as art critic: Lora Anne Palladino, "Pietro Aretino: Orator and Art Theorist," Ph.D. diss. (Yale University, 1981); David Rosand, "Titian and the Critical Tradition," in *Titian: His World and His Legacy*, ed. David Rosand (New York: Columbia University Press, 1982), 1–39; Norman E. Land, *The Viewer as Poet: The Renaissance Response to Art* (University Park: Pennsylvania State University Press, 1994), 128–50.

36. The origins of Renaissance art literature in rhetorical convention have been explored most acutely by Michael Baxandall, *Giotto and the Orators: Humanist Observers of Painting in Italy and the Discovery of Pictorial Composition 1350–1450* (Oxford: Clarendon Press, 1971). But, as we shall see, Leon Battista Alberti, in the first humanist treatise devoted to the art of painting (1435), reveals a keen appreciation of pure drawing.

37. Cennino Cennini, *Il libro dell'arte o trattato della pittura*, ed. Fernando Tempesti (Milan: Longanesi, 1984), caI.

38. Leon Battista Alberti, *De pictura* (1435), ed. Cecil Grayson (Rome and Bari: Gius. Laterza and Figli, 1975), ¶31.

39. For a basic survey of this tradition, see H. van de Waal, "The *Linea Summae Tenuitatis* of Apelles: Pliny's Phrase and Its Interpreters," *Zeitschrift für Aesthetik und allgemeine Kunstwissenschaft* 12 (1967): 5–32. More recent literature on the topic will be found in Rosand, *Drawing Acts*, 345, note 13.

40. Leonardo da Vinci, *Treatise on Painting*, ed. McMahon, ¶115 (c. 50v).

41. This is Dolce on Raphael: "... le sue cose tutte movono sommamente, si trova in loro quella parte che avevano, come scrive Plinio [*Natural History*, XXXV.79], le figure di Apelle: e questa è la venustà, che è quel non so che, che tanto suole aggradire, così ne' pittori come ne' poeti, in guisa che empie l'animo d'infinito diletto, non sapendo da qual parte esca quello che a noi tanto piace" (Dolce, *Dialogo*, ed. Roskill, 174–75). For the distinction between *grazia* and *venustà* as applied to Raphael and for the mannerist implications of the latter term, see Daniel Arasse, "Raffaello senza venustà e l'eredità della grazia," in *Studi su Raffaello (Atti del Congresso Internazionale di Studi)*, ed. Micaela Sambucco Hamoud and Maria Letizia Strocchi (Urbino: Quattro Venti, 1987), 703–14, and "The Workshop of Grace," in *Raphael: Grace and Beauty*, ed. Nitti et al., 57–68; and, for further consideration of the term

in its Raphaelesque context, Patricia Emison, "Grazia," *Renaissance Studies* 5 (1991): 427–60. Also relevant is the discussion by Pierluigi De Vecchi, "Difficulty/Ease and Studied Casualness in the Work of Raphael," in *Raphael: Grace and Beauty*, 29–38.

42. Vasari, *Vite* (1550), ed. Bellosi and Rossi, 121–22. Further on the "O" of Giotto within the traditions of virtuoso display, see Ernst Kris and Otto Kurz, *Legend, Myth, and Magic in the Image of the Artist: A Historical Experiment* (New Haven: Yale University Press, 1979), 91–99; and, for its alphabetic implications, see Paul Barolsky, *Why Mona Lisa Smiles and Other Tales by Vasari* (University Park: Pennsylvania State University Press, 1991), 10–12.

43. Francisco de Hollanda, *Vier Gespräche über die Malerei geführt zu Rom 1538*, ed. Joaquim de Vasconcellos (Vienna: C. Graeser, 1899), 119.

44. Paolo Pino, *Dialogo di pittura* (1548), ed. Paola Barocchi, in *Trattati d'arte del Cinquecento*, I (Bari: Giuseppe Laterza and Figli, 1960), 117.

45. Ibid., 116.

46. Dolce, *Dialogo*, ed. Roskill, 130–31.

47. Heinrich Wölfflin, *Classic Art: An Introduction to the Italian Renaissance* (1898), trans. Peter and Linda Murray (London: Phaidon Press, 1953), 254.

48. Blunt, *Artistic Theory in Italy*, 98.

49. This, certainly, was the deeper vision offered by the participants in the Columbia symposium of 1978, *Castiglione: The Ideal and the Real in Renaissance Culture*. As we wrote in the preface to that publication, summarizing our own experience in teaching the *Courtier*: "In reading and rereading Castiglione's dialogue with our students, we continued to discover how beautifully rich and complex it was, how highly nuanced and ominously perceptive, how profoundly moving a reflection of and response to life. Serving as a gauge for so many aspects of Renaissance culture—from language and literature to art and music, courtiership and politics to humor and feminism, Neoplatonic idealism to the most cynical realism—the *Courtier* in the full integrity of its whole, in the contradictions of its dialogic structure, offered the most satisfying image of experience, of the precariousness of life and of the tenuous balance necessary for survival. We found in the text levels of the highest linguistic self-consciousness opening into the most profound situations of drama . . ." (viii).

PUBLICATIONS OF ROBERT W. HANNING

1960s

The Vision of History in Early Britain: From Gildas to Geoffrey of Monmouth. New York: Columbia University Press, 1966; 2d printing, 1970.

"Development and Awareness" (*Ecclesiam suam—II*). *Commonweal* 80.21 (18 September 1964): 634–37.

"Handel: Dead or Alive." *The Second Coming* 1.2 (1961): 62–64.

"*Havelok the Dane:* Structure, Symbols, Meaning." *Studies in Philology* 64 (1967): 586–605.

"Medieval Romance and the Critic's Quest." *Colloquium* 6 (Fall 1966): 1–9.

"Off the Bookshelf: *Canterbury Tales.*" *Report* 2.6 (March 1965): 25.

"Uses of Names in Medieval Literature." *Names* 16.4 (1968): 325–38.

1970s

The Individual in Twelfth-Century Romance. New Haven: Yale University Press, 1977.

The Lais of Marie de France. Cotranslated with Joan M. Ferrante. New York: Dutton, 1978. Reprints, Durham, N.C.: Labyrinth Press, 1982; Grand Rapids, Mich.: Baker Book House, 1995.

Sixteenth-Century English Poetry and Prose: A Selective Anthology. Coedited with Paul Delany and P. J. Ford. New York: Holt, Rinehart and Winston, 1976.

"Ariosto, Ovid, and the Painters: Mythological *Paragone* in *Orlando Furioso* 10–11." In *Ariosto 1974 in America*, edited by Aldo Scaglione, Maristella Lorch, and James Mirollo, 99–116. Ravenna: Longo, 1976.

Benoit Lacroix, *L'historien au moyen âge. History and Theory* 12.4 (1973): 419–34. [Review article]

"*Beowulf* as Heroic History." *Medievalia et Humanistica*, n.s. 5 (1974): 77–102.

"The Community of Risk: A Review of Daniel Berrigan's *The Trial of the Catonsville Nine.*" *Social Policy* 2.2 (1971): 55–58.

"*Engin* in Twelfth-Century Romance: An Examination of the *Roman d'Eneas* and Hue de Rotelande's *Ipomedon.*" *Yale French Studies* 51 (1974): 82–101.

"From EVA and AVE to Eglentyne and Alisoun: Chaucer's Insight into the Roles Women Play." *Signs* 2 (1977): 580–99.
"Mony Turned Tyme: the Cycle of the Year as a Religious Symbol in Two Medieval Texts." In *Saints, Scholars, and Heroes: Studies in Honor of Charles W. Jones*, edited by Margot H. King and Wesley M. Stevens, 282–98. Collegeville, Minn.: St. John's Abbey and University Press, 1979.
"Renaissance Studies." Coauthored with David Rosand. *Columbia University Seminar Reports* (Seminar on General and Continuing Education in the Humanities) 2.1 (1974).
"Sharing, Dividing, Depriving: The Verbal Ironies of Grendel's Last Visit to Heorot." *Texas Studies in Literature and Language* (1973): 203–13.
"The Social Significance of Twelfth-Century Chivalric Romance." *Medievalia et Humanistica*, n.s. 3 (1972): 3–29. German translation "Die gesellschaftliche Bedeutung des höfischen Romans im 12. Jahrhundert." In *Der altfranzösische höfische Roman*, 189–228. Darmstadt, 1978.
"Sources of Illusion: Plot Elements and Their Uses in Ariosto's Ginevra Episode." *Forum Italicum* 5 (1971): 514–35.
"The Theme of Art and Life in Chaucer's Poetry." In *Geoffrey Chaucer: A Collection of Original Articles*, edited by George Economou, 15–36. Contemporary Studies in Literature. New York: McGraw-Hill, 1976.
"View From the Ivory Tower: In Response to Rosemary Park." In *Small Comforts for Hard Times: Humanists on Public Policy*, edited by Florian Stuber and Michael Mooney, 321–32. New York: Columbia University Press, 1977.
"'You Have Begun a Parlous Pleye': The Nature and Limits of Dramatic Mimesis as a Theme in Four Middle English 'Fall of Lucifer' Plays." *Comparative Drama* 7 (1973): 22–50. Reprint in *The Drama of the Middle Ages*, edited by Clifford Davidson, C. J. Gianakaris, and John H. Stoupe, 140–68. New York: AMS Press, 1982.

1980s

Castiglione: The Ideal and the Real in Renaissance Culture. Coedited with David Rosand. New Haven: Yale University Press, 1983.
W. T. H. Jackson, *The Challenge of the Medieval Text: Studies in Genre and Interpretation.* Coedited with Joan M. Ferrante. New York: Columbia University Press, 1985.
"Appropriate Enough: Telling 'Classical' Allusions in Chaucer's *Canterbury Tales*." In *Florilegium Columbianum. Essays in Honor of Paul Oskar Kristeller*, edited by Karl-Ludwig Selig and Robert Somerville, 113–23. New York: Italica, 1987.
"Arthurian Evangelists: The Language of Truth in Thirteenth-Century Prose Romances." *Philological Quarterly* 64 (1985): 347–86.

"The Audience as Co-creator of the First Chivalric Romances." *Yearbook of English Studies* 11 (1981): 1–28.

"*Beowulf* and Anglo-Saxon Poetry." In *European Writers: The Middle Ages and the Renaissance*, edited by W. T. H. Jackson, vol. 1, 51–87. New York: Scribner's, 1983.

"Castiglione's Verbal Portrait: Structures and Strategies." In *Castiglione: The Ideal and the Real in Renaissance Culture*, edited by Robert W. Hanning and David Rosand, 131–41. New Haven: Yale University Press, 1983.

"Chaucer and the Dangers of Poetry." *CEA Critic* 46 (1984): 17–26.

"Chaucer's First Ovid: Artistic Transformation and Poetic Tradition in the *Book of the Duchess* and the *House of Fame*." In *Chaucer and the Craft of Fiction*, edited by Leigh A. Arrathoon, 121–63. Rochester, Mich.: Solaris, 1986.

"The Classroom as Theater of Self: Some Observations for Beginning Teachers." *ADE Bulletin* 77 (Spring 1984): 33–37.

"Courtly Contexts for Urban *Cultus:* Responses to Ovid in Chrétien's *Cliges* and Marie's *Guigemar*." *Symposium* 35 (1981): 34–56.

"The Criticism of Chivalric Epic and Romance." In *The Study of Chivalry: Resources and Approaches*, edited by Howell Chickering and Thomas H. Seiler, 91–113. Kalamazoo, Mich.: Medieval Institute Publications, 1988.

"Deciphering the Middle English Narrative Poem. Two Approaches" [Review-article of John Ganim, *Style and Consciousness in Middle English Narrative*, and Lynn Staley Johnson, *The Voice of the 'Gawain' Poet*]. *Modern Language Quarterly* 45 (1984): 395–403.

"Distrust Low Library, but do it benevolently." *Columbia Spectator*, 15 November 1983, 5.

"'I shal Finde It in a Maner Glose': Instances of Textual Harassment in Medieval Literature." In *Medieval Texts and Contemporary Readers*, edited by Martin B. Schichtman and Laurie A. Finke, 27–50. Ithaca, N.Y.: Cornell University Press, 1987.

"Poetic Emblems in Medieval Narrative." In *Vernacular Poetics in the Middle Ages*, edited by Lois A. Ebin, 1–32. Kalamazoo, Mich.: Medieval Institute Publications, 1984.

"Roasting a Friar, Mis-taking a Wife, and Other Acts of Textual Harassment in the *Canterbury Tales*." *Studies in the Age of Chaucer* 7 (1985): 3–22.

"Sir Gawain and the Red Herring: The Perils of Interpretation." In *Acts of Interpretation* (E. Talbot Donaldson Festschrift), edited by Mary J. Carruthers and Elizabeth D. Kirk, 5–23. Norman, Okla.: Pilgrim Books, 1983.

"'The Struggle Between Noble Designs and Chaos': The Literary Tradition of Chaucer's Knight's Tale." *The Literary Review* 23 (1980): 519–41. Reprint in *Geoffrey Chaucer's The Knight's Tale. Modern Critical Interpretations*, edited by Harold Bloom, 69–89. New York: Chelsea, 1988.

"Suger's Literary Style and Vision." In *Abbot Suger and Saint-Denis*, ed. Paula Gerson, 145–50. New York: Metropolitan Museum of Art, 1986.

"'Ut enim faber . . . sic creator': Divine Creation as Context for Human Creativity in the Twelfth Century." In *Word, Picture, Spectacle,* edited by Clifford Davidson, 95–149. Kalamazoo, Mich.: Medieval Institute Publications, 1984.

"Witless Christians or Christian Witness? The 'Social Gospel' and Its Detractors." *Columbia Catholic Forum* 1.1 (1983): 2–6.

1990s

"'And countrefete the voys of every man / He koude, whan he wolde telle a tale': Toward a Lapsarian Poetics for the *Canterbury Tales.*" *Studies in the Age of Chaucer* 21 (1999): 29–58. [Biennial Chaucer Lecture.]

"Come in out of the Code: Interpreting the Discourse of Desire in Boccaccio's *Filostrato* and Chaucer's *Troilus and Criseyde.*" In *Chaucer's Troilus and Criseyde: Subgit to Alle Poesie. Essays in Criticism,* edited by R. A. Shoaf, 120–37. Albany: State University of New York Press, 1992.

"The Crisis of Mediation in Chaucer's *Troilus and Criseyde.*" In *The Performance of Middle English Culture. Essays on Chaucer and the Drama in Honor of Martin Stevens,* edited by Lawrence Clopper, James Paxson, and Sylvia Tomasch, 143–59. Cambridge: Boydell and Brewer, 1998.

Introduction to volume 2 of *Medieval Scholarship: Biographical Studies on the Formation of a Discipline.* Coauthored with Joan M. Ferrante. Vol. 2: *Literature and Philology,* edited by Helen Damico with Donald Fennema and Karmen Lenz, xiii–xxvi. New York: Garland, 1998.

"*Inventio Arthuri:* A Comment on the Essays of Geoffrey Ashe and D. R. Howlett." *Arthuriana* 5.3 (1995): 96–100.

"Love and Power in the Twelfth Century, with Special Reference to Chrétien de Troyes and Marie de France." In *The Olde Daunce. Love, Friendship, Sex, and Marriage in the Medieval World,* edited by Robert R. Edwards and Stephen Spector, 87–103. Albany: State University of New York Press, 1991.

"'Parlous play': Diabolic Comedy in Chaucer's Canterbury Tales." In *Chaucerian Comedy: Critical Essays,* edited by Jean Jost, 295–319. New York: Garland, 1994.

"The Talking Wounded: Desire, Truthtelling, and Pain in the *Lais* of Marie de France." In *Desiring Discourse: Studies in the Literature of Love, Ovid to Chaucer,* edited by Cynthia Gravlee and James Paxson, 40–61. Selinsgrove, Pa.: Susquehanna University Press, 1998.

"Telling the Private Parts: 'Pryvetee' and Poetry in Chaucer's *Canterbury Tales.*" In *The Idea of Medieval Literature. New Essays on Chaucer and Medieval Culture in Honor of Donald R. Howard,* edited by James M. Dean and Christian K. Zacher, 108–25. Newark, Del.: University of Delaware Press, 1992.

"A Theater of Domestication and Entrapment: The Cycle Plays." In *Approaches to Teaching Medieval English Drama*, edited by Richard Emmerson, 116–21. New York: MLA Publications, 1990.

"*Troilus and Criseyde* 4.210: A New Conjecture." *Chaucer Yearbook* 4 (1997): 79–84.

"Words to Fill an Empty Tomb: The Holy Sepulcher and a 'Cipollan' Reading of Three *Decameron* Novelle." In *Tradition and Ecstasy: The Agony of the Fourteenth Century*, edited by Nancy Van Deusen, 291–318. Ottawa: Institute of Mediaeval Music, 1997.

2000–

Lapsarian Poetics: Coping with an Imperfect World in the Decameron and the Canterbury Tales (manuscript near completion).

"Before Chaucer's *Shipman's Tale*: The Language of Place and the Place of Language in *Decameron* 8.1, 8.2." In *Place, Space, and Landscape*, edited by Laura L. Howes. Special issue of *Tennessee Studies in Literature*, forthcoming.

"The Body of/as Evidence: Desire, Eloquence, and the Construction of Society in *Decameron* 7.8." In *Rhetoric and Experience: Studies in Memory of Robert O. Payne*, edited by John Hill and Deborah Sinnreich-Levi, 269–93. Madison, N.J.: Fairleigh Dickinson University Press, 2000.

"Custance and Ciappelletto in the Middle of It All: Problems of Mediation in the 'Man of Law's Tale' and *Decameron* 1.1." In *The Decameron and the Canterbury Tales: New Essays on an Old Question*, edited by Brenda Deen Schildgen and Leonard Koff, 177–211. Cranbury, N.J.: Associated University Presses, 2000.

"*Decameron* and *Canterbury Tales*." In *Approaches to Teaching Boccaccio's Decameron*, edited by James H. McGregor, 103–19. New York: Modern Language Association, 2000.

CONTRIBUTORS

SUZANNE CONKLIN AKBARI is Associate Professor of English and Medieval Studies at the University of Toronto.

WILLIAM ASKINS is Professor of English and Humanities at the Community College of Philadelphia.

CHRISTOPHER BASWELL is Professor of English at the University of California, Los Angeles.

JOSEPH A. DANE is Professor of English at the University of Southern California.

GEORGE D. ECONOMOU is Professor of English Emeritus at the University of Oklahoma.

JOAN M. FERRANTE is Professor of Comparative Literature at Columbia University and former president of the Medieval Academy and of the Dante Society of America.

JOHN M. GANIM is Professor of English at the University of California, Riverside.

SEALY GILLES is Associate Professor of English at Long Island University.

WARREN GINSBERG is Distinguished Professor of English and Head of the English Department at the University of Oregon.

CHARLOTTE GROSS is Professor of English at North Carolina State University, Raleigh.

NICHOLAS HOWE is Professor of English at the University of California, Berkeley.

LAURA L. HOWES is Associate Professor of English at the University of Tennessee.

H. MARSHALL LEICESTER, JR., is Professor of English Literature, Cowell College, University of California, Santa Cruz.

NANCY F. PARTNER is Professor of History at McGill University.

MONIKA OTTER is Associate Professor of English and Comparative Literature at Dartmouth College.

MARGARET AZIZA PAPPANO is Assistant Professor of English at Queen's University, Ontario.

SANDRA PIERSON PRIOR is a Senior Scholar at Columbia University, where she recently retired as Associate Professor of English and Comparative Literature and Director of the Composition Program.

ELIZABETH ROBERTSON is Professor of English at the University of Colorado at Boulder.

DAVID ROSAND is Meyer Schapiro Professor of Art History at Columbia University.

SARAH SPENCE is Professor of Classics at the University of Georgia.

ROBERT M. STEIN is Associate Professor of Language and Literature at Purchase College, SUNY, and Adjunct Professor of English and Comparative Literature at Columbia University.

SYLVIA TOMASCH is Professor of English and Chair of the English Department of Hunter College, CUNY.

PETER W. TRAVIS is Professor of English and Chair of the English Department at Dartmouth College.

INDEX

Page numbers in italics refer to illustrations